INTERVIEWS AND RECOLLECTIONS *Series*

Philip Collins (*editor*)
DICKENS: INTERVIEWS AND RECOLLECTIONS (2 volumes)
THACKERAY: INTERVIEWS AND RECOLLECTIONS (2 volumes)

Morton N. Cohen (*editor*)
LEWIS CARROLL: INTERVIEWS AND RECOLLECTIONS

A. M. Gibbs (*editor*)
SHAW: INTERVIEWS AND RECOLLECTIONS

J. R. Hammond (*editor*)
H. G. WELLS: INTERVIEWS AND RECOLLECTIONS

David McLellan (*editor*)
KARL MARX: INTERVIEWS AND RECOLLECTIONS

E. H. Mikhail (*editor*)
BRENDAN BEHAN: INTERVIEWS AND RECOLLECTIONS
(2 volumes)
W. B. YEATS: INTERVIEWS AND RECOLLECTIONS (2 volumes)
LADY GREGORY: INTERVIEWS AND RECOLLECTIONS
OSCAR WILDE: INTERVIEWS AND RECOLLECTIONS (2 volumes)
THE ABBEY THEATRE: INTERVIEWS AND RECOLLECTIONS
SHERIDAN: INTERVIEWS AND RECOLLECTIONS
JAMES JOYCE: INTERVIEWS AND RECOLLECTIONS

Harold Orel (*editor*)
KIPLING: INTERVIEWS AND RECOLLECTIONS (2 volumes)

Norman Page (*editor*)
BYRON: INTERVIEWS AND RECOLLECTIONS
DR JOHNSON: INTERVIEWS AND RECOLLECTIONS
D. H. LAWRENCE: INTERVIEWS AND RECOLLECTIONS
(2 volumes)
TENNYSON: INTERVIEWS AND RECOLLECTIONS
HENRY JAMES: INTERVIEWS AND RECOLLECTIONS

Martin Ray (*editor*)
JOSEPH CONRAD: INTERVIEWS AND RECOLLECTIONS

R. C. Terry (*editor*)
TROLLOPE: INTERVIEWS AND RECOLLECTIONS

Series Standing Order

If you would like to receive future titles in this series as they
are published, you can make use of our standing order
facility. To place a standing order please contact your
bookseller or, in case of difficulty, write to us at the address
below with your name and address and the name of the
series. Please state with which title you wish to begin your
standing order. (If you live outside the UK we may not have
the rights for your area, in which case we will forward your
order to the publisher concerned.)

Standing Order Service, Macmillan Distribution Ltd,
Houndmills, Basingstoke, Hampshire, RG21 2XS, England.

SHAW

Interviews and Recollections

Edited by

A. M. GIBBS

MACMILLAN

First published 1990

Published by
THE MACMILLAN PRESS LTD
Houndmills, Basingstoke, Hampshire RG21 2XS
and London
Companies and representatives
throughout the world

Typeset by Wessex Typesetters
(Division of The Eastern Press Ltd)
Frome, Somerset

Printed and bound in Great Britain by
WBC Ltd, Bristol and Maesteg

British Library Cataloguing in Publication Data
Shaw: interviews and recollections.—
(Interviews and recollections).
1. Shaw, Bernard—Biography
2. Dramatists, English—20th century
—Biography
I. Gibbs, A. M.   II. Series
822'.912   PR5366
ISBN 0–333–28717–7

Contents

List of Plates

Acknowledgements

Those who embark on study of the vast subjects of Shaw's biography and his manifold associations and activities sometimes feel involuntarily engaged with no less a topic than the history of the world from 1856 to 1950. Fortunately, the long journey from beginning to completion of the *Shaw: Interviews and Recollections* project has not been a solitary one, and I am glad to acknowledge here the extensive assistance I have received from many individuals and institutions.

First, I must gratefully acknowledge the help of Mr Dan H. Laurence, who in the preliminary stages of research generously allowed me access to his bibliographical records of Shaw interviews, and gave me invaluable advice as to other sources of relevant materials. The editorial commentary in this work is everywhere indebted to Mr Laurence's scholarly editions of Shaw's letters and works and to his *Bernard Shaw: A Bibliography*. I am also much indebted to four people who have been employed as research assistants on the project at different stages of its development. Dr Simon Trezise assisted greatly with the early collection of materials in the United Kingdom. Dr Jeremy Steele had a long association with the project and made major contributions to the tasks of gathering, selection and organisation of materials, and to research for the editorial commentary. Dr Lyndy Abraham worked with admirable skill and expedition on the unearthing of numerous and often elusive items of information necessary for the completion of the commentary, carried out the checking of the final typescript and prepared the index to the work. Dr Bernadette Masters provided invaluable assistance in the correcting of the page proofs and the carrying out of other final editorial tasks. I am also grateful for the expert assistance given by the Macmillan editorial staff and Longworth Editorial Services.

Research for this work has been carried out in many institutions in the United Kingdom, the United States and Australia. I am especially grateful to the following for their help: the former Administrator–Registrar of the Royal Academy of Dramatic Art, Mr Richard O'Donoghue, for allowing access to the Currall Collection of newspaper cuttings about Shaw; the staff of the Southern Historical Collection and Manuscripts Department of the Library of the University of North Carolina at Chapel Hill for access to the Henderson Collection; Mr Andrew Leigh, Administrator, the Old Vic; the staffs of: the British Library and the British Library Newspaper Library, Colindale; the Senate

House Library, University of London; the Theatre Museum, Victoria and Albert Museum; the Humanities Research Center, University of Texas at Austin; the New York Public Library; the Fisher Library, University of Sydney; the Macquarie University Library.

My thanks are due to the Australian Research Grants Scheme and the Macquarie University Research Grants Committee for financial support for the project, and to the Council of Macquarie University for granting me two periods of leave to enable me to carry out research.

From the beginning of the preparation of this work I have been deeply indebted to my wife, Donna, for help and well-judged advice.

Macquarie University

A. M. GIBBS

The author and publishers wish to thank the following who have kindly given permission for the use of copyright material:

The Bodley Head, for the extract from *The Romantic '90s* by Richard Le Gallienne;

Campbell Thomson & McLaughlin Ltd and Taplinger Publishing Co. Inc., for the extract from *Irish Literary Portraits*, edited by W. R. Rodgers;

Jonathan Cape Ltd, on behalf of the Executors of the Augustus John Estate, for the extract from *Chiaroscuro: Fragments of Autobiography*;

Chapman & Hall Ltd, for the extract from *Table-talk of G. B. Shaw* by Archibald Henderson;

Century-Hutchinson, for the extract from *Confessions of a Writer* by V. Brome;

Collins Publishers, for the extracts from *Robert Loraine: Soldier, Actor, Airman* by W. Loraine;

Constable Publishers, for the extracts from *Today We Will Only Gossip* by Beatrice Lady Glenavy;

Curtis Brown, for the extract from James Drawbell's *The Sun Within Us*, copyright by James Drawbell (1963);

Daily Mail, for the extracts from the articles by Frederick George Prince-White;

J. M. Dent & Sons Ltd Publishers, for the extract from C. H. Herford's *Philip Henry Wicksteed: His Life and Work*;

Janet Dunbar, for the extracts from her *Mrs G. B. Shaw: A Biographical Portrait*;

E. P. Dutton, for the extracts from *George Bernard Shaw: Man of the Century* by Archibald Henderson;

Faber and Faber Ltd, for the extract from H. G. Wells's *Experiment in Autobiography*, vol. II;

Victor Gollancz Ltd, for the extract from *Thirty Years with G.B.S.* by Blanche Patch;

Alfred A. Knopf Inc. and Laurence Pollinger Ltd, for the extract from *Frieda Lawrence: The Memoirs and Correspondence*, edited by E. W. Tedlock;

Hamish Hamilton Ltd, for the extract from *Author Hunting by an Old Literary Sportsman* by Grant Richards;

Hamish Hamilton and A. M. Heath, for the extract from *Conversations with Max* by S. N. Behrman;

Harcourt Brace Jovanovich, Inc. and the Hogarth Press, for the extracts from *The Diary of Virginia Woolf*, vol. 4: *1931–1935*, edited by Anne Oliver Bell, copyright © 1982 by Quentin Bell and Angelica Garnett;

Harcourt Brace Jovanovich, Inc. and the Hogarth Press, for the extract from *Beginning Again: An Autobiography of the Years 1911–1918*, copyright © 1963, 1964 by Leonard Woolf;

William Heinemann Ltd, for the extract from *Chronicle of a Life* by S. Trebitsch, translated by E. Wilkins and E. Kaiser;

Jermyn Publications Ltd, for the extracts from Lady Rhondda, 'Recollections of GBS' in *Time and Tide* (1950);

Mrs Catherine M. Johnson-Flynn, for the extracts from 'Encounters with GBS', by A. E. Johnson, in *The Dalhousie Review* (Spring 1951);

London Express News and Feature Services, for the extracts from articles by Sir Arthur Beverley Baxter, E. M. Salzer and Dorothy Royal;

Mrs Frances McElwaine, for the extract from *The Pageant of the Years* by Sir Philip Gibbs;

Macmillan Publishers Ltd, for the extracts from Rex Harrison's *Rex: An Autobiography*;

William Morris Society, for the extracts from R. Page Arnot's *Bernard Shaw & William Morris*;

Motor, for the extract from 'Mr Bernard Shaw on Motoring' by Stuart MacRae;

New Statesman, for the extract from Clifford Sharp;

Peters, Fraser and Dunlop Group Ltd, for the extract from C. E. M. Joad's *Shaw* (Gollancz, 1949), and the extract from *Editor* by Kingsley Martin (Hutchinson, 1968);

Peters, Fraser and Dunlop Group Ltd, for the extracts from *The New Statesman and Nation* by J. B. Priestley;

Charles Skilton, for the extracts from *Shaw the Villager and Human Being* by Allan Chappelow;

the Society of Authors, on behalf of the Bernard Shaw Estate, for the extracts from interviews and articles by George Bernard Shaw;

The Spectator, for the extract from St John Ervine's *Bernard Shaw*;

Miss Olivia Swinnerton, for the extract from Frank Swinnerton's *Swinnerton: An Autobiography*;

University of North Carolina at Chapel Hill, the Archibald Henderson Collection of George Bernard Shaw, Rare Book Colle. ion, for the extract from *Memoirs of GBS* by Edward McNulty;

Unwin Hyman Ltd, for the extracts from *William Archer* by C. Archer, and the extracts from *Portraits from Memory and Other Essays* by Bertrand Russell;

Virago Press, for the extracts from *Diary of Beatrice Webb*, vol. II, edited by Norman and Jeanne MacKenzie;

A. P. Watt Ltd, on behalf of Ruth Lumley Smith, for the extracts from *Sybil Thorndike Casson* by Elizabeth Sprigge;

A. P. Watt Ltd, on behalf of Michael B. Yeats, and Macmillan London Ltd, for the extract from *Autobiographies* by W. B. Yeats.

Every effort has been made to trace all the copyright-holders but if any have been inadvertently overlooked the publishers will be pleased to make the necessary arrangements at the first opportunity.

Introduction

In the course of a professional writing career which spanned more than seventy years in the last quarter of the nineteenth and the first half of the twentieth centuries, Bernard Shaw became one of the most widely celebrated literary figures of his age.

His career as a playwright began late: he was thirty-six when his first play, *Widowers' Houses*, was produced. But by the end of the first decade of the twentieth century he had clearly established himself as the foremost playwright of his day in the English-speaking world. Before the turn of the century Shaw had become very well known in political, literary and artistic circles and more widely as a popular platform orator. He had joined the Fabian Society in 1884, and soon became conspicuous as one of its leading members and its most eloquent spokesman. He had written major essays on Ibsen and Wagner, some of the best topical music and theatre criticism in the English language, and ten plays.

Shaw was a man of prodigious energy and extraordinarily wide-ranging interests and activities. His creative writings include five novels, several short stories and over fifty plays, many of the latter being accompanied on publication with lengthy prefaces. His music and theatre criticisms are collected in two three-volume works.[1] He wrote extensive political and economic treatises, topical tracts, essays and introductions, and made nearly 4,000 contributions to periodicals. Dan H. Laurence, as editor of his correspondence, conservatively estimates that he wrote more than a quarter of a million letters and postcards.[2] He grew up with the modern age, and, living through a period of profound social and political upheaval and change and rapid technological development, took a lively and knowledgeable interest in everything that went on around him. He was a born controversialist, and his ability to deliver trenchant, entertaining and unorthodox opinions on almost any proposed topic, from Belisha beacons at pedestrian crossings to the first cause of the universe,[3] made him a natural and much prized quarry for journalists.

A collage made up of a few of the images of Shaw which emerge from some of the many striking and amusing recollections gathered in the present work might show him: flying through the air after a bicycle collision with Bertrand Russell; almost drowning in the sea with Robert Loraine; putting down H. G. Wells in a Fabian Society debate; amazing Virginia Woolf with a cascade of talk in Hyde Park; telling the young

Ralph Richardson that he was overacting in the role of Bluntschli in *Arms and the Man*; riding in a tank at the Front in France towards the end of the First World War; flying upside down in a two-seater biplane, and telling the pilot on landing that 'the world is like that young man'; and, as a ninety-year-old man, farewelling Kingsley Martin in the lane outside the Shaw house at Ayot St Lawrence with a vigorous rendition of an aria from Verdi. Those who have recorded their recollections of Shaw come from a wide social and vocational spectrum, including people from the theatre, broadcasting and film worlds, politicians and civil servants, authors of all description, academics, administrators, artists, publishers, editors, journalists, soldiers, airmen, private secretaries, tradespeople and servants. The recollections included in this work have been drawn from a variety of sources, including autobiographies and memoirs, diaries, letters and periodical articles. A general principle of selection has been that the recollections record first-hand associations and actual meetings with Shaw, or direct observations of him on public and private occasions.

As a means of coping with the increasing demand for interviews with him as his celebrity grew (and no doubt to ensure a large measure of control over what was published in his name) Shaw came to adopt the practice of having 'interviewers' present him with sets of typewritten questions, leaving spaces in between for his handwritten replies. He was quite happy for journalists to present the results as records of *viva voce* conversations, complete with fabricated accounts of visits and settings. He used interviews freely as a means of publicising forthcoming productions of his plays. The majority of the 'interviews' in the latter category, both questions and answers, were entirely written by Shaw himself.[4] The twenty-seven interviews relating to individual plays which have been gathered in the Bodley Head *Collected Plays* are omitted from the selection made for the present work. Consideration of space has made it necessary to represent some of the longer interviews and recollections included here by substantial excerpts, rather than by the full texts. Omissions from the full texts are indicated by the usual symbol '. . .'. The interviews and recollections have been selected from an immense quantity of available material. This work is intended to provide a generous sample of items in both categories, covering the full range of Shaw's various interests and activities as they developed in the course of his career. The interviews and recollections are arranged chronologically within the topic areas indicated by part titles.

Referring to gramophone recordings of his own voice, Shaw once wrote: 'I can get any number of different voices, none of them mine, by running the instrument at different speeds . . . however I play about with the machine, I never get *me*.'[5] Those who look for an essential self, the 'real' Bernard Shaw amongst the myriad of impressions of him which have been left by his contemporaries, may well find a similar difficulty. There are very many highly favourable impressions. Significantly, those who worked closely with Shaw in his domestic life generally found him, in the words of the Scottish housekeeper who came to Ayot St Lawrence after the death of Charlotte Shaw in 1943, 'a vur-r-r-ee fine man . . . charming . . . to the last'.[6] He appeared to many an unusually courteous, considerate, good-humoured and generous person. Yet there were others, even amongst his close friends, who found him frequently infuriating, and even detestable. 'A man who I know slightly and much hate' was the verdict of one early commentator.[7] Samuel Butler found himself both repelled and attracted, and Max Beerbohm thought him 'cold'.[8] 'A world made up of Bernard Shaws would be a world in moral dissolution',[9] Beatrice Webb roundly declared to her diary, in one of the many perceptive and observant comments she made there on her friend and fellow-worker. There was undoubtedly a streak of callousness in Shaw's nature, which showed itself especially in his early relations with women and in some of his later pronouncements on political and social issues. People closely acquainted with Shaw have described him as essentially a shy person. Obviously he courted, and up to a point enjoyed, the enormous public attention he attracted, and he had a fairly large share of vanity. But testimonies to his shyness are consistent with the sense, sometimes conveyed in recollections, that Shaw tended to use his brilliant conversational powers as a wall around the self, keeping intimacy at bay. Certainly, he was almost invariably the one doing most of the talking.

Whichever judgements about him prevailed in people's minds, it is clear that meetings and associations with Shaw generally made a deep impression. It is not easy to calculate the extent of the influence of any individual on the spirit of an age. But there is no doubt that for many of his contemporaries Shaw was an extraordinarily invigorating and liberating influence. His arrival on the intellectual scene of the late nineteenth and early twentieth centuries seems to have been rather like that of Lona Hessel in Ibsen's *The Pillars of Society*, when she comes to a house of stale conventions and unhealthy secrets and flings open the doors and windows to let in some fresh air.

NOTES

1. *Our Theatres in the Nineties*, 3 vols (London: Constable, 1948); *Shaw's Music*, ed. Dan H. Laurence, 3 vols (London: Max Reinhardt, the Bodley Head, 1981).
2. See *Collected Letters 1874–1897*, p. xi.
3. See below, pp. 208 and 409.

4. Shaw sometimes drafted interviews in other categories in this way. For accounts of this practice see below, pp. 103–6; and for further discussion of Shaw's methods of dealing with interviews see Dan H. Laurence, '"What's Your Opinion, Mr Shaw?"', *The Library Chronicle of the University of Texas at Austin*, n.s., no. 8, Autumn 1974, pp. 53–9.

5. W. R. Titterton, 'My Second Childhood, by Bernard Shaw', *Sunday Graphic*, 28 June 1936.

6. See below, p. 452.

7. See below, p. 46.

8. See below, pp. 273, 274.

9. *The Diary of Beatrice Webb*, vol. III: *1905–1924*, ed. Norman and Jeanne MacKenzie (London: Virago, 1984) p. 257. The remark quoted here occurs after Beatrice Webb's caustic account of Shaw's intervention in the Casement affair (see below, pp. 239–40).

Part 1
Growing Up

INTRODUCTION TO PART 1

George Bernard Shaw was born at 3 Upper Synge Street (later renamed 33 Synge Street), Dublin, on 26 July 1856. He was the son of George Carr Shaw (1814–85) and Lucinda Elizabeth Shaw (née Gurly, 1830–1913). Bernard Shaw (as he preferred to be named) had two elder sisters, Lucinda Frances (1853–1920) and Elinor Agnes (1855–76). From about 1866 the Shaws shared a house at 1 Hatch Street, Dublin, and a summer residence, Torca Cottage, Dalkey Hill, with a Dublin conductor and music teacher, George Vandeleur Lee. In 1873 Mrs Shaw left Dublin with her daughter Agnes (followed shortly afterwards by Lucy) to join Lee in London in a new career of music teaching. Shaw remained in Ireland with his father, working in the land agent's firm of C. Uniacke Townshend & Co., until April 1876, when he joined his mother and Lucy in London. His sister Agnes had died of tuberculosis at Ventnor on the Isle of Wight a few days before Shaw's departure from Dublin.

Apart from a brief period, from November 1879 to July 1880, when he worked for the Edison Telephone Company, Shaw had no regular employment during his early years in London. But he was far from idle at this time, and it was in many ways an important period of literary apprenticeship. By November 1876, through the agency of Vandeleur Lee, he obtained a commission as ghost writer of musical columns for the satirical weekly *The Hornet*, a job which continued until September of the following year. Between March 1879 and November 1883, he wrote five novels which adumbrate many themes and character portrayals in his plays. He also embarked during this period on a programme of further self-education in music and art, and set about teaching himself French and Italian.

The Shaws of Dublin

A SYMPOSIUM

From 'George Bernard Shaw', in *Irish Literary Portraits*, ed. W. R. Rodgers

(London: BBC, 1972) pp. 119–27. The following discussion of Shaw, his family and early life in Dublin, formed part of a programme broadcast by the BBC in September 1954. The speakers included: Denis Johnston (b. 1901), playwright, BBC director and university professor; St John Greer Ervine (1883–1971), playwright, novelist, dramatic critic and author of *Bernard Shaw: His Life, Work and Friends* (1956); Frank O'Connor, pseudonym of Michael O'Donovan (1903–66), journalist, author of short stories, novels and plays, and a director of the Abbey Theatre during the 1930s; Lady Constance Geraldine Hanson, patroness of the arts and friend of the Shaw family, who held a literary salon in the days of Oliver St John Gogarty; her mother, Mrs Ada Tyrrell, poet and wife of a Regius Professor of Greek at Trinity College, Dublin; Father Leonard, an Irish priest, on the staff of St Mary's College, Twickenham, when Shaw consulted him about *Saint Joan*; and Dr Thomas Bodkin, who was associated with Dublin's National and Municipal Galleries and became curator of the Birmingham Art Gallery during the 1930s.

W. R. Rodgers (1909–69), poet and a Presbyterian minister before he joined the BBC in 1946, compiled the programme from separately recorded interviews. He supplied a linking commentary, some of which has been silently omitted.

JOHNSTON: It always formed a regular pattern. If you told Shaw that you intended to examine his past, and write about him, he would immediately forbid you to do so; but if you went on and said you were going to do it, whether he helped you or not, he then immediately went to the other extreme, and loaded you down with information about his past. Of course this may just have been natural *bonté* on his part, but on the other hand it seems to me much more likely that he wished you not to dig out the facts for yourself, and that he thought that he could prevent you from doing so by telling you himself.

ERVINE: That I think is true – the astonishing thing about GBS, as I am discovering now that I'm writing his life, is that although he seemed to be telling you a great deal about himself, he told you nothing at all. There are a whole lot of things about GBS – his early life – which are undiscoverable now.

JOHNSTON: To another Dubliner, one of the most fascinating things about Shaw is the fact that only in his old age did he ever reveal what to him appears to have been a terrible secret, the fact that for a short time he attended Marlborough Street school, in his early youth, and he could never bring himself to mention this perfectly respectable and reputable fact, for a period of seventy years.[1] Now it's true that he did mention it at the end, but only at the end. And what an extraordinary sort of mental block of social and religious prejudice this reveals in his mind, a block that I really think can only be appreciated by an Irish Protestant.

ERVINE: Well, that's understandable enough – you ought to understand it as much as I do. Remember, GBS belonged to the upper classes – he didn't as some people imagine rise up from the proletariat – he belonged to the landed gentry, but an impoverished branch of the landed gentry. And to him, a Protestant and a member of the ascendancy, to be sent to a school mainly populated by Roman Catholics, generally the children of publicans, was a disaster.

JOHNSTON: It's his childhood that we've got to know about, not what he says about himself, and in my belief there were other secrets in his childhood that he has not yet revealed at all.

What was the skeleton in the Shavian cupboard? What was he hiding, and why? Frank O'Connor, you, I think, have a theory about it.

FRANK O'CONNOR: I think he was hiding the fact that he, his sister and his mother had abandoned his father.[2] The old man isn't mentioned at all in his work until very late on – in the preface to *Immaturity*.[3] Suddenly you get the beginning of the man trying to come to grips with the thing that's strangling him. When he begins writing about his father, he writes about him from a funny point of view, but each reference to his father, as he goes on in life, becomes more mature in its realisation of what was really happening. His father was a drunkard – his mother and his sister left his father and went to live in London.

Well, every skeleton has a human being in the cupboard. You, Ervine, must know as much as anybody about the human conditioning of Shaw's boyhood.

ERVINE: You've got to remember he lived in a very queer home. His father was greatly older than his mother. He was a curiously spineless, and yet very impressive, man. He tippled rather a lot. Mrs Shaw didn't love him, never had loved him, and GBS grew up in a loveless home, with a mother who, I think, disliked him because he had a physical resemblance to his father. It was an impoverished home and in some respects an unfortunate home, but he didn't like to talk about that part of his life, he never mentioned it to me. And I knew him so well, that I could ask him questions that it would have been impertinent to ask anybody else. He didn't talk very much about his life until he was about thirty. He had a hatred of poverty so profound that he wouldn't even acknowledge its existence.

'To have been brought up in poverty is to have the chill of it in one's bones all one's life.' That is what Shaw actually said to you, isn't it? That explains the streak of meanness in his old age?

ERVINE: You see, it wasn't only that they were poor, but there was this lack of love in the home. And it's a frightful thing for a child to grow up in a loveless home.

'My mother,' said Shaw, 'never made the least attempt to win my affections.' 'If I were run over by a dray,' he told Lady Gregory, 'she'd say, "Oh, poor

fellow!" but if a beautiful rose were crushed she'd go out of her mind with grief.'

Lady Hanson recalls a long family acquaintanceship with the Shaws in Dublin. It began with a dispute between her mother and Lucy Shaw.

LADY HANSON: The Shaw family lived in Synge Street, which, as all Dubliners know, is round the corner from Harrington Street, then a less noisy and unlovely thoroughfare than it is today. Both families employed the same laundress (it was before the time of public laundries). A table-cloth, missing from the Harrington Street list, was traced to the house in Synge Street, so, directed by the washerwoman, my mother, then about twelve years old, called to claim the missing property. Lucy, who was much the same age, resisted the claim and there ensued a tug-of-war between the two. The ownership must somehow have been decided amicably because the conflict ended and a friendship was formed between the two girls which lasted as long as Lucy lived. She was the master-mind in the group of young people – daring and independent. Her companion, my mother, looked up to her in humble admiration of her brilliance and original opinions.

There was a little boy, George Bernard, who wore a holland tunic and went by the name of 'Sonny'. He was always rather apart from the others and would be seen sitting at the piano, picking out airs with one finger or absorbed in the construction of a toy theatre. My mother remembers him declining to join a party assembled on the front steps, who were engaged in eating sticks of raw rhubarb. As an article of diet, he could not but have approved of it, but he may have disliked the publicity of the proceeding! . . .

SEAN MACREAMOINN: Mr William Meegan of Dalkey told us his memories of Shaw at this time . . . .

WILLIAM MEEGAN: We got on all right, only when he'd take my bird we'd fight then. We used to be catching birds and he'd take mine, and then we'd have a scuffle. Sure, he was a good few years older than me, and he'd have the better of it – he was bigger and stronger than I was. He was a strong lump of a fellow with a red face. We used to call him bullock soup, not because he was as red as a bullock, but because he'd been boasting out of the soup the cook used to give him. Och, I remember him well!

Lady Hanson's mother, Mrs Tyrrell, remembers 'Sonny' Shaw playing with a cardboard theatre. What age was he then, Mrs Tyrrell?[4]

MRS TYRRELL: Oh, he was about ten. Mrs Shaw was an accomplished woman. I think it was her brains that Shaw inherited. The father was an old silly. I remember playing bears under the table.

And what was Sonny like?

MRS TYRRELL: Oh, he was a very nice-looking boy, he was very dignified.

And a certain Mr Fry,[5] who as a boy ran the streets of Dublin with Shaw, bore out that point –

MR FRY: He was a very correct boy – we got on well together. I played with him, I shot marbles with him, I lashed tops with him, I boxed the fox with him,[6] I robbed the orchard with him. We were never caught – it was a terrible thing being caught robbing an orchard in them days. You'd get five years for taking an apple!

Yes, Shaw was always the dignified playboy. Mr Kerwan recalls his landlady talking about the elderly GBS and her memory of him as a small boy.

MR KERWAN: Well, the first thing she told us was that 'It may have been yesterday or the week before that he passed down the street on the other side and never so much as looked across at the house.' That was rather difficult to believe in itself, because we knew that Shaw very seldom was in Dublin at the time. But we asked her why he should look across. She explained that he had lived there when he was a boy and she was a little girl. And the other thing she had against him was that he'd locked her in a wardrobe and frightened the life out of her!

'My home life,' Shaw said, 'was a torture.' He talked much about this, later in life, to an Irish friend.

FATHER LEONARD: He told me that his father was a drunkard and he said that when he was a very small child he did not realise about people being drunk, but when he did wake up for the first time to the fact that his father was drunk he said to his mother, 'Father is drunk,' and she said to him, 'Is he ever anything else?'

'I have never believed in anything since,' said Shaw. 'Then the scoffer began.'

LEONARD: I think that incident made a deep impression on him as a child and I think it partly accounted for his attitude towards the family.

'My family, though kindly, might be called loveless,' said Shaw. 'But what did that matter to a child who could sing A te O cara *and* Suone la tromba intrepida *before he was perfect in the church catechism.'*

LEONARD: Music was really one of the great passions of his life at that time. His love for music was one of the deepest things in his whole character. I remember him saying that he thought some of the most beautiful religious music that was ever written was the music in the tempest scenes in *The Magic Flute*. And there was one thing that amused me very much when he told me that in the funeral march in the second movement of the 'Eroica',[7] the English critics couldn't understand at all why that gay little tune comes on towards the end of the second movement: he said it was perfectly clear to him because when he was a boy his Uncle George was superintendent of Mount Jerome cemetery, and Shaw used to attend quite a number of funerals, and when they got as far as Harold Cross – up to that the funeral procession had been proceeding very sombrely – the jarveys whipped up the horses and they went off at a gay trot. Then, when they came near the cemetery, they relapsed into the funeral march; so it was perfectly clear to him, he said, the meaning of that movement – it was probably the same at funerals in Vienna.

'My father,' said Shaw, 'found something in a funeral which tickled his sense of humour, and this characteristic I have inherited. The gift of ridicule which I inherited is my most precious possession.'

LADY HANSON: I think GBS wrote heartlessly about the father and I think he owes a great deal more than he admitted or perhaps realised.

But it was to his mother that Shaw owed his interest in music. Dublin, says Lady Hanson, was at that time a centre of musical activity.

LADY HANSON: Mrs Shaw was a highly trained musician who sometimes, as an amateur, sang the leading role in grand opera and composed and published songs, forgotten now, which had a success. There was a fine living to be made by orchestra conductors and teachers of singing. The most popular and successful was Vandeleur Lee, whose special method for producing and preserving the voice GBS often recalled and believed to be unique. . . .

I think there was very little family affection between them. None of the family went to the father's funeral in Dublin. I think Lucy happened to be in Dublin at the time,[8] perhaps with her touring company, but it meant nothing to her. I can't remember ever having heard her make a reference to her father. He was abandoned by them all.

'For the very solid reason,' said Shaw, 'that he could not support them. In leaving him they took off his shoulders a burden he was unable to bear and glad to discard. I believe it was the happiest time of his life.' Peace, perfect peace, with loved ones far away.

O'CONNOR: What the biographers all overlook is that Shaw did not leave him and go to London. Shaw stayed on with him and worked in a lawyer's office. And that went on for about a year and then Shaw did leave him[9] and finally the old man died in a house in Leeson Street. I've forgotten the name of the people in whose house he died. . . .

'I left Ireland,' said Shaw, 'because I realised there was no future for me there . . . Dublin was a desert.' Unlike Joyce, he had no afterthoughts. More than thirty years passed before he set foot in the city again.

ERVINE: He hated Dublin. There's no doubt about that and he made that perfectly plain in one of his letters to Mrs Patrick Campbell, written comparatively late in his life when he was staying with Sir Horace Plunkett;[10] he described himself driving into Dublin and hating every house he saw on the way. He loathed the place. And I think myself it is a loathsome city.

For the Irishman, too far east is best. 'No man prefers the city that conquered him to the city he conquered,' said Shaw. All the same he carried much of Dublin with him: its scepticism and an accent which, as Dr Bodkin says, was unmistakably Dublin.

DR BODKIN: Someone brought him into the Athenaeum and I was sitting there with Max Beerbohm, whom I'd only met for the first time on that particular afternoon, and D. S. MacColl, who was a dear and old friend of mine.[11] The two of them, before Shaw arrived, had commented on the fact that my speaking voice and accent were very like his. 'Oh', I said, 'well, why not? We've both had the same sort of middle-class Dublin upbringing and he was born in South Frederick Street, or somewhere of the sort, and I was born in North Great Denmark Street.' They mentioned this to Shaw, who was quite obviously hurt that anyone could suppose he spoke with such a patently Dublin brogue as I did.

Lady Hanson recalls, later on, going with her mother to visit the Shaws in Fitzroy Square.[12]

LADY HANSON: I remember he sat on the floor at mamma's feet and he ate ripe cherries the whole time. He was very pleasant and nice to her, and she was asking him if he remembered this person and that person, and what became of so and so, and he would put her off in some cynical fashion, because he hated to be reminded of his Dublin days. That was obvious.

NOTES

1. One of the four schools attended by Shaw was the Central Model Boys' School, Marlborough Street. Shaw describes his reaction to being sent there in the chapter entitled 'Shame and Wounded Snobbery', in his *Sixteen Self Sketches* (London: Constable, 1949) pp. 20–9. According to Shaw the school was 'undenominational and classless in theory but in fact Roman Catholic' (p. 22).

2. This needs some qualification. Mrs Shaw returned to Dublin in 1874 to supervise the transfer of her son and husband from 1 Hatch Street to lodgings at 61 Harcourt Street (see *Bernard Shaw: Collected Letters 1874–1897*, ed. Dan H. Laurence [London: Max Reinhardt, 1965] p. 7; hereafter cited as *Collected Letters 1874–1897*). It is true, however, that George Carr Shaw died alone in lodgings at 21 Leeson Park Avenue, Dublin, in April 1885, and that no members of the family attended his funeral.

3. Published in 1930. Shaw did, however, write about his father in 'interviews' printed in 1896 and 1901; see below, pp. 24–5 and 30.

4. A fuller version of Mrs Tyrrell's recollections of Shaw is supplied in Frank Harris, *Contemporary Portraits*, 4 vols (London: Methuen, 1915–24) II, 42–3:

> I can tell you very little more than you know yourself of George's youth after the age of twelve or fourteen, as his family left Ireland to live in London about then. My first memory of George is a little boy in a Holland overall sitting at a table constructing a toy theatre. 'Sonny' the other Shaws called him, then. We lived a few doors from them, and our mothers being both singers, was the bond between us. Even at that early age – George was about ten – he had a superior manner to his sisters and me, a sort of dignity withal, and I remember feeling rather flattered when he condescended to explain anything that I asked him; though we girls were a year or two older.
>
> I should say, as well as I can judge between the two men, Oscar Wilde and GBS, that George is a good man *all through* and Oscar had only good *impulses*, though with more sentiment than George; more romance in fact, which is always a charm to me. I know George to have been the best of sons and brothers; he is generous, not alone to worthy objects, but to the unworthy as well. I often think that the luxury of having unlimited money is that one can give to both.

5. This name may be a mistake for Foy (see next recollection).

6. The nature of this activity (presumably a children's game) is obscure.

7. Beethoven's Third Symphony.

8. Lucy Shaw married the actor Charles Robert Butterfield on 17 December 1887; after a long separation they were finally divorced in 1909.

9. After nearly three years (see introductory note).

10. This was a letter dated 3 April 1913, in which Shaw wrote: 'I drove into Dublin today and cursed every separate house as I passed' (see *Bernard Shaw and Mrs Patrick Campbell: Their Correspondence*, ed. Alan Dent [London: Victor Gollancz, 1952] p. 106). Sir Horace Plunkett (1854–1932) was Shaw's host on several of the latter's visits to Ireland.

11. Both (Sir) Max Beerbohm (1872–1956), author and cartoonist, and Dugald Sutherland MacColl (1859–1948), painter, critic and gallery director, had connections with Shaw via the *Saturday Review*: Beerbohm succeeded him as drama critic in 1898, while MacColl was the paper's art critic from 1896 to 1906.

12. The Shaws moved to 29 Fitzroy Square, in Bloomsbury, on 5 March 1887. Shaw left after his marriage in 1898, but his mother remained there until 1907.

Boys at Play

JOSEPH FOY

From 'Mr Foy Tells of GBS (Orchard-raider)', *Empire News* (Irish edn), Manchester, 19 November 1950. Mr Foy is probably to be identified with the man named above (p. 7) as Mr Fry. His recollection may be complemented by Shaw's reported answer to Patrick O'Reilly, a Dublin dustman who had organised the erection of a plaque on Shaw's birthplace. On a visit to Shaw in the late 1940s, O'Reilly asked him if he remembered the Pottle, a narrow alleyway in Dublin (near which Swift had lived). 'Yes, indeed, I remember it well,' Shaw replied. 'I often played marbles from Synge Street, up the Pottle into the Coombe and back by the "Barn" past my father's mill at Rutland House. I remember, too, robbing an orchard at the back of Portobello Bridge on the way home' (Desmond M. Fisher, 'Shaw's Other Dustman', *American Mercury*, March 1954, p. 121).

On Tuesday next at midday a sprightly old man will sit in a public house in Dublin telling his friends there of the days he spent playing with George Bernard Shaw. He is probably the only man alive who knew Shaw as a boy.

Joseph Foy was born nearly ninety-three years ago not far from Shaw's birth-place in Synge Street, Dublin, and they played together in petticoats.

Mr Foy remembers games of 'three-hole' marbles with Shaw and the two of them falling into a stream on their way from an orchard they had raided.

He knew young GBS for only a few years, however, and when Shaw left Dublin to live at Dalkey, eight miles away, Mr Foy lost trace of him.

But every Tuesday he goes to 86 Bride Street, Dublin, in the shadow of St Patrick's Cathedral, to talk of old Dublin and of his old friends.

It was only when Shaw died that Mr Foy revealed that he had known him as a boy.

'He was a stern lad,' he told me, 'and a good sport. He never cheated in any of our games, and I liked him a lot. But I could never get to know Shaw's father very well. He was a strange man.

'I wish I had met GBS before he died. We could have had grand times talking about Dublin.'

Stories and Dreams: I

LADY SCOTT

From *Self-Portrait of an Artist: From the Diaries and Memoirs of Lady Kennet, Kathleen, Lady Scott* (London: John Murray, 1949) pp. 160–1. Lady Scott (1878–1947), sculptor, widow of Captain Scott, the Antarctic explorer, married Hilton Young, later Lord Kennet of the Dene, in 1922. She had known Shaw since about 1903 and saw him quite often from 1917 onwards. Their friendship was fostered by her visits to Lamer, near the Shaws' country home at Ayot St Lawrence, Hertfordshire. Lamer, which belonged to Apsley Cherry-Garrard, a member of

Scott's last Polar expedition, is the scene of the following diary entry, dated 9 December 1917.

Shaw came to tea and we had a quiet evening. Shaw told stories of his dreams, and how since he was quite little he has always told himself a story each night before he goes to bed, and some, he said, go on as serials, but others he tells himself over and over again. After dinner we danced and gave Shaw a lesson, both practical and demonstrative.

Stories and Dreams: II

LADY GREGORY

From *Lady Gregory's Journals* vol. I, ed. Daniel J. Murphy, Coole Edition xiv (Gerrards Cross: Colin Smythe, 1978) p. 106. Lady Augusta Gregory (1852–1932), playwright, translator and folklore collector, joined W. B. Yeats in 1898 in successful efforts to found an Irish theatre. Shaw wrote *John Bull's Other Island* for them in 1904 (the year which saw the opening of the Abbey Theatre in Dublin). In *Our Irish Theatre* (1914) Lady Gregory mentioned having heard Shaw speak after a public lecture in 1897, but she probably met him through Yeats. By the time she began the *Journals* in 1916 she was a close friend of the Shaws, and the following recollection, dated 9 November 1919, is taken from an account of one of her numerous visits to Ayot St Lawrence.

Talking of the Dublin statues, he says he had, when a child, a dream one night that he went out and went through the garden, and at the end of it opened a gate and saw the sky all filled with wonderful light, and in the centre was God. And he was in the form of the statue of William III in College Green.

Educational Confessions

From Bernard Shaw, 'Educational Confessions', *The Schoolmistress*, 17 November 1927.

What was your favourite subject at school? Has this or some other subject influenced you most in your after-school life?

I had no favourite school subject. No subject was made interesting to me. My interests, which were keen, lay outside that dreary prison.

What was your favourite game?

I had no choice. We played rough, *unorganised* games, like Police and Robbers; and I enjoyed roaring and rushing about and struggling.

What book most impressed you as a child?

An impossible question. I read everything I could lay my hands on that was readable, which of course excluded school books. The earliest literary sensations I can recall are *The Pilgrim's Progress* and *The Arabian Nights*.

Did you 'rag' your treachers?

No. I left school before the ragging age. Boys under fifteen don't rag, as far as I know them.

Would you like to have your school-days over again?

Good God. NO! Would anybody like to serve a sentence of penal servitude twice over? But then my home was not a prison. The boys who liked school dreaded their parents more than their teachers.

Did you find examinations a source of anxiety?

Not in the least. I never prepared for them, and could not understand the boys who did. I instinctively saved my brains from destruction by resolute idleness, which, however, made school tedious and meaningless to me.

Is the modern freedom better for the child than the old-time discipline?

I don't know. In the schools I attended there was neither freedom nor discipline. They told you to learn lessons and sit quiet, and hit you or kept you in if you didn't do it. They did not even hit you hard enough to matter. Clearly that was not real discipline.

Could you draw a tolerable map of England without access to an atlas? Is this worth being able to do?

1. No. 2. Not under ordinary circumstances except for self-satisfaction. It does not happen to appeal to me.

Where does the education of today fail in your opinion?

Because it is only a disguise for relieving parents of the worry of children by caging them and taming them like wild animals, mostly by cruel methods, and because it ends in Latin verse, which is only a vested interest in torture.

Do you accept the principle of secondary education for all?

It depends on what you call secondary. A minimum of technical education (the three R's, for example) is necessary to qualify for citizenship in a modern city. Beyond that people will seek all the knowledge they are capable of without compulsion; and it is most important that they should have the fullest opportunities as easily and cheaply as possible.

To what extent, if any, should the education of the modern girl differ from that of the modern boy?

Not at all in the compulsory stages (all boys should be taught to mend their clothes and cook); but in the voluntary stages the sexes would find their own differentiation.

What can the nation reasonably expect to get for its expenditure on education?

At present, the moral and intellectual imbecility, the illiteracy of pen and speech, that it actually does get. With a reasonable, sincere, and really available system of education, the nation might reasonably expect to become educated after a generation or two.

Shaw's School Days

R. THURSTON HOPKINS

From R. Thurston Hopkins, 'George Bernard Shaw on his School Days and Non-Age', *Books of the Month*, December 1928. R. Thurston Hopkins (d. 1958), journalist and author of topographical, biographical and other popular works, named 'ghost hunting' as his recreation in *Who's Who*. His article is in some respects unreliable, but the following recollections seem worth recording, even if his account of their origins is specious.

Shaw went to the Wesleyan Connexional School at Dublin.[1] An old boy of this school thus described him to me as he remembers him in 1866: 'There was always a look of other-worldness about young Shaw. There was a certain hauteur about his manner that compelled attention. It seemed that he had never been young and his face as a boy was the same as the portraits which are published today. He was always feverishly hungry for information but he looked upon the school system of learning lists of names and dates as senseless. Out of school hours he held little meetings in the playground and delivered lectures in art and life to the small boys. Even as a boy he combined an extravagant fancy with a curious sort of coldness, and I can still see him giving a lecture on the uselessness of arithmetic and brilliantly defending his theory when the headmaster tackled him.'

Many years ago I ventured to interview Shaw. I tackled him at a Fabian meeting, taking with me a note book containing a series of questions which I intended to ask him. There were about twenty questions in all but I think that Shaw cleverly evaded most of them. But another journalist was more fortunate and I remember seeing the following answers and questions in his note book:

'What book in childhood made the deepest impression on your mind?'

'I have no more recollection of my first book than I have of my first meal. I read everything that came my way but I had to be encouraged by my mother to persevere at *Robinson Crusoe* until he reached the desert island, after which he carried me with him unaided. I acquired a very boyish (not childish) taste for Shakespeare from the snippets printed beneath Selous' illustrations.[2] Children's books, from the accursed *Swiss Family Robinson* onwards, I always loathed and despised for their dishonesty, their hypocrisy, their sickly immorality, and their damnable dulness. My moral sense, like my literary taste, was sound.'

NOTES

1. The Wesleyan Connexional School, later Wesley College, was Shaw's first school, which he attended in 1867–8. In a letter written in 1944, he described it as 'utterly incompetent', continuing:

I was taken away from it because my clerical uncle, who had grounded me in Latin Grammar quite successfully in my childhood, examined me and discovered that I had learnt nothing and forgotten a good deal at the Wesleyan. The school was not then the co-educational Wesley College of today. It was in an old private house, next door to the mansion of Sir Benjamin Lee Guinness, with a big schoolroom at the back of the playground, where the stables used to be. It was the cheapest of the Dublin Protestant schools of any social pretentions, and could not afford to give adequate attention to the number of dayboys and boarders it took on. The classes were too large: the teachers, untrained in pedagogy (they had never heard of such a word) were mostly young men waiting for a ministry. There was really no teaching. Latin and Greek were the only subjects that were taken seriously: history, geography, arithmetic and Euclid, were in the curriculum; but education meant Caesar, Virgil and Homer. The method of teaching was never to teach, but to set lessons and sums without a word of explanation. In the large classes the utmost examination possible in the lessons meant one question for each boy in alphabetical order, or at most two. If you could answer the questions or do the sums or construe the few lines that fell to your lot, you passed unscathed: if not, or if you talked in class or misbehaved, you were marked in your judgement book for caning by the headmaster. Manners and dress

were not taught: the boarders (we dayboys called them the skinnies) could
appear with their shoes unlaced and their collars unpresentable without
rebuke. Such discipline and study as there was, were learnt and enforced at
home: for we were all snobbishly respectable, and would not speak to one
unfortunate outcast whose father was a pawnbroker.   (Shaw to John Araben,
1 November 1944: copy in the Currall Collection, Royal Academy of Dramatic
Art; original in the Humanities Research Center, the University of Texas at
Austin)

The clerical uncle referred to was William George Carroll, who instructed his
two sons and Shaw in 'the declensions and conjugations and irregular verbs'
(Shaw, Sixteen Self Sketches [London: Constable, 1949] p. 20).
    2. Henry Courtney Selous (1811–90), painter of portraits, landscapes and
historical and literary subjects, illustrated many books, including Outlines to
Shakespeare's Tempest (1836) and Cassell's Illustrated Shakespeare (1864).

Shaw and The Arabian Nights

FREDERICK SINCLAIR

From Frederick Sinclair, 'The Splendid Torchbearer: some Notes on the Life of
George Bernard Shaw – Playwright, Philosopher and Prophet', St Pancras Journal,
November–December 1950. Frederick P. Sinclair (d. 1953) was Borough
Librarian at St Pancras from 1934 to 1953 and editor of the St Pancras Journal (for
Shaw's association with St Pancras, see below, pp. 69–70). Sinclair describes his
first encounter with Shaw at a meeting to gain support for a children's library
with Dickensian associations c. 1921.

Shaw asked what books were going to be stocked in this proposed
children's library: if they were to be 'improving' books of the kind
considered good for children he would have nothing to do with the
idea. He then told of having discovered, as a child, the first volume of
Burton's translation of The Arabian Nights in a country house belonging
to his mother's aunt. The book was missed from its place in a cupboard
and when found, in his bed, was taken away and hidden with the other
volumes of the work. The young Shaw would not rest until he had
found the original volume and its fellows, which he then eagerly
devoured in secret. In telling this personal story Shaw pointed out that,
as a boy, he thoroughly enjoyed The Arabian Nights, ignoring the –
to him – incomprehensible coarse passages; and having made the
acquaintance of the book in such circumstances, he could always go
back to it without bothering about the 'broad parts'. He inferred, from

the experience, that it was wise to put the world's classics in their
original English versions in every children's library.

Shaw as a Boy

EDWARD McNULTY

Edward McNulty, 'George Bernard Shaw as a Boy', *Candid Friend*, 6 July 1901.
Matthew Edward McNulty (1856–1943) was a fellow-pupil at a school in Aungier
Street, the last of the four Shaw attended – he left in 1871 – and was probably
Shaw's only close school friend. After McNulty moved to a job in Newry, the
friendship flourished in letters (subsequently destroyed; see below, p. 31) until
McNulty returned to Dublin in 1874. The two remained friends after Shaw's
move to London. A forty-nine-page typescript, 'Memoirs of GBS', by McNulty,
which includes copies of Shaw's letters to him, is held in the Rare Book Collection
of the University of North Carolina at Chapel Hill. The article in the *Candid
Friend* presents an abbreviated version of McNulty's account of his friendship
with Shaw in the typescript. Corrections made by Shaw to McNulty's recollections are preserved in the margin of a typescript copy of the *Candid Friend* article
in the Currall Collection, Royal Academy of Dramatic Art. These marginal
comments are reproduced below.

4 Mistakes.

When I first met Shaw he was in *Eton jacket,
knickerbockers, long stockings* and *laced-up boots*.
He sat at the desk directly in front of mine, and
I showed my interest in him by striving to kick
him in the ankles. Failing in this attempt, I
pulled his hair. He turned and smiled at me.
I followed up these advances by drawing a
caricature of him, and passing it over to him.
He took it, and remained quiet for some time
with his head bent. I began to wonder what he
was doing, when he handed me back the paper
over his shoulder: then I saw that he had drawn
on the other side a caricature of myself. I had
been until then the acknowledged caricaturist
of the school. I recognised, however, that my
rival had appeared.

Soon after Shaw's advent, a discussion arose
about the best way to take a ball with a long
hop. Some said that the proper thing to do was
to step back and 'block'. I contended that a

better way was to step forward and take the ball with a swipe as it rose. The playground of our Dublin school was small, unsuited to cricket, and overlooked from the opposite side of the street by a Catholic chapel. I took the bat, and Shaw bowled the ball with a long hop. I stepped forward and let drive with all my might. There was an awful crash. I had sent the ball through the stained-glass window of the chapel. There was an awe-struck silence in the playground: we all knew what would be thought of this sacrilegious outrage concocted in a Protestant school. Suddenly came an unearthly scream of laughter, and we saw Shaw rolling on the ground in hysterics of delight.

This broken window legend was current in the school long before I went to it. I never played cricket there nor saw any one else attempt it.

I had my revenge later when we started a Shakespearean Club. Our first and last attempt was *Hamlet*, and, as we could only perform during the recreation half-hour, we proposed to divide the play over a week. Owing to the latitidue allowed the performers and the derisive criticisms from the audience, the play stretched out three weeks. Shaw was Ophelia, and, as I was the Ghost, I indulged freely in the luxury of sepulchral laughter at Shaw's attempts to simulate the female voice with a shrill falsetto.

All invented. The duel scene in *Romeo & Juliet* was our only achievement.

Instead of going home, like the other boys, after school, we used to walk to the National Gallery; smaller, but better lighted, than its London sister. Here we spent long hours. Our favourite pictures in the large hall were Raphael's 'St Cecilia'; 'The Crucifixion', by Annibale Carracci; six pictures by Canaletto; a small Fra Angelica [sic]; 'Portrait of a Gentleman', by Tintoretto; and a landscape by Ruysdael. In another room were photographs of Angelo's work from the Sistine chapel. Shaw was an enthusiastic admirer of Angelo, and, when I demurred to the exaggerated muscular development of the figures, he explained that it was merely Angelo's masculine love of strength run amok.

Shaw was then devoured with ambition to be an artist. He never attempted landscape, but used to draw figures with extreme care: too much care, since his lines were sometimes, as a consequence, stiff. The first occasion, when he brought me up to his little private room, which was at the top of a high house, he produced a wonderful collection of prints and studies which he had picked up at the bookstalls.

It was a glorious treasure, and we lingered over it fondly. Some time later, in this queer little room, he proposed that I should pose as a nude model, and that he would do the same for me. I declined, because the door was close to and opposite the window, and I was afraid of catching cold.

Shaw's mother was the foremost amateur singer in Dublin, and her house the centre round which musical Dublin revolved. *Yet the musical education of the boy destined to write* 'The Perfect Wagnerite' *was entirely neglected. He was not even taught his notes. But he taught himself.* He told me with triumph, one day, that he could read notation, and brought me into the drawing-room to prove his statement. We were alone, and he had approached the piano, when a maid hurried in, exclaiming:

'Oh! Master George, you are late for dinner!'

Master George said:

'I won't have any today, thank you.'

The consternation of the maid was painful to witness. She said:

'Your mamma is out. What will she say when she comes back and finds that you had nothing to eat?'

But his mind was made up. He wanted to show me that he could really play the piano, and this idea made dining hateful. The maid went out, and returned with another. Both girls knelt before him, and implored him to take his dinner, but in vain. Eventually they went out in despair, and then Shaw placed music on the piano and played with one finger the serenade from *Don Giovanni*. He had learned to hum the air from hearing it sung, then strummed it on the piano and compared it with the printed

This is true; but the anecdotic sequel is romance.

notes. In this way, he became so good a pianist
that, in later years, when he played the Wald-
stein sonata,[1] I actually recognised it. His favourite operas were *Don Giovanni* and *Faust*;[2] he
adored Mozart and reverenced Bach.

His first serious literary effort was entitled
'Strawberrinos: or, the Haunted Winebin'. It was
in MS, illustrated by the author. He presented me
with the one and only copy. I deeply regret
having lost this valuable manuscript, but I recollect that Strawberrinos, the hero, had a series
of breathless adventures which were constantly
anti-climaxed by the arts of a sardonic demon.
The refrain to the demon's song in the great
incantation scene was:

> Fill the magic cup!
>   Drink it with a will;
> If it doesn't save your life
>   It is pretty sure to kill –
> A saline draught and a big blue pill!

The chorus, with menacing forte, repeated: 'A
big blue pill!'

Wrong. The
Dalkey cottage
was not taken
until I was ten
or thereabouts.

Shaw was *born in a villa* on Dalkey Hill, which
overlooks the Bay of Dublin. To this place we
often walked. In many fields about, there were
notice-boards: 'Trespassers will be prosecuted'.
We invariably crossed a field when it displayed
this notice, not from a spirit of bravado, but
because of our conviction that, though men
might use land, they should not own it. The
establishment of the Fabian Society was simply
Shaw's roundabout way of reviving, in the
minds of the people, the elemental instinct of
universal ownership. An historic event occurred
during our passage through one of these forbidden fields. Shaw began discussing our future.

That we should both become famous, we
always accepted as a matter of course, and I had
arranged, in my own mind, that our sphere
should be literature.[3]

'My father can't afford to let me study art in
Italy,' said Shaw regretfully. 'I don't know what
I shall make my name in.'

'Literature, of course,' I said.

'I don't care much about that,' said he. 'I rather think I shall start a new religion.'

I was horrified. I pictured him wandering about with tattered cloak, long hair and wild eyes; mounting on wayside barrels, and shrieking spiritual subtilties at open-mouthed rustics.

'Oh, no,' I said, imploringly. 'There are enough, too many, religions. Become famous in literature. Promise me!'

My pathetic appeal was successful. After some serious discussion, Shaw graciously surrendered, and we glorified the decision with a box of chocolate.

At the age of thirteen, we finally parted with the supernaturalism of Christianity, and, later, gratefully exchanged the delusions of metaphysics for the more restful illusions of writers like Tyndall, Huxley, and Darwin.

I am always interested, and sometimes amused, at the various attempts to explain GBS. He, too, spends much care and ink in endeavouring to explain himself. But more of him will be found in the character of Julius Cæsar, in *Plays for Puritans*, than in all the rest of his writings; and the value of this revelation is enhanced by the fact that Shaw himself is unaware of it.

NOTES

1. Beethoven's difficult piano sonata Opus 53.

2. In January 1905 Shaw told Archibald Henderson that amongst the parts his mother had sung in Dublin were 'Donna Anna in *Don Giovanni*' and 'Margaret in Gounod's *Faust*', and that, as the operas produced by Vandeleur Lee 'were all rehearsed in our house, I whistled & sang them from the first bar to the last whilst I was a small boy' (see *Bernard Shaw: Collected Letters 1898–1910*, ed. Dan. H. Laurence [London: Max Reinhardt, 1972] p. 499; hereafter cited as *Collected Letters 1898–1910*).

3. McNulty became a bank manager, but realised his literary ambitions to the extent of publishing four novels and three plays. Two of the plays (*The Lord Mayor* and *The Courting of Mary Doyle*) were successfully produced at the Abbey Theatre.

An Exam Paper

From G. Bernard Shaw, *Nine Answers* (privately printed [sixty-two copies] for Jerome Kern, 1923). In September 1896 Shaw wrote answers to nine questions submitted by Clarence Rook (d. 1915), author and journalist, who had interviewed him the previous year about *Candida* (see *The New Budget*, 4 April 1895). Rook put his questions in the form of a mock 'Examination Paper', headed 'Corvus [i.e. Rook]: De vita et operibus Georgii Bernardi Shaw.' Then, with Shaw's blessing, he took the questions and answers as the basis for constructing an 'interview', published in the *Chap-Book* (Chicago), 1 November 1896. *Nine Answers* thus reproduces the autobiographical material exactly as it left Shaw's hands, without Rook's skilful sophistications. The questions, originally set out together, have here been placed at the head of each answer, and the last five questions and answers, which fall outside the scope of this Part, have been omitted.

1. *Name the places of Shaw's birth and education.*

Dublin is my chief birthplace.
Date, 26 July 1856 (hearsay only: I do not remember the occasion).
Education, NONE.
    On reflection, this is not true. My mother was a very active musician – an amateur singer. She belonged to a choral and orchestral society, which performed several big works, and subsequently half a dozen operas, in all of which she took a leading part. The works were rehearsed in our house, within earshot of me, or at big rehearsals at which I could be present when I chose. The fact that before I was fifteen, I knew at least one important work by Handel, Mozart, Beethoven, Mendelssohn, Rossini, Bellini, Donizetti, Verdi and Gounod right through from cover to cover, so that I sang and whistled their themes to myself exactly as other boys whistled music-hall songs, entitles me to withdraw my hasty answer above and claim to have been a very highly educated boy. If you want to know how I subsequently extended those musical possessions of mine, I refer you to an excellent article of mine entitled 'The Religion of the Pianoforte'. (*Fortnightly Review*, I think, about a couple of years ago.)[1]
    Further, there is in Dublin a modest National Gallery, with the usual collection of casts from the antique. Here boys are permitted to prowl. I prowled. A well-known Dublin musician, Joseph Robinson,[2] allowed me to call on him periodically and borrow a volume of Duchesne's outlines of the old masters – twenty volumes of them, I think.[3] When I

had any money – which hardly ever happened, I bought volumes of the Bohn translation of Vasari, and read them with immense interest.[4] Result, at fifteen, I knew enough about a considerable number of Italian and Flemish painters to recognise their work at sight. Yes, on the whole, I got some education, thanks to Communism in pictures.

Again, we had, for our summer residence, a cottage high up on a hill commanding the northern bight of Dublin Bay, from Howth to Dalkey Sound, on one side, and the southern bight, from Dalkey Island to Bray Head, on the other. There is not two penn'orth of really grand mountain or tree in that landscape, but I have never seen more beautiful skies, even in Italy; and I always look at the sky.

Consequently my University has three colleges – the musical society, the National Gallery, and Dalkey Hill.

The reason I hastily said that I had no education was that the word brought to my mind no less than four schools, where my parents got me out of the way for half the day.[5] In these creches – for that is exactly what they were – I learnt nothing. How I could have been such a sheep as to go to them when I could just as easily have flatly refused, puzzles and exasperates me to this day. They did me a great deal of harm, and no good whatever. However, my parents thought I ought to go; and everybody else thought I ought to go; and I thought I ought to go, being too young to have any confidence in my own recalcitrant instincts. So I went; and if you can in any public way convey to these idiotic institutions my hearty curse, you will relieve my feelings infinitely. I may add that I was incorrigibly idle and worthless as a schoolboy, and proud of the fact.

2. *Recount the mode of his ingress into literary activity.*

I was driven to write because I could do nothing else. In an old novel of mine – *Cashel Byron's Profession* – the hero, a prizefighter, remarks that it's not what a man would like to do, but what he *can* do, that he must work at in this world. I wanted to be another Michel Angelo, but found that I could not draw. I wanted to be a musician, but found I could not play – to be a dramatic singer, but had no voice. I did not want to write: that came as a matter of course without any wanting. I began, after the fashion of the sons of commercially unsuccessful middle-class men, by spending from my fifteenth to my twentieth year in an office – the office of an eminent Irish land agent (of all professions! – in Ireland, it *is* a profession, pursued under fire occasionally) who honourably appreciated the fact that I was intelligent; that I did not steal his money; and perhaps also that I did not take the faintest interest in his business, knowing well that my destiny did not lie in that direction.[6] At twenty, I resigned my prospects as a man of business, and blindly plunged into London. My published works at this time consisted of a letter written when I was sixteen or seventeen to *Public Opinion*, in which I sought to stem the force of the first great Moody and Sankey revival by the announcement that I, personally, had renounced religion as a delusion.[7] London was not ripe for me. Today, after twenty years, it has hardly caught my tone yet. For nine years there was not a break in the clouds. When people reproach me now with the unfashionableness of my attire, they forget that to me it seems like the raiment of Solomon in all his glory by contrast with the indescribable seediness of those days when I trimmed my cuffs to the quick with a scissors, and wore a tall hat, and soi-disant black coat, green with decay. I wrote novel after novel – five long ones in all, besides plenty of articles and essays. No publisher would touch them: no editor would look at me. However, it did not matter: I knew perfectly well that I had produced nothing of real value. I had been thrown back on myself since my earliest childhood, and my self sufficiency was proof against all discouragement. It is perfectly easy to be poor so long as you don't borrow money. You can never borrow enough to pay you for the friends you lose by the transaction. I should have starved – having quite made up my mind, on closing my career as an incipient land agent, that I would never again do a day's honest work on any compulsion whatever – but for my father, who was ending his days impecuniously in Dublin, and my mother, who had taken to teaching singing in London, and some scraps of an inheritance of hers.[8]

Perhaps it will help you to visualise if I mention that my father was derived from the prosperous bourgeois class. His father was some combination of notary and stockbroker unknown in modern life. He died prematurely, leaving a widow with about twenty children, whose sole inheritance was a tradition of their own very extra-special gentility. On this unsubstantial capital they throve, everything considered, most astonishingly. I had unlimited uncles and aunts, and myriads of cousins. Without disliking them personally, I had a theory that they were snobs and humbugs, a conception which I extended later on to the whole class to which I belonged. Their chief merit was a remarkable aptitude for playing all sorts of wind instruments by ear. Thus, my father was an amateur of the trombone, and could play 'Home, Sweet Home' on the penny whistle or on the flute in its primitive form, uncomplicated by the Boehm system of fingering.[9] He was the most unlucky, incompetent and impecunious of mortals. Even his post in the civil service – attained, doubtless, by the assertion of his claim as a SHAW to social consideration – got abolished by 1850, which will give you a notion of how surpassingly useless as a sinecure it must have been. He sold his pension, and embarked with the proceeds in a wholesale corn business (his birth not permitting him to stoop to retail trade), and spent the rest of his life in contemplating his warehouse and mill in melancholy wonder that other men with warehouses and mills made money out of them, whilst he became poorer and poorer. In a furtive, unconvivial way, he drowned his sorrow in the bowl from time to time. My mother, who was an able person (she is alive and on view at Fitzroy Square), came from the landed gentry class, which cut her off with £1,500 on her making an idiotic marriage.

Behold me, then, in London in an impossible position. I was a foreigner – an Irishman – the most foreign of all foreigners when he has not gone through the university mill. I was, as aforesaid, not uneducated; but unfortunately what I knew was exactly what the educated Englishman did not know; and what he knew I either didn't know or didn't believe. I was provincial; I was opinionated; I was unpresentable; my destiny was to educate London, and yet I had neither studied my pupil nor related my ideas properly to the common stock of human knowledge. At first I earned a little by devilling for a music critic, whose paper died – partly of me. He followed it to the grave.[10] Then London absolutely refused to tolerate me on any terms. As the nine years progressed, I had one article accepted – by G. R. Sims, who had just started a short-lived weekly paper of his own.[11] It brought me fifteen shillings. Full of hope and gratitude I wrote a really brilliant contribution. That finished me at once. On another occasion a publisher showed me some old blocks which he had bought up with the intention of having verses fitted to them and using them as a school prize book. I wrote a parody of the sort of thing he wanted, and sent it to him as a friendly joke. To my stupefaction he thanked me seriously and paid me five shillings. I was touched, and wrote him a serious verse for another picture. He took it as a joke in questionable taste, and my career as a versifier ended. Once I got a £5 job; but as it was not from a publisher or editor, but from a lawyer who wanted a medical essay – evidently for use as an advertisement for some patent medicine – I was unable to follow up this success. Total, £6 in nine years. And yet I have been called an upstart.

In a certain *World* article, republished in part in the preface to my play *Widowers' Houses*, William Archer has described his discovery of me in the British Museum Reading Room with Karl Marx's *Capital* on the table before me, and the orchestral score of Wagner's *Tristan und Isolde* on the folding desk.[12] This was in 1885 (I came to London in '76). By that time I had given up humiliating editors and publishers by exposing them to the stupidity of failing to see any merit in me. Archer, regarding this as mere inertia on my part (not without some reason), took my affairs in hand with such success that the *Pall Mall Gazette*, then edited by Stead, began to send me books to review;[13] and the appointment of art critic to the *World*, which Archer was for the moment doubling with his regular part of dramatic critic, was transferred to me.[14] I suddenly began to make money – nearly £100 a year after a while. Archer proposed collaboration in a drama which he had planned in a most workmanlike manner on the technical lines of 'the well made play' of Scribe and the French school.[15] I took it in hand and produced two acts so outrageously off the 'well made' lines that Archer at once ceased to wonder why I had not been a success. The play was abandoned for six or seven years, when I fished it out, added a third act to it, and had all the honours of a production by the Independent Theatre under J. T. Grein, a remarkable mixture of hooting and applause from the audience (upon which I retorted in a speech before the curtain), and quite a fortnight's press discussion of the play, and of Mr James Welch, the young actor who had made his reputation as Lickcheese, the slum rent collector. However, I anticipate. The question as to my ingress to literary activity is now answered. For about four years, I criticised every picture show in London, and reviewed heaps of books. In 1888 the *Star* was founded, and I joined the political staff. Here my impossibility broke out worse than ever. Not one of my articles seemed feasible. At last I proposed, as a compromise, that I should be allotted a column of the paper every week to fill with some non-political matter – say, music.[16] This column, which was signed 'Corno di Bassetto' (the Italian title of an old fashioned musical instrument called the basset horn) was a mixture of triviality, vulgarity, farce and tomfoolery with genuine criticism. Now that I had learnt to write and to criticise, my old knowledge of music, practically useless to me before, filled my hands with weapons. It happened that the most important paper in London, as an organ of musical criticism was the *World*, Edmund Yates having always recognised the journalistic value of the subject,[17] and kept a whole page at the disposal of the late Louis Engel, the best hated musical critic in Europe.[18] In 1891 or thereabouts Engel got into a scrape with one of his pupils, and had to leave the country. His post fell to Corno di Bassetto; and I wrote a page of the *World* on music every week, until, on Yates' death in 1894, I gave up this labour of Hercules (you have no conception of what musical criticism means, done as I did it) and was succeeded by Mr Robert Hichens, of *Green Carnation* fame.[19] As a critic I had now only one more critical continent to conquer – dramatic criticism. By this time I knew that what I wanted was the right editor – one with the qualities of Yates, and one or two of his faults as well, perhaps. At the beginning of 1895, I accepted the post of dramatic critic from Frank Harris, who had just revived the *Saturday Review*.[20] The drama being less of a special cult than music, my fame immediately increased with leaps and bounds. You now have the answer to question 4 as well as question 2. For nine years past I have, as Corno di Bassetto first and 'GBS' afterwards, written about 2000 words a week on music and the drama, including the Shaw philosophy, religion and politics. It was the magic formula 'GBS' that broke down the rigid tradition of anonymity on the *Saturday Review*. But for four or five years previously I had, for the *World*, and (for one season only) for *Truth*,[21] anonymously criticised all the picture exhibitions, whilst for the *PMG* [*Pall Mall Gazette*] I produced numbers of book reviews. My twenty years in London therefore pan out this way. A couple of years (1876–8) of casual activities, including the devilling for the musical critic (appallingly bad). Five years (1879–83) of absolutely unsuccessful novel writing at the rate of one great work per year, the titles being *Immaturity*, *The Irrational Knot*, *Love among the Artists*, *Cashel Byron's Profession* and *An Unsocial Socialist*. About five years (1885–9) of literary and pictorial criticism, printed and paid for. Nine years (1888–96) of musical and theatrical criticism as above. And behold me at last figuring as a brilliant beginner.

For full particulars of the fate of the novels, see a very amusing article of mine some years ago in the *Novel Review*, formerly *Tinsley's Magazine*.[22] I have since let *Cashel Byron* and *An Unsocial Socialist* go out of print.

3. *When and how did he become a vegetarian?*

I became a vegetarian in 1880 or 81. It was at that period that vegetarian restaurants began to crop up here and there, and to make vegetarianism practically possible for a man too poor to be specially catered for. My attention had been called to the subject, first by Shelley (I am an out-and-out Shelleyan), and later on by a lecturer. But of course the enormity of eating the scorched corpses of animals – cannibalism with its heroic dish omitted – becomes impossible the moment it becomes conscious instead of thoughtlessly habitual. I am also a teetotaller, my family having paid the Shaw debt to the distilling industry so munificently as to leave me no obligations in that direction. I flatly declare that a man fed on whiskey and dead bodies cannot do the finest work of which he is capable.

A propos of Shelley, an article of mine entitled 'Shaming the Devil about Shelley', in the *Albermarle Review* [*sic*] of the Shelley Centenary Year, is worth looking at.[23] It was at the Shelley Society's first big meeting that I made a speech, once much quoted, in which I announced myself as, like Shelley, 'a socialist, an atheist, and a vegetarian'.[24] Shaw-ism is, however, distinctly and fundamentally a religion.

4. *It has been stated that Shaw has tried his hand at every kind of criticism – musical, artistic and dramatic – with amazing results. Comment and explain.*

See answer to 2.

NOTES

1. 'The Religion of the Pianoforte' was published in the *Fortnightly Review* in February 1894.

2. Joseph Robinson (1816–98) was the founder of the Dublin Antient Concert Society and a professor at the Irish Academy of Music. He established the Dublin Musical Society in 1876.

3. Jean Duchesne's *Musée de peinture et de sculpture* was published in 16- and 17-volume editions between 1829 and 1834.

4. Henry G. Bohn published Mrs Jonathan Foster's translation of Vasari's *Lives of the Most Celebrated Painters, Sculptors and Architects* in five volumes of his cheap Standard Library in the early 1850s.

5. The four schools were: the Wesleyan Connexional School, private school at Glasthule, near Dalkey, the Central Model Boys' School in Marlborough Street and the Dublin English Scientific and Commercial Day School in Aungier Street.

6. Shaw became a junior clerk in the firm of Uniacke Townshend & Co. in November 1871. When the cashier absconded in February 1873, Shaw was given his job as stopgap, but he did it so well that he was confirmed in the position. However, an inexperienced nephew of Mr Townshend's was later appointed cashier, which helped Shaw decide to resign. He left on 31 March 1876.

7. Dwight L. Moody and Ira D. Sankey, American evangelists, conducted a mission in Dublin early in 1875. Shaw's letter, misleadingly summarised here, appeared in the London weekly *Public Opinion* on 3 April 1875, and can be found reprinted in the centenary biographies of St John Ervine and Archibald Henderson.

8. Shaw dealt with his early years in London at some length in the Preface to *Immaturity* (1930). He did in fact take commercial employment once more: between 14 November 1879 and 5 July 1880 he worked for the Edison Telephone Company, but did not re-apply for his position when the firm merged with its rival.

9. The essential design of the modern concert flute was worked out by Theobald Boehm (1794–1881), a German goldsmith who turned to flute playing and manufacturing. His developed instruments called for a change from the traditional fingering.

10. The music critic was Vandeleur Lee, who was clearly anxious to help Shaw, as he passed on the fees to him as well. Shaw wrote opera and concert notices for the *Hornet* from November 1876 until September 1877. The paper in fact survived until February 1880, and Lee did not die until November 1886.

11. The article, entitled 'Christian Names', was published by George Robert Sims (1847–1922) in his paper *One and All* on 11 October 1879 (see *Collected Letters 1874–1897*, p. 21).

12. William Archer (1856–1924), critic, playwright and translator of Ibsen, 'discovered' Shaw c. 1883 and become one of his closest and best loved friends. His article in the *World* of 14 December 1892 was occasioned by the first performance of *Widowers' Houses*. A later version of the discovery may be found below, pp. 87–8. Despite differences of temperament and outlook, and Archer's sometimes remarkable imperceptiveness about Shaw's qualities as a dramatist, the friendship lasted until Archer's death, though its intimacy declined.

13. William Thomas Stead (1849–1912), a brilliant and unconventional journalist, took over the *Pall Mall Gazette* from John Morley in 1883 and edited it until 1889. Shaw contributed over 100 book reviews in three and a half years, after Archer passed on a novel to him in May 1885.

14. For Archer's account of the transfer, see below, p. 88. Shaw acted as art critic on the *World* from February 1886 until December 1889.

15. Eugène Scribe (1791–1861) was a prolific and successful dramatist, with an exceptional talent for plot construction and an instinct for theatrical effect, but little else. As originator and exponent of 'the well made play' he was much admired by Archer. The eventual result of the abortive collaboration with Archer was Shaw's first play, *Widowers' Houses*: see below, pp. 120–1 and 122–3, for accounts by Archer and J. T. Grein of its development and first staging.

16. See below, pp. 88–90, for an equally misleading account of Shaw's translation to music critic by T. P. O'Connor, founding editor of the *Star*.

17. Edmund Yates (1831–94), novelist and journalist, founded the *World* in 1874 and remained editor-in-chief until his death. Shaw's music criticism appeared in it between May 1890 and August 1894. Again Archer seems to have secured him the position (see below, p. 88).

18. Shaw's poor opinion of Engel is evident in his 1887 review of Engel's *From Mozart to Mario* (reprinted in *Shaw's Music*, ed. Dan H. Laurence, 3 vols [London: Max Reinhardt, the Bodley Head, 1981], I, 481–4).

19. Robert Hichens (1864–1950) was the author of the anonymously published satire, *The Green Carnation* (1894).

20. For Harris's version of Shaw's appointment, see below, pp. 90–3.

21. Shaw resigned from *Truth* in May 1890, refusing to puff a painter favoured by the editor.

22. Shaw's article appeared in the February 1892 issue of the *Novel Review*.

23. The article appeared in the *Albemarle* in September 1892.

24. For accounts of Shaw's dramatic intervention at this meeting by two others present, see below, pp. 45–6.

'Who I Am, and What I Think'

From G. Bernard Shaw, 'Who I Am, and What I Think', *Candid Friend*, 11 May 1901. Extracts from a continuation in the following week's issue may be found below, pp. 95–6. The editor, Frank Harris, introduced the piece thus: 'I asked Mr Shaw to tell me of the formative influences of his life and career, and sent him, at his request, a series of questions, some of which he has answered.' Harris became closely acquainted with Shaw when he employed him as a dramatic critic on the *Saturday Review* from 1895 to 1898 (see below, p. 90), and it is not surprising to find him exploiting Shaw's reputation in the second and third issues of his new magazine. Revised and abridged versions of the *Candid Friend* interview were published in two later autobiographical works: *Shaw Gives Himself Away* (London: Gregynog Press, 1939) and *Sixteen Self Sketches* (London: Constable, 1949).

Won't you begin by telling me something of your parents and their influence on your life?

It is impossible to give you the Rougon-Macquart view of myself in less than twenty volumes.[1] Let me tell you a story of my father. When I was a child, he gave me my first dip in the sea in Killiney Bay. He prefaced it by a very serious exhortation on the importance of learning to swim, culminating in these words: 'When I was a boy of only fourteen, my knowledge of swimming enabled me to save your Uncle Algernon's life.' Then, seeing that I was deeply impressed, he stooped, and added confidentially in my ear – and, to tell you the truth, I never was so sorry for anything in my life afterwards.' He then plunged into the ocean, enjoyed a thoroughly refreshing swim, and chuckled all the way home. Now, only the other day, Mr Granville Barker,[2] in rehearsing the part of Napoleon in my play, *The Man of Destiny*, said to me that the principle of the whole play was anti-climax. Mr Henry Norman[3] once said of me that no man could butter a moral slide better than Shaw. That was before he became serious and went into Parliament. Now I protest that I do not aim at anti-climax; it occurs as naturally in my work as night follows day. But there is no doubt some connection between my father's chuckling and the observations of Granville Barker and Norman. My father was an ineffective, unsuccessful man, in theory a vehement teetotaller, but in practice often a furtive drinker. He might have been a weaker brother of Charles Lamb.[4] My mother you can interview for yourself if you want to know about her. But her musical activity was of the greatest importance in my education. I never learnt anything at school, a place where they put 'Cæsar' and 'Horace' into the hands of small boys and expected the result to be an elegant taste and knowledge of the world. I took refuge in total idleness at school, and picked up at home, quite unconsciously, a knowledge of that extraordinary literature of modern music, from Bach to Wagner, which has saved me from being at the smallest disadvantage in competition with men who only know the grammar and mispronunciation of the Greek and Latin poets and philosophers. For the rest, my parents went their own way and let me go mine. Thus the habit of freedom, which most Englishmen and Englishwomen of my class never acquire and never let their children acquire, came to me naturally.

When did you first feel inclined to write?

I never felt inclined to write, any more than I ever felt inclined to breathe. I felt inclined to draw: Michel Angelo was my boyish ideal. I felt inclined to be a wicked baritone in an opera when I grew out of my earlier impulse towards piracy and highway robbery. You see, as I couldn't draw, I was perfectly well aware that drawing was an exceptional gift. But it never occurred to me that my literary sense was exceptional. I gave the whole world credit for it. The fact is, there is nothing miraculous, nothing particularly interesting even, in a natural faculty to the man who has it. The amateur, the collector, the enthusiast in an art, is the man who lacks the faculty for producing it. The Venetian wants to be a soldier; the Gaucho wants to be a sailor; the fish wants to fly, and the bird to swim. No, I never wanted to write. I know now, of course, the value and the scarcity of the literary faculty (though I think it over-rated); but I still don't want it. You cannot want a thing and have it, too.

What form did your literary work first take?

I vaguely remember that when I was a small boy I concocted a short story and sent it to some boys' journal – something about a man with a gun attacking another man in the Glen of the Douns. The gun was the centre of interest to me. Some years ago, Arnolds, of Covent Garden, published a couple of really original Irish novels called *Misther O'Ryan* and *The Son of a Peasant*, by Edward McNulty.[5] McNulty was a school-fellow of mine for a short time. Then I drifted into an office in Dublin, and he drifted into the Newry branch of the Bank of Ireland. We had struck up one of those romantic friendships that occur between imaginative boys; and from the ages of fifteen to twenty we kept up a voluminous correspondence between Dublin and Newry, exchanging long letters by return of post.[6] That correspondence worked off the literary energy which usually produces early works. I believe my first appearance in print was on the occasion of the visit of the American evangelists, Moody and Sankey, to Dublin. Their arrival created a great sensation on this side of the Atlantic; and I went to hear them. I was wholly unmoved by their eloquence, and felt bound to inform the public that I was, on the whole, an Atheist. My letter was solemnly printed in *Public Opinion*, to the extreme horror of my numerous uncles. I perpetrated one more long correspondence, this time with an English lady whose fervidly imaginative novels would have made her known if I could have persuaded her to make her own name public, or at least to stick to the same pen name, instead of changing it for every book.[7] Virtually, my first works were the five novels I wrote from 1879 to 1883, which nobody would publish.[8] They got into print later on as pure padding for Socialist magazines, and are now raging in America, in unauthorised editions, as the latest fruits of my genius. I came to London in 1876; and between 1876 and 1879 I did a little devilling at musical criticism, and began a Passion Play in blank verse, with the mother of the hero represented as a termagant;[9] but I never carried these customary follies of young authors through; I was always, fortunately for me, a failure as a trifler. All my attempts at Art for Art's sake broke down; it was like hammering tenpenny nails into sheets of notepaper.

When did you begin to be interested in political questions? In what way did these affect your work?

Well, at the beginning of the eighties I happened to hear an address by Henry George at the Memorial Hall in Farringdon Street.[10] It flashed on me then for the first time that the 'conflict between Religion and Science' – you remember Draper's book?[11] – the overthrow of the Bible, the higher education of women, Mill on Liberty, and all the rest of the storm that raged round Darwin, Tyndall, Huxley, Spencer and the rest, on which I had brought myself up intellectually, was a mere middle-class business. Suppose it could have produced a nation of Matthew Arnolds and George Eliots! – you may well shudder. The importance of the economic basis dawned on me: I read Marx,[12] and was exactly in the mood for his reduction of all the conflicts to the conflict of classes for economic mastery, of all social forms to the economic forms of production and exchange. But the real secret of Marx's fascination was his appeal to an unnamed, unrecognised passion – a new passion – the passion of hatred in the more generous souls among the respectable and educated sections for the accursed middle-class institutions that had starved, thwarted, misled and corrupted them from their cradles. Marx's *Capital* is not a treatise on Socialism; it is a jeremiad against the bourgeoisie, supported by such a mass of evidence and such a relentless Jewish genius for denunciation as had never been brought to bear before. It was supposed to be written for the working classes; but the working man respects the bourgeoisie, and wants to be a bourgeois; Marx never got hold of him for a moment. It was the revolting sons of the bourgeoisie itself – Lassalle, Marx, Liebknecht, Morris, Hyndman, Bax,[13] all, like myself, bourgeois crossed with squirearchy – that painted the flag red. Bakunin and Kropotkin,[14] of the military and noble caste (like Napoleon), were our extreme left. The middle and upper classes are the revolutionary element in society; the proletariat is the Conservative element, as Disraeli well knew, Hyndman and his Marxists, Bakunin and his Anarchists, would not accept this situation; they persisted in believing that the proletariat was an irresistible mass of unawakened Felix Pyats and Ouidas.[15] I did accept the situation, helped, perhaps, by my inherited instinct for anti-climax. I threw Hyndman over, and got to work with Sidney Webb[16] and the rest to place Socialism on a respectable bourgeois footing; hence Fabianism. Burns[17] did the same thing in Battersea by organising the working classes there on a genuine self-respecting working-class basis, instead of on the old romantic middle-class assumptions. Hyndman wasted years in vain denunciations of the Fabian Society and of Burns; and though facts became too strong for him at last, he is still at heart the revolted bourgeois. So am I, for the matter of that; you can see it in every line of my plays. So is Ibsen;

so is Tolstoy; so is Sudermann; so is Hauptmann[18]; so are you, my CANDID FRIEND (else you would be 'The Hypocrite'); so are all the writers of the day whose passion is political and sociological. And that is the answer to your question as to how my politics and economics affect my work. What is a modern problem play but a clinical lecture on society; and how can one lecture like a master unless one knows the economic anatomy of society? Besides, at their simplest, politics save you from becoming a literary man. Feeding a man on books exclusively is like feeding a lap-dog on gin; both books and gin are products of distillation, and their effect on the organism is much the same.

To what do you owe your marvellous gift for public speaking?

My marvellous gift for public speaking is only part of the GBS legend. I am no orator, and I have neither memory enough nor presence of mind enough to be a really good debater, though I often seem to be one when I am on ground that is familiar to me and new to my opponents. I learnt to speak as men learn to skate or to cycle – by doggedly making a fool of myself until I got used to it. Then I practised it in the open air – at the street corner, in the market square, in the park – the best school. I am comparatively out of practice now, but I talked a good deal to audiences all through the eighties, and for some years afterwards. I should be a really remarkable orator after all that practice if I had the genius of the born orator. As it is, I am simply the sort of public speaker anybody can become by going through the same mill. I don't mean that he will have the same things to say, or that he will put them in the same words, for naturally I don't leave my ideas or my vocabulary behind when I mount the tub; but I *do* mean that he will say what he has to say as movingly as I say what I have to say – and more, if he is anything of a real orator. Of course, as an Irishman, I have some fluency, and can manage a bit of rhetoric and a bit of humour on occasion; and that goes a long way in England. But 'marvellous gift' is all my eye.

What was your first real success? Tell me how you felt about it. Did you ever despair of succeeding?

Never had any. Success in that sense, is a thing that comes to you, and takes your breath away. What came to me was invariably failure. By the time I wore it down I knew too much to care about either failure or success. Life is like a battle; you have to fire a thousand bullets to hit one man. I was too busy firing to bother about the scoring. As to whether I ever despaired, you will find somewhere in my works this line: 'He who has never hoped can never despair.'[19] I am not a fluctuator.

Where did you live in your developing period, and how? By journalism?

My parents pulled me through the years in which I earned nothing. My mother came to London, and became a professional musician late in life to keep things together. It was a frightful squeeze at times; but I never went back to the office work I did from fifteen to twenty, and finally I got journalistic work enough to fill the larder. As to my developing period, I hope it's not over. At all events leave me the illusion that it isn't.

NOTES

1. *Les Rougon-Macquart* is a cycle of twenty novels by Emile Zola, published between 1871 and 1893 and sub-titled 'Histoire naturelle et sociale d'une famille sous le second Empire'. It was intended as a study of the transmission of family characteristics (mainly vicious), recurring and developing through five generations of the Rougon-Macquarts.

2. Harley Granville Barker (1877–1946), who was to play a crucial role in establishing Shaw on the London stage, had first met him in 1900 and acted in Stage Society productions of *Candida* and *Captain Brassbound's Conversion* before the end of the year. *The Man of Destiny* was produced at the Comedy Theatre on 29 March 1901.

3. Henry Norman (1858–1939) was for several years a member of the editorial staff of the *Pall Mall Gazette* and afterwards of the *Daily Chronicle*. He was Liberal MP for South Wolverhampton from 1900 to 1910.

4. In this comparison Shaw perhaps had in mind Lamb's genteel poverty, his facetious humour and his fondness for alcohol.

5. Published respectively in 1894 and 1897.

6. None of this early correspondence has survived. See *Collected Letters 1874–1897*, p. 19.

7. Elinor L. Huddart published novels under pseudonyms and anonymously. A collection of her letters to Shaw is held in the Department of Manuscripts, British Library (MS Add. 50535–37).

8. The first of the novels to appear in print was *An Unsocial Socialist*, published serially in the periodical *To-Day* in 1884. *Cashel Byron's Profession* was also published serially in *To-Day* in 1885–6. *The Irrational Knot* and *Love Among the Artists* were published serially in Mrs Annie Besant's magazine, *Our Corner*, in 1885–7 and 1887–8 respectively. *Immaturity*, written in 1879, remained unpublished until 1930. Numerous editions of the novels were published in New York and Chicago around the turn of the century.

9. *Passion Play*, otherwise entitled *Household of Joseph*, was written in 1876. The MS is held in the British Library (MS Add. 50593).

10. Henry George (1839–97), American economist, was the author of several works on economics and politics, of which *Progress and Poverty* (1879) is the best known. Shaw heard him speak on Land Nationalisation and Single Tax at the Memorial Hall in Farringdon Street on 5 September 1882.

11. John William Draper (1811–82), chemist, was the author of a work entitled *History of the Conflict between Science and Religion*, which went through numerous editions after its first publication in 1874.

12. Shaw began reading Marx's *Das Kapital* in the French translation of Gabriel Deville soon after it was published in 1883.

13. Ferdinand Lassalle (1825–64) and Wilhelm Liebknecht (1826–1900) were prominent figures in the development of socialism in Europe. Henry Mayers Hyndman (1842–1921) was a disciple of Marx and leader of the Social Democratic Federation. His Marxian theories were frequently criticised by Shaw (see below, pp. 48–52). William Morris (1834–96), the designer and poet, and E. Belfort Bax (1854–1926), Shaw's predecessor as music critic on *The Star*, were co-founders of the Socialist League.

14. Mikhail Aleksandrovich Bakunin (1814–76) and Pyotr Alekseyevich Kropotkin (1842–1921) were prominent theoreticians of anarchism.

15. Félix Pyat (1810–89), radical journalist and member of the Paris Commune of 1871, was distrusted by other revolutionaries because of his inherited fortune and aristocratic bearing. Ouida was the pseudonym of Marie-Louise de la Ramée (1839–1908). She wrote popular novels of fashionable life, which often reflect a spirit of rebellion against conventional morality.

16. Sidney James Webb, later Baron Passfield (1859–1947), lawyer, political economist, social reformer and historian, was one of the early and most influential members of the Fabian Society, which he joined on 1 May 1885, some eight months after Shaw. Their lifelong friendship had begun when they met at the Zetetical Society in October 1880.

17. John Elliot Burns (1858–1943) became one of Battersea's first representatives on the London County Council in 1889 and was elected MP for Battersea in 1891. He campaigned strongly for the Social Democratic Federation in the 1880s, but his later leanings towards the Liberals, and his advocacy of state socialism within the existing political framework, alienated him from the Hyndmanites. He had notable success in bringing less skilled workers into the Labour movement.

18. Hermann Sudermann (1857–1928), German novelist and playwright; Gerhart Hauptmann (1862–1946), Silesian-born German playwright.

19. Caesar's answer to Apollodorus's question, 'Does Caesar despair?' (*Caesar and Cleopatra*, Act IV).

Part 2
Fabian Socialist and Platform Speaker

INTRODUCTION TO PART 2

Judging from the many accounts of his platform performances, Shaw's celebrity as a lecturer and debater was fully deserved. Contemporaries remember him as a cool, audacious, eloquent and witty speaker, with exceptional talents for lucid exposition and lively illustration. In debate he was quick-witted, disarmingly courteous and powerfully persuasive. His mastery of the art of public speaking, however, was not easily acquired. His first attempts in the early 1880s were bedevilled by acute nervousness and a tendency to forget his best points in the midst of a speech. The perseverance with which he laboured to overcome these problems – driven by what seems a quite compulsive desire to succeed – could have served as a model for contemporary guides to self-improvement:

> I persevered doggedly. I haunted all the meetings in London where debates followed lectures. I spoke in the streets, in the parks, at demonstrations, anywhere and everywhere possible. In short, I infested public meetings like an officer afflicted with cowardice, who takes every opportunity of going under fire to get over it and learn his business.[1]

Shaw first gained practice in public speaking at meetings of a society called the Zetetical, founded in 1878 to 'furnish opportunities for the unrestricted discussion of Social, Political and Philosophical subjects'. Encouraged by James Lecky, a friend with interests in music and phonetics, Shaw joined the Zetetical Society in October 1880, and there met shortly afterwards one whom he was later to describe as 'the ablest man in England: Sidney Webb'.[2] During the 1880s Shaw was also a member of two other debating and discussion societies, the Dialectical, founded in the wake of J. S. Mill's *On Liberty* (1859), and the Bedford, founded by the Rev. Stopford A. Brooke (1832–1916), Irish man of letters, Fabian socialist and Unitarian minister at Bedford Chapel, Bloomsbury. In addition, he was a prominent member of three literary societies, the Browning, the New Shakespeare and the Shelley Societies, all founded by F. J. Furnivall (1825–1910), the early proponent and editor of the *Oxford English Dictionary*, and founder and director of the Early English Text, Chaucer and Ballad Societies.

Shaw's first public lecture on socialist themes, entitled 'Thieves', was delivered at the Invicta Working Men's Club, Woolwich on 4 May 1884.[3] From then until a breakdown in health followed by his marriage in 1898, public lecturing, at venues ranging from street corner to drawing room, was a normal part of Shaw's weekly activities. He continued to accept invitations to lecture and debate after his marriage, until his final retirement from public performances in 1941.

Shaw attended some of the early meetings of H. M. Hyndman's Marxist Social Democratic Federation, and once applied for membership. But he withdrew his application on discovery of the Fabian Society (founded in 1883–4) to which he was elected on 5 September 1884. The ideological differences between the essentially middle-class Fabian Society, with its gradualist approach to social and political change, and the more proletarian, revolutionary and anarchist SDF, widened over the years and were the cause of frequent clashes.

Shaw declined several offers of nomination for parliamentary candidature, but served in local government as a St Pancras vestryman and borough councillor from 1897 to 1903, and stood unsuccessfully for the London County Council in 1904.

NOTES

1. Bernard Shaw, *Sixteen Self Sketches* (London: Constable, 1949) pp. 57–8.
2. Ibid., p. 65.
3. See *Collected Letters 1874–1897*, pp. 81–8.

'Kindred Particles'

SYDNEY OLIVIER

From a letter by Lord Olivier to Archibald Henderson, 8 June 1931, in Henderson, *Bernard Shaw, Playboy and Prophet* (London and New York: D. Appleton, 1932) pp. 144–5. Sydney Haldane Olivier, later Baron Olivier (1859–1943) entered the Colonial Office after graduation from Oxford, topping the entry competition (Sidney Webb was second). He subsequently held many important public service positions. He joined the Fabian Society with Webb on 1 May 1885, and was secretary from 1886 until 1890. Shaw wrote of him: 'Olivier was an extraordinarily attractive figure, and in my experience unique; for I have never known anyone like him mentally or physically: he was distinguished enough to be unclassable. He was handsome and strongly sexed, looking like a Spanish grandee in any sort of clothes, however unconventional' ('Some Impressions', a Preface to *Sydney Olivier: Letters and Selected Writings,* ed. Margaret Olivier [London: George Allen & Unwin, 1948] p. 9).

I think it must have been in the autumn of 1883 that I first met Shaw. . . . The only assortment of young middle-class men who were at that time thinking intelligently, in England, about social and economic conditions, gravitated into close contact with one another, like kindred particles in a fluid, and consolidated into an association out of whose propaganda, later, originated the British Parliamentary Socialist Labour Party. Starting myself from the viewpoint of John Stuart Mill and Auguste Comte I became in 1882 friends with H. H. Champion,[1] with whom I was associated in founding the Land Reform Union,[2] specially inspired by Henry George's *Progress and Poverty.* That society brought George to England subsequently for a lecturing tour.

Sidney Webb was a colleague and friend of mine in the Colonial Office: at that time an individualist Radical. I remember H. H. Champion, at a committee meeting of the Land Reform Union, speaking to us of an amazing chap he had met (I think at a meeting of the Zetetical Society, a sceptical association of which Sidney Webb was at that time a member), whom we must, he said, get hold of. This man was a Socialist (we were then publishing the monthly *Christian Socialist* – with very little intelligent Socialism in it) and appeared to combine all the appropriate eccentricities of a conscientious intellectual revolutionary: Atheism, vegetarianism, Jaegerism[3] and malnutrition – having a dead-white complexion and orange patches of whisker about his cheek and chin (a face, as Champion described it, 'like an unskilfully poached egg'), but being extraordinarily witty and entertaining. Then I heard of this flaming phœnix from Webb to the like effect.

Thomas Davidson came to England, and at a meeting of Champion's house exhorted us to espouse the New Life, and to emigrate to Southern California (the then projected colony of Topolobampo was suggested) to found a new Colony to recreate the world.[4] But we didn't: we formed the Fabian Society instead: and it was in the early days of that Society that I came to know Shaw well. He, Sidney Webb and I used to walk once a fortnight, evenings, all the way up to Hampstead Heath together and back again, for meetings of a discussion club, the Hampstead Historic Club,[5] in which we and our friends overhauled the economic evolution of Europe and all its gospels of Social Reform, from Thomas More to Karl Marx, and practically elaborated the Fabian formulation of Socialism which took shape later in the Fabian Essays of 1889.

Needless to say we delighted in Shaw's society – his talk was a continual entertainment; and he regarded it, we tolerantly considered, as his duty to talk wittily, if only for practice. And the transparent generosity and liberality of his character had an irresistible charm. But Webb and I were university graduates, I from Oxford, and we often judged Shaw's education and his appreciation of academically and socially established humanities to be sadly defective. . . . On the face of his conversation I thought his apprehension and sympathies in regard to a good deal of the springs of human conduct perversely shallow and limited, and his controversial arguments often cheap and uncritical: an attitude of priggish superiority which he no doubt fully appreciated, and at which he poked fun (in the character of Cokane) in his first play, *Widowers' Houses*. But two things impressed me to a contrary estimation of his critical make up: the extraordinary ability and acuteness, within their scope, of his early novels and his understanding and extensive knowledge of music, an art of which I was feebly and amateurishly appreciative, but sufficiently to make me envy his critical mastership.

NOTES

1. Henry Hyde Champion (1859–1928) had resigned his army commission to take up socialist agitation. He was the first Hon. Secretary of the SDF, proprietor of the Modern Press, editor of *To-Day*, and a successful leader of strike action in the London docks in 1889. In 1893 he migrated to Australia, where he wrote leaders for the Melbourne *Age* and acted as Shaw's literary agent.

2. The Land Reform Union, set up in April 1883 with the *Christian Socialist* as its journal, was a Georgeite splinter from the Land Nationalisation Society formed a year earlier. In August 1883 Shaw was trying to get Sidney Webb to join it.

3. Shaw was an enthusiastic supporter of the theories of Dr Gustav Jaeger (1832–1917), a health culturist who advocated woollen clothes and bedding.

4. Thomas Davidson (1840–1900), Scottish-born philosopher and wandering scholar, spent many years of his life in North America. At meetings held in London in 1882–3 he inspired the founding of a society called the Fellowship of the New Life, which in January 1884 gave birth to the Fabian Society, with a more practical and outward-looking programme.

5. The first meetings of the Hampstead Historic Society were held in the autumn of 1884 at Wyldes Farm, Hampstead, the consciously 'rural' home of Charlotte Wilson and her stockbroker husband, Arthur. Mrs Wilson (1854–1944) was one of the first women students at Cambridge, an anarchist and a prominent early Fabian. Shaw missed the first meeting on *Das Kapital* and Webb, who had attended it, urged him and Olivier to come to the second on 12 November.

An Evening in Belsize Square

C. H. HERFORD and E. I. FRIPP

From C. H. Herford, *Philip Henry Wicksteed: His Life and Work* (London and Toronto: J. M. Dent, 1931) pp. 207–9. For several years Shaw and Webb were members of the 'Economic Circle'. Meetings had begun early in 1884 and from October that year took place at the Belsize Square home of Henry R. Beeton, a London stockbroker. Another member was Edgar Innes Fripp, then a student at Manchester New College, London, later a Unitarian minister and Shakespearean scholar. According to Herford (p. 206), Fripp was the only one to take careful notes at the time. The meetings were led by the Rev. Philip Wicksteed (1844–1927), lecturer, political economist, Ibsen pioneer and Dante scholar, and were particularly concerned with the ideas of the economist William Stanley Jevons (1835–82). Wicksteed had published a critical review of *Das Kapital* in the October 1884 issue of *To-Day*; Shaw defended Marx the following January and Wicksteed's rejoinder appeared in the April issue. So the likely date of the evening described below is April 1885 or shortly afterwards. Wicksteed and Shaw continued to have a warm regard for each other in later years, and when Shaw brought out his *Common Sense of Municipal Trading* in 1904 he sent Wicksteed a copy inscribed 'To my father in economics'.

The transfer of the meetings to Mr Beeton's house nearly coincided in time with the appearance of Wicksteed's notable review of Marx, already noticed. This arrested the attention, as we know, and challenged the criticism, of the Fabian Socialists, and his antagonist in that controversy, Mr Bernard Shaw, presented himself, one evening, at the debate, and set upon it, as it was his way to do, the indelible stamp of his impish wit. He was led there, he has told the present writer, by a desire to understand the drift of Wicksteed's 'last word in their debate'. The scene deserved a record which, thanks to Mr Fripp, it may here receive. The problem under discussion that evening was the element of choice in value, exchange, and purchase, and was carried on, as usual, with the help of the chalk and the blackboard. 'I remember Mr Shaw's advent somewhat vividly,' writes Mr Fripp. 'He stood up with red hair and beard, in a grey suit (most of the company being in evening dress), and chaffed both Wicksteed and the rest of us with an audacious wit, sometimes too pointed to be entirely relished. "You fellows," he declared, "have been talking a great deal about 'choice'. You would know better what choice is, if, like me, you had every night to 'choose' between a bit of fire and a bit of supper before you went to bed." And as to "curves", the "curves of supply and demand" had much less to do with a man's control of the market, than the curves of his profile. He himself had earned only £100 in the previous twelve months, whereas, with our host's resolute curve of the chin, he would be making £10,000 a year. And he proceeded to illustrate his point, amid the embarrassed laughter of the company, by drawing their own profiles in lively caricature on the blackboard.'

These, however, were only preliminary flourishes of the cap and bells; and they did not prevent Wicksteed, then or later, from doing justice to the serious thinking and purpose which Mr Shaw's coruscations have often served rather to conceal than to illuminate. At these meetings, in any case, where economists so distinguished as Foxwell, Graham Wallas[1] and others were present, the two *coryphæi* of the discussion were Wicksteed and Shaw; and Mr Fripp declares that their encounters were the most brilliant he has ever heard.

NOTE

1. Herbert Somerton Foxwell (1849–1936) became Professor of Political Economy at University College, London, in 1891. Graham Wallas (1858–1932) was a student at Oxford with Sydney Olivier and worked as a schoolmaster and university extension lecturer before joining the staff of the London School of Economics in 1895. He became a member of the Fabian Society in 1886 and together with Webb, Shaw and Olivier formed a group which determined its early course.

Marx in the Original

SIDNEY WEBB

From *The Letters of Sidney and Beatrice Webb*, ed. Norman MacKenzie, 3 vols (Cambridge: Cambridge University Press, 1978) I, 93. On 17 August 1885 Webb wrote to Graham Wallas proposing to join him for a holiday in Germany, where Wallas was living to learn the language.

I have begun to teach German to G. B. Shaw, the embryo-novelist. He knows 'and' and 'the' only. We began Marx, *Kapital*, vol. 2 – not the easiest of books. We read two pages in two hours, accompanying each word with a philological dissertation. It was really very *interessant* to me.

'A Good Shelleyan': I

T. J. WISE

From Doris Arthur Jones, *The Life and Letters of Henry Arthur Jones* (London: Victor Gollancz, 1930) p. 221. Shaw's provocative declaration that he was 'like Shelley, a Socialist, Atheist and Vegetarian' (see *Sixteen Self Sketches* [London: Constable, 1949] p. 58) was made at the first regular meeting of the Shelley Society on 14 April 1886. In his own recollection Shaw claimed that two of 'the pious old ladies' whose subscriptions kept Furnivall's literary societies going were so scandalised by his speech that they 'resigned on the spot' ('Notes by George Bernard Shaw', Appendix I in Wilfred Partington, *Thomas J. Wise in the Original Cloth* [London: Robert Hale, 1946] pp. 315–16). Henry Arthur Jones (1851–1929) was one of the leading British playwrights of the Victorian and Edwardian periods. He had, in fact, met Shaw at William Archer's house on 4 May 1885. Shaw wrote highly respectful, if often incisively critical, reviews of Jones's plays in the *Saturday Review*, and the friendship between the two survived frequent quarrels before a serious rift over Shaw's attitude towards the First World War (see below, p. 231). Thomas James Wise (1859–1937) was a celebrated bibliographer and Honorary Fellow of Worcester College, Oxford, later exposed as a forger, on a grand scale, of nineteenth-century pamphlets.

T. J. Wise told me a story of the first occasion on which HAJ set eyes on GBS. It was in 1885, at a meeting of the Shelley Society in the Botanical Theatre at University College, Gower Street. My father and Mr Wise were sitting next to one another on the platform, and, after the official speeches had been made, members of the audience were invited to speak. A tall lank figure in grey flannels, with a flaming head and beard, shot up from the middle of the hall and said, 'Ladies and gentlemen, I am an atheist (pause), a vegetarian (pause) and a Socialist (pause)' – Henry Arthur nudged Mr Wise and said, 'Three damned good reasons why he ought to be chucked out.'

'A Good Shelleyan': II

PHILIP MARSTON

From Charles Churchill Osborne, *Philip Bourke Marston* (London: The Times Book Club, 1926) pp. 26–7. Marston (1850–87) was a poet blinded by an accident in childhood. Osborne came to know him late in his life, and compiled a brief memoir. Marston's account of the Shelley Society meeting is contained in a letter to Osborne on 17 April 1886.

On Tuesday, we all went to the Shelley Society and heard Buxton Forman[1] expound *Queen Mab*, and tell us how it was written, and that kind of thing. I do think these societies are such nonsense. As for paying a guinea to belong to one, No thank you. By-the-bye Buxton Forman cannot speak at all, and that made it difficult for one to keep one's eyes open; and as for *Queen Mab*, I wonder if you agree with me in thinking that the less people talk about it the better. I shall never forget the wave of overwhelming disappointment which came against me when I first read it, and took it to be representative of the Shelley of whom I had heard so much. But I went on and need hardly say was rewarded. Then, a man called Bernard Shaw, who frankly declared himself at the start an atheist and a socialist, a man who I know slightly and much hate, an Irishman who speaks with a strong accent, arose in his glory and said that he regarded *Queen Mab* as a much greater work than the *Cenci*.[2] I wanted to get up and murder him, and could not even hiss. I think I am not wrong in saying that a man who asserts that is either a fool or a buffoon. Then, Aveling[3] addressed us, and we were all very glad when it was over. If the other people who were present at the Shelley Society were as well content afterwards as I and a friend were eating tripe and onions I am glad. It needed something pretty strong to take the taste of Shaw out of one's mouth.

NOTES

1. Harry Buxton Forman (1842–1917), civil servant, editor and biographer of Shelley and author of several other works on nineteenth-century poets and poetry.
2. The Shelley Society gave the first stage performance of *The Cenci* privately the following month (7 May) at the Grand Theatre, Islington. Shaw acted as press agent.
3. Edward Bibbins Aveling (1851–98), translator of *Das Kapital* and common-law husband of Marx's daughter, Eleanor.

Out of doors Orator

D. J. O'DONOGHUE

From D. J. O'Donoghue, 'George Bernard Shaw: some Recollections', *Irish Independent*, 17 February 1908. David J. O'Donoghue (1866–1917), journalist, biographer and editor, was the author of numerous works on nineteenth-century Irish subjects. His collection *The Humour of Ireland* (1894) contained extracts from Shaw's music criticism written under the name of 'Corno di Bassetto'.

It is just twenty-two years ago that I first laid eyes on the brilliant writer who now dominates the English theatrical world. I saw a small group of people collected round a speaker – evidently a Socialist – and approached to listen. I heard the Chairman call upon 'Comrade' Bernard Shaw for an address, and immediately the gaunt figure of the man whose name was becoming familiar as a Fabian and a novelist and critic ascended the platform. Imagine a very tall man, in a hideous snuff-coloured suit, with flaxen, almost golden hair, a flaming red beard, and a peculiarly sardonic expression, an ivory-like complexion contrasting badly with the suit and the hair, and you have a fairly correct picture of the perplexing personality whose name is now a household word with all who are interested in literature and drama.

He spoke for a full hour, and having heard a good many out-of-doors orators, I was struck with his absolute originality and curious refinement of speech. He then possessed a good deal of the 'Rathmines accent',[1] which he has never entirely lost, and his speech was a remarkably witty performance, mainly directed against certain Liberal politicians.

As always, he was careful to explain that he was an Irishman, trying to make an impression upon the thick wits of John Bull with only indifferent success. The crowd, which had swelled considerably, were agape with the audacity of the speaker, and interrupted barely at all. The cool assumption of the orator that the English were naturally stupid and inferior, and were, therefore, walked upon without protest by every exploiter, political and commercial, quite silenced the audience. The Socialists present – about six altogether – loudly applauded. At the end one or two listeners questioned Shaw, who was even more insolent and amusing than in his address. In repartee he has been always at his best, and those who went to hear him always waited till the end, sure of 'a good time' if there were any opposition. . . .

After this I frequently went to hear Shaw. His meetings were mostly in the open air, for the Socialists were too poor to hire halls, and Hyde Park, or Clapham Common, or some other well-known open space was usually the place where, Sunday after Sunday, the inimitable 'GBS' was likely to be heard.

NOTE

1. Rathmines, originally a village south of Dublin, was absorbed into the city in the early nineteenth century and became a fashionable area. See also below, p. 337.

Shaw versus Marx and Hyndman

DAN RIDER

From Dan Rider, *Adventures with Bernard Shaw* (London: Morley & Mitchell Kennerley Junior, [1929]) pp. 15–20. Dan Rider, a bookseller, was a member of the Bermondsey Branch of the SDF and often called at the office of the Central Branch in the Strand – the scene of the first part of his recollection. The incidents are probably to be assigned to the second half of the 1880s, when Shaw's work at the Hampstead Historic Society and the Economic Circle had made him critical of Marx, and when his controversies with Hyndman in print were most vigorous.

Without naming his source, Hesketh Pearson included a summary of this part of Rider's book in *GBS: A Postscript* (London: Collins, 1951) pp. 40–2. Some doubt is cast on the account of Hyndman's behaviour at the debate by one of Shaw's comments on the summary: 'All this is absurdly wrong. Hyndman was a man of considerable personal distinction, a public school and university man, quite incapable of behaving himself in the way you represent.' Shaw's other comments to Pearson (ibid., pp. 42–3) tend to bear out the substance of Rider's recollections, however.

Several times had I noticed a tall thin young fellow in the room with a bicycle which he had carried up the stairs. He was very fair and rather unkempt with a straggling and unusually poor crop of ginger whiskers. He had a slouch hat and a well-worn Norfolk suit of light-brown. I rather pitied him. He looked as though he were having a bad time and couldn't afford a shave. I summed him up as an insurance canvasser, as he always had a small notebook sticking out of his pocket. But as soon as he joined the talking group of older men he livened them up like a catfish in a tank of cod. There was no doubt that he could give and take, and get in a lot of common sense between whiles. I was not curious. I didn't ask his name. Somehow I didn't care as much for these fine talking Socialists as I did for my friends the navvies and the bricklayers' labourers. Yet I felt attracted towards this man, who seemed a bit of an outsider. He had a sense of humour and a witty and biting tongue, and he hugely enjoyed using it.

One lunch hour, several of us were seated round the smoky little fire, feeling depressed by the weather, which was cold and damp and foggy; and gradually becoming more depressed in listening to Herbert Burrows holding forth on theosophy, which he had just discovered.[1] Burrows was one of the best, and we were all very fond of him, but when he got going on theosophy he was more foggy than the weather outside. Suddenly the door burst open and there appeared my insurance canvasser looking fed up to the eyes with things. Nobody took any notice of him, nor even made way so that he could come into the fireside circle. From the chimney corner where I was sitting I watched him closely. After a few minutes he started to tackle Burrows, turning and twisting his arguments and assertions into the most fantastic fooleries, and before long he had got them all shouting at him, whilst he remained as cool as a cucumber. When he saw that the temperature had nearly reached boiling point he turned on his heels and left us as abruptly as he came.

Immediately there was a lull in the storm, and in a meek little voice I broke the silence by timidly inquiring who the man was?

'Why, that's Shaw! George Bernard Shaw! You don't mean to say you don't know him! He's the biggest bally fool that God ever made. He can't think straight for two minutes on end. Why, he even thinks he knows more than Karl Marx! Just think of it! He says Marx is wrong! That shows you what he is. He's mad. He's looney . . . fair dotty . . . right up the pole. Take no notice of him. He's always like that.'

In this way was I overwhelmed by the comrades, whilst Burrows was quietly nursing his wounds.

'You will forgive me for saying so,' I replied, coming out of my shell, 'but I like that man. He has more life and go in him, and more wit and humour than anyone I have yet met in the Socialist movement. Couldn't you see that he was pulling your leg?'

'That's the trouble,' they rejoined. 'He isn't serious. He's always acting the giddy goat. He's a dangerous man.'

'I am sorry, gentlemen,' said I, as I rose to go, 'but I must differ from you. It is you who are too serious. Your lack of humour will kill this movement. Mark my words, that man will go far. Dangerous indeed! Isn't that the quality we need when we are out fighting?'

It was part of my duties to arrange the lectures for the branch on Sunday evenings, and when the next list of lectures was being prepared I saw to it that Shaw was included in our invitations.

The evening came round. I did not expect a big meeting as Shaw was not considered to be anything in particular, and to make matters worse the weather was as bad as it could be, rain coming down all day in sheets. Our meeting-hall was not of the most attractive, being a converted coffee-shop in the midst of the then slum area of Bermondsey Square. Punctually, however, to the minute, Bernard Shaw arrived. The audience, including myself, numbered four. Shaw was not at all perturbed. He walked up to the raised platform and took a seat at the speaker's table and quietly went over his notes. It was perishing cold, so we gathered round the stove in the middle of the room and smoked our pipes to the accompaniment of the smoke that puffed out of the stove in gusts, and gradually filled the room. First one half-drowned comrade came in and joined us; then another, until after half an hour we mustered eight good men and true.

Shaw then suggested we might make a start, so the chairman opened the meeting and Shaw began his address. He spoke with great ease and fluency. His sentences were well constructed and telling, and I was surprised and (to tell the truth) rather disappointed to find he did not play the buffoon. He applied himself seriously and logically to destroying the theory of Karl Marx. We all sat deep in thought, cuddling up to the stove and puffing away at our pipes. As the ventilation of the room was as defective as the stove pipe, the air became misty and we all of us got more or less drowsy. Still Shaw kept on pumping it out, and laying into Marx as hard as he could. The chairman kept on nodding and nodding until at last his head came to rest in his hands upon the table, and he fell into a sweet slumber soothed by the voice of the lecturer. Suddenly Shaw ceased speaking and resumed his seat: the lecture was over. Missing the sound of the voice beside him, the chairman woke with a start, and jumping to his feet and rubbing his eyes he gave off the chairman's conventional speech about everybody having enjoyed a most intellectual evening. He then asked for questions. The atmospheric conditions had so overcome us that we could not have asked a question to save our lives. Whereupon the chairman wound up the meeting with the usual florid vote of thanks, assuring the lecturer that he had given us a great intellectual treat and that all present had agreed with every word he had said. . . .

I had almost forgotten this episode when I saw a debate announced to take place at the Central Branch one Sunday evening between H. M. Hyndman and George Bernard Shaw upon 'Marx's *Das Kapital*'.

This was a night not to be missed. Hyndman was a dear old boy, but in many ways quite impossible. His creed might have been 'Marx is the only God, and Hyndman is his only prophet'. There were all the elements for a battle royal, and in that we were not disappointed. Shaw took the floor first, and led off quietly with his arguments well marshalled, and bit by bit unmercifully picked the great Marxian idol to pieces. Then Hyndman took his turn and tried to gather up the pieces and stick them together again. Upon the second round being called, Shaw sprang into the arena with great spirit. Up to now there had been only sparring, each opponent measuring the reach of the other, but now Shaw began forcing the pace and hitting hard, with a brilliant display of upper-cuts. He was feeling very good when he came out with the triumphant declaration 'Marx is as dead as mutton. I, Bernard Shaw, have killed him'. He then narrated how some months before in that very hall he had thrown out a challenge that he would convert all the Social Democratic branches to his views on the Marxian gospel. And he went on to tell how he had kept his word, and had lectured upon this subject at all their branches, and never met with any opposition: his criticism of Marx, in fact, was so much the accepted opinion of all thinking men, as these Social Democrats were, that at one meeting, actually at the most important of their branches, the chairman was so bored at the common place nature of his arguments that, failing to find anything to disagree with, he went to sleep; and the audience passed him [Shaw] a unanimous vote of thanks for having given them an intellectual treat; and an intellectual treat was the clear expression of a man's own belief.

This was more than Hyndman could endure. Jumping to his feet, and stroking his flowing beard, and shooting out his cuffs, and looking for all the world like Moses when he saw the Jews worshipping the Golden Calf, he shouted out, 'That's a lie, and you know it. We are debating a serious matter, and you refuse to treat it seriously. I appeal to the meeting against such tomfoolery.'

'But it is the truth,' said Shaw with suppressed laughter, standing calmly amid the excitement with folded arms.

'It's a lie! It's a lie! I tell you it's a lie!' shouted Hyndman, now beside himself with rage.

'Withdraw! Withdraw!' howled the meeting at Shaw, who stood unmoved.

At that moment I butted in, but I could not make myself heard above the din. So mounting on a chair, I shouted out, 'What Shaw says is true. I was at the meeting he speaks of, and the chairman did go to sleep, and everybody did agree with him.'

Of course I was pulled down and told to shut up. But I went home that night feeling very pleased with myself. It was great fun. Nobody believed Shaw, except me. Hyndman was so angry he wouldn't speak to me for months.

NOTE

1. Herbert Burrows (1845–1922) was a leading member of the SDF, a theosophist and author with Annie Besant of *A Short Glossary of Theosophical Terms* (1891).

Shaw under Attack

H. M. HYNDMAN

From Henry Mayers Hyndman, *Further Reminiscences* (London: Macmillan, 1912) pp. 264–5. The hero of this story of Hyndman's, James Macdonald, was a tailor by trade and a unionist member of the SDF. However, the tone of the story may be misleading as to the real nature of the relationship between Shaw and Hyndman. Shaw told Hesketh Pearson that despite their clashes his friendship with Hyndman was 'never broken', and pointed out that he was in the chair at a public dinner to celebrate Hyndman's seventieth birthday. He added that the description of Tanner in *Man and Superman* was modelled on Hyndman's appearance (see Pearson, *GBS: A Postscript* [London: Collins, 1951] p. 42).

Our friend Bernard Shaw once found in [Macdonald] a very ugly customer indeed.

This was at a conference on unemployment, held in Old Holborn Town Hall, or the Trade Union Hall hard by, I forget which. Macdonald opened the discussion. Shaw thought he had closed it with one of his clever, satirical speeches directed towards the destruction of all enthusiasm in the gathering, whether this was intentional on Shaw's part or not. The chairman, whoever he was, thought also that the business of the meeting had concluded with Shaw's speech and Shaw himself was quite convinced it had. Not so Macdonald. He claimed the right to reply. This was challenged by the chairman supported by Shaw. Some dissension arose thereupon, but Macdonald very properly insisted upon his right and obtained his hearing. Then Shaw for once in his life had the opportunity of listening to such a rush of conclusive argument, thorough exposure and bitter ridicule turned upon himself, as he has only experienced in speech or in writing a few times in his life.

Macdonald was in no humour to spare a man who brought heartless chaff and fine-chopped literary ribaldry into a discussion upon such a terrible subject to the whole working-class as unemployment. As Macdonald spoke you could see the families starving, and their homes made desolate by the relentless and ruthless system of profitmongery that Shaw thought a fitting subject for jest. The audience sat at first in breathless silence and then Macdonald turned on Shaw. He simply ripped up Shaw's middle-class quips, and pseudo-economic fantasies, and threw the fragments at him, one after the other. He laughed heartily at Shaw's assumption of superiority and obvious overrating of himself, and made the whole of those present laugh with him not with Shaw. Winding up in a serious vein he showed why, as a member of the working class and a skilled tradesman himself, he knew that the question of unemployment lay at the root of all real change for the better, so long as capitalism and wagedom dominated society. Not the most skilled, thrifty and sober worker and wage-earner present but by a turn of bad trade or a bout of ill-health might be reduced to almost hopeless misery, and be forced to join the great army of those whom Shaw's class had sucked wealth out of when toiling and stigmatised as loafers and wastrels when the 'labour-market' was overstocked. I have never heard what Shaw thought of the trampling that befel his devoted carcase on this occasion, and I am convinced that his contemptuous attitude and joking were merely a pose. But he has never tried this sort of thing again with a working-class audience since Macdonald thus fell foul of him and offered up his smart witticisms as a sweet-smelling sacrifice on the altar of genuine conviction.

Socialist Visions

ERNEST RHYS

From Ernest Rhys, *Wales England Wed: An Autobiography* (London: J. M. Dent, 1940) p. 85. Ernest Rhys (1859–1946), who was to be the founding editor of the J. M. Dent Everyman's Library series, was at this time a freelance critic and poet in London. Arthur H. Mackmurdo (1851–1942), architect, had in 1882 founded the Century Guild, which for several years published a lavish quarto miscellany called *The Hobby Horse*. Mackmurdo shared chambers in Fitzroy Street with

Herbert P. Horne (1865–1916), who edited the miscellany and was a friend and neighbour of Rhys in Chelsea. The evening Rhys recalls probably belongs to 1887 (the Shaws had been at 29 Fitzroy Square since 5 March).

Another group, in some ways even more attractive, was that of the Hobby-Horse Men I have described, who were doing in art and letters what the Fellowship of the New Life was aiming at in philosophy and religion. To their evenings came a strange assortment of young poets, artists and rebels, and one night Arthur Mackmurdo, who was the chief prop of the Hobby-Horse house in Fitzroy Street, brought in with him George Bernard Shaw, the first glimpse I had had at close quarters of that incorrigible Fabian. Later the same evening Oscar Wilde came in, and he and Shaw had a characteristic passage of arms, both gay and bitter. When the Hobby-Horse meeting broke up, instead of going back direct to Chelsea, I followed Shaw to Fitzroy Square, where he was living at that time with his mother, and to my surprise he talked seriously, even emotionally, about the Socialist campaign, and the work to be done in London and in the country at large. What was needed, he said, if I remember aright, was some man who would have something of the religious fervour of Hyndman with something added akin to the cultured suasiveness of Stopford Brooke. We must have walked round and round Fitzroy Square a dozen times, talking of these things, and afterwards I went home with a curious sense of a movement, a revolutionary rising which would upset many of our conventions and bring a new dispensation, political and economic, into the London world.

At Kelmscott House: I

ERNEST RHYS

From Ernest Rhys, *Everyman Remembers* (London: J. M. Dent, 1931) p. 49. The coach house at William Morris's Hammersmith home, Kelmscott House, was converted into a hall for lectures, concerts and plays. The famous Hammersmith Sunday evening lectures were begun by Hyndman in 1884 and continued until Morris's death in the autumn of 1896. Morris first became aware of Shaw when he read the serialised instalments of Shaw's fifth novel *An Unsocial Socialist* in the pages of *To-Day*. By January 1885 Shaw was closely acquainted with the Morris family and circle and was acting in a play with Morris's daughter, May, with whom he was for a time in love. Rhys's recollection can be roughly dated from the fact that he records seeing shortly afterwards Morris's play *The Tables*

Turned, performed at Kelmscott House on 15 October 1887, with Morris himself playing the part of the Archbishop of Canterbury. On the night described below, Morris 'in a very impatient revolutionary mood' was speaking out for action.

Bernard Shaw as he stepped to the front of the platform made an absolute contrast to Morris. His sandy or reddish-yellow hair and sparse sandy whiskers framed a face that looked dead-white as compared with Morris's florid complexion. He was much taller too, and his way of speaking was cool, collected, provocative. He seemed to take a pleasure in planting malicious little darts, or in uttering taunts which roused Morris to something like humorous fury. The platform of the hut, I may say, had been hastily constructed and the planks were loose; and as Morris tramped up and down one feared at every moment they might collapse. Also, he had an odd way as he glanced at his opponent of thrusting his hands behind his back with an awkward gesture, as if afraid he might be tempted to make a personal attack upon the provoking, cynical, plausible Irishman.

But at the end of the battle, the two combatants went off together happily enough to sup at the poet's house.

At Kelmscott House: II

H. H. SPARLING

From Archibald Henderson, *Bernard Shaw, Playboy and Prophet* (London and New York: D. Appleton, 1932) p. 280. Henry Halliday Sparling (1860–1924) was Morris's assistant and protégé and married May Morris in 1890. They were divorced in 1898 and Shaw believed that the marriage had foundered as a result of his staying several weeks with them at the end of 1892 (see below, p. 160). Sparling never forgave him, according to Hesketh Pearson (*Bernard Shaw: His Life and Personality* [London: Collins, 1942] p. 101). The Eight Hours Movement (to shorten the working day) began to interest the Fabians in 1889, when it gathered momentum after the London dock strike. Webb was active in the campaign and Shaw spoke for it in a two-day public debate in January 1891.

On one occasion, according to the story told me by the late H. H. Sparling, friend and fellow-worker with Morris, Shaw lectured at Kelmscott House on Compulsory Eight Hours. 'He was more cadaverous then than he has been since,' Sparling explained, with a grin, 'and was decidedly uninspired. He had no real sympathy with Ben Tucker of *Liberty*,[1] and had probably taken up the subject under the influence of

Sidney Webb. At any rate, he droned on and on, reiterating "compulsory eight hours" and looking ill fed, until a comical idea struck Morris, who began to chuckle silently. A moment later Morris, who was presiding, "thought aloud" suddenly, in a tense growl which reverberated throughout the little hall: "Compulsory eight hours, indeed! Compulsory *guts* for Bernard Shaw!"'

NOTE

1. Benjamin Ricketson Tucker (1854–1940), American journalist and anarchist, was the editor of *Liberty*, a radical weekly which he published in Boston between 1881 and 1892. His unauthorised reprint in *Liberty* on 11 April 1885 of Shaw's article 'What's in a Name? (How an Anarchist might put it)' was the first publication of a Shaw work in America.

Shaw at Cambridge

LOWES DICKINSON

From *The Autobiography of G. Lowes Dickinson and Other Unpublished Writings*, ed. Dennis Proctor (London: Gerald Duckwork, 1973) pp. 144–5. Goldsworthy Lowes Dickinson (1862–1932), humanist, historian and philosophical writer, was a Fellow of King's College, Cambridge, where he lectured on political science from 1896 to 1920. At the time of Shaw's visit, having taken a first in classics and gained a fellowship with a dissertation on Plotinus, he had turned to medicine, which he was soon to abandon. Shaw lectured on 'Socialism: its Growth and Necessity' at a meeting of the Cambridge Fabian Society at King's College on 18 February 1888. The meeting was chaired by the historian and Cambridge celebrity, Oscar Browning (1837–1923). Also in the audience was the art critic Roger Fry (1866–1934), then a science undergraduate at King's College. He reported to his mother: '[Shaw] spoke wonderfully well, he only looked at it from the purely scientific standpoint of a political economist and there was none of the inflammatory gas which is too common among Socialist orators' (*Letters of Roger Fry*, ed. Denys Sutton [London: Chatto & Windus, 1972] p. 120).

About this time I had arranged that the then leaders of that Society should come to King's College and lecture. There came Webb, Shaw, Clerk, Bland,[1] Olivier. Webb I remember becoming involved by M'Taggart[2] in philosophy, and scored off in a kind of debating way which did not go deep but naturally rather annoyed him. Bland talked football to the young men. But the real event was Bernard Shaw, the most amusing of men, whom, I fear, we treated rather badly, for after a long evening in my then very cold rooms we saw him to bed about 2 a.m., and after that, I rather think, he was visited by some drunken revellers. At lunch next day he described inimitably his Irish relations, especially an uncle who thought he was in Heaven, and hung himself up in a basket from the ceiling dressed in gauze. Seeing we had pianos in our rooms, and shared one another's commons, Shaw pronounced that we were already Socialists, in his sense. His lecture was brilliant. It was attended by Professor Westcott, afterwards Bishop of Durham;[3] and he requested me to find out from Shaw what his moral basis was. I inquired, and received on a post card the following message: 'Ask the old boy what his is, and tell him mine's the same.'

NOTES

1. Clerk is apparently a mistake for William Clarke (1852–1901), political journalist and lecturer, who had attended on the birth of the Fabian Society and was a member of the Executive from 1888 to 1891. Hubert Bland (1856–1914), socialist author, was one of the original Fabians and served continuously on the Executive and as Treasurer until 1911.
2. John M'Taggart Ellis M'Taggart (1866–1925), philosopher and Fellow of Trinity College, Cambridge, was at this time an undergraduate at Trinity.
3. The Rt Rev. Brooke Foss Westcott (1825–1901), Bishop of Durham from 1890, was Regius Professor of Divinity and a Fellow of King's College at the time of Shaw's visit.

'A Live Socialist'

HENRY SIDGWICK

From A. S. and E. M. Sidgwick, *Henry Sidgwick* (London: Macmillan, 1906) pp. 497–8. Henry Sidgwick (1838–1900) was Professor of Moral Philosophy at Cambridge and author of works on ethics and political economy. Shaw delivered a paper, 'The Transition to Social Democracy', at a meeting in Bath of the British Association for the Advancement of Science on 7 September 1888. The paper was published in *Our Corner* in November 1888 and in *Fabian Essays in Socialism* the following year. Sidgwick's account of the paper comes from his journal entry for 8 September. Shaw recalled the occasion as follows: 'Henry Sidgwick, a follower of Mill, rose indignantly . . . and declared that I had advocated nationalisation of land; that nationalisation of land was a crime; and that he would not take part in a discussion of a criminal proposal. With that he left the platform' (Appendix I, 'Memoranda by Bernard Shaw', in Edward R. Pease, *The History of the Fabian Society* [London: A. C. Fifield, 1916] pp. 258–9).

The most interesting thing at my Section (Economic Science) was the field-day on Socialism which we had yesterday. The Committee had invited a live Socialist, redhot 'from the Streets', as he told us, who sketched in a really brilliant address the rapid series of steps by which modern society is to pass peacefully into social democracy. The *node* of the transition was supplied by urban ground-rents (it is interesting to observe that the old picture of the agricultural landlord-drone, battening on social prosperity to which he contributes nothing, is withdrawn for the present as too ludicruously out of accordance with the facts). It is now *urban* ground-rent that the municipal governments will have to seize, to meet the ever-growing necessity of providing work and wages for the unemployed. How exactly this seizure of urban rents was to develop into a complete nationalisation of industry I could not remember afterwards, but it seemed to go very naturally at the time. There was a peroration rhetorically effective as well as daring, in which he explained that the bliss of perfected socialism would only come by slow degrees, with lingering step and long delays, and claimed our sympathy for the noble-hearted men whose ardent philanthropy had led them to desire to cut these delays short by immediate revolution and spoliation. It was, indeed, a mistake on their part; the laws of social development did not admit of it; but if we were not quite lost in complacent selfishness we should join him in regretting that this shorter way with property was impossible.

Altogether a noteworthy performance: – the man's name is *Bernard Shaw*: Myers says he has written books worth reading.[1]

NOTE

1. Frederic W. H. Myers (1843–1901) was a Fellow of Trinity College, Cambridge, a President of the Society for Psychical Research and a close friend of Sidgwick's.

Shaw and the Fabian Style

STEPHEN SANDERS

From W. Stephen Sanders, *Early Socialist Days* (London: Hogarth Press, 1927) pp. 43–5. William Stephen Sanders (1871–1941), who had started work as a farmer's boy at the age of eleven, was a member of the Battersea branch of the

SDF, which had its headquarters at Sydney Hall, York Road. He was elected to the London County Council in 1904 and to Parliament in 1929, and served as Secretary of the Fabian Society from 1914 to 1920. His first meeting with Shaw can be dated to mid-1887 by his reference to Shaw's controversy with Hyndman, which took the form of letters printed in the *Pall Mall Gazette* on 7, 11, 12 and 16 May.

I have a pleasant memory of my first meeting with Bernard Shaw. It occurred a few weeks after I had placed my name on the roll of Sydney Hall. Shaw was in the committee-room waiting for the assembling of the gathering he was to address. (The only Socialist organisation of that day which practised the 'bourgeois' virtue of punctuality was the Fabian Society.) His mind was evidently full of his recent controversy with Hyndman concerning the theory of value, for he drew me, a young and bashful neophyte, into a conversation on this difficult and elusive subject. Or, to be exact, he talked to me about it and I listened, grateful for the opportunity of hearing the views of the brilliant writer and speaker. He gave me then the impression of his personality, which I have retained ever since: intense intellectual keenness, combined with innate courtesy and kindliness of spirit.

There is nothing of the 'irritable genius' about Shaw. He does not make you feel that he thinks you are either a fool or a knave if you happen to disagree with him. A questioner or an opponent at a lecture or a discussion, no matter how unskilful or crude he may be, is treated by Shaw as an earnest seeker after light and a possible convert. He can, however, when the occasion demands it, administer a rebuke by means of a touch of irony without inflicting a rankling wound to the self-esteem of the delinquent. I was witness of an instance of the Shavian method of reproving bad public manners, which took place at a lecture he gave in the early nineties to the Playgoers' Club.[1]

Among those who took part in the discussion was the late Harry Furniss.[2] He was in every way the antithesis of Shaw, being short, stout, pompous, and completely self-satisfied. His remarks were intended to be a criticism of Shaw's views; his tone was bombastic, arrogant, and bordered on the offensive. In closing, he expressed regret that he was unable to agree with the lecturer, especially as they had both attended the same educational establishment. Shaw rose to reply to the attack, unruffled, polished, and, as always, studiously courteous. He concluded by saying that he shared Mr Furniss's regret that they did not agree, and that it was true they had both been to the same school, adding: 'I trust, ladies and gentlemen, you recognise the style!'

NOTES

1. Shaw took part in a debate on 'Criticism, Corruption and the Remedy' at the Playgoers' Club on 22 April 1894. In a letter of 30 April to R. Golding Bright

Shaw wrote: 'Even my little platform performance at the Playgoers' Club was the result of about fifteen years practice of public speaking. . . . In London all beginners are forty, with twenty years of obscure hard work behind them' (*Collected Letters 1874–1897*, p. 433).

2. Harry Furniss (1854–1925), illustrator, humorous lecturer and *Punch* cartoonist, had been a fellow-pupil at Shaw's first school, the Wesleyan Connexional.

Propagating Socialism

G. F. McCLEARY

From G. F. McCleary, 'Some Early Recollections of GBS', *Fortnightly Review*, February 1953. Dr George Frederick McCleary (1867–1962), author of works on public health, social welfare and population theory, became Medical Officer of Health in Battersea in 1901. He was a pioneer of child and maternity welfare services and lectured on public health administration at the London School of Economics. He married the sister of Sydney Olivier's wife, Margaret.

I first met Shaw early in 1892. It was at a luncheon party, and the company included Graham Wallas and H. W. Massingham, then editor of the *Star*.[1] I had never seen Shaw before, and was struck by his etiolated appearance. His eyes were pale blue, his face was white, his hair, faintly red, looked well brushed and sleek, but his beard, rather more reddish than the hair of his head, was untrimmed and straggling. He was tall and very lean, and I had the impression that he was a man of ascetic life and delicate, fastidious taste. He seemed to radiate vivacity and evidently enjoyed talking.

He discussed how best to make converts to socialism, and maintained that it was essential to convince a possible convert that socialism would be to his personal advantage. 'No one,' said Shaw, 'is going to be a socialist unless he feels sure that socialism will be a good thing for him. I should not be a socialist if I were not sure that socialism would be a good thing for me.' I asked him whether he laid this down as a rule of universal application. 'Certainly,' he replied, 'you must always demonstrate personal advantage. But,' he continued – and here there came over his face that expression of delight which usually appeared when he was going to say something he would specially enjoy saying – 'when you have removed every vestige of doubt on that point, you must on no account fail to add: "and now let us cast aside all personal considerations and immolate ourselves upon the altar of self-sacrifice."'

Massingham remarked that these statements hardly explained why Shaw should devote so much time and energy to the unpaid advocacy of socialism, to which Shaw replied: 'I find it very amusing.' . . .

My next meeting with Shaw was in the spring of 1895 when he and I spent a weekend at Sydney Olivier's house in Surrey. Shaw, who had bicycled down, was companionable and unassuming, making no attempt to play the great man. He was surprised to find that I read Artemus Ward.[2] 'I thought,' he said, 'nobody of your generation ever read Artemus Ward. My generation read him and I still read him.' He proceeded to quote from the works of Artemus and to compare him with other humorists. Later in the day he discussed Sidney Webb's project of founding a school of economics in London, and disagreed with Webb's idea that the teaching should be given by scholars of established reputation as authorities on their various subjects, irrespective of what political views they might hold. Shaw contended that the object of the school should be to teach socialism.[3] 'What is the use,' he said, 'of getting men like Marshal[4] and Foxwell to lecture at the school? They are not going to advance socialism.' Fortunately, when the London School of Economics and Political Science took shape some years later, it was Webb's view and not Shaw's that was adopted.

NOTES

1. Henry William Massingham (1860–1924), journalist, was assistant editor of the *Star* during Shaw's association with the paper, but editor only from July 1890 to January 1891. He later became editor of the *Daily Chronicle* (1895–9) and the *Nation* (1907–23). Between 1891 and 1893 he was an active Fabian.

2. Artemus Ward was the pseudonym of Charles Farrar Brown (1834–67), American humorous moralist. Using a comical phonetic spelling he created (in the pages of the Cleveland *Plain Dealer*, 1858–9) the persona of a travelling showman anxious to exhibit waxworks of various historical 'figgers', tame bears and a kangaroo. He became a popular contributor to the New York *Vanity Fair* and London *Punch*, and a very successful lecturer.

3. The London School of Economics and Political Science held its first classes in the autumn of 1895. It was Webb's project: he was determined to divert a legacy left by Henry Hutchinson, a Derby solicitor, away from the Fabian Society's normal activities to establish something more permanent, and he kept his intentions secret as far as he could. In terms of Hutchinson's ambiguously worded will, Shaw certainly had grounds for his argument.

4. Alfred Marshall (1842–1924) was Professor of Political Economy at Cambridge from 1885 to 1908. Like Foxwell, he had attended meetings of the Economic Circle.

The Birth of the ILP

JAMES SEXTON

From *Sir James Sexton, Agitator: The Life of the Dockers' MP: An Autobiography* (London: Faber & Faber, 1936) pp. 128–30. James Sexton (1856–1938), son of Irish hawkers, became a leader of the dockers after bitter experiences in the Liverpool docks. He was MP for St Helens from 1918 to 1931, when he was knighted. The conference he describes took place at Bradford in January 1893 and saw the foundation of the Independent Labour Party. Shaw and William De Mattos (1851–1905) were the delegates of the London Fabians. Although most of the provincial Fabian groups soon became ILP branches or associated themselves with the ILP, the London parent body remained aloof.

Outstanding in the Fabian ranks was the figure of their bearded chieftain, George Bernard Shaw. He was in what seemed queer company to me and my colleagues, for he was ever a fighter, and that was the last thing the Fabians could claim to be. Possibly he found in their negative beliefs a sort of political vegetarianism!

Both in the Press before the Conference, and at the Conference itself, he declaimed with all his power against what he called the 'unnecessary and mischievous intervention of a new party', which was bound, he feared, to queer the pitch for the Fabians and their policy of peaceful penetration of the enemy's ranks until they should awake some fine morning to discover that, all unbeknownst to them, they had become Socialists.

We knew his debating strength, we dreaded the effect it might have upon the Conference, and took steps to keep him out of the arena. Hyndman demanded a scrutiny of credentials, and those of GBS were challenged on the ground that he was presumably a self-elected delegate. Thereon it was held that he could take no part in the proceedings. This move was not without danger of having repercussions, for I feel fairly certain that if Shaw had thus lamentably sinned, he was not the only offender, and that a closer scrutiny might have revealed a good many other delegates eligible for classification in the same category.

But it was no easier then that it is now to make Shaw go the way you want him to go, and though we decided that he was not for us, he certainly remained with us. He accepted the decision of the Conference to the extent of withdrawing from the floor of the house, which was actually an old chapel, but he promptly took up a strong enfilading position in the gallery, from which he bombarded us so violently with his interruptions that on the following day we admitted him to our deliberations in sheer self-defence.

We spent three glorious days nominally discussing three principal propositions, but actually in fiery denunciation of the capitalistic system, its products, by-products and residuals. We were all agreed upon almost everything, but we felt we were strengthening each other's faith, and at any rate we got rid of a lot of steam and heat which might otherwise have caused some of us to explode.

'Young Bernard'

W. R. TITTERTON

From W. R. Titterton, *So this is Shaw* (London: Douglas Organ, 1945) pp. 9–11, 13. William Richard Titterton (1876–1963), theatre critic, music-hall singer and author, became a regular publisher of 'interviews' with Shaw. His particular recollections of Shaw as a speaker probably belong to the mid-1890s, though his composite impressions cover a wider time-span.

I think that the first time I saw him was at the Dock Gates, Blackwall, in East London.[1]

Sometimes the ILP or the SDF had possession, and then I revelled in the purple eloquence of Tom Mann[2] or H. M. Hyndman with its assurance that the social revolution was coming in the spring.

One day when I got there, a tall and very upright man, very neatly dressed, with a flaming red beard, a laughing eye and a quizzical smile, was speaking. And the crowd was in a mixed mood.

Sometimes it laughed, but more often it growled. And the speaker seemed to welcome the growls more than the laughter. He had one thumb in the arm-hole of his waistcoat. From time to time he looked into his free hand, which, I was not to know, held a watch. He seemed altogether at his ease.

The man fascinated me. He was at once so truculent and so urbane; so reasonable and so provocative. And, while he debunked all the revolutionary tailoring of the comrades, I had the sense to see that he was the most revolutionary of us all.

Shaw tells me that a certain plain-clothes policeman was of the same mind, or was sent by somebody who agreed with me, for the detective followed him round. He would pay attention for a while, and then become bored.

Well, at the first encounter outside the Dock Gates, I asked one of the comrades who the speaker was, and he said, with a queer mixture of respect and dislike, 'Bernard Shaw,' and added: 'talking nonsense as usual'.

I nodded, said 'Oh, him!' for I thought small potatoes of the Fabians; and, reinforced with a sense of superiority, I set myself to listen.

I found Shaw most inspiriting – and most irritating. For example, he mentioned Karl Marx's *Das Kapital*; there was a roar of applause; and then Shaw said with a happy smile, 'Of course, none of you have read it.' He was an acid, eating away all our soft parts. But I liked the feel of the acid.

Not long after this I joined the Fabian Society, and I went to the Clifford's Inn meetings because of Shaw. Fabianism I regarded as feeble stuff. We young revolutionaries asked for the wine of life, and they gave us a tract on municipal beerhouses.

But there was nothing feeble about Shaw. He always seemed to me the perfect revolutionary, the perfect soldier; always mindful of the commissariat and the ammunition, but never unmindful of the war.

In fact, he was always fighting, always trailing his coat. We, the comrades, were content at our meetings with saying what we would do to the bloated capitalists when we rose. That is, we fired blank cartridges at an absent enemy. But he fired ball cartridges at his audience, and every shot went home. He rose to speak, whether at Clifford's Inn, the Albert Hall, a tuppenny-ha'penny branch meeting, or the street corner, blithely imperturbable, aggressively urbane, and *slew* – without malice as without mercy – but with a pious joy. . . .

But it is as a speaker that I remember him best. There he stands, slim, trim, alert and gallant – yes, gallant every inch of him, his hands veiled now in the pockets of his well-cut, rough tweed jacket. His head is cocked sideways provocatively, his red beard juts out like a challenge, his face looks as if it came fresh from the wash and a rough towelling, his eyebrows – by art or by nature – have an archly diabolical lift.

Out comes a hand, he gazes into the cup of it. Up comes the head, a shaft flies, with a silent, friendly gush of laughter he registers his point; a huge echo of laughter from the house follows. . . . The face becomes serious, a hand grasps the red beard, you are being scolded, or the world is – it amounts to the same thing, for Shaw will not let you contract out of the obligations of the world. Scolded? The scourge bites; it is wielded with calm, almost insolent calm, yet with a white-hot passion for justice in every blow.

The pose relaxes, the trim figure swaggers – jauntily, yet with sure restraint. Hands and eyebrows make play. Out comes an epigram – a flock of epigrams – the hall roars. But the speaker himself remains calm and cool, supremely self-controlled. He ends on the very tick of his climax, yet as though casually subsiding with no more to say.

A perfect piece of acting! Is the man a mere poseur? Only a fool would think that, and a good many fools have said it.

NOTES

1. A popular meeting place of left-wing political groups with a rostrum for speakers.

2. Tom Mann (1856–1941), a skilled engineer and prominent unionist, was one of the champions of the dockers in the 1889 dock strike. He was an early member of the SDF and became Secretary of the ILP.

'What is it to be a Fabian?'

From Percy L. Parker, 'What is it to be a Fabian? An Interview with Mr George Bernard Shaw', *Young Man*, April 1896. Percy Livingstone Parker (1867–1925), journalist and editor of works by George Fox and Wesley, was sub-editor of the *New Age* at the time this interview appeared.

The question I first put to Mr Shaw was a very modest one, remembering that the Fabians had published a volume of essays and innumerable tracts to answer it – 'What is it to be a Fabian?'

'Well,' replied Mr Shaw, 'a Fabian is a Socialist who is not a Socialist at all, you know. We have always said that a man was of no use to us until he had got over his Socialism. What I mean by that is, that we do not want in the Fabian Society a man who has got economic theories, or a social creed, to which he wants to square the world and human nature, and all the rest of it. We want a man who keeps his eye definitely on certain concrete reforms which we want to bring about. We want the man who is so far an economist that he thoroughly understands the way in which competitive private property in land, and private enterprise in industry, throw a large part of the nation's wealth into idle hands; who is dead against it; and who, in short, wants to get rid of unearned incomes. If a man is that much of a Collectivist he is Socialist enough for us.'

'What are the concrete reforms you desire?'

'We want to take the supply of the general necessities of life – food, clothing, travelling, housing, and all the things that are necessary to enable a man to live – out of the region of speculative and private enterprise, and to organise it collectively. We aim at the reorganisation of society by the emancipation of land and industrial capital from individual and class ownership, and the vesting of them in the community for the general benefit. In this way only can the natural and acquired advantages of the country be equitably shared by the whole people. The Society works for the transfer to the community of the administration of such industrial capital as can be managed socially. For, owing to the monopoly of the means of production in the past, industrial inventions and the transformation of surplus income into capital have mainly enriched the proprietary class, the worker being now dependent on that class for leave to earn a living. By these means rent and interest will be added to the reward of labour, and practical equality of opportunity will be maintained.

'Socialism in practice, however,' continued Mr Shaw, 'works itself out in instalments; such as the shortening of the working day; the establishment of the "moral minimum" instead of competitive wages; the gradual extension of municipal management to gas, water, tramways, the building of houses, and so on. In parochial activity it works out in the provision of allotments, public libraries, reading-rooms, drainage, the provision of labourers' cottages, and so on.'

'"So on" is rather an elastic phrase, isn't it? You have used it twice.'

'Yes, that is so. I am only giving you the thin end of the wedge, and only that so far as it has been greased by modern progressive politicians. But I can foresee no point in the social evolution where the spring from the one instalment of Socialism to the next need shock the public conscience or produce any keener consciousness of a break with the old order than, for instance, the freeing of the turnpikes or of the Thames bridges. At present we are perfectly familiar with the idea of the municipalisation of water, which has already been effected in many provincial towns. By the time we are ready for the municipalisation of bread and milk, the public will be just as much out of humour with the underground bakery and the private dairy as they are now with the water companies.

'Our great obstacle now is the fact that the masses of the people are not Socialists, and do not care enough about the bettering of their own condition to try and understand the social synthesis which the Socialist has to grasp.'

'What differentiates the Fabian Society from other Socialist bodies?'

'Our distinctive point has always been that we are not a sectarian society. Up to the time of the foundation of the Fabian Society all Socialist societies were founded with the idea of enlisting in their own ranks the whole of the working classes, and being thus made irresistible, omniscient and omnipresent, establishing a democratic republic. The

Fabians recognised almost from the first that that was not how things were going to be done in England. They accordingly adopted their famous policy of "permeation" or the policy of propagating Fabian ideas outside the Society wherever there was a human brain for them to lodge in. Our idea has not been to reform the world ourselves, but to persuade the world to take our ideas into account in reforming itself.'

'And how will your policy be ultimately realised?'

'Well, if you want to know where the really serious part of the business will come in, the guillotine, or rather, that "expropriation of the expropriators" of which Karl Marx speaks, then you must look to the activity of the income-tax collector. We already expropriate them to the tune of the regulation eightpence in the pound, and also by death duties which twenty years ago would have appeared revolutionary. There is no reason to doubt that we shall go on in that direction. But nothing worse will happen than vigorous grumbling on the part of the idle rich, and their gradual conversion to the necessity of bringing up their descendants to work for their living.'

'Of course the Fabian realises the part which individual initiative must always play in the development of society, and the number and importance of the political and other questions of which Socialism affords no solution whatever?'

'Certainly he does. Take the case of Home Rule, for instance. The Social Democrat is a Socialist and a Democrat. As a Socialist he is an Internationalist, calling on the proletarians of all lands to unite as far as possible under a common communal organisation. As such he is clearly bound strenuously to resist the splitting off, on national lines, of the English from the Irish proletariat. On the other hand, as a Democrat, he is bound to admit the right of the Irish nation to be governed by the form of government it prefers. Consequently he is bound to be an enthusiastic Home Ruler. There you have an example of Social Democracy giving you two opposite solutions of the same question. The same may be said of the question of woman's suffrage. The whole range of foreign policy, and Imperial Federation too, presents difficulties of the same kind as the Home Rule problems. As a matter of fact there is no Fabian foreign policy, although all Socialists profess an international brotherhood – which, in "Mr Jagger's" phrase, is "Pious but not to the purpose".

'It is worth adding, in consequence of these difficulties and the vague and imaginary character of the views held by some of the most fanatical Socialists, that when Socialism is reduced to a series of practical political measures, each of these measures is fiercely combated, and contemptuously disparaged as "a mere palliative", or "a capitalist red herring", by many Socialists. That is why I have said that the chief obstacle to the establishment of Socialism in England is the Socialists.

'Generally speaking I should say that the Fabian is a Socialist who recognises the practical difficulties which I have been pointing out to you. Such a Socialist joins the Fabian Society just as naturally as a revolutionary, visionary Socialist joins the Social-Democratic Federation.'

'What do you think will be the future of the Fabian Society?'

'The sort of annihilation that a drop of cochineal undergoes when it is dropped into a tumbler of water. The redness of the water destroys the individuality of the cochineal. Although to many people our views appear peculiar and extraordinary, yet I do not think that the enlightened, broadminded politicians of today will hesitate to believe that the time may come when all England will be so Fabianised in its ideas that the need for any special organisation will cease.'

Vestryman and Borough Councillor

A. G. EDWARDS

A. G. Edwards, 'GBS brought Wit, Vigour, and Good By-laws to St Pancras', *Local Government Service*, May 1947. Shaw ran unsuccessfully for the St Pancras Vestry (municipal council) in 1894. He was elected unopposed in 1897, and served as vestryman and borough councillor until 1903. A. G. Edwards was an officer of the Vestry at the time. The Vestry had 120 members, the Council seventy. Shaw's term as vestryman was interrupted by his marriage and long illness (1898–9), but as councillor he was assiduous in attending all council and committee meetings. He was made the first Freeman of the Borough of St Pancras in October 1946.

In 1893, I was a member of the Fabian Society and saw and heard GBS many times. So when, in 1897, he became a member of the St Pancras Vestry – predecessor of St Pancras Metropolitan Borough Council – of which I was an official, I knew that things would hum. He was not elected by vote, but became a vestryman through the instrumentality of the political 'boss' of the Tottenham Court Road Ward – a very conservative ward – who did a deal with the Progressive opponent to allow three of his nominees to stand unopposed in return for three Progressive nominees.

In those days, many thought Shaw a dangerous revolutionary, and some thought him a clown. But in municipal affairs, he proved to be a thoroughly practical and diligent administrator – though never a popular one. The present council, not having known him, recently made him the first Freeman of St Pancras.

In his first three years as a vestryman he did little that was spectacular. In the next three, as a borough councillor – the vestries became boroughs in 1900 – he was most active, especially on public health, by-laws and municipal insurance. I was present in the council chamber in November, 1900, when the first mayor was to be elected. The parties had agreed on the choice of Mr Edmund Barnes; all was ready for a unanimous vote, and the Robe and Chain of Office (the latter provided by the late Sir John Blundel Maple, MP) were waiting. But when the motion was moved, up stood GBS, full of opposition and, against all precedent, made an eloquent thirty-five minute speech in which, after recounting Mr Barnes's public career and past deeds, he concluded: 'and this is the sort of man you are thinking of making the first citizen of St Pancras!' I need hardly add that GBS's own nominee was silently defeated – but it was an enjoyable afternoon.

When the new council started work, questions arose as to the selection of aldermen and whether they and the councillors should wear red robes and badges. GBS vigorously opposed the wearing of robes, declaring that the councillors would look like a row of pillar-boxes. He taunted them with the fact that they had not bought their robes themselves, and when one grumpy old alderman retorted that he *had* bought his, Shaw promptly rejoined with: 'Yes, perhaps you. Nobody would have felt it worth while to buy yours.'

Later, when there was a number of cases of smallpox, the health committee recommended that all sanitary inspectors should be vaccinated. Shaw, a rabid anti-vaccinationist (he had himself been vaccinated and had subsequently contracted smallpox) vigorously opposed. It was impudence, he said, for a committee of laymen to seek to compel trained health experts to protect themselves; the sanitary inspectors were responsible men and should be allowed to do what they thought best without dictation from their employers. One old doctor shouted that the members should take no notice of 'that scoundrel over there' but the 'scoundrel' got the recommendation referred back, never to come up again.

Shaw was appointed as a delegate to a conference at Shoreditch to consider the advisability of forming a Municipal Mutual Insurance Scheme. He wrote a long, detailed report to the St Pancras Council and strongly recommended it to join the scheme. As most of us now know, it has proved an unqualified success.

Later, he was made chairman of a special by-laws committee. He devoted much time and thought to this and made a complete revision of the by-laws. Many of these affected officials, and it was always noticed how careful he was to safeguard their freedom.

One by-law, making it compulsory for officials to live in the borough, he threw out, and another, fixing office hours at 9 to 5.30 and 9 to 2 on Saturdays, he altered to 9 to 5 and 9 to 1. Alas, the 5 was spotted and 5.30 restored – but one o'clock on Saturdays remained. I am told that these by-laws still stand as he revised them more than forty-five years ago.

Once, when something affecting children was under discussion, I noted a remark of his: 'The children of England are the children of a rich country and therefore should be well off' – which seemed to me a revealing philosophy of life.

He was always outspoken and vehement on behalf of any reform of the municipal machine and gave six of the best years of his life to the cause of running and improving local government.

At the close of his experiences in local government, he published his book *The Common Sense of Municipal Trading*, which remains today the finest case ever put up for municipal enterprise.

An Aberrant Candidate: I

'Too Many Electors sit at Home "Reading my Books"', *St James's Gazette*, 5 March 1904. In the 1904 London County Council elections Shaw and Sir William Geary, Bt (1854–1944), barrister and author, were the Progressive candidates for South St Pancras. They were defeated at the polls held on the day the following interview was published. The Education Acts passed by Balfour's Conservative government (in which Sidney Webb had been closely involved) were a key issue in the elections. The 1902 Act had made the counties and county boroughs responsible for the whole range of education, while the 1903 Act did the same for the LCC in London. One provision of the Acts – the funding of voluntary schools from the rates – had particularly upset the Nonconformists, who resented giving any aid to Anglican schools. In a widespread campaign of passive resistance some objectors refused to pay their rates.

'Well, Mr Shaw, can you fulfil your promise to convert the Nonconformists of South St Pancras to your enthusiasm for the Education Act?' an interviewer inquired of Mr George Bernard Shaw.

'The Act itself will convert them. Just think a little. Do you realise that the Act sweeps away the wretched old restriction of public education to elementary education; gives us command of the whole educational machine, from the kindergarten up to the university; enables us to establish unsectarian training colleges; rescues nearly quarter of a million children from having their education sacrificed to the poverty of voluntary schools; and provides us with grants worth nearly £200,000 a year to do the work that has hitherto been done by begging £80,000 a year from private subscribers.'

'Then why do the passive resisters object to it so strongly?'

'Because, sir, they read party newspapers instead of reading the Act. They are Liberals; and therefore they feel bound to assume that every Act passed by a Conservative Government is the result of a criminal conspiracy between the peers, the publicans, and the Church. Have they ever objected to pay for the Catholic services in our asylums and prisons, where the very wafer that undergoes the miracle of transubstantiation in the Mass is paid for out of rates collected from Protestants of all denominations [?] Why, they pay for the Established Church of Malta, which is Roman Catholic. Does any sane man suppose that in a country like ours, which tolerates all creeds, his public contributions can be ear-marked for expenditure on his particular sect only? It is an insult to the Free Churches to suggest that they are so incapable of citizenship – for that is what such objections come to. Besides, the school buildings which the denominations are giving us will more than pay for the catechisms and crucifixes. The passive resister may urge us to repudiate the gifts of the Greeks; but in that case the ratepayer will have to find five millions to replace the refused schools. Eh?'

'The ratepayer is always the difficulty, I suppose?'

'Of course he is. Why should he – or she – not be? The rates are outrageous. In St Pancras the people who are opposing me put the local rate up by sixpence in the pound at a single jump through sheer financial incapacity, in spite of all my remonstrances. Half the ratepayers in St Pancras are lodging-house keepers who are rated as if they were millionaires because they live in large houses and pay high rents.'

'Your remedy is taxation of ground values, I suppose?'

'Oh, much more than that. Complete exemption of people who are really poor, as in the case of the income tax. Abatements for moderate incomes. Heavy taxation not only of ground values, but of all the thoroughly unearned incomes that are derived indirectly from ground values.'

'I suppose there is no opposition to you on that point.'

'Oh, isn't there! My anti-Progressive opponents have taken up that glove, and are boldly standing for "No Taxation of Ground Values."'

'Are you and Sir William Geary going to win?'

'Yes, easily, if the intelligent people in the constituency can be induced to vote. But 3,000 of them sat at home last time – reading my books, I suppose – and did nothing. If that happens again, the old vestry gang will dispose of me as easily as a donkey disposes of a thistle. But it will not be my fault, nor Sir William Geary's.'

An Aberrant Candidate: II

BEATRICE WEBB

From *The Diary of Beatrice Webb*, vol. II: *1892–1905*, ed. Norman and Jeanne MacKenzie (London: Virago, 1983) p. 318. Beatrice Webb (1858–1943) was the daughter of Richard Potter, a wealthy industrialist and entrepreneur. A protégée of Herbert Spencer, she was already active as a social researcher when she met Sidney Webb in January 1890. They were married in July 1892 and thenceforward formed a formidable team, indefatigably researching and writing together, and manoeuvring for political influence. Beatrice published some extracts from her voluminous diaries herself; a more generous selection is now in progress. What follows is taken from her entry for 7 March 1904. She had noted on 27 February that 'party organisers have long ago given up the seat as lost' and that it 'would be a forlorn hope to any other Progressive candidate' (ibid., p. 315). Shaw had in fact polled 1,460 votes, while the lower of his two successful Moderate opponents polled 1,808.

GBS beaten badly, elsewhere the Progressives romping back with practically undiminished members. As to the first event, we are not wholly grieved. GBS with a small majority might have been useful, with an overwhelming one [he] would simply have been compromising. He certainly showed himself hopelessly intractable during the election, refused to adopt any orthodox devices as to address and polling cards, inventing brilliant ones of his own, all quite unsuited to any constituency but Fabians or Souls.[1] Insisted that he was an Atheist, that though a teetotaller he would force every citizen to imbibe a quartern of rum to cure any tendency to intoxication, laughed at the Nonconformist conscience and chaffed the Catholics about Transubstantiation, abused the Liberals and contemptuously patronised the Conservatives – until nearly every section was equally disgruntled. His bad side is very prominent at an election – vanity and lack of reverence for knowledge or respect for other people's prejudices; even his good qualities – quixotic chivalry to his opponents and cold-drawn truth ruthlessly administered to possible supporters – are magnificent but not war. Anyway, we did our best for him, Sidney even puffing him outrageously in the *Daily Mail*, and he and Charlotte are duly grateful. He will never be selected again by any constituency that any wire-puller thinks can be won.

NOTE

1. The Souls were a group of 'Society' men and women with artistic interests who were at pains to distinguish themselves from the usual upper-class circles.

Shaw at Manchester

NEVILLE CARDUS

From Neville Cardus, *Second Innings* (London: Collins, 1950) p. 110. Sir Neville Cardus (1889–1975), music critic and cricket writer, was born in Manchester. The Ancoats Brotherhood grew out of another society, 'The Jacobs', formed in the late 1850s by Charles Rowley (1840–1933) and eight other members of a cricket club. Rowley, who was born in Ancoats, a slum area of Manchester, and never went to school, was energetically concerned not only to improve housing and sanitation there, but to open opportunities for cultural and intellectual life. The Sunday meetings of the Brotherhood became famous. Shaw addressed them on 21 October 1906, and the report of his speech two days later in the Manchester *Daily Dispatch*, headlined 'GBS overhauls the Ten Commandments', provoked a scandalised reaction (see *Collected Letters 1898–1910*, pp. 670–3).

Every week between October and March, I walked four miles to Ancoats on Sundays and four miles back. It was at the 'Ancoats Brotherhood' that I first heard Egon Petri play Beethoven's Opus 3;[1] on the same occasion Bernard Shaw spoke about the Ten Commandments, and he was not then regarded as respectable. As he stood on the platform, arms akimbo, in tweeds and with still the red flame of Socialism in his beard, he told us to burn down the Manchester Town Hall and the Cathedral, for some reasons I can't remember but they were strictly reformative; and having digressed a while from the theme of his discourse, said, 'But now, ladies and gentlemen; let's return to our old friend God.' I didn't know at the time that this was a cheap joke; we revelled in the outrageousness of it, we had been repressed so long in our public discussions of the Almighty. Even the atheists of the period shilly-shallied, as Lady Bracknell might have observed: they called themselves agnostics. I remember nothing else of Shaw's talk that day except that I was electrified by the tempo, charmed by the accent and twinkle, astounded that anybody could say so much without a manuscript, an hour of it and not a fumble, not the omission of a semi-colon, of speech.

NOTE

1. Egon Petri (1881–1962), German pianist, was Busoni's most important pupil and exponent, and particularly admired for his Bach and Liszt.

Shaw, Wells and Fabian Politics

S. G. HOBSON

From S. G. Hobson, *Pilgrim to the Left: Memoirs of a Modern Revolutionist* (London: Edward Arnold, 1938) pp. 106–7. Samuel George Hobson (1864–1940), socialist author and promoter of Guild Socialism, joined the Fabian Society in 1891 and served on the Executive from 1900 until he resigned from the Society in 1910. H. G. Wells joined the Society in 1903, but grew impatient with its philosophical basis and methods. On 9 February 1906 he delivered a lecture to the Society on 'The Faults of the Fabian'. A Wells committee was subsequently set up 'to consider what measures should be taken to increase the scope, influence, income and activity of the Society' (Hobson, *Pilgrim to the Left*, p. 105). Wells conducted himself badly in the whole affair, and at a meeting held on 7 December 1906 to consider his committee's report and the Executive's reply, he moved an amendment which virtually demanded that the Executive resign and deliver up the Society to him. Shaw made himself spokesman for the Executive at the next meeting on 14 December, and in a masterful speech demolished Wells, forcing him to withdraw the amendment. Wells finally resigned from the Society in 1908. Looking back on the affair much later, he wrote: 'no part of my career rankles so acutely in my memory with the conviction of bad judgement, gusty impulse and real inexcusable vanity, as that storm in the Fabian teacup' (H. G. Wells, *Experiment in Autobiography: Discoveries and Conclusions of a Very Ordinary Brain (since 1866)*, 2 vols [London: Victor Gollancz and the Cresset Press, 1934] II, 660–1).

At the final meeting Shaw blew up the wearisome business with a characteristic joke. 'Ladies and gentlemen,' he said, 'Mr Wells in his speech complained of the long delay by the "Old Gang" in replying to his report. But we took no longer than he. During his Committee's deliberations he produced a book on America.[1] And a very good book too. But whilst I was drafting our reply I produced a play.'[2] Here he paused, his eyes vacantly glancing round the ceiling. It really seemed that he had lost his train of thought. When we were all thoroughly uncomfortable, he resumed: 'Ladies and gentleman: I paused there to enable Mr Wells to say: "And a very good play too!"' We got no farther. We laughed, and went on laughing. Shaw always has been an adept at the unexpected; never did he put his gift to such practical purpose. He stood on the platform waiting. Wells, also on the platform, smiled self-consciously; but the audience went on laughing. Finally, when we were too exhausted to laugh longer, Wells withdrew his amendment, and we all went trooping out in search of refreshment. Keats was snuffed out by an article; Wells was squelched by a joke.

NOTES

1. *The Future in America* (London: Chapman & Hall, 1906).
2. *The Doctor's Dilemma*, which Shaw began writing in August 1906 and completed on 3 September. The play was first presented at the Court Theatre on 20 November 1906.

Shaw and the Life Force

FENNER BROCKWAY

From Fenner Brockway, *Inside the Left: Thirty Years of Platform, Press, Prison and Parliament* (London: George Allen & Unwin, 1942) p. 22. Archibald Fenner Brockway (b. 1888), socialist, pacifist, author and parliamentarian, was a leading figure in the ILP. He was made a life peer in 1964. In *Outside the Right* (1963), he indicates that the meeting described below took place in 1910 at a converted shop in Goswell Road, the home of the Finsbury branch of the ILP.

One evening Bernard Shaw came. I was a Shaw worshipper, and was thrilled by this opportunity of meeting him at close quarters. His theme was an appeal for economic equality on the ground that only when class divisions are abolished will natural selection take place in the mating of human beings, and until that happens the superman and the super-race will not be delivered. I can still see Shaw as he stood on the shallow platform at the end of our shop-hall – crowded to suffocation, of course – tall, slight, straight-backed, arms folded across his chest, throwing out his stream of challenging sentences with the confidence of a god, taking a delight in uttering ideas which shocked. There was still a little red in his beard and hair then, and he spoke with extraordinary vigour, on and on for an hour and a half, the crisp sharp sentences, so definite, so ruthless in their destruction of old idols, so clear and bold in the creation of new gods, poured out with a rapidity that held us all spell-bound.

Even the industrial section, rather contemptuous of the Fabian Nursery intellectuals, were conquered. The rest of us were entranced.

At the end we asked Shaw questions. I must still have been a rather subjective youth, for the question I put was this: 'Mr Shaw, we are young and we want to make the best use of our lives. What is your advice?' His answer came in a flash: 'Find out what the Life Force is making for and make for it, too.' How many times since have I used that answer in perorations to Socialist speeches!

Time to Retire?

BEATRICE WEBB

From *The Diary of Beatrice Webb*, vol. III: *1905–1924*, ed. Norman and Jeanne MacKenzie (London: Virago, 1984) p. 154. The extract below is taken from the entry for 7 March 1911. The Webbs were to begin a journey round the world in June and Sidney had suggested that he stand down from the Fabian Executive during their absence. Thereupon Shaw, who was not alone in feeling that the Society had drifted since the Wells episode, suggested that he and the other long-serving members should retire too (Shaw had been on the Executive continuously since 1885). In the event Webb stood and topped the poll in the April elections, but Shaw, Hubert Bland (in poor health) and three others did retire.

The Fabian Society is going through a crisis, not of dissent, but of indifference. Sidney thought that, as he was leaving England, he had better resign [from the Executive] for a year. Thereupon GBS not only announces his intention of resigning, but persuades some half-a-dozen others of the Old Gang to resign also. All with the view to making room for young men who are not there! Clifford Sharp,[1] who is a loyal and steadfast member of the Executive, is in despair, and Sidney is remaining on if GBS and the others persist in going. Charlotte Shaw told Sharp that GBS had got sick of the Fabian Society and cared for nothing but his own productions, that he felt himself too important to work in harness with anyone else. It is largely her fault, as she has withdrawn him from association with us and other Fabians in order not to waste his intellectual force in talk and argument.

NOTE

1. Clifford Dyce Sharp (1883–1935), a protégé of the Webbs and centrally involved in their 1909–11 Poor Law campaign, served on the Fabian Executive from 1909 to 1914.

Debate as Entertainment: I

FRANK SWINNERTON

From Frank Swinnerton, *Swinnerton: An Autobiography* (London: Hutchinson, 1937) pp. 84–5. The following sketch of Shaw in debate by Frank Arthur Swinnerton (1884–1982), novelist and critic, is taken from contrasted memories of his three 'platform heroes' of the Edwardian era. The others were Hilaire Belloc (1870–1953) and G. K. Chesterton (1874–1936), friends, fellow-Catholics, and both versatile and productive writers who looked back to the Middle Ages with idealising vision.

Shaw, a much wirier figure, was when we heard him reddish in beard and whitish in face (the converse is now true). He was a better debater than Chesterton; the best debater in London. He had the more incisive mind, the more scathing tongue, the less simple faith. When he stood facing an audience with his arms folded or, at Kensington Town Hall, with his hands wide apart on the platform rail, he had every assembly at his mercy. In the first half-hour they often wriggled; they shrugged; they shook heads; but in the end they were conquered by his voice and his persuasiveness. He knew all about municipal politics, because he had been a member of the St Pancras Council; he knew all about Shakespeare and the 'Drahma' because he was a 'drahmatist'; he knew all about economics, 'gahs', Ibsen, Wagner, Socialism, Chesterton and Belloc, doctors, lawyers, politics, respectability, absurdity, and everything else. At any rate, he knew much more about all those things than the audience did, or he could talk more entertainingly about them; and if a member of one audience produced a few facts Shaw could always deal with those with the utmost verve. The same words, when printed and thus susceptible of analysis, were at times found to be inflated with 'gahs'; but he was the most delightful of speakers, who leapt to his feet like an athlete, ascended the platform, faced the audience, and enjoyed talking as much as the other fumblers hated it; and his spoken victories were innumerable.

At Chesterton's lecture on Puck, Shaw, who had just then roused what is called in the Press a storm of indignation by speaking his mind (in terms unlike those of the respectful obituarists) about a dead actor,

Sir Henry Irving, was called upon to address us. Another man rose simultaneously and said 'I protest against Mr Shaw being allowed to speak'. There was a moment's pause of consternation; and then the entire audience, with a single voice, shouted 'Shaw! Shaw!' and the other man, having made his protest, sat down overwhelmed with ignominy. Shaw, cocking his head, began at once upon a note of severe rebuke. 'Really, ladies and gentlemen, I'm surprised at you. It's well known that I'm an abominable fellow; and yet you insist upon my speaking to you . . .'. What followed dealt wholly with the subject of Chesterton's lecture, which I believe to have been, not 'Puck' (that was only the title) but the English Character or the Comic Spirit or some other general topic well suited to the characteristic displays of both speakers; and it was observed that the protesting member of the audience remained in his seat until the close.

Again, in lecturing on Shakespeare (this also was a matter that aroused the usual 'storm'), he began by remarking candidly: 'I hope you will be more fortunate than the last audience I intended to address on Shakespeare. On that occasion the chairman, in introducing me, made an elementary mistake in economics. I had to correct him. It took me the whole evening; and I never got to Shakespeare at all.'

Debate as Entertainment: II

ARNOLD BENNETT

From *The Journal of Arnold Bennett* (New York: The Literary Guild, 1933) pp. 471–2. Enoch Arnold Bennett (1867–1931), journalist, novelist and playwright, had returned in 1912 from ten years' residence in France, having reached the zenith of his popular success and critical esteem. This journal entry is dated 28 January 1913. Shaw was still debating with Belloc as late as 1925.

Political debate between G. B. Shaw and Hilaire Belloc as to connection between private property and servitude. At Queen's Hall.

Went with Vaughan.[1] Crammed, at concert prices. Not a seat unsold. Shaw very pale with white hair, and straight. His wife beside him. Effect too conjugal for a man at work. Sidney and Beatrice Webb next to them. Effect also too conjugal here. Maurice Baring[2] supporting Belloc, both very shabby. Maurice with loose brown boots and creased socks. They spoke thus: Belloc thirty minutes, Shaw thirty, Belloc twenty, Shaw twenty, Belloc ten, Shaw ten. Time was kept to three minutes. Belloc's first was pretty good. Shaw's first was a first-class performance, couldn't have been better; the perfection of public speaking (not oratory); not a word wrong. But then afterwards the impression that it was a gladiatorial show or circus performance gained on one, and at the end was a sense of disappointment, as the affair degenerated into a mere rivalry in scoring. Still I have never seen Shaw emotional before, as he was then. Curious trick of audience, as of all audiences, of applauding sentiments with which they were already familiar, and receiving anything relatively new in silence.

NOTES

1. Probably to be identified with Thomas Vaughan, 'partner in God knows how many theatres', whom Bennett's journal mentions in November and December 1920.

2. Maurice Baring (1874–1945), poet and man of letters, had hitherto spent much of his working life abroad as a diplomat and foreign correspondent.

Shaw at Oxford

C. E. M. JOAD

From C. E. M. Joad, *Shaw* (London: Victor Gollancz, 1949) pp. 29–31. Cyril Edwin Mitchinson Joad (1891–1953) was Head of the Department of Philosophy at Birkbeck College, London, from 1930 to 1946. He wrote numerous works on philosophical and other subjects as well as his study of Shaw, and was a popular broadcaster on the wartime 'Brains Trust'. Shaw lectured at Oxford on 'The Nature of Drama' early in March 1914 and was reported at some length in the *Oxford Times* of 6 March.

I first saw Shaw in 1913, my third year at Oxford, when he visited the University to give a public lecture in the Schools on the origin of the drama. The University had turned out in force, some to do him honour, more out of curiosity, and the place was packed. I had a seat in the embrasure of a window, high up in the wall. As the tall, erect figure, stiff as a ramrod, came striding down the central aisle, the place shook with applause. Glowing with hero-worship, I gazed with rapture, more particularly upon the hair which still bore traces of red, the rampant moustache and the beard, every hair of which seemed to bristle with vitality. . . .

I cannot remember what Shaw said, but I do remember the voice. . . . It was extremely musical and the articulation was as near perfect as makes no matter, with the result that one could hear every word that Shaw said. Now, audibility, which is the first requirement in a public speaker, is also the one most rarely fulfilled.

This melodious voice was very pleasant to listen to, so pleasant that it enabled its owner to make assertions which, coming from any other speaker, would have been immediately challenged, and to rebuke and even on occasion outrageously to insult his audience without causing a riot. You took the rebukes and the insults in your stride, because the intonation in Shaw's voice took them so obviously for granted. The voice was so fresh, so easy, so bland, so confidential, as if it wanted you to share its confidences, its intonation conveyed so persuasive a suggestion of there being no deception, of Shaw having, as it were, nothing whatever up his oratorical sleeve that, had there been all the deception in the world, you would nevertheless not only have been taken in, but would have been glad to have been taken in.

At the same time, the voice was indifferent, casual, almost nonchalant, as if Shaw did not care a row of pins whether you agreed with him or not. It was this habit of his of conveying what were then the most outrageous sentiments – as, for example, that everybody's income ought to be equal irrespective of work done, or that incorrigible criminals or invalids ought to be painlessly eliminated – that first took my breath away and then filled me with inexpressible gratification. The voice was used with the artistry of a master, so that while in retrospect I do not doubt that the owner's intention was to produce precisely the conviction that the voice did in fact produce – namely, that what was so obvious to the speaker must be equally obvious to everyone in the audience who was not a congenital idiot – this intention was carefully concealed.

'Scotch Lecturing'

LADY GREGORY

From *Lady Gregory's Journals*, vol. I, ed. Daniel J. Murphy, Coole Edition xiv (Gerrards Cross, Colin Smythe, 1978) pp. 253–4. Lady Gregory was visiting the Shaws at Ayot St. Laurence. She arrived on 18 May 1921.

GBS and Charlotte came to meet me, he back from his Scotch lecturing; had immense audiences. I asked what his moral purpose was in speaking to the Scotch – what he was doing for them. He said he wasn't doing them any good, that was the worst of it. He had gone to lecture for the Fabian Society of Edinburgh, and when in Scotland some time ago he had had an audience of working-men and tried to help them; now he had a paying audience of the well-to-do; but he must have set up that Fabian Society for ever and ever. . . .

We have been for a motor drive. I asked if he was ever nervous lecturing. He said not now, but at the beginning his hands used to tremble so much he could hardly hold the notes (just like me at my lecture for the Theatre at Fagan's on Thursday!). He used the same lecture all through Scotland, quotes some preacher – Whitefield[1] – 'No sermon is any good till you have preached it forty times.'

NOTE

1. George Whitefield (1714–70), Calvinist Methodist leader, published sermons, autobiography and other writings. He preached with great success in Scotland in 1741 and 1742. He enjoyed extraordinary popularity as a preacher, and is said to have delivered more than 18,000 sermons.

A Shaw Flop

FENNER BROCKWAY

From Fenner Brockway, *Towards Tomorrow* (London: Hart-Davies, MacGibbon, 1977) p. 62. Brockway stood unsuccessfully as ILP candidate for Lancaster in 1922 and Shaw was one of a distinguished band who came there to speak on his behalf in the large Ashton Hall.

I met Shaw at the station and left him at the Railway Hotel to rest; when I called to take him to the meeting he was brushing his artificial teeth. Lifting a plate in one hand and waving his toothbrush in the other he exclaimed: 'Young man, you are witnessing an historic act. When man made teeth better than God the barrier between barbarism and civilisation was pierced.' Shaw's speech at the Ashton Hall was a flop; he never got going and the audience was bored. He saved it by his last sentence. 'Ladies and Gentleman,' he declared, his voice vibrant at last, 'you will be able to inform your incredulous grandchildren that you heard Bernard Shaw when he was dull.' There were some in the audience who thought GBS was deliberately dull for the sake of his conclusion, but in fact he was deeply ashamed. He declined to face the ILP members at a social we had arranged after the meeting. I took him to the hotel and put him on the night train to London: 'I shall recover reading my own incomparable writing,' was his last remark. He proposed to correct proofs through the night journey.

Part 3
In Print: Journalism, Publishers, Printers

INTRODUCTION TO PART 3

In 1898, when he took over from Shaw the position of drama critic for Frank Harris's *Saturday Review*, Max Beerbohm wrote of his predecessor: 'With all his faults – grave though they are and not to be counted on the fingers of one hand – he is, I think, by far the most brilliant and remarkable journalist in London.'[1] William Archer said of Shaw's qualities as a music critic, that he had 'a peculiar genius for bringing day-by-day musical criticism into vital relation with aesthetics at large, and even with ethics and politics – in a word, with life'.[2] The same is true of the splendid series of weekly theatre reviews with which Shaw concluded his career as a regular journalist in the years 1895–8. It was in the sphere of journalism that Shaw first made his mark as a literary figure, and both as music and drama critic his approach and style were revolutionary.

Shaw first appeared in print on 3 April 1875 when a letter of his from Dublin was published in the London weekly, *Public Opinion*. Although he first earned money for his writing the following year in London, when Vandeleur Lee paid him for ghosting music criticism in the *Hornet*, he had little success or income as a journalist until he met William Archer. In 1885 Archer secured him book reviewing in the *Pall Mall Gazette* and music criticism in the *Magazine of Music* and the *Dramatic Review* (to which he contributed weekly unsigned notices through most of the year) and in 1886 he engineered his appointment as the *World's* art critic.[3] But Shaw's fame as a reviewer of the arts did not begin to establish itself until he undertook a weekly column, 'Musical Mems', in the *Star* in February 1889. In May 1890 he transferred it to the *World*, exchanging his pseudonym 'Corno di Bassetto' for his initials. Within months of giving up the music column in August 1894, GBS accepted Frank Harris's invitation to become dramatic critic for the *Saturday Review*. When he collected his play reviews in *Dramatic Essays and Opinions* (1907), his 'Author's Apology' warned the reader that 'what he is about to study is not a series of judgements aiming at impartiality but a siege laid to the theatre of the nineteenth century by an author who had to cut his own way into it at the point of the pen and throw some of its defenders into the moat'. Although he retired from regular journalism in 1898 Shaw continued throughout his life to be a frequent contributor to newspapers and periodicals, either as a correspondent or as a writer of occasional articles. He hugely enjoyed public controversies, and other journalists sought his opinion on an extraordinary range of topics.

Shaw took a keen interest in all aspects of the publishing and printing trades. A devotee of William Morris in his ideas about book production, he was rigorous and demanding in his dealings with publishers and printers about the physical appearance of his own works. His extensive correspondence with publishers began late in 1879 with the first of several unsuccessful attempts to place his novel *Immaturity*. His first play, *Widowers' Houses*, was published by Henry & Co. in 1893, and his first collection, the two-volume *Plays Pleasant and Unpleasant*, was brought out by Grant Richards in 1898. But by 1903 Shaw had decided that Richards did not promote his books with enough energy. He had *Man and Superman* printed on his own account, and arranged with Archibald Constable & Co. to publish it on commission. He kept to the arrangement for the rest of his life, as it gave him an unusual degree of control over the issue of his work. The Webbs were already using a similar system with the same printer (R. & R. Clark of Edinburgh) and Shaw must have been influenced by their example.

NOTES

1. Max Beerbohm, 'Why I ought not to have become a Dramatic Critic', *Saturday Review*, 28 May 1898.
2. Quoted in Archibald Henderson, *George Bernard Shaw: His Life and Works* (London: Hurst & Blackett, 1911) p. 230.
3. See above, pp. 25–7, for Shaw's 1896 account of his early journalistic career.

Shaw 'Discovered': I

H. M. HYNDMAN

From Henry Mayers Hyndman, *Further Reminiscences* (London: Macmillan, 1912) pp. 202–3. Archibald Henderson reports Hyndman saying in 1907 that he approached Greenwood on Shaw's behalf in 1883, and so was 'the first person in England to discover Shaw' (Henderson, *Bernard Shaw, Playboy and Prophet* [London and New York: D. Appleton, 1932] p. 265). Frederick Greenwood (1830–1909), a distinguished and influential conservative journalist, began the *St James's Gazette* in May 1880.

I thought if there was one man in London who would understand Shaw and would see the value of his writing it would be Frederick Greenwood. I gave Shaw, therefore, a letter of introduction to my old friend, feeling confident that, so far as journalism of a high class was concerned, Shaw would find an appreciative and congenial opening in the *St James's Gazette*, which Greenwood was then editing. Nothing came of this. What happened I do not precisely know. But I was much surprised, for there was no more acute judge of exceptional literary talent than Greenwood, and Shaw had certainly plenty to say and could say it well.

Years afterwards, when Greenwood was staying with us at Brasted, I asked him, casually, as we walked up and down the lawn together, whether he remembered my letter about Shaw, and how it was that Shaw never wrote for the *St James's*. 'The fact is, Hyndman, Shaw is quite unhuman, and I never could stand that.' I did not pursue the matter much farther at the time; but I believe what really upset Greenwood, though why it should have done so, as a matter of Shaw's writing, I do not know, was the indifference displayed by one of the characters in a novel of Shaw's to the death of his wife.[1]

NOTE

1. Sidney Trefusis in *An Unsocial Socialist*.

Shaw 'Discovered': II

WILLIAM ARCHER

From C. Archer, *William Archer: Life, Work and Friendships* (London: George Allen & Unwin, 1931) pp. 119–35. Charles Archer's biography of his brother draws on autobiographical writings by William, the manuscripts of which do not appear to have survived. William here outlines the beginnings of his friendship with Shaw and the work he was able to turn Shaw's way from the mid-1880s.

In the winter of 1881–2,* Archer wrote long after, 'I used to go almost every day to the British Museum Reading Room in London. I frequently sat next to a man of about my own age (twenty-five)* who attracted my attention, partly by his peculiar colouring – his pallid skin and bright

*This is clearly a slip of the pen. We should read '1882–3' and 'twenty-six'.

red hair and beard – partly by the odd combination of authors whom he used to study – for I saw him, day after day, poring over Karl Marx's *Das Kapital* and an orchestral score of Wagner's *Tristan und Isolde*. How we first made acquaintance I have forgotten;[1] but one did not need to meet him twice to be sure that George Bernard Shaw was a personality to be noted and studied. . . . At any rate we became fast friends. . . .

'The post of art-critic of the *World* fell vacant,[2] and Edmund Yates asked me to undertake it. I told him I knew nothing about painting: he said that did not matter. I did the work laboriously and infamously for some weeks, until my conscience could endure it no longer. I then got Shaw to do a specimen article, which I sent to Yates, and thus easily secured him the post. He didn't know much more about painting than I, but he thought he did, and that was the main point. I had, as a matter of fact, already forced upon him a good deal of work as a reviewer of books.[3] Then the post of musical critic fell vacant, and I secured it for Shaw, by the simple process of telling Yates the truth: namely, that he was at once the most competent and the most brilliant writer on music then living in England.'

NOTES

1. The date and circumstances of their meeting are elusive, but shortly before his death Shaw stated that they were introduced by Henry Salt (see his Preface to Stephen Winsten, *Salt and His Circle* [London: Hutchinson, 1951] p. 13).
2. Towards the end of 1885; Archer was already dramatic critic for the *World*.
3. For the *Pall Mall Gazette*; see above, p. 28, n. 13.

The *Star* and 'Corno di Bassetto'

T. P. O'CONNOR

From T. P. O'Connor's regular column in *TP's and Cassell's Weekly*, 12 July 1924. Thomas Power O'Connor (1848–1929) successfully combined journalism and politics. He entered Parliament in 1880 and represented the same Liverpool constituency from 1885 until his death. He founded a number of papers and journals – the *Star*, a radical evening paper, being the first. It was launched on 17 January 1888, with Shaw on the editorial staff. Here and elsewhere O'Connor followed Shaw's version of events (see above, p. 26), but the truth is that Shaw took his own way out of the political impasse by resigning his editorial position after less than a month, on 9 February. He continued to contribute occasional pieces, but though he started to act as second string to the regular music critic, E. Belfort Bax, in August 1888, he did not take over the position until Bax resigned the following February.

Mr Shaw, whose name up to that moment I had scarcely heard, was recommended to me by Mr H. W. Massingham, my assistant editor, as a suitable man to write editorials.

I accepted the advice, and Mr Shaw began writing for me, not leaders, but sub-leaders. The articles were naturally brilliant, but they were the articles of a Socialist, and my paper was a Liberal paper. Like so many Socialists of that period and of this, Mr Shaw had apparently much more animosity against the Liberals than against the Conservatives, and I would find some morning, to my surprise and horror, an attack on a Liberal leader, and by choice on one who was among my closest personal as well as political friends.

John Morley[1] at that time was the special aversion of Mr Shaw and also, I think, of Mr Sidney Webb. And one day Mr Morley himself brought me a copy of the *Star* with a very venomous little thrust at him which rather worried me. The truth was that I was writing so much for the paper myself, and in such a hurry – for the first edition of an evening paper in those days came out at about 10 a.m. – that I hadn't time left to supervise what my colleagues did.

The situation became impossible. On the one hand, I could not expect Mr Shaw to write anything he did not believe in; and, on the other hand, I could not reconcile myself to the idea of losing so good a man. I have always, besides, hated sending a journalist out of a job; I had gone through too terrible hardships myself ever lightly to expose any other journalist to such possibilities.

It was not I but Mr Massingham who suggested the solution. He told me that Shaw, among other gifts, had that of music. He not only knew all about music, but also could play – I think it was the piano. I jumped at the idea, and Mr Shaw was appointed to write a weekly musical article at the price of three guineas a week.[2]

I little knew what I was doing. The articles began to appear, and the world soon knew that there was a new and strange portent in the realm of musical criticism. Never before and never since – except from Mr Shaw himself – was there such musical criticism. Mr Shaw but mildly describes the quality of his articles when he describes them as personal.

Personal! They were appallingly personal. I have a dim recollection of one article in which Mr Shaw dropped from his criticism of some symphony to say that he had been hypnotised by the wild eye of the man with the piccolo, who at the same moment sent forth from his piccolo a wild shriek. After that Mr Shaw could hear no more.

Articles of this kind soon began to attract notice, and they attracted the notice, among other people, of the proprietors of the *World*, then a popular and prosperous journal. Mr Shaw was offered a position on that paper. It was then, and not from me, that he got the six pounds a week of which he has spoken. And perhaps it was the position he attained which led up to the next great step in his career, namely, the possibility of getting the theatrical managers to consider his many but all unacted plays. And then his genius getting its chance led him to his great but well-deserved fame and fortune.

NOTES

1. John Morley, later Viscount Morley (1838–1923), politician, journalist and man of letters, was at this time MP for Newcastle. He was a leader of the radical wing of the Liberals and advocated Home Rule for Ireland, but as a strong individualist he opposed socialism.
2. Shaw was in fact paid two guineas a week and O'Connor's refusal to pay him more was a leading reason for his move in May 1890 to the *World*, which offered him five.

From Drama Critic to Dramatist: I

FRANK HARRIS

From Frank Harris, *Contemporary Portraits*, 4 vols (London: Methuen, 1915–24) II, 3–8. Frank Harris (1856–1931), journalist, author and adventurer, had edited the *Evening News* and the *Fortnightly Review* before he bought the *Saturday Review* in September 1894. He set about improving its quality and circulation by engaging the best contributors he knew and for four years made it the most brilliant weekly in London. Shaw, who had begun his weekly contributions in January 1895, gave notice in April 1895 of his intention to retire at the end of the season, but was forced by ill-health to hand over to Max Beerbohm in May. Harris sold the *Review* later that year. Shaw remained appreciative of the opportunity Harris had given him and never cast him off during the long years of his decline.

The idea of connecting Shaw the Socialist orator with the high Tory *Saturday Review* pleased me; the very incongruity ter. pted and his ability was beyond question. Now and again I had read his weekly articles on music and while admiring the keen insight of them and the satiric light he threw on pompous pretences and unrealities, I noticed that he had begun to repeat himself, as if he had said all he had to say on that theme.

What should I ask him to write about ? What was his true vein? He had as much humour as Wilde – the name at once crystallised my feeling – that was what Shaw should do, I said to myself, write on the theatre; in essence his talent, like Wilde's, was theatrical, almost to caricature, certain, therefore, to carry across the footlights and have an immediate effect.

I wrote to him at once, telling him my opinion of his true talent and asking him to write a weekly article for the *Saturday Review*.

He answered immediately; a letter somewhat after this fashion:

'How the Dickens you knew that my thoughts had been turning to the theatre of late and that I'd willingly occupy myself with it exclusively for some time to come, I can't imagine. But you've hit the clout, as the Elizabethans used to say, and, if you can afford to pay me regularly, I'm your man so long as the job suits me and I suit the job. What can you afford to give?'

My answer was equally prompt and to the point:

'I can afford to give you so much a week, more, I believe, than you are now getting. If that appeals to you, start in at once; bring me your first article by next Wednesday and we'll have a final pow-wow.'

On the Wednesday Shaw turned up with the article, and I had a good look at him and a long talk with him. Shaw at this time was nearing forty; very tall, over six feet in height and thin to angularity; a long bony face, corresponding, I thought, to a tendency to get to bedrock everywhere; rufous fair hair and long, untrimmed reddish beard; grey-blue English eyes with straight eyebrows tending a little upwards from the nose and thus adding a touch of Mephistophelian sarcasm to the alert, keen expression. He was dressed carelessly in tweeds with a Jaeger flannel shirt and negligent tie; contempt of frills written all over him; his hands clean and well-kept, but not manicured. His complexion, singularly fair even for a man with reddish hair, seemed too bloodless to me, reminded me of his vegetarianism which had puzzled me more than a little for some time. His entrance into the room, his abrupt movements – as jerky as the ever-changing mind – his perfect unconstraint – all showed an able man, very conscious of his ability, very direct, very sincere, sharply decisive.

'I liked your letter,' Shaw began, 'as I told you; the price, too, suits me for the moment; but – you won't alter my article, will you?'

'Not a word,' I said. 'If I should want anything changed, which is most unlikely, I'd send you a proof and ask you to alter it; but that is not going to occur often. I like original opinions even though I don't agree with them.'

After some further talk, he said:

'Very well then. If the money appears regularly you can count on me for a weekly outpouring. You don't limit me in any way?'

'Not in any way,' I answered. . . .

Shaw was a most admirable contributor, always punctual unless there was some good reason for being late; always scrupulous, correcting his proofs heavily, with rare conscientiousness, and always doing his very best.

I soon realised that the drama of the day had never been so pungently criticised; I began to compare Shaw's articles with the *Dramaturgie* of Lessing,[1] and it was Shaw who gained by the comparison.

His critical writing was exactly like his speaking and indeed like his creative dramatic work; very simple, direct and lucid, clarity and sincerity his characteristics. No pose, no trace of affectation; a man of one piece, out to convince not to persuade; a bare logical argument lit up by gleams of sardonic humour; humour of the head as a rule and not of the heart. His writing seemed artless, but there is a good deal of art in his plays and art too, can be discovered both in his speaking and in his critical work, but whether there is enough art to serve as a prophylactic against time, remains to be seen.

His seriousness, sincerity and brains soon brought the actor-managers out in arms against him. Naturally they did not condemn his writing, but his dress and behaviour. Two or three of them told me at various times that Shaw was impossible.

'He often comes to the theatre in ordinary dress,' said one, 'and looks awful.'

'You ought to thank your stars that he goes to your theatre at all,' I replied. 'I certainly shall not instruct him how to clothe himself.'

'What I object to,' said another, 'is that he laughs in the wrong place. It is dreadful when a favourite actor is saying something very pathetic or sentimental to see a great figure in grey stretch himself out in the front stalls and roar with laughter.'

'I know,' I replied grinning, 'and the worst of it is that all the world laughs with Shaw when he shows it the unconscious humour of your performance.'

An amusing incident closed this controversy. One night a manager told Shaw he could not go into the stalls in that dress. Shaw immediately began to take off his coat.

'No, no,' cried the actor-manager; 'I mean you must dress like other people.'

Shaw glanced at the rows of half-dressed women: 'I'm not going to take off my shirt,' he exclaimed, 'in order to be like your clients,' and forthwith left the house.

The dispute had one good result. Shaw asked me to buy his tickets. 'I hate the whole practice of complimentary tickets,' he said. 'It is intended to bind one to praise and I resent the implied obligation.'

Of course, I did as he wished and there the trouble ended.

At rare intervals I had to tell Shaw his article was too long and beg him to shorten it. For months together I had nothing to do except congratulate myself on having got him as a contributor; though at first he was strenuously objected to by many of my readers who wrote begging me to cancel their subscriptions or at least to cease from befouling their houses with 'Shaw's socialistic rant and theatric twaddle'.

NOTE

1. Gotthold Ephraim Lessing (1729–81), German dramatist and critic, published his *Hamburgische Dramaturgie* in 1767–8, while he was literary adviser and critic to a short-lived German National Theatre in Hamburg. In a series of papers on theatrical problems he tried to break away from French classicism.

From Drama Critic to Dramatist: II

From C. R., 'Mr Shaw's Future. A Conversation', *Academy*, 30 April 1889. C. R. probably represents Clarence Rook (see above, p. 22).

'We are anxious about your future,' I remarked to Mr Bernard Shaw.

'There is really no news about my future,' said Mr Shaw, 'except that I am going to throw up dramatic criticism.'

'Good gracious! Why?' I asked.

Mr Shaw, who does not even sit in a chair as other men sit, twisted himself rapidly round a sprained foot – the result of overmuch cycling.

'Well, I've been writing dramatic criticism in the *Saturday Review* for nearly four years, and really I've said all I've got to say about actors and acting. If I went on I should only repeat myself; I've begun to do that already. After all, when you have written two or three articles about Beerbohm Tree you have said all there is to say about Beerbohm Tree. It doesn't take very long to say all you think of Irving.[1]

'I shall lose my pulpit,' continued Mr Shaw, 'and that is a pity. But I fancy the world is rather tired of being preached at. Besides, I suspect it is beginning to find me out. For years I was supposed to be brilliant and sparkling and audacious. That was quite a mistake. I am really slow, industrious, painstaking, timid. Only I have continually been forced into positions that I am bound to accept and go through with. I am not clever at all.'

Mr Shaw sat upright and looked at me with complete candour in his eyes, and I made a gesture of polite dissent.

'I am a genius,' pronounced Mr Shaw, sitting upon his shoulder-blades.

'After all,' proceeded Mr Shaw, 'I have accomplished something. I have made Shakespeare popular by knocking him off his pedestal and kicking him round the place, and making people realise that he's not a demi-god, but a dramatist.'

'Then do you think of going in for Parliament?'

Mr Shaw writhed round his disabled foot.

'I haven't much voice,' he said; 'but I daresay I might get a place in the chorus at the opera. And I should be doing quite as much good there, and have a deal more fun, than in the chorus at Westminster. Think of the incredible waste of time! And you must remember that for the last ten years I – I and a few of my associates – have practically directed public policy. There's no reason at all for my going into Parliament. But the Vestry – now there is some sense in a Vestry. It does something. Really, my dear fellow [Mr Shaw nursed his foot in his lap], you ought to be on a Vestry. If you take it humorously, you can laugh at the amazing difficulties it finds in doing the simplest things. If you take it seriously, you learn how things ultimately get done. . . .

'I have always made it a rule, you know, to be mixed up with practical life; that is where I score and the purely literary man fails. The people who write Adelphi melodramas know life – of a kind.[2] They know the bar-loafing blackguard, and the sort of thing he likes. I know life – the life of action – affairs. The literary man can't write a play, because he knows nothing at all of life. The literary man ought to serve on a Vestry. For my own part I have found my experience of affairs invaluable in the writing of plays.'

'Then are we to regard you in the future as a dramatist?'

'I am just in the middle of the first act of a new play.'

'What is it about?'

'Well, this time I am going to give Shakespeare a lead. Cleopatra is the heroine, but Cæsar, and not Antony, is the hero. And I want to see Forbes Robertson and Mrs Patrick Campbell in it.'[3] . . .

Mr Shaw dug both his hands deep into his pockets, and turned on to one side.

'Criticism is a poor thing to spend your life over,' he said. 'Four years over the painters of London, four years over the musicians, and four years over the actors – that is quite long enough to express any views you may have. It's an awful labour done as I do it. And you can't make money at that sort of work. Now, you wouldn't think that *Arms and the Man* was a great success. I don't suppose anyone made much out of it, as things go. But from first to last it has brought me £800. And that was when my percentage of profits was low. *The Devil's Disciple*, which has been running in America, has drawn £25,000; and on that I get 10 per cent. I should have to write my heart out for six years in the *Saturday* to make as much. It was quite easy to write, too. A young woman I know wanted to make a portrait of me, sitting on the corner of a table, which is a favourite attitude of mine. So I wrote the play in a note-book to fill up the time. I write all my plays on scraps of paper at odd times – on omnibuses and places like that.'

NOTES

1. (Sir) Henry Irving (1838–1905) at the Lyceum and (Sir) Herbert Beerbohm Tree (1852–1917) at the Haymarket, and from 1897 at Her Majesty's, were the dominant London actor–managers in the late Victorian period. Shaw was sharply critical of Irving in the *Saturday Review* and Irving never produced *The Man of Destiny*, which Shaw had written for him and Ellen Terry. Tree, however, created Higgins in the first English production of *Pygmalion* at His Majesty's in 1914.

2. The Adelphi Theatre in the Strand presented a famous series of melodramas in the 1880s and 1890s, starring William Terriss (1847–97), for whom Shaw wrote *The Devil's Disciple.*

3. (Sir) Johnston Forbes-Robertson (1853–1937) appeared as Caesar in the first American production of *Caesar and Cleopatra* in 1906, and in the first English production the following year, but Mrs Patrick Campbell (1865–1940) did not play Shaw until she undertook Eliza in the first English production of *Pygmalion*.

Shaw's Verdict on Journalism

From G. Bernard Shaw, 'Who I Am, and What I Think. II', *Candid Friend*, 18 May 1901. The interviewer was Frank Harris (see above, p. 29).

'What do you think of journalism as a profession?'

'Daily journalism is a superhuman profession: excellence in it is quite beyond mortal strength and endurance. Consequently, it trains literary men to scamp their work. A weekly *feuilleton* is at least possible: I did one for ten years. I took extraordinary pains – all the pains I was capable of – to get to the bottom of everything I wrote about. There is an indescribable levity – not triviality, mind, but levity – something spritelike about the final truth of a matter: and this exquisite levity communicates itself to the style of the writer who will face the labour of digging down to it. It is the half truth which is congruous, heavy, serious, and suggestive of a middle-aged or elderly philosopher. The whole truth is often the first thing that comes into the head of a fool or a child; and when a wise man forces his way to it through the many strata of his sophistications, its wanton, perverse air reassures him instead of frightening him. Ten years of such work, at the rate of two thousand words a week or thereabouts – say, roughly, a million words – all genuine journalism, dependent on the context of the week's history for its effect, was an apprenticeship which made me master of my own style. But I don't think it was practicable journalism. I could not have kept up the quality of my work if I had undertaken more than one *feuilleton*; and even that I could not have done without keeping myself up to the neck all the rest of the week in other activities – gaining other efficiencies and gorging myself with life and experience as well. My income as a journalist began in 1885 at £117 0s. 3d.; and it ended at about £500, by which time I had reached the age at which we discover that journalism is a young man's stand-by, not an old man's livelihood. So I am afraid that even weekly journalism is superhuman except for young men. The older ones *must* scamp it; and the younger ones must live plainly and cheaply, if they are to get their work up to the pitch at which they can command real freedom to say what they think. Of course, they do nothing of the sort. If they did, journalism would train them in literature as nothing else could. Would, but doesn't. It spoils them instead. If you want a problem stated, a practised journalist will do it with an air that is the next best thing to solving it. But he never solves it: he hasn't time, and wouldn't get paid any more for the solution if he *had* time. So he chalks up the statement, and runs away from the solution.'

'What is your honest opinion of GBS?'[1]

'Oh, one of the most successful of my fictions, but getting a bit tiresome, I should think. GBS gets on my nerves and bores me, except when he is working out something solid for me, or saying what I want said. GBS be blowed!'

'What is your definition of humour?'

'Anything that makes you laugh. But the finest sort draws a tear along with the laugh.'

NOTE

1. Shaw had signed GBS below his theatre reviews for Harris and his music column in the *World*.

Publishing *Plays Pleasant and Unpleasant*

GRANT RICHARDS

From Grant Richards, *Author Hunting by an Old Literary Sportsman: Memories of Years spent mainly in Publishing, 1897–1925* (London: Hamish Hamilton, 1934) pp. 13–14, 124–5, 128–9, 134. Grant Richards (1872–1948), author and publisher, had worked with W. T. Stead on the *Review of Reviews* before he opened his own publishing firm on 1 January 1897. Late in 1896 he wrote to Shaw proposing to publish his plays; Shaw's response was hardly encouraging but he subsequently agreed to meet Richards after a theatrical first night. This briefly conducted meeting opens the following selections from Richard's account of the gestation of *Plays Pleasant and Unpleasant*. The two volumes were finally published in April 1898, and issued simultaneously in Chicago by Herbert S. Stone. The *Plays Unpleasant* volume included Shaw's first three plays, *Widowers' Houses*, *The Philanderer* and *Mrs Warren's Profession*. *Plays Pleasant* included *Arms and the Man*, *Candida*, *The Man of Destiny* and *You Never Can Tell*.

The chief things Shaw had to say to me as we strode into Tottenham Court Road . . . was that I was crazy to think of printing his plays, that to do so would ruin me in no time, that there was no sufficient public for them yet; and so on and so on. It seemed to me more than doubtful whether he was even attempting to hear what I had to say. We were walking too fast. Shaw was wearing his large, shovel, felt-hat and his baggy brown Jaeger suit and his poultice tie; I was in dress-clothes. We must have looked more than a little odd. He would hardly allow me to get an oar in. However, whenever I did have a chance I chipped in with a fresh appeal to what I considered common horse-sense. GBS, however, would have none of it, and continued to impress his views on me until, after a time relenting, he left me at his own door in the spirit of on your own head be it if you insist; do not expect me to speak up for you in the Bankruptcy Court. What did all this pessimism matter to me? In theory at least George Bernard Shaw had agreed that I should produce the Plays. The fact that J. T. Grein as Henry & Co. had already produced *Widowers' Houses* without attracting many buyers,[1] counted for very little in my mind, did not in any way reduce the elasticity of my steps, as I walked home to Flood Street, Chelsea, from Fitzroy Square. Having the promise of Bernard Shaw on my first list of announcements, I had indeed made sure that I should succeed in putting myself on the map. . . .

With *Plays Pleasant and Unpleasant* the period of gestation was a long one. We spent time discussing the agreement. Not that GBS was not at work. I am sure he was. And he would raise fresh points. I wanted the books to be in their way beautifully printed; he had the same wish, but would have them printed by a Union house. I suppose I doubted whether a Union house could do justice to my ideal. I had few notions of what made a Union house. I do not think I had a Union house on my list. The problem shifted to the question of fair wages, and R. & R. Clark were approved. . . .

In the meantime I was plugging away at the Edinburgh printers and working at proofs. I little knew what those proofs were to let me in for. Those were the days when William Morris was revolutionising modern printing by his Kelmscott Press. Shaw, up to his eyes in Socialist propaganda with Morris, was intensely interested in his artistic enterprises, and was enchanted by his books and his rules for making printed pages pictorial in themselves. Better printers than R. & R. Clark of Edinburgh under the late Edward Clark and Peter Begg were not to be found; and I had, I thought, proved my own good taste in the design of books already published. But the Morris revolution, with Shaw as its fiercest fanatic, burst on us like a typhoon. We were willing to learn; and the new margins, the elimination of 'mutton quads' and all the rest of it, justified themselves in the result;[2] but our docility was sorely tested, as will presently appear. Even the rate at which Clark worked was not good enough for Shaw. He writes again, no doubt led on by the fact that I had been spending a quiet fortnight at St Moritz, which had in those days no such excited winter season as it has now:

> The Argoed, Penallt, Monmouth
> 26 August 1897
>
> This letter of yours comes well, Grant Richards, from a man who has been bounding idly up the Jungfrau and down the Matterhorn to an exhausted wretch who, after a crushing season, has slaved these four weeks for four hours a day at your confounded enterprise. I have sent three plays to the printer, transmogrified beyond recognition, made more thrilling than any novel; and he has only sent me proofs of one, of which it has cost me endless letters and revises to get the page right, to teach him how to space letters for emphasis, and how to realise that I mean my punctuation to be followed. . . .

Plays Pleasant and Unpleasant did manage to come out early in 1898. I was as proud as Punch. The look and feel of it gave me intense pleasure. But it did not make me rich. As I have shown, its rate of sale was entirely incommensurate with the amount of notice it attracted and with the reputation it helped to make for its author.

NOTES

1. *Widowers' Houses*, published in May 1893 as no. 1 in the Independent Theatre series, had sold only 150 copies in its first year (see *Collected Letters 1874–1897*, pp. 423–4). J. T. Grein, responsible for its 1892 première (see below, pp. 122–3), had an interest in Henry & Co.
2. Morris's idea was to dispose of the margins so that the two facing pages of each opening looked like one picture. 'Mutton quads' is printer's slang for an em space, i.e. a patch of white. Morris wanted his pages to look as black and even in tone as possible.

A Printer Corrected

W. D. ORCUTT

William Dana Orcutt, 'Celebrities Off Parade: George Bernard Shaw', *Christian Science Monitor*, 28 June 1934. William Dana Orcutt (1870–1953), book designer and author, was associated with the University Press, Cambridge, Mass., when in 1903 he was offered the chance of setting *Man and Superman* in type to secure the American copyright. (The requisite copy was deposited on 12 August 1903 but the book was not issued commercially in America – by Brentano – until June 1904.) In the following article he drew extensively on a letter from Shaw dated 28 August 1903, given in full in his book *Celebrities Off Parade* (1935), and reprinted in Shaw, *Collected Letters 1898–1910*, pp. 352–5.

One day, about 1900, I received a telephone call from a widely known Boston publisher.[1] He said, in effect, that an unknown British author had submitted a manuscript which the editor felt was too socialistic in its treatment to be acceptable. The author had requested, so the telephone message continued, that, if not desired for publication, the Boston house should arrange to have the manuscript put into type in order to obtain an American copyright.

'We don't care to have anything to do with it,' the publisher stated flatly; 'but before returning the manuscript we thought perhaps you might be interested.'

'Who is the unknown author?' I inquired.

'It's a man named Shaw.'

'What is the rest of his name?' I persisted.

'Wait a minute and I'll look it up.'

Presently the information came: 'His name is George Bernard Shaw. Did you ever hear of him?'

I smiled quietly to myself. I had recently returned from England, where I had become aware of the growing power of this new personality.

'Yes,' I replied. 'I happened to lunch with him in London a few weeks ago, as a fellow-guest of Cobden-Sanderson.[2] I think I'll take a chance on the unknown Mr Shaw.'

Thus came into my hands the manuscript of *Man and Superman*, and so I began business relations with George Bernard Shaw. Our relations, personal and business, continued for several years to be a stimulating experience. His personality in those early days was no different from that with which the world has since become familiar. His ideas on typography, as on everything else, were not only clearly defined but absolutely set, and no amount of argument could move him.

Shaw has always been an ardent champion of the work of William Morris at the Kelmscott Press, and his attitude toward other printers, especially American, showed little less than contempt. On one occasion he took me caustically to task for using more than one size of type upon one of his title-pages, but removed the sting from his criticism by adding, 'After all, any other printer would have used sixteen instead of two, so I bless you for your restraint.'

We had another set-to on the use of apostrophes. 'Don't use them,' he insisted, 'in such words as *Ive*, *youve*, *lets*, *thats*, where the meaning is quite unmistakable. Until we have a phonetic alphabet to distinguish between long and short *e* I suppose I must yield on such words as *Ill*, *hell*, *shell* for *I'll*, *he'll*, and *she'll*, but we shall never get rid of these senseless disfigurements that have destroyed all the old sense of beauty in printing until people have been forced to have some consideration for a book as something to look at as well as something to read.'

We were hopelessly at odds over Morris's use of artificial florets to fill in the white spaces at the end of paragraphs, his overloading his text with Burne-Jones decorations,[3] and his determined insistence on securing beauty at the expense of readability. As *objets d'art*, no one admires William Morris's books more than I, but somehow I can't overcome a conviction that, after all has been said and done, a book is intended to be read.

Shaw pleaded with me to forswear my ideas and embrace the Morris principles. 'There is no reason,' he insisted, 'why you should not make yourself famous through all the ages by turning out editions of standard works on the Morris lines, whilst other printers are exhausting themselves in dirty felt end papers, sham Kelmscott capitals, leaf ornaments in quad sauce, and wondering why no one in Europe will pay twopence for them.'

In spite of my shortcomings, I must have grown in favour, for he became solicitous for me to meet Emery Walker, of the Doves Press, and Sydney Cockerell, at one time William Morris's secretary.[4] 'They both regard an American printer as a monster,' Shaw admitted to me frankly – 'thanks to your sham Kelmscotts and other horrors – but they are very amiable men. Approaching them, as you would, as a repentant prodigal, really desirous of spreading the light in Darkest America, you would find out from them all there was to find out about printing in the world.'

Thus, when I receive a complimentary comment from some booklover on some typographic design that has found favour, or when I discover the slightest trace of complacency creeping into my work, I get out my old notebooks and the Shaw correspondence, and, with due humility, put myself back into my proper place.

NOTES

1. The American publisher Harry Houghton, head of Houghton Mifflin.
2. Thomas James Cobden-Sanderson (1840–1922), bookbinder and co-founder of the Doves Press.
3. (Sir) Edward Coley Burne-Jones (1833–98), painter, was a close friend of Morris from their undergraduate days at Oxford, and was much interested in the work of the Kelmscott Press. He drew the illustrations for the Kelmscott Chaucer.
4. (Sir) Emery Walker (1851–1933), process-engraver and typographer, had founded the Doves Press with Cobden-Sanderson in 1900 after working with Morris at the Kelmscott Press. Shaw had first met him in Morris's socialist circle at Hammersmith in the mid-1880s. (Sir) Sydney Carlyle Cockerell (1867–1962), bibliophile and museum director, served as secretary to Morris and the Kelmscott Press from 1892 to 1898, and was a partner in Walker's engraving business from 1900 to 1904.

'Printing for Bernard Shaw'

WILLIAM MAXWELL

From William Maxwell, 'Printing for Bernard Shaw', *Listener*, 10 November 1949. William Maxwell (1873–1957), in his day the doyen of the printing trade in Scotland – 'Mister William Maxwell/The typographical crack swell', as Shaw jokingly described him (see *Edinburgh Evening News*, 28 September 1949) – was managing director of the Edinburgh firm of R. & R. Clark. He was associated with the firm for fifty-seven years before his retirement in 1949.

GBS scorns the precaution of the registered post. . . . His new books and plays come in instalments through the ordinary post in unsealed envelopes. He writes his original MS in shorthand; his secretary transcribes on green paper which he likes as being restful to the eyes.

Why does he send his manuscript to me direct and not through a publisher? In this (as in many other ways) he is unique. He is the only living British writer, so far as I know, who has his books printed at his own expense. When they have been printed and bound his publisher markets them. We have been co-operating with him in this way for the last fifty-one years.

I remember when GBS decided to have a collected limited edition of his works in some thirty-odd volumes,[1] he told me he would insist on this being set by hand. I told him it would not be set by hand. I argued long and then took a risk. I told him I would show him a hand-set and a machine-set page side by side and let him choose. When the pages were ready I took them to him and did not, of course, indicate which was which. Shaw got out a magnifying glass, and various other gadgets, and retired to another room to examine the pages. Eventually he decided in favour of the one that happened to be machine-set. Even then he was not won round to the idea of machine-setting. And it was not until one of the most eminent typographers of the day [Emery Walker] had confirmed his choice of page that Shaw gave way.

Shaw's nimble wit and repartee, cynical sometimes, sarcastic sometimes but never unkindly, are to me a perpetual joy. He is now in his ninety-fourth year and when he had a fall recently I wrote saying I hoped he had suffered no bad effects. His reply by postcard was characteristically brief. It ran to seven words only and said: 'Which fall? I fall twice every day'. Another Shavian story I particularly like is one he told me when he was staying with me in Edinburgh. He was a music critic in the nineties and he had been invited to a soirée in the house of a noted hostess. She had a new violinist to entertain her hundreds of guests and when the show was over she asked Shaw what he thought of her protégé. He said that the violinist reminded him of Paderewski.[2] 'But,' said the lady, 'Paderewski is not a violinist.' To which Shaw replied, 'Exactly.'

NOTES

1. This began to appear in 1930.
2. Ignacy Jan Paderewski (1860–1941), Polish pianist and composer, made his London debut on 9 May 1890 and became a favourite with British audiences.

The Journalist's Quarry: I

FRANK RUTTER

From Frank Rutter, *Since I was Twenty-five* (London: Constable, 1927) pp. 81–2. Frank V. P. Rutter (1876–1937), who was to establish himself as an art critic and author, was in 1900 a young Cambridge graduate trying to make his way into journalism. He was helped by Thomas Cox Meech (d. 1940), barrister, journalist and author, then editing the *Morning Herald*.

Then, as now, there was a Housing Problem, and as it was to the front in the spring of 1900, Meech suggested I should find somebody to interview on the subject.

Now I had met George Bernard Shaw. He and my eldest brother had been together on the old St Pancras Vestry, and one afternoon when I went there to meet Thornton he had introduced me to Shaw.

Shaw was not then the world-famous dramatist he is now, but even then he was a 'big noise', as the Americans say, and I knew he would be a fine man to interview on the subject. On the strength of this one meeting and the casual introduction I wrote to Shaw, telling him what I wanted and asking if he would consent. Two days later I received a long envelope enclosing a type-written 'interview' on the Housing Problem, far wittier and more intelligent than I could possibly have manufactured even with his verbal aid, and – best of all – a note inside saying, 'Make what use you like of the enclosed and come to tea at 4 p.m. on Thursday when we can talk of other things.'

Could anything be kinder or more generous? Not only to make a youngster a present of a column of valuable copy, but – lest he might feel that he was being got rid of – to follow it up with a friendly invitation. But that is the real Shaw, the kindest-hearted man in the world, as well as the wittiest. Those who know his books know something good: those who know the man know something even better.

Of course I went to tea, and so began an acquaintance which I am proud to claim today. What we talked about – or rather what Shaw talked about – I forget, but I know he kept me chuckling for more than an hour and I can still see the light dancing in his eyes and the demure smile which never left his lips for long.

Two fragments of his conversation I have never forgotten. To me as a novice in the writing trade he had been giving some sound advice, and I remember he wound up with, 'Get talked about, that's the great thing. It doesn't matter what people say so long as they say something.' Profoundly true! The other fragment that survives consists of his parting words when at last I rose to go – 'If you want to see me, join the Fabian Society. You'll always find me there.'

The Journalist's Quarry: II

HANNEN SWAFFER

From Hannen Swaffer, article in *Weekly Illustrated*, 29 September 1934. Hannen Swaffer (1879–1962), journalist and dramatic critic, had joined the staff of the *Daily Mail* in 1902. The occasion of the 'interview' he describes was the performance of a one-act play *Punch: A Toy Tragedy* by (Sir) James Matthew Barrie (1860–1937). It featured Superpunch, made up to resemble Shaw, and ran as part of a Barrie triple-bill at the Comedy Theatre for three weeks in April 1906.

I can remember Shaw when, as a young reporter in Fleet Street, I had to go to interview him so that I could ask him the most foolish of questions, ones that I notice, with the cynicism born of years, are still asked him by the present generation of reporters.

Besides, you know, reporters do not always print what Shaw tells them. They merely quote the silly little bits.

Nearly thirty years ago, Barrie wrote a one-act play about Shaw. I was sent along to his Adelphi flat to ask him, why I did not know, whether he were going to write a play about Barrie! Shaw, if he were not really a kindhearted man, would have kicked me out. Besides, he always liked publicity.

'Have you brought along the £300?' he said.

I made the necessary noises, explaining my misunderstanding in reply.

'If I write an article for William Randolph Hearst,' went on Shaw, 'he pays me £300. If Alfred Harmsworth wants an article, in the form of an interview, he ought to pay £300.[1] He is quite rich. Why should I give it to him for nothing?'

I explained that I lived by asking people things, that I could not pay them.

'Well, if I don't get the £300,' replied Shaw, 'will you get it? I don't mind if you get it. But why should Alfred Harmsworth get it?'

This shows the insistent way in which, in those days, Shaw would explain the evils of capitalism to the young. He exposed Commerce by proving he was the better business man.

Once having made his point, however, Shaw relented.

'Let's see, your columns hold twelve hundred words, don't they?' he said. Shaw knew a lot of things. 'How much do you want? Half a column? Come back in half-an-hour.'

When, half-an-hour later, I returned, I was handed six hundred words typed and signed.

I am afraid the statement was the sheerest bunk. I remember that, in it, Shaw said that an author had to see his press cuttings and that press cutting agencies charged a lot of money, so, in future, Barrie was going to write about him and he was going to write about Barrie, and then they could both save money on press cuttings by sharing them, for all the comments about each would be about both.

NOTE

1. The American William Randolph Hearst (1863–1951) and the Irish-born Alfred Charles William Harmsworth, later Viscount Northcliffe (1865–1922), were both immensely successful newspaper publishers. Harmsworth and his brother Harold had opened a new era in Fleet Street with the launching of the *Daily Mail* in 1896.

The Journalist's Quarry: III

G. R., 'Away from the News', *Daily Mail* (Continental edition), 9 November 1950. Neither the author nor the setting of this incident have been identified, but 'more than forty years ago' places it in the first decade of the century.

Only on one occasion did I meet GBS. The encounter was brief and not at all brotherly. He had come to pay a visit to friends in the Midland city where I was a very young journalist. Some question or other had been raised by him and was being hotly discussed. (I now forget what the topic was.) By arrangement, I was sent to interview him.

At the house, the front door was opened promptly when I rang. 'Are you the reporter?' I was asked by a domestic servant. 'Yes,' was, I thought, the best answer. 'Wait!' I was told and the door was, rather emphatically, banged in my face.

Well, like a quite modest edition of *Casabianca*,[1] I stood – on the doorstep. It had begun to rain and there was but little shelter. Ten minutes passed. Fifteen. Twenty. At twenty-five I felt like throwing a handful of gravel at the lighted window where the fire-light was flickering on the curtains. Half an hour, I was just going to ring and knock violently when the door opened.

'Mr Shaw,' the domestic servant said haughtily, 'will now receive you.' 'Good! Half an hour in the rain.' I remarked, a trifle sniffingly, I imagine, 'I might have sat in that hall chair without spreading any infectious disease throughout the house.'

The domestic servant threw open a door and pompously announced: 'The reporter, sir!' I was ushered into a pleasantly-heated parlour-sort of room. (It was late autumn.)

The great GBS was seated at a desk beside the fire; he had his back to the door. For some minutes he took not the slightest notice of my entry. He was scanning the last page of a manuscript of three or four pages. Then the famous man rose and held it out to me. I took it.

'Why,' I asked, 'was it necessary to keep me waiting for a good half hour after the time fixed, and in –'

'Because I can write the interview much better than you can.' (Of that I could not have the slightest doubt.)

'– and in the rain,' I went on. But GBS took no notice. He went back to his desk. I was not even shown out of the house; I was allowed to find my own way back into the rain.

Well, I was young then. (The little incident happened more than forty years ago.) On my wet way back to the office I pondered my revenge. Over the interview, next day, there appeared, in italics, the little story of how the interview was obtained.

A couple of weeks later I met Shaw's host.

'You had better steer wide of GBS in future,' he remarked. 'You made him wild.'

I did not have to do any steering. Fate took the matter in hand, and I never met him again – to my regret, for I am sure he would have been provocative and pleasant.

NOTE

1. An allusion to 'Casabianca' by Felicia Dorothea Hemans (1793–1835), a poem based on an incident at the battle of the Nile (1798), which begins, 'The boy stood on the burning deck,/Whence all but he had fled.'

The Journalist's Quarry: IV

NEVILLE VEITCH

From Neville Veitch, memoir of Shaw in the *Newcastle Journal*, 3 November 1950. The encounter Veitch describes took place when Shaw visited Newcastle in April 1921 to see *Man and Superman* at the People's Theatre.

On his arrival the writer, as an awed youth, wormed his way into the presence with an equally young reporter from the *Newcastle Journal* who had begged the editor for this his first big assignment.

His first impression was of more than six feet of rough tweeds sitting on a bench in a gas-lit café drinking milk. On approaching for an interview, we were confronted with a jutting beard and a lowering stare.

'How much do you earn?' said a businesslike voice. The modest 1921 salary of a junior reporter was mentioned.

'How much space do you expect to fill?' We mumbled something about a possible half page.

'Well,' said the beard, 'I also am a professional writer, and if I wrote that I would get £50 for it.'

Here followed an accurate and detailed description of newspaper writing, its remuneration, its value as publicity, and its opportunities for propaganda.

'So I am sorry, gentlemen, it is economically impossible for me to give you an interview and the conversation is now at an end.'

We crept to the door to be hailed by a new voice – dare we say with a hint of blarney in it? 'Young man, how long have you been a reporter?'

'Three months.'

'Well,' with an outrageous twinkle and a quite undisguised brogue, 'I have been one forty years and in your place I would now have quite enough in the last half-hour to do half a page on Bernard Shaw.

'And Bernard Shaw has no objection to your using everything he has said.'

The *New Statesman*: I

BEATRICE WEBB

From *The Diary of Beatrice Webb*, vol. III: *1905–1924*, ed. Norman and Jeanne MacKenzie (London: Virago, 1984) p. 188. The following extract opens the entry for 5 July 1913; the *New Statesman* had first appeared on 12 April. The Webbs wanted to start a reformist political weekly to follow up the *Crusade*, the organ of their Poor Law campaign, published between February 1910 and February 1913. Clifford Sharp had edited the *Crusade* and was an obvious choice to edit the new paper. He remained editor until 1931. Shaw put up £1,000 of the £5,000 initial capital and was a director until he resigned in October 1916, disagreeing with the direction the paper had taken. However, trouble arose early on from his refusal to sign his contributions.

GBS has in fact injured the *New Statesman* by his connection with it; we have had the disadvantage of his eccentric and iconoclastic stuff without the advantage of his name. Lots of people will think any article brilliant that they know is by him, whilst dismissing his anonymous contribution as tiresome and of no account, or as purely mischievous. And in all the details of his arrangements he is grossly inconsiderate, refusing to let Sharp know whether or not he was going to write, and what he was going to write about, until, on the day the paper goes to press, there appears on Sharp's table two or three columns – sometimes twice that amount – on any subject that he (Shaw) happens to fancy. Sharp has now decided that if Shaw insists on these terms we are better without him. Meanwhile, persons who subscribed for their weekly portion of Shaw are angry and say they were got to subscribe on false pretences. The *New Statesman* is in fact the one weekly in which Shaw's name never appears, and it is Shaw's name that draws, not his mind. He may become more considerate: he means to be kindly, but he is spoilt – spoilt by intense vanity and intellectual egotism. He will not co-operate on terms of equality.

The *New Statesman*: II

CLIFFORD SHARP

From Clifford Sharp, 'Early Days', *New Statesman and Nation*, 14 April 1934.

Apart from his frequent abusive letters, which we always, of course, enjoyed and which may, possibly, after all, have been of some good to my soul,[1] Shaw was at all times generosity itself in his readiness to help in every possible way without ever casting even the shadow of a question upon my right to the last word. But all the same to a young and wholly inexperienced editor his contributions were a source at first of almost continual embarrassment. We saw eye to eye about next to nothing, except perhaps Ireland, Municipal Trading and the death duties. We did not even agree about the Income Tax, for that involved the question of whether authors' royalties should be treated as income or as capital increment.

The root of the trouble was that GBS flatly refused to sign any of his contributions. He declared that it was the first chance he had ever had of using the editorial 'we' and that he was going to make hay while the sun shone. Often, knowing that he had not to put his name to it, he would send me an article containing the most outrageous nonsense. More often, of course, he sent first-class stuff, but whatever subject he wrote upon he never considered for a moment anything that might previously have been said about it editorially. He used to complain that I inserted 'not's' into his sentences. He was right. I sometimes had to.

One day I thought I had got a safe subject for him. Cecil Chesterton (younger brother of G. K., killed 1918) was being prosecuted by Godfrey Isaacs (brother of Sir Rufus) for criminal libel.[2] C. C. had certainly 'asked for it' with all his great powers of fluent and damaging invective, and in court he could not produce a leg to stand upon. I knew, however, that Shaw would defend Chesterton and wished that he should. But when the article came I found that it was based upon a complete misapprehension both of the facts and of the law. I sent it back to Shaw and explained the errors by telephone. He promised to put it right and let me have it first thing next morning – press day. In the morning I found the MS duly waiting for me. I found also that not only were all the original errors still there but that more had been added and the whole of them, as it were, doubly underlined. Something had to be done at once. A blank page or more had been left for the article and had somehow to be filled within thirty minutes or so. Squire[3] and I set to work. Shaw's article was written in three long paragraphs, like a *Times* leader. We took the first paragraph almost as it stood, Squire wrote an entirely different second paragraph, and I wrote the third – using of course bits of Shaw. I have just re-read it. In its final form it was an admirable article.

We lunched at 10 Adelphi Terrace next day and Webb came too. After a prolonged argument GBS admitted that we seemed to be right as far as the facts and the law went, but he insisted that one day we should realise that he had been right all along as to the underlying intention of the prosecution. The Government meant to put Cecil in gaol somehow and he (GBS) wanted to checkmate their unamiable plans.

After this episode Shaw wrote little for the paper. He realised, I suppose, that the idea of his using the editorial 'we' without accepting public editorial responsibility was not a workable proposition. He was always very friendly and jolly about it, however. One day Israel Zangwill[4] sent me a letter criticising a criticism which we had published of a new play of his. Naturally I declined to print the letter. No point of fact was at issue, and a paper which once began to permit authors to use its correspondence columns to start discussions of their own works would soon find itself in a mess. Mr Zangwill, however, wrote and complained to Shaw. Shaw sent me a copy of his reply. I can quote only from memory, but it ran roughly thus. 'My dear Z., You complain that Sharp won't print your letter. That's nothing. You're not a proprietor; I am; and he won't print my articles.'

NOTES

1. Sharp had quoted from a letter Shaw wrote him in November 1915: 'Forgive my perpetual cavilling; but somebody must complain; it is for the good of your soul.'

2. Sir Rufus Isaacs (1860–1935), Attorney-General in the Liberal government, was involved in the Marconi scandal; he and several other government members had speculated in the shares of a company associated with the Marconi company, which had been awarded a government contract. Cecil Chesterton (who had been a prominent Fabian) and Hilaire Belloc were prosecuted for allegations of corruption published in their paper, the *New Witness*.

3. (Sir) John Collings Squire (1884–1958), poet and man of letters, was the first literary editor of the *New Statesman*. The doctored article appeared on 14 June 1913.

4. Israel Zangwill (1864–1926), novelist, playwright and Zionist.

Shaw and Wells at Odds

KINGSLEY MARTIN

From Kingsley Martin, *Editor* (London: Hutchinson, 1968) pp. 86–7. Basil
Kingsley Martin (1897–1969) had lectured at the London School of Economics
and written leaders for the *Manchester Guardian* before he took over the editorship
of the *New Statesman and Nation* in 1931. When he published H. G. Wells's
account of an interview with Stalin in 1934, he invited comment from Shaw,
who had met Stalin on a visit to Russia with Lady Astor in 1931. Shaw obliged
'in a manner that was certain to infuriate H. G.'. A lively correspondence,
involving many others, ensued and Martin proposed to collect it all in a
pamphlet. Wells was more openly enthusiastic about this than Shaw, who
claimed it would show his old friend had 'made a perfect ass of himself'.

We were just going to press when H. G. sent a final letter. He had
discovered an old article by Shaw in the *Daily Herald*; Shaw's views
about Stalin and revolution had then been very much the same as those
of Wells ten years later. I sent it to the printer for the *NS*, but Wells
insisted that it must also go into the pamphlet. It so happened that
Shaw was having one of his rare illnesses at the time and I explained to
H.G. that I could not include it in the pamphlet unless GBS had had a
chance of seeing it and replying to it. Wells became extremely cross and
silly. GBS was ill, was he? Well, he had diabetes and rheumatism and
goodness knows what else, and he didn't run away from controversy. I
must remember what a greater publisher than I had said, 'Publish and
be damned'.[1] Next morning his secretary rang me up to say that if his
new letter was not included in the pamphlet H.G. would not consent to
the pamphlet appearing at all. I rang Shaw's number and Mrs Swaw
replied. GBS, she said, was ill and it was too bad to have Wells' letter in
the paper because when GBS woke up – and she was afraid I might
have awakened him by telephoning – he would want to write a reply
and he wasn't really well enough. I rang off, much abashed. Half an
hour later she rang me up again in the happiest of moods. GBS was
sitting up in bed writing a reply to Wells. He was delighted and said
that H.G.'s letter had given him a chance finally to wipe the floor with
him. Would I like to fetch the letter myself? So I went round and found
GBS looking like Father Christmas, in bed with a very pink face and
very white whiskers. (He had originally, as H.G. remarked, had very
red hair and a very white face.) He was very pleased with himself and

asked me to read the letter there and then. He had added a footnote to his reply. In an earlier letter he had referred to Wells 'trotting into the Kremlin'. Wells had replied:

> Shaw can have all the glory of saying that I 'trotted' into the Kremlin while, by implication, he and Lady Astor, with the utmost grace, strode, swam, stalked, danced, slid, skated, or loped in, and conversed in some superior imperial fashion of which no record survives.

Shaw replied in his footnote:

> I cannot withdraw the word 'trotted' as descriptive of Wells' entry into the Kremlin. A man's mood is always reflected in his locomotion. Wells did not strut; that would have been vulgar; and Wells is not vulgar. He did not stalk or prance for he is not tall enough for such paces. He did not merely walk; he is too important for that. Having eliminated all possible alternatives, I conclude that he trotted. If not, what *did* he do?

Later it was suggested to me that Wells would be hurt by this reference to his height. Shaw was tall and handsome, Wells was tubby. Adler[2] would have seen in this the basic reason for Wells' irritability. I rang Mrs Shaw and said I was sure that GBS would not wish to tread on so sensitive a corn. He enjoyed teasing Wells, but wouldn't want to hurt him. She agreed and went to consult GBS. I remember her voice on the phone now: 'He thinks we are rather silly but he has made an amendment to please us and the sentence should now read *'he did not stalk nor prance in the Shavian manner'*.

In these comic rows Shaw usually scored because to him it was all a fine game of wits, while Wells was always deeply and personally involved.

NOTES

1. Attributed originally to the first Duke of Wellington (1769–1852), when threatened with the publication of compromising letters and memoirs.

2. Alfred Adler (1870–1937), Austrian psychiatrist, who pioneered work on feelings of inferiority and their treatment.

Supporting *Time and Tide*

LADY RHONDDA

From Lady Rhondda, 'Recollections of GBS', *Time and Tide*, 11 November 1950. Margaret Haig Thomas, Viscountess Rhondda (1883–1958) inherited her title and considerable business interests from her father in 1918. Two years later she founded the weekly political review *Time and Tide*, taking over the editorship in 1926, and devoted the rest of her life and some £250,000 to it. Shaw would not accept payment for his contributions.

I met him first in the twenties. It was his generosity that brought us into touch with one another.

Time and Tide in its steep-climbing days in the late twenties and early thirties owed perhaps more to Bernard Shaw than to any other one person outside the office and its regular contributors. He had written his first article for it during the first few months of its existence. But our real acquaintance dates from some years later than that. It begins, as it should, with a grateful letter from me, in reply to a post-card from him agreeing to take the Chair at a debate between G. K. Chesterton and myself, on the subject of some articles which I had written in *Time and Tide*.

Most generous people are even more ready to help a second or a third time than a first. GBS certainly was. Taking the Chair was not only the beginning of our acquaintance it was also the beginning of helping *Time and Tide*.

It was early in 1929, shortly after I had taken on the editorship of *Time and Tide*, that I decided to start a circulation drive with a bumper issue of the paper and very rightly thought that my best plan would be to try to centre it around an article by Shaw. I must have been aware of the shamelessness of my proceeding for I remember that it was something of an effort to write and ask him. He responded that he was coming down to Fleet Street to see me. And one winter afternoon at about three o'clock he arrived, climbing the long, tall, narrow stairs of the old house overlooking St Bride's at the top of which *Time and Tide* was then housed, and appeared in my little room.

I told him that I should never have dreamed of daring to ask him to write if this had not been so very exceptional an occasion. To which he replied that no one ever did ask him to write except on very exceptional occasions, but that, nevertheless, the requests for articles mounted up to a fair-sized pile of letters every week.

But he wrote for us all the same, an extravaganza entitled *The King and his Doctors* (that was the winter of George V's dangerous illness). It sent our circulation soaring.

From then on we published articles and letters from him nearly every year and often several times in a year right up to 1940. After 1940 he wrote very little for the paper for we disagreed about the war. I had a letter from him dated January 5, 1940:

> I somehow felt that I ought to give *T & T* a lift by my name in the bills when the war knocked all the weeklies to pieces for the moment; but as I am not taking your line about the war I could not see how to butt in without getting across you.
>
> However, I think you might use the enclosed if you care to. It may freshen up the correspondence by starting a new hare. . . . If it jars, don't hesitate to throw it into the basket: I have written it as a sort of Christmas card for you personally: so it need go no farther.
>
> I am greatly surprised to find myself alive in the nineteen-forties. I never counted on it.

We printed the article he enclosed, with a footnote to explain how strongly we disagreed with it and it was followed by one or two other pieces that year but after that we published scarcely anything more, though, of course, I continued to meet the Shaws as usual.

We had already begun to disagree on matters of world policy before the war. There was indeed one occasion in 1935 when I was so outraged by his views on the Abyssinian war,[1] that I printed our usual 'Notes on the Way' disclaimer in type about half as large as the title. I lunched at Whitehall Court shortly afterwards. 'Surely,' Charlotte inquired mildly, 'that disclaimer was in larger print than usual?' 'Indeed it was,' I replied. But the Shaws never minded a thing like that. They were above all tolerant. Very often I used to go along to their flat in Whitehall Court. It was a happy place. The sun always seemed to shine there. Six or eight people would come to eat a good luncheon around a small table in a narrow little slip of a room, and afterwards sit and talk in the pleasant atmosphere of the big corner room overlooking the Thames. The people one met there were always interesting. That was the passport to the Whitehall flat.

NOTE

1. Shaw supported Mussolini's invasion of Abyssinia in October 1935 as a civilising mission.

Shaw and *Forward*

EMRYS HUGHES

From Emrys Hughes, 'George Bernard Shaw', *Forward*, 11 November 1950. Emrys Hughes (1894–1969), author and Labour MP for South Ayrshire from 1946 until his death, edited the Glasgow-based weekly *Forward* between 1931 and 1946.

He enjoyed writing to *Forward* during the war for he liked helping the unorthodox papers and people that were, like him, out of step.

In those years he wrote more frequently to *Forward* than anywhere else, unless it was in the Letters to the Editor column of *The Times*.

When I wrote asking him to comment on anything he invariably promptly obliged, usually in his own handwriting or carefully corrected typescript and even occasionally, when in a hurry to get the post, in his clear meticulous shorthand.

On one occasion he had written some advice to de Valera. I sent it to Dublin and hopefully waited for a reply.[1]

None came, but over the Irish wireless a few days later came a blistering reply. Shaw wrote a come-back but it was not up to his usual and he realised it. He wrote, 'Chuck it in the waste-paper basket and write something yourself.' But I knew better than to take over his controversies.

It was indeed a wonder to note how carefully the old man watched the news and kept up with events. *Forward* readers may remember an article on a Labour Party Conference that he wrote, 'The Battle of the Vans and the Vins'. He wrote his own headlines and they were usually as good as the articles. They were widely quoted in America and indeed in those days were a veritable gift from the gods.

Only on one occasion did he receive any payment. After a series of lengthy articles I felt conscience-stricken (and we were paying too much in income tax) so I sent him a cheque for five pounds.

He replied, 'Why are you throwing your money about like this? I don't want it.' I never sent him anything after this.

I was, however, able to do him a good turn in wartime. I introduced him to Scots shortbread made by John McGavin, the Cumnock baker. John McGavin scoured the Ayrshire countryside to get the butter for

Bernard Shaw's shortbread and kept the cheques with Shaw's signatures as treasured souvenirs.

NOTE

1. Probably a reference to an article by Shaw in *Forward* of 7 December 1940: at this stage of the war he was advocating that Eire accept British occupation of her ports. Eamon de Valera (1882–1975), the Irish premier, counter-attacked in an Associated Press interview (printed in the *Irish News* of 12 December) and Shaw replied, in *Forward* on 21 December. Shaw's articles, together with an earlier questionnaire and two later, more conciliatory articles, are collected in Shaw, *The Matter with Ireland*, ed. David H. Greene and Dan H. Laurence (London: Rupert Hart-Davis, 1962) pp. 281–9.

Part 4
Plays and Players,
1892–1914

INTRODUCTION TO PART 4

Before the completion of *Widowers' Houses* in October 1892, Shaw had tried his hand at the writing of two other plays, which survive in unfinished form under the titles *Passion Play* and *The Cassone*.[1] *Passion Play* (first called *Household of Joseph*) was begun and abandoned by the twenty-one-year-old Shaw early in 1878. Written in reasonably competent, but undistinguished, blank verse, it contains a few fore-shadowings of later Shavian themes and some knockabout comedy – which sits uneasily with the high poesy elsewhere – in the depiction of a violently quarrelsome Holy Family. *The Cassone*, which exists only as a series of disjointed passages of dialogue, was intended to be 'a suggestive comedy of modern society',[2] dealing *inter alia* with the relations between the sexes and the institution of marriage.

Widowers' Houses, a play about slum landlordism and the forces of corruption in bourgeois society, underwent a long period of gestation. Originally intended to be written in collaboration with William Archer, who suggested the project in 1884, it was subsequently taken over entirely by Shaw, and completed for production by J. T. Grein's Independent Theatre in December 1892. Thereafter, Shaw's output of plays was rapid and prolific. Before the turn of the century he had completed the seven plays which were published in the *Plays Pleasant and Unpleasant* volume and all three of those published in *Three Plays for Puritans*. In 1901 he celebrated the arrival of the new century with his most ambitious work up to that time, *Man and Superman: A Comedy and a Philosophy*. The play included Shaw's first extensive exploration in drama of his ideas about creative evolution, and included the sensational appearance on stage, in Act II, of a touring motor-car, complete with the chauffeur-mechanic, well-read graduate of the London Polytechnic and Wellsian New Man, Henry Straker. *Man and Superman* had to wait for its first production until 1905, when it was presented at the Royal Court Theatre with Harley Granville Barker as Tanner and Lillah McCarthy as Ann Whitefield. The lengthy 'Don Juan in Hell' dream scene (omitted in the 1905 production) was first performed separately at the Royal Court in 1907.

Shaw's reputation as a dramatist was much enhanced by productions of his plays in the highly successful seasons at the Royal Court Theatre, under the management of J. E. Vedrenne and Granville Barker in the years 1904–7. Ten of Shaw's plays, including the new works, *John Bull's*

Other Island (1904), *How He Lied to Her Husband* (1904), *Major Barbara* (1905) and *The Doctor's Dilemma* (1906), were presented at the Royal Court during this period. After the Royal Court seasons, Shaw made increasingly bold experimentation in the discussion-play form, with *Getting Married* (1908) and *Misalliance* (1909). In *Fanny's First Play* (1911), which had a run of over 200 performances in its first production, Shaw settled old scores with some of his newspaper theatre critics by introducing easily recognisable caricatures of them into his play. This period of Shaw's career was crowned with the two delightful comedies, both written in the first half of 1912, *Androcles and the Lion* and *Pygmalion*. Three other, lesser-known works were completed before the outbreak of the First World War.

NOTES

1. Texts of these works are included in *The Bodley Head Bernard Shaw: Collected Plays with their Prefaces*, ed. Dan H. Laurence, 7 vols (London: Max Reinhardt, The Bodley Head, 1970–4), vol. VII. (Hereafter referred to as *Collected Plays*.) Laurence also includes in this volume another pre-1892 piece, a dramatic sketch written in French and addressed as a letter to Mrs Pakenham Beatty on 7 October 1884.
2. See *Collected Plays*, vol. VII, p. 484.

Widowers' Houses: I

WILLIAM ARCHER

From C. Archer, *William Archer: Life, Work and Friendships* (London: George Allen & Unwin, 1931) pp. 136–7. William Archer supplied plot material for the play on which he and Shaw were to collaborate in 1884. Early in October 1887 Shaw gave Archer an MS of the first two acts of their play, entitled *Rhinegold*, and read it to him, but Archer's contemptuous reaction led him to put the draft aside until 1892, when he completed it as *Widowers' Houses*.

'Of course,' writes Archer, 'Shaw and I used often to discuss the stage, and the possibility of his writing for it. He told me that he had a great genius for dialogue, but was not very strong in the matter of invention and construction. At that time I rather fancied myself as a constructor of plots, so I offered to provide him with a scenario which he should work up. He agreed to this collaboration, and I cast about for a story.

In spite of my self-confidence, I did not invent the germ of the plot: I borrowed it – shall we say? – from an early play of Emile Augier's, entitled Ceinture Dorée.[1] I developed it after the style of T. W. Robertson,[2] with a serious and a comic heroine; and I placed the scene of the first act in a hotel garden on the Rhine: the title was to be Rhinegold. Having handed the scenario to Shaw, I heard no more about it for six weeks or two months. I saw him every day at the British Museum, laboriously and very slowly writing shorthand in a reporter's notebook; but I had no idea what he was about.' Then one day he is surprised by Shaw producing two acts in which the whole of the plot has been used up, and asking for more. 'I told him,' Archer says, 'that this was quite absurd – that my plot was an organic whole, and that to ask me to add to it was like asking a sculptor to add a few more arms and legs to a statue which was already provided with its full complement. . . . [sic] So I had to leave him, as we say in Scotland, to "make a kirk or a mill of it"; and when at last the manuscript was placed in my hands, behold! my Rhinegold had become Widowers' Houses, and my sentimental heroine . . . [sic] was transmuted into a termagant who boxed the ears of her maid-servant. Still, however, it is possible to discern in the play fragments of my idea, and to trace its relationship to Ceinture Dorée.'

NOTES

1. Emile Augier (1820–89), French playwright, had his greatest successes with solidly made dramas of social life, rooted in conventional middle-class morality. La Ceinture Dorée, a three-act comedy, was published in 1855.

2. Thomas William Robertson (1829–71), actor turned dramatist, produced a series of successful plays in the 1860s, moving towards greater realism. The best known, Caste, is typical in setting a sentimental, youthful interest in a more cynical and worldly frame. The term 'cup-and-saucer school' goes back to a remark on his work by the Athenaeum critic, and reflects his liking for contemporary domestic interiors.

Widowers' Houses: II

SYDNEY OLIVIER

From a letter by Lord Olivier to Archibald Henderson, 8 June 1931, in Henderson, Bernard Shaw, Playboy and Prophet (London and New York: D. Appleton, 1932) p. 211.

I was surprised one day when he told me that he had been trying his hand at a new sort of stuff, some of which he showed me, written lengthwise in a reporter's note-book in his exquisite hand-writing, unaffected by the vibration of railway travelling, and which I realised to be dramatic dialogue. It was the beginning of *Widowers' Houses*. . . . [*sic*] I was surprised, because the quality of British playwriting and the deadly artificiality and narrow conventions of native contemporary British drama were so repellent to me, that I could not imagine any man of the intelligence of Shaw or myself or of any critical conscience conceiving that there was any possibility of any one of original talent or literary or artistic impulse finding scope for expressing himself in that medium.

Widowers' Houses: III

J. T. GREIN

From J. T. Grein, 'GBS's First Play Revived', *Illustrated London News*, 14 August 1926. Jacob Thomas Grein (1862–1935), theatre critic and founder of the Independent Theatre Society, sponsored the first production of *Widowers' Houses* on 9 December 1892 at the Royalty Theatre. Only two performances were given.

As in a glass darkly I remember that nocturnal walk towards Hammersmith in 1892 with GBS, then already renowned as a Fabian, a novelist (*Cashel Byron's Profession*) and as a musical critic. We were then in the revolutionary days of our drama. Ibsen was ramming the old walls; the besieged were pouring the boiling tar and molten lead of vituperation on the beleaguerers.[1] What was wanted was a British Captain to ally with the foreign posse. George Moore promised his then one and only play, *The Strike at Arlingford*, in due course, when we felt sure of our footing.[2] Arthur Symons, Frank Harris, John Gray had swelled our contingent with one-act original plays.[3] But we wanted the strong card and the new man, and he was found that night *en route* for Hammersmith.

'I have written a play,' he said, and so I jumped with joy at the thought. He added, in that provoking way of his, 'But you will never produce it.' He then went on to tell me that William Archer had something to do with its inception, but had no belief in it, wanted it 'scrapped'. 'Never mind,' I said, 'it is by you; that is sufficient. I will promise to produce it even if I don't know yet what it is all about.' It seemed rash, but I knew my man: from him could only come originality. Then came the MS, at first in scraps; it took me – always a slow reader – three days to wade through it. I was deeply impressed by the housing question, but a little afraid of the scene in which Blanche assaults the housemaid. Would the audience stand that in the 'lady-like' Victorian days of 1892? However, I was pledged, and would forge ahead. Later, he sent me his revised and complete script – I have it still – beautifully engrossed in that Gothic, diamond-pointed handwriting of his – and so for casting and rehearsal.

In those days it was not so easy to find actors for *théâtres à côté*, so we had to seek and plead to get our cast together, and, in the aspect of today, we had willy-nilly to make the best of our material. But, try as we would, we could not find the right Lickcheese. We rehearsed and rehearsed at the Bedford Head, a public-house, but we had *Hamlet* minus the Prince of Denmark. Then one day, when we were all in despair, for the first night was drawing nigh, suddenly in the midst of rehearsal a woolly little head popped through the door, and to the little head was attached the quicksilvery body of a little man – 'Any actor wanted here?' he exclaimed, and with one voice, author, producer, actors bade him come in. He was the right man, the *rara avis* we had tried to find. On the night of 9 December 1892, at the Royalty Theatre, two men became famous for all time. GBS the author, and James Welch, the wonderful comedian, whose Lickcheese was a blend of pathos and humour, a diminutive yet compelling personality of exquisite harmony.[4]

The play had an uproarious reception; the author made a flamboyant speech; the old school of critics and the new vied with one another in abuse and praise; but the fact was patent – a new man had come to court, and one who, like the *preux chevalier*, feared neither convention nor public opinion. For all that, no manager could be found to adopt the play. It was an attack on capitalism and landlordism – it would be caviare to the great public of London; perhaps it would tend to riot.

NOTES

1. The Independent Theatre was launched with a production of Ibsen's *Ghosts* in March 1891. The play had an extremely hostile reception from critics.
2. *The Strike at Arlingford*, the second of seven plays by George Moore (1852–1933), Irish novelist, was produced by the Independent Theatre on 21 February 1893. His first play *Worldliness* (apparently lost) was written c. 1874.
3. The plays referred to here are John Gray's *The Kiss*, an English version of Théodore de Banville's *Le Baiser*, and *The Minister's Call*, Arthur Symons's adaptation of Frank Harris's novel *A Modern Idyll*.
4. James Welch (1865–1917), comic actor from Liverpool, began his career at the Globe Theatre, London, in 1887. Apart from Lickcheese, his other Shavian

roles were Major Petkoff in the first production of *Arms and the Man* (1894) and the Waiter in *You Never Can Tell* (1900).

Widowers' Houses: IV

G. LOWES DICKINSON

From *The Autobiography of G. Lowes Dickinson and Other Unpublished Writings*, ed. Dennis Proctor (London: Gerald Duckworth, 1973) pp. 158–9.

In 1892 I tell how I went to see his first play *Widowers' Houses* at its first appearance; and I am a little surprised at my verdict.

> It was a socialist tract against slum-landlords and possibly effective from that point of view: – as a play miserably dreary and unconvincing, all the personages unintelligible and repulsive caricatures, and even the dialogue not very clear. I don't like my powder and jam mixed in that inartistic way.

This sounds like the sort of criticism I am always hearing from intellectuals and lovers of the drama. I haven't read the play in question, or seen it, since, so I don't know what I should think now of my comments. I remember, however, one thing; that after the performance there was a great deal of noise and hissing,[1] and that after some time the manager appeared to say that Mr Shaw had left the theatre. Whereupon Mr Shaw appeared upon the stage, very pale, and began a speech: 'I hope,' he said, 'that the time is coming when a play like this will be impossible.' 'It's impossible now,' from the gallery. 'It's not impossible now, for it's just been performed,' from Shaw. And so on.

NOTE

1. In May 1921 Shaw told Lady Gregory, 'The first night of my *Widowers' Houses* I came in to see half the House applauding, half booing, but I didn't mind. And I have never felt nervous at the performance of my own plays. The only times in my life I felt really nervous was at the Opera in Dublin when my mother sang – though she always did well, yet I used to suffer from anxiety' (*Lady Gregory's Journals*, ed. Daniel J. Murphy, Coole Edition xiv [Gerrards Cross: Colin Smythe, 1978] p. 256).

Arms and the Man: I

R. PAGE ARNOT

From R. Page Arnot, *Bernard Shaw and William Morris* (London: William Morris Society, 1957) pp. 14–16. The following recollection formed part of a lecture delivered by Robert Page Arnot (b. 1890), left-wing author and labour historian, at a joint meeting of the Shaw and William Morris Societies on 11 May 1956.

I have a vivid memory of a conversation with Shaw just forty years ago. It was the middle of the 1914–18 war. Five years before that O. H. Mavor, known as the playwright James Bridie,[1] told me how in the King's Royal Rifles camp he had asked the sergeants' mess of that crack regiment what author in their opinion knew most about soldiers and soldiering: and received as answers not any of the names that might have been expected, like Rudyard Kipling, but the confident unanimous reply 'Bernard Shaw'. So therefore one day I asked Shaw how he came to write *Arms and the Man*. This, to my recollection, is what Shaw related:

'I wanted to write a play to destroy the romantic idea of a soldier as a sort of knight in armour. It was when we had all been reading Mommsen with his picture of Julius Caesar as against the perfect knight Vercingetorix.[2] I got the notion that if I could show a cavalry charge against a battery of machine guns it would be a dramatic illustration of my argument. I asked everybody who seemed likely to know if this had actually happened since the maxim gun. Nobody knew. At last I asked Sidney Webb, to whom I should have gone at first, and of course he knew the answer. Webb said: "Wasn't there something like that in the Serbo-Bulgarian war?"[3]

'What war?'

'The Serbo–Bulgarian war.'

'Never heard of it.'

Then I went and read it up in the British Museum and it was all as Webb had said. So I laid my play in Bulgaria.'

But there was more to it than that. Shaw went on to tell how after he had done a first draft he went to Stepniak[4] to ask him to read his play and advise him if he had got Bulgaria right.

'Stepniak said: "I really know little about Bulgaria. But there is a comrade who does. He has only come recently: and before he became a revolutionary he was an officer with the Tsar's navy and as such was in the Serbo-Bulgarian war.[5] He can tell you. I'll send him round."

'Soon afterwards the Russian ex-naval officer came to see me. He was very formal. He said, in rather halting English: "My friend Stepniak has asked me to meet you as a socialist who has written a play about the Serbo-Bulgarian war, about which I know something. I am willing to do what my friend Stepniak asks. So if you will read your play to me, very, very slowly, I shall listen."

'He was a magnificent figure, a tall, broad-shouldered, fair-haired Russian, with moustache and flowing beard, flashing eyes, perfect teeth. As soon as I saw him, I made him my model for Sergius.

'So I began to read *Arms and the Man*. I said: "I shall read the stage directions first." He bowed and said: "That will be perfectly all right."

'I began with the rich man's house, a large three-storied mansion.

RUSSIAN: Stop, Stop!
SHAW: But I have only begun.
RUSSIAN: Stop! There are no three-storied houses in Bulgaria. There are hardly any two-storied houses.
SHAW: In the library of this house . . .
RUSSIAN: Stop! There are no libraries in Bulgarian houses.
SHAW: This is obviously the house of a rich man, actually a general in the Bulgarian army.
RUSSIAN: Stop! There are no generals in the Bulgarian army.
SHAW: Very well. *Colonel* Petkoff.
RUSSIAN: Stop! There are no colonels in the Bulgarian army.
SHAW: All right. *Major* Petkoff.
RUSSIAN: Stop!
SHAW: O come, surely there must be colonels and majors.
RUSSIAN: My dear Sir, it is very difficult to make a Bulgarian into a private soldier. It is almost impossible to make a Bulgarian into an officer.[6] I know this for a fact. I was the Admiral of the Bulgarian fleet, a flotilla on the Danube. You cannot conceive of a Bulgarian colonel. But I believe we did make one or two of them into majors in the end – but only after the *pourparlers* for an armistice had begun.

'And so it went on all the time. So I remade the play, using what he had told me in the dialogue.'

NOTES

1. James Bridie was the pseudonym of Dr Osborne Henry Mavor (1888–1951), Scottish doctor and dramatist, and part-founder of the Glasgow Citizens' Theatre.

2. Theodor Mommsen (1817–1903), German scholar and historian, produced formidable and influential studies of Roman history and Roman law. He strongly admired Julius Caesar. Vercingetorix was Caesar's chief adversary in his conquest of Gaul.

3. Serbia made an unprovoked attack on Bulgaria in November 1885, but was worsted in a short, sharp campaign and saved only by Austrian intervention.

4. Sergius Stepniak was the pseudonym of Sergei Kravchinsky (1852–95), a Russian nihilist who had settled in London; Shaw often saw him at William Morris's house.

5. E. A. Serebryekov, who had jumped ship and escaped to England on learning he was suspected of nihilist affiliations.

6. Before the war the Bulgarian army had been largely officered by Russians, who were withdrawn when mobilisation was decreed.

Arms and the Man: II

W. B. YEATS

From W. B. Yeats, *Autobiographies* (London: Macmillan, 1955) pp. 281–4. Yeats and Shaw had a mutual friend in Florence Farr (1860–1917) who had created Blanche in *Widowers' Houses*. She became manageress of the Avenue Theatre in 1894, and set out with a group of others to flout convention with the production of *avant-garde* plays. Their season opened with Dr John Todhunter's *The Comedy of Sighs* and Yeats's *The Land of Heart's Desire* in a double bill, but Todhunter's play was a failure and was replaced by *Arms and the Man*, with Florence Farr as Louka, on 21 April. It ran until 7 July.

Shaw . . . had planned an opening that would confound his enemies. For the first few minutes *Arms and the Man* is crude melodrama and then just when the audience are thinking how crude it is, it turns into excellent farce. At the dress rehearsal, a dramatist who had his own quarrel with the public, was taken in the noose; at the first laugh he stood up, turned his back on the stage, scowled at the audience, and even when everybody else knew what turn the play had taken, continued to scowl, and order those nearest to be silent.

On the first night the whole pit and gallery, except certain members of the Fabian Society, started to laugh at the author, and then, discovering that they themselves were being laughed at, sat there not converted – their hatred was too bitter for that – but dumbfounded, while the rest of the house cheered and laughed. In the silence that greeted the author after the cry for a speech one man did indeed get his courage and boo loudly. 'I assure the gentleman in the gallery,' was Shaw's answer, 'that he and I are of exactly the same opinion, but what

can we do against a whole house who are of the contrary opinion?'[1]
And from that moment Bernard Shaw became the most formidable man
in modern letters, and even the most drunken of medical students knew
it. My own play, which had been played with *The Comedy of Sighs*, had
roused no passions, but had pleased a sufficient minority for Florence
Farr to keep it upon the stage with *Arms and the Man*, and I was in the
theatre almost every night for some weeks. 'O yes, the people seem to
like *Arms and the Man*,' said one of Mr Shaw's players to me, 'but we
have just found out that we are all wrong. Mr Shaw did really mean it
quite seriously, for he has written a letter to say so, and we must not
play for laughs any more.'[2] Another night I found the manager
triumphant and excited, the Prince of Wales and the Duke of Edinburgh
had been there, and the Duke of Edinburgh had spoken his dislike out
loud so that the whole stalls could hear, but the Prince of Wales had
been 'very pleasant' and 'got the Duke of Edinburgh away as soon as
possible'. 'They asked for me,' he went on, 'and the Duke of Edinburgh
kept on repeating, "The man is mad," meaning Mr Shaw, and the Prince
of Wales asked who Mr Shaw was, and what he meant by it.' I myself
was almost as bewildered, for though I came mainly to see how my
own play went, and for the first fortnight to vex my most patient actors
with new lines, I listened to *Arms and the Man* with admiration and
hatred. It seemed to me inorganic, logical straightness and not the
crooked road of life, yet I stood aghast before its energy as today before
that of the 'Stone Drill' by Mr Epstein or of some design by Mr Wyndham
Lewis.[3] Shaw was right to claim Samuel Butler for his master,[4] for Butler
was the first Englishman to make the discovery that it is possible to
write with great effect without music, without style, either good or bad,
to eliminate from the mind all emotional implication and to prefer plain
water to every vintage, so much metropolitan lead and solder to any
tendril of the vine. Presently I had a nightmare that I was haunted by a
sewing-machine, that clicked and shone, but the incredible thing was
that the machine smiled, smiled perpetually. Yet I delighted in Shaw,
the formidable man. He could hit my enemies and the enemies of all I
loved, as I could never hit, as no living author that was dear to me
could ever hit.

Florence Farr's way home was mine also for a part of the way, and it
was often of this that we talked, and sometimes, though not always,
she would share my hesitations, and for years to come I was to wonder,
whenever Shaw became my topic, whether the cock crowed for my
blame or for my praise.[5]

NOTES

1. This has some claim to be the most frequently repeated (and misappropri-
ated) Shavian anecdote, and even eyewitnesses do not agree – cf. the following

extract. The booer was Reginald Golding Bright (1874–1941), who wrote to Shaw soon afterwards and was later of service to him as a journalist and dramatic agent.

2. See letters of Alma Murray, who played Raina, in *Collected Letters 1874–1898*, pp. 435–8.

3. Percy Wyndham Lewis (1882–1957), writer and artist, was the protagonist of the short-lived Vorticist movement (c. 1912–15), which sought to relate English art to machinery and the industrial process. The 'Rock Drill' by (Sir) Jacob Epstein (1880–1959), American-born sculptor, was one of its best-known products.

4. The wide-ranging work of Samuel Butler (1835–1902) included scientific controversy, and his profoundest influence on Shaw was actually in the realm of ideas about evolution. Shaw first came across Butler's criticism of Darwin's theories of natural selection when he reviewed Butler's *Luck or Cunning?* for the *Pall Mall Gazette* (31 May 1887). They met through Emery Walker in 1889; for Butler's opinion of Shaw, see below, pp. 273–4.

5. For an analysis of the literary relations of Yeats and Shaw, see A. M. Gibbs, 'Yeats, Shaw and Unity of Culture', *Southern Review* (Australia), September 1973, pp. 189–203.

Arms and the Man: III

YORKE STEPHENS

From an interview with Yorke Stephens under 'Music and the Drama', *Daily Chronicle*, 10 November 1906. Yorke Stephens (1860–1937), Irish actor, created Bluntschli, and his memories of the 1894 rehearsals suggest that Shaw's directing skills and technique were in the process of development (cf. Eva Moore below, p. 134). Stephens also created Valentine in the Stage Society production of *You Never Can Tell* on 26 November 1899.

'Even then, at rehearsal, it was amazing what a grasp Mr Shaw had, if not of stage technicalities, at any rate of what he wished to evolve out of them. One felt always that he knew exactly what he wanted you to do – which is not always the case with authors. Then the "scrip" was, as I daresay you know, minute to the very limit of possibility in the matter of stage-directions – and even soul-directions.

'With it all it may be said that Mr Shaw was not very great at showing the way. Indeed, it would have been too bad to ask him to try. You just either understood him or did not. I am happy in believing that I was one of those who did. Anyhow, he told me at the end of the run that "we were made for each other". . . .

'As for the first night of *Arms and the Man* – who will ever forget it? The whole house was bewildered. They didn't know when to laugh, or where, or how. Of course, a good many people in the stalls were used to Mr Shaw, but the pit and the gallery were in a complete quandary. I think the gallery "booed" at the finish, simply because they didn't know what else to do. At any rate, they veered completely round after Mr Shaw's famous speech to the one man who cheered: "My dear fellow, I am of your opinion, but what are we among so many?" After that they cheered him to the echo.

'For the rest of the run,' continued Mr Stephens, 'every evening was a still more puzzling ordeal. The play created a certain sensation, there is no doubt about that, but the great outer public simply couldn't understand – or didn't take the trouble to understand – what it was driving at.'

Candida

From '*Candida*: a Talk with Mr Bernard Shaw', *Realm*, 5 April 1895. The copyright performance took place on 30 March 1895. But though the play was given some provincial performances by the Independent Theatre from 1897 onwards, it did not reach London until 1 July 1900, when the Stage Society produced it.

Now, Mr Shaw, as himself avers, writes plays more by accident than design. An idea occurs to him on a bus; and presently the idea has – quite fortuitously – spread itself into a play. It was about the latest accident – *Candida* – that we were talking – and about its author.

'I am the most conventional of men,' sighed Mr Shaw, somewhat regretfully.

'And yet,' I suggested, 'there is an impression abroad that any work of yours is likely to be unconventional.'

'Has it ever occurred to you,' said Mr Shaw, 'that the conventional play has never been written?'

'I suppose the conventional reply would be that the conventional play is "all over the stage".'

'Not at all. The play "all over the stage" is the play in which the convention is violated. It is not the convention, but the violation of it, which is the subject of the play. That is what the playwright and the public wallow in. The convention is really only an assumption that what the characters are doing is extremely wrong. It is never explained or argued for a moment why it's wrong, or what the conventional position really is. The author assumes it, the public assumes it, all for the sake of a bit of tragedy – and there you are. Now, it occurred to me that, as the really conventional play remained to be written, I was just the sort of man to write it.'

It was a hard saying. I pleaded for more light.

'In *Candida*,' explained Mr Shaw, 'the convention is the subject of the play.'

'What convention?'

'I beg your pardon – the wife-and-mother convention. The strongest and best position a woman can occupy, you know, is that of a wife and a mother.'

'Then, you accept the convention as valid?'

'Of course, there is a truth in that, as in every other convention. Not that every woman is in her right place as a wife and a mother. Some women in that predicament are in a hopelessly wrong position. They are married to the wrong man; they have no genius for motherhood; there are a thousand and one ways in which they may be out of their plane. But my heroine happens to be precisely in the right position. That, you perceive, is an absolutely original and yet a completely conventional situation for a heroine.'

'But do you find it a thrillingly dramatic one?'

'That's a home question, in more senses than one. And a question that must be answered by the public. For myself, I have found it, as a dramatist, a sufficiently dramatic situation. I have found in it a motive which completely satisfies my dramatic sense.'

'And what of the plot? Does the heroine never get out of this original and conventional situation?'

'If I told you the plot, you would think it the dullest affair you had ever heard. There is a clergyman and his wife – who is Candida, the heroine.'

'Who is the villain of the piece?'

'I never deal in villainy. The nearest thing I have got to it is a minor poet, who falls in love with the heroine.'

'Ah! And then what happens?'

'Some conversations. That's all.'

'Absolutely nothing more than that?'

'No more than that. But such conversations!'

'Doesn't the heroine even run away with the minor poet – or – or anything?'

'No – nothing. She stays at home with her husband. Rather a good idea – isn't it?'

'Yes – conventional in real life, and novel on the stage. Really, I suppose lots of wives stay with their husbands. Only, it's a point that the modern drama has missed.'

Thereupon it struck me that I might clear up a matter which has been bothering people a good deal for the last few years. There is no category for Mr Bernard Shaw. We like to be able to stick a label on a man, put him in a pigeon-hole, and be certain of always finding him there.

'Some time ago,' I said, 'I remember asking you what you were – a musical critic, a dramatic critic, a demagogue, a dramatist? Independent candidates stand a poor chance for Walhalla.[1] On which ticket are you going for election?'

'I am all of them by turns,' replied Mr Shaw. 'Not long ago I was a musical critic, as you know. But when I began to write plays I recognised the necessity of getting into a position to slate other people's plays. So I became a dramatic critic. Beyond that, nothing is changed. I am still a leader of the democracy, which still persists in taking no notice whatever of my teachings.'

'Now, – speaking for a moment as a dramatic critic – what do you consider the chief faults of Mr G. Bernard Shaw, the playwright?'

Mr Shaw took counsel with his beard.

'It is very difficult to say,' he said at length, – 'very difficult indeed. Speaking from my own point of view, of course I start miles ahead of anyone else, and keep there. But from the point of view of the public – well, perhaps, one of my faults is that I do not preach enough: I am not sufficiently didactic. The public want a dramatist to tell them ten minutes beforehand what he is going to do, then to do it, and then, ten minutes afterwards, to tell them what is the right moral to draw from it. The public,' continued Mr Shaw, leaning forward confidentially, 'want to be bored, and I am never a bore. That is one of my greatest failings. For the public are quite uncomfortable when they look for the moral in (say) *Arms and the Man* and can't find one.'

'Except, perhaps, that a true story seldom has any moral. Have you any other failings?'

'The only other is a kindred one. It comes from my lack of experience in writing for the stage. When I get a good idea I have not had sufficient practice to work it for all it is worth and exhaust it. I have to run away from it, as it were, and take refuge in being brilliant and sparkling. With experience comes dulness. When I have written enough plays to grow dull I shall succeed. But at present I have only been a dramatist to amuse myself.'

'And a demagogue to amuse other people?'

'Exactly.'

NOTE

1. Walhalla (the home of dead heroes in Scandinavian mythology) figures largely in Wagner's *Ring* operas and so may be a Shavian fingerprint on the interview.

The Devil's Disciple

JESSIE MILLWARD

From Jessie Millward (in collaboration with J. B. Booth), *Myself and Others* (London: Hutchinson, 1923) pp. 117–18. Jessie Millward (1861–1932) was the stage partner and mistress of William Terriss (1847–97), the leading actor of Adelphi melodramas. Shaw wrote *The Devil's Disciple* for Terriss and had finished a draft by the end of November 1896. The play was first produced by Richard Mansfield in America in October 1897. Two months later Terriss was murdered at the stage-door of the Adelphi.

[Terriss] loathed having plays read to him – 'I would not have a MS read to me if there were millions in it,' he once wrote to a friend; 'send it on and I will run through it' – and when Mr Shaw wrote to ask if he might read a play to Mr Terris and myself I feared the worst. I persuaded Mr Terris to consent, but my fears were justified. From the very first things went badly.

Mr Shaw arrived about three o'clock and I was much struck by his appearance: to my unsophisticated eyes he looked more like a farmer than a famous playwright.

He sat down and in a business-like way began to read, and in a little while, to my horror, I saw that Mr Terriss, who was sitting in a big chair beside the fire, was beginning to nod. Taking advantage of a pause while the dramatist was turning over a leaf, I suggested to Terriss that we should change places, saying that I felt rather cold. We changed places, and the reading went on.

But in ten minutes or so Terriss was indubitably asleep.

Mr Shaw read on, and when he reached the end of the second act he stopped for a moment. The sudden silence woke Terriss.

'No, Shaw, no,' he said, shaking his head. 'I'm afraid it won't do. I don't like the end. It isn't suited to Miss Millward and myself.'

'Mr Terris,' said Mr Shaw, 'I have not finished the play, and I am not going to finish it.'

Feeling that if ever there was an uncomfortable moment this was one, I rang for tea.

'Have a whisky and soda?' suggested Terriss.

'Thank you, I never drink anything but water,' replied Mr Shaw. Worse and worse!

Luckily it was now nearly four o clock, and when I was acting I always dined at four, so I asked the two men to stay to dinner. They both gloomily accepted.

We sat down to table. The maid handed some dish to Mr Shaw.

'No, thank you,' he said. 'I never eat meat.'

This seemed absolutely the last straw, and I don't think I completely recovered until he rose to go.

Before leaving he turned and fired a parting shot.

'I didn't have you in my mind for the part, Mr Terriss,' he said coldly. 'I wanted Miss Millward, and I hope that some day she will play in one of my pieces.'

You Never Can Tell

EVA MOORE

From Eva Moore, *Exits and Entrances* (London: Chapman & Hall, 1923) p. 108. Eva Moore (1870–1955) played Dolly in rehearsals for an eventually abandoned production of *You Never Can Tell* in the spring of 1897 – described humorously and anonymously by Shaw in chapter 16 of Cyril Maude, *The Haymarket Theatre* (London: Grant Richards, 1903). The first public performances waited until May 1900, when Yorke Stephens and James Welch presented six matinées at the Strand Theatre.

GEORGE BERNARD SHAW: I once rehearsed for a play of his at the Haymarket Theatre. I remember he used to sit at rehearsals with his back to the footlights, tilting his chair so far on its hind legs that it was only by the intervention of heaven that he did not fall into the orchestra. There he sat, always wearing kid gloves, firing off short, terse comments on the acting, and rousing everybody's ire to such an extent that the fat was in the fire, and finally the production was abandoned, after five weeks' rehearsal!

John Bull's Other Island

From C. K. Shorter, 'George Bernard Shaw – a Conversation: Concerning Mr

Shaw's New Play, *John Bull's Other Island'*, *Tatler*, 16 November 1904. Clement King Shorter (1857–1926), journalist and author, founded the *Tatler* in 1903. Shaw's acquaintance with him goes back to the first year of the *Star* in 1888, when Shorter was contributing a column of literary gossip. *John Bull's Other Island* had had its first performance at the Court Theatre on 1 November.

CKS: They seem all agreed that *John Bull* is not a play at all and that you have thrown all attempt at construction overboard. Even Walkley[1] calls it a Shavian farrago.

GBS: Walkley is too thorough an Englishman to be dramatically conscious of what an Englishman is, and too clever and individual a man to identify himself with a typical averaged English figure. I delight in Walkley: he has the courage of his *esprit*; and it gives me a sense of power to be able to play with him as I have done in a few Broadbent strokes which are taken straight from him.

CKS: But *is* it a play; and did you purposely abandon all care for construction?

GBS: My dear CKS, I never achieved such a feat of construction in my life. Just consider my subject – the destiny of nations! Consider my characters – personages who stalk on the stage incarnating millions of real, living, suffering men and women. Good heavens! I have had to get all England and Ireland into three hours and a quarter. I have shown the Englishman to the Irishman and the Irishman to the Englishman, the Protestant to the Catholic and the Catholic to the Protestant. I have taken that panacea for all the misery and unrest of Ireland – your Land Purchase Bill[2] – as to the perfect blessedness of which all your political parties and newspapers were for once unanimous; and I have shown at one stroke its idiocy, its shallowness, its cowardice, its utter and foredoomed futility. I have shown the Irish saint shuddering at the humour of the Irish blackguard – only to find, I regret to say, that the average critic thought the blackguard very funny and the saint very unpractical. I have shown that very interesting psychological event, the wooing of an unsophisticated Irishwoman by an Englishman, and made comedy of it without one lapse from its pure science. I have even demonstrated the Trinity to a generation which saw nothing in it but an arithmetical absurdity. I have done all this and a dozen other things so humanely and amusingly that an utterly exhausted audience, like the wedding guest in the grip of the Ancient Mariner, has waited for the last word before reeling out of the theatre as we used to reel out of the Wagner Theatre at Bayreuth after *Die Götterdämmerung*. And this they tell me is not a play. This, if you please, is not 'constructed'. Why? I will tell you. Because the play did not begin with two and a half acts of explanations by stage servants, stage solicitors, 'character parts', and 'comic relief', all leading up to Larry catching his bosom friend, Broadbent, in the act of making love to his adored Nora – this is what is called a strong and original situation – with a blow, a struggle, a duel arranged for the last act between friends whose hearts bleed for their broken friendship, but who must kill each other because the free list would consider any other course unnatural, and – but I need not go on with it; you know the sort of thing. What is to be done with men whose heads are full of such stuff?

NOTES

1. Arthur Bingham Walkley (1855–1926) was appointed dramatic critic of *The Times* in 1900, having previously covered drama for the *Star* since its inception. He is the addressee of the Epistle Dedicatory of *Man and Superman*.

2. The 1903 Land Act was the most effective of a series designed to encourage Irish landlords to sell their land to tenants.

Dramatic Purposes

From 'HFS', 'Our Saturday Talk. VI – Mr Bernard Shaw', *Saturday Westminster Gazette*, 26 November 1904.

'People talk all this nonsense about my plays,' said Mr Shaw, 'because they have been to the theatre so much that they have lost their sense of the unreality and insincerity of the romantic drama. They take stage human nature for real human nature, whereas of course real human nature is the bitterest satire on stage human nature. The result is that when I try to put real human nature on the stage they think that I am laughing at them. They flatter themselves enormously, for I am not thinking of them at all. I am simply writing natural history very carefully and laboriously; and they are expecting something else. I can imagine a Japanese who had ordered a family portrait of himself, and expected it to be in the Japanese convention as to design, being exceedingly annoyed if the artist handed him a photograph, however artistic, because it was like him in a natural way. He would accuse the photographer of making fun of him, and of having his tongue in his cheek.

'But there is a deeper reason for this attitude of mind. People imagine that their actions and feelings are dictated by moral systems, by religious systems, by codes of honour and conventions of conduct which lie outside the real human will. Now it is part of my gift as a dramatist that I know that these conventions do not supply them with their motives. They make very plausible *ex post facto* excuses for their conduct; but the real motives are deep down in the will itself.

'And so,' continued Mr Shaw, 'an infinite comedy arises in everyday life from the contrast between the real motives and the alleged artificial motives; and when the dramatist refuses to be imposed upon, and forces his audience to laugh at the imposture, there is always a desperate struggle to cover up the scandal and save the face of the conventional by the new convention that whoever refuses to play the conventional game is a cynic and a satirist, a *farceur*, a person whom no one takes seriously.'

'Is it not a little hard on people to have the workings of their innermost souls laid bare?' I asked. 'Do you expect them to like being represented as hypocrites and humbugs?'

'You misunderstand me altogether,' said Mr Shaw, with a slight touch of irritation. 'It is not my object in the least to represent people as hypocrites and humbugs. It is conceit, not hypocrisy, that makes a man think he is guided by reasoned principles when he is really obeying his instincts. The ordinary citizen is a most extraordinarily conceited person, especially in England, because English people are not nearly so intellectually self-conscious as the Irish or the Latin races, and, consequently, they are extremely offended when it is assumed that they are subject to the common and inevitable inconsistencies and bogus apologetics to which the able and cultivated man confesses as a matter of course. They are madder than Don Quixote,' added Mr Shaw, laughing, 'because they imagine themselves as chivalrous in their shops and offices and villas as he did on Rozinante's back in the Sierra.

'Another mess that some of the critics get into over my plays is that they imagine I am contradicting myself when my characters contradict one another. According to these innocents, all the persons in *John Bull* are only mouthpieces for Shaw. Larry is Shaw; and Keegan is Shaw; and Hodson is Shaw; and Matt Haffigan is Shaw. And the differences between these characters are therefore, if you please, my inconsistencies, my insincerities, my levities. The fact is, some critics live so completely outside the political and sociological world, and even the moral and religious world, that the moment they are shown a character whose world is wider than the Divorce Court they exclaim "Hallo! here is Shaw" – Shaw being the only man they ever met or heard of who cared about politics or sociology, morals or religion, and who was unspeakably bored by the Divorce Court. That is why Stead has beaten them so completely at their own game at his first trial in his fifty-fifth year.[1] I don't, of course, mean the half-dozen able critics who are also men of the world. I mean the stuffy little set of theatrical newsmen who write as if they had been born in a box-office and had never got out of it into the fresh air.'

'But is it the business of a playwright to ventilate opinions on politics and religion?'

'The business of a dramatist is to make experience intelligible. Shakespeare's notion that it was to hold the mirror up to nature was the blunder of a playwright who was a mere observer, not a thinker. Hold the mirror up to nature (which Shakespeare, to do him justice, never did) and you will get nothing but an unintelligible confusion, like a snapshot of Cheapside. The dramatist's business is to bring order, intelligibility, and significance out of that confusion. The minor dramatist can only deal with some little part of it – mostly its petty concupiscences, unfortunately; but I profess to handle the whole mass – politics, morals, religion, and all.'

'Then you profess to write on the highest plane of the drama?' I asked.

'Yes; certainly,' replied Mr Shaw. 'I am trying to do the sort of work that Euripides and Goethe did and Ibsen does. I remember years ago, in St James's Hall, when Beethoven's Ninth Symphony was being played, a young man who had listened to the first movement in bewildered consternation got up and said in an agonised voice: "Look here, *is* this the Moore and Burgess Minstrels?"[2]

'Now my line is the Ninth Symphony line, and when people expect from me a Moore and Burgess entertainment they have simply come to the wrong shop. They are offended at my saying this: no doubt they think I ought to give myself the airs of the gentlemen who dabble in minor poetry, and to simper and deprecate my work and pretend that I am a humble follower of greater men. But if you ask a plumber or carpenter about his job you will not find any of that false modesty about him.

'Well, that is my feeling about my work. I never let a play out of my hands until it is as good as I can make it, and until it is sufficiently light to be digested without any difficulty.

'But the only thanks that people give me for not boring them is that they laugh delightedly for three hours at the play that has cost many months of hard labour, and then turn round and say that it is no play at all and accuse me of talking with my tongue in cheek. And then they expect me to take them seriously!'

NOTES

1. W. T. Stead's 'First Impressions of the Theatre' had appeared in his *Review of Reviews* in July 1904; until he was fifty-four the only play he had seen was the Oberammergau passion play.

2. The Moore and Burgess Minstrels, perhaps the most famous of the 'black' minstrel companies in late Victorian London, were based at the small St James's Hall in Piccadilly, beneath the main concert hall.

Man and Superman and Other Plays

LILLAH McCARTHY

From Lillah McCarthy, *Myself and My Friends* (London: Thornton Butterworth, 1933) pp. 55–6, 58–60, 84–5, 165, 170–1. Lillah McCarthy (1875–1960) played Ann Whitefield in the first public performance of *Man and Superman* at the Court Theatre in May 1905. (The play, written in 1901–3, was given a copyright performance at the Bijou Theatre, Bayswater, on 29 June 1903.) Between 1905 and 1918 she played many leading roles in Shaw plays, at the Court Theatre and elsewhere. She had first come to Shaw's notice in May 1895, when he reviewed her performance as Lady Macbeth in an amateur production at St George's Hall, London. (She recalls him on this occasion as 'nothing but two eyes staring out of a white face surrounded by a halo of red hair' [p. 33].) His criticism was an amusing mixture of damning remarks and praise: he concluded that 'her Lady Macbeth was a highly promising performance, and that some years of hard work would make her a valuable recruit to the London stage' (Bernard Shaw, *Our Theatres in the Nineties*, 3 vols [London: Constable, 1932] I, 133). However, her memory of the verdict was that she should go into the country for *ten* years to learn her business.

One day brother Dan, become also a good craftsman,[1] looks up from the paper he is reading in the sitting-room of our lodgings, and exclaims: 'Your red-headed man has written a play.' 'Who?' I said. 'Why, that dramatic critic of the *Saturday Review* who gave you such a wigging.' 'Not Bernard Shaw?' I asked. 'That's the chap,' says he. I said no more. It was an omen; for, almost to the day, the ten years were up.

I wrote to Shaw and told him that I had done what he said I must and was come back, and might I go and see him. The answer was a summons to the Shaws' flat in Adelphi Terrace. I obeyed. I climbed the stairs, past the gate with iron spikes, and with a self-possession I did not feel, announced myself. He looked at me, gave a broad smile, and said: 'Why, here's Ann Whitefield.' At first I thought that he had mixed me up with some other girl, but as he talked it dawned upon me that Ann Whitefield must be the woman in his new play. Presently he got up, shook hands, and said, 'Yes, you're Ann. Good-bye'; and, wondering and hoping, I went away. . . .[2]

Shaw's method was to read the play over to the company, after having read it to a group of personal friends. The parts were then handed to us, and we were allowed to stumble through them. His own conceptions of the characters were withheld. He never harassed us with interruptions in the raw beginning stage. But as he listened to us his pencil was never still; and at the end of each rehearsal we would get plenty to ponder over in the shape of brilliant and brief little personal notes.

He would wait for a week before he came up on to the stage to interfere with our work. Then began a revelation of his knowledge of the theatre and of acting. With complete unselfconsciousness he would show us how to draw the full value out of a line. He could assume any role, any physical attitude, and make any inflection of his voice, whether the part was that of an old man or a young man, a budding girl or an ancient lady. With his amazing hands he would illustrate the mood of the line. We used to watch his hands in wonder. I learned as much from his hands, almost, as from his little notes of correction. The care with which Shaw approached the details of his production is indicated in a letter which he wrote to me before *Man and Superman* was presented.

Yes, I think that will do very well; only don't have any light-blue ribbon with the white muslin; use violet or purple.

Mrs William Morris wore a black mantle with violet lining at her husband's funeral; that was what gave me the idea of the dress in the first act. Ann should not produce an impression of artless simplicity; there should be a certain pomegranate splendour lurking somewhere in the effect – just a touch even in the muslin dress – I trust your judgement in this matter; do what you like.

GBS[3]

Before I appeared as Ann I finished Shaw's season of *John Bull's Other Island*.[4] During the rehearsals of the new play we often lunched together at the little Queen's Restaurant, near to the Court Theatre. The lunches were of apples, cheese, macaroni, salads, and, to crown them, a chilly milk and soda. He throve upon this fare. I ate it because everything he did seemed right to me; but it always left me hungry. . . .

Shaw has done more than anyone to rescue the theatre from 'theatricality' and he has done it because he is a realist; one who will not avert his face from truth even though tradition and art bid him look the other way.

The old tricks of production never count with him. He snatches his characters, his way of dressing them, his conception of their movements, from the streets, from anywhere, from people he actually knows. Here is an instance. We were preparing for the death scene in *The Doctor's*

Dilemma. When Dubedat, the artist, dies, Jennifer, his wife, goes from the room whilst the doctors bend over him. She returns, not in black and sombre clothes, but in a lovely flaming gown and a jewelled head-dress. London is shocked.

But Dubedat, poor spineless genius, had stared over the edge of physical life and, almost with his dying breath, he had recited his creed:

> I believe in Michael Angelo, Velasquez and Rembrandt; in the might of design, the mystery of colour, the redemption of all things by Beauty everlasting.

> It was not a creed that could be served by a widow draped in mourning. I must return to the body of my husband in gorgeous raiment. . . .[5]

Whilst the play was in manuscript he brought *Androcles and the Lion* and read it to me.[6] I was deeply impressed by it; its fun was more spontaneous than in any of his previous plays. Of course Shaw's reading is so perfect that it casts a glamour over everything he reads aloud. His voice is under perfect control, and his unerring dramatic sense, which finds expression on every occasion even in private life, gives to any play that he reads a vividness so dazzling that even if it were a bad play it would seem to be a masterpiece. . . .

Recollections of comic moments during the production of the play help to soften the sorrow which I shall always feel at the failure of *Androcles.* The playing of the Lion offered a pretty problem for Shaw. Neither Shaw nor I knew anything about lions or their ways; so off we went to the Zoo on a sunny August morning. I had been told that lions like eau-de-Cologne and therefore provided myself with a bottle-full and several old handkerchiefs as well. The keeper took us into the back of the cage. The lion roared. Shaw talked gently to it. The lion roared louder still. I saturated a handkerchief with eau-de-Cologne and threw it between the bars of the cage. The lion sniffed, sneezed and all Regent's Park echoed with its roaring. ''E's never roared like that before,' said the keeper, looking reproachfully at Bernard Shaw. The lion tore the handkerchief to ribbons and threw the pieces in GBS's face: a British lion!

NOTES

1. Dan McCarthy (1869–?), the first BA graduate from London University, was a schoolmaster and private tutor before becoming a professional actor.

2. Shaw recorded his own account of this visit in 'An Aside' prefaced to *Myself and My Friends* (p. 5).

3. Lillah McCarthy had earlier given a rather different view of Shaw at rehearsal in an interview published – with his imprimatur – in *Everybody's Weekly* (17 September 1927).

> Shaw was not altogether a pleasant producer to work with, because he took all the good work for granted, and just pointed out the weak spots and showed how to get them right. The reward of being perfect was to be absolutely ignored, or perhaps corrected for a misplaced comma.
>
> Even when something was wrong he would say nothing until he had found out how to get it right. He never criticised unless a scene was hopeless; and then he made fun of it and of everybody, including himself. In fact he was the just man made perfect at rehearsal – the ideal producer; and you can't imagine how trying any sort of perfection is to the artistic temperament.

4. She took over the part of Nora from Ellen O'Malley.

5. Lillah McCarthy goes on to describe how Shaw interested himself in the design of the head-dress. The painter Neville Lytton (see below, p. 283) modelled it on an elaborately piled and bejewelled style worn by his wife, Judith. It was first seen on the stage of the Court Theatre on 20 November 1906.

6. The part of Lavinia was written for Lillah McCarthy. Shaw read the play to her and Granville Barker, then her husband, on a Sunday morning in April 1912. They produced it the following year.

Man and Superman: I

CHARLES RICKETTS

From *Self-Portrait taken from the Letters and Journals of Charles Ricketts, RA*, collected and compiled by T. Sturge Moore, ed. Cecil Lewis (London: Peter Davies, 1939) pp. 127, 128–9. Charles Ricketts (1866–1931), designer, painter, sculptor and author, designed scenes and costumes for a production of the Dream scene in *Man and Superman* at the Court Theatre in 1907. He later designed for *The Dark Lady of the Sonnets* (1910), *Annajanska and the Wild Grand Duchess* (1918) and *Saint Joan* (1924).

31 December [1905] Miss [Florence] Farr and Bernard Shaw to tea, to discuss the possibility of staging his Don Juan scene in *Man and Superman*. Shaw has aged, he was voluble and amusing on his arrival. . . .

The chatter was distinctly vital and vivacious. Shaw said the *Vision of Hell*[1] is too long. How could it be otherwise? – it contains the whole ethics of a new Religion! Like all men of letters, speaking of beauty, he viewed it as a sort of agreeable compromise, and the essence of moderation, instead of its being a supreme form of controlled exaggeration. I wanted Donna Anna to be a type of exaggerated femininity, in an Infanta hoop and a perfect collection of Virgins, Holy Hearts and 'Memento Moris' in nests of lace, with the white napkin and black gloves; Don Juan to be a creature of silver and purple, also in a sort of half-mourning; and the Commendatore to be in Roman armour, buskins, ruffs and sash, in a true mock-heroic get-up, with a touch of comedy. This frightened Shaw; he wanted nothing that would take from the dignity of the figure, the comedy should be in the words, etc.

Shaw spoke of an amazing essay sent to him by Tolstoï against *King Lear*,[2] in which he not only falls foul of the true faults of the play, but makes terrible blunders in fact, and this amazing statement: 'All Shakespeare's characters talk the same bombast, they are all mouthpieces for Shakespeare, instead of being persons. Now the truly great artist always gives character to his people. We view them, whatever the language, as separate living persons.' This gives one an idea of the value of the rest. Shaw returned the essay to Tolstoï, pointing out fallacies. In the discussion of the quality and force in Shakespeare's language which followed, Shaw spouted some bombast of Shakespeare's with extraordinary feeling for its beauty when spoken; he maintained that Shakespeare gave passages like these to hold the attention of the public, just like his clowning scenes.

NOTES

1. Act III of *Man and Superman*.
2. 'What is Art?' (1897).

Man and Superman: II

ESMÉ PERCY

From Esmé Percy, 'Bernard Shaw: a Personal Memory', *Listener*, 26 May 1955. Esmé Percy (1887–1957), actor and producer, first met Shaw, by chance, 'late in 1905 or early in 1906'. From 1911 he frequently played Tanner, as well as many other Shavian roles, and in 1924 he was appointed general producer to Charles Macdona's Bernard Shaw Repertory Company. He was the first to produce *Man and Superman* in its entirety (on 11 June 1915 at the Lyceum Theatre, Edinburgh) playing Tanner and Don Juan himself.

When I first went to see Shaw about doing *Man and Superman* in its entirety, he was living at no. 10 Adelphi Terrace, now, alas, no more. . . . He was in his most ebullient mood – he said, 'Man alive, have you no more sense than a dormouse? Do you imagine you'll get an audience to sit the play out unless you Bayreuth it?' And I did, as far as having a lengthy interval allowing for dinner between the second and third acts. He then went into details about the lighting of the Hell scene. In those days direct lighting was still in its infancy. Shaw said to me 'When I did the Hell scene on its own at the Court Theatre, the problem of lighting the figures only and keeping the rest of the stage in complete darkness seemed impossible, until I switched on my torch to make a note, and there, all of a sudden was one figure alone visible, and the rest in complete darkness; and so, like many far more important discoveries, this one was solved by an accident.' Maybe that was the beginning of direct spot lighting. 'And now,' said Shaw, 'as to the devil, leave all the posing to him; your youthful chubbiness and Latin appearance would be admirable for Juan Tenorio. And now for Ana, all she has to do is listen with the arrested attention of a marionette – no easy task. God help you – don't blame me for disaster.' Shaw was wrong. Whenever I have played the entirety of *Man and Superman*, capacity houses were the order of the day.

Major Barbara: I

GILBERT MURRAY

From Gilbert Murray, 'The Early GBS', *New Statesman and Nation*, 16 August 1947. George Gilbert Aimé Murray (1866–1957), Greek scholar and internationalist, held chairs at Glasgow (1889–99) nd Oxford (1908–36). Several of his translations of Euripides were produced at the Court Theatre under the Vedrenne–Barker management. In 1889 he had married Lady Mary Henrietta Howard (1865–1956). Her mother, the Countess of Carlisle (1845–1921), certainly furnished Shaw with ideas for Lady Britomart in *Major Barbara*, while Cusins was modelled on Murray himself.

I may mention the history of *Major Barbara*, in which I served as a model much as Sir Almroth Wright did in *The Doctor's Dilemma*.[1] I had been reading the *procès* of Joan of Arc in Michelet[2] when I happened to meet GBS in the Court Theatre, where one of my Greek plays was being produced by Granville Barker. I suggested to him that a closely historical account of that trial or the trial of Mary Queen of Scots would make an effective play of quite a new kind; but Shaw hardly listened; he said 'I can't. I'm doing a play called *Murray's Mother in Law.*' About a year later he turned up at my house at Oxford. 'Were you a foundling?' he asked. 'No!' 'Do you mind my saying you were a foundling?' 'Not in the least.' Then he explained that he had brought the play, *Murray's Mother in Law*, which was now called *Major Barbara*, to read to us, to see if there was anything in it to hurt the feelings of my wife's family: 'I don't mind about *you.*' He read it in his own inimitable way, bubbling with laughter, like a boy, and also showing delicately the most varied shades of feeling. I think I enjoyed his reading of his plays more than any performance of them. At the end of Act II my wife and I were thrilled with enthusiasm, especially at the Salvation Army scenes. Act III in which the idealists surrender to the armament industries, was a terrible disappointment to us and, I think, unsatisfying to Shaw himself. He tried to justify his general line of solution, but muttered: 'I don't know how to end the thing.' He did to some extent alter it.

How far Barbara is like my wife, Cusins like me, or Lady Britomart like Lady Carlisle, it is not for me to say, but Cusins's combination of financial sharpness with arithmetical incompetence is derived, I hope, not from a general observation of my habits, but from a particular incident. I had been advised that I ought to get an improvement in my contract with a publisher, and in the course of the discussion with him had incidentally to choose between 10 per cent and a penny in the shilling. My wits suddenly left me, and I could not think which was the larger percentage, but providentially I guessed right and chose 10 per cent. I went to lunch with Shaw directly after, and my account of the whole affair amused him.

I heard him read some other plays afterwards, notably *Pygmalion* and *Too True to be Good*, always with delight and wonder; and he once or twice heard me read my versions of Greek plays, of which he was always a friendly and most understanding critic. A breaker of forms and conventions himself, I think he particularly enjoyed what he found in Greek tragedy, the highly conventional forms combined with vivid emotion and free philosophic thought.

NOTES

1. Sir Colenso Ridgeon, the protagonist of *The Doctor's Dilemma*, was based on the bacteriologist Sir Almroth Wright (1861–1947) and his experience of choosing patients at St Mary's Hospital, Paddington, which appears in the play as St Anne's.
2. Jules Michelet (1798–1874), French romantic historian, whose pivotal study of Joan of Arc appeared in the fifth volume of his monumental *Histoire de France*.

Major Barbara: II

ANNIE RUSSELL

From Annie Russell, 'George Bernard Shaw at Rehearsals of *Major Barbara*', a talk given at the St Ursula Club, New York, 28 April 1908. Printed in the *Shaw Review*, May 1976, from an MS in the Theatre Collection, New York Public Library. Annie Russell (1864–1936), Liverpool-born actress who had made her reputation in New York, played Major Barbara in the first production of the play, which opened at the Court Theatre on 28 November 1905.

This Bernard Shaw will be arrogantly satisfied that if anything is lacking it will most certainly be in the actors. He will be odious to the unimportant members, of course, and I shall detest him. So I thought as I climbed up the long stairs of the theatre where the company was assembled to hear the first reading. Mr Shaw was presented to me and I received my first surprise. Instead of the Mephistophelian, aggressive, untamed, uncouthly clothed person I had formed an imaginary portrait of – from goodness knows what set of impressions or descriptions I had accepted as true – I met instead a charming, courteous gentleman clothed with exquisite neatness and elegance in quiet tones of light brown, which harmonised well with his sandy and grey hair and beard. He had kindly, humorous eyes, and such a delightful smile. He said some commonplace thing or other in a sympathetic, well modulated voice, then proceeded to the reading of *Major Barbara*. During the reading of the play, the matter so different to the manner of the author continually struck me with such force of humour and wonder that I frequently lost the thread of attention to the play. Was it possible that that gentle-mannered man with the fine head and ascetic face was reading his own thundering denunciations against Society, the Church, Politics, Journalism, the Salvation Army, and all the rest, which he attacks so boldly with such scorching scorn, humorous contempt and utter fearlessness? Yet there he sat, his long slender body erect, reading on in his tuneful Irish voice, without excitement or over-emphasis, looking so unresponsible for his daring fulminations. 'The Church of England exists by selling itself to the Rich.' 'I'd rather be a murderer than a slave.' 'Poverty is the worst of crimes' and Barbara's sacred line – 'My God, why hast thou forsaken me?' – how *would* we actors *dare* to speak such lines before a general audience? Then suddenly the supercharged atmosphere would clear with a lightning flash of his irresistible wit, bewildering one as to his mental position. He seemed to be playing a sort of intellectual bowling match. Through which of his characters did he mean to express his own convictions? Any one of them might have stood in Shaw's own ethical position, for each declared with equal force his special doctrine. . . .

As I climbed the many stairs to the rehearsal room next morning I heard Mr Shaw ahead of me saying to Mrs Filippi, Major Barbara's mother,[1] who was heavily and wearily toiling up: 'Oh, Miss Filippi, let me take hold of your hand and draw you up. It often helps Mrs Shaw.' This little thoughtful, kind act started my day well with him, started and continued during the entire month of our rehearsals. Never once did he fail in kindliness, courtesy or patience and I do assure you he was tried over and over again. . . .

There are days when this benumbed mood infects many members of a company. The stage director grows desperate and irritable and hopeless and impolite, which, of course, only makes matters more hopeless. Mr Shaw always met such days with seeming calm, patience and good humour. There was one who tried him particularly – the hero, Major Barbara's father.[2] A superb actor but one whose intelligence was not – well – not *nimble*. He would continually interrupt rehearsal to demand lengthy explanations of perfectly obvious things, but would resent necessary illumination on profound ones. We called him the Giant's baby, not only on account of his great size. One day he brought the rehearsal to a standstill because a scene which was going on while he was apart writing a stage cheque did not give him sufficient time to write the cheque as he would in real life. 'But,' argued Mr Shaw, 'the audience is not paying attention to you just then and would not be conscious how much time it took to write the cheque.' But no, the Giant's baby stubbornly persisted that he must have time to write that cheque precisely as he would in real life. Bernard Shaw insisted that he could not lengthen the scene by a word. We were all annoyed at this foolish deadlock, but Mr Shaw smiled delightfully and said: 'Ah, Calvert, you see what comes of your playing Othello and blacking yourself all over.' . . .

How hard we all worked towards the first performance and with what enthusiasm and perfect spirit of camaraderie and consideration for the sensitive acting temperament. I have never seen actors so cleverly handled. No one was taught to act, but each was encouraged to give out the very best he was capable of. It was all done by a suggestion, a reasoning out of debatable matter, a selection of the best way offered by actor or author. No one was expected to do a thing merely because it was commanded by the stage director, but because the actor clearly understood *why*. Instead of the belittling process, which humiliates and congeals, they were encouraged to feel proud of their powers and free to express them. This is one reason why the Court Theatre of London, where we played *Major Barbara*, has the reputation of 'discovering' so many good actors. Many who have played for years elsewhere without particular success have achieved great distinction there.

NOTES

1. Rosina Filippi (1866–1930) played Lady Britomart.
2. Louis Calvert (1859–1923) played Andrew Undershaft. The previous year he had created Broadbent in *John Bull's Other Island*.

Major Barbara: III

ALFRED SUTRO

From Alfred Sutro, *Celebrities and Simple Souls* (London: Duckworth, 1933) pp. 117–18. Alfred Sutro (1863–1933), playwright and translator of Maeterlinck, remembers the first performance of *Major Barbara*.

I was at the first performance of that play; all the intelligentsia of London were there, and the first two acts were received with rapturous enthusiasm. Going into the lobby, after the curtain had fallen on Act II, I met Shaw, and warmly congratulated him on what I declared was a masterpiece, and the best play he had written, 'If the last act is as good as the other two,' I said – Shaw stopped me. 'The last act plays for an hour,' he chuckled, 'and it's all talk, nothing but talk!' My face fell; I was sorry. 'Don't you worry,' said Shaw, as he patted me on the shoulder, 'you'll see – they'll eat it!'

Well, they didn't. The curtain rose on an audience that had been hugely entertained, that was happily and confidently expectant; but, alas, there were streams, rivers, cataracts of talk, talk that caught us up, engulfed us and drowned us; the intense boredom in front seemed to infect the actors on the stage, and a little fluffiness on the part of the principal, the unending, talker, did not help matters. Never was the end of a play received with more rapturous relief, but, as the audience filed out, the brilliance of the first two acts was held to atone, in some measure, for the spate of talk that had flooded the last one.

Major Barbara: IV

BEATRICE WEBB

From *The Diary of Beatrice Webb*, vol. III: *1905–1924*, ed. Norman and Jeanne MacKenzie (London: Virago, 1984) p. 14. Beatrice Webb had taken the retiring Prime Minister, A. J. Balfour, who admired Shaw, to the première of *Major Barbara*, which she described next day (29 November) as 'a dance of devils – amazingly clever, grimly powerful in the second Act – but ending, as all his plays end (or at any rate most of them), in an intellectual and moral morass'. The following extract is taken from her entry for 2 December.

Today I called at the Shaws' and found GBS alone in his study. He was perturbed, indeed upset, by the bad acting, as he thought, of Undershaft and generally of all in the last scene, and by a virulent attack on the play in the *Morning Post*. Calvert, he said, had completely lost his nerve over Undershaft, could not understand or remember his part and was aghast at what he considered its blank immorality.

I spoke quite frankly my opinion of the general effect of his play – the triumph of the unmoral purpose. He argued earnestly and cleverly, even persuasively, in favour of what he imagines to be his central theme – *the need for preliminary good physical environment before anything could be done to raise the intelligence and morality of the average sensual man.* 'We middle-class people, having always had physical comfort and good order, do not realise the *disaster to character* in being without. We have, therefore, cast a halo round poverty instead of treating it as the worst of crimes, the one unforgivable crime that must be wiped off before any virtue can grow.' He defended Undershaft's general attitude towards life on the ground that until we divested ourselves of feeling (he said 'malice'), we were not fit to go to the lengths needed for social salvation. 'What we want is for the people to turn round and burn, not the West End, but their own slums. The Salvation Army with its fervour and its love might lead them to do this and then we really should be at the beginning of the end of the crime of poverty.'

I found it difficult to answer him, but he did not convince me. There is something lacking in his presentment of the crime of poverty. But I could honestly sympathise with his irritation at the suggested intervention of the censor, not on account of the upshot of the play, but because Barbara in her despair at the end of the second act utters the cry: 'My

God, my God, why hast thou forsaken me?' A wonderful and quite rational climax to the true tragedy of the scene of the Salvation Army shelter.

Androcles and the Lion

HESKETH PEARSON

From Hesketh Pearson, 'Memories of GBS and Granville Barker: Hesketh Pearson on the Original Production of *Androcles and the Lion*', *Listener*, 24 February 1949. Hesketh Pearson (1887–1964), actor and biographer, was the author of two biographical studies of Shaw. *Androcles and the Lion* was first produced at the St James's Theatre in September 1913, Pearson taking the small part of Metellus.

[Granville Barker's] method as a producer was Shaw's: but his taste for acting was quite different. He described Shaw's plays as 'Italian opera', while Shaw called Barker's low-toned acting 'serious relief'. Shaw produced his own plays as a rule; but for some forgotten reason he left *Androcles* to Barker and turned up only at the last rehearsal. By that time it was not an Italian opera but a French one: Debussy instead of Verdi. To give an example from my own part. In the last act Metellus checks Lavinia for telling Caesar that the Christians forgive him. Barker had said that I should do it with a kind of scandalised dignity. But Shaw disagreed: 'Good gracious! You mustn't behave like an offended patrician. You must treat her as if she had committed sacrilege. Jump at her! Fling yourself between them! Shut her mouth! Assault her!' While Shaw was busy upsetting the work of weeks, I noticed Barker looking on with an air of amused but weary acquiescence, rather like a mother who is pleased to see her son enjoying himself but wishes he could do it with less noise and destruction. Shaw's knowledge of acting, founded in Barry Sullivan, Ristori and Salvini,[1] all superhuman stars, resembled Shakespeare's. Barker, twenty years younger, had never seen such acting as theirs. He loved Shakespeare, but hated Shakespearian actors. His main object at rehearsals was to make the players think, so that they understood the play as well as their parts and were not content with merely learning their words and speaking them effectively.

When writing his *Life* I reminded Shaw of his antics at the dress rehearsal of *Androcles* and received a broadside. 'You jumping idiot!' he exclaimed, using the first term of endearment that came to his mind, 'what happened was that you were under-acting in the gentlemanly manner of the fashionable cup-and-saucer school then still prevalent. My method of dealing with this was to suggest an outrageously exaggerated reading of the line in question. The exaggeration was to prevent the actor from simply imitating me. The effort to comply usually got the gentlemanly novice about right. The Robertson cup-and-saucer drawing-room style was as hopeless in my plays as in Shakespeare's. Barker was not cup-and-saucer, but he was fastidious and low-toned, whereas I was blatantly declamatory, short of senseless ranting, which I could not endure. I often had to say, "Sing it: make music of it". Barker's *Androcles* production was all right: I had only two points to alter, though I may have seemed to be knocking the whole thing to pieces. Only one of the points was of any importance.'

NOTE

1. The Irish actor Barry Sullivan (1821–91) was Shaw's boyhood idol in Dublin, making a lasting impression with his forcible and vigorous style in tragedy. Adelaide Ristori (1822–1906) and Tommaso Salvini (1829–1915) were both Italians who made international reputations, Salvini being especially noted for his playing of Shakespeare's tragic heroes.

Pygmalion: I

PEGGY WOOD

From Peggy Wood, *Actors – and People: Both Sides of the Footlights* (London: D. Appleton, 1930) pp. 17–19. Peggy Wood (1892–1978), American actress and singer, who had played Candida in New York in 1925, called on Shaw while he was staying at Stresa in Italy in 1927. When the talk turned to *Pygmalion*, Shaw recalled the first English production, which opened at His Majesty's Theatre on 11 April 1914, with Mrs Patrick Campbell (1865–1940) as Eliza and Sir Herbert Beerbohm Tree (1853–1917) as Higgins.

'But I must tell you of some of the difficulties and trials of the early days of *Pygmalion*. We nearly never got it on,' he added.

'You mean the censor felt a little shaky about your using a certain word?'

'Oh, that, of course! But added to that we had Mrs Campbell's conviction during rehearsals that this was the worst part she had ever

played and that it would ruin her career. She couldn't get out of playing
it, and she couldn't make head or tail of it. Towards the final rehearsals
she began to take it out on the furniture and every time she came near
anything movable she shoved or pulled it viciously out of her way. As
a consequence the rest of the cast were stumbling over stools and chairs
and sofa cushions strewn over the stage in most unexpected places.

'However,' he continued, 'my friend the stage carpenter and I
remedied that at the dress rehearsal by stealing into the theatre on the
night before and nailing down everything lighter than a grand piano!

'The next day I sat far back in the gloom of the theatre and hugged
myself every time she tried to yank a poor inoffensive chair up by the
roots!

'But, of course, this did not improve her state of mind and the second
act curtain fell upon Mrs Campbell advancing to tell us with all the
command of language which is hers at such a moment that this was
without doubt the silliest play and the worst part of her entire career
and that come what might, she would rather die than play it. The
curtain rose for Tree's and my notes and criticisms, Mrs Campbell's
mouth opened to begin her denunciation when suddenly a strange
woman burst out of the wings with outstretched hands crying, 'Stella!
Stella! This is the best thing you have ever done. My dear, you are made
all over again!' It was some friend of Tree's whom he had asked to the
rehearsal, some blessed woman whose name I never knew.

'Mrs Campbell's expression changed slowly, she smiled as the woman
caught both her hands in an ecstasy of praise. The day and the play
were saved.

'Now I don't vouch for this, for I don't remember a thing about it,
but Tree, who always loved to tell stories on me, swore I leaped up on
the stage and did a war dance around Mrs Campbell howling, "I told
you so! I told you so!"'

Whereupon he illustrated by springing from his chair and dancing
around it, clapping his hands like a delighted child, his beard waving
and his coat-tails flapping.

Pygmalion: II

MRS PATRICK CAMPBELL

From Mrs Patrick Campbell (Beatrice Stella Cornwallis-West), *My Life and some*

Letters (London: Hutchinson, 1922) pp. 269–70. Mrs Campbell always called Shaw 'Joey'. Her account of their affair, preceding her appearance in *Pygmalion*, is given below (pp. 174–7).

If an artist has a personality that *will* force its way through, spoiling the effect of Joey's brilliant dialogue, he shudders and laughs murderously. 'Tree, old chap, must you be treacly?' he said at a rehearsal of *Pygmalion* before the company and 'stage hands'; nobody laughed; they knew death should have been Joey's punishment.

And he thought to cheer me when he remarked, 'Good God; you are forty years too old for "Eliza"; sit still, and it is not so noticeable.'

To 'sit still' with your hands folded in your lap for three-quarters of an hour, a glare of indignation in your eyeballs, while somebody else for the same length of time stands with his back to the fire, and another sits in an armchair – nobody budging except for some practical purpose of turning up a light, or picking up a newspaper, or ringing a bell – is Joey's idea of perfect stage management.

His genius and passion for debate often cut across the rhythmical movement of his drama, harming the natural sequence of emotion, and making the artist feel his own imagination is but an interruption.

Don't think: I have thought for you, is Joey's attitude to us poor players.

Pygmalion: III

EMIL DAVIES

From A. Emil Davies, *I Wander* (London: Watts, 1942) pp. 73–4. Albert Emil Davies (1875–1950), who served on the Fabian Executive from 1911 to 1947 and rose to be Chairman of the London County Council (1940–1), was the City editor of the *New Statesman* from its inception until 1931. Early in May 1914 the Webbs asked him to join a weekend party, which included Shaw and Clifford Sharp, at the Beacon Hotel, Hindhead. His record of the conversations he had with Shaw then is based on shorthand notes he made immediately afterwards.

Naturally, I mentioned *Pygmalion*, which was then running most successfully at His Majesty's. Shaw said they were taking £300 per performance and that the running cost of the house was £1,600 a week. Tree was not suited to the part and did not act it very well: he was, however, a character. He originally wished to play the part of the dustman.

The manner in which the critics had taken up his introduction of the word 'bloody' was ridiculous. Bearing in mind that it was a woman who had been a flower-girl with a passion for taxi-cabs, who now for six months had been able to gratify her taste in that direction as much as she pleased, and then a young man calmly suggests that she should walk, what other expression would she be likely to use?

The day after the play's appearance Tree took fright and suggested that they should omit the word; but Shaw insisted. He added laughingly that he had had a good deal of trouble with Mrs Patrick Campbell about the way in which she should utter it. He said that she began to use the expression in just the way a fine lady would, which made it sound indeed a horrible expletive! He explained this to her, whereupon she said, 'Am I to do it in the Siddons[1] manner?' with which he acquiesced.

I asked him if it was true that he had had to add a happy ending with a marriage to the German version,[2] and he said 'No'. All that had been done in the German version was to make Eliza Dolittle [sic], as she goes out, ask the Professor what size or colour gloves he requires – something which showed her devotion to him.

NOTES

1. Mrs Sarah Siddons (1755–1831), the most celebrated tragic actress of her time.
2. Siegfried Trebitsch's German version of *Pygmalion* was the first to be staged (on 16 October 1913 at the Hofburg Theatre, Vienna).

Pygmalion: IV

ALEXANDRA KROPOTKIN

From Alexandra Kropotkin, 'Pleasant Memories of Bernard Shaw', *New American Mercury*, January 1951. Alexandra Kropotkin (b. 1887) had known Shaw since she was a child through her father, the Russian revolutionary and social philosopher, Prince Peter Kropotkin. An associate of William Morris, he became a leader of the anarchist movement after he settled in London in 1886. Alexandra translated several of Shaw's plays in collaboration with her husband, Boris Lebedeff.

Immediately after the first production of *Pygmalion* in London, I asked Shaw to let us translate it into Russian. He thought that the gradual changes of Liza's speech, from pure Cockney to pure Oxford English, would be untranslatable. 'You are quite insane,' said Shaw. Not at all we insisted. In Russia, we told him, educated people and uneducated people do not talk any more alike than they do in England. Russia has just as many variations of accent and vocabulary. Shaw signed a contract with us.

Putting *Pygmalion* into Russian was a fantastically tough job, but our results were successful. The play was accepted by the *Maliy Teater* – the *Small Theatre* – one of the two State theatres in Moscow. From Alexander Sanine, brilliant director of the Maliy, came an enthusiastic cable announcing that he would rush to London to discuss the Moscow project with Shaw.

Sanine arrived, saw the London production, and insisted that when he met Shaw, they must have space enough to approximate a stage. We arranged a late lunch at an Italian restaurant in Soho, where the proprietor, an ardent Shaw admirer, was willing to let us turn his place topsy-turvy as soon as the luncheon crowd had left. The minute lunch was over, Sanine began shoving chairs and tables around. A row of tables represented the stage, a row of chairs represented the front row of the audience.

Pygmalion, as everyone knows, opens with a rainstorm scene. People who have just attended a Covent Garden performance are waiting for carriages and cabs. Sanine had definite ideas about the rain. Speaking Russian, he said, 'It is a sudden storm. At your theatre here in London, the rain is wrong. It comes down straight. A sudden storm is *slanting* rain.'

I translated for Shaw. He took a seat in what was supposed to be the front row of the audience. 'If you slant the rain,' he said, 'you'll get these front-row people soaking wet.'

Sanine and Shaw argued the point at top speed in their respective languages, with me translating as fast as I could. Presently the two men changed places, Shaw climbing up on the stage of tables, Sanine taking a front-row chair. On the stage, Shaw had one of the water carafes from the restaurant. Gleefully he sprinkled Sanine with *slanting rain*. 'All right!' capitulated the Russian impresario. 'In Moscow there will be no front row. Second row will be first row.'

Shaw greeted this solution with one of his rare outbursts of laughter. Turning to my father, who had come along for the fun, Shaw said, 'Well, Peter, you must admit there is something to be said for a theatre controlled by the State. Where, in this country, could a director do away with the front row of seats?'

Father abominated the words state-controlled, state-owned. To tease Shaw, advocate of State socialism, Father said, 'Why shouldn't the public get wet? It's all for art. And the Stage is better art than the State.'

By this time Sanine was through with the rain. He had his pockets full of notations, and he settled down to business. What, he wanted to know, did Eliza Doolittle think her fate was going to be after Professor Higgins tried his linguistic experiments on her? What did Higgins intend to do with her eventually? Intensely solemn, intensely Slavic, for an hour Sanine plied Shaw with questions. My father coped with the translating of complicated psychological analyses covering each and every character in the play. At last Sanine reached his final question. 'What happens to the characters in *Pygmalion* – after the play is over?'

Shaw was sitting there with his arms crossed, his chin pulled down on his chest, a favourite pose of his. Rather sadly he said, 'Liza marries Freddy.'

'No, no, no!' I wailed. 'Please, GBS, please don't say that! Freddy is such a silly ass.'

Shaw, most undemonstrative of men, laid a hand on my shoulder. 'You're not much of a realist, are you?' he said very gently. 'Liza has to eat, and Freddy will give her a comfortable life. Higgins doesn't really care a great deal what becomes of her.'

Part 5
Philanderer and Married Man

INTRODUCTION TO PART 5

Shaw was highly attractive to women and he enjoyed flirting with them – characteristics which both endured into his old age. Beatrice Webb, an avid observer of his philandering, wrote in her diary for 25 July 1894: 'Shaw lives in a drama or comedy of which he himself is the hero – his *amour propre* is satisfied by the jealousy and restless devotion of half a dozen women, all cordially hating each other.' His first documented love affair was with Alice Lockett, a nurse, in the early 1880s, but though it lasted for three years or more, and some of his letters to her may be read in *Collected Letters 1874–1897*, no record by her or any third party seems to be available. The same applies to Jenny Patterson, a widow more than fifteen years older than him, to whom he relinquished his virginity on his twenty-ninth birthday, and who competed passionately for his attention and affections for several years thereafter. Other important figures in his amatory progress, such as the actresses Florence Farr and Janet Achurch, are absent from this chapter for similar reasons, and the memoirs of others are understandably discreet. But enough remains to form a strong impression of a man, inured to emotional isolation in childhood, who sought and thrived on women's affections but drew back from committing his own.

Shaw met his future wife Charlotte at the Webbs' on 29 January 1896 and married her two and a half years later. Their partnership, though apparently sexless by Charlotte's wish, was in many ways highly successful. Shaw told Alexandra Kropotkin that he was able to encourage young people because 'Charlotte has organised my life so that I can work as much as I do and still have some leisure. Without Charlotte, I would have worked less, and would have less time for friends.' Yet it is hard to avoid feeling that they inhabited different emotional worlds. When he read a diary and some of her letters to T. E. Lawrence, he was taken aback to discover how much of her had escaped him. And if he was intellectually and sometimes sexually restless, she was spiritually and physically restless. His relief at her death was not altogether due to the heavy strain of her last illness. It was also relief from constraint, and Hesketh Pearson reports him saying more than once then that he should never have been married (*GBS: A Postscript* [London: Collins, 1951] pp. 101, 103).

'A Bump of Veneration'

MAY MORRIS

From May Morris, *William Morris: Artist, Writer, Socialist*, 2 vols (1936; reissued New York: Russell & Russell, 1966) II, 186–7. When Shaw began to frequent William Morris's house at Hammersmith in the mid-1880s, he naturally met Morris's daughter May (1862–1938). In his reminiscence 'William Morris as I knew him', prefaced to this second volume of May's memoirs of her father, he tells of an occasion when their eyes met and he 'was immediately conscious that a Mystic Betrothal was registered in heaven' (p. xxvii). Although he did nothing about it (claiming he could not afford to marry) he was stupefied when May married the less eligible Henry Sparling in 1890. However, he continues, the 'violated Betrothal' avenged itself when he stayed with the couple two years later and by his presence exposed the weakness of the marriage, which never recovered (see above, p. 55). May's only reference to their relationship is the following equivocal recollection, involving an elderly Chartist, E. T. Craig.

Craig had been a sturdy and valiant fighter; he watched the young movement with keen interest and would make speeches at our meetings in a fife-like voice which sometimes recovered its old chest register in a sort of bellow that beat upon one's ear-drums. He would come and sit in the garden at Kelmscott House and we would gather round him and hear tell of those old Co-operative days,[1] or listen to his expositions on phrenology. I remember one time when we were having our characters described by the bumps on our heads, Shaw, who was one of the company and also undergoing examination, naughtily asked if he had a bump of veneration. 'A bump?' shrieked the old gentleman, 'why, it's a 'ole there!' and struck his stick into the ground to emphasise the answer. This was one of the light moments of those hard-working days that one may be forgiven for slipping in among heavier matter.

NOTE

1. The Co-operative movement, which began in Britain in 1844, aimed for a more equitable system of 'production, distribution, education and government'. The opening of a retail shop and payment to members of a dividend from profits ensured its rapid growth.

Shaw the 'Loafer'

ANNIE BESANT

From Annie Besant, *An Autobiography* (1893; 2nd edn London: T. Fisher Unwin, 1908) p. 303. Annie Besant (1847–1933) was a freethinker, closely associated with Charles Bradlaugh and his *National Reformer*, when she first heard Shaw speak in May 1884, with the consequences she describes below. Her feeling of injury 'at having been entrapped into such a blunder' may well have extended to the intimacy that developed between them after she joined the Fabian Society in 1885, for Shaw seems to have been responsible for its termination two years later. Her autobiography is silent on the whole affair. In 1889 she was converted to theosophy and subsequently settled in India.

At this time also I met George Bernard Shaw, one of the most brilliant of Socialist writers and most provoking of men; a man with a perfect genius for 'aggravating' the enthusiastically earnest, and with a passion for representing himself as a scoundrel. On my first experience of him on the platform at South Place Institute he described himself as a 'loafer', and I gave an angry snarl at him in the *Reformer*, for a loafer was my detestation, and behold! I found that he was very poor, because he was a writer with principles and preferred starving his body to starving his conscience; that he gave time and earnest work to the spreading of Socialism, spending night after night in workmen's clubs; and that 'a loafer' was only an amiable way of describing himself because he did not carry a hod. Of course I had to apologise for my sharp criticism as doing him a serious injustice, but privately felt somewhat injured at having been entrapped into such a blunder.

A Fascinating Fabian

EDITH NESBIT

From Doris Langley Moore, *E. Nesbit: A Biography* (1933; rev. edn London: Ernest Benn, 1967) p. 113. Edith Nesbit (1858–1924), poet and novelist best remembered for her children's books, was the wife of Hubert Bland and, like him, an early

Fabian. Alice Hoatson, a journalist, joined their household as companion-help about 1885; she bore Hubert two children, whom Edith brought up as her own. Edith's letter quoted here probably dates from 1885 as well, and is a prelude to her infatuation with Shaw, which, in his own phrase, elicited from him 'nothing but a heartlessness which he knew how to make amusing' (ibid., p. 23).

The said Society is getting rather large now and includes some very nice people, of whom Mr Stapleton[1] is the nicest and a certain G. B. Shaw the most interesting. GBS has a fund of dry Irish humour that is simply irresistible. He is a very clever writer and speaker – is the grossest flatterer (of men, women and children impartially) I ever met, is horribly untrustworthy as he repeats everything he hears, and does not always stick to the truth, and is *very plain* like a long corpse with a dead white face – sandy sleek hair and a loathsome small straggly beard, and yet is one of the most fascinating men I ever met. Everyone rather affects to despise him. 'Oh it's only Shaw'. That sort of thing you know, but everyone admires him all the same. Miss Hoatson pretends to hate him, but my own impression is that she is over head and ears in love with him.

NOTE

1. J. Glode Stapleton did not especially distinguish himself in the Fabian Society. Though Edith Nesbit liked him, she was aggravated by his constant talk of spiritualism.

'Mr Shaw'

ELLEN TERRY

From Ellen Terry, *The Story of My Life* (London: Hutchinson, 1908) pp. 320–2. (Dame) Ellen Terry (1848–1928), for many years Henry Irving's leading lady at the Lyceum, first came into contact with Shaw in June 1892, when he replied to a letter she had sent to the *World*, asking that its music critic (Shaw) attend a recital by Miss Gambogi, a protégée of hers. But their correspondence, published in 1931 and famous ever since, did not begin in earnest until 1895. In many ways their epistolary romance suited Shaw perfectly and he shrank from spoiling it by personal contact. They did not meet until 16 December 1900, at the Stage Society première of *Captain Brassbound's Conversion*, written the previous year. Shaw had designed the part of Lady Cecily in the play for her, and she finally acted it at the Court Theatre in March 1906.

At this time Mr Shaw and I frequently corresponded. It began by my writing to ask him, as musical critic of the *Saturday Review*, to tell me frankly what he thought of the chances of a composer-singer friend of mine. He answered 'characteristically', and we developed a perfect fury for writing to each other! Sometimes the letters were on business, sometimes they were not, but always his were entertaining, and mine were, I suppose, 'good copy', as he drew the character of Lady Cecily Waynflete in *Brassbound* entirely from my letters. He never met me until after the play was written.

The first time he came to my house I was not present, but a young American lady who had long adored him from the other side of the Atlantic took my place as hostess (I was at the theatre as usual); and I took great pains to have everything looking nice! I spent a long time putting out my best blue china, and ordered a splendid dinner, quite forgetting the honoured guest generally dined off a Plasmon biscuit and a bean!

Mr Shaw read *Arms and the Man* to my young American friend (Miss Satty Fairchild) without even going into the dining-room where the blue china was spread out to delight his eye. My daughter Edy was present at the reading, and appeared so much absorbed in some embroidery, and paid the reader so few compliments about his play, that he expressed the opinion that she behaved as if she had been married to him for twenty years![1]

The first time I ever saw Mr Shaw in the flesh – I hope he will pardon me such an anti-vegetarian expression – was when he took his call after the first production of *Captain Brassbound's Conversion* by the Stage Society. He was quite unlike what I had imagined from his letters.

When at last I was able to play in *Captain Brassbound's Conversion*, I found Bernard Shaw wonderfully patient at rehearsal. I look upon him as a good, kind, gentle creature whose 'brain-storms' are just due to the Irishman's love of a fight; they never spring from malice or anger. It doesn't answer to take Bernard Shaw seriously. He is not a man of convictions. That is one of the charms of his plays – to me at least. One never knows how the cat is really jumping. But it *jumps*. Bernard Shaw is alive, with nine lives, like that cat!

NOTE

1. Shaw's visit took place on 5 November 1896 and he described it to Ellen Terry later that evening (*Collected Letters 1874–1897*, p. 695). The play he read was *You Never Can Tell*. Satty (Sally) Fairchild, a Bostonian, had become a friend during one of Ellen Terry's American tours. Edith Craig (1869–1947), Ellen's daughter, was at this time an actress.

Nipping the Bud

MALCOLM MUGGERIDGE

From Malcolm Muggeridge, *Chronicles of Wasted Time*, vol. I: *The Green Stick* (London: Collins, 1972) pp. 147–8. Malcolm Muggeridge (b. 1903), journalist and author, married Katherine Dobbs, a niece of Beatrice Webb, in 1927. His speculations about Beatrice's diaries suggest that her feelings about her husband's friend were deeply ambivalent. Shaw threatened her security because as 'an irregular artistic person' he appealed to an aspect of herself that was rigorously suppressed in her marriage. Shaw described the extraordinary tension between them in a letter of 31 August 1895 to Janet Achurch, an actress with whom he enjoyed another triangular relationship in the 1890s (see *Collected Letters 1874–1897*, pp. 554–5). He told Janet then that the understanding between Sidney Webb and himself was fuller and easier than that between Sidney and Beatrice.

Webb was her gargoyle; the *reductio ad absurdum* of love and lovers; a Blue Book Abelard, or computer Casanova: Sancho Panza to their friend Shaw's Don Quixote. Maybe, I sometimes used to reflect, Shaw would have provided a compromise mate for her; something between the monocle and the pince-nez. She told me once that, the first time they were alone together, Shaw 'simply threw himself upon me'. It was something, she went on, lest I should suppose this experience had any significance in her eyes, or, for that matter in his, that he did to every woman, and she had so sternly rebuffed him that nothing of the kind ever happened again. If the thought had crossed her mind that the tall, red-bearded, pale-faced jester would have been a more diverting companion than the partner she chose, and *Plays Pleasant and Unpleasant* a more diverting *oeuvre* than the forbidding tomes the Webb partnership produced, about which she always spoke disparagingly, she took a characteristic and terrible revenge by ensuring that Shaw was married, not to one of the luscious actresses like Ellen Terry, or advanced ladies like Annie Besant that he occasionally fancied, and she so disliked (she made the word 'advanced' somehow more detestable by accentuating the second syllable and shortening the 'a'), but to Charlotte Payne-Townshend, an Irish lady of great plainness and considerable wealth. He met her at the Webbs' house; it was Mrs Webb who made the match, and resolutely cut off his retreat when he tried to make a getaway.[1]

NOTE

1. Muggeridge's final remark can hardly be squared with the facts: see below, pp. 168–70.

The End of an Affair: I

BEATRICE WEBB

From *The Diary of Beatrice Webb* vol. II: *1892–1905*, ed. Norman and Jeanne MacKenzie (London: Virago, 1983) pp. 110–11. In the following entry for 9 March 1897 Beatrice Webb describes a call she paid on Bertha Newcombe, a Fabian and professional artist, whom some of Shaw's friends had earlier expected him to marry. On at least two occasions in 1894–5 Beatrice had arranged for them to join her holiday parties together. But in August 1895, while Shaw was staying in Wales with the Webbs (Bertha being excluded), he made it clear to Janet Achurch that he had no intention of marrying Bertha, and his letter suggests that he had tried to convince her of this too.

As I mounted the stairs with Shaw's *Unsocial Socialist* to return to Bertha Newcombe I felt somewhat uncomfortable as I knew I should encounter a sad soul full of bitterness and loneliness. I stepped into a small wainscotted studio and was greeted coldly by the little woman. She is petite and dark, about forty years old but looks more like a wizened girl than a fully developed woman. Her jet-black hair heavily fringed, half-smart, half-artistic clothes, pinched aquiline features and thin lips, give you a somewhat unpleasant impression though not wholly inartistic. She is bad style without being vulgar or common or loud – indeed many persons, Kate Courtney for instance, would call her 'lady-like'[1] – but she is insignificant and undistinguished. 'I want to talk to you, Mrs Webb,' she said when I seated myself. And then followed, told with the dignity of devoted feeling, the story of her relationship to Bernard Shaw, her five years of devoted love, his cold philandering, her hopes aroused by repeated advice to him (which he, it appears, had repeated much exaggerated) to marry her, and then her feeling of misery and resentment against me when she discovered that I was encouraging him 'to marry Miss Townshend'. Finally, he had written a month ago to break it off entirely: they were not to meet again. And I had to explain with perfect frankness that so long as there seemed a chance for her I had been willing to act as chaperone, that she had never been a personal friend of mine or Sidney's, that I had regarded her only as Shaw's friend, and that as far as I was concerned I should have welcomed her as his wife. But directly I saw that he meant nothing I backed out of the affair. She took it all quietly, her little face seemed to shrink up and the colour of her skin looked as if it were reflecting the sad lavender of her dress.

'You are well out of it, Miss Newcombe,' I said gently. 'If you had married Shaw he would not have remained faithful to you. You know my opinion of him – as a friend and a colleague, as a critic and literary worker, there are few men for whom I have so warm a liking; but in his relations with women he is vulgar, if not worse; it is a vulgarity that includes cruelty and springs from vanity.'

As I uttered these words my eye caught her portrait of Shaw – full-length, with his red-gold hair and laughing blue eyes and his mouth slightly open as if scoffing at us both, a powerful picture in which the love of the woman had given genius to the artist.[2] Her little face turned to follow my eyes and she also felt the expression of that man, the mockery at her deep-rooted affection. 'It is so horribly lonely,' she muttered. 'I daresay it is more peaceful than being kept on the rack, but it is like the peace of death.'

There seemed nothing more to be said. I rose and with a perfunctory 'Come and see me – someday,' I kissed her on the forehead and escaped down the stairs. And then I thought of that other woman with her loving easygoing nature and anarchic luxurious ways, her well-bred manners and well-made clothes, her leisure, wealth and knowledge of the world. Would she succeed in taming the philanderer?

NOTES

1. Beatrice's sister Catherine (1847–1929), who married the Liberal MP Leonard Courtney.

2. Bertha Newcombe painted Shaw several times; a portrait entitled 'The Platform Spellbinder' (now lost) has been most often reproduced and is probably the one referred to here.

The End of an Affair: II

BERTHA NEWCOMBE

A note by Bertha Newcombe, reprinted in *Collected Letters 1874–1897*, p. 546. In

1928, after she had read Shaw's letter mentioned in the previous headnote, Bertha Newcombe wrote this note for Ashley Dukes, who was then planning to edit and publish the Shaw–Achurch correspondence. The substance of the note was printed earlier in Janet Dunbar, *Mrs GBS: A Biographical Portrait* (London: Harrap, 1963).

As, in a letter from The Argoed[1] dated 24 August 1895 Shaw refers to his acquaintance with me I think it only just that I should be allowed to state, what seems to me after nearly forty years to be a fairly true account of our friendship. Shaw was, I should imagine, by preference a passionless man. He had passed through experiences and he seemed to have no wish for and even to fear passion though he admitted its power & pleasure. The sight of a woman deeply in love with him annoyed him. He was not in love with me, in the usual sense, or at any rate as he said only for a very short time, and he found I think those times the pleasantest when I was the appreciative listener. Unfortunately on my side there was a deep feeling most injudiciously displayed & from this distance I realise how exasperating it must have been to him. He had decided I think on a line of honourable conduct – honourable to his thinking. He kept strictly to the letter of it while allowing himself every opportunity of transgressing the spirit. Frequent talking, talking, talking of the pros & cons of marriage, even to my prospects of money or the want of it, his dislike of the sexual relation & so on, would create an atmosphere of love-making without any need for caresses or endearments.

But in what he says in this letter, he is not fair to me. Love-making would have been very delightful doubtless, but I wanted, besides, a wider companionship, and as I was inadequately equipped for that, except as a painter of some intelligence, he refused to give more than amusement.[2] Shaw has not a gift of sympathetic penetration into a woman's nature. He employs his clever detective power and pounces on weaknesses & faults which confirm his pre-conceived ideas. He imagines he understands. I objected to my emotions being divided into compartments and still retain my opinion that the emotion of love can be a fusion of body, spirit & mind.

Nevertheless I acknowledge now that the hand of Providence with Shaw's consent & guidance intervened with good results on his behalf in warding off any possibility of a marriage with me.

NOTES

1. The Argoed was a holiday house near Tintern in the Wye valley, acquired by Beatrice Webb's father in 1865.

2. Shaw had written: 'She has no idea with regard to me except that she would like to tie me like a pet dog to the leg of her easel & have me always to make love to her when she is tired of painting.'

A Disturbing Friendship

BEATRICE WEBB

From *The Diary of Beatrice Webb*, vol. II: *1892–1905*, ed. Norman and Jeanne MacKenzie (London: Virago, 1983) pp. 100–1, 112–13, 114–16, 123. Charlotte Payne-Townshend (1857–1943) grew up on a large Irish estate and always held a strong affection for Ireland. She and her extremely pretty sister were known as Miss Payne-Townshend and Miss Plain-Townshend. After her sister married and her father died in 1885, Charlotte moved to London with her mother, a domineering, self-centred and self-pitying woman, who left her with an aversion to marriage and bearing children. Her mother's death in 1891 released her to find her own path with a substantial income. She met the Webbs in the autumn of 1895 and they lost no time in diverting her interest and money towards the nascent London School of Economics. The following year Beatrice suggested they should take a country house together to entertain their friends. She designed Charlotte for Graham Wallas, but he bored her and she showed a marked preference for Shaw. Beatrice's entry for 16 September 1896, the last day of their stay at Stratford St Andrew Rectory in Suffolk, introduces Charlotte and her developing relationship with Shaw.

For the last fortnight, when the party has been reduced to ourselves and Shaw, and we have been occupied with our work and each other, they have been scouring the country together and sitting up late at night. To all seeming, she is in love with the brilliant philanderer and he is taken, in his cold sort of way, with her. They are, I gather from him, on very confidential terms and have 'explained' their relative positions. Though interested I am somewhat uneasy. These warm-hearted unmarried women of a certain age are audacious and are almost childishly reckless of consequences. I doubt whether Bernard Shaw could be induced to marry: I doubt whether she will be happy without it. It is harder for a woman to remain celibate than a man.

[The next three extracts, from entries dated 1, 8 and 24 May 1897, were written at a holiday house on the North Downs near Dorking, which the Webbs were sharing with Charlotte for three months.]

I am watching with concern and curiosity the development of the Shaw–Townshend friendship. All this winter they have been lovers – of a philandering and a harmless kind, always together when Shaw was free. Charlotte insisted on taking a house with us in order that he might be here constantly, and it is obvious that she is deeply attached to him. But I see no sign on his side of the growth of any genuine and steadfast affection. He finds it pleasant to be with her in her luxurious surroundings, he has been studying her and all her little ways and amusing himself by dissecting the rich woman brought up without training and drifting about at the beck of impulse. I think he has now exhausted the study, observed all that there is to observe. He has been flattered by her devotion and absorption in him; he is kindly and has a cat-like preference for those persons to whom he is accustomed. But there are ominous signs that he is tired of watching the effect of little words of gallantry and personal interest with which he plied her in the first months of the friendship. And he is annoyed by her lack of purpose and utter incapacity for work. If she would set to, and do even the smallest and least considerable task of intellectual work, I believe she could retain his interest and perhaps develop his feeling for her. Otherwise he will drift away, for Shaw is too high-minded and too conventionally honourable to marry her for the life of leisure and luxury he could gain for himself as her husband.

Silly these philanderings of Shaw's. He imagines that he gets to know women by making them in love with him. Just the contrary. His stupid gallantries bar out from him the friendship of women who are either too sensible, too puritanical or too much 'otherwise engaged' to care or bandy personal flatteries with him. One large section of women, comprising some, at any rate, of the finest types, remains hidden from him. With the women with whom he has *'bonne fortune'* he also fails in his object, or rather in his *avowed* object – vivi-section. He idealises them for a few days, weeks or years, imagines them to be something utterly different from their true selves, then has a revulsion of feeling and discovers them to be unutterably vulgar, second-rate, rapscallion, or insipidly well-bred. He never fathoms their real worth, nor rightly sees their limitations. But in fact it is not the end he cares for; it is the *process*. His sensuality has all drifted into sexual vanity, delight in being the candle to the moths, with a dash of intellectual curiosity to give flavour to his tickled vanity. And he is mistaken if he thinks that it does not affect his artistic work. His incompleteness as a thinker, his shallow and vulgar view of many human relationships, the lack of the sterner kind of humour which would show him the dreariness of his farce and the total absence of proportion and inadequateness in some of his ideas, all these defects come largely from the flippant and worthless self-complacency brought about by the worship of rather second-rate women. For all that, he is a good-natured agreeable sprite of a man, an intellectual cricket on the hearth always chirping away brilliant paradox, sharp-witted observation and friendly comments. Whether I like him, admire him or despise him most I do not know. Just at present I feel annoyed and contemptuous.

For the dancing light has gone out of Charlotte's eyes – there is at times a blank haggard look, a look that I myself felt in my own eyes for long years.[1] But throughout all my misery I had the habit of hard work and an almost religious sense of my intellectual mission. I had always my convent to fly to. Poor Charlotte has nowhere to turn. She can only wander listless through the world, with no reason for turning one way rather than another. What a comfort to be a fanatic. It is Bernard Shaw's fanaticism to turn everything inside out and see whether the other side won't do just as well if not better; it is this fanaticism which gives him genuine charm. He has a sort of affectionateness too, underneath his vanity. Will she touch that?

Glorious summer days. . . . Charlotte sits upstairs typewriting Shaw's plays. Shaw wanders about the garden with writing-book and pencil, writing the *Saturday* [*Review*] article, correcting his plays for press or reading through one of our chapters. With extraordinary good nature he will spend days over some part of our work, and an astute reader will quickly divine those chapters which Shaw has corrected and those which he has not – there is a conciseness and crispness in parts subjected to his pruning-knife lacking elsewhere.

[Shaw and Charlotte spent most of August and September 1897 staying with the Webbs in Monmouth; this extract comes from the entry dated 27 September.]

Shaw and Charlotte's relationship is disturbing. Shaw goes on untroubled, working hard at his plays and then going long rides with her on a tandem cycle. But she is always restless and sometimes unhappy, too anxious to be with him. He is sometimes bored, but he is getting to feel her a necessary part of his 'entourage' and would, I think, object to her breaking away from the relationship. He persuades himself that by keeping her occupied he is doing her good. If it were not for the fact that he is Shaw I should say that he was dishonourable. But as he has always advertised his views of marriage and philandering from the house-tops, every woman ought to be prepared for his logical carrying out of these principles.

NOTE

1. Beatrice was remembering the disappointed love for Joseph Chamberlain which clouded her young womanhood.

The Marriage Announced

W. A. S. HEWINS

From a letter by W. A. S. Hewins to Sidney Webb, 30 May 1898 (BLPES). William Albert Samuel Hewins (1865–1931), political economist, was the first director of the London School of Economics (1895–1903) and later a Conservative MP (1912–18). The Webbs were away on a round-the-world voyage from March 1898 until the end of the year. On 12 March Charlotte had set off for Italy to escape the impasse of her relationship with Shaw. Her project was a study of Rome's municipal administration. She was haled back by news of Shaw's diseased foot, arriving in London on 2 May. Shaw's invalid condition precipitated their marriage, which took place at the Covent Garden registry office on 1 June. Some idea of family reaction may be gained from a letter by Charlotte's cousin, Edith Somerville (of *Irish RM* fame), who amongst other uneasy speculations wrote: 'he can't be a gentleman and he is too clever to be really in love with Lottie, who is nearly clever but not quite. However it may be better than it seems' (Maurice Collis, *Somerville and Ross: A Biography* [London: Faber & Faber, 1968] p. 127).

You have probably heard from other sources that Bernard Shaw & Miss Payne-Townshend are going to be married. By the time you get this the wedding will have taken place. As soon as Shaw is strong enough they will go to the nearest registry and thence to the station. Miss P. T. is very busy nursing Shaw and looking for some 'bowery hollow crowned with summer seas'[1] where he can recover his strength. She told me about it only a day or two ago. I was not greatly surprised. When I have seen Shaw coming from her rooms the idea has frequently crossed my mind that if they were young & their expressed dislike of one of the oldest institutions a mere mannerism they might give up the platonic friendship for a closer relation. It will be interesting to see them begin life on a new basis. Though I think it impossible in the nature of things for people who defer marriage so late ever to rise to the loftier heights of wedded love, they may, & probably will, find 'happy ease' and refreshment on the lower slopes. They cannot win the more than double strength of convictions jointly reached & tested in the fire of common sorrows. But probably they don't wish to do so. I thought Miss P. T. went to Rome to study the municipality, but it seems she went because she couldn't make up her mind to marry Shaw. It is a quaint & humourous [sic] proceeding to try to smother one's lover under municipal reports.

But she should have gone to Germany. When she went to Italy she was lost. Even the official language is redolent of the softer passions.

NOTE

1. An adaptation of l. 431 in 'The Passing of Arthur' from Tennyson's *Idylls of the King*.

A 'Most Devoted Married Couple'

BEATRICE WEBB

From *The Diary of Beatrice Webb*, vol. II: *1892–1905*, ed. Norman and Jeanne MacKenzie (London: Virago, 1983) pp. 154, 166. Shaw's recovery was retarded by a series of accidents and broken limbs. So, when the Webbs returned to England in December 1898, they immediately went down to Hindhead in Surrey to stay with the Shaws. Beatrice, however, did not resume her private diary until this entry, dated 5 February 1899.

With regard to our friends and relations, we found only two persons whose lives had been completely changed during our absence – our two friends GBS and Charlotte have married each other. Shaw has become a chronic invalid, Charlotte a devoted nurse. They live in an attractive house up at Hindhead. He still writes but his work seems to be getting unreal: he leads a hothouse life, he cannot walk or get among his equals. He is as witty and as cheery as of old. But now and again a flush of fatigue or a sign of brain irritation passes over him. Charlotte, under pressure of anxiety for the man she loves, has broadened out into a motherly woman and lost her anarchic determination to live according to her momentary desires. There are some compensations for the sadness of the sudden cutting-off of his activity.

[When Shaw and Charlotte finally settled back in London in October 1899 (after a Mediterranean cruise) Shaw decided to move into the flat at 10 Adelphi Terrace which Charlotte had originally rented to subsidise the London School of Economics. Beatrice's impression of them is dated 30 October.]

The Shaws have taken up their residence in Charlotte's attractive flat over the School of Economics, and Sidney and I meet there on Thursdays to dine sumptuously between our respective lectures. Charlotte and Shaw have settled down into the most devoted married couple, she gentle and refined, with happiness added thereto, and he showing no sign of breaking loose from her dominion. What the intellectual product of the marriage will be I do not feel so sure: at any rate he will not become a dilettante, the habit of work is too deeply engrained. It is interesting to watch his fitful struggles out of the social complacency natural to an environment of charm and plenty. How can atmosphere be resisted?

Box and Cox

SIEGFRIED TREBITSCH

From Siegfried Trebitsch, *Chronicle of a Life*, trans. Eithne Wilkins and Ernst Kaiser (London: Heinemann, 1953) pp. 122–4. Siegfried Trebitsch (1869–1956), Austrian novelist and playwright, who was to do invaluable work in translating and promoting Shaw's plays in Germany and Austria, was alerted to their existence by William Archer on a visit to London in the spring of 1901. When he returned in the autumn, he called on Shaw with a letter of introduction from Archer, and his account of the visit affords a glimpse of the Shaws' team work in the early years of their marriage.

First of all I was received by Mrs Shaw, a lady who made an uncommonly likeable impression at the very first glance and whose understanding gaze revealed the intense vigour of her mind. Asking me to sit down, she told me that her husband would appear in a moment, and chatted with me about matters of no importance. I realised that this conversation was a pretext in order to be able to observe the visitor without his being aware of it and to form a proper picture of him: either to get rid of him again as quickly as possible or to introduce him to her husband. We had just got slightly warmed up when George Bernard Shaw, who had meanwhile read Archer's note, made an impatient appearance in the doorway and held out his hand to me. His wife now vanished as soundlessly as she had appeared. . . .

After I had held forth for quite a while about his plays and had then somewhat shyly begun to work up to the real subject of my visit, he interrupted me with the words: 'Upon my word, you have made a pretty thorough study of my works! And what is it you are really after? What do you mean to do with me?'

At this I said roundly and boldly that I was determined to translate his plays into German and had set myself the aim of conquering the German stage for him.

Shaw jumped up and ran upstairs in a flash. I heard him call out: 'Charlotte, here's a young lunatic Archer's sent me whom I won't be able to make see reason! You come and try to calm him down. Perhaps you'll manage it.'

Once again Mrs Shaw came in, and now, in some embarrassment, I expounded my intentions to her. She nodded in smiling agreement, apologised for her impatient husband, and spoke words of encouragement to me. But to him, upstairs, she called out: 'The young man seems uncommonly sensible. Come down and listen to what he has to say.' Hesitantly, the man so summoned now returned and sat down beside us, his penetrating gaze fixed on me.

'He is quite right,' Mrs Shaw said, taking my part. 'Why should the German theatre, which has made Shakespeare into a German poet, not also give you the satisfaction that is still denied you in your own country?' Shaw smiled incredulously, and exclaimed: 'So you want to be my Schlegel and Tieck,[1] do you?'

NOTE

1. August Wilhelm von Schlegel (1767–1845) and Johann Ludwig Tieck (1773–1853) produced the classic German translations of Shakespeare's plays.

'Dearest Liar'

MRS PATRICK CAMPBELL

From Mrs Patrick Campbell, *My Life and Some Letters* (London: Hutchinson, 1922) pp. 248–51, 264–8. Mrs Patrick Campbell, a formidable actress, had made her name in the title-role of Pinero's *The Second Mrs Tanqueray* (1893). Shaw seems to have met her first in 1897, but their intimacy did not begin until he asked her to undertake Eliza in *Pygmalion* in June 1912. She was ill for months after being injured in a taxi collision in July, and Shaw became seriously fascinated. Their liaison posed the most serious threat to Shaw's marriage that it was ever to face: Charlotte was appalled when she overheard a telephone conversation between them in May 1913. The relationship reached its turning-point in August when Shaw followed her to Sandwich, where she had wished to be alone by the sea, and she fled from him. Her account of it, which depends heavily on the quotation of letters (here omitted), is understandably less than frank and probably coloured by their quarrel over the inclusion of the letters.

There was one who, perhaps through the intelligent grasp of his genius, understood a little the nerve rack of my illness. Himself living in dreams, he made a dream-world for me. Only those who can understand this can understand the friendship Bernard Shaw gave to me by my sick-bed – the foolish, ridiculous letters he wrote me, and his pretence of being in love with me.

He revelled in the mischievous fun and in the smiles he brought to my face. He did not care a snap of the fingers at the moment what anybody else might say or think.

In the early days of our acquaintance we had had conversations something like this: –
I: What about God?
HE: *I* am God.
I: Don't be silly.
HE: Where would you be without your face?
I: I'm not going to talk to you any more.
HE: Scorn me, scorn me; I don't mind. Two hundred years hence, the world will say that you were my mistress, and — — was our son!

There is a certain 'maiden modesty' about Joey* which, to my mind, is his inimitable charm; but both his genius and his charm are at the mercy of his Irish mischievousness – disarming and enraging.

To be made to hold his tongue is the greatest insult you can offer him – though he might be ready with a poker to make you hold yours.

His want of consideration for other people's feelings is not from a lack of gentlemanliness; it is the necessary sport of his brilliant impudence.

But woe betide – should another say a word that belittles! In a trice, the belittled one is lifted high as the sky: mental catch-if-you-can and leap-frog, are the hobby of his genius.

Is it the song of life that Joey sings, with its tragedy and finality?

Or is it the song – accompanied by many delicious and sometimes glorious 'tra-la-las' – of his pertinent intellectual triumph over some human weakness: the song of the would-be Superman?

I have sometimes thought that perhaps it is only his human heart he hides and fears.

* I always called Mr Bernard Shaw 'Joey'.

Though he wrote and talked as if no other consideration existed in the world except his regard for me, his work, his endless political lectures and committees, and his very well regulated house came before everything. Whatever might betide, Charlotte (Mrs Shaw) must not be kept waiting ten minutes. To me, accustomed to the irregularities and emergencies of the theatre, which make all meals movable feasts to be put off or hurried on at a moment's notice, Joey's inflexible domesticity seemed absurd; especially as he would have me believe he only ate apples, carrots and potatoes.

When my recovery was complete and I was at work again, I learnt that his sister Lucy was an invalid. I said I would like to go and see her: his comment was, 'Go; she will tell you lies about my childhood; the relatives of great men always do.' I became very attached to Lucy; he was pleased, but insisted that I must not on any account kiss her, for fear of infection.

This struck me as fantastic – an incurable invalid to be made to feel she was too infectious to kiss! Had I murmured 'noblesse oblige', he would have grunted 'theatrical effect at any price'. I always kissed Lucy.

Joey and I had some 'words' at the theatre – probably over negotiations about *Pygmalion* – and I spent nearly an hour telling him nothing would ever make a gentleman of him; the next day he wrote as follows: –

> 25 June 1913
> . . . I was in heaven yesterday. Spoke to the Queen. A dear woman and frightfully beautiful.
> She just slanged me in the most shocking way for a full hour: and I adored her and burnt endless candles to her all the time. In the end my prayers touched her. And now I have a halo inside like this.
> GBS

At rehearsal, in pressing my hand on a rough wooden table, I had managed to get a splinter under my thumbnail. The next day I went to see Lucy: Joey and her doctor were there: they took me to a chemist, where a surgical instrument was found to remove the splinter.

Joey exclaimed with enthusiasm – as my nail was being slowly lifted and the splinter withdrawn, the veins in my neck swelling in my effort to resist the pain – 'By Jove! what a throat, "Michael Angelo"!'

This time I felt Joey's admiration was sincere.

Strong feeling exalted him – but the slightest contretemps would turn his fantastic adoration into almost alarming abuse.

When my illness was over, the real friendship which exists today was between us.

This funny incident happened when I was nearly well again, but not yet able to walk.

Joey insisted that he could make me walk in five minutes and jump in ten. We went for a drive to Richmond Park, and on the way he told me about physical exercises, and the force of will on the play of human muscles. We drew up before a low bench, he got out, helped me out, and said, 'Watch me'. With this he doubled himself up, his Aquascutum playing in the wind, and said 'You jump like this' as he leapt on to the seat. I bent and tried to spring, but it was no use; I could not move. Again gesticulating and explaining, he leaped a second time triumphantly on to the seat! Mr John Burns, MP, passed by at this moment in an open brougham.[1]

I have never heard whether Mr Burns has alluded to this extraordinary exhibition.

One day two lovely American girls came to see me. Joey called at the same time. I was out. When I returned all three were lying face downwards on the floor. He was explaining the beauty and profit of some Swedish exercises.

I remember a young society lady asking him at my house humbly and politely if she might act a play of his for a charity performance. 'No: no one can play my plays who cannot walk a tight-rope!' She replied sweetly, 'I can do double splits', and straightway did them. Joey stared in amazement.

Some years later, in his play *Pygmalion*, he succeeded in making me exclaim 'bloody' nightly before a thousand people – he thought to conquer my pre-Raphaelite instinct.

I invented a Cockney accent and created a human 'Eliza Doolittle' for him: and because the last act of the play did not travel across the footlights with as clear dramatic sequence as the preceding acts – owing entirely to the fault of the author – he declared I might be able to play a tune with one finger, but a full orchestral score was Greek to me.

Some wept at the finish of this play, for no one knew what had happened to the two characters they had grown to love.

After all – Elijah went to heaven in a chariot – you must end your story somehow.

NOTE

1. John Burns (1858–1943), MP for Battersea from 1892 to 1918, was at this time President of the Local Government Board in the Liberal government. Shaw

had known him since the 1880s, when he was a prominent socialist and unionist, and he was the model for Boanerges in *The Apple Cart*.

Shaw Reviews Mrs Pat

LADY RHONDDA

From Lady Rhondda, 'GBS and Mrs Pat', *Time and Tide*, 22 November 1952. Mrs Campbell's intention to publish some of Shaw's letters in her autobiography strained their friendship severely. Shaw casually gave his permission, but when he realised what he had let himself in for, he tried desperately to get all of them excluded (he was especially apprehensive of the effect on his wife). He edited a proof of the chapter but even so uncut versions appeared in a New York paper. Subsequently he withstood all Mrs Campbell's efforts to get permission to publish the entire correspondence. It finally appeared after his death in 1952, when it occasioned Lady Rhondda's article.

GBS once told me quite a lot about his relations with Mrs Campbell. He had come to my flat one day at tea-time, not very long after his wife died. He sat there talking for a couple of hours with his mind travelling back over the past. Among the people he spoke of was Mrs Pat. I had known both him and his wife fairly well for many years and what he told me was exactly what I should have expected. He was certainly a polygamist on paper, but only, I would have judged, on paper.

He spoke that afternoon of Mrs Campbell's *My Life and Some Letters*, which had been published in 1922. It was a bit awkward, he said. He had given permission for the publication in it of some of his letters, as she was very badly off and the letters would help to sell the book. But when he agreed he had understood that a number of other letters of the same type (she wasn't, he said, the kind of woman to whom any man could write any other sort) from other extremely notable people would be published. Permission to print these had, however, been withdrawn without his knowledge and when the book came out it looked as if he had been about the only man in Mrs Pat's life. Nothing could have been further from the truth.

He had replied to the book in *The Apple Cart*. In the scene between Magnus and Orinthia he had given an accurate description of his relationship with Mrs Campbell. Some of the passages were, in fact, an almost verbatim record of what had passed between them, as Mrs Pat well knew.

Blind Spots

ALEXANDRA KROPOTKIN

From Alexandra Kropotkin, 'Pleasant Memories of Bernard Shaw', *New American Mercury*, January 1951.

His own judgement of people was usually very shrewd, except where women were concerned. It always seemed to me that the intricacies of the female mind – or perhaps I should say of female character – were beyond his understanding. He was sincerely grieved to see that the famous Beatrice Webb (Mrs Sidney Webb) and I did not get on together. . . . Once he complained to me, 'I should have thought that you and Beatrice would hit it off very well.'

'She thinks I'm frivolous,' I replied. 'And I find her so patronising, I have an almost irresistible impulse to talk to her in Cockney slang.'

Mrs Shaw said to me, most unexpectedly, 'Why don't you?' and Shaw looked at his wife in immense astonishment.

Shaw once told me he didn't understand why I got on well with the magnificent Mrs Patrick Campbell, since Mrs Pat was not exactly noted for her sweet attitudes toward other women. 'You don't admire her acting,' Shaw grumbled to me. 'You imitate her quite wickedly. But when I see you together, you both seem to be having a good time.'

'Of course we do,' I answered. 'She is delightfully witty, and I adore being malicious with her.'

Shaw shook his head. He, the great master of malice, simply couldn't understand this feminine twist.

'My Husband'

CHARLOTTE SHAW

From H. F. Wheeler, 'Wife reveals Bernard Shaw', *Boston Post*, 29 April 1914. Charlotte made a private visit to America with the actress Lena Ashwell in April

1914, thereby removing herself from the embarrassment of Mrs Campbell's appearance in the English première of *Pygmalion*. She rarely spoke to the press and this interview may be unique. It bears no trace of the previous year's turmoil.

'Few persons understand Mr Shaw. He is a great man, a dreamer of wonderful dreams, an idealist and an individualist who is always striving and working to lift others to the high plane of his own thoughts and beliefs.

'He is not the blatant, bombastic person of the popular conception. He is bashful and retiring, quiet and reserved by nature. But he does not let this part of his nature overrule him. He sweeps it aside by might of will when he must, and when he thinks it is the only way to propagate his ideas and beliefs. At all other times – most of the time, too – and because it is natural, he is a man the direct opposite of what the world thinks.

'Mr Shaw is a Socialist and believes implicitly in all the doctrines and tenets of Socialism. He has been a Socialist for thirty years and became one after he had listened to the words and teachings of Henry George, one of your famous Americans. Mr George had been lecturing in England and my husband and Sidney Webb, Hubert Bland and Edward Pease became so interested in his theories that they formed that great Socialist organisation now known as the Fabian Society. . . .

'Since then my husband has preached and written Socialism, and this, with the fact that he is an atheist, a vegetarian, a firm believer in women's rights, going so far as to espouse the feminist movement, and his fearless pen, have all tended to form the popular opinion of him.

'He has been a vegetarian for thirty years, because he does not believe in the killing of animals. A horror of slaughter houses and butcher establishments made him one, and he has always remained one.

'Are you a vegetarian, too?' asked the reporter. Mrs Shaw smiled.

'I was for a time,' she answered in her well-modulated voice. 'But then I tasted of the flesh pots. My early bringing up had not made me fitted to be a vegetarian. You know a vegetarian has a wonderful palate – apparently I didn't have – and is most sensitive to taste. Mr Shaw gets more taste and keen enjoyment out of a meal of rice and macaroni than most persons do out of mutton.'

Mrs Shaw did not seem inclined to consider vegetarianism a very serious subject, though, and passing it by, spoke enthusiastically of her husband's belief in the rights of women.

'Mr Shaw goes so far,' she continued, 'as to believe that all government should be by women. He believes women are more capable of management than men and he is a thorough feminist. Women, he says, should be placed on all governing boards.'

A Genius, But . . .

LAWRENCE LANGNER

From Lawrence Langer, *GBS and the Lunatic* (London: Hutchinson, 1964) pp. 30–1, 59–60. Lawrence Langner (1890–1962), patent specialist and theatre director, was born in Swansea and went to America in 1911. In 1918 he founded the Theatre Guild, which gave the world première of *Heartbreak House* in New York in November 1920. He first met the Shaws in London shortly afterwards (see below, pp. 296–7).

I was constantly amazed at Shaw's courtly old-fashioned manners. If Mrs Shaw started to leave the room, Shaw would leap from his chair, dash like a sprinter to the door with his beard waving so as to arrive ahead of her, and he would hold it open with a deep bow until she had passed into the hall. When I first met her, Shaw introduced her in the grand manner, like an impresario displaying a prima donna, a role which did not fit Mrs Shaw in the least. He ostentatiously seated her in a chair and showed her the photographs of the production, which she admired. However, when Shaw pointed out his objection to the doors with the rounded tops,[1] she replied simply, 'What difference does it make?' to which the great man made no reply. I was to learn from many years' friendship with Mrs Shaw that 'the Genius', as she lovingly called him, was guided by her excellent common sense, which often served as an antidote to his tendency to explode fireworks on all occasions.

[Langner now describes an occasion in Birmingham, during performances of *Back to Methuselah* in October 1923, when he and Mr and Mrs St John Ervine were listening to Shaw talking about *Saint Joan* for some two hours.]

All of us were exhilarated by his lively stories, which happily seemed endless; and while he held forth, Mrs Shaw, seated on a low chair at one corner of the fireplace, appeared to be engrossed in her knitting, pausing only to smile now and again, like a kindly mother whose grown son was distinguishing himself before an appreciative audience. During one of the lulls in the conversation, which were infrequent and came only when GBS had reached the end of one anecdote and waited for the chorus of 'How wonderful!' before going on to the next, Nora Ervine leaned over to Mrs Shaw, looked at her knitting and asked with some concern, 'Whatever are you making, Mrs Shaw?' 'Nothing,' replied Mrs Shaw in a whisper. 'Nothing, really. But I've heard the Genius tell these same stories at least a hundred times, and if I didn't have something to do with my hands, I think I'd go stark raving mad!'

One might imagine from this little story that there was not the greatest understanding and sympathy on Mrs Shaw's part toward her husband. But that would be erroneous. She regarded him with amused admiration and never lost her sense of humour about him. Mrs Shaw's influence was always directed to the more human, emotional side of GBS's work, and I felt that had it been even stronger, GBS might have written many more plays of the stature of *Saint Joan*, for her warm human quality was a good antidote for his tendency to theorise on political, social and every other subject under the sun. 'All Italian women are stupid', he once remarked in her presence at Stresa.[2] 'How can you say that?' she replied. 'You know only three or four Italian women, and you can hardly speak enough Italian to carry on an intelligent conversation with any of them.' The Genius subsided.

NOTES

1. Shaw had said that the Theatre Guild set for *Heartbreak House* should have looked more like a ship's cabin, objecting that rounded door tops were never found on ships.

2. Langner stayed with the Shaws at Stresa on Lake Maggiore in August 1927.

Lunching with the Shaws: I

DORA RUSSELL

From Dora Russell, 'Shaw – a Personal Impression', *Civil Liberty*, Winter 1950. Bertrand Arthur William Russell (1872–1970), 3rd Earl Russell (from 1931), mathematician and philosopher, married Dora Black, his second wife, in 1921. Shaw had known Russell, through the Webbs, since 1895.

Soon after my marriage to Russell, I was taken to lunch with the Shaws. Possibly it is not strange that my most vivid recollection of this meeting is not of Shaw, but of Charlotte and her relation to him. With what surprise, in the pleasant large room in the flat at Adelphi, I met in Mrs

Shaw the image of my former headmistress, erect, gracious, somewhat forbidding! With an eager young poetess for the fifth, we sat down to lunch. Charlotte and I faced each other in silent communion as the wit and laughter of our two irrepressible brilliant husbands sparkled and crackled across the table. I recalled Ann's 'go on talking' from the end of *Man and Superman*, and reflected on the wives of great men. As we left, Shaw remarked that the poetess had intended to read him her poems all afternoon. But she had already vanished. Charlotte had seen to that.

One day, not long after Russell and I had started our school, a car drove up bringing Beatrice Webb and Bernard Shaw on an unexpected visit. Russell was not at home. Feeling most inadequate, I conducted the visitors through the children's dining room. It was just before tea, when children are at their wildest. They found this tall bearded visitor most attractive. As Shaw muttered, 'Let's get out of here', I hastily led the way to the staff dining room, where, as I dispensed tea and apologised for Russell's absence, Mrs Webb and Shaw lectured the staff and myself on the care and education of children, and then went away. We could not help reflecting that both were childless.

Lunching with the Shaws: II

BERTRAND RUSSELL

From Bertrand Russell, *Portraits from Memory and Other Essays* (London: George Allen & Unwin, 1956) pp. 72–3.

Lunching with Mr and Mrs Shaw at Adelphi Terrace was a somewhat curious experience. Mrs Shaw was a very able manager and used to provide Shaw with such a delicious vegetarian meal that the guests all regretted their more conventional menu. But he could not resist a somewhat frequent repetition of his favourite anecdotes. Whenever he came to his uncle who committed suicide by putting his head in a carpet-bag and then shutting it,[1] a look of unutterable boredom used to appear on Mrs Shaw's face, and if one were sitting next her one had to take care not to listen to Shaw. This, however, did not prevent her from solicitude for him. I remember a luncheon at which a young and lovely poetess was present in the hopes of reading her poems to Shaw. As we said good-bye, Shaw informed us that she was staying behind for this purpose. Nevertheless, when we departed we found her on the mat, Mrs Shaw having manoeuvred her there by methods that I was not privileged to observe. When I learnt, not long afterwards, that this same lady had cut her throat at Wells because he refused to make love to her, I conceived an even higher respect than before for Mrs Shaw.

Wifely solicitude towards Shaw was no sinecure. When they and the Webbs were all nearing eighty, they came to see me at my house on the South Downs. The house had a tower from which there was a very fine view, and all of them climbed the stairs. Shaw was first and Mrs Shaw last. All the time that he was climbing, her voice came up from below, calling out, 'GBS, don't talk while you're going up the stairs!' But her advice was totally ineffective, and his sentences flowed on quite uninterruptedly.

NOTE

1. Shaw's paternal Uncle William, whose story he told in the Preface to *Immaturity*.

Subtle Sovereignty

LILLAH McCARTHY

From Lillah McCarthy, *Myself and My Friends* (London: Thornton Butterworth, 1933) pp. 173–4. Lillah McCarthy had married the botanist Sir Frederick Keeble in 1920.

When he married, Shaw was badly run down, but Charlotte, his wife, changed all that. How she has done it is a mystery to those who do not know her, for Charlotte almost always seems to let him go his own way; but the way GBS goes is her way – at all events in large matters.

The Shaws were staying with us not so very long ago. He was just finishing his book on 'Socialism for Ladies'.[1] One of us asked him if, after dinner, he would tell us what new ideas he had on socialism. 'Of course I will,' said Shaw. But after dinner his mood had changed. He did not want to talk about socialism. Then Charlotte said very gently: 'GBS! You promised to talk to us about socialism and you must.' Without further demur he did. Shaw's wonderful health, sustained by all sorts of farinaceous fare and by his abstemiousness, and his untiring energy owe much to his common-sense way of looking at things. Though he scoffs at science, he has a scientific mind, and though he laughs at scientific experiments, he has himself found out by experiment what food agrees with him. But his health and vigour owe much to the care, constant although it seems so casual, with which Charlotte watches over him. She seems unobservant; but misses nothing, and her care is exercised without constraint.

NOTE

1. *The Intelligent Woman's Guide to Socialism and Capitalism* was published on 1 June 1928.

The Shaws at Malvern

BEVERLEY NICHOLS

From Beverley Nichols, *All I Could Never Be: some Recollections* (London: Jonathan Cape, 1949) pp. 145–7. Beverley Nichols (1898–1983), playwright, novelist, composer and dramatic critic, met Shaw at the first Malvern Festival in 1929. His play *The Stag* was one of the works chosen for inclusion in the Festival, having been first produced at the Globe Theatre in April 1929.

During the festival, Shaw, his wife and I were all staying at the same hotel. It was a tepid place, but the food was good, the beds were comfortable, and it was of a stunning respectability. It was mostly patronised by elderly female hypochondriacs, who rustled down to dinner as though they were going to the stake, sipped Malvern water through pruney-prismy lips, and occasionally, in their more abandoned moments, suggested that somebody should pass the salt.

Into this curious setting Shaw would stalk, every evening at seven-thirty, followed by his wife. It seemed to be an unwritten convention among the other guests that nobody should look at him. The pruney-prismy ladies averted their eyes, as though they had suddenly been confronted by a nude, and the elderly colonels pressed their noses deep into their copies of *The Times*, lest it should be thought that they were guilty of celebrity-hunting. Never had there been such an impressive exhibition of British tact. I did not attempt to emulate this politeness; I could never keep my eyes off him. For really, he was very good to look at. The cleanliness of the man! He was like snow and new linen sheets and cotton wool and red apples with the rain on them. One felt that he must even smell delicious, like hay or pears.

Shaw evidently appreciated the convention that respected his anonymity; as he strode into dinner each night he was always clasping a travel-book. Mrs Shaw, in her turn, clutched a volume of economics. As they sat down, the travel book would be opened on his side of the table, and propped up against a bottle of Malvern water. On the other side, the procedure was identical. Never a word did they speak during dinner, and I have often thought that if more husbands and wives would follow their example there would be fewer unhappy marriages.

Meditation

CYRIL SCOTT

From Cyril Scott, 'Impressions of Bernard Shaw', *Mark Twain Journal*, Summer 1954. Cyril Scott (1879–1970), composer, pianist and writer, was a guest of the Shaws for a fortnight at a Torquay hotel in the early days of the First World War. Both before and after this he lunched fairly often with them, and last saw Shaw in 1938.

Mrs Shaw had died, but as she had suffered so much before the end, he took her death like the philosopher he was. She had been a good companion to him, yet not an entirely uncritical one. She told him in front of me, I remember on one occasion, that some of his plays ought to be burnt! He merely laughed. Mrs Shaw was something of a mystic, and informed me when we were in Torquay that she used to meditate for the best part of an hour every morning before breakfast. GBS was indulgently tolerant about it all but unbelieving. Perhaps he came to think differently before he died.

Charlotte and her Marriage

LADY RHONDDA

From Lady Rhondda, obituary memoir of Charlotte Shaw, *Time and Tide*, 18 September 1943. Charlotte had died on 12 September, after being crippled by osteitis deformans.

There cannot have been many happier marriages than theirs. That was the background which, whilst it never in any way obtruded itself (nothing about Mrs Shaw was obtrusive) coloured every knowledge of them.

Mrs Shaw was the kind of person one noticed and thought about a good deal. That is not true of the wives of all great men, perhaps not of most of them. But she was a person one would have still thought about if she had never married Shaw. She had a great deal of personality. She had integrity, charm, unusual honesty, great tact, capacity, kindness and intelligence. She had also a full-size social conscience. A conscience which I am quite sure she could never have faced, if she had not made full use of her opportunities and talents. She was, as every one knows, a friend of the Webbs and already a Socialist before she met Shaw. And she had already come near to taking up more than one career. She had at one time very nearly decided to study at the London School of Medicine for Women with a view to becoming a doctor. I am not sure whether it was her marriage which prevented this.

She would have made, I imagine, a success of any career she had decided to take up, but having decided to become the wife of GBS she must have known as surely as everyone else who ever met them knew, that she had chosen as useful a career as she could have found. She was responsible to society for seeing that a great genius functioned to the fullest possible capacity. However much her marriage might mean to her privately (and every available evidence suggests that it meant everything) she was certainly perfectly well aware that she had a public as well as a private responsibility. And I doubt if she could have felt satisfied without it. She was fortunate in that the two so completely coincided.

There are drawbacks to every career, and there must have been for her certain drawbacks to being the wife of a genius. She was an unusually reserved woman who valued privacy more than most. She had a horror – almost a Victorian horror – of publicity, and she had to spend a considerable part of her time in leading a life which was, I used to think, rather like that of a Queen Consort. It is true that she had a number of the attributes of a Queen. Her views might be those of an advanced Fabian, but her manners were the *soignée* manners of a lady of the eighteen-eighties. She had graciousness, courtesy, complete poise. Yes, she played the part of a Queen to perfection (I have always imagined that she served as part-model for the Queen in *The Apple Cart*), but she certainly had a greater loathing of publicity than it could be convenient for royalty to have.

Charlotte's Will

From 'Shaw and the Problems of a £154,000 Will', *News Chronicle*, 17 February 1944. The bulk of Charlotte's estate was left in trust for her husband's benefit; only after his death was it to be used for grants to secure 'masterpieces of fine art' for the Irish people, and for other purposes which caused something of a furore when the will was published.

Mr Bernard Shaw, hale and hearty at eighty-seven and dressed in a grey Norfolk suit, gave me a breezy interview of five minutes at his home here today when I spoke to him about his wife's will.

Mrs Shaw has left £154,967, most of it to the people of Ireland.

The money is to be used for education in 'self-control, elocution, deportment, the arts of personal contact, and other arts of public, private, professional and business life.'

I saw Mr Shaw in his lounge. He paced up and down impatiently and was anxious to terminate an interview which had only just begun.

'All you can say is this,' he said, stroking his flowing white beard. 'THAT WILL DOESN'T COME INTO OPERATION UNTIL I'M DEAD.'

Mr Shaw roared these words at me with such vigour that I could not fail to hear them.

'All Ireland has been getting at me about this will,' he went on, 'and I do want you to make that clear. I wouldn't care if the will came into operation straight away, but there it is.

'It's no good your asking me about Mrs Shaw's attitude towards Ireland. Don't ask me; ask her spirit. What she observed in Ireland I observe in England.'

Mr Shaw was referring to the wording of Mrs Shaw's opinion, expressed in the will, that many people are handicapped by vulgarities of speech and other social defects.

He had no idea how the will would be administered. 'That's a job,' he said, 'for the trustees – when I'm dead.'

By this time he was standing at the door. There was an ominous silence, a fixed glare at me and then out it came: 'I am trying to put you out politely.'

Mr Shaw saw me to the front door, to the front gate, and opened the car door for me. Few great men have ended an interview with such determination – or such charm.

Part 6
'Anything Except Sport'

INTRODUCTION TO PART 6

The quotation which provides the title of this Part was Shaw's succinct statement under the heading 'Recreations' in his entry in the 1930 edition of *Who's Who*. He had no interest in the various team sports popular in England, Australasia and South Africa, and, of course, was actively hostile to blood sports. Yet Shaw engaged with gusto in a wide range of recreational activities. Apart from some periods of serious illness and persistent migraine headaches, he remained extraordinarily fit throughout his life, his regimes of diet and exercise being of a kind that most acknowledge as desirable but few care to follow. He was a keen and energetic walker, and even into quite advanced old age would have younger men panting to keep up with him on walks in the countryside surrounding Ayot St Lawrence, over the Malvern Hills or in the streets of London. He was also a strong and 'insatiable'[1] swimmer. In the 1890s, with Sidney and Beatrice Webb, he avidly took up the new craze of cycling, and after the turn of the century became equally enthusiastic about motor cars. He was quite a reckless person in physical ways. He had many spectacular spills from bicycles (one following a collision with Bertrand Russell). He was a fairly skilful car driver, but had several accidents, and developed a tendency to mistake the accelerator pedal for the brake. One of the following recollections records a narrow escape from death by drowning when Shaw was swimming in rough surf with Robert Loraine.

Shaw professed to dislike holidays, which he invariably used as times for keeping up with correspondence. But in his late twenties and thirties he visited Europe on several occasions, and would often spend time in the country with the Webbs and other fellow Fabians. After their marriage, Charlotte, who was fond of travelling, frequently persuaded Shaw to take holidays and tours in various parts of England, Ireland, Scotland and Europe. The sea cruises which the Shaws took in the early 1930s are recalled in a later chapter.[2] This part begins with an interview about a very early sporting interest of Shaw's, which fits with the polemical side of his character, and which was the profession of the hero of one of his early novels.

Music was one of Shaw's earliest and most abiding forms of recreation. Born into a household in which the playing and singing of music was a part of everyday life, Shaw in his teens developed the custom of playing the piano and accompanying himself as he sang. He knew by heart the

entire scores of many of the classical operas, and had a large repertoire
of other music. He had early ambitions to become a painter and, as his
letters sometimes reveal, he could produce a lively sketch. But, in the
field of visual arts, his main recreational interest was photography. He
bought his first camera in 1898, and remained keenly interested in all
aspects of photography for the rest of his life.

NOTES

1. Sydney Olivier's description. See below, p. 196.
2. See vol. II, ch. 2.

Boxing

NORMAN CLARK

From Norman Clark, '"Come to Lunch!" – G. Bernard Shaw: Exclusive Interviews', *Cassell's Magazine*, April 1929. Norman Clark (b. 1892), former amateur
welterweight champion, became a referee and secretary of the British Boxing
Board of Control. He wrote several books on boxing and one on Kant's
philosophy. The conversation reported here took place when he first met Shaw
c. 1917. Shaw's interest in boxing was kindled by his friend Pakenham Beatty
(1855–1930), an enthusiastic amateur and an aspiring poet, whom he met in the
late 1870s. Beatty introduced him to Ned Donnelly, a respectable 'Professor of
Boxing', who kept a gymnasium near the Haymarket Theatre. Both young men
entered for the Amateur Boxing Championship in March 1883 (a month after
Shaw had completed his pugilistic novel *Cashel Byron's Profession*) but neither
was chosen to compete. Shaw's interest was revived by seeing Georges
Carpentier fight in 1919 – a contest he reported with great spirit in the *Nation*
(13 December). In the 1920s he also followed the careers of the heavyweight
champions Jack Dempsey and Gene Tunney (partly on film) and Tunney later
became a friend.

I asked Shaw if he ever went to boxing contests nowadays.
   'Oh, very rarely,' he replied with a smile. 'Before I wrote *Cashel Byron*
I used to frequent the old Queensberry contests at Lillie Bridge, and the
early Boxing Association contests at the old St James's Hall which grew
out of them,[1] with a poet friend of mine, who, like all poets, had an
incorrigible passion for fighting. The chief arenas then,' Shaw explained,
'were Bob Habbijam's School of Arms and Bill Richardson's Blue Anchor
(immortalised in my *Admirable Bashville*[2]); but I never went to these

places. The NSC,[3] did not then exist, and I have never witnessed a fight in it. The most brilliant boxer of that day was Jack Burke;[4] but he was killed in a bicycle accident. It was an exhibition spar of his that suggested the exploits of *Cashel Byron*.

'Then there would be Ned Donnelly, the Royal Professor,' I suggested, 'who when commanded to spar before the King, immediately bought a new top hat and frock coat.'

'I knew him,' said Shaw. 'He taught all my friends. Ned Skene, in *Cashel Byron*, owes something to him.'

[Shaw was then led to recall a fight in which a lightweight trounced a heavyweight by superior speed and skill.]

I suggested that an exhibition like that perhaps made him feel boxing was rather a brutal sport.

'Oh, boxing is rarely more distressing than running a mile or rowing in the Boat Race,' Shaw answered. 'It was the bloody-minded newspaper reporters who gave that impression, just as it was the people who clamour against the cruelty of the Ring who are incidentally the best propagandists for its box-office. A bruise soon healed, and the jaw knock-out, far from being painful, was the most perfect form of anaesthetic. No; I gave up going to boxing because I found the second-rate boxing one usually sees so tedious; whilst as to mere slogging exhibitions, which have neither the brutal realism of a genuine fight nor the interest of a skilled game – these reduced me to such a condition of deadly boredom that even disgust would have been a relief.'

NOTES

1. The Amateur Boxing Association was formed in 1880 and held its first championship meeting at St James's Hall, Piccadilly, the following year.

2. Shaw's blank-verse dramatisation of *Cashel Byron's Profession*. The Blue Anchor was in Shoreditch and the publican, Bill Richardson, a retired prize-fighter and trainer, staged fights in a back room.

3. The National Sporting Club (1891–1929), which governed professional boxing in Britain.

4. The career of Jack Burke (d. 1913) culminated in a record-breaking contest in New Orleans in 1893, when he fought for seven hours and ten minutes spread over 110 rounds.

Swimming: I

SYDNEY OLIVIER

From a letter by Lord Olivier to Archibald Henderson, 9 June 1913, in Henderson, *Bernard Shaw, Playboy and Prophet* (London and New York: D. Appleton, 1932) p. 707. Olivier and Shaw attended the Zurich Socialist Congress early in August 1893, Shaw reporting on it for the *Star*.

Shaw was, and I believe still is, an insatiable swimmer. On our journey together to Zürich in 1893, as delegates to the International Social Congress, after we had battled before breakfast with the rushing flood of the frigid Rhine at Basel, he insisted during our next halt at Bern on committing our bodies to the still more impetuous Aar, with a speed of about five miles an hour and a temperature of about forty degrees in its turbid snow-waters. At Zürich, the lake was more than tepid. So incandescent however was the temperature of the Congress room, that when (as Morley Roberts, who was there with us, reminded me the other day when we met again in Jamaica[1]), we used to rush, in the lunch interval, to the bathing house, the water seemed agreeably bracing. Shaw maintained that the lake used to hiss and boil as our red hot bodies plunged into it.

NOTE

1. Morley Roberts (1857–1942) was a widely travelled journalist and novelist. Olivier had been in Jamaica in 1929–30 as chairman of the West Indian Sugar Commission.

Swimming: II

ROBERT LORAINE

From Winifred Loraine, *Robert Loraine: Soldier, Actor, Airman* (London: Collins,

1938) pp. 93–4. The English-born actor Robert Loraine (1876–1935) had already established himself on the American stage when he first met Shaw in the summer of 1905, through his enthusiasm for *Man and Superman*. He produced the play in New York that autumn with immense success, playing Tanner himself. In August 1907 he stayed with the Shaws on holiday at Llanbedr in Wales, where they were also taking part in the first of the annual Fabian summer schools. The following account of a narrow escape from drowning is taken from Loraine's diary, extensively used by his widow in writing his biography. Shaw gave an account to H. G. Wells (see *Collected Letters 1898–1910*, pp. 708–12).

'Once,' says Robert, 'there had been a great storm in the night and the sea was still so rough when we arrived for our swim, we decided to go for a walk instead.

'Another look at the curling waves, however, made GBS think the combers so inviting that we nipped out of our clothes and were soon diving under the breakers with glee. We rolled for a while in the surf. Then Shaw wanted to try and swim out. After a good deal of buffeting we managed to get past the inshore line of waves to steadier water farther out. Shaw went on and on. I followed. After a while we turned towards the land again, and were amazed to find we were far farther out than we had ever thought possible. What was more alarming still, we soon realised that we were being carried away by an irresistible current set up by the tide that had just turned.

'Purposefully, side by side, we struck out for the shore. I became seriously concerned about Shaw's safety. This was stupid, because he is a better swimmer than I, his lean physique has more endurance; and it was absurd for me to think of helping him; I should only have been an encumbrance. Still, I felt that at all costs he must be saved. It would have been a disaster for the world to lose him. As I struggled, I thought fantastically that Shaw would be handicapped by the weight of his brain.

'Then, shortness of breath and desperation at the distance still had to be swum, told me I was quite incapable of rendering assistance. My lungs were going from distress to agony, and as I despaired of reaching land, I tried to get it over and drown. After each attempt to sink I found myself automatically striking out again to save my life. In one of these attempts to cease swimming and go under – floating was out of the question in that foaming water – my foot struck a jagged end of rock. The sharp pain and sensation of something solid brought fresh hope and stimulated me to a last effort. Miraculously I found myself standing on solid ground in the middle of the sea, up to my knees in water. We had struck a sandbank or possibly an old causeway. I staggered ashore and flopped on to the sand gasping. Shaw came to land side by side with me.

'We lay gasping for some time. When we recovered our breath, Shaw said very coolly: "That was a near thing", and went off to fetch his sandshoes, which were drying where our swim began. When he came back I asked him whether visions of his past life had come before him, as they say the drowning have them. He shook his head. "Nor I—" I said.'

Swimming: III

LILLAH McCARTHY

From Lillah McCarthy, *Myself and My Friends* (London: Thornton Butterworth, 1933) p. 88. Lillah McCarthy's memories are centred on the decade preceding the First World War.

Shaw is a very strong swimmer. I am not. Many times he would give me lessons. When he is teaching some exercises or art, away from the theatre, he is both patient and kind. He would tell me to put one hand upon his shoulder and just swim, on and on. We would find ourselves well out to sea. Then a change would come over Shaw, a sea change. He is vigorous on land but when he is swimming in the sea, he becomes for once tranquil. He would say to me as we swam: 'We are in another world'. If I were afraid when I saw the land slipping farther and farther away, he would say: 'Have no fear, Lillah, gently and slowly does it.'

Swimming: IV

LAWRENCE LANGNER

From Lawrence Langner, 'The Sinner-Saint as Host: Diary of a Visit to GBS at Stresa', *Saturday Review of Literature* (New York), 22 July 1944. When Langner and his wife Armina stayed with the Shaws at the Regina Palace Hotel, Stresa, in August 1927, they were woken the first morning at seven by Shaw asking them to swim with him.

GBS was waiting for us. It was his custom each morning to cross the lake in a motor boat, then moor this boat off the estate of Albert Coates, the conductor,[1] swim for the shore, and end up with a sunbath on a grassy meadow which sloped down to the beach. We boarded the motor boat dressed in our bathing suits, crossed over towards the other side of the lake, and at what seemed to me to be an enormous distance from the shore, GBS dived in off the side of the boat. As his head and shoulders emerged from the lake and he shook the water out of his white hair and beard, the sun caught his pink cheeks and blue eyes, and he looked for all the world like Father Neptune emerging from the waves.

'Come on in, it's fine!' he shouted.

Armina, like most California-bred girls, was somewhat of a mermaid, and in she dove, showing off with a very effective scissors-stroke. I cautiously lowered myself down the side of the boat, looking nervously at the shore which seemed to be miles away. I suppose the motor boat will keep moving slowly behind us, I thought, throwing discretion to the winds and timidly striking out in the direction of Father Neptune and the Mermaid. I kept going for a while, as the waves waved wildly, and the other swimmers swam rapidly ahead of me towards the shore. I looked back to reassure myself that the motor boat was following me. It was not. The Italian boatman had stopped his engine and was settling down to a comfortable siesta. I was torn between the choice of drowning or calling for help. I called for help. The motor boat started up, GBS and Armina swam back, and between the three of them I was heaved out of the water and ignominiously ferried to the shore. Some years later, when recounting this incident, GBS remarked that it was the greatest compliment ever paid him.

'Lawrence Langner,' he said, with a twinkle in his eye, 'followed me to such an extent that, when I jumped into Lake Maggiore, he jumped in after me without being able to swim a stroke, evidently thinking that my mere presence would save him from drowning.'

NOTE

1. Albert Coates (1882–1953) had begun his career in Germany and Russia, but settled in England in 1919 and became a leading conductor of concerts, operas and recordings.

Swimming: V

IAN COSTER

From Ian Coster, *Friends in Aspic* (London: John Miles, 1939) pp. 130–1. Ian Coster, a young journalist from New Zealand who wanted to meet Shaw, sought him out at the Royal Automobile Club, where for years he regularly swam before breakfast, only giving up the practice in the late 1930s. Elsewhere Coster makes it clear that his report on Shaw's routine must be dated after the Shaws had exchanged their Adelphi Terrace flat for one in Whitehall Court in 1927.

George Bernard Shaw stepped up to the weighing machine and jauntily checked his loss or gain. Then he took off from the five-feet springboard at the deep end in a passable dive, legs straight, feet together. A neat enough header needing a trifle more lift. He came up slowly and went into a leisurely breaststroke, his head well up, his beard draggling. He swam four lengths, changing over to an overarm stroke but carrying his legs too deep. This natatorial display could easily have been surpassed by Byron or George Borrow, but it gave the swimmer a deep, placid enjoyment. He looked a contented Neptune forgetful of turbulent seas and mermaid minxes.

Photography: I

From Helmut Gernsheim, 'GBS and Photography', *Photographic Journal*, January 1951. Helmut Erich Robert Gernsheim (b. 1913), German-born photo-historian and author, who had settled in England in 1937, approached Shaw for information in 1949 and finally secured written answers to his questions on 19 September.

What, or who, led you to take up photography, and about what date?

I always wanted to draw and paint. I had no literary ambition: I aspired to be a Michael Angelo, not a Shakespear [sic]. But I could not draw well enough to satisfy myself; and the instruction I could get was worse than useless. So, when dry plates and push buttons came into the market, I bought a box camera and began pushing the button. This was in 1898.

Was photography, to you, a creative art or did you regard the camera merely as an instrument for recording the appearance of persons and places?

I wanted to make both pictures and portraits. I did not argue about it.

With what camera did you work, and approximately how many photographs do you think you took?

First a box camera. Then a long extension Sanderson with an 18-inch spectacle lens costing ninepence, and involving long exposures and calculated focusing, but giving pictures of extraordinarily [*sic*] natural-ness. I did this under instruction from a friendly physicist named Bolas.[1] Also some pinhole work. These processes were commercially impossible. Then rectangulars, anastigmats, a Dallmeyer–Bergheim telescopic, Kodak, Leica, Contax, etc., etc.

For how many years was photography your hobby?

There is no 'was' about it. I took a dozen photographs last week.

Do you think there has been any progress in artistic photography since the days of your own activity in this field?

No. The changes have been in materials and processes. Nobody has yet beaten Mrs Hay Cameron, or Frederick H. Evans, or Langdon Coburn.[2]

Was your oft-quoted comparison of the photographer with the cod based on personal experience?[3]

Yes.

Do you still hold your opinion that 'Some day the camera will do the work of Velasquez and Pieter de Hoogh, colour and all'?[4]

All that belongs to the days when photography was not ranked as a fine art, and when I, then a professional critic of painting, astonished the cliques by writing a notice of a photographic exhibition as if it were the Royal Academy, and criticising Robinson as if he were Millais.[5]

Do you uphold your dictum of 1901 that 'The camera has hopelessly beaten the pencil and paint-brush as an instrument of artistic representation'?[6]

Substitute 'mere' for 'artistic' and such an idiocy might be partly true. But nothing can falsify a representation more grossly than a lens, which can distort features and make molehills of mountains as no draughtsman could.

NOTES

1. Thomas Bolas, who had designed the first 'detective' or disguised camera for police use in 1881.
2. Julia Margaret Cameron (1815–79) produced some of the finest photographic portraits ever made, though they form only a small portion of her twelve-year output. The bookseller Frederick H. Evans (1852–1943) was a gifted amateur photographer, much admired by Shaw. They became friends after an approach from Evans in 1895 to publish some of Shaw's music criticism in volume form. For Coburn, see following headnote.
3. 'The photographer is like the cod, which produces a million eggs in order that one may reach maturity (from the preface Shaw supplied for the catalogue of Coburn's exhibition shown in London and Liverpool in 1906).
4. Quoted from Shaw's review of the Salon and Royal Photographic Society exhibitions in *Amateur Photographer*, 11 and 18 October 1901: he seems to have taken Velasquez and de Hoogh as types of excellence in, respectively, portrait painting, and the painting of domestic interiors and townscapes.
5. Henry Peach Robinson (1830–1901) tried to emulate the traditions and techniques of painting by building up compositions from a number of negatives. He was the most influential exponent of 'High Art' photography, supporting his work with prolific writings. (Sir) John Millais (1829–96) helped found the Pre-Raphaelite movement, and became an extremely successful and fashionable painter.
6. See n. 4 above.

Photography: II

ALVIN COBURN

From *Alvin Langdon Coburn, Photographer: An Autobiography*, ed. Helmut and Alison Gernsheim (London: Faber & Faber, 1966) pp. 26, 28, 40, 42. Alvin Langdon Coburn (1882–1966), American-born photographer of independent means who settled in Britain, did most of his best work, including some magnificent portraits, in the first two decades of the century before he turned to religious mysticism, though he did take up photography again in the 1950s. He wrote to Shaw in July 1904, mentioning their mutual friend F. H. Evans and requesting a sitting. Shaw's reply from his recently rented country house at Welwyn details a cornucopia of equipment he could lend his visitor (see *Collected Letters 1898–1910*, pp. 435–6). However, Coburn preferred to use his own.

Unfamiliar with English customs, I chose August Bank Holiday for my journey, not realising that there would be no available conveyances, apart from the train. On arrival at Welwyn station I recognised Shaw on the platform from descriptions: a very tall man with red hair and beard, wearing a knitted Jaeger suit. He was carrying a long pole on which he proceeded to sling my heavy camera-case, and each taking hold of one end we brought it to his house. Shaw was a perfect model,[1] and I made at least fifty photographs of him at one time or another. The friendship which began on 1 August 1904 lasted throughout the years and was one of the pleasantest factors in my life in London.

[Encouraged by Shaw, Coburn visited Paris in April 1906 to photograph Rodin, who was then executing a commission from Charlotte Shaw for a bust of her husband.]

On 21 April I accompanied Mr and Mrs Shaw to the unveiling ceremony of Rodin's sculpture 'Le Penseur' outside the Panthéon. The next morning GBS surprised me by suggesting that after his bath I should photograph him nude in the pose of 'Le Penseur'. I had photographed him in almost every conceivable way, he said, so now I might as well complete the series as 'The Thinker' – his true role in life. As for nudity, GBS said to Frank Harris 'though we have hundreds of photographs of Dickens and Wagner, we see nothing of them except their suits of clothes with their heads sticking out; and what is the use of that?' I think GBS was quite proud of his figure, and well he may have been, as the photograph testifies. When exhibited under the title 'Le Penseur' at the London Salon of Photography it aroused considerable comment in the press. Reporters asked me if it were really a photograph of Shaw, and they asked him the same question, but I referred them to him for verification and he referred them to me, so they remained mystified. During his lifetime the photograph was never published, although GBS had no objection to this, saying I could do what I liked with it. . . .

Shaw gave me a letter of introduction to Mrs Patrick Campbell in which, referring to my photograph of him as 'Le Penseur', he suggested that I should photograph her in the same way: 'Coburn has just photographed me "in the altogether".' I did photograph the famous actress, but of course clothed.

NOTE

1. In an earlier article (*Photoguide Magazine*, December 1950) Coburn had characterised Shaw as 'picturesque in person, and enough of an actor to know the value of a pose. He keeps up a running stream of conversation while the work is in progress'.

Motoring: I

JEROME K. JEROME

From Jerome K. Jerome, *My Life and Times* (London: Hodder & Stoughton, [1926]) p. 163. Jerome Klapka Jerome (1859–1927), journalist and man of letters, knew Shaw as a fellow-dramatist by the first decade of the century, if not earlier. On 16 March 1909 Shaw sailed with his wife and sister-in-law for five weeks' motoring through Algeria and Tunisia, taking his first car, a 28–30 h.p. De Dietrich delivered the previous December, and his chauffeur, Albert Kilsby, who was to remain with him until 1917.

Shaw is one of the kindest of men, but has no tenderness. His chief exercise, according to his own account, is public speaking; and his favourite recreation, thinking. He admitted to me once that there have been times when he has thought too much. He was motoring in Algiers, driving himself, with his chauffeur beside him, when out of his musing came to him the idea for a play.[1]

'What do you think of this?' he said, turning to his chauffeur; and went on then and there to tell the man all about it.

He had usually found his chauffeur a keen and helpful critic. But on this occasion, instead of friendly encouragement, he threw himself upon Shaw and, wrenching the wheel out of his hands, sat down upon him.

'Excuse me, Mr Shaw,' the man said later on; 'but it's such a damn good play that I didn't want you to die before you'd written it.'

Shaw had never noticed the precipice.

NOTE

1. Shaw drafted *Press Cuttings* on this holiday; he also wrote to Edward McNulty about a completely different idea for a play – a comedy based on their relative fortunes (see *Collected Letters 1898–1910*, pp. 840–1).

Motoring: II

FRED DAY

From reminiscences by Fred Day in *Shaw the Villager and Human Being: A Biographical Symposium*, ed. Allan Chappelow (London: Charles Skilton, 1961) pp. 37–41. Fred Day was engaged by the Shaws as chauffeur in May 1919 and stayed on until Shaw died.

My first journey with Mr Shaw was up to London. I well remember that drive. The car was slow and had a badly slipping clutch. He took me to a garage where I had to pick up things to take home. When we got there he said to me, 'I won't want you any more today; if I were you I should go home, pick up your wife and children, and take them for a drive.' To which I replied, 'I think I will get the car going a bit better first, sir.'

Mr Shaw at that time was an ardent motor-cyclist. He had a two-stroke machine. He came to me one day and said, 'Can you ginger her up a bit?' – to which I replied that I would try. I took the engine down, overhauled it and put it back again, put a mixture in the petrol tank and sent him out. He came back all smiles and said, 'She is running away with me'. But it didn't last long. He went out with her one day and I don't know what happened, but he came back and said, 'The bike got me down and got on top of me. Someone pulled it off me, and I got up and came home.' He didn't use it much after that. . . .

As a motorist, Mr Shaw was a very good driver, but at times rather reckless. On one occasion when we were coming home round the narrow lanes to Ayot, we met a small car. I thought there was plenty of room to pass, but we hit the car. As we got past it our car went across the road and started to go over the bank. I pulled the wheel out of Mr Shaw's hand, got the car back on to the road, and shut off the engine. Then we went to see what had happened to the other car. We found the front axle broken right off. We got it to the side of the road – none of the people were hurt. Another car came along and took two of the passengers home. Mr Shaw took the lady who had been driving to Ayot with us and arranged to pay all expenses, after which I had to take her home. It was then that I found out that the steering of our own car was all wrong. It took a long time to get it right again.

I shall always remember an amusing incident which happened in Scotland around 1922. We were touring, moving from one hotel to another. Mr Shaw would always drive till lunch-time, after which I drove for the rest of the day. On this particular morning Mr Shaw was in one of his most reckless moods and going very fast. Mrs Shaw, sitting in the back, was very nervous and was glad when we got to the lunch stop. After lunch we went on. I was driving at a nice regular speed. Mrs Shaw suddenly put her head through the partition window and remarked, 'I call this a nice comfortable speed to drive.' To which Mr Shaw retorted, 'Yes, we will get out and walk presently.' . . .

If ever anything happened on the road Mr Shaw was always ready to take the blame. I remember one time when we were staying at Malvern, the following incident occurred. We were going to lunch with Mrs Shaw's niece. On our way through Birmingham on a Sunday morning there was a continuous stream of traffic coming toward us. Suddenly a motor-cycle combination shot right out in front of our car. I cried, 'Brake, sir!' Before we could stop we had crashed into it. The sidecare was ripped off the bike; the passenger lay in the middle of the road. I got Mr Shaw to pull to the side of the road and stop. Neither of the occupants was very much hurt. Mr Shaw asked the man if he had enough money to get home. He said he hadn't much, so Mr Shaw gave him five pounds and told him to get his machine repaired and let him have the bill. Mr Shaw then wanted to go on, but I told him we would have to wait till the police came to take particulars, which we did. . . .

Mr Shaw continued to drive until about 1937, but it was a very anxious time for me. I was fully occupied trying to keep him out of trouble when driving. In 1933 I got him to get a Lanchester ten, which was the simplest thing to drive. He got on all right for a time, but one day, when he was driving it into the garage, I said: 'Stop! That will do, sir.' But instead of stopping he put his foot on the accelerator and crashed into the hot water pipes, bringing them all down.

Motoring: III

STUART MACRAE

From Stuart Macrae, 'Mr Bernard Shaw on Motoring', *Motor*, 18 July 1939. The occasion of this article was the delivery of a new 25–30 h.p. Rolls-Royce Wraith at Ayot St Lawrence on 8 July (Macrae's celebration of Shaw's first Rolls-Royce had appeared in the *Motor* on 22 October 1935). Shaw first took part in a photographic session, airily discounting the falling rain.

At last the photographer was satisfied, and the car was taken to the garage. Mr Shaw looked suitably impressed when the bonnet was raised.

'How many cylinders has it got?' he asked.

'Six, sir,' said the expert.

'Only six! It looks as if it ought to have at least sixteen. A wonderful piece of work the modern car – or so a neighbour of mine assures me. He bought a very expensive one, and it took him thirteen months to start it. . . . [*sic*] What are those things in front?'

'Those are the twin horns.'

'Twin horns! . . . Funny things, horns. I remember I had one called a Gabriel horn.[1] I thought rather a lot of it until one day when I was going up somebody's drive I let it off to advise them I was coming. When I arrived they asked me if I'd run over a donkey at the gate. I hadn't realised that was the kind of row it made.'

'Are you going to drive this car yourself, Mr Shaw?' I asked.

'I doubt it. I suppose it's easy enough to handle, but my reaction is getting slow, you know. I don't know why on earth they let me have a driving licence at my age. I'm not safe. They should refuse to renew it. Besides, I think too much of Day, my chauffeur, to risk his life by taking the wheel. He's a married man with children.

'Mind you, I used to drive quite a lot. I had my first car in 1908 – a Lanchester.[2] Later on I was the proud possessor of a straight-eight Lanchester with a harmonic balancer, which I always took to be some kind of musical instrument. In between I owned a Vauxhall and a Lorraine-Dietrich. I told you about that one last time you were here.' Mr Shaw in October 1935, had dwelt upon its virtues.

'The trouble with my driving is that I'm easily put off. In the early days of motoring I hired a car to go down to the coast, and it collapsed on the way. That put me off. Another time, when I'd just changed my car, I thought I'd try running the new one home from the station. I did everything just the same as usual, and found myself shooting out of the yard at thirty-five miles an hour instead of my customary fifteen. Of course, that put me off.

'Then one day I was going along a narrow lane near here, when the car I was driving encountered one coming from the opposite direction driven by a lady. I don't know whose fault it was, but it put me off just the same. So nowadays, except now and then when I run the little car down to the village, I'm content to be driven. Anyway, I generally want to read when I'm motoring.'

NOTES

1. An allusion to the Angel of the Annunciation (Luke I: 26 ff.), as in 'Gabriel-bell'.
2. An error (see above, p. 204).

Motoring: IV

From 'Roads Safe for You', *Passing Show*, 23 March 1935. Shaw's written answers to questions submitted by Frank D. Long were published alongside an interview with Leslie (later Lord) Hore-Belisha (1893–1957), Minister of Transport from 1934 to 1937, who was conducting an energetic campaign to improve road safety. It included provision of pedestrian crossings marked by yellow-globed beacons that took his name.

The Minister of Transport has the idea that a form of public selfishness needs to be curbed as a first step towards a perfect road service. Would you say he is taking the wisest course?

Nothing can induce me to say that any Minister is taking the wisest course. If he were capable of that he could never get elected to the House of Commons.

Are the people frequenting crowded roadways selfish from want of thought or are they maliciously indifferent?

They are careless, or pre-occupied, or fifty other things. I never go out now without having hair's-breadth escapes at every crossing.

Are vehicle drivers greater offenders than pedestrians?

As a motorist I say no, as a pedestrian I say yes.

Are we, living in a mechanical age, becoming contemptuous of machines and forgetting or ignoring their power to harm?

We don't bother about them until they hoot at us. Therefore the most startling hooters are necessary. The driver who 'honks' unnecessarily is a nuisance; but the driver who had no horn to 'honk' with in an emergency would be a public danger.

Do you feel safer for the existence of Belisha crossings and Belisha beacons?

Yes, motorists approach them with fear and trembling.

Which appals you most – the number of accidents, or the apparent common negligence?

I am not appalled. But when I contrast the precautions taken to prevent people trespassing on the railways, where the track of the train is immutably fixed, and the freedom of all the world to stroll about roads crowded with vehicles rushing at fifty miles an hour anywhere they can squeeze through, with unbridged roads galore, I see that only a race that can step lively and grow eyes in the back of its head can survive in any considerable number.

Is the modern youth intent upon speed at the expense of his 'road sense' and human obligations?

There is no such thing as the modern youth. There are youths and youths. Some produce accidents by driving too fast and others by driving too slow. Most of them drive sensibly. If they didn't we should all be dead.

Do you see any connection between the craze for amusement and indifference to public safety on the highways?

No. It is not amusing to drive over people. I have done it; and I know. I have not been run over; but I cannot imagine that it is amusing.

Do you think any good purpose could be served by swelling the school curriculum to include lessons on roads and their uses?

Certainly. It might replace the Classics at Oxford with great advantage.

Have you noticed whether we are better behaved in our roadways than foreigners are in theirs?

The world cannot be classified into English people and foreigners. I have driven in many countries and not noticed any difference. Epidemics of fast driving occur in all neighbourhoods. I always speed up indignantly when I find other cars passing me. . . .

Is our system of roads adequate for modern needs?

No; it needs a lot of straightening, widening and bridging. Also roads for motors exclusively, like rail-roads, with or without tolls, like the Italian autostradas.

Up in the Air: I

ROBERT LORAINE

From Winifred Loraine, *Robert Loraine: Soldier, Actor, Airman* (London: Collins, 1938) pp. 90–1. Shaw went up in a balloon – the 'Norfolk', piloted by Percival Spencer – on 3 July 1906. His companions were his sister-in-law Mary Cholmondeley, Granville Barker and Robert Loraine, who left an account in his diary. It was this ballooning exploit that Shaw remembered when he told Charles Graves (brother of Robert) in 1929:

> Personally I don't consider flying at all thrilling. The earth looks like one of those dreadful lithographic maps you see at the beginning of a directory. I expected also that the clouds would look as they do wreathing the feet of a Madonna in some old painting. In actual fact, of course, they are far beneath you. I know, because I once went up in a balloon.
> When we reached 9,000 feet I found I was getting sleepy. That altitude seemed to have a deadening effect on the mind, at least in a balloon, although it might be different in an aeroplane. (*Daily Mail*, 19 September 1929)

'Ascending from Wandsworth Gas Works,' says Robert's diary, 'we were soon floating above the clouds at about 9,000 feet, exhilarated but somewhat awed by our first experience of altitude. After about forty minutes' drifting, very pleasant and seraphic with nothing happening, except that Shaw would peer through a hole in the boarding at his feet which made him feel rather sick, we discussed landing. We wondered what our reception would be on coming down in somebody's garden. I thought the people would be rather interested to receive visitors from the air, and especially flattered when they discovered Shaw's identity. "Don't be so certain," said Shaw. "They may think my works detestable." Mr Spencer, the aeronaut, assured us that no matter where we landed or who we might be, we should be overwhelmed by the warmth of our welcome owing to the unusual nature of our arrival.

'In due course we came down on a field near Cobham Common, and after assisting to deflate the balloon, we turned to find ourselves surrounded by people who seemed to have appeared from nowhere. We were just going to tell them all about it, when a purple-faced individual came rushing towards us waving a shooting-stick. This he had the grace to hide when he saw Mrs Cholmondely, but he was suffocating with fury, and the welcome he gave us was a curt direction as to the quickest way off his property.'

Up in the Air: II

H. C. BIARD

From H. C. Biard, *Wings* (London: Hurst & Blackett, [1934]) pp. 56–7. Henri Charles Biard, a distinguished pilot and a winner of the Schneider Trophy seaplane race, was working in 1916 at a flying school at Hendon, on the outskirts of London, when on 20 May he was asked to take a celebrated writer for a joy-ride.

I went along to meet my prospective passenger, and was introduced to Mr George Bernard Shaw.

We disposed ourselves in a two-seater biplane – quite a modern affair, with a covered-in bodywork in which the great man's legs were decently hidden. I took him up to about a thousand feet, circled over the flying-ground, did a few minor stunts, opened the throttle full out to show him a turn of speed, and came down again. He stood the display without turning a hair. He seemed chiefly interested in the fact that, when one is flying upside-down in the loop, there is no particular sensation of invertedness. Mr Shaw commented on this as he climbed out of his seat.

'The world is like that, young man!' he remarked gravely. He then fished in the depths of his pockets, solemnly presented me with ten shillings, and added, 'I hope you will use it properly!'

Holidays: I

THOMAS OKEY

From Thomas Okey, *A Basketful of Memories: An Autobiographical Sketch* (London: J. M. Dent, 1930) pp. 125–7, 129. Thomas Okey (1852–1935) had a remarkable career, beginning as a basket-maker in London and ending as Professor of Italian at Cambridge University. In the 1890s he organised Continental expeditions for the Art Workers' Guild; the first, to northern Italy, lasted from 16 September to 4 October 1891. Shaw was one of the party, probably introduced by friends in

William Morris's circle. He went to Italy again with the Guild in September 1894.

Mr Shaw's rigid vegetarian principles gave me at first some trouble at the Italian hotels where we put up. Italians cannot understand any one, except on religious grounds, refusing to eat meat when able to include it in his diet. Mr Shaw, in the early stages, was actually suffering from insufficient food (even *maccaroni al sugo* he refused – the gravy was repugnant to him), until at length I hit upon the expedient of seeing the head-waiter on our arrival at the hotel, and explaining to him that one member of our *comitiva* was under a vow. This was at once understood, and for the remainder of the *Italienische Reise* Mr Shaw travelled as a devout Catholic under a vow to abstain from flesh, wine and tobacco. The expedition in 1894 saw Mr Shaw again among its members. These were the days when *Arms and the Man* had been staged at the Avenue Theatre. Few of us, however, had any suspicion that we had with us the future great dramatist of the twentieth century.

One incident I now remember. At Genoa Mr Shaw asked me to get him entrance to the great Carlo Felice theatre. Much of the time there he spent examining the construction, arrangements, and measurements of the stage – an incident whose significance became intelligible in later years. Yet another memory of our visit. Among the sculpture at Genoa we came upon a realistic representation in marble, by a famous Italian artist, of Jenner vaccinating a child's arm.[1] As Shaw's eyes met the figure a thrill of horror and indignation shook his frame and an impulse seized him to act the image-breaker. That Shaw's anti-vaccination propaganda, apart from statistical and other reasons, is due to his intense humanitarian feelings, is indubitable.

The accommodation at Pavia, then rarely visited, being limited, the demands of a considerable party of men were met by allotting the largest room* available in the Albergo, where we put up, to sleep three of our travellers – Bernard Shaw, Sydney Cockerell and Emery Walker. After all, did not Charles I, Queen Henrietta Maria and their three children sleep in one bedroom at Hampton Court?

It was not long ere on a survey of the walls of the chamber indications of the presence of other inhabitants of the couches were manifest to those quartered there. . . . War to the death was proclaimed; the horrified trinity of sleepers straightway devised a plan of campaign. Descending on the supply of Keating[2] ammunition available in the city they bought it up and erected defensive ramparts around each of the three beds: they reckoned without the strategical resources of the enemy who, climbing the ceiling, dropped thence on their victims as they lay.

---

* It probably was in normal times the dormitory of the staff.

NOTES

1. Edward Jenner (1749–1823) pioneered vaccination against smallpox. Shaw contracted smallpox in 1881 although he had been vaccinated in childhood.
2. A brand of insecticidal powder.

Holidays: II

LILLAH McCARTHY

From Lillah McCarthy, *Myself and My Friends* (London: Thornton Butterworth, 1933) pp. 87–8. Lillah McCarthy is recalling holiday incidents in the decade preceding the First World War.

One weekend I said to Shaw: 'Where and how do you take your holidays?' He almost leapt at me as he answered: 'Holidays, woman! I never took one in my life.'

I felt as if I had suggested an unmentionable sin; but the holidays came. In those days as now, The Beetle and Wedge at Moulsford[1] was amusing and pleasant, and we used to stay there for weekends and spend much time on the river. Shaw as an oarsman was not conspicuous for style. I had been trained by a diamond sculls man, and had learned to feather my oars; but Shaw had no use for feathers. Speed is everything he said; style does not matter. He would make rapid strokes and show me how powerful he was. But I also was clever. I used to row downstream and leave him to the hard work of rowing home again upstream. I watched him maliciously, straining and panting, and do not believe that he ever noticed my ruse.

Shaw is the best companion in the world. He has not forgotten how to play, he loves foolishness, and never forces conversation when he is alone with his friends. One summer found us at Tor Cross, in Devonshire. Lady Bonham Carter, then Violet Asquith,[2] was of the party. We used to bathe before breakfast and do our exercises on the beach wearing the lightest of bathing costumes.

After breakfast, we would spread ourselves upon Violet Asquith's sumptuous blue rug. One morning, we sat thus, our backs to the sea, with the sunshine scorching down upon us. Violet Asquith was prone upon the rug with a book. I also was reading or dreaming. GBS, of course, was working: reading one of his manuscripts. We forgot that the sea has tides. Suddenly we were reminded by being thrown upon our faces by a wave, and what a helter-skelter! I, laughing at Shaw grabbing in the water for his manuscript, and Violet Asquith grabbing for her floating rug.

NOTES

1. An hotel on the Thames between Reading and Oxford.
2. Violet Bonham Carter (1887–1969) was the only daughter of Herbert Asquith, Liberal Prime Minister from 1908 to 1916. She identified closely with her father and took a prominent part in public life, becoming a life peeress in 1964.

Holidays: III

BEATRICE WEBB

From *The Diary of Beatrice Webb*, vol. II: *1892–1905*, ed. Norman and Jeanne MacKenzie (London: Virago, 1983) p. 80 and *The Diary of Beatrice Webb*, vol. III: *1905–1924*, ed. Norman and Jeanne MacKenzie (London: Virago, 1984) p. 194. These two extracts, taken from entries dated 9 September 1895 and 2 January 1914, reveal changes in Shaw's holiday style brought about by his marriage and increasing age and wealth. He learned to ride a bicycle with a holiday party led by the Webbs at Beachy Head in April 1895. That summer, cycling, including Shaw's collision with Bertrand Russel (p. 278 below), figured largely in a seven-week holiday with the Webbs at The Argoed. It was interrupted by the Trades Union Congress at Cardiff, which Shaw covered for *The Star*, and ended with a three-day ride back to London.

Trades Union Congress. On Sunday week Sidney, Shaw and I left here about ten o'clock on our cycles, rode through the exquisite valley of Raglan, Usk to Newport, thence along the coast to Cardiff, our first long ride (forty miles) arriving at the great Park Hotel hot, dusty and pleasantly self-complacent with our new toy and its exploits. It is certainly attractive – riding through the beautiful country, trundling slowly up hills and rushing down, with feet up, every incline. The only disadvantage being the intolerable thirst you suffer as a novice. One's 'bike' is a great addition to the pleasure of life – we have still to prove that it does not detract from one's desire, if not one's capacity, for work.

A fortnight's walking and motoring tour in Cornwall and Devon, with GBS. . . . It has been a delightful and luxurious holiday, our first intention of tramping round the coast, with knapsack and mackintosh being transformed, by the advent of GBS, into walking over ten or thirteen miles of picked country with the motor car in attendance to take us, when tired, to the most expensive hotel in the neighbourhood.

Holidays: IV

LADY GLENAVY

From Beatrice Lady Glenavy, *Today We Will Only Gossip* (London: Constable, 1964) pp. 127–8. Beatrice Elvery married Gordon Campbell, later Lord Glenavy, in 1912. Their early friends in London included D. H. Lawrence and Frieda, Katherine Mansfield and Middleton Murry, and 'Kot' – Samuel Koteliansky, a Russian Jew who settled in London about 1910 and remained a crucial figure in Beatrice's life until his death in 1955. Clonard, the Campbells' house on the outskirts of Dublin, had been fired in the Irish civil war at the end of 1922. The following memories must be dated to 1923, when the Shaws stayed at Parknasilla during August and September.

It was shortly after we had moved back to Clonard that we spent a few weeks at Parknasilla, in Kerry. Bernard Shaw and Mrs Shaw were also staying in the hotel. They had a private sitting-room, where Shaw was writing *Saint Joan*. Both were very friendly with the other visitors and Shaw was popular with the children, who looked on him as a nice elderly gentleman very interested in cameras.

We had a car and we used to take them for long drives over the mountains. We passed many places showing signs of the 'Troubles': blown-up bridges, burnt-out houses and the remains of ambushes on the roads. Shaw was very interested in the street-ballads that had come out of those times. I remember we were all out in a boat on the Kenmare river, with Shaw rowing, when he asked us about them. We sang:

> In Mountjoy Gaol on Monday morning
> High upon the gallows tree
> Kevin Barry gave his young life
> For the cause of liberty.[1]
> Another martyr for Old Ireland,
> Another murder for the Crown,
> Cruel laws to crush the Irish
> For to break their spirits down.

He liked the comic ones best and sang with us, to the tune 'Yankee Doodle':

> de Valera had a cat
> Who sat upon the fender,
> Every time she heard a shot
> She shouted 'No surrender'.[2]

Kot had often spoken of Shaw as 'that old music-hall entertainer', though he would add 'he made himself into a great journalist'. I could not help remembering Kot's phrase one day at the bathing-place when Shaw took the lifebelt that hung there and gave us a demonstration in the sea of how dangerous a thing it was, showing us all the different ways it could trap you and drown you. At times it seemed as if the lifebelt had really got the better of Shaw. With his two feet sticking up through it, it seemed unlikely that his head would ever appear again. There was a lot of laughter, but Mrs Shaw looked really quite anxious.

NOTES

1. Kevin Barry, a student member of the IRA hanged towards the end of 1920, was the first Irishman executed by the British after the First World War.
2. Eamon de Valera was political leader of republican opposition to the compromises embodied in the Anglo-Irish Treaty of 1921, which established the Irish Free State and provoked the civil war of 1922–3. Ironically, the slogan 'No Surrender' goes back to the siege of Londonderry in 1689, when Protestants successfully held out against the Catholic forces of James II.

Holidays: V

From 'GBS in Shetland. An Interesting Interview . . .', *The Shetland News*, 20 August 1925. The Shaws spent four days in Shetland, after a motoring holiday in Scotland and a visit to Orkney. A good part of this interview, given the evening before they left, was taken up with Shaw's vision of harnessing tidal power and industrialising the island – a suggestion to which he returned in a 1943 letter to *The Times* (published 9 March).

Mr Shaw . . . first of all compared the flatness of Orkney with the hilly nature of Shetland, and said there was not a single place where one could put down a billiard ball without it running into the sea. 'But,' he added, 'the place is altogether delightful. In other countries you have little corners and places just as beautiful where you can go to, but here the whole thing is before you and at hand. Once outside the town there is the most wonderful landscapes, and lake and ocean scenery. Your islands have a certain character of their own. Your people have good looks, good manners and a very gentle speech. They have not yet become thieves like some people but they may improve in that respect!' . . .

Asked regarding Shetland as a holiday resort, Mr Shaw said that, leaving out the industrial possibilities of the place, he thought the islands resembled a great deal the Scottish Highlands and Western Ireland. 'Human beings should not be allowed to try to get a living out of it in the ordinary way by farming, which is heartbreaking work. You cannot get enough out of it. There are great masses of peaty soil, exactly the same as in certain parts of Scotland and Ireland, where people have to go and work elsewhere periodically. Frankly, I think the islands should be turned into a sanatorium, not only for the British Isles, but for the rest of the world.

'I was astonished to find there are only two hotels in Lerwick. There are, of course, houses for visitors in the country districts. The old tradition referred to in Scott's *Pirate* still survives,[1] that anybody is entitled to go into any house as a matter of course, and is hospitably entertained. I found such places at Spiggie and Reawick. There is nothing to indicate that these houses take in people, but I knocked at the door, was taken in and given a very good meal. I paid for it, of course, but not unreasonably.'

Mr Shaw specially commented on the roads. He said the roads in Shetland are very much better than those in the north of Scotland, and added that a great deal of money must be spent on them. 'They are very narrow,' he said, 'especially for motor traffic, and when cars meet: but their charm lies in their tortuous winding along the hill-sides and valleys, always opening up some new and beautiful view.'

Mr Shaw was quite enthusiastic about the excellence of the Shetland potatoes. 'I grow some myself in my garden,' he said, with a laugh, 'which probably cost me five shillings each, but here they are plentiful and magnificent. Your butter and milk, also, are splendid, and your buttermilk is simply gorgeous. The men of Tipperary are reared on buttermilk and potatoes, and they are the biggest men in Ireland – and the most quarrelsome! . . .'

He vividly compared the cleanness, quietude and peacefulness of Shetland with the hideous noise and over-crowding of English seaside resorts. 'The English Channel,' he proceeded, 'is only a dirty ditch and that is the water that ebbs and flows at many English watering places. Here there is an ideal and beautiful watering place every three miles along the coast. It is altogether wonderful.' . . .

Another thing that both Mr and Mrs Shaw commented on was the freshness of the air and the mildness of the climate: it was soft and balmy, they said, and could scarcely fail to be very healthy.

NOTE

1. Sir Walter Scott's *The Pirate* (1822), which Shaw had just reread, is set in seventeenth-century Zetland (Shetland).

Music: I

HENRY HYNDMAN

From Henry Mayers Hyndman, *Further Reminiscences* (London: Macmillan, 1912) pp. 209–11. Shaw's enthusiasm for Wagner informs much of his music criticism and ultimately led to *The Perfect Wagnerite* (1898), a treatise on the *Ring*.

One day we were walking together when Shaw burst forth about Wagner. He took it for granted, as *more suo* he has done ever since, that I knew nothing about the composer, his works, or music generally, for that matter.

His verbal panegyric of that day has appeared in print since then more than once. I listened – yes, I did, I listened – with silent attention. What he said was very good. I agreed with nearly all of it except the usual exaggerated belittlement of every other musician, without which no genuine Wagnerian seems to have fulfilled his mission. It was pointed out to me in much detail and with no lack of sarcasm how utterly incapable I, who knew nothing of Wagner, must be of understanding the nobler contrasts and harmonies of orchestration, how much I lost by this incapacity to rise to the level of the highest combination of the aesthetic and the intellectual in the world of sound. As to the Italian school, that was a thing of the past. I ventured to hint that Mozart's *Don Giovanni*, though written by a Viennese, was really of the old Italian school in its highest perfection, and that I would rather hear *Don Giovanni* – such were my philistine and reactionary proclivities – than the *Meistersingers* any day.

[As Shaw's eulogy continued after this momentary interruption, Hyndman could not help thinking of a scathing French criticism of the first

MUSIC: II   219

production of Wagner's *Ring* and 'was even imprudent enough to laugh quietly'.]

   That settled it. He began afresh. Then I knew what real objurgation meant. All the marvellous Hibernian facility of diction, all the unlimited Shavian choice of vituperative words seemed to be concentrated in one scathing flood of contemptuous denunciation against myself. It swept me along, it tumbled me about, it stripped me of all raiment, denuded me of any self-respect, and landed me a battered and forlorn creature – to my great surprise, walking apparently whole and in my right mind, by Shaw's side along the Thames Embankment. Finding that I was not quite obliterated, that I lived and moved and had my being, and that Shaw was out of breath, I ventured to utter a few still small words myself. 'But, my dear Shaw,' I said, 'I know Wagner's music intimately well, and I was playing his overtures in the orchestra before you were breeched.' It was quite true; but of course he did not believe it, and so we parted at the door of the house he had come to call at.

Music: II

SYDNEY OLIVIER

From a letter by Lord Olivier to Archibald Henderson, 8 June 1931, in Henderson, *Bernard Shaw, Playboy and Prophet* (London and New York: D. Appleton, 1932) p. 209. Shaw taught himself to play the piano about the age of sixteen, after the departure of his mother and Vandeleur Lee from Dublin left him without the profusion of music that had surrounded him. Kate Salt was the sister of James Leigh Joynes, who had originally introduced Shaw to Henry Salt (see below, p. 259). Shaw's relationship with her was intimate though not sexual; he called himself a 'Sunday husband'. The duet-playing took place in the Salt's cottage in Surrey from the late 1880s and then in London, where Kate also acted intermittently as unpaid secretary before Shaw's marriage.

Shaw, I may observe, though not an artistic pianist, had evolved for himself somewhat original and very spirited technique and succeeded in playing effectively, as his Irish compatriot explained that he played the violin, 'by main strength'. When he visited our friends the Salts, he and Mrs Katherine Salt, through whose fingers her half German musical temperament poured gloriously, used to thunder duets together for hours: he maintaining a running fire of remonstrance and correction throughout the performance. The combination between the naturally-gifted critic and the naturally-gifted artist was very interesting.

Music: III

G. F. McCLEARY

From G. F. McCleary, 'Some Early Recollections of GBS', *Fortnightly Review*, February 1953. Though he followed a medical career, Dr McCleary had studied at the Royal College of Music and was an Associate of the Royal College of Organists. The first visit to the Oliviers he mentions was in the spring of 1895 (see above, p. 61), the second must be dated at least to 1901 and probably later (Shaw wrote *The Admirable Bashville* in one week early in 1901).

On the first evening of our visit to the Oliviers, I was asked to play the piano and complied with extreme reluctance, especially as the work particularly requested was the second Act of *Tristan*. However, there was nothing for it but to comply. I got through about half of the Act, and continued the ordeal with some other pieces, including a song by Grieg in A followed by a Handel fugue in F sharp minor. During the whole performance I felt acutely that I must be inflicting much un-deserved discomfort upon Shaw, one of the most severe of musical critics, who with the rest of the company was out of sight in a conservatory opening into the room where I was playing. He took the song and the fugue to be a prelude and fugue by Mendelssohn, and, as I was told later, he said it was enough to make Wagner turn in his grave to have Mendelssohn played after his *Tristan*. He called to me: 'Why did you play that Mendelssohn stuff?'[1] I replied that I had played nothing by Mendelssohn. 'Surely,' he persisted, 'you played a prelude and fugue by Mendelssohn.' When I explained what I had played he was much chaffed by the company, but he took it in excellent part and came to the piano and talked to me very pleasantly.

Some years later I again met Shaw at the Oliviers' house, where the daughters and some young friends gave a creditable performance of *The Admirable Bashville*, which Shaw came down to see – one of his innumerable acts of kindness and encouragement to young people. Before dinner I played one of Elgar's *Enigma Variations* – the *Nimrod* Variation, a noble sound portrait of Elgar's friend, A. J. Jaeger.[2] When the last chord had been played, Shaw came into the room and asked what the piece was. I told him, and he said he had been listening to it as he was coming downstairs and could find nothing distinguished or original in it. He added: 'I know very little of Elgar's music, but I suppose that with his high reputation he must be a good composer.'[3]

NOTES

1. Although the creative spans of Handel and Mendelssohn are separated by a hundred years and more, Shaw's mistake is better understood in the light of Mendelssohn's close study of Handel and J. S. Bach (exact contemporaries) and his emulation of Bach's fugal technique.

2. August Jaeger (1860–1909) worked for Novello, the music publishers, and gave Elgar vital encouragement.

3. Elgar's reputation was only established by the *Enigma Variations* (1899) and *The Dream of Gerontius* (1900), i.e. some years after Shaw had stopped attending concerts professionally. Shaw later became a warm admirer and close friend of Elgar, and the *Nimrod* variation was amongst the music he chose for his funeral.

Music: IV

LADY SCOTT

From *Self-Portrait of an Artist: From the Diaries and Memoirs of Lady Kennet, Kathleen, Lady Scott* (London: John Murray, 1949) pp. 166, 265.

29 June [1918] I went to Lamer alone. Shaw came to dinner. He amazed me. I have known him for fifteen years, and this was the first time I knew he sang. He went almost all through the score of *Rheingold*[1] on the piano, singing in a charming baritone voice. He plays amazingly well. He is a marvellous man.

7 February [1929] Bernard Shaw came to lunch. He often does nowadays, which is fun, with Suggia,[2] Hudson [of *Country Life*] and George [Lord Sandwich]. Shaw chid Suggia for having such a cumbrous instrument as a cello. Why not a nice little fiddle? It reminded him of the old removals-man who was weighed down by a grandfather's clock he was carrying, and a young man stopped him and said, 'Excuse me, but, at your age, wouldn't you find a wristwatch more convenient?'

NOTES

1. The first of Wagner's four *Ring* operas.
2. Guilhermina Suggia (1885–1950), Portuguese cellist of international reputation, and subject of a famous portrait by Augustus John.

Music: V

FERRUCCIO BUSONI

From Ferruccio Busoni, *Letters to his Wife*, trans. Rosamond Ley (London: Edward Arnold, 1938) pp. 279–80. Ferruccio Busoni (1866–1924), Italian–German composer and pianist, was anti-Romantic in his musical attitudes; he rejected Wagner and advocated intensive study of J. S. Bach and Mozart. He mentions reading Shaw (*The Devil's Disciple*) as early as 1907 – an interesting index of Shaw's spreading reputation in German-speaking countries. In the autumn of 1919 he was staying in London and had some hope of getting Shaw to write him an opera libretto. They met on 31 October.

Yesterday afternoon, G. B. Shaw came to tea (which he did not drink). He is now sixty-three, very tall, and in appearance he might be a brother of old Hase, a wittier, more lively, and sharper brother. He talks too much and he cannot cloak his vanity. . . .

During tea he spoke chiefly about music, and evidently wished to display his knowledge. He loves Mozart with understanding. 'Mozart was my master, I learnt from him how to say important things, and yet remain light and conversational.' 'How do you make that tally,' I asked, 'with your admiration for Wagner?'

'Oh, there is room for many different things in the world. And it was necessary at that time to protest against senseless misunderstandings. But I confess, much as I love Tristan, I could wish that Tristan might die a little sooner.'

'Why,' I asked, 'have you never *written* that?'

But he did not know how to answer that.

Then he began to praise Elgar, and his intimate knowledge of the orchestra.

'He showed me' (said S.), 'how one could make a place in *Leonora*,[1] which never sounds well, acceptable.' He described how Elgar corrects it, which is bad.

'Excuse me' (I said again), 'but I should do so and so, as one can see it done in Mozart's compositions.' (And I explained my example.)

'I had not thought of that,' he said, somewhat abashed.

He does not seem to have considered *the nature* of opera. 'He couldn't write a libretto, he would write just as he always wrote.' I said 'It would attract me to try and write music for the scene in hell in *Man and Superman*.'

'That would be waste of work' (said S.), 'because it could bring in no profit.'

'That is not what attracts me,' I said.

'Oh, but you *must* reckon with that, everybody has to reckon with it. Of course, I am now a famous artist (he added, half jokingly), I can allow myself to ride hobby horses' (or something similar).

Now that was not very nice, and still less tactful.

NOTE

1. Presumably a reference to one of the overtures, known as *Leonora I, II* and *III*, which Beethoven wrote and rejected for his opera *Fidelio*.

Music: VI

MARK HAMBOURG

From Mark Hambourg, *From Piano to Forte: A Thousand and One Notes* (London: Cassell, 1931) p. 280. Mark Hambourg, Russian-born pianist who settled in Britain, was best known for his playing in the big Romantic tradition. He had met Shaw as a child prodigy and met him again at a postwar luncheon party, where he reports Shaw protesting at asparagus being served, as it was 'full of uric acid'.

After lunch I had some talk with Shaw, and he tried to convince me that the art of the modern pianoforte was nothing compared with that of the harpsichord. The latter was to his mind the perfect expression of keyboard music. He said he hated the modern pianoforte; it reminded him of a battle-cruiser. To which I answered that we should have been badly off during the late war without battle-cruisers. 'I don't agree,' said Shaw; 'on the contrary, if it had not been for the battle-cruisers we might have had nothing but peace.'

Music: VII

SIEGFRIED TREBITSCH

From Siegfried Trebitsch, *Chronical of a Life*, trans. Eithne Wilkins and Ernst Kaiser (London: Heinemann, 1953) pp. 275–6. Trebitsch is here recalling a time in the mid-1920s when he and his wife were guests of the Shaws at Ayot St Lawrence for several weeks.

The evenings were particularly stimulating, because Shaw was very musical and remained very fond of music into his extreme old age. After dinner he would sit down at the piano and play. He insisted that my wife, who had quite a good voice, though not a very highly trained one, should sing to his accompaniment. That always went off quite well and entirely satisfied the audience's modest demands, until Shaw suddenly launched into *Tristan* and my wife vainly tried to hold her own as Isolde. In order to set her a good example – as though that could have helped – he himself began to shriek in the highest and loudest of voices, without succeeding in convincing us that this was a satisfactory cast for *Tristan*.

Music: VIII

KINGSLEY MARTIN

From Kingsley Martin, *Editor* (London: Hutchinson, 1968) pp. 106–7.

Perhaps my most vivid memory of him was on a visit after the war when he told us how music had always meant much to him ever since he learnt to sing grand opera in his teens, and how he had always sung to his wife before she went to bed. He added: 'When my wife was alive, she always made me go to bed at ten o'clock for the good of my health. Since she died, I stay up till midnight or even after and I have never been better in my life.' No. He had never been better in his life than he was at ninety! He walked out with us to the car in the road and found in it our marmalade cat which he called 'Pussykins' and with whom he conversed as he always did with cats and other animals, finding, as he said, that they apparently enjoyed the conversation as much as he did, even though they might not fully grasp its content. And then as I turned the car round, I heard a surprising sound. I stopped to see Shaw standing in the middle of the lane and singing, at the top of his bell-like voice, an aria from Verdi. He turned round and said: 'My voice is no penny whistle now!' That it had never been. It was a voice that exposed shams, cleared the way, that liberated us from bad conventions and confused ideas. To me his death was very much as if I had been living in a room with the window open and suddenly found it shut. The room had become much darker and a lot stuffier.

Part 7
First World War

INTRODUCTION TO PART 7

The outbreak of the First World War was a turning point in Shaw's life, and in his relations with the British public. By 1914, Shaw had clearly established his position as the outstanding dramatist of his day in England, and had become an internationally celebrated figure. *Pygmalion*, the crowning achievement of this period of his career, opened in London's leading playhouse, His Majesty's, having already had successful seasons in Vienna and Berlin. The play delighted London audiences, and the sensation caused by its Cockney heroine's use of the swear-word 'bloody' on an English stage was front-page news. Seven months later, however, there appeared a non-dramatic work by Shaw which was to cause as much fury and hostility as *Pygmalion* had pleasure. Shaw's pamphlet, *Common Sense about the War*, was first published as a supplement to the *New Statesman*, on 14 November 1914. Shaw's argument about the war is that it was essentially concerned with the balance of power in Europe, and that the German violation of Belgian neutrality was no more than a convenient pretext for Britain's entry into the struggle. He detested the jingoistic fervour which accompanied the recruitment campaigns, and argued that militaristic Junkerism was as much a characteristic of the English squirearchy as of the Prussian aristocracy. Predictably enough, though the justness of some of his arguments was acknowledged by a few at the time, Shaw's views were widely condemned as dangerously perverse. H. G. Wells summed up the opinion of many when he wrote, in a letter to the *Daily Chronicle*: 'He [Shaw] is at present . . . an almost unendurable nuisance.'[1] As the war went on, Shaw became more and more convinced of the need for a British victory. By 1917 he had returned sufficiently to favour among official circles to be invited to the Front in France. He described the invitation at the time as 'either a compliment or a design on [my] life'.[2]

Undaunted by the hostile reception of *Common Sense*, Shaw continued to engage in controversy during the war years. He wrote in support of the Irishmen involved in the Easter uprising in 1916, and later in the same year made several vain attempts to prevent the hanging of the pro-German Irish traitor, Roger Casement. Shaw also involved himself in anti-conscription activities.

Shaw's major creative achievement during the War was *Heartbreak House*, a play conceived in 1913, and written during 1916–17. It was first performed in New York in 1920. During the war he also wrote several short plays, *Augustus Does His Bit*, *The Inca of Perusalem* and the amusing *O'Flaherty VC*, a play whose hero decides that life is quieter at the Front than at home with his ultra-patriotic mother and acquisitive former girlfriend. The short story about the Kaiser, *The Emperor and the Little Girl*, was also a product of the war years.

In his private life, as in his public career, the war years were a turbulent period for Shaw. His flirtation with Mrs Patrick Campbell, begun before the war, continued on its stormy path. His views about the war brought him into conflict with many old friends. Both his inner and outer worlds were transformed during the war, with profoundly significant results as far as the future course of his career as a writer was concerned.

NOTES

1. Published 31 December 1914; quoted in Stanley Weintraub, *Bernard Shaw 1914–1918: Journey to Heartbreak* (1971; London: Routledge & Kegan Paul, 1973) p. 78.
2. Weintraub, *Bernard Shaw 1914–1918*, p. 213.

Friends as Foes

SIEGFRIED TREBITSCH

From Siegfried Trebitsch, *Chronicle of a Life*, trans. Eithne Wilkins and Ernst Kaiser (London: Heinemann, 1953) p. 229. Shaw's last prewar communication to Trebitsch in fact took the form of a telegram. But it was transmitted via Ostend in Belgium and did not reach Vienna for several weeks. Shaw and Trebitsch were later able to circumvent the censorship by sending letters through Switzerland.

Many of us, after all, had our best friends abroad and could never be got to see them as suddenly metamorphosed into damnable enemies. . . . as for Shaw, his last postcard, which reached me on the last day of peace, said: 'You and I at war, and enemies? What nonsense!'

In our cellar we still had the crate that had contained Rodin's bust of Shaw – his splendid gift to me – and since he was the only foreign writer whose plays anyone still tried to perform, I could not drop the habit of writing to him, the last time being, I believe, through a member of the British Consulate, which was still in existence. Then suddenly I received a summons to the Ministry of Foreign Affairs, which I instantly obeyed, only to learn that I was under strict orders to abandon all attempts at correspondence with an 'enemy alien', whoever it might be, until the conclusion of hostilities, if I did not want to expose myself to consequences quite as unpleasant as anything I would be causing the recipient of my letters.

A Friendship Broken

DORIS JONES

From Doris Arthur Jones, *The Life and Letters of Henry Arthur Jones* (London: Victor Gollancz, 1930) p. 310. Jones was to play a leading role in Shaw's expulsion from the Dramatists' Club in the autumn of 1915, on account of his attitude to the war. He continued to attack him long after the war was over, despite Shaw's refusal to take offence.

My father's friendship with Shaw was one of the most delightful and cordial of all his many friendships. He had for Shaw a deep and strong attachment, and for more than twenty years GBS's companionship and their intercourse had been a constant pleasure and stimulation to him. He often referred to the times when GBS was a journalist and used to stay with him. But soon after the War broke out Henry Arthur was amazed and disgusted at GBS's attitude. Writing to me from New York in 1914, he said: 'Shaw continues his crazy attacks. I never felt more angry with any man. He is trying to keep up the strife between England and Ireland. I do not think I can meet him in the future.' In 1915 he wrote: 'No use talking or thinking about the War. It's awful, and Shaw is only anxious to get an advertisement out of it.'

He felt that Wells and Shaw were the spokesmen of the most dangerous and fallacious political creeds, and that it was his duty as a patriot to combat their influence with every means at his disposal. He was nourished and sustained in this conviction by the enormous body of approval and encouragement he received from all over the world. A great many prominent English men and women supported him in his campaign, and he received hundreds of letters from unknown correspondents, who thanked him for the public service he was rendering England.

'The Illusions of War'

R. PAGE ARNOT

From R. Page Arnot, *Bernard Shaw and William Morris* (London: William Morris Society, 1957) pp. 22–3. Although he mistakenly attributes it to the previous year, R. Page Arnot is recalling 'The Illusions of War', the opening lecture of the 1915 Fabian autumn series, given by Shaw on 26 October at King's Hall, Covent Garden. It was his first lecture appearance that year and was largely censored from the Press.

At the Fabian lectures in the Kingsway Hall that autumn Shaw in his speech shook some of the audience back into sanity. When he spoke of jingoes who sacked and gutted the shops with German-sounding names in the East End of London and of the ravings against all Germans that were being uttered by panic-stricken men and women carried away in the torrent of Chauvinism, he got little enough response for a while from his audience. So he paused, and then said:

'Many of you must know the great play of Euripides, the *Bacchae*, which has been translated into beautiful English verse by my friend Dr Gilbert Murray. You will remember how the women in that play, the Bacchantes, under the influence of the god Dionysus, go mad, and roam the countryside in the darkness, seeking to tear the wild beasts of the mountain limb from limb, with hand and mouth. The King Pentheus tries to stop the orgy and is himself torn in pieces: and his mother, also among the Bacchantes, finds in the morning that she is holding not the head of a wild beast she has killed, but the head of her own son.

'There are women in Britain today who have gone mad in the pursuit of the wild beasts, who are killing Germans with their mouths. On the morrow when they awake after their frenzy they will find in their laps the heads of their slaughtered sons.'

The effect of these words on the audience was that of an electric shock. It almost resembled the effect upon the Athenians of that play of Aeschylus, when, as we are told, men fainted and women fell into the pangs of travail.[1] Shaw to rescue them from the emotional upheaval he had caused then turned once more to his reasoned statement along lines which he had set out with such courage in his *Common Sense about the War*.

NOTE

1. The *Eumenides* of Aeschylus, in which the first appearance of the chorus in terrifying masks and costumes induced great fright in the spectators.

The Causes of the War

From Albert J. Beveridge, 'British War Opinion', *Collier's*, 12 June 1915. Albert Jeremiah Beveridge (1862–1927), American lawyer, Senator (1899–1911) and historian, spent part of 1915 in Germany as a war correspondent. In March that year he obtained a series of interviews to represent the diversity of opinion within Britain about the reasons for her entering the war, remarking on the absence of similar controversy in France and Germany. Later he submitted his texts to each speaker for revision.

In his assessment of the causes of the war Shaw tended to discount the immediate impulse and uncertain outcome of events and to emphasise long-term fears and tensions, arguing rather deterministically that what had happened was bound to happen, and indeed had been intended to happen. But while the two major European power blocs (Germany/Austro-Hungary and France/Russia/Britain) were likely to come into conflict sooner or later, the understanding between France and Britain was not binding, and their secret Military Conversations, which began in 1906, were precautionary rather than aggressive. Shaw viewed the neutrality of Belgium as a technicality, but it was respected by France and Britain and was crucial to the Belgians, who rebuffed British military overtures in 1912 to preserve their neutral purity. The British government would have split down the middle over entering the war if Germany had not invaded Belgium.

'[W]e Americans would like to know what *you* say "the row is about", as one cab driver put it. What do you think caused it?' I asked.

'A general fear of one another,' answered Mr Shaw. 'Everybody was afraid that if he did not destroy his neighbour, his neighbour would destroy him.'

'The reason which we Americans believe caused Great Britain to declare war is the violation of Belgian neutrality,' I remarked.

'That was the formal plea on which we declared war,' answered Mr Shaw. 'But really the broken treaty of 1839 had nothing to do with it.[1] Plenty of treaties have been broken since 1839 without war. The real reason was: Grey had secretly pledged us to support France if the Austro-German alliance ever came to blows with the Franco-Russian alliance.

'All the European diplomatists had made up their minds that a European war between these two combinations was inevitable,' continued Mr Shaw, 'Our diplomatists decided that we must be in that war. They chose our side – the French side – on the ground that if the Germans vanquished France and Russia they could vanquish us afterward.

'So they concerted all the neccessary military and naval plans and arrangements with the French diplomatists. And when the Serbian affair brought about the war[2] we were of course bound by these arrangements.'

'But,' I remarked, 'I have heard that the Liberal party went into power as a peace party. I have been told that peace was its central principle.'

'Not exactly,' said Mr Shaw. 'When the party came into power in 1906 it was divided between modern Imperialism and the old nonintervention policy of peace, retrenchment and reform. The difference was compromised by including three Liberal Imperialists – Asquith, Grey and Haldane[3] – in the Cabinet. They were reenforced by Churchill, a blazing militarist Junker.[4]

'But,' went on Mr Shaw, 'the difficulty was that, though these Ministers were convinced of the necessity of our taking sides in the European quarrel, and backing France by arms, they would have broken up their party if they had said so openly and revealed their entry into the Franco-Russian *entente*. They had even to deny that they were committed to war by any secret arrangement.'

'Do you mean that they publicly told a lie?'

'Not at all – technically,' Mr Shaw responded. 'Mr Asquith had taken care of that. He insisted on Sir Edward Grey asking the French to note particularly that the arrangements did not bind us to anything.[5] The French, who understand the electioneering exigencies of democracy as well as any politicians on earth, gravely noted the statement. Thus Mr Asquith was perfectly in order in stating repeatedly that we were bound by no secret engagements. And Sir Edward Grey confirmed him.

'That,' said Mr Shaw, 'is how the Liberal party and the nation were led up to the guns blindfolded,' and his calm voice cut like a knife.

'According to that,' I remarked, 'Germany's violation of Belgian neutrality had nothing to do with England's entering the war.'

'Nothing whatever,' answered Mr Shaw, 'except to furnish Mr Asquith with a perfectly presentable and correct pretext for entering on a war to which he was already secretly pledged, Belgium or no Belgium.

'Of course,' continued Mr Shaw, 'the secret arrangements with France had to come out; but as the revelation was accompanied by the announcement that we were virtually at war with Germany, the consternation and excitement and war fever prevented the Liberals from realising at once how they had been humbugged – though, by the way, three members of the Cabinet resigned.'[6] . . .

'In America,' I remarked, 'it has been said that England was surprised, pained, and outraged when Germany attacked France through Belgium.'

'Surprised!' said Mr Shaw. 'Why, everybody knew for ten years that Germany would march through Belgium in case of war with France! There were Germany's strategic railways built right up to Belgium's frontiers! What other object could they have? The British Government had long since taken action accordingly. Not only were our fleets disposed and stationed according to plans agreed upon in pursuance with Grey's pledge to France, but our Government fixed things up with Belgium so that Great Britain and France could meet the German attack in Belgium when the war came.'

'But was not this to be done only in case Germany first invaded Belgium?' I inquired.

'There would have been no occasion to do it in any other case,' explained Mr Shaw. 'Naturally, if Germany had attacked through Alsace, the British army would not have gone to Liège. And please note that when England and France were about to pledge themselves not to enter Belgium they did so only on condition that Germany did not attack through Belgium.

'In other words, they refused to respect the neutrality of Belgium unless Germany respected it also. There was nothing in these pledges. There never is, because international law – as far as there is such a thing – admits that a violation of neutrality by one power dispenses all the rest from respecting it. That is why neutrality is nonsense.

'When the Germans took Brussels,' went on Mr Shaw, 'they discovered documents recording the negotiations; and there is now no secret about them. You can be as indignant as you like in theory about the devastation of Belgium, the innocent victim of all the policies and ambitions of her big neighbours; but you need not waste any virtuous indignation over the technical breach of neutrality.'

'Why this combination against Germany?' I asked.

'The old story – the balance of power and our command of the sea – you know that we regard the sea as our private property,' replied Mr Shaw, laughing – but his eyes did not laugh. 'Some years ago Count Kessler[7] organised an expression of good feeling between England and Germany. First came a sort of manifesto signed by all the illustrious names in Germany, which should be reprinted on every copy of Lissauer's 'Hymn of Hate'.[8] It breathed nothing but esteem and admiration for the English character and the contributions of the English to culture and science. According to it, Germany saw us as a nation of Shakespeares, Newtons, and Wellingtons.

'We responded with an equally ecstatic document. I remember it very well. As a matter of fact, I drafted it; and it may interest you to know why my name did not appear among the signatories.[9] The reason was that I put into it a test sentence to discover what its real political value was. That sentence was to the effect that far from regarding the growth of the German fleet with suspicion and jealousy, we saw in it only an additional bulwark of our common civilisation.

'Well, not a single signature of any political weight could we get except on condition that this sentence was expunged. Expunged it was accordingly. They were rather surprised when I refused to give my name to the document I had myself drafted for them; but I had tested it for humbug, and it had not passed the test.'

NOTES

1. Article VII of the Treaty of London affirmed that Belgium was 'an independent and perpetually neutral state' under the collective guarantee of Britain, France, Prussia, Russia and Austria. The treaty was a British initiative, achieved under Palmerston's direction, and had been reaffirmed by Gladstone at the time of the Franco-Prussian War.

2. The Austrians had used the assassination of their Crown Prince by a Serbian extremist as a pretext for declaring war on Serbia. Opposing alliances brought Russia and Germany into the conflict.

3. Herbert Henry Asquith, later Earl of Oxford (1852–1928), was Chancellor of the Exchequer until 1908, when he became Prime Minister. Sir Edward Grey, later Viscount Grey (1862–1933), served as Foreign Secretary until May 1916. Richard Burdon Haldane (1856–1928) was Secretary for War until 1912, when he was created Viscount and became Lord Chancellor.

4. (Sir) Winston Leonard Spencer Churchill (1874–1965) did not enter the Cabinet until 1908 (as President of the Board of Trade). From 1911 to 1915 he was First Lord of the Admiralty.

5. The original 'no commitment' formula had been reaffirmed in a letter approved by the British Cabinet in 1912, under pressure from the anti-war group within it.

6. In fact only John Burns and Lord John Morley resigned (on 2 August). Two other ministers resigned on 3 August but rejoined the government the same day.

7. Count Harry Kessler (1868–1937), German politician, humanist and amateur of the arts, had been educated in England.

8. 'Hassgesang gegen England', composed early in the war by the Jewish writer Ernst Lissauer (1882–1937), who later regretted it.

9. Shaw's correspondence in January 1906 with the sponsors of the English letter, Emery Walker and the artist William Rothenstein, suggests a slightly different record (see *Collected Letters 1898–1910*, pp. 600–1).

The Conscription Issue

From C. Ward-Jackson, 'Mr Bernard Shaw on: Is Conscription Necessary or Advisable?', *New Age*, 16 March 1916. The publication of this written interview in England was *ex post facto*, as conscription had been introduced in January 1916: it had, however, appeared earlier in the *New York American* (28 November 1915). At the beginning of the war Britain was the only nation in Europe to depend on voluntary enlistment for its armed forces. Elsewhere in the interview Shaw made it clear that he favoured relaxation of the harsher forms of military regimentation and discipline to attract recruits, rather than conscription – at the same time reverting to his old ideal of compulsory public service at all times, with the rights of the individual nevertheless preserved.

Do you think that if Conscription or Compulsory Service is adopted in Great Britain the masses will believe that it is 'part of a servile scheme that reaches far beyond the War' – that it is an attempt of the capitalist class to smash Trade Unionism and Democracy by placing all under a worse system even than Prussian Militarism, because, in their opinion, it will have the hypocrisy of patriotism and national sacrifice behind it? . . .

I don't know what the masses will believe; but they would find all that you say a fairly good working hypothesis. Capitalist class is, however, rather too general an expression. It includes our country-house class, which the Germans call the Junker class. It includes the vagabond idle rich. It includes the financiers, the employers, and to some extent the professional class. Of these the country-house class is the most ignorant socially; for it alone imagines that Trade Unions are mere crude rebellious conspiracies, and Democracy mob rule. The financiers and professionals may share these ridiculous delusions to the extent to which they share the social ignorance of the country houses, which means to the extent to which they are the younger-son offshoots of the country houses; but there is a big wedge of the capitalist class which knows better. In the big industries it is easier and, in the long run, cheaper to deal with organised than with unorganised labour; and in any case compulsory service would clearly make for organisation and discipline among the workers instead of against it. For example, the German working class is enormously better organised politically, syndically, and co-operatively than the British working class. Obviously, if you are afraid of a class, and want to keep it helpless and unorganised, the very last thing you will give it is military training. Consequently the capitalists who know the world best, and don't want to change it, are against compulsory service and in favour of Democracy, which opens all doors to the adroit political adventurer and closes them to the mere noodles from the châteaux and the Faubourg St Germain.[1] As to the idle rich, they are incapable of schemes of any sort, and neither know nor care anything about national service or Trade Unionism. So you see the capitalist class, as you call it, is by no means unanimous on the point; and if it becomes unanimous, or allows the Coalition to carry it, the result may surprise it very disagreeably. Remember that the German Social Democrats are not opposed to military service, though they are to its abuses. And except perhaps in our Guards, where the discipline is Prussian even to the slow march which is our Paradeschritt, military service is more easy-going in England than in Germany.

Also, in this event, are you of opinion that strikes, riots and, ultimately, a violent revolution will be the result if military despotism, under any pretext, is imposed upon our people?

I think that if we go on as we have been going on hitherto all these calamities will be the result, whether or no.

Finally, do you think that Great Britain is strong enough to win this war without Conscription and National Service?

Yes, if she is strong enough to win it *with* them. And she is so strong in material resources and in strategical position that if she loses it will serve her right. I will go so far as to say that an unlimited supply of soldiers to either side might quite conceivably lead to its defeat. In America, during the nineteenth century, the scarcity of labour led to a tremendous development of invention and business faculty, on the reputation of which the American hustlers are still living. Our manufacturers would not invent and would not think, because they could always fall back on multitudinous cheap labour. In just the same way military general staffs will not invent or think as long as they can snow their enemies under with piles of corpses. Cut off the supply of corpses, and the generals will have to use their brains. If we had fewer men there would be no Dardanelles adventures. And if we can afford to waste more men than the Germans, and *do* waste them, the Germans may have cause to be thankful for being outnumbered.

NOTE

1. The Faubourg St Germain is a district in the centre of Paris, developed as a fashionable residential suburb in the eighteenth century.

The Casement Affair: I

BEATRICE WEBB

From *The Diary of Beatrice Webb*, vol. II: *1905–1924*, ed. Norman and Jeanne MacKenzie (London: Virago, 1984) p. 256. Sir Roger Casement (1864–1916) served with distinction in the British Consular Service, retiring shortly after being knighted in 1911. He then devoted himself to the cause of Irish nationalism, and after reaching Germany from America in October 1914 tried unsuccessfully to raise an Irish Brigade from British prisoners of war. In 1916 he left Germany for Ireland by submarine to try and stop the planned Easter Rising, and failing that, to take part in it, but was arrested within hours of landing on 20 April and brought to London. He was convicted of high treason on 29 June and hanged on 3 August. His friend Alice Stopford Green (1847–1929), historian, made herself responsible for organising his defence. Like him, she had grown up in Ireland and was a nationalist of romantic cast. The Webbs were neighbours of hers in Westminster and Beatrice asked her to lunch with the Shaws in the hope of securing funds for Casement's defence. Beatrice's diary entry for 21 May describes the occasion.

Charlotte is a wealthy Irish rebel, and I had noticed that when Casement's 'treason' was mentioned, her eyes had flashed defiance and she had defended his action. And GBS had publicly urged clemency and had also defended Casement's action. But GBS as usual had his own plan. Casement was to defend his own case, he was to make a great oration of defiance which would 'bring down the house'. To this Mrs Green retorted tearfully that the man was desperately ill, that he was quite incapable of handling a court full of lawyers, that the most he could do was the final speech after the verdict. 'Then we had better get our suit of mourning,' Shaw remarked with an almost gay laugh. 'I will write him a speech which will thunder down the ages.' 'But his friends want to get him reprieved,' indignantly replied the distracted woman friend.

The meeting turned out to be a useless and painful proceeding. The Shaws were determined not to pay up – not 'to waste our money on lawyers'. GBS went off to write the speech which was 'to thunder down the ages'. Alice Green retired in dismay, and I felt a fool for having intervened to bring Irish together in a common cause. Alice has been heroic: her house has been searched, she herself has been up before Scotland Yard, she is spending her strength and her means in trying to save the life of her unfortunate friend. The Shaws don't care enough about it to spend money; and Shaw wants to compel Casement and

Casement's friends to 'produce' the defence as a national dramatic event. 'I know how to do it,' was GBS's one contribution to the tragedy-laden dispute between the weeping woman friend and the intellectual sprite at play with the life and death of a poor human. The man is both kindly and tolerant, but his conceit is monstrous, and he is wholly unaware of the pain he gives by his jeering words and laughing gestures – especially to romantics like Alice Green.

The Casement Affair: II

CHARLOTTE SHAW

From a letter by Charlotte Shaw to T. E. Lawrence, 15–16 September 1927, in Janet Dunbar, *Mrs GBS: A Biographical Portrait* (London: Harrap, 1963) p. 285. Sydney Cockerell had introduced 'Lawrence of Arabia' to the Shaws: the rapport between them was immediate and Lawrence became a particularly intimate friend of Charlotte's. He had written to her about Casement and she determined to set down all she knew.

[I]t was not difficult to persuade GBS to do everything in his power. We got a little knot of people together – Casement's solicitor, Gavin [sic] Duffy,[1] and others. So few! alas! (war time – it was!) We had many meetings. GBS wrote out what he thought Casement ought to do. That was, not to employ counsel; to *defend himself* (he was a fine speaker): not to deny anything, to acknowledge facts and to say they did not make him guilty: that his country had declared herself free and that he had a right to work for his country's freedom and be treated as, what he was, a prisoner of war.[2]

Casement wouldn't take his advice: he was just not big enough.

He sent most grateful messages but said he was in the hands of his legal advisers and that they said they must conduct the case, but that he, Casement, should make a statement afterwards from the dock.

They did for him. When the trial came of course precisely what we feared happened. F. E.[3] was damnable: treated the whole with consummate insolence, *de haut en bas*. Casement's counsel, Sullivan (a man I knew, to my sorrow, over other things) made an excited speech for hours and hours and hours – bored everyone to tears – and then broke down and fainted. They passed sentence, and then – Casement got up and made the speech GBS had sketched for him. He made a profound sensation with it, and several of the jury said afterwards that if they had heard all that before retiring the verdict would have been different. Of course it was too late and could do nothing to change the result.

NOTES

1. George Gavan Duffy (1882–1951), lawyer and politician, had built up an extensive legal practice in London. For Casement's defence he briefed his cousin, Serjeant A. M. Sullivan of the Irish Bar, a spirited nationalist. After the trial Duffy returned to Ireland and took a leading part in establishing the Irish Free State.

2. In 1922 twenty-five copies of Shaw's draft speech were privately printed as *A Discarded Defence of Roger Casement* – collected in Shaw, *The Matter with Ireland* (1962).

3. Frederick Edwin Smith, later 1st Earl of Birkenhead (1872–1930), lawyer and Conservative politician, had been closely involved with armed Ulster resistance to Home Rule in 1913–14. As Attorney-General at the time of Casement's trial he led the prosecution.

British Insularity

'G. Bernard Shaw on what we think of the Foreigner', *Everyman*, 14 July 1916. Shaw wrote answers to questions put by the editor of *Everyman*, Charles Sarolea.

What do you think of the present attitude of the British public towards the foreigner and his Governments?

The British public is not really conscious of any other public or any other interests. To it the universe consists of a great central fact called, according to its size, Peckham, England or the British Empire. Its atmosphere contains blacks, who ought to be treated kindly when they behave themselves; Huns, who ought to be exterminated: and Allies, who provide us with useful auxiliary troops, and ought to be protected and encouraged within proper limits. But the true Briton does not strike attitudes at such things. Attitudinising is a foreign habit, like eating frogs and snails.

If the British public took up a sensible attitude, what do you think would be the first thing it would demand?

It would drop down dead, slain by the novelty of the sensation.

Can you name any actual instances when an informed British opinion could have been of any practical use in foreign affairs?

Yes. This war is due to our insular ignorance of the terrifying dangerousness to the military imagination of the situation of Germany with France on one frontier and Russia on the other. We should have done either of two things: guaranteed Germany against an attack from the West in the event of an attack by Russia on the Central Empires, or declared that if Germany attacked France she would have to fight us too. If we had done the first, the war would have been confined to the Eastern half of Europe. If we had done the second, there would probably have been no war at all.[1] We did neither, and the result has been Armageddon. We simply did not take any interest in the situation of Germany, or any other Continental Power. We were satisfied that as we felt all right they must feel all right if they were reasonable people. And we have not yet recovered from our scandalised surprise at Germany losing her head and making a desperate attempt to break by force the ring that encircled her. All that is the result of pure ignorance of foreign affairs, and, of course, reckless indifference to them.

Does national modesty of itself make for peace?

Modesty does not make for anything but itself. It is, in politics, only a pious kind of swank, or an excuse for shirking responsibility, or the card player's trick of looking glum over a handful of trumps. Germany and England would stand out as the most conceited nations on earth if they were not so completely outdone in that quality by Ireland. It is not modest to sing 'Rule, Britannia', and it is not modest to retort 'Deutschland über Alles'. And it is not immodest to sing 'O God, our help in ages past' and 'Ein feste Burg ist unser Gott'. On the whole, I am inclined to back the hymn against the patriotic song. But the sensible thing in war is not to keep bothering about your own character, but to count your guns, keep your powder dry, and claim no more than they will run to. In peace, national modesty would be fatal. If any civilised nation today were to become modest enough to see itself as it really is, it would utter a shriek of horror and run violently down a steep place into the sea.

What can you predict will be the state of British opinion after the war?

As usual, bumptious when it is not blithering with sentiment or blubbering in baseless panic. In short, it will be reading the halfpenny picture papers.

Will war cure bellicosity, or ignorance, or anything else?

War will cure nothing. The business of war is to inflict wounds, not to heal them.

Do you think that the war will make the British public want anything violently after it is over?

Yes, beer.

NOTE

1. Shaw's first recommendation ignored the possibility that Austro-Hungary, backed by Germany, might be the aggressor in the East (as was the case), while the second would have been invalidated by the *idée fixe* of German military planning, which staked all on an enveloping attack on France through Belgium, too rapid and overwhelming to be affected by the anticipated British intervention.

Work in Progress

LADY GREGORY

From *Lady Gregory's Journals*, vol. i, ed. Daniel J. Murphy, Coole Edition xiv (Gerrard's Cross: Colin Smythe, 1978) p. 11. The source entry, dated 19 November 1916, was written during a brief visit to Ayot St Lawrence. There was snow outside but Lady Gregory found the house 'warm and bright with fires in every room and pots of chrysanthemums'.

Last night GBS read me a story he had written. He had been asked for one for a Gift Book to be sold for the Belgian Children's Milk Fund and had refused, saying the Society of Authors objected to these Gift Books. But the lady[1] came again to say she had got leave from the Society of Authors to print it, if she gave them a percentage. He was quite taken aback and said he hadn't promised it, but in the end sat down and wrote it straight off. Then the lady brought it back in a few days to say she wouldn't put it in the Gift Book but Mrs Whitelaw Reid had offered £400 for it to put in the *New York Tribune*.[2] So the Belgian children will get plenty of milk for that.

He read it and it is beautiful and touching, about a child and the Kaiser. He said that his idea was to show that the Kaiser is not quite a demon. . . . He read also the first act of a play, very amusing, 'The House in the Clouds' (afterwards *Heartbreak House*!) but says he doesn't know how to finish it, it is so wild, he thought bringing my 'fresh mind' to bear on it might be a help.[3]

NOTES

1. Muriel Carmel Goldsmid, who in 1910 had married Leslie Haden-Guest, a Fabian colleague of Shaw's.
2. 'The Emperor and the Little Girl', written for the Vestiaire Marie-José, had appeared in the *New York Tribune Magazine* on 22 October and was collected in *Short Stories, Scraps and Shavings* in 1932. Belgium was very largely occupied by Germany for most of the war.
3. *Heartbreak House* was not finished until the following May.

At the Front 1917: I

PHILIP GIBBS

From Sir Philip Gibbs, *The Pageant of the Years: An Autobiography* (London: Heinemann, 1946) pp. 195–7. (Sir) Philip Armand Hamilton Gibbs (1877–1962), journalist and author, was one of five official correspondents appointed to the British Expeditionary Force in 1915. For the next three years he covered the Western Front for the *Daily Chronicle* and *Daily Telegraph*. In a conversation reported by Sewell Stokes in *Pilloried!* [1928], he said he had suggested Shaw visit the Front because he wanted to meet him, adding that it was extremely difficult to get him invited anywhere once he arrived. Shaw crossed to France at the end of January 1917 and stayed nearly ten days instead of the expected three.

Another distinguished man who came out was George Bernard Shaw. I had something to do with his coming because General Charteris, Chief of Intelligence,[1] asked me one day if I could suggest some famous writer who would do a series of articles likely to be of value from a propaganda point of view. In a moment of wild inspiration I ventured to suggest Bernard Shaw, never thinking that the idea would be accepted, because he had written things about the war which were very shocking to traditional minds. To my deep surprise he arrived in due course, and I was appointed as his companion during his visit to the Front. I enjoyed the experience, and every hour I spent with him increased my admiration for him as a man of genius, charm of personality, and high distinction. He said many wise and witty things, and I regret that I did not note them down. Of course he could not deny his instinctive urge to shock the conventional and rigid minds by remarks which seemed like blasphemy to their humourless way of thinking. I remember going with him to lunch with one of our generals, who hated having him as his guest and regarded him as next door to a traitor. Courtesy, however, overcame his ill-temper and he turned to Shaw, who was having a lively conversation with his ADCs and asked a polite question.

'Well, Mr Shaw, when do you think this war will be over?'

'Well, General,' said Bernard Shaw, 'we are all anxious for an early and dishonourable peace.'

This reduced the General to silence for quite a time but the ADCs set up a howl of mirth.

I discovered one well-kept secret of Bernard Shaw's. He was a lover of England, and deeply anxious for our victory. He gave this away one day when we were going up to the Vimy Ridge.

'Gibbs,' he said, 'one's thoughts about this war run on parallel lines which can never meet. The first is that all this is a degradation of humanity, a great insanity, and a crime against civilisation. It ought never to have happened. It's dirty business for which we all ought to be ashamed. That's the first line of thought: and the second is that *We've got to beat the Boche!*'

Going into Arras one morning, when the enemy was sending over some shells into that city as usual, Bernard Shaw adjusted his steel hat and glanced at me humorously under his spidery eyebrows.

'If the Germans kill me today,' he said, 'they'll be a very ungrateful people.'

He had in his mind, no doubt, all the plays which had been produced in Germany to the delight of their audiences, who were more enthusiastic in their admiration for Shaw than, for a long time, anyhow, the theatre-goers of England.

GBS was very easy in his way with officers and men, and it was surprising what a lot of knowledge he had about the technical side of war, especially about aviation. He could talk to young pilots about planes, and wind pressure, and other technical subjects, in a way that astonished them and me. To whatever subject he turned his fine brain he became its master, or at least seized upon the essential facts and principles in a penetrating way. Upon his return to England he wrote a series of articles about his experiences in the war zone which maddened his critics even by his title which was 'Joy riding at the Front'.[2]

They were, as I must admit, utterly useless as propaganda, and written with a flippancy which was not in the best of taste in the middle of a war which was taking a frightful toll of youth. But Shaw wanted again to shock people out of the slush and sentiment which had taken possession of many minds who evaded the grim realities. He shocked them all right.

NOTES

1. Brigadier-General John Charteris (1877–1946).
2. The articles appeared in the *Daily Chronicle* on 5, 7 and 8 March 1917 and were collected in *What I Really Wrote about the War* (1930).

At the Front 1917: II

CHARLOTTE SHAW

From a letter by Charlotte Shaw to Mary Cholmondeley, 16 February 1917, in Janet Dunbar, *Mrs GBS: A Biographical Portrait* (London: Harrap, 1963) pp. 253–6. Charlotte's sister had asked for a full account of Shaw's military adventures.

He was asked the first morning what he most wanted to see, & he said Ypres. They said it was a very 'unhealthy place' but if he really must go they would see what could be done. So he was motored to Ypres. There he found the 'Town Major' who was a gigantic Irishman, who took them in charge & said 'If you want to see it all, I'll show you, though I expect I'll be stopped by my own police – but we'll get round.' So they drove off to the principal square where the Cloth Hall is – or was. GBS was very much struck by the fact that though all the houses are gutted the walls are nearly all standing – because shells explode vertically & do almost no execution laterally. . . . Another thing GBS noticed was that you go straight from the streets into the trenches. At the end of a road you will see a hole, or a door, & by that you go into the lines.

Well: when they were getting near the big square – bang! a shell exploded in front of the car! I have never been able to ascertain exactly how far in front! But anyway it frightened the chauffeur & he stopped. The Town Major yelled 'Go on man, go right on. A shell never comes in the same place twice.' So they went on. Then they saw what had been the Cloth Hall.

Then he was taken to see the tanks, & had a ride in one! He says they go about three miles an hour, but when you are inside you fancy you are tearing over the ground, the engines are so powerful & make such a commotion. . . .

Then there came an invitation for GBS to lunch with the C. in C. & all the arrangements made for that day had to be countermanded. They had a very cheery lunch, I gather, & after lunch Sir Douglas,[1] to the great disgust of his people, who had made other arrangements for him, said he should take GBS off with him in his car to see some experiments that were being made of the new inventions. So they had a long drive alone together in an immense Rolls-Royce *closed* car & GBS says it was the only time in all those bitter drives in that Arctic weather that he had a rug over his knees! They appear to have had quite a heart-to-heart talk, & to have discussed everything!

[Later Shaw visited his actor friend Major Robert Loraine, then commanding 40 Squadron at Trézennes.]

They live in huts, & when he got there GBS really knew what cold meant. When he was dressing in the morning in his hut his money froze to his fingers! & he could not button any button without holding his fingers in a jug of hot water they brought him. The men's clothes freeze to the ground. He says Loraine is completely taken up with office work & organisation, that he never flies now. . . .

The next day GBS drove to Boulogne in Loraine's car – about an hour & a half – & there was the guest of a great friend of ours, Sir Almroth Wright (the original of Ridgeon in *The Doctor's Dilemma*) who is superintending a big hospital there; &, incidentally, making many discoveries. The men in the hospital were practically the only wounded GBS saw. He seems to have escaped horrors, & only saw one dead man the whole time. But he saw a regiment of men coming back from the trenches – they had been there for sixteen days & were coming back for a rest – he was greatly struck by their exhaustion. He said practically every one of them had their mouths wide open & gave the impression they were too exhausted to keep them closed.

NOTE

1. Sir Douglas Haig: see below, p. 248.

At the Front 1917: III

C. D. BAKER-CARR

From C. D. Baker-Carr, *From Chauffeur to Brigadier* (London: Ernest Benn, 1930) p. 209. Brigadier-General Christopher D'Arcy Baker-Carr (1878–1949), a career soldier and battalion commander at the time of Shaw's visit, was shortly to take command of the Tank Corps First Brigade. Shaw was one of the very few civilians allowed to view the tank depot.

It was my great pleasure and privilege to give GBS his first, and probably his last, ride in a tank.

   With boy-like glee he watched the machines ascending and descending steep banks, going over their 'jumps', and generally being put through their paces. He eagerly accepted my invitation to be a passenger and he sat on the improvised seat with a smile of perfect happiness on his face, while the tank jolted and bumped over the hard, uneven ground. After the ride was finished, he descended and was, with some difficulty, discouraged from pressing a Treasury note on the driver of the tank.

At the Front 1917: IV

DOUGLAS HAIG

From *The Private Papers of Douglas Haig 1914–1919*, ed. Robert Blake (London: Eyre & Spottiswoode, 1952) pp. 194–5. Field-Marshal Sir Douglas (later Earl) Haig (1861–1928) was British Commander-in-Chief on the Western Front from December 1915 until the end of the war. His note of Shaw's visit is dated 1 February.

Mr Bernard Shaw (the Author and Playwriter) came to lunch. An interesting man of original views. A great talker! On sitting down to lunch, I at once discovered he was a vegetarian. As if by magic, on my ordering it, two poached eggs appeared, also some spinach and also macaroni, so he did not fare badly.

At the Front 1917: V

DAVID POWELL(?)

From Winifred Loraine, *Robert Loraine: Soldier, Actor, Airman* (London: Collins, 1938) p. 237. When he reached Loraine's airfield, Shaw found two of his short wartime plays in production (*O'Flaherty VC* still awaited a public performance).

The author of the note below was probably David Watson Powell (1878–1935), a Cambridge graduate and regular soldier, seconded to the Royal Flying Corps.

[Shaw] attended a dress rehearsal of his play, *The Inca of Perusalem*, which was acted by the men. *O'Flaherty VC* was done by the officers. Says Major Powell MC: 'I sat behind him in the empty Mess at this rehearsal. He laughed throughout the performance and enjoyed himself enormously. I thought it a curious sight to see an author laughing at his own jokes, and at the end leant over and said to him: "I'm glad you appreciate our poor efforts at your play, sir." He could scarcely speak for laughing. "D'you know," he said, "if I had thought the stuff would prove to be as poor as this, I'd never have written it."'

At the Front 1917: VI

HEYWOOD BROUN

From [Heywood Broun], 'What the Soldier Thinks of Shaw', *Literary Digest* (New York), 25 August 1917. Heywood Campbell Broun (1888–1939), socialist, journalist and author, worked for the *New York Tribune* from 1912 to 1921. He came across Shaw's signature in the visitors' book of the château reserved for guests at British Headquarters, and sent a report of the ensuing conversation to the *Tribune*, whence it reached the *Digest*.

The hand was tiny. In a sense Shaw is economical of words. He writes many, but he writes them small. This time economy was complete. There was no preface to the signature, and no handbook or footnotes. The visitor had simply written 'G. Bernard Shaw' and allowed it to stand without explanation or comment. The officers supplied that.

'Awful ass!' said one who had met the playwright at the Front. 'He was no end of nuisance for us. Why, when he got out here we found he was a vegetarian, and we had to chase around and have omelets fixed up for him every day.'

'I censored his stuff,' said another. 'I didn't think much of it, but I made almost no changes. Some of it was a little subtle, but I let it get by.'

I inquired and learned that the blue pencil which cut the copy of G. Bernard Shaw had not been preserved. It seemed a pity.

'I heard him out here,' said a third officer, 'and he talked no end of rot. He said the Germans had made a botch of destroying towns. He said he could have done more damage to Arras with a hammer than

the Germans did with their shells. Of course, he couldn't begin to do it
with a hammer, and, anyway, he wouldn't be let. I suppose he never
thought of that. Then he said that the Germans were doing us a great
favour by their air-raids. He said they were smashing up things that
were ugly and unsanitary. That's silly. We could pull them down
ourselves, you know, and, anyhow, in the last raid they hit the post-
office.'

'The old boy's got nerve, though,' interrupted another officer. 'I was
out at the Front with him near Arras, and there was some pretty lively
shelling going on around us. I told him to put on his tin hat, but he
wouldn't do it. I said, "Those German shell-splinters may get you," and
he laughed and said if the Germans did anything to him they'd be
mighty ungrateful, after all he'd done for them. He doesn't know the
Boche.'

'He told me,' added a British journalist, '"when I want to know about
war I talk to soldiers". I asked him: "Do you mean officers or Tommies?"
He said that he meant Tommies.

'Now you know how much reliance you can put in what a Tommy
says. He'll either say what he thinks you want him to say or what he
thinks you don't want him to say. I told Shaw that, but he paid no
attention.'

Here the first officer chimed in again. 'Well, I stick to what I've said
right along. I don't see where Shaw's funny. I think he's silly.'

The officer who was showing the visitors' book turned over another
page. 'There's Conan Doyle,' he said.

At the Front 1917: VII

STANLEY RYPINS

From Stanley Rypins, 'Bernard Shaw Remembered', *Virginia Quarterly Review*,
Winter 1957. Stanley Rypins, later Professor of English at Brooklyn College,
New York, was a twenty-four-year-old Rhodes scholar at Oxford University
when he first met Shaw in November 1915. Their last meeting before he went
back to America took place soon after Shaw's visit to the Front.

Shortly after his return, walking home from a Fabian Society lecture
with Shaw along the blacked-out Strand, I got his reaction. 'Of course,'
he insisted, 'I still detest war. But it's extremely exhilarating. One gets
keyed up to a pitch of nervous exictement which makes life away from

the firing line dull by contrast. It's like living in an oxygenated chamber.'
A pause. 'How quiet it seems here!' Another pause. 'I've been invited
to visit the trenches again, the Italian front this time; but I hesitate to
go, it's so demoralising.' He never did go.

Writers' Gathering

ARNOLD BENNETT

From *The Journal of Arnold Bennett* (New York: The Literary Guild, 1933) p. 633.
On 24 July 1917 Bennett went to dine with J. M. Barrie, Shaw's neighbour in
Adelphi Terrace. Thomas Hardy, then seventy-seven, was staying with his wife
at Barrie's flat, and at dinner Bennett found him 'very lively; talked like
anything'.

Later in the evening Barrie brought along both Shaw and the Wellses
by phone. Barrie was consistently very quiet, but told a few A1 stories.
At dusk we viewed the view and the searchlights. Hardy, standing
outside one of the windows, had to put a handkerchief on his head. I
sneezed. Soon after Shaw and the Wellses came Hardy seemed to curl
up. He had travelled to town that day and was evidently fatigued. He
became quite silent. I then departed and told Barrie that Hardy ought
to go to bed. He agreed. The spectacle of Wells and GBS talking firmly
and strongly about the war, in their comparative youth, in front of this
aged, fatigued and silent man – incomparably their superior as a creative
artist – was very striking.

The War in Retrospect

From Archibald Henderson, *Table-talk of GBS: Conversations on Things in General
between Bernard Shaw and his Biographer* (London: Chapman & Hall, 1925) pp. 147–
50, 154–8, 163–5. Archibald Henderson (1877–1963), sometime student of
Einstein, taught mathematics at the University of North Carolina for nearly fifty
years. He 'discovered' Shaw in 1903 and wrote to him a year later proposing to
undertake a biography. Eventually he produced three – in 1911, 1932 and 1956 –
as well as a large number of articles on Shavian topics. *Table-talk*, despite its title

and presentation, was the product of written question and answer, augmented and revised by Shaw himself.

HENDERSON: To what extent did you attack the Government during the war?

SHAW: I protest I did not attack it at all, though everyone else did, especially the hyperpatriots. But I know what you are driving at. I was fiercely determined, like Ramsay MacDonald,[1] that the diplomatists and militarists who brought about the war should not get credit for having saved the world from the peril which they had in fact created. They were pretending – or allowing green horns and journalists to pretend for them – that the war was a war to end war, an act of pure defence against an unprovoked attack by Germany, a crusade against tyranny, oppression, imperialism and foreign domination led by a peaceful, unambitious, unaggressive, idyllic England; and in that faith many gallant young men enlisted, fought and died.

If that pretence had not been exposed, the victory would have established reactionary government in England for fifty years instead of for five. I did all I safely could to expose it, and to make the country understand that it was fighting for its life to escape the ruin its militarist governing class had brought upon it, and that, having no moral case against the Germans (all the parties were equally guilty) it must keep its powder dry for a military success.

But I could not say very much. The danger of discouraging enlistment during the voluntary period, and of weakening the national *moral*, was too serious. I did not let myself go until the war was over, during the election of 1918, when I had a great oratorical campaign. After a speech of mine at Stourbridge, in support of the late Mary Macarthur,[2] a soldier said to me: 'If I had known all that in 1914, they would never have got khaki on *my* back.' My reply was: 'That is precisely why I did not tell you in 1914.'

HENDERSON: What effect, if you please, did *Common Sense about the War* produce in England?

SHAW: None, beyond giving some relief and satisfaction to the people who were bursting with impatience at the reckless folly, spite, and ignorant romance and mendacity that were being stuffed down their throats by the press, and by the fussy bores who found that they could get listened to and make themselves important by what they imagined to be patriotism. I had to get cards printed to acknowledge the resolutions that were passed all over the country thanking me. The sale, I think, was 75,000 copies. . . .

HENDERSON: Were you right in *Common Sense about the War*? Have you been justified by events?

SHAW (*with animation and triumph*): Completely, even where I had been guessing. Within a few months of its publication *The Times* and the *Pall Mall Gazette* were going far beyond anything I had ventured to say. Great offence had been given by my contemptuous dismissal of the pretence that we had not been prepared for the war – that we were innocent lambs suddenly and wantonly attacked by a German wolf who had been preparing for years. The silly people who were spreading this sentimental fairy tale forgot that they were accusing the War Office, the Admiralty and the Foreign Office of gross blindness and neglect of duty. Lord Haldane hastened to explain that General French[3] had been sent to study the country in Flanders years before the war broke out, and claimed rightly that the War Office had fulfilled to the letter the military arrangements it had made with France and Belgium in view of the war as early as 1906. Mr Winston Churchill claimed that the British navy had gone into the war with five years' accumulation of ammunition made expressly for it. Lord Fisher's autobiography revealed the pressure put on the British Government to attack and destroy the German fleet – to 'Copenhagen' it – without notice in the days of Edward VII, who had finally to ask Fisher to be good enough to stop shaking his fist in the royal face.[4] . . .

HENDERSON: I seem to recall a violent outburst of popular feeling aroused by one of your speeches following the sinking of the *Lusitania*?[5]

SHAW: The violent outburst was against the sinking of the *Lusitania*, not against me. I did not conceal my contempt for the people who had taken the frightful slaughter of our soldiers in Flanders as if it were a cinema show got up to please their patriotism, but who went stark raving mad when one of their favourite pleasure boats – actually with first-class passengers on board – was blown up. But they were too mad to mind me. The truth is that the *Lusitania* catastrophe – much too big a word for it, by the way – was the first incident in the war that was small enough for their minds to take in: they suddenly realised at last that the Germans were out to kill them, and that the war was something more serious than reading dispatches from correspondents at the Front about 'our gallant fellows in the trenches'. Their frivolity infuriated me; but no newspaper dared rebuke their silly heartlessness as it deserved; and I did not tell them off until the war was over, in the preface to *Heartbreak House*. . . .

HENDERSON: Would the world today be better off if the war had been prolonged and the Allies had dictated a peace from Berlin?

SHAW (*emphatically*): Good Lord, no! Look at the peace they dictated from Versailles! That was bad enough in all conscience. What more could they have done if they had gone to Berlin but annex Germany? That, if it could have worked at all, might have been better for the Germans, as the motive for plunder would have been broken.

HENDERSON: Is the world today 'safe for democracy'? In a word, do you think that, on the whole, the effects of the war have been beneficial to mankind?

SHAW (*countering*): Do *you* think the effects of the San Francisco earthquake have been beneficial to California as a whole?[6] It demonstrated the stability of steel-framed skyscrapers and shook down great numbers of rotten and unsanitary buildings, besides removing many people who have not been perceptibly missed. Well, the war shook down the Tsardom, an unspeakable abomination, and made an end of the new German Empire and the old Apostolic Austrian one. It settled the Irish question; it gave votes and seats in Parliament to women; and it gave prohibition its dead lift over the final obstacles in your country. It is conceivable that another war, if frightful enough, might even reform our spelling. But if society can be reformed only by the accidental results of horrible catastrophes – if these results are the precise opposite of what was intended by those who brought about the catastrophe – what hope is there for mankind in them? The war was a horror; and everybody is the worse for it except the people who were so narrowly selfish that even a war improved them.

NOTES

1. James Ramsay MacDonald (1866–1937), early Fabian and future Prime Minister, became extremely unpopular because of his sustained criticism of Britain's entry into the war (though he supported efforts to win it). He had resigned from the chairmanship of the Parliamentary Labour group on 5 August 1914.
2. Mary Reid Macarthur (1880–1921), pioneering women's labour organiser, came close to winning the Stourbridge division of Worcestershire for Labour.
3. Field Marshal Sir John French (1852–1925) was Haig's predecessor as Commander-in-Chief on the Western Front. Much more of the prewar study of frontier terrain had in fact been done by Sir Henry Wilson (1864–1922), the linchpin of Anglo-French military cooperation.
4. Admiral of the Fleet John Arbuthnot Fisher (1841–1920), created Baron in 1909, was First Sea Lord in 1903–10 and 1914–15. The mentions of this plan in his *Memories* (London: Hodder & Stoughton, 1919; see pp. 4–5, 33–5 and 182) are less colourful than Shaw's report of them. Recalling Nelson's successful

attack on the Danish fleet at Copenhagen in 1801, Fisher says he urged a 'first-strike' against the German fleet at Kiel in a secret conversation with Edward VII c. 1908.

5. The British liner *Lusitania*, returning to Liverpool, was sunk off the south coast of Ireland by a German torpedo attack on 7 May 1915. Of the 1,959 people on board 1,198 were drowned, including 128 American citizens.

6. San Francisco was devastated by an earthquake in 1906.

Part 8
Earlier Recollections

INTRODUCTION TO PART 8

The recollections in this chapter encompass the period from Shaw's first appearances in London literary, philosophical and political circles in the early 1880s until the mid-1920s. Shaw developed during this time from a pallid, impecunious and rather priggish young man, with a burning zeal for social reform, into a prosperous, world-renowned playwright at the top of his profession, and a public figure whose name was a household word. Despite his controversial views about the First World War, Shaw had become, by the early 1920s, a national institution and popular sage.

The earlier recollections reveal sharp differences in the way in which Shaw was viewed by his contemporaries of this period. Recollections such as those of Samuel Butler and Max Beerbohm show what intense feelings of hostility and irritation Shaw could arouse even after he had reached a high point of popularity as a dramatist. Others, such as William Archer and Gilbert Murray, present strongly favourable accounts; and many recall with delight his wit, humour and spontaneous liveliness. But a strain of ambivalence runs through many of these early accounts of Shaw. Bertrand Russell, in his finely balanced memoir, provides a concise example, in his comment on Shaw that, 'as an iconoclast he was admirable, but as an eikon rather less so'.

'A Tall, Thin Young Man'

HENRY SALT

From 'Salt on Shaw', Appendix I in Stephen Winsten, *Salt and His Circle* (London: Hutchinson, 1951) pp. 205–6, 209, 212, 214–15. Henry Stephens Shakespear Salt (1851–1939), educated at Eton and King's College, Cambridge, taught at his old school for several years before resigning to devote himself to causes he believed in. He was a member of the Fabian and Shelley Societies, founder and secretary of the Humanitarian League, champion of vegetarianism and animals' rights, and a writer on English and American literature. He was introduced to Shaw in about 1880 by James Leigh Joynes (1853–93), a friend from Eton and Cambridge and then his colleague and brother-in-law, a socialist and member of the SDF

who blazed the trail Henry followed away from Eton. Shaw's friendship with
the Salts was particularly warm; his Preface to Winsten's book begins: 'I was
always happy at the Salts.' Winsten showed him Henry's memoir before it was
printed, and his marginal corrections are reproduced below, with Henry's
'incorrect' statements enclosed in square brackets.

[Joynes] introduced to us a tall, thin young man whose
black coat, and somewhat staid, almost penurious appearance, were remembered by us afterwards from their
contrast with the exuberant Jaeger suits that distinguished
the GBS of the nineties. Of his cleverness there could be
no doubt.

From this meeting an intimate friendship resulted; and
from the time when we left Eton, at the end of 1884, for
some fourteen years we saw him very often. He said at a
later date that it was 'the Shelleyan nexus', and our
common admiration of De Quincey, that had chiefly
brought us together; my wife's love of music was another
bond between us, and many were the evenings when he
came to our rooms [in Gloucester Road] for duets.[1] . . .

He lived with his mother, who was a music teacher, in
Fitzroy Square; and we gathered from what he used to tell
us that the household was by no means in affluence. On
one occasion when Mrs Shaw had been away for a week,
and had left him sufficiently provided for that time and no
more, an old [friend] unexpectedly arrived and [claimed
his hospitality, with the result that he was reduced, during
the remaining days, to] a diet of bread and apples. Mrs
Shaw was a charming old lady, full of vivacity and wit;
and it was evident that GBS, in spite of the levity of his
talk, was very fond of her.

flame
underpaid her
cabman, Shaw
tipped him so
handsomely
that for the rest
of the week he
was reduced to

Shaw was never more delightful than when staying with
us in our cottage at Tilford, or later at Oxted; and his
pretended dislike of the country added a zest to his visits.
A very wet weekend at Tilford, with a Sunday walk to
Gallows Hill on Hindhead, gave him a subject for a
lugubrious article in the *Pall Mall Gazette* (28 April 1888),
in which he anathematised the rural life, and brought on
himself a severe reproof from the editor of a Farnham
paper whose strong point was not a sense of humour.[2] . . .

On these visits to the country Shaw would be entirely
natural and unaffected. He was often very tired after his
labours in London; and I have seen him sit at the breakfast-
table with a forlorn expression, turning perhaps the pages

of the Army and Navy Co-operative Society's catalogue, and sadly shaking his head if a remark were made to him. No greater contrast to the GBS on the war-path could have been imagined. We had the real pleasure of seeing that he felt at home. He wrote to me, years after: 'My old visits to Oxted were quite unlike my other experience of the sort, and occupied a place of their own in my life.'[3] In my *Seventy Years among Savages*[4] I have spoken of the exemplary manner in which he played his part in the household duties, such as the 'washing up' after meals. He had his own way of making his bed: no one else might touch it. . . .

I several times accompanied him on day-trips to the homes of Socialist or literary acquaintances. At one, a newly furnished villa in the suburbs, the floors had just been stained by the ladies of the family with bullocks' blood. Shaw said nothing, until the question of a *name* for the house was mooted, when he suggested, with emphasis, 'Goreville'.

Our most notable excursion was when we went to Putney, at the invitation of Mr Watts-Dunton, to a vegetarian lunch at 'The Pines', and there met the author of *Atalanta in Calydon*.[5] On this occasion GBS was recklessly talkative as usual, Swinburne silent and constrained; and the impression left on my mind was that the poet viewed the Socialist with a feeling akin to dismay. . . .

His affectation of a sense of greatness, long before the general public was aware of him, was most entertaining. I heard a lady say to him: 'Shaw, when you are famous —'. He interrupted, with pretended amazement: 'When I am famous!' Asked if he ever read any books, he replied emphatically, 'None'; but immediately continued: 'Except my own; which I read with ever-increasing admiration.' But he was not always thus flattered in private circles. I remember, when he had just written *Candida*, how he read it to a few friends in our rooms, and at the end, as we were giving our various opinions, Edward Carpenter said curtly: 'No, Shaw. It won't do.'[6]

NOTES

1. Shaw described himself at the age of twenty-six as a young man 'full of Darwin and Tyndall, of Shelley and De Quincey, of Michael Angelo and

Beethoven' (*Collected Letters 1898–1910*, p. 476). Salt wrote monographs on Shelley and De Quincey. Kate Salt shared Shaw's interest in Wagner, and their duet-playing is described above (pp. 219–20). After Henry's resignation from Eton, the Salts moved first to a cottage at Tilford, then to a house at Oxted (both in Surrey) and then to rooms in Gloucester Road, London. Shaw was a frequent visitor to all three places in the years before his marriage.

    2. The article was entitled 'A Sunday on the Surrey Hills'. Shaw was criticised when it was reprinted in the *Farnham Herald*, 16 September 1899.

    3. Shaw was writing shortly after Kate Salt's death in February 1919. The letter is given in *Salt and His Circle*, pp. 136–8.

    4. (London: George Allen & Unwin, 1921) p. 75.

    5. *Atalanta in Calydon*, a drama in classical Greek form, had won celebrity for the poet Algernon Charles Swinburne (1837–1909) when it came out in 1865. For the last thirty years of his life Swinburne lived with the critic Theodore Watts-Dunton (1832–1914).

    6. Edward Carpenter (1844–1929), poet and socialist author, after a brief career as a Cambridge don turned to literary work, market gardening and sandal-making on a small farm near Sheffield. He was known as 'the noble savage' in the Salt circle. Shaw described Carpenter and himself as Kate Salt's 'Sunday husbands' (see his Preface to *Salt and His Circle*, pp. 9–10).

'Arrantly Bohemian'

HUBERT BLAND

From Archibald Henderson, 'The Real Bernard Shaw', *Mumsey's Magazine*, January 1908. Hubert Bland describes Shaw's manner of dress in the early days of the Fabian Society, c. 1884.

'When I first knew Bernard Shaw,' said Herbert Bland, the journalist, author, and Fabian, 'his costume was unmistakably, arrantly Bohemian.' We were walking through the gardens of Mr Bland's beautiful place at Eltham, in Kent, awaiting the appearance of his wife, the poet and novelist E. Nesbit. 'Shaw wore a pair of tawny trousers, distinguished for their baggy appearance, a long cutaway coat which had once been black, but was then a dingy green, cuffs which he was now and then compelled, cruel though it was, to trim to the quick, and a tall silk hat, which had been battered down so often that it had a thousand creases in it from top to crown. Ah, that was a wonderful hat!' Mr Bland laughed heartily over the recollection, 'Shaw had to turn it around when he put it on, because it was broken in the middle, and if he wore it in the usual way it would fall limply together when removed from his head.'

At Fitzroy Square

SYDNEY OLIVIER

From a letter by Lord Olivier to Archibald Henderson, 8 June 1931, in Henderson, *Bernard Shaw, Playboy and Prophet* (London and New York: D. Appleton, 1932) p. 212. Olivier recalls the later 1880s, when he was a clerk in the Colonial Office.

I was at this time employed in a Downing Street public office in which clerks of my privileged class began their work at the aristocratic hour of 11 a.m. (We did *not* leave at 5 p.m.!); and on my walk down to Westminster from my North London lodgings I frequently dropped in at the house in Fitzroy Square (No. 29) where Shaw lived with his mother, acquaintance with whom was as delightful and invigorating as his own society. Shaw, after his early morning labours at the office of T. P. O'Connor's *Star*, used to be breakfasting about that time, and I could not resist partaking greedily of the extremely delicious wholemeal bread and butter, with chocolate, on which he discriminatingly supported himself.

Caliban and the Philharmonic Society

KATHARINE TYNAN

From Katharine Tynan, *Twenty-Five Years: Reminiscences* (London: Smith, Elder, 1913) p. 313. Katharine Tynan (1861–1931), Irish novelist and poet, visited England for four months in the summer and early autumn of 1889. She was probably introduced to the Morris circle by W. B. Yeats.

Another day in that September I went down and had tea with May Morris in the garden of Kelmscott House, where she sat under a big mulberry tree in the old garden which was rapidly being built in. George Bernard Shaw's mother joined us at tea. Like her son, she was very witty, very satirical, and yet neither wit nor satire left anything painful behind. You were amused: you laughed when the rapier flashed in your eyes: afterwards you felt it was sword-play, with neither intention nor desire to wound. I remember that she expressed strong Irish Protestant sentiments, which were perhaps hardly well-founded. The meeting brought me back five years to the first time I saw and heard Bernard Shaw at a meeting of the Browning Society, when my neighbour whispered to me that he was very brilliant and had a great future. I can only remember that he discussed 'Caliban upon Setebos', and his remarking that if Caliban was now alive he would belong to the Philharmonic Society.[1]

NOTE

1. At this meeting of the Browning Society, held on 25 April 1884, Shaw spoke after the Positivist author James Cotter Morison (1832–88) had delivered a paper on Browning's 'Caliban upon Setebos'.

'Such wit as we had never heard'

ROGER FRY

From *Letters of Roger Fry*, ed. Denys Sutton, 2 vols (continuous pagination) (London: Chatto & Windus, 1972) vol. II, pp. 633–4. The following is a draft of a letter to Shaw written by Fry c. 1928.

It must be about forty years since I first met you at Cambridge when you came to lecture on Socialism.[1] I was an aspiring first or second year man excessively proud of being asked to lunch to meet so terrific a figure. I looked upon the distinctly satanic aureole which then shone round you with dreadful veneration. I felt the awful delight of one daring to participate in forbidden mysteries. I remember that you dazzled us not only with such wit as we had never heard but with your stupendous experience of the coulisses of the social scene on which we were beginning to peer timidly and with some anxiety. All my friends were already convinced that social service of some kind was the only end worth pursuing in life. I alone cherished as a guilty secret a profound scepticism about all political activity and even about progress itself and

haw and Edward McNulty, 1874 (the earliest photograph of Shaw) (T. McKay and Co.)

2. William Archer (photograph by Shaw)

3. Beatrice Webb (photograph by Shaw)

4a. Shaw on the Stump, January 1900 (British Library)

4b. Shaw at sea, c. 1905 (British Library)

5. W. B. Yeats (British Library)

6. Lady Gregory (British Library)

7. Lillah McCarthy, as Ann Whitefield, 1905 (Victoria and Albert Museum)

8. Crowd leaving a performance of *Pygmalion*, April 1914 (Victoria and Albert Museum)

Shaw, aged sixty (British Library)

10a. Shaw aboard the *Empress of Britannia*, 1931 (British Library)

10b. Shaw at Pompeii, 1932 (British Library)

10c. Shaw in Russia, 1931 (British Library)

11. Portrait by Augustus John, 1915 (Mrs Vivien White/Fitzwilliam Museum, Cambridge)

12. Virginia Woolf, 1902 (National Portrait Gallery)

13a. (*right*) Esmé Percy (British Library)

13b. (*below*) Sybil Thorndike as Saint Joan and R. Horton as Dunois, 1924

14a. (*above*) Shaw with his new Rolls-Royce, 1935 (T. McKay and Co.)

14b. (*below*) Shaw with Gabriel Pascal, in the garden at Ayot St Lawrence (T. McKay and Co.)

15. Shaw on the balcony at Whitehall Court (T. McKay and Co.)

16. Lady Astor with Shaw on his 73rd birthday (T. McKay and Co.)

had begun to think of art as somehow my only possible job. I like to recall my feelings when that afternoon you explained incidentally that you had 'gone into' the subject of art and there was nothing in it. It was all hocus-pocus. I was far too deeply impressed by you to formulate any denial even in my own mind; I just shelved it for the time being. Those were the first experiences of your shockingness. My next was when I had gone back for two very uncomfortable years to the parental hearth – a peculiarly flamboyant and tediously pretentious one in the Bayswater Road. I met you on a bus going eastward from that desirable region and you took the occasion to explain to me what a colossal farce British Justice was. Up to then my respect for my father had led me to take his word for it that nothing so pure as British Justice had ever been known on earth.[2] Again I shelved it, and if in the intervening forty years I have been led to think you were quite wrong about art these have taught me how right you were about British Justice, which at the time had seemed to me an almost wilful paradox. So in those forty years I seem to have always been disagreeing with you and sometimes converted; sometimes my heart has been hardened – yes, I daresay I disagree more than ever but none of all this has ever interfered with my feelings to you as a man.

NOTES

1. In February 1888; see above, pp. 56–7.
2. Fry's father, Sir Edward Fry (1827–1918), was a distinguished jurist who held the posts of Judge of the High Court, Chancery Division, and Lord Justice of Appeal.

'A Group of Qualities'

BEATRICE WEBB

From *The Diary of Beatrice Webb*, vol. II: *1892–1905*, ed. Norman and Jeanne MacKenzie (London: Virago, 1983) pp. 36–7, 355–6. Beatrice Webb's earliest attempt to describe Shaw, dated 17 September 1893, was written at The Argoed, at the end of a holiday which Shaw had partly shared while helping to revise the Webbs' *History of Trade Unionism*. It is here juxtaposed with an extract from an entry some twelve years later (14 October 1905).

Bernard Shaw I know less well than Graham Wallas, though he is quite as old a friend of Sidney's. Marvellously smart witty fellow with a crank for not making money, except he can make it exactly as he pleases. Persons with no sense of humour regard him as a combined Don Juan and a professional blasphemer of the existing order. An artist to the tips of his fingers and an admirable *craftsman*. I have never known a man use his pen in such a workmanlike fashion or acquire such a thoroughly technical knowledge of any subject upon which he gives an opinion. But his technique in specialism never overpowers him – he always translates it into epigram, sparkling generalisation or witty personalities. As to his character, I do not understand it. He has been for twelve years a devoted propagandist, hammering away at the ordinary routine of Fabian Executive work with as much persistence as Wallas or Sidney. He is an excellent friend – at least to men – but beyond this I know nothing. I am inclined to think that he has a 'slight' personality – agile, graceful and even virile, but lacking in *weight*. Adored by many women, he is a born philanderer – a 'Soul', so to speak – disliking to be hampered either by passions or by conventions and therefore always tying himself up into knots which have to be cut before he is free for another adventure. Vain is he? A month ago I should have said that vanity was the bane of his nature. Now I am not so sure that the vanity itself is not part of the *mise en scène* – whether, in fact, it is not part of the character he imagines himself to be playing in the world's comedy. A vegetarian, fastidious but unconventional in his clothes, six foot in height with a lithe, broad-chested figure and laughing blue eyes. Above all a brilliant talker, and, therefore, a delightful companion. To my mind he is not yet a *personality*; he is merely a pleasant, though somewhat incongruous, group of qualities. Some people would call him a cynic – he is really an *Idealist* of the purest water (see his *Quintessence of Ibsenism* and his plays).

The smart world is tumbling over one another in the worship of GBS, and even we have a sort of reflected glory as his intimate friends. It is interesting to note that the completeness of his self-conceit will save him from the worst kind of deterioration – he is proof against flattery. Where it will injure him is in isolating him from serious intercourse with intimate friends working in other departments of life. Whenever he is free there is such a crowd of journalists and literary hangers-on around him that one feels it is kinder to spare him one's company, and that will be the instinct of many of his old friends engaged in administration, investigation or propaganda.

What a transformation scene from those first years I knew him: the scathing bitter opponent of wealth and leisure, and now! the adored one of the smartest and most cynical set of English Society.

Sartorial Shaw

AUGUSTIN HAMON

From Augustin Hamon, *The Twentieth Century Molière*, trans. Eden and Cedar Paul (London: George Allen & Unwin, 1916) pp. 88–90. Augustin Hamon (1862–1945) was a French socialist author who at Shaw's insistence became his French translator in 1904. *The Twentieth Century Molière*, a study of Shaw and his work, was first published in Paris in 1913. Here Hamon begins by describing Shaw's appearance when they met in 1894.

Twenty years ago, when I first made his acquaintance at the house of a mutual friend, a member of the Fabian Society, Shaw's pointed beard and his hair, parted in the middle, were of a light red colour. His deep-set eyes were blue, clear and merry, sometimes glinting like steel when he fixed his gaze upon you and seemed to search the bottom of your soul; his forehead was wide, lofty, straight; he had an almost persistent, sardonic smile; all this combined to give him a singularly mephistophelian expression. His face was pale, and since then has paled yet more, while his beard has become grey, softening the irony of his expression. His hand is long, with taper fingers, rather small for a man of his height.

In 1894 Shaw was no longer extremely poor; . . . He dressed . . . with an eye at once to comfort, hygiene and artistic considerations, as did his friends and rivals in Socialism and literature. He wore a soft shirt, unstarched, saying, 'I prefer this to a white breast-plate covered with a filthy layer of glazed starch'.

His necktie was usually of a soft green, brown or red. He wore a suit of brown tweeds of loose and easy cut, harmonising in tint with his shirt and necktie, with his broad-brimmed soft felt hat, also brown, and with his brown boots with massive soles, intended, he tells us, not for mountaineering, but 'for the hard floors of the London galleries' and for the London pavements, since he was a great walker. . . . In 1906, when he visited Paris to sit to Rodin for his bust, he wore a fine-spun golden brown suit. With his soft cream-coloured shirt and his dull-green tie, the effect was that of a symphony in brown, forming an artistic and agreeable contrast to the pallor of his face and the grizzled red of his hair and beard.

'Easiest of Visitors'

LADY MARGARET OLIVIER

From a letter by Lord Olivier to Archibald Henderson, 8 June 1931, in Henderson, *Bernard Shaw, Playboy and Prophet* (London and New York: D. Appleton, 1932) p. 787. Sydney Olivier married Margaret Cox in 1885: they had four daughters. He enclosed in a letter of his own these reminiscences by his wife, which probably belong to the 1890s.

Mr Shaw was very popular with my children. I remember when we were living at Limpsfield in Surrey, returning one day from a walk to find him sitting on the grass, resigned and patient, amid several aggressive children who, he declared, had been beating him with drain pipes.

And another scene I remember. I think he had been with us for the night and I, having to go out, had left him, as I hoped, to spend a quiet morning. On returning I heard music in the house, and going into the room I found him seated at the piano with children on each side pressing as close against him as they could and all together singing loudly and cheerfully the ballad of 'Barbara Allen'. They were steadily working through our *Old English Song Book*.

He was one of the kindest and easiest of visitors. One Sunday evening (my nurse, I suppose, being absent) he quickly noticed that, he being there, I was wondering how to get up to put the children to bed, and solved the difficulty at once by saying: 'Well now I think you would like to get rid of us for a little while – we'll stroll down and see the Peases' – and he carried my husband off to see our neighbours.[1] Blessed tact! And on similar occasions he would insist on washing up after supper.

NOTE

1. 'The Peases' were the family of Edward Reynolds Pease (1857–1955), one of the founders of the Fabian Society, Secretary from 1890 to 1913 and author of *The History of the Fabian Society* (1916).

'A liking that has lasted'

H. G. WELLS

From H. G. Wells, *Experiment in Autobiography: Discoveries and Conclusions of a Very Ordinary Brain (since 1866)*, 2 vols (London: Victor Gollancz and the Cresset Press, 1934) vol. II, pp. 539–41. The 'eventful evening' to which Wells refers was the first night of Henry James's *Guy Domville* at the St James's Theatre on 5 January 1895. Shaw was there for the *Saturday Review*, and Wells for the *Pall Mall Gazette*. The play was a complete failure, though Shaw wrote sympathetically about some aspects of it in his review (see Shaw, *Our Theatres in the Nineties* [London: Constable, 1948] I, 6–9).

On that eventful evening I scraped acquaintance with another interesting contemporary, Bernard Shaw. I had known him by sight since the Hammersmith days[1] but I had never spoken to him before. Fires and civil commotions loosen tongues. I accosted him as a *Saturday Review* colleague[2] and we walked back to our respective lodgings northward while he talked very interestingly about the uproar we had left behind us and the place of the fashionable three-act play amidst the eternal verities. He laid particular stress on the fact that nobody in the audience and hardly any of the caste [*sic*], had realised the grace of Henry James's language.

Shaw was then a slender young man of thirty-five or so,[3] very hard-up, and he broke the ranks of the boiled shirts and black and white ties in the stalls, with a modest brown jacket suit, a very white face and very red whiskers. (Now he has a very red face and very white whiskers, but it is still the same Shaw.) He talked like an elder brother to me in that agreeable Dublin English of his. I liked him with a liking that has lasted a life-time. In those days he was just a brilliant essayist and critic and an exasperating speaker in Socialist gatherings. He had written some novels that no one thought anything of, and his plays were still a secret between himself and his God.[4]

From that time onward I saw him intermittently, but I did not see very much of him until I went into the Fabian Society, six or seven years later. Then he was a man in the forties and a much more important figure. He was married and he was no longer impecunious. His opinions and attitudes had developed and matured and so had mine. We found ourselves antagonistic on a number of issues and though we were not quite enough in the same field nor near enough in age to be rivals, there was from my side at any rate, a certain emulation between us.

We were both atheists and socialists; we were both attacking an apparently fixed and invincible social system from the outside; but this much resemblance did not prevent our carrying ourselves with a certain sustained defensiveness towards each other that remains to this day. In conversational intercourse a man's conclusions are of less importance than his training and the way he gets to them, and in this respect chasms of difference yawned between Shaw and myself, wider even than those that separated me from Henry James. I have tried to set out my own formal and informal education in a previous chapter. Shaw had had no such sustained and constructive mental training as I had been through, but on the other hand he had been saturated from his youth up in good music, brilliant conversation and the appreciative treatment of life. Extreme physical sensibility had forced him to adopt an austere teetotal and vegetarian way of living, and early circumstances, of which Ireland was not the least, had inclined him to rebellion and social protest; but otherwise he was as distinctly over against me and on the aesthetic side of life as Henry James. To him, I guess, I have always appeared heavily and sometimes formidably facty and close-set; to me his judgements, arrived at by feeling and expression, have always had a flimsiness. I want to get hold of Fact, strip off her inessentials, and, if she behaves badly put her in stays and irons; but Shaw dances round her and weaves a wilful veil of confident assurances about her as her true presentment. He thinks one can 'put things over' on Fact and I do not. He philanders with her. I have no delusions about the natural goodness and wisdom of human beings and at bottom I am grimly and desperately educational. But Shaw's conception of education is to let dear old Nature rip. He has got no farther in that respect than Rousseau. Then I know, fundamentally, the heartless impartiality of natural causation, but Shaw makes Evolution something brighter and softer, by endowing it with an ultimately benevolent Life Force, acquired, quite uncritically I feel, from his friend and adviser Samuel Butler. We have been fighting this battle with each other all our lives.

NOTES

1. In his student days Wells had attended William Morris's Sunday evening meetings in Hammersmith, at which Shaw was a frequent speaker (see above, pp. 54–6, and *Experiment in Autobiography*, I, 238–9).
2. Wells had been engaged to review novels for the *Saturday Review* in 1894.
3. Shaw was thirty-eight at the time of his meeting with Wells.
4. *Widowers' Houses* and *Arms and the Man* had both been produced before this time.

'Pleasures of the Intellect'

GILBERT MURRAY

From Gilbert Murray, 'A Few Memories', *Drama*, Spring 1951.

Shaw . . . retained for me that peculiar halo which seems to surround the friends of one's real youth. I knew him first when I was in my early twenties and he in his thirties, an amazing young man with a red beard, bold views on music and philosophy and most other subjects, and a number of plays which no prudent manager would produce. What hopes we had then, and what ideas! We were both teetotallers, both vegetarians, both great 'world-changers', to use a recent keyword of Shaw's, but, unlike other world-changers, neither of us at all noticeably grumbly or unamiable.

He advised me once about a play of mine, *Carlyon Sahib*.[1] I had sent it for an opinion to William Archer, and he showed it to Shaw. Archer had suggested some re-writing; Shaw differed. 'No, no; what's the good of re-writing? It is a good play with bad parts, as it is. So are all good plays! No. Write another and another; when you have written a dozen, you'll know ever so much more about it.' How like him!

I saw a good deal of him at Fabian meetings, and still more during the Vedrenne–Barker management at the Court Theatre, when Euripides and Shaw and St John Hankin and Galsworthy filled the bill month by month.[2] He was, of course, a beautiful producer. No rehearsal was ever stale or dull. He never spared people's feelings and never hurt them either, because he somehow established an atmosphere in which one knew that all the worst was openly said, and nothing but friendliness and good will left behind. . . .

Shaw was never much of a democrat. He was a fastidious intellectual, but of course of an Irish type. I have known few people whose pleasures were so almost exclusively pleasures of the intellect. What he liked was conversation, wit, imagination, a new idea, a new experience, a new book of philosophy, and of course a good deal of music and a little poetry. Give him those, and he was content. He wanted no particular sensual pleasures, and even pains did not distract him much. I once went to see him at Hindhead when he was covered with bruises owing to a particularly bad fall downstairs.[3] I thought he would be in bed; but no, they told me: he was in the garden. I looked about and heard a distant chuckle. There he was in a hammock, writing away, wrapped in bruises and bandages, and chuckling gaily at the result. His wit and humour were real and inexhaustible. The great majority of comedians have not quite enough real wit to carry them through; when it runs thin they eke it out with a bit of indecency or perhaps spite, and get their laugh with most audiences. But Shaw, though he speaks freely of everything, never falls back on such mean second bests. Has there ever been a satirist so free from personal malice?

He would make violent political attacks, of course, and denounce innocent public men as fools or villains. But that was for public reasons, and, when charged with intolerance, he made the surprising answer: 'Who am I that I should be just?' This is not so absurd as it sounds. He never wrote as a judge, always as an accuser or an advocate. He attacked the things he considered wrong, showed them up as ridiculous, illogical, oppressive; he vividly over-stated his case against them. It was for others to pronounce judgement. I once came away with him from hearing a speech of Sir Edward Grey's. It had been just in Grey's manner; a moderate, unadorned, fair and absolutely convincing statement. Shaw thought it very poor indeed.[4] It had none of the qualities that he valued; no wit, no eloquence, no happy phrase, no new point of view or illuminating paradox. It was, in fact, the just judge speaking, not the brilliant advocate.

NOTES

1. Shaw saw the play in manuscript early in 1895; it was published in 1900.

2. A production of the *Hippolytus* of Euripides in Murray's version inaugurated the Vedrenne–Barker seasons at the Court Theatre in October 1904. Two more of his Euripides translations, *Electra* and *The Trojan Women*, were staged later. St John Hankin (1869–1909), journalist and playwright, had *The Return of the Prodigal* and *The Charity that began at Home* produced, while John Galsworthy (1867–1933), novelist and playwright, contributed *The Silver Box*.

3. Murray was probably referring to the accident at Haslemere on 17 June 1898, when Shaw fell from his crutches down the stairs and broke an arm. However, the Shaws did not move to nearby Hindhead until November.

4. Shaw was hostile to Grey and deeply suspicious of his motives; Murray, on the other hand, produced a reasoned defence in *The Foreign Policy of Sir Edward Grey 1906–1915* (Oxford: Oxford University Press, 1915).

'Dissatisfaction'

SAMUEL BUTLER

From *Samuel Butler's Notebooks: Selections*, ed. Geoffrey Keynes and Brian Hill (London: Jonathan Cape, 1951) pp. 45–6. Henry Salt wrote of the 'almost filial respect' with which Shaw treated Butler, his mentor on evolutionary theory (see Stephen Winsten, *Salt and His Circle* [London: Hutchinson, 1951] p. 216, and cf. Bertrand Russell's comments below, p. 279). Shaw also gave Butler practical help by introducing him in 1901 to Grant Richards, who later that year published the satirical fantasy *Erewhon Revisited*, as well as a revised edition of its predecessor *Erewhon*. In 1903, after Butler's death, Shaw assisted Richards with the publication of *The Way of All Flesh*, Butler's autobiographical novel. However, the following note, set down on 2 January 1897, indicates that Shaw's admiration was scarcely reciprocated.

I have long been repelled by this man though at the same time attracted by his coruscating power. Emery Walker once brought him up to see me, on the score that he was a great lover of Handel. He did nothing but cry down Handel and cry up Wagner. I did not like him and am sure that neither did he like me.

Still at the Fabian Society when I had delivered my lecture – 'Was the *Odyssey* written by a Woman?'[1] – (not, heaven forbid, that I belong to or have any sympathy with the Fabian Society) he got up at once and said that when he had heard of my title first he supposed it was some mere fad or fancy of mine, but that on turning to the *Odyssey* to see what had induced me to take it up, he had not read a hundred lines before he found himself saying, 'Why, of course it is a woman'. He spoke so strongly that people who had only laughed with me all through my lecture began to think there might be something in it after all. Still, there is something uncomfortable about the man which makes him uncongenial to me.

The dislike – no this is too strong a word – the dissatisfaction with which he impressed me has been increased by his articles in the *Saturday Review* since it has been under Frank Harris's management – brilliant, amusing, and often sound though many of them have been. His cult of Ibsen disgusts me, and my displeasure has been roused to such a pitch as to have led me to this note, by his article 'Better than Shakespeare' in this morning's *Saturday Review*.[2] Of course Bunyan is better than Shakespeare in some respects, so is Bernard Shaw himself, so am I, so

is everybody. Of course also Bunyan is one of our very foremost classics –
but I cannot forgive Bernard Shaw for sneering at Shakespeare as he
has done this morning. If he means it, there is no trusting his judgement –
if he does not mean it I have no time to waste on such trifling. If Shaw
embeds his plums in such a cake as this, they must stay there. I cannot
trouble to pick them out.

NOTES

1. Butler's lecture was given before some twenty Fabians in Graham Wallas's
rooms on 24 April 1893. Shaw was in the chair.
2. Shaw's provocative article says of Shakespeare: 'All that you miss in
Shakespeare you find in Bunyan, to whom the true heroic came quite obviously
and naturally' (*Saturday Review*, 2 January 1897; collected in Shaw, *Our Theatres
in the Nineties* [London: Constable, 1948] III, 2).

'A Cold Man'

MAX BEERBOHM

From S. N. Behrman, *Conversations with Max* (London: Hamish Hamilton, 1960)
pp. 19–21, 162. (Sir) Max Beerbohm (1872–1956), caricaturist, essayist, critic and
novelist, succeeded Shaw as theatre critic for the *Saturday Review* in May 1898.
In 1910 he settled in Italy at Rapallo, where the American playwright S. N.
Behrman (1893–1973) visited him a number of times in the last four years of his
life. All but the last paragraph below dates from their first meeting in June 1952.

'Well, he had a powerful brain, don't you know, but he was a cold
man,' Max said. 'It's true I never had anything but kindness from him.
Though I had written, in the *Saturday*, several sharply critical articles
about him, it was Shaw who, in the absence of Frank Harris – Harris
was on holiday, or whatever, in Athens – approved Runciman's[1] slipping
me in, rather, to the post of drama critic. Shaw was not vindictive.
There was no element of vindictiveness in him. This is an admirable
quality. In his case, it may have emanated, don't you know, from his
absolute conviction – a conviction so manifest that it did not require
assertion – that there was no one living who was worthy of his animosity.
He was – Max paused on the brink of an epithet, then decided to take
the plunge. 'He was a coarse man. I remember his inviting me to lunch
in his flat at Adelphi Terrace to meet Mark Twain. Barrie was there,

three or four others. At the end of a very agreeable lunch, Shaw jumped up, said he had an appointment with his dentist, and rushed off, leaving us alone with his guest. It was somewhat embarrassing, don't you know. Might he not have told us in advance that he had an engagement, so that we should be prepared?[2] In his plays, I really enjoy only his stage directions; the dialogue is vertical and, I find, fatiguing. It is like being harangued; it is like being a member of one of those crowds he used to exhort on street corners. He uses the English language like a truncheon. It is an instrument of attack, don't you know. No light and shade, no poetry. His best work, I think, appears in his books of drama and music criticism and his stage directions. When I was living with my mother and sisters in London – I had just come down from Oxford – Shaw made an immense journey by bicycle to see me, because he had heard that I had done some caricatures. He came to be caricatured. I had indeed done some caricatures, I was beginning to achieve a little reputation as a caricaturist, but I hadn't really, at that time, done anything very good, you know. Still, Shaw would rather have had a presentment by anybody, no matter how incompetent, no matter how malicious, than no presentment at all.[3] One day, I visited Madame Tussaud's, in preparation for an essay I was writing on that gruesome establishment. To my astonishment, I was confronted by the waxen effigy of GBS.[4] A few days later, I dined with him and twitted him about it. He rather flushed with embarrassment, don't you know, but he said that Madame Tussaud had wished to add him to her chamber of horrors and that he felt that it would be snobbish to refuse. Considering that it was the proudest day of his life, I think his account of it was rather touching, don't you? Shaw was not, in those early days, very attractive – dead white, and his face was pitted by some disease. The back of his neck was especially bleak – very long, untenanted, dead white. His hair was like seaweed. In those days, you were lucky not to see GBS from the back. But in later years, with that wonderful white beard, he became very handsome and impressive-looking. In a day when *everybody* carried a walking-stick, I used to see him, in Hampstead, strolling *without* a walking stick, just to be conspicuous. Instead, he was eternally accompanied by female Fabians in jibbahs[5] and amber beads. When he died, he stipulated that his ashes be sprinkled among the roses in the garden at Ayot.' Max leaned forward, in distress. 'Imagine! Among the *roses!*' It took Max a moment to get over this affront to the roses, and then he went on, as if in explanation, 'GBS had no sense of beauty. That is why he couldn't appreciate Henry Irving. One night at dinner at Philip Sassoon's,[6] I found myself sitting next to Mrs Shaw. GBS was a safe distance down the table, don't you know, and I ventured to say this to her. After spraying GBS with every variety of praise, I murmured, "But you know, Charlotte, GBS has no aesthetic sense. He is not an artist." She leapt at this! She said that she was always telling GBS that. She said that what he *really* was was a reformer.'

Max . . . found less understandable than anything else about Shaw his remark when he was asked whether he missed any of his contemporaries who had died. 'No,' said Shaw. 'I miss only the man I was.' Max's comment on this was 'When I think of the gay and delightful people he knew . . .'. He shook his head in bewilderment. Prophets with idiosyncrasies like Shaw's couldn't, for Max, prophesy anything good.

NOTES

1. John F. Runciman (1866–1916), a Fabian, was music critic and Harris's deputy on the *Saturday Review*.

2. Mark Twain (Samuel Clemens, 1835–1910), who came to England in 1907 to receive an honorary degree at Oxford. Shaw had been introduced to him by Archibald Henderson when they arrived at St Pancras Station on 17 June. The Shaws' lunch took place on 3 July. Later on the same day Shaw wrote to Clemens explaining his sudden departure as follows: 'Just a line to excuse myself for running away today. A domestic bargain was made to the effect that I should not keep you to myself; so I cleared out to give Charlotte and Max a good turn. I had my reward at the dentist's' (*Collected Letters 1898–1910*, p. 697).

3. In fact Shaw became one of Beerbohm's favourite subjects: he produced over forty caricatures of him, as well as a number of others in which he was a subsidiary figure. The earliest were published in 1896.

4. Beerbohm's essay 'Madame Tussaud's', written in 1897, does not mention the effigy of Shaw.

5. Jibbah is an Egyptian form of Arabic jubbah, a long-sleeved cloth coat worn in Muslim countries.

6. Sir Philip Sassoon, 3rd Bt (1888–1939), politician, connoisseur and trustee of the National and other galleries.

Twain and Shaw

MARION BARTON

From a letter by Marion Barton to the *New York Times*, 19 April 1933, reprinted in the *Independent Shavian*, Spring 1972. Shaw's speech in the Metropolitan Opera House, New York, on 11 April 1933 drew forth this recollection from an American lady who had visited the House of Commons in the summer of 1907.

Down below us in the pit Campbell-Bannerman[1] graciously fumed and thumped away at his pet theme, abolition of the House of Lords (even four years of Armageddon failed to abolish the Lords). Joseph Chamberlain hammered wedges into his favourite obsession, world-wide free trade. And the bored Irishmen, abetted by John Burns, sprawled insolently, their feet crossed on the tops of the chairbacks in front of them, and yawned or booed or nonchalantly stroked their flaming red four-in-hands, conspicuous as flags.

Suddenly a little bell rang in my brain. A thrill passed around the sombre old chambers as if switched on by a powerful button. And over there opposite the ladies' cage into the men's gallery ambled a pair of stringbeans – Mark Twain and Bernard Shaw.

Both gaunt frames elegantly togged in white flannels, both ascetic faces set in a bush of floppy white hair, only then Shaw's was still streaked with enough red to look washed-out-sandy. And there in the front row they lolled – sentient, alert, sublime as gods. As the drone of inanities from the pit below wafted up to them they too began to fidget. First they nudged each other. Next they chuckled. Then their pallid faces flushed. Presently, like toy balloons, their cheeks puffed out with tight-lipped laughter. And then they exploded and sat there quaking with uncontrollable, silent merriment.

NOTE

1. (Sir) Henry Campbell-Bannerman (1836–1908), reformist Liberal politician, had been Prime Minister since December 1905.

Iconoclast and Eikon

BERTRAND RUSSELL

From Bertrand Russell, *Portraits from Memory and Other Essays* (London: George Allen & Unwin, 1956) pp. 71–5, 100. Despite his claim to have first met Shaw at the 1896 International Socialist Congress (held in St Martin's Hall, London, between 28 July and 1 August) there was an earlier meeting when they were on holiday with the Webbs in Monmouth in September 1895. (For Shaw's version of their bicycle smash then, see *Collected Letters 1874–1897*, pp. 558–9.) He is unlikely to have heard of Shaw before publication of *The Quintessence of Ibsenism* in September 1891 (although it was based on a paper read to the Fabian Society on 18 July 1890).

I heard of him first in 1890, when I, as a Freshman, met another Freshman who admired his *Quintessence of Ibsenism*, but I did not meet him until 1896 when he took part in an International Socialist Congress in London. I knew a great many of the German delegates, as I had been studying German Social Democracy. They regarded Shaw as an incarnation of Satan, because he could not resist the pleasure of fanning the flames whenever there was a dispute. I, however, derived my view of him from the Webbs, and admired his Fabian essay in which he set to work to lead British socialism away from Marx.[1] He was at this time still shy. Indeed, I think that his wit, like that of many famous humorists, was developed as a defence against expected hostile ridicule. At this time he was just beginning to write plays, and he came to my flat to read one of them to a small gathering of friends. He was white and trembling with nervousness, and not at all the formidable figure that he became later. Shortly afterwards, he and I stayed with the Webbs in Monmouthshire while he was learning the technique of the drama. He would write the names of all his characters on little squares of paper, and, when he was doing a scene, he would put on a chess board in front of him the names of the characters who were on the stage in that scene.

At this time he and I were involved in a bicycle accident, which I feared for a moment might have brought his career to a premature close. He was only just learning to ride a bicycle, and he ran into my machine with such force that he was hurled through the air and landed on his back twenty feet from the place of the collision. However, he got up completely unhurt and continued to ride. Whereas my bicycle was smashed, and I had to return by train. It was a very slow train, and at every station Shaw with his bicycle appeared on the platform, put his head into the carriage and jeered. I suspect that he regarded the whole incident as proof of the virtues of vegetarianism. . . .

Shaw's attack on Victorian humbug and hypocrisy was as beneficent as it was delightful, and for this the English undoubtedly owe him a debt of gratitude. It was a part of Victorian humbug to endeavour to conceal vanity. When I was young, we all made a show of thinking no better of ourselves than of our neighbours. Shaw found this effort wearisome, and had already given it up when he first burst upon the world. It used to be the custom among clever people to say that Shaw was not unusually vain, but only unusually candid. I came to think later on that this was a mistake. Two incidents at which I was present convinced me of this. The first was a luncheon in London in honour of Bergson,[2] to which Shaw had been invited as an admirer, along with a number of professional philosophers whose attitude to Bergson was more critical. Shaw set to work to expound Bergson's philosophy in the style of the Preface to *Methuselah*.[3] In this version, the philosophy was hardly one to recommend itself to professionals, and Bergson mildly interjected, 'Ah, no-o! It is not qvite zat!' But Shaw was quite unabashed, and replied, 'Oh, my dear fellow, I understand your philosophy much better than you do.' Bergson clenched his fists and nearly exploded with rage; but, with a great effort, he controlled himself, and Shaw's expository monologue continued. . . .

Shaw, like many witty men, considered wit an adequate substitute for wisdom. He could defend any idea, however silly, so cleverly as to make those who did not accept it look like fools. I met him once at an 'Erewhon Dinner' in honour of Samuel Butler and I learnt with surprise that he accepted as gospel every word uttered by that sage, and even theories that were only intended as jokes, as, for example, that the *Odyssey* was written by a woman. Butler's influence on Shaw was much greater than most people realised. It was from him that Shaw acquired his antipathy to Darwin, which afterwards made him an admirer of Bergson. . . .

Shaw had many qualities which deserve great admiration. He was completely fearless. He expressed his opinions with equal vigour whether they were popular or unpopular. He was merciless towards those who deserve no mercy – but sometimes, also, to those who did not deserve to be his victims. In sum, one may say that he did much good and some harm. As an iconoclast he was admirable, but as an eikon rather less so. . . .

I once remarked to Shaw that Webb seemed to me somewhat deficient in kindly feeling. 'No,' Shaw replied, 'you are quite mistaken. Webb and I were once in a tram car in Holland eating biscuits out of a bag. A handcuffed criminal was brought into the tram by policemen. All the other passengers shrank away in horror, but Webb went up to the prisoner and offered him biscuits.' I remember this story whenever I find myself becoming unduly critical of either Webb or Shaw.

NOTES

1. Russell must have been thinking of Shaw's second contribution to the 1889 *Fabian Essays*, 'The Transition to Social Democracy', with its advocacy of gradual rather than violent change.

2. This incident seems rather to have taken place at an evening meeting of the Aristotelian Society in October 1911. At the time Russell was working on a paper on the French philosopher Henri Bergson (1859–1941), with whose ideas he had little sympathy.

3. Shaw's Preface to *Back to Methuselah* (1921) contains a popular exposition of ideas on creative evolution, mainly based on Lamarck and Samuel Butler, in which Bergson's *élan vital* is equated with the Life Force.

Advice to School Children

RICHARD LE GALLIENNE

From Richard Le Gallienne, *The Romantic '90s* (London: G. P. Putnam's Sons, 1926) pp. 143–6. Richard Le Gallienne (1866–1947), man of letters and poet, was book reviewer for the *Star* when his *English Poems* came out in 1892. Shaw was pressed to review the volume for his old paper and to Le Gallienne's chagrin he slated it. Le Gallienne places the following incident 'at the time we were neighbours at Hindhead', where the Shaws lived from November 1898 to August 1899.

The tiny schoolhouse there was presided over by an accomplished lady, herself with a pretty wit, who was anxious to interest her children in the wild life of the surrounding countryside, and had, therefore, got up a juvenile natural history club, which she asked Mr Shaw to address. Happening to meet Mr Shaw during the afternoon, he invited me to go with him to the meeting, to give him my moral support, he said; for he pretended, incredible as it may sound, to be nervous, as, in fact, I am inclined to think he really was. Inured to all manner of audiences, hostile, indifferent and devoted, he had never yet talked to boys and girls. What on earth was he to say to them? As we entered the little schoolroom he noticed on the wall one of those game-preservation notices, giving particulars of the 'close' periods, during which no one might hunt certain birds and beasts, under heavy penalties. Mr Shaw detached the notice from the wall, and, when the schoolmistress had duly introduced him to his quite infantile audience, he rose with it in his hands. He began by reading certain passages. Then, turning to the children, he remarked that probably they had got the idea from what he had read that the grown-up people made such laws because of their great love for animals, because they couldn't bear the thought of their being killed. Nothing of the sort, my dear children, proceeded the arch-rebel against social hypocrisies, nothing of the sort! Their real meaning was, he continued, that they wanted you and me – and he adopted a confidential tone, as, so to say, a fellow youngster with themselves – to leave the birds, and rabbits, and other wild things alone, so that when the shooting season commenced there would be all the more of them – for the grown-ups to shoot! It was not because they loved animals – but because they liked shooting them! This was the gist of his theme, which was received by the youngsters, with peals of laughter, becoming still more uproarious as he went on to say that this was a sample of all the laws made by grown-ups for the young, and when from this he proceeded to deduce that the first duty of a child was to disobey its parents, and grown-ups generally, there was no controlling the delight of those happy little boys and girls. Never, of course, had they heard such talk before. Here was a friend of their young hearts indeed! When Shaw ended there was a small riot in that schoolroom, and the mistress held up her hands in amused dismay.

But, as I said, she was witty herself, and she rose to the occasion in a spirited reply. It was all very well, she said, for Mr Shaw to talk like that to her young charges, but he had to deal with them for that night only, while she had them the whole year round, and it would take weeks for her to bring them back to law and order once more. So Mr Shaw sowed the good seed of rebellion, in season and out, and I am sure he never won an audience so completely as he won those Hindhead children.

A Terrible Walk

GERALD CUMBERLAND

From Gerald Cumberland, *Set Down in Malice: A Book of Reminiscences* (London: Grant Richards, 1919) p. 17. Gerald Cumberland was the pseudonym of Charles Frederick Kenyon (1879–1926), critic and playwright, who visited Shaw at Pickards Cottage, Guildford – one of a series of rented country retreats – early in 1902. He came to discuss a book on Shaw (which was rejected by his publishers). His account presents a teasing and testing Shaw, and Shaw's condescension is perceptible in his own description of Kenyon as 'rather a decent type of the viewy provincial', whom he 'rather liked' (*Collected Letters 1898–1910*, p. 273).

Almost immediately after [lunch], we started on our walk.

Never shall I forget that terrible walk. I believed then, as I believe now, that Shaw was deliberately pitting his powers of endurance against my own – the powers of endurance of a middle-aged vegetarian against those of a young meat-eater. He walked with a long, easy stride, swinging his arms, breathing deeply through his wide nostrils. His pace, which never for a moment did he attempt to accommodate to mine, was at least five miles an hour. He forgot, or he did not choose to remember, that I had that morning travelled by the slow midnight train from Manchester, that I had crossed London, that I had reached Guildford by a weary Sunday train from Waterloo, and that I had just eaten an enormous lunch. I panted and struggled half a pace behind him. I became stupendously hot. I made unexpected and unathletic sounds, like a man who is being smothered. Blissfully unconscious of all this was Shaw. . . . I wonder? . . . No; blissfully conscious of all this was Shaw.

Hero Worship

ROBERT LORAINE

From Winifred Loraine, *Robert Loraine: Soldier, Actor, Airman* (London: Collins, 1938) pp. 81–2. The following extract joins diary entries written by Robert Loraine in the summer of 1905 after his first meeting with Shaw at a matinee of *Man and Superman* at the Court Theatre, and after a visit to the Shaws' rented country house near Welwyn a few days later.

He has sharp bright-blue penetrating seer's eyes, . . . with the impish twinkle of a schoolboy. A transparent delicate alabaster skin, which gives him the appearance of being not at all of common clay, but having the minimum of earth and maximum of fire in his composition. A lightning conductor, a visitant, who makes other men look not so clean nor fresh as he.

I had expected his voice to have reverberations of the thunder, but it is high-pitched, clear and flexible as a violin's. He says: 'In a minute', not 'in a minnit', and speaks with the most persuasive variant of English I have ever heard, a satin-Irish brogue. . . . his wit and wisdom seem to me to be like the fresh and uncontaminated outlook on life of a baby, miraculously made supremely articulate. . . . [*sic*] I have a foolish self-assertive independence which fights against the idea of hero-worship, yet I was never free from the impression when Shaw was speaking to me that he might at any moment ascend to Heaven like Elisha on a chariot of fire.

As he walked back with me to the station a yokel called out: 'Hallo, Ginger Whiskers!' – at him. I could have thrashed the boy for his impudence – it seemed like sacrilege – but Shaw prevented me.

'A Capital Fellow'

WILFRID SCAWEN BLUNT

From Wilfrid Scawen Blunt, *My Diaries: Being a Personal Narrative of Events, 1888–1914*, 2 vols (London: Martin Secker, 1919–20) II, 141–2. Wilfrid Scawen Blunt (1840–1922), poet, playwright, traveller and supporter of nationalist struggles, who was crippled by illness in his later years, was a great admirer of Shaw's plays, declaring *Arms and the Man, John Bull's Other Island* and *Fanny's First Play* to be 'the most amusing plays ever written in any language' (*My Diaries*, II, 379). In 1899 his only child Judith had married the artist Neville Stephen Lytton, later 3rd Earl of Lytton (1879–1951), who in 1906 painted Shaw in imitation of Velasquez's portrait of Pope Innocent X. The following diary entry is dated 10 April 1906.

Neville sent me word this morning that Bernard Shaw was sitting to him for his portrait, and I looked in (his house is next to mine), and spent an hour with him, seated in an ancient cinque-cento chair, a grotesque figure, with his trousered legs showing through the lace cotta transparent to his knees. He is an ugly fellow, too, his face a pasty white, with a red nose and a rusty red beard, and little slatey-blue eyes. Neville's portrait is wonderfully like. Shaw's appearance, however, matters little when he begins to talk, if he can ever be said to begin, for he talks always in his fine Irish brogue. His talk is like his plays, a string of paradoxes, and he is ready to be switched on to any subject one pleases, and to talk brilliantly on all. He was talking about his marriage when I entered. 'I should never have married at all,' he said, 'if I had not been dead at the time. I tumbled off my bicycle, and the surgeons made a hole in my foot which they kept open for a year, and me in bed. I thought I was dead, for it would not heal, and Charlotte had me at her mercy. I should never have married if I had thought I should get well. Then I tumbled again, this time downstairs from top to bottom. When I found myself on the floor in the hall with every bone broken I felt satisfied. I could not do more and I took to my bed again.'[1] These particulars were *à propos* of my having said that there were two quite happy moments in one's life, the first when one took to one's deathbed, and the other when one got up from it. He told us next his experiences in public speaking, and how shy he had been, and described his first open-air speech in Hyde Park when he had practised on three loafers lying on their backs on the grass, and how one of them without getting up had called out 'ear! ear!' He said the great art of speaking was to get somebody to interrupt you with a question, and for you to misunderstand it, and he gave some funny instances. I then got him to give his views on land reform, which he said was a very simple matter. You had only to get all the agricultural labourers to migrate into the towns, where they would make themselves useful by loafing in the streets and attending music halls, the only thing they understood, and by sending the townspeople down into the country to cultivate it by electricity and explosives. If he had a farm he thought he would plough it by firing cannon up and down it – amusing rubbish, which I fancy concealed a complete ignorance of the agricultural branch of the socialistic case. Shaw is a capital fellow all the same, and one I should like if I knew him better. He showed himself personally kind and of much practical dexterity when I got him to help me to my feet from the sofa on which I was, when the sitting was over.

NOTE

1. Writing to Beatrice Webb on 21 June 1898, Shaw told her, 'I found my objection to my own marriage had ceased with my objection to my own death'. He also recounted his fall downstairs four days earlier (see *Collected Letters 1898–1910*, pp. 49–52).

Shaw, Rodin and Rilke

SIEGFRIED TREBITSCH

From Siegfried Trebitsch, *Chronicle of a Life*, trans. Eithne Wilkins and Ernst Kaiser (London: Heinemann, 1953) pp. 187–90. Rainer Maria Rilke (1875–1926), German poet and a close friend of Trebitsch, was Rodin's secretary at the time Shaw sat for his bust in Paris (16 April–8 May 1906). In a letter to William Rothenstein he characterised Shaw as an extraordinary model, *'qui pose avec la même énergie et sincérité qui font sa gloire d'écrivain'* (William Rothenstein, *Men and Memories 1900–1922* [London: Faber & Faber, 1932] p. 108). Anthony M. Ludovici, who shortly succeeded Rilke as Rodin's secretary, recalled that the sculptor expatiated at length on the Christ-like appearance of Shaw' head, declaring it to be *'une vraie tête de Christ'* ('Further Personal Reminiscences of Auguste Rodin II', *Cornhill Magazine*, January 1926).

Rilke knew, of course, that I had come partly to see Shaw and because of Shaw, and spoke of this model of Rodin's – and, what was more, without using those threadbare expressions 'mocker, talker, preacher, juggler with words'. On the contrary, he had fully recognised Bernard Shaw's immense seriousness and told me how instructive these sittings always were, especially for him; how that great writer looked up to the sculptor with all the modesty of one who felt he was himself a learner; and how honoured, indeed almost flattered, Shaw felt at being immortalised by Rodin's chisel, much more certainly than he would be through his own work. Later he was to say, with a smile: 'Some day my name will be in the encyclopaedias followed by the phrase: sat for the celebrated sculptor Auguste Rodin.'

I thought it more appropriate to call on Shaw and his wife for the first time in their hotel on the Quai d'Orsay and let him take me along with him to a sitting, instead of suddenly popping up in Rodin's studio at Rilke's side. This first meeting in Paris was extremely stimulating. Shaw was never tired of talking about Rodin and his sittings and invited me to come to one of them the next day, saying he and my friend Rilke had already prepared the Master for this visit.

I well remember that silent sitting, with three people present who hardly dared to breathe, while the fourth, the artist at work, filled the studio with his raging activity, his gigantic movements and exclamations, which were not always quite intelligible and doubtless were meant only for himself. What delighted me as much as it astonished me was the great understanding Bernard Shaw showed for Rainer Maria Rilke, whom he called the *prima materia* of a poet who in innocence and goodness excelled even myself. . . .

Now the bust of Shaw was finished, and there were no more evenings to be spent together at the theatre or in conversation. Among other things, I had gone with Shaw to the Grand Guignol, that theatre of dread and horror.[1] The plays, most of them by de Lorde,[2] interested Shaw very much, but the more blood-curdling and frightful they became, the more of an effort he had to make not to burst out laughing. Nothing could frighten him; he was not frightened even when, coming out of the theatre one evening, we suddenly met with formations of police and small units of armed cavalry outside the Madeleine, because, as sensation-hungry evening newspapers had claimed, the outbreak of a revolution was imminent.[3] Even this sight aroused Shaw's mirth, and he said: 'Oh, no, there's no previously announced revolution. This is only the next instalment of the horror-play we have just been seeing.'

NOTES

1. The Théâtre du Grand Guignol was the main centre of a popular form of nineteenth-century French cabaret entertainment, named after the Lyons

marionette, Guignol. The shows comprised short plays depicting scenes of horror, violence, sadism, rape and murder. Shaw went on 30 April and told Granville Barker he had seen four of the five plays, 'all fairly amusing, especially a farce with a guillotine in it' (Collected Letters 1898–1910, p. 621).

2. André de Lorde (1871–1942) was a prolific author of Grand Guignol plays.

3. This was in fact the evening of the Grand Guignol visit: the 'revolution' took the form of a demonstration next day, 1 May, witnessed by the Shaws. Shaw believed that clashes with police and troops were engineered by the Government to win support in the coming election.

Impressions

DESMOND MacCARTHY

From Desmond MacCarthy, Shaw (London: MacGibbon & Kee, 1951) pp. 213–17. Sir Desmond MacCarthy (1877–1952), author and critic, was one of the most perceptive of the early reviewers of Shaw's plays. He first met Shaw in 1906 when Harley Granville Barker took him to lunch at Adelphi Terrace, and his memories of that occasion open the following extracts, which are drawn from 'A Personal Memoir' appended to a collection of his Shaw reviews and essays.

Two impressions of that visit have remained with me. Harley must have said that he and I were going to visit Meredith[1] for I remember saying to Shaw, after describing Meredith, that it must be a terrible humiliation for a man who gloried in physical excellence to suffer from such a disease as locomotor ataxy, that terrible jerking stammer of the hands and feet. Shaw assented briefly. Soon after, happening to look out of the window and catching sight of a large building with big windows, obviously not a block of flats, I asked him what it was. His face contracted with intense and painful sympathy and he said: 'It is a place where they torture animals. I can hardly bear the sight of it'. Now the serenity of his sympathy with the sufferings of an old man of genius and this poignant response to the pain inflicted on animals with a view to discovering remedies for human beings seemed to me to reveal a strange sense of proportion that I was often to encounter in one form or another in Shaw's works.

As I walked away I said to myself 'What is it that has made my first meeting with this man of genius different from my first meetings with others?' and I must have covered a good deal of ground before the answer flashed upon me. He had not flattered me. All the others, by graciously receiving my homage, had in a certain measure done that. Moreover I also felt that in the case of Shaw I should be recalled only when to do so was relevant to some matter which was preoccupying him; that I should be kept in a pigeon-hole and that his thoughts would never stray, as it were, accidentally in my direction.

I was destined to see him at intervals, some of them few and far between, up to 1940. My connection with the *New Statesman* as its dramatic critic and later as its literary editor (1920–1927) occasionally brought me in contact with him. I have little doubt that it was on his recommendation that I was first taken on. At a weekend party given by the Webbs at a hotel near Beachy Head to the future staff of the *New Statesman*, Shaw was also present. He arrived late in the evening and explained that he had been delayed by his mother's funeral.[2] One of his first remarks as he settled down on the sofa before the fire was to the effect that the military understood well the kind of music that was wanted at a funeral; on the way to the grave a solemn dead march and on the way back from it a gay and rousing tune. Then with that sensitiveness that was marked in him to the impression that he might be making on others, he added after a pause: 'But don't think that I am a man who forgets the dead'. This I am sure was perfectly true, but there was something in him that made him take death more lightly than all but the very heartless, his own included, I expect.

But what I loved in Shaw was his instinctive chivalry, which, I have no doubt, exaggerated beyond all bounds his horror at using a helpless guinea-pig, dog or rabbit to discover remedies for human suffering. I was to run up against indications of this chivalry as frequently as his generosity in helping people with money. (By the way I never appealed to. him on behalf of others in vain and once his contribution was so large that, to his amazement, I sent half of it back. He told me that I was a fool and that I would soon be writing to him again, but our unfortunate friend died too soon for that so I did save some of his money.)

The absence in him of personal touchiness was remarkable. I knew that I should never lose his goodwill whatever I wrote about his plays though he might think me a fool for my pains.

What puzzled some people about Shaw was that although in print and conversation he had far fewer inhibitions than most men about conveying intimate information to do with himself and his life, he also gave the impression that he was not more intimate with old friends than with acquaintances or indeed, one may say, with the public. I remember going to see Conrad soon after Shaw had visited him for the first time.[3] Conrad had been shocked and almost insulted by what he considered on Shaw's part an abuse of intimacy. 'What do you think he told me? He told me that his father drank like a fish! Imagine my feelings on being presented with this revelation of his private life on our first meeting!' Conrad no doubt was a romantically fastidious Pole who instinctively took account of the milestones on the road to intimacy and it was precisely the milestones that Shaw ignored. That by the way is also a characteristic of the saint who may make no distinction in communication between those to whom they are deeply attached and human beings in general. But for all that it is disconcerting to human beings to feel that they must always be equidistant from one whom they admire. It is a trait which suggests a complete spiritual independence even perhaps of affection.

Next to his wife his closest friendship was probably with the Webbs.

NOTES

1. In return for Barker's arranging the lunch with Shaw, MacCarthy had promised to take him to see the novelist and poet George Meredith (1828–1909).

2. Mrs Shaw's funeral took place at Golders Green Crematorium on Saturday, 22 February 1913, with only Shaw, Granville Barker and the undertaker in attendance. That evening, however, Shaw was in Oxford for a performance of *The Philanderer*; the *New Statesman* gathering was a fortnight later.

3. This visit to the Polish novelist Joseph Conrad (1857–1924) was probably the one made early in 1902 of which Conrad wrote: 'GBS towed by Wells came to see me reluctantly and I nearly bit him' (*Letters from Joseph Conrad 1895-1924*, ed. Edward Garnett [1928; rpt. New York: Charter Books (Bobbs-Merrill), 1962] p. 181).

'Uncanonical Saint'

AUGUSTUS JOHN

From Augustus John, *Chiaroscuro: Fragments of Autobiography* (London: Jonathan Cape, 1952) pp. 69–71. In May 1915 Shaw and the artist Augustus Edwin John (1878–1961) were fellow guests of Lady Gregory at Coole Park in the west of Ireland. John, ill at first, was cured by Shaw's chauffeur and then set about painting Shaw. Three portraits survived John's hectic revisions: Shaw kept one and later gave another to the Fitzwilliam Museum, Cambridge, while the third eventually passed into the Royal collection. Elsewhere in his reminiscence John mentions Shaw's driving – 'faultless if a trifle slow' – his enthusiasm for colour photography and their visit to the church once attended by Samuel Butler in Shrewsbury.

I had come with no less serious a purpose than to paint Bernard Shaw. But with my newly regained health, I felt ready for anything, and faced my task with confidence. Shaw's head had two aspects, as he pointed out himself: the concave and the convex. It was the former that I settled on at the start. I produced two studies from that angle and a third from the other. In the last he is portrayed with his eyes shut as if in deep thought. Although he had just consumed his midday vegetables, there was no question of nodding: he had avoided a surfeit.

'What!' exclaimed my model, when I informed him of my fee, 'do you mean to say you work for so paltry a sum?' But before I had time to revise my charges, the cheque was written and handed over. GBS was always kind and helpful to the young, especially when they showed talent and honesty of purpose. Perhaps as an old campaigner he kept a good look out for possible recruits; nor did he forget them, as his occasional postcards testify. Without being exactly a recruit myself, our differing outlooks in no way precluded friendship: perhaps they even enhanced the charm of intimacy by adding an element of the unknown.

In the evenings we sometimes collected in the drawing-room. Shaw would, when so disposed, seat himself at the piano and sing a succession of pieces in his gentle baritone. His effortless, unassuming and withal accomplished performance was welcomed by everybody. His conversation, however (at any rate, in my experience), was sometimes apt to be irritating. The style proper to privacy is not that suitable to the platform, but this practised orator seemed sometimes to overlook the distinction. Mrs Shaw and Lady Gregory, each in her amiable way, adopted a humorous, appreciative but slightly aloof attitude, as if in the presence of a difficult, precocious but an essentially lovable wonder-child. What the society of Coole lacked, I thought, was the participation of some innocent, even naif, but rather contentious person to act as feeder to the Master: with that we should all have had more fun. As it was, the monologues, unenlivened by opposition, gained only in length what they lost in piquancy. Is not inconsequence the fuel of wit? Unanimity, besides being the cause of moral discomfort, inhibits repartee. Pomposity, however, could never be charged against GBS, and he would have been the last to encourage 'the foolish face of praise'. . . .

When the time came to leave, Shaw offered me a lift homewards. I was glad to accept as I calculated this would mean closer contact with the country and people than the railway journey afforded. On nearing any town of importance, GBS, well aware of what he was in for, prepared himself suitably, with an eye to the photographers, who, apprised of his approach, posted themselves with their cameras in readiness to shoot, as our car, in slow motion, passed majestically along the main street. . . .

I parted from my kindly hosts at their house at Welwyn. What I have sketched here was more than an ordinary episode: it was a great occasion, for I had come to know in intimacy a true Prince of the Spirit, a fearless enemy of cant and humbug, and in his queer way, a highly respectable though strictly uncanonical saint.

On Being Shaw's Secretary

ANN ELDER

From a letter by Ann M. Elder Jackson to Archibald Henderson, 5 May 1955, in Henderson, *Bernard Shaw: Man of the Century* (New York: Appleton-Century-Crofts, 1956) p. 807. Ann M. Jackson (née Elder) succeeded Mrs Georgina Musters as Shaw's secretary in 1912. She had been recommended by Mrs Musters herself, and remained in the position, with one interruption of service in 1918–19, until 1920, when she married and left to join her husband in India.

Later, when I was properly installed as his secretary, . . . he taught me how to fill in cheques, and insisted that I always put stamps on letters in the extreme top right hand corner of the envelope 'or the good angels will not love you'. Then I was handed a bunch of little hand-made green papers with one word 'Pygmalion' written at the top in his own beautiful longhand and underneath the beginning of that play in the leisurely Pitman shorthand which he consistently used for plays, letters and articles. This was the first play I had to transcribe for him. Then came *Overruled* which it was his intention to call *Trespassers Will be Prosecuted*; but the title was already taken, as was also *Keep off the Grass*, another choice. Very happy years they were. The last big play with which I was concerned was *Back to Methuselah*.

I do not think I ever enjoyed any part of my life . . . more than my years with GBS. He was a most delightful and unexacting employer, thoughtful and considerate. He enjoyed sharing his enjoyment; and, when dictating a letter, would glance across at his secretary to make sure that a point which merited appreciation was receiving it. I admired him very much.

The Idealist

WILLIAM ARCHER

From William Archer, 'The Psychology of GBS', *Bookman*, December 1924. Shortly after this article appeared Archer underwent an operation. He died on 27 December 1924, and what he had written took on the aspect of a public valediction from one of Shaw's oldest and dearest friends. His private valediction, in a letter written on 17 December, may be found in St John Ervine's *Bernard Shaw: His Life, Work and Friends* (London: Constable, 1956) p. 504.

For many years it was impossible to mention the name of Bernard Shaw without being confronted with the question 'Is he ever serious?' or 'Does he expect people to take him seriously?' The question was not inexcusable, for he has said countless things regarding which he himself would have been puzzled to decide what element of seriousness lurked beneath the surface of reckless, irresponsible humour. But a very small acquaintance with his writings ought to have assured any discerning reader that at bottom he is intensely in earnest. I am tempted to call him the most uncompromising, not to say fanatical, idealist I have ever met. His life has been dominated by, and devoted to, a system of interwoven ideals to which he is immovably faithful. His sense of right and wrong is so overmastering that he carries it into regions – such as that of personal hygiene – which most people are apt to regard as morally indifferent. And his ideals, if sometimes a little crankish, are for the most part high and humane. He sometimes fights for them with a ferocity that appears like unscrupulousness: but this appearance is due to the fact that his perceptions are warped by the intensity of his feelings: the mirror of his mind does not accurately image the external object. His will is always intent on the good as he sees it; and that I take to be the essence of a high morality. Having known him for forty years, I say without hesitation that his greatest moral failing, in my judgement, is (or was) a certain impishness, a Puck-like *Schadenfreude*, to which he would sometimes give too free play. Apart from this, there is no man for the fundamentals of whose character I have a more real respect. I own myself deeply indebted to him for many lessons taught me in the years of our early intimacy; though he never succeeded in imbuing me with his inflexible devotion to ideals.

Part 9
Plays and Players, 1916–25

INTRODUCTION TO PART 9

The period 1916–25 saw the creation of three of Shaw's most ambitious and large-scale theatrical works, *Heartbreak House*, *Back to Methuselah* and *Saint Joan*, as well as some minor plays. Contrary to Shaw's statements, in the Preface to the play and elsewhere, that *Heartbreak House* was begun before a shot was fired in the First World War, there is clear evidence that the actual composition was begun in March 1916 and completed in May of the following year. Three years elapsed before it was first produced. The play had a mixed reception from English critics at the time of its first London production though it was a success in New York and has since come to be seen as one of his most outstanding works. Two slight one-act plays, *Augustus Does His Bit* and *Annajanska, the Bolshevik Empress* were written in 1916 and 1917 respectively, and in 1918 Shaw turned to the writing of his mammoth five-part cycle of plays on evolutionary themes, *Back to Methuselah*. The daunting task of production was undertaken first by the Theatre Guild, New York, in 1922 and in the following year by Barry Jackson's Birmingham Repertory Company. In the meantime Shaw had produced a comic version of a play, *Frau Gittas Sühne*, by his German translator, Siegfried Trebitsch, under the title *Jitta's Atonement*. In April 1923 he began the composition of *Saint Joan*, and completed the play in less than four months. Despite early complaints about its length at the first 1923–4 production in New York, *Saint Joan* was an outstanding success on both sides of the Atlantic.

The immediate postwar years also marked the formation of several important new theatrical associations for Shaw. Lawrence Langner, the energetic and enterprising co-founder and director of the New York Theatre Guild, was responsible for the world premières of all three of the major works of the period, and many years later devoted an entire book, *GBS and the Lunatic*, to reminiscences of his association with Shaw. Dame Edith Evans, Sir Cedric Hardwicke, Reginald Denham and Ernest Thesiger played their first Shavian roles in this period. Dame Sybil Thorndike and Sir Lewis Casson had been acquainted with Shaw since the days of the Vedrenne–Barker season at the Royal Court, but their collaboration with him in the first English production of *Saint Joan* established the beginning of a long-lasting professional association.

This Part concludes with extracts from an interview on the subject of playwriting which Shaw gave to Archibald Henderson in 1925.

Shaw's view of *Heartbreak House*

ST JOHN ERVINE

From St John Ervine, 'Note on *Heartbreak House*' (copy of a BBC Third Programme talk script sent by Ervine to Ivo L. Currall; London: Currall Collection, Royal Academy of Dramatic Art, n.d.). One of Shaw's very late works, the puppet play, *Shakes versus Shav*, supports Ervine's remarks here about the special regard that Shaw had for *Heartbreak House*. In the course of the play, in response to a challenge from Shakes, Shav conjures up a tableau from *Heartbreak House* of *'Captain Shotover seated, as in Millais' picture called North-West Passage, with a young woman of virginal beauty'*, and exclaims: 'Behold my Lear' (*Collected Plays*, vol. v, p. 12).

His attitude to *Heartbreak House* was entirely different from his attitude to the rest of his work. He would discuss any other play at length, but *Heartbreak House* very remarkably silenced him, not because he felt dubious about it, but because it stirred a reverence in him which he had never felt for anything else he had written. I say this with some diffidence lest I should be misunderstood. I shall have failed in my purpose if I make you feel that he was vain about the play in any foolish fashion. In his heart, he was a humble man, vain only on platforms and in the presence of people who expected him to show off. There was no such mood in him when he thought of *Heartbreak House*. It affected him profoundly because he felt that it had been inspired as nothing else of his had been.

A Crisis

LAWRENCE LANGNER

From Lawrence Langner, *GBS and the Lunatic* (London: Hutchinson, 1964) pp. 29–30. Langner's association with Shaw began in 1920 when the New York Theatre Guild obtained the rights to stage the world première of *Heartbreak*

House in a season beginning 19 November 1920. At the end of the month Langner visited Shaw in England seeking to obtain a contract for the Theatre Guild to produce all of his plays in the States, and bringing with him photographs of the production of *Heartbreak House*. The stage directions of *Heartbreak House* call for a room *'built so as to resemble the after part of an old-fashioned high-pooped ship with a stern gallery'*, and specify that Hesione Hushabye has *'magnificent black hair'*. The contrasting hair colour of two of the leading female characters, Hesione and Ellie Dunn, is a significant motif in the play. Lee Simonson (1888–1967), designer and artist, was one of the founding directors of the Guild, and designed sets for *Heartbreak House, Back to Methuselah, The Apple Cart* and *The Simpleton of the Unexpected Isles*. Effie Shannon (1867–1954), distinguished American actress, embarked on her long stage career before she had reached the age of seven. Amongst her pre-1921 roles was that of Blanche in a New York production of Shaw's *Widowers' Houses* in 1907.

After a few minutes, Shaw came in, lean, white-bearded and erect, looking rather like Father Christmas on a hunger strike, minus only the red cloak and the bell. His face was pink and red, his eyes alive and keen and his manner very cheerful and sprightly. He greeted me warmly, put me at my ease and after discussing the production of the play, asked to see the photographs I had brought with me. His sharp blue eyes scanned the very handsome set Lee Simonson had provided – 'Quite good,' he said rather severely, in the manner of a schoolmaster appraising an examination paper, 'only the room should look more like a ship's cabin. Simonson has made the tops of the doors rounded instead of flat. Doors on ships are never rounded.' I murmured apologies, and said that it hadn't hurt the play – no one had noticed the tops of the doors anyway, they were so engrossed in his dialogue! His severity relaxed until he came across the picture of Effie Shannon. 'Isn't she playing the part of Hesione?' he asked sharply. My heart momentarily stopped beating. The vision of being permitted to produce more Shaw plays began to fade. I nodded, and the sharp blue eyes regarded me angrily. 'But she has blond hair – you must have cut one of the lines!' 'Well, not exactly,' I replied. 'We just mumbled it – what would you have done?' The fate of my mission hung in the balance. Shaw smiled. 'That's all right,' he said, and the crisis was passed.

Heartbreak House and the Critics

BEVERLEY BAXTER

From an untitled article in the *Sketch*, 22 November 1950. Sir Arthur Beverley Baxter (1891–1964), Canadian-born editor and journalist, joined Lord

Beaverbrook's *Daily Express* in 1920, and subsequently became its Managing
Editor and, in 1929, Editor-in-Chief and Director. After seeing the poor press
reception of *Heartbreak House* at the opening of the 1921 London production at
the Court Theatre, Baxter went to a performance and thought the play to be a
work of 'exquisite quality'. Going backstage afterwards he undertook with the
producer, J. B. Fagan, to arrange for Shaw to meet and debate with his critics
at a matinee performance of the play. James Bernard Fagan (1873–1933),
playwright and director, took over the management of the Court in 1918. He
opened the Oxford Playhouse in 1923 and later became director of the Festival
Theatre, Cambridge.

The *Daily Express* . . . published a signed news-story by me called: 'Shaw
to Meet His Critics' together with the information that applications for
seats should be made to the newspaper. At the same time, tickets were
sent to all the critics.

The response was enormous. We could have filled the theatre twenty
times over. Everybody who was anybody wanted to be there, and even
those who wrongly imagined that they were somebody were equally
clamorous. Everything had gone to plan until two days before the
matinée, when Fagan called me on the telephone. 'Shaw says he won't
come.' That was all – but it was enough!

Vanity, vanity, all is vanity. What in the Dickens was to be done? My
newspaper would look like a fool, and newspapers are sensitive on that
point. Lord Beaverbrook would certainly have something to say. The
idiocy of the whole thing hit me like a wet towel.

At ten o'clock that night I took up the telephone and called Shaw at
his house in the Adelphi. The great man answered the phone himself
and in a voice that was parched with nervousness I told him who I was
and asked him why he would not come. 'Well, my bhoy,' he said in a
rich Irish brogue, 'for one thing you never asked me. But tell me now.
Why are you doing this?'

I told him that *Heartbreak House* was a great play, a great play, a great
play. It must have sounded like a cracked record, but he listened. Then
he asked me what other plays of his I had seen, and I told him how
Robert Lorraine [*sic*] had brought *Man and Superman* to Toronto. Then I
returned to the cracked record again.

'You're a queer fellow,' said Shaw, 'but hire a car and call for me here
and we'll go to the matinée together.'

That night London belonged to me. No condemned man reprieved
on his way to the gallows could have felt a greater sense of relief.

So on the day we drove to Sloane Square, where a great crowd had
gathered, and fought our way to the box which had been reserved. The
place was packed with celebrities and nearly all the critics were there.
When the play was over the audience called for Shaw and he stood up
in the box.

'You have come to see *Heartbreak House* this afternoon,' he said. 'Whether you like it or not is another question. However, do not worry. Three hundred years hence you will come to see it again.'

A lot of people laughed. The old joker was true to form, up to his pranks as usual. But Shaw was supremely if contemptuously in earnest. In the public forum he was announcing his own immortality. Then he went down to the stage, where some refreshments had been arranged, and some of the critics joined him. But nothing much happened, there was no debate, and finally it all fizzled out. Next day a number of the critics generously wrote in their newspapers that their second thoughts were more favourable. Others refused to alter their verdicts. On the whole the play had been given many thousands of pounds' worth of publicity.

With what result! Next night the theatre was empty. The play closed on the Saturday, the extra week having cost J. B. Fagan money that he could not afford. London was not ready for a play that would force it to think.

Some time afterwards a book came to my house. It was a first edition of *Back to Methuselah*, and in it were inscribed these words: 'To Beverley Baxter in heartfelt appreciation for his intervention on behalf of *Heartbreak House*', followed by Shaw's signature.

Heartbreak House at Oxford

REGINALD DENHAM

From Reginald Denham, *Stars in my Hair: Being Certain Indiscreet Memoirs* (New York: Crown Publishers, 1958) pp. 111–12. Reginald Denham (b. 1894), actor, author and director, began his acting career at His Majesty's Theatre in 1913. In 1919–20 he played under J. B. Fagan's management at the Court and Duke of York Theatres. In 1922 he acted in several Shaw plays at the Everymans Theatre, and the following year was appointed Director of the Oxford Players by Fagan. *Heartbreak House* was chosen for the company's first production in October 1923. The venue was a museum not far from St John's College which Fagan had converted into a small playhouse.

The Oxford Playhouse opened to a great send-off. The paint was not even dry as the curtain went up. The play was Shaw's *Heartbreak House*. The grand old man himself came to rehearsal, if you can call it such.

He acted all the parts from memory and played the audience as well, laughing uproariously at his comedy lines. Hardly anybody in the cast spoke at all. Our apron stage, however, with its small, box-like inner stage, had him completely baffled. He couldn't suggest any of the movements that had been carried out in the original production, so he didn't return to the afternoon rehearsal.

He came back a week later to see the final performance. The circumstances attending his visit are not without humour. It was a Saturday night and the hall was largely filled with undergraduates. Obviously they couldn't help noticing that the famous national possession, the Shaw beard, was in their midst. Word of his august presence soon got around to the actors back-stage. So the players overplayed and overwaited for laughs, and the audience overlaughed out of politeness. The result was distinctly debilitating. At the end of the play there were loud yells for 'Author'. For a long time he refused to go up on the stage. But some undergraduates eventually forced him there more or less physically.

He stroked his beard as he stood among us and looked unusually grave. Finally he raised his hand for silence and spoke. 'Ladies and gentlemen,' he said, 'this has been one of the most depressing evenings I have spent in the theatre. I imagined I had written a quiet, thoughtful, semi-tragic play after the manner of Chekhov.[1] From your empty-headed laughter, I appear to have written a bedroom farce. All that remains for me to do is to give the actors, and particularly the director, my most heavy *curse*. Good night.'

Then he strode up into the tunnel and disappeared.

For a moment or two the audience sat in stunned silence. Then suddenly they recovered and their guffaws became war-whoops. But the old firebrand meant it all right. He was livid with rage.

NOTE

1. In the Preface to the play Shaw writes of Chekhov and Tolstoy as having anticipated his portrayal of 'Heartbreak House'. *Heartbreak House* is sub-titled *A Fantasia in the Russian Manner on English Themes*.

Back to Methuselah: I

CHARLES RICKETTS

From Charles Ricketts, *Self-Portrait taken from the Letters and Journals of Charles Ricketts, RA,* collected and compiled by T. Sturge Moore, ed. Cecil Lewis (London: Peter Davies, 1939) pp. 294–5. Charles Ricketts (1866–1931), designer, painter, sculptor and author, designed sets and costumes for Shaw plays in the early 1920s. The meeting he describes here took place on 8 May 1918. Shaw had begun writing *Back to Methuselah,* the work referred to in the conversation, in March of that year. Mrs Lee Mathews was an accomplished pianist and musician who held 'charming chamber concerts' at her home in London in the early decades of the twentieth century (see Ricketts, *Self-Portrait,* p. 175).

Shaw met me on the stairs as I was leaving the music-room at Mrs Lee Mathews'. He said, 'Tell me, is the war inspiring you? Are you doing big things?' 'No, my dear chap, it is a nightmare, a bore. I view it as I would an earthquake.' 'I am like you – at least, any attempt of mine has been disastrous.' I said, 'But in your case it might not have been so, your work is in touch with reality, mine as a painter is in a backwater; for years I have absorbed only what interested me, or was needful to my work. Were I young, I might respond to events, but I am too old by this time; if I did, it would be too late, life is too short.' 'Curious,' said Shaw, 'I am at work on that subject – the shortness of life. I deal with the future, the secret of longevity has been discovered, men have time for adventure, discovery and work. There are very funny things: my hero, or one of them, is a survivor in the Colonies from our times; he hates all he sees, yet people are kind to him, he is given a home as he is unable to fend for himself; he takes up a sheet of notepaper to write to his wife, and discovers from it he is in a madhouse.' We were descending the stairs. I said, 'Life is too short, I wonder if time slows down later?' Shaw said, 'Yes, I think it does. I am sixty-three, and I feel from time to time that bland sensation one experiences in autumn afternoons – one becomes a spectator as one was in childhood.'

Back to Methuselah: II

LADY GREGORY

From *Lady Gregory's Journals 1916–1930*, ed. Lennox Robinson (London: Putnam, 1946) pp. 202–4. The following accounts of Shaw's reading of various parts of *Back to Methuselah* are recorded in Lady Gregory's journal entries for 3 March 1919. She was staying with the Shaws at Ayot St Lawrence.

Last night . . . he gave an account of a wonderful and fantastic play he is writing beginning in the Garden of Eden before Adam and Eve, with Lilith who finds a lonely immortality impossible to face and so gives herself up to be divided into Man and Woman.[1] He read a scene in it (on the pier at Burren) about a thousand years in the future with the Irish coming back to kiss the earth of Ireland and not liking it when they see it.[2]

GBS read me his play beginning in the Garden of Eden. The first act a fine thing, 'a Resurrection Play' I called it. The second, two hundred years later, an argument between Cain, Adam and Eve, the soldier against the man of peace. I told him I thought it rather monotonous, an Ossianic dialogue,[3] and he said that he thought of introducing Cain's wife, 'the Modern Woman', or perhaps only speaking of her in the argument.[4] I said even that would be an improvement as Cain is unnecessarily disagreeable and one could forgive if he is put, by aspersions on his wife, in a passion, for one can forgive where there is passion. It is like drunkenness – 'Ah, you can't blame him, he was drunk', when a man has cut your head open. He laughed and agreed or seemed to.

NOTES

1. In Act I of the first play of the cycle, 'In the Beginning', the Serpent tells Eve this story of Lilith dividing herself into Adam and Eve.
2. The reference is to part IV of the cycle, 'Tragedy of an Elderly Gentleman'.
3. I.e. in the manner of the bardic Ossianic poems of James Macpherson (1736–96).
4. Cain's wife, Lua, is the subject of several passages of dialogue in Act II of 'In the Beginning'. She is described as a manipulative *femme fatale*.

Back to Methuselah, a Reading

C. E. M. JOAD

From C. E. M. Joad, *Shaw* (London: Victor Gollancz, 1949) pp. 35–6. In 1919 and the early 1920s the Fabian Society held summer schools in Penlea on the Devonshire coast near Dartmouth. Shaw stayed in a chalet about 100 yards from the main building of the school.

It was, I think, the Summer School of 1920 that was rendered memorable by Shaw's reading of *Back to Methuselah*. Shaw, who never appeared until midday, spent the mornings writing, and sometimes in the evening he would read to the assembled School what he had written. The reading was most impressive. Shaw sat in front of a reading-desk with a candle on either side of him, the rest of the hall being in darkness. Much has been written about Shaw's histrionic powers. We have been told how, at rehearsals, he would put the actors through their paces, demonstrating to them by gesture and intonation exactly how their parts should be played. We have heard how deeply these Shavian performances impressed those who were privileged to see them, and how actors who had begun by resenting the implied suggestion that they did not know their own business succumbed in the end to their recognition of Shaw's superiority of insight and judgement, no less than to his invincible good humour. But anybody who has not actually heard Shaw read one of his plays can have no conception of the charm and power of his presentation.

Shaw's voice, of course, was an enormous asset; apart from its intrinsic melodiousness, it was wonderfully flexible, and he could convey the slightest *nuance* of meaning by changes of intonation. There stand out more particularly in my mind the reading of the first play of the *Back to Methuselah* pentateuch and the intensity of meaning which Shaw put into the Serpent's utterances, more especially those in which he supplies Eve with the appropriate words for the conceptions to which she is feeling her way. 'Imagination is the beginning of creation. You imagine what you desire; you will what you imagine; and at last you create what you will.'[1] As I write, it is Shaw's tones that I hear and not those of the many competent actors whom I have subsequently seen in the part.

NOTE

1. *Collected Plays*, vol. v, p. 348.

Producing *Back to Methuselah*

LAWRENCE LANGNER

From Lawrence Langner, *GBS and the Lunatic* (London: Hutchinson, 1964) pp. 31, 49–50. *Back to Methuselah* was first presented by the Theatre Guild at the Garrick Theatre, New York, in February and March 1922. Shaw's comment below on the project of producing the whole of the *Back to Methuselah* cycle inspired the title for Langner's book. The actor Albert Bruning (1859–1929) played the parts of Franklyn Barnabas in Part II, 'The Gospel of the Brothers Barnabas' and the Elderly Gentleman in Part IV, 'Tragedy of an Elderly Gentleman'.

We talked about *Back to Methuselah* and the best way to present it. Shaw's idea was to have all five plays produced consecutively, so that the audience would have to take the entire dose in one helping. On leaving, he said he would send me the printed proof sheets, and I asked for a contract. 'Don't bother about a contract,' he said, as I stood at the door taking my leave. 'It isn't likely that any other lunatic will want to produce *Back to Methuselah*!'

And he was right, as usual. . . .

After the opening of the last play of the cycle, I left for Europe, and called on GBS with the intention of securing his permission to cut 'An Elderly Gentleman' so that the play would have a chance for a New York run. I was met very cordially by Shaw, and also by Mrs Shaw, who stayed and chatted with us while we looked over the photographs of the production. 'Look, Charlotte,' he said to Mrs Shaw as he examined the pictures of Albert Bruning as the Elderly Gentleman, 'they've given the actor a make-up so that he looks like me! Why, the Elderly Gentleman was an old duffer. Why on earth did you suggest me?' 'Because he talked on and on and on,' I replied. 'Besides, he said he could not live in a world without truth, by which we of course assumed you had written yourself into the character.'

This was a bad beginning for an interview in which I wished to persuade him to cut the play, but encouraged by Mrs Shaw, I persevered. 'The reason I object to cutting my plays is this,' said GBS. 'I write a certain amount of deadly serious dialogue, and when I have given the audience as much as they can possibly take, I throw in some humour as a reward. Now when my plays are cut, the actor or other person who does the cutting always takes out the serious dialogue, and leaves the funny parts, so that the whole purpose of the play is defeated. Besides,' he said, 'you can never trust an actor to cut a play.' 'But I suggest you cut this yourself,' I replied, 'and I'll cable the changes to New York.' 'You shouldn't have given the two plays in one evening,' was the retort. 'But people can't come in the afternoon,' I replied, 'and it's so long, they really suffer.'

Then GBS began to suffer too. 'This goes against all my principles,' he said, looking at Mrs Shaw.

'GBS,' she said, 'perhaps the Americans don't always know what the Elderly Gentleman is talking about. There's that long piece about John Knox and the Leviathan;[1] hardly any English people know about that either.'

I unashamedly and unscrupulously followed Mrs Shaw's lead and suggested that there was a great deal more in the play that wasn't understood by Americans – or by anybody else either. 'Besides,' I added, 'at least half a dozen times the Elderly Gentleman starts to leave the stage. Each time the audience settles back delighted, but each time he turns around and comes back for another ten minutes of monologue.'

'After all,' said Mrs Shaw, 'you did intend him to be an old duffer, and it is hard to listen to an old duffer going on and on.' GBS squirmed and twisted, but finally gave in. 'Very well,' he said. 'We'll go over it line by line.'

'I have some cuts suggested,' I said, quickly offering him the printed version on which I had marked my deletions. In a few minutes he grew so interested in cutting the play that he took out at least half as much again as I had originally hoped for. An hour later I left, trying to stop looking too pleased with myself, for I had been told in New York that I would be wasting my time, as no one had ever been able to persuade Shaw to cut one of his plays before. And I doubt very much whether I would have succeeded without the help of Mrs Shaw.

NOTE

1. The Elderly Gentleman refers to a work called *Leviathan* written by one Jonhobsnoxious, a facetious amalgamation of the names of the Scottish divine, John Knox (c. 1514–1572) and the philosopher, Thomas Hobbes (1588–1679), author of *Leviathan* (1651) (see *Collected Plays*, vol. v, p. 550).

Rehearsing *Back to Methuselah*

CEDRIC HARDWICKE

From Cedric Hardwicke, *A Victorian in Orbit: The Irreverent Memoirs of Sir Cedric Hardwicke as told to James Brough* (London: Methuen, 1961) pp. 109–10. *Back to Methuselah* was presented at the Birmingham Repertory Theatre on four consecutive nights starting 9 October 1923. Sir Cedric Hardwicke (1893–1964), actor, joined the Birmingham Repertory Theatre in 1922. He played many leading Shavian roles, including Captain Shotover in *Heartbreak House* and King Magnus in *The Apple Cart*. In *A Victorian in Orbit* (p. 17) he records that Shaw once told him: 'You are . . . my fifth favourite actor, the first four being the Marx Brothers'. In *Back to Methuselah* he played the roles of Haslam in Part II, the Archbishop in Part III and the He-Ancient (opposite Edith Evans as the She-Ancient) in Part V.

What most concerned us was that Shaw was returning to Birmingham for rehearsals. We flayed ourselves by remembering everything we had heard about the biting remarks he made about actors, and his alleged habit of reducing leading ladies to tears. . . .

He turned up at the theatre, in the timeless Jaeger suit, and inspected us assembled on the stage with feelings that were sinking with apprehension through the floorboards. None of us had any idea that he walked with difficulty and in pain, after having cracked some ribs a few days earlier, clambering over rocks on a visit to Ireland.[1] He immediately showed himself to be the most sympathetic and genial of men, an inspiring director, and no mean actor himself.

His rehearsal manners were impeccable. Where Tree[2] and others had left in the middle of a scene with no thought for the interruption they were causing, Shaw was all eyes and ears and sustained concentration, devoted to the task of 'making the audience believe that real things are happening to real people'. He could act out any role, the result of his years as a dramatic critic when he watched every actor and actress of any consequence, going back as far as Barry Sullivan,[3] that superhuman player of the old, bravura school. Down to the last gesture, he could reproduce the dying Hamlet as portrayed by Sullivan, whom he told me he rated as three times the actor Irving could have hoped to be.[4]

Shaw's rehearsal methods were founded on experience and developed by the cold logic of his mind. With his manuscript beside him, he had worked out in advance all important stage business, so that he knew not only what he wanted every speech to convey, but also precisely where it was to be spoken. The position of each piece of furniture and every prop was determined beforehand; when actors addressed each other, they were at the most effective distance apart. If one of us had to hang up his hat, the peg would be within easy reach. No time was wasted in fumbling for our places on stage, or trying out one position after another, until hit-or-miss chance solved the problem. As a result of his care and foresight, everything was calm, cool and unarguably correct. We were made to feel that we could not possibly improve on his business, and the impression was well founded. Any director who attempts to stage a Shaw play without following his stage directions, finds himself in trouble. They cannot be improved upon. I know, because I have tried the experiment as a director myself.

NOTES

1. For an account of this accident, on the coast of County Kerry, see *Collected Letters 1911–1925*, pp. 850–1.

2. Sir Herbert Drafer Beerbohm Tree (1853–1917), actor and theatre manager, was responsible for the first production in English of Shaw's *Pygmalion*.

3. Thomas Barry Sullivan (1821–91), Irish actor, whom the young Shaw had seen playing at the Royal Theatre in Dublin.

4. Sir Henry Irving (1838–1905), the celebrated actor–manager, was frequently a butt of critical attack by Shaw.

Jitta's Atonement

LAWRENCE LANGNER

From Lawrence Langner, *GBS and the Lunatic* (London: Hutchinson, 1964). *Jitta's Atonement* was first performed at the Shubert-Garrick Theatre, Washington on 8 January 1923. Siegfried Trebitsch's play *Frau Gittas Sühne*, of which Shaw's work is a very free adaptation, was first performed at the Burgtheater, Vienna on 3 February 1920.

When I was in London in the summer of 1922, Shaw told me of the unhappy plight of his Austrian translator, Siegfried Trebitsch, now ruined by the war, who had written a drama called *Jitta's Atonement*. To earn some money for him, Shaw had translated it into English. 'But how could you translate it when you don't know German?' I asked. 'I have a smattering,' he replied. 'Besides,' he added, with a twinkle, 'translating isn't just a matter of knowing the language. The original play was a tragedy – which was all right for Austria where they like tragic endings – but it would never go that way in England and America, so I turned it into a comedy!' Shaw then offered this play to the Guild.

Saint Joan in Composition

LADY GREGORY

From *Lady Gregory's Journals 1916–1930*, ed. Lennox Robinson (London: Putnam, 1946) pp. 211–12, 215. The following recollections are dated 19 and 23 May 1923. The composition of *Saint Joan* was begun on 29 April, and completed on 24 August 1923.

GBS drove me home and talked of his Joan of Arc play. He has not read Mark Twain,[1] is afraid of being influenced by him. He has read a little of Anatole France[2] and is reading the evidence at the trial, it was published some years ago. He does not idealise her as Mark does, and defends the Church, 'it didn't torture her'. I think there will be something good about the English soldiers. . . .

   GBS just before I left read me a new scene he had written in the morning, the Relief of Orleans, in a scene between Joan and Dunois and a boy. 'The wind', long waited for, comes and is shown to the audience by the waving of the pennon. I said if I had been writing it for 'Kiltartan'[3] I would have made the little boy sneeze. (And when I was going, after the play was put on, GBS said, 'You will have your sneeze.' So I did!)

NOTES

   1. Mark Twain's *Personal Recollections of Joan of Arc by the Sieur Louis de Conte* (London: Chatto & Windus, 1896) was presented on the title page as a translation of an original French document edited by him, in order to prevent the public from thinking it was another of his comic novels.
   2. Anatole France's controversial two-volume work *La Vie de Jeanne d'Arc* was published in 1908.
   3. 'Kiltartan' was the name used by Lady Gregory for her own style of writing in the rendering of Irish folk idiom.

Saint Joan

SYBIL THORNDIKE

From Elizabeth Sprigge, *Sybil Thorndike Casson* (London: Victor Gollancz, 1971) pp. 154–6, 159–60, 163–4, 165. Dame Sybil Thorndike (1882–1976), celebrated English actress, played Saint Joan in the first London production of the play at the New Theatre in March 1924. Her husband Sir Lewis Casson (1875–1969) co-directed the play with Shaw and played the part of the chaplain, de Stogumber. Shaw read the play to a small group at Ayot St Lawrence in the winter of 1923. In addition to Dame Sybil and Sir Lewis, the group included Sir Bronson James Albery (1881–1971), then manager of the New Theatre, the Antarctic explorer Apsley Cherry-Garrard (1886–1959) and Charlotte Shaw. Asked what she thought of the part of Joan, in an interview given to the *Evening Standard* on 1 March 1924, Sybil Thorndike replied: 'I think so much of it that I do not care if I never have another part'. Dame Sybil here records her response to the reading at Ayot and her recollections of the production.

We simply could not believe our ears. It seemed to me the most wonderful first scene that I had ever heard. Very daring, very startling. 'No eggs! No eggs! Thousand thunders, man, what do you mean by no eggs?'[1] It was extraordinary – and then the way he developed the mystery in that first scene. So daring and true, with that girl who was exactly as I had imagined her. When that first scene came to an end Lewis and I didn't say a word to one another. We both just felt, 'Oh, wonderful!' We could tell that Bronson Albery had certain doubts about it, but we had none.

Shaw read divinely. Like an actor, but much bigger size than most actors. Yes, a big-size actor. I felt, 'This is too good, it can't go on and be the real Saint John I've always wanted.' But it did, and I got more and more excited. And then at the end of the Loire scene, where the wind changes so dramatically, Shaw said, 'Well, that's all flapdoodle. Now the real play starts', and went into the tent scene with Warwick, Cauchon and de Stogumber, the Chaplain – one of the best scenes, I think, in all theatrical literature. He got the whole argument of the play into this scene, and one could see why he had wanted so passionately to write it. He made it clear that Joan did for France then what we hope somebody may yet do for the world. All the little warring factions in France she linked together. She made the nation. Shaw called her the first Nationalist and, although she was a devout Catholic, 'one of the first Protestant martyrs'. He also brought out the fact that she was a born general – she actually invented a new way of using artillery.

As the play progressed Lewis and I were more and more thrilled. The trial – I'd read the Records of it, and Joan's lines were word for word what she said. Except for the last big outburst, which was sheer poetry and pure Shaw. His two great speeches – the loneliness of God, at the end of the cathedral scene, and the great cry against imprisonment in the trial scene, those are the ones, and when people say Shaw wasn't a poet they should just read those speeches and consider whether they could have been written by anyone except a poet.

When it came to the Epilogue Lewis and I were in tears. Bronson Albery wasn't too keen on it – hardly anybody was. They said it was redundant, when the trial scene ended so marvellously – 'You have heard the last of her'. 'The last of her? Hm, I wonder.' People said that was the right finish, but Shaw said, 'No, that's not the finish. Now we've got to see what the modern world says. If she came back now it would be exactly the same.' . . .

Well, then we went into rehearsal. Oh, I shall never forget those rehearsals! Shaw was so inspiring, always a better actor than any of us. He took the morning rehearsals and Lewis took the afternoon ones and undid, Shaw said, everything he had done in the morning. But according to Lewis he was interpreting Shaw to us rabble. And actually he did have to translate some of Shaw's intonations into English for us. But besides this Lewis had got Shaw's tunes – the tune of every line. I remember Shaw telling me to say the words 'Dear-child-of-God' and 'Be-brave-go-on' just like the chimes. Shaw had such a sense of rhythm that any player with an instinct for music had only to hear the lines with a musician's ear to learn them with a minimum of effort. But this didn't mean anything falsely musical, any more than Shaw's Shakespearean speech meant ham – no, not ham in the least, just bigly spoken and not elocuted. Of course I had to speak in a dialect, because Shaw said he wasn't going to have one of those ladylike Joans. He made me invent a dialect, a sort of Lancashire cum the West cum this and that – what Nigel Playfair[2] used to call Lumpshire. I even used a bit of my Cornish maid's odd speech. In fact, I used something of her country-girl nature too.

I simply lived in that part. I have never had anything in the theatre which has given me as much as Saint Joan did. Something more than just theatre. It confirmed my faith, it confirmed something in my life that I've always known intuitively from my father's saintliness and my mother's ridiculousness, and all the things I had to say were things I wanted to say. That was marvellous, and Shaw said to me over and over again, 'Yes, you've got it – just what I wanted. I don't have to tell you anything, you know it.' But he did tell me, lots. And I loved him –

almost as much as I loved Gilbert Murray. One thing he said to us in rehearsal reminded me of what Edy Craig had said, when she was producing *The Hostage*.[3] 'Don't talk about God in holy voices, as if you are atheists.' And he liked us to be rather motionless, to stand about rather still, a thing he seldom did himself. . . .

We all thought the dress rehearsal was pretty exciting, but Shaw was horrified. 'You've spoilt my play,' he said, 'dressing yourselves all up like this. Why don't we do it just as it was in rehearsal? Sybil in her old jersey and the rest of you just as you were. You looked much better than all dressed up with that stuff on your faces.' He really was in despair, but we promised him that we would rehearse in our costumes and get rid of the dressed-up look. 'It won't be a costume play by the time we've done with it.' . . .

Ricketts was awfully funny with Shaw. He had a tiny little voice, and it got tinier and higher as he talked. 'You're so ignorant, Shaw,' he would say as we were all discussing the staging of *Saint Joan*. 'Your wife knows much more than you do.' . . .

When we read the notices that morning Lewis said, 'Well, we are good for six weeks on Shaw's name', and when we went up to the theatre a few hours later we couldn't get near the box office. And we played for six months choc-a-bloc.

I saw Shaw a couple of days later in Leicester Square, looking like a dark angel with the sleeves of his coat flapping. I chased after him – he always moved at a great rate.

'We're a success,' he said. 'What shall we do now?'

'A play about Elizabeth and Richard III – both together,' I said.

'Very well.' He laughed. 'And you and Ernest Thesiger[4] can play both parts turn and turn about.'

NOTES

1. The first lines of the play, spoken by Captain Robert de Baudricourt.
2. Sir Nigel Playfair (1874–1934), actor, manager and director.
3. Edith Geraldine Ailsa Craig (1869–1947), actress and director, produced Claudel's *The Hostage*, with Dame Sybil Thorndike in a leading role, in 1919.
4. See following recollection.

A Coy Dauphin

ERNEST THESIGER

From Ernest Thesiger, *Practically True* (London: Heinemann, 1927) pp. 141–2.
Ernest Thesiger (1879–1961), actor, recalls here his flirtatious response to Shaw's
inviting him to play the Dauphin in the 1924 production of *Saint Joan*, a role in
which he was brilliantly successful. Thesiger subsequently played a number of
important roles in later plays of Shaw.

At last he himself asked me to sit next to him, and said that he had
hoped that I would have acted in *Saint Joan*. 'I have never really wanted
to act in any of your plays,' I said. 'I have always thought that a Shaw
play could be best performed by several gramophones with *very* loud
speakers.' 'That is one of the reasons why I wanted you in my play,' he
answered. 'It is of the utmost importance that what I write should be
heard, and you, at any rate, are always audible.' 'There are surely
enough loud-voiced parrots,' I said, 'without engaging an artist,' and I
changed the conversation. There is nothing so exhilarating as being
offered what you most want and then flirting with a refusal. Moreover,
I knew that not only did I like Bernard Shaw very much better than I
had expected to, but that he also liked me.

After lunch, Mrs Shaw came up to me and said that they were both
very much disappointed that I was not going to play the Dauphin, but
that she quite understood the position. 'But if Mr Shaw really wanted
me,' I said, 'there would be no "position". I am quite certain that he
has a veto on the casting of his plays, and that he has only to insist
upon my being engaged, for the whole thing to be settled.'

That evening a telephone message engaged me to play in *Saint Joan*.

My part appealed to me enormously, but I was very nervous lest my
reading of it should not be in the least what Shaw wanted. So I was
considerably alarmed when after the first rehearsal he came up to me
in a most solemn manner and with that fascinating brogue of his said:

'There is one thing I want you to do about this part.'

Humbly I said that I would try to do anything he wished, upon which
he continued: 'I want you to go home to bed and stay there till the first
night. You already know as much about the part as I do.'

Shaw on Writing Plays

ARCHIBALD HENDERSON

From Archibald Henderson, 'Dramatists Self-Revealed. G. B. Shaw', [1925], unpublished typescript in the Currall Collection, Royal Academy of Dramatic Art. This questionnaire formed the basis for a heavily embroidered two-part article which Henderson published in the *Fortnightly Review*, under the title 'George Bernard Shaw Self-Revealed' (*Fortnightly Review*, n.s. CXIX [April and May 1926]). A fuller discussion of play-writing and other topics between Shaw and Henderson is recorded in Henderson's book, *The Table-talk of GBS* (London and New York: Harper, 1925).

1. *What principal factors must be borne in mind in writing a play?*

The aspect and mechanical limitations of the stage only. The born playwright has 'theatre sense' and bears them in mind automatically. They do not hamper his imagination, because all human faculties accept the limits of possibility without protest if they are conscious of them: that is, in this case, if they have theatre sense. For instance, no writer feels trammeled because his hero may have only one head and two legs, and cannot be in two places at once. In the same way the genuine playwright does not feel trammeled because he has to work under conditions which are not imposed on the novelist. . . .

2. *In writing a play, do you start from one central or dominant or controlling idea?*

In writing a play you start anyhow you can. You may even have a plot, dangerous as that is. At the other extreme you may not see a sentence ahead of you from the rise of the curtain to its fall. You mostly start with what is called a situation, and write your play by leading up to it and taking its consequences. The situation may be a mere incident, or it may imply a character or a conflict of characters. That is, it may be schoolboyishly simple or sagely complex. Even a repartee may be the seedling of a play. Then there is the chronicle play, in which you just arrange history for the stage. Akin to this is the play founded on fact, when you arrange some incident in real life for the stage; but this involves a fictitious introduction and a fictitious finish; so that your slice of life is treated as a situation. Examples from my own plays are *Heartbreak House*, which began with an atmosphere and does not contain a word that was foreseen before it was written. *Arms and the Man*, *The Devil's Disciple* and *John Bull's Other Island* grew round situations.[1] The first fragment of *Man and Superman* that came into my head was the repartee: 'I am a brigand: I live by robbing the rich.' 'I am a gentleman: I live by robbing the poor',[2] though it afterwards developed into a thesis play, which is always a Confession of Faith, or a Confession of Doubt, on the author's part.

The Philanderer began with a slice of life,[3] *Back to Methuselah* is prophecy, in the scriptural, not the race tipster's sense. Sometimes the grand scene of the play is left out when you come to it. That happened in *Pygmalion*:[4] the only person who spotted it was Barrie. *Caesar and Cleopatra* and *Saint Joan* are, of course, chronicles. The only play which I planned and plotted was *Captain Brassbound's Conversion*, which was neither the better nor the worse for that ceremony.[5] The only rule that I can give is that it matters very little what starts the play: what is important is to let it take you where it wants to without the least regard to any plans you may have formed. The more unforeseen the development the better. Nobody knows or cares about your plans and plots, and if you try to force your play to conform to them you will distort your characters, make the action unnatural, and bore and frustrate the audience. Trust your inspiration. If you have none, sweep a crossing. No one is compelled to write plays.

3. *What mental procedure takes place when you write a play?*

Imagination. If I could tell you more than that I should be famous, not as a playwright, but as the greatest psychologist that ever lived. But the object of the mental procedure is plain enough. It is to select from the unmeaning mass of events which you can record by cinematographing a crowded city street – a spectacle which leaves you as ignorant and bewildered as it has left many a bootblack who has seen it day after day for years – a set of imaginary but possible persons and a series of imaginary but possible actions which make life intelligible and suggest some interpretation of it.

When the great dramatists are driven by their evolutionary appetite for knowledge to do this, and to have invented the theatre and the art of acting and the dramatic form in literature to communicate their lesson to the world, then smaller men use the theatre for smaller ends, to raise a laugh, to tell naughty stories in dramatic form, to tomfool or sentimentalise according to their taste and depth and that of the paying public; but the root of the business is one desire for larger and clearer consciousness of the nature and purpose of that wonderful mystery life, of which we find ourselves the tormented and erratic, but still aspiring vehicles.

4. *Do you visualise the characters?*

No. I can neither draw them nor paint them. My sense of them is not a visual one: if it were I should be another Hogarth. My sense of my characters is one of the unspecified senses. It has nothing to do with sight, sound, taste, smell or touch. Two intimate friends of mine have just died. I knew them both for forty years. But I cannot tell you the colour of their eyes.

5. *Do you draw your dramatic characters from real individuals?*

Sometimes. But the use one makes of the living model varies from close and recognisable portraiture to suggestions so overloaded with fiction that the most ingenious detective could not penetrate the disguise. Among well-known people of whom I have made use are Mrs Besant, Cunninghame Graham, Gilbert Murray, the late Countess of Carlisle, Sidney Webb, Sir Almroth Wright, Stopford Brooke, Bishop Creighton and Lord Haldane,[6] to say nothing of practically avowed caricatures of A. B. Walkley, Mr Asquith, Mr Lloyd George and the Kaiser.[7] In one case I thought I was using a certain public man as a model; but I became conscious years later that I had really used another. Cokane, in *Widowers' Houses*, was a man I had never seen; but my mother told me stories about him; and her father's solicitor was never tired of imitating him. Sartorius was an Irish stationer to whom I never spoke: his imposing manner proclaimed his character. Bohun, in *You Never Can Tell*, is a variation on Jaggers in Dickens's *Great Expectations*. The critic in *The Philanderer* was Clement Scott, the sentimentalist of the *Daily Telegraph*. I omit cases of writing parts for particular performers. Sometimes my imaginary characters turn up later in real life. But all this part of my business is very fanciful. The chief use of models is to correct or prevent too much family likeness between one's characters, and excessive mannerism in drawing them.

6. *Do you ever create characters which are composites of several individuals?*

I probably never did anything else. But I have never done it consciously.

7. *Do you always first draw up a scenario?*

No. I cannot too often repeat that a play is a natural growth, and not the filling up of a form. Of course what is called a well-made play – the nineteenth-century Parisian article – can be built up like a ferro-concrete house; but the real thing grows and shapes itself and is a joy for ever, whilst the watching of a ferro-concrete building, though interesting for the first time, soon becomes a bore.

NOTES

1. *Arms and the Man* develops from the situation in which a fleeing soldier takes refuge in an enemy household and is given protection in her bedroom by the daughter of the house. The situation was suggested to Shaw by a scene in Verdi's opera *Ernani*, which is based on the historical play *Hernani* by Victor Hugo. In a letter to William Archer of 22 June 1923, Shaw wrote: '*The Devil's Disciple* began with the situation of the arrest of Dudgeon, *John Bull's Other Island* with the Irishmen laughing at the accident to the pig and the motor car and the Englishman taking it seriously' (*Collected Letters 1911–1925*, p. 837).

2. This became part of the opening exchange between Tanner and the brigand, Mendoza, in Act III of *Man and Superman*. I have suggested elsewhere that Tanner's reply may have been based on a passage in a story by William Morris (see A. M. Gibbs, *The Art and Mind of Shaw: Essays in Criticism* [London: Macmillan, 1983] p. 138, n. 14).

3. Act I of *The Philanderer* was founded on a 'shocking scene' which occurred on the evening of 4 February 1893. Shaw was visiting Florence Farr when the extremely jealous Jenny Patterson burst in on them and became abusive and violent (see *Collected Letters 1874–1897*, pp. 295–6).

4. The scene of Eliza's triumph at the ambassador's reception was omitted in the original version of *Pygmalion*. Shaw later created a reception scene for the film scenario.

5. But Shaw had earlier told William Archer that his working to a plan made the first act 'smell a little of the workshop' (*Collected Letters 1911–1925*, p. 837).

6. Shaw made use of these people as follows: Mrs Besant (Mrs Clandon in *You Never Can Tell*, and possibly Raina in *Arms and the Man*); Cunninghame Graham (Sergius in *Arms and the Man*); Gilbert Murray (Cusins in *Major Barbara*); the Countess of Carlisle, Murray's mother (Lady Britomart in *Major Barbara*); Sidney Webb (Bluntschli in *Arms and the Man*); Sir Almroth Wright (1861–1947), distinguished Irish-born bacteriologist (Sir Colenso Ridgeon in *The Doctor's Dilemma*); Bishop Mandell Creighton (1843–1901), Bishop of London (the Bishop in *Getting Married*); Richard Burdon Haldane, Viscount Haldane of Cloan (1856–1928), lawyer and statesman (the Waiter in *You Never Can Tell*).

7. A. B. Walkley is satirised in the character of Mr Trotter, one of the several theatre critics invited to see the play-within-the-play in *Fanny's First Play*. Herbert Henry Asquith, 1st Earl of Oxford and Asquith (1852–1928), British Prime Minister from 1908 to 1916, and Lloyd George are caricatured in Part II of *Back to Methuselah* as H. H. Lubin and Joyce Burge. Kaiser Wilhelm II (1859–1941), German emperor, was the model for the Inca in *The Inca of Perusalem*.

Part 10
World Travels

INTRODUCTION TO PART 10

Before the 1930s Shaw had travelled no further than North Africa. But his journey to Russia in 1931 was the prelude to a period of voyaging that took him to South Africa in 1931–2 and again in 1935, around the world in 1932–3, to New Zealand in 1934, and to the Pacific in 1936. Undoubtedly Charlotte's restlessness had a good deal to do with this change in their lifestyle (she always enjoyed travelling more than he did) and their increasing age made her at least anxious to escape a part of the English winter. Yet Shaw, who had told a young admirer in 1924 to remember in the midst of its vexations that 'travel is for recollections and not for experiences', came to find a positive value in removing himself from the routine weekly shuttle between his London flat and Ayot St Lawrence. Eleven years later he wrote to the same correspondent: 'I now take my holidays on ships going as far round the world as possible, as I find that in this way alone can I work continuously and rest at the same time.'[1] Evidently shipboard life suited him and encouraged him to write, for he was freed from the incessant demands of being a celebrity at home. But whenever he landed he became the celebrity again, and though he delighted in his world-wide acclaim and expected it, after a certain point the attention annoyed and exhausted him.

Naturally, journalists in the countries Shaw visited sought his views on world affairs and he dispensed them readily enough. In the following selection, however, preference has been given to those of his pronouncements that have a more specific local reference.

NOTE

1. *To a Young Actress: The Letters of Bernard Shaw to Molly Tomkins*, ed. Peter Tomkins (London: Constable, 1960) pp. 62, 164.

Russia: I

H. W. L. DANA

From H. W. L. Dana, 'Shaw in Moscow', *American Mercury*, March 1932. Henry Wadsworth Longfellow Dana (1881–1950), American lecturer and author, spent six months in Russia in 1931 working on a book about Soviet drama, and was in Moscow when Shaw made his only visit to Russia, lasting nine days and including his seventy-fifth birthday on 26 July. The visit had been suggested to him by Philip Henry Kerr, 11th Marquess of Lothian (1882–1940), journalist and Liberal statesman, and the party also included Viscount and Lady Astor and their son David (but not Charlotte). Nancy Witcher Astor (1879–1964), American-born politician and hostess, was the first woman to sit in the House of Commons; she was Conservative MP for the Sutton division of Plymouth from 1919 to 1945. She seems to have made friends with Shaw in 1927 (his name first appears in the visitors' book at Cliveden, the Astors' country house, at Christmas that year).

When it entered the station and slowed down, they saw standing in the narrow doorway of the railway carriage a tall, thin man in a brown suit, with brown cloth gloves, and a brown, soft felt hat, which he waved over his head in response to the welcoming cheers. . . . His healthy pink face was wreathed in a genial smile. His blue eyes sparkled with malicious enjoyment. He seemed to be saying: 'Here I am at last and I like you!' All doubts disappeared. Shaw was a friend among friends.

As we walked along the platform toward the still larger crowd that was waiting impatiently outside, I took the occasion to introduce to Mr Shaw a young compatriot of his, an Irish youth of eighteen. In answer to Mr Shaw's questions, he said that he had come to Moscow for ten days, had already stayed ten weeks, and had decided to stay for ten years. Shaw answered enthusiastically: 'If I were your age I would do the same!' And we felt he really meant it.

Through the cheering masses of workers outside the station, we made our way to the Hotel Metropole, where Shaw and his party were staying.

From there, as soon as he had taken his bath and brushed up a bit, Mr Shaw asked to be conducted at once to the mausoleum of Lenin[1] in the Red Square. Entering the dark red marble tomb, he stood for a long time looking at the embalmed body of Lenin lying there. It was interesting to watch in juxtaposition the heads of two of the brainiest men of our age, one preëminent in politics and the other in literature, here in death and life brought face to face. Perhaps no foreigner ever lingered so long looking at the figure of the dead Lenin. At length, in answer to my question, Shaw made his comment on the finely chiselled features that he had been gazing at: 'Pure intellectual type.' Commenting on the hands of Lenin, he pointed out that he had evidently never worked with his hands and then added with characteristic Shavian exaggeration: 'His ancestors evidently never worked with their hands for six hundred years', – a statement which is probably not true of any mortal. . . .

From the tomb of Lenin, Shaw asked to be taken into the Kremlin. Passing through the heavy gateway in the crenellated walls, we entered the former fortress of the Tsars, which had become the centre of the government of the workers. Far from humbly acquiescing to all that was said and to all that he was shown, Shaw reacted in a way that kept his guides continually guessing. When from the terrace of the Kremlin they pointed out to him the great gilded dome of the nearby Church of the Saviour, a mid nineteenth century monstrosity, which had dwarfed the towers of the Kremlin during recent decades and which they were now tearing down, Shaw pretended to be shocked and cried out, 'What you need is not an Economic Five-Year Plan, but an Æsthetic Five-Year Plan.' Yet a little later, when they showed him how carefully they have preserved the beautiful earlier Russian churches of the thirteenth, fourteenth and fifteenth centuries, and how the crosses were still intact on the domes and the imperial two-headed eagles on the towers of the Kremlin, Shaw took the other tack and playing with a new paradox, declared, 'You Russians are not thorough-going revolutionists at all. In England, Henry VIII did a better job in destroying monasteries, and Cromwell in Ireland. We English are really the thorough-going revolutionists. You in Russia are only half-way revolutionists!'

The bewildered Russians did not know how to take Shaw's sallies and began to feel that perhaps he was right and that they had not been thorough enough in their attack on religion. They were equally puzzled a few minutes later when he climbed up on top of the big old cannon of the Kremlin and posed as a pacifist. . . .

[In the afternoon of this first day Shaw made a tour of public parks, ending as follows.]

We had climbed a hill from which we got a view over the far extended playing ground, across the river crowded with boats and swimmers, to the city of Moscow with its towers and domes. We were descending the hill cautiously by wooden steps, keeping hold of the railing. Suddenly I saw Mr Shaw running down the hill ahead of us and waiting laughing for us at the bottom. On the eve of his seventy-fifth birthday

he seemed magnificently fit. At the end of the day, when the others
were puffing, they often suggested going back to the hotel, saying, 'We
mustn't tire out Mr Shaw'; but it was obvious that it was they who were
tired and not he. Throughout his nine days' stay he showed an
inexhaustible curiosity. He insisted on seeing the things and the people
he himself wanted to see. . . .

The following day Shaw asked to see the workers at work, and visited
a great electric plant. He watched with keen interest the merry zeal with
which the men worked. When the lunch-hour came, they gathered
around him and asked him for a speech. He was lifted on to a motor
lorry as a rostrum. Once more, as he had fifty years ago in his early
Socialist days, he found himself speaking from what he used to call the
cart's tail. Some of the shock troops among the workers who had
received the Lenin Medal for getting work done quicker than the others,
were introduced to him. Shaw remarked:

> In England a worker who gets his work done quicker than his fellow
> workers would receive from them not a medal but a thumping. What
> is the difference? If our workers produce more, that merely enables
> some shareholder to stay longer on the Riviera. When you work faster
> you are enabling the Five-Year Plan to be finished sooner. Your work
> is building up Socialism. When I return to England, I shall try to
> persuade English workers to do as you have done, and establish a
> system where they are working for public service and not for the
> private profits of a few individuals. . . .

One day Shaw went to a talking film studio and had recorded there his
voice and features while making a speech on Lenin. A few days later
we went to see this talking film tried out. Shaw sat in the front row of
chairs in the projection room, watching himself appear on the screen
with boyish delight. He saw his film self come and bow with a merry
smile, take off his brown cloth gloves, lay them on the table, and
throwing back his head, begin his speech. . . .

Shaw went on in his talking film to make a comparison of the two
great tombs of the world today: the tomb of Napoleon in Paris and that
of Lenin in Moscow. He declared that the tomb of Lenin had today
become more important than that of Napoleon, and said:

> I do not know whether there will ever be a man to whom so much
> significance will be given as the future will give to Lenin. If the
> experiment which Lenin started succeeds, it will be the opening of a
> new world era. If the experiment fails, then I shall have to take leave
> of you when I die with something of melancholy; but if the future is
> the future as Lenin saw it, then we may smile and look forward to
> the future without fear. . . .

Another day Shaw went to the horse races. He said whimsically to his Communist companions, 'You don't believe in competition: So I suppose there will only be one horse.' They had named one of the horses in his honour 'Shaw'. But Shaw took so little interest in the race that when his namesake was running he dozed off, or perhaps pretended to doze, while he was preparing his next speech. . . .

The last evening came the interview with Stalin,[2] which Shaw had particularly demanded, and which no one had dared to refuse. Most foreigners had only been granted twenty minutes. Shaw came back triumphant, crying that he had broken all records and that Stalin had talked with him for two hours and twenty minutes. The reporters gathered around Shaw as he was about to enter the elevator. They were clamouring to hear something about the interview with Stalin. Shaw pretended that he was going to make a great revelation. They drew close around him. He began: 'I will tell you something about Stalin: Stalin has a black moustache' – and Shaw's elevator ascended, leaving the reporters gaping.

Later, still playing with the paradox he had used about Lenin, Shaw gave me something of his impression of Stalin. He said:

I expected to see a Russian working man and I found a Georgian gentleman. He was not only at his ease himself, but he had the art of setting us at our ease. He was charmingly good humoured. There was no malice in him, but also no credulity.

NOTES

1. Vladimir Ilyich Lenin, the leader of the Bolshevik revolution, had died on 21 January 1924, at the age of fifty-three.
2. Joseph Visarionovitch Stalin (1879–1953), son of a cobbler from Georgia, had established the supremacy of his power by 1928, when the first of the Five-Year Plans was introduced.

Russia: II

RHEA CLYMAN

From a letter by Rhea G. Clyman in the *American Mercury*, May 1945. Rhea Clyman was an American reporter based in Moscow at the time of Shaw's visit; her letter was written in response to another critical of a brief article of hers in the February issue of the *Mercury*.

The Shaw visit lasted ten days, and I was with Mr Shaw most of the time. He liked having me around; even at seventy-six, which he was then, he had an eye for the ladies. Also as I had been in Russia for three years and had learned the language, he wanted to hear all I could tell him about actual conditions. . . .

Mr Shaw did not like banquets, but he did like visiting churches. Professor Lunacharsky and Constantine Umansky, later ambassador in Mexico,[1] who were attached to the Astor–Shaw party as guides and interpreters, did their utmost to prevent this by arranging a full day's round of visits. However, with the aid of George Walker, British Embassy's first secretary, we managed to contrive it; between the hours of five and seven in the afternoon, when Mr Shaw was supposed to be resting, Walker would come into the hotel and take Lunacharsky or Umansky, whoever happened to be on duty, off for a drink in the bar, and I would slip upstairs and get Mr Shaw out the back way, and we would go off on a round of churches. It gave Mr Shaw great satisfaction, I remember, to discover that, despite, the anti-God campaign which was then going strong, the churches were still well patronised.

NOTE

1. Anatoly Vasilyevich Lunacharsky (1875–1933) had been the first Soviet Commissar for Enlightenment (Education) until he was removed from the post in 1929. A cultured and moderate man himself, he believed that pre-Revolutionary culture should be absorbed, not rejected out of hand. Konstantin Aleksandrovich Umansky (1902–45) had worked as a Tass correspondent in Rome, Paris and Geneva, and in 1931 had just returned to Russia to begin a successful diplomatic career, which would take him to the United States as ambassador in 1939.

Russia: III

JULIAN HUXLEY

From Julian Huxley, *Memories* (London: George Allen & Unwin, 1970) p. 204. Shaw's itinerary included a visit to Leningrad, where he was glimpsed by (Sir) Julian Huxley (1887–1975), biologist and author, then on an official tour of Russian scientific institutions.

In the Hermitage picture gallery we found another English party – Lady Astor (Nancy), escorted by her son and Bernard Shaw. They passed in front of a huge painting depicting a female saint giving suck from her ample breasts to a hungry beggar. 'You couldn't do that, Nancy,' said GBS to his flat-chested companion, and they passed on giggling.

Russia: IV

EUGENE LYONS

From Eugene Lyons, *Assignment in Utopia* (London: Harrap, 1938) p. 429. Eugene Lyons represented the American United Press agency in Russia. Experience of the Soviet system had eroded his earlier optimism, and his hostile view of Shaw's conduct in Russia typifies the majority reaction in western countries. Shaw himself dismissed claims that he had seen only what he was meant to see when he addressed an ILP summer school shortly after his return to England. 'The things I wanted to see were precisely the things I did see. I didn't want to see poverty and other remains of the capitalist system they have not been able to remove. I said I can see that within twenty minutes of my home in London' (*Manchester Guardian*, 6 August 1931).

It was a fortnight of clowning that ran us ragged. Since I reported for British United Press as well as the mother agency, I could not afford to miss a Shavian wheeze or sneeze. My secretary camped in the Metropole lobby, someone else trailed the party on its sight-seeing trips. Deftly Shaw skimmed the surface, careful not to break through the lacquer of appearances; if Lady Astor asked too many questions he neatly slapped her wrist. He judged food conditions by the Metropole menu, collectivisation by the model farm, the GPU by the model colony at Bolshevo,[1] socialism by the twittering of attendant sycophants. His performance was not amusing to the Russians, I happen to know. It was macabre. The lengthening obscenity of ignorant or indifferent tourists, disporting themselves cheerily on the aching body of Russia, seemed summed up in this cavorting old man, in his blanket endorsement of what he would not understand. He was so taken up with demonstrating how youthful and agile he was that he had no attention to spare for the revolution in practice.

NOTE

1. The GPU were the secret police; they ran a penal settlement for homeless boys at Bolshevo, which Shaw visited and approved.

Russia: V

CATERINA ANDRASSY

From Caterina Andrassy, 'GBS in Moscow', *New Statesman and Nation*, 3 March 1951. Caterina Andrassy recalls the reception in honour of Shaw's seventy-fifth birthday given by the Soviet government in the former Club of the Nobility. It had been preceded by a party in the British Embassy.

After an interminable period of waiting, Bernard Shaw at last appears. He is wearing a Norfolk jacket and a shirt without a tie. He has tried his best to look Bolshevik, but he has not succeeded in losing his strikingly Anglo-Saxon air. . . .

Lunacharsky delivers a speech in Russian. We don't understand a word of it, but there is no doubt that he is appropriating Shaw, turning him into the precursor of the proletarian dictatorship, the 'Voltaire' of the Russian Revolution,[1] the destroyer of individualism and inspirer of the new collective ideology. Shaw seems rather worried about what is said about him and, with one eyebrow raised, giving him a Mephisto-phelean expression, he listens attentively to the translation of the interpreter seated behind him. But still more so are his English travelling companions who, wiping the sweat off their brows, wait uneasily for what their great 'enfant terrible', will say or do next.

In an impressive silence Bernard Shaw rises and addresses the audience.

'Tovarichi . . .' his voice is drowned in a storm of enthusiasm which he endeavours to diminish by adding that it is the only word he knows in Russia. He tries to assume his customary ironic tone; but somehow less successfully than at other times. One cannot help feeling that he is deeply touched by the spirit of the people – although he tries to conceal it. It is not the usual Bernard Shaw – his jokes lack their habitual flavour.

'My travelling companions are all capitalists, very rich capitalists indeed,' he continues. At this Lady Astor claps her hands in genuine pleasure, and the audience, not understanding English and imagining that it must be something revolutionary, again reacts with a new burst of applause. 'They were very worried coming to Russia. . . .'

He goes on, but his wit dries up. And then suddenly: 'I can't talk to you as I generally do, I see in your eyes something I have never met in the audience of other countries.'

After this he goes on in a changed voice. There is nothing left of the sardonic Shaw; an unusual earnestness has taken hold of him.

'England should be ashamed that it was not she who led the way to Communism. We let Russia, an industrially backward country, do what we should have done.'

I see Lord Astor nervously twitching his short moustache.

'It is a real comfort to me, an old man, to be able to step into my grave with the knowledge that the civilisation of the world will be saved. . . . It is here in Russia that I have actually been convinced that the new Communist system is capable of leading mankind out of its present crisis, and save it from complete anarchy and ruin. . . .'

How many things have changed since then.

NOTE

1. The energetic crusade by Voltaire (1694–1778) against all forms of tyranny and persecution by the privileged powers of Church and State was held to have prepared the ground for the French Revolution.

South Africa, 1932: I

From 'Breakdown of Morality', *Cape Times* (Cape Town), 12 January 1932. Escaping the northern winter, the Shaws docked at Cape Town on 11 January 1932, their destination apparently determined by the adroit salesmanship of Rex Naisby from the South African tourist bureau in the Strand (see *South Africa* [London], 11 November 1950). Their visit was prolonged by a motor accident in which Charlotte was injured. While she convalesced, he wrote *The Adventures of the Black Girl in her Search for God*. Most of the lengthy interview he gave to the *Cape Times* on his arrival was, understandably, devoted to broader issues, but he hazarded some local comment near the beginning.

Asked if he would discuss any South African problem, Mr Shaw said he had been particularly struck by that of the 'black proletariat'.

'It seems to me to create an appalling problem,' he said. 'The white man with a trade or a profession or owning property is in a strong position, but when you have "poor whites" up against black men with a lower standard of living, what can you do with them? Simply drop them into the water?'

Mr Shaw made some trenchant observations on morals and religion: 'There has been a tremendous moral change in Britain since the war.

The subject of my latest play (*Too True to be Good*)[1] is the breakdown of morality in the war. You cannot turn morality upside down for four years and say, "Evil, be thou my good".

'The professional soldier admittedly has an inverted morality; he has to have. But it is no use imagining you can throw a whole people into a war and then get down to normal again when it is over.

'The average modern Christian does not realise he is not a Christian, and does not know what it is to be a Christian. Yet he is making Christians of the negroes.

'One does not know what is going to happen. Civilisation is like a tree. It grows to a point and then perishes. We do not know that the next civilisation may not be a black civilisation. There is a danger in natives taking their Christianity with intense seriousness, because they will find out their teachers only profess to be Christians. The best thing would be to develop their intelligence and make them sceptics.'

True religion, according to Mr Shaw, is to be found only in Russia.

'Where will you get genuine religious fanaticism?' he asked. 'You get it in Russia. They have a religion and they believe in it. The man who is religious is working for something outside himself. The Russian serves the good of the State, the Commune. He carries out the Christian doctrine that "all are equal" – he may say "before Marx". No one believes here that the black man is the equal of the white, that the professional man is the equal of the retail shopkeeper, equal in the sight of God – but the Russians do believe it. The child there is taught to work for the State and the community.'

NOTE

1. *Too True to be Good* had been written between March and June the previous year.

South Africa, 1932: II

From 'GBS advises South Africa', *Daily Telegraph*, 21 March 1932. The Shaws finally sailed from Cape Town on 18 March and the *Telegraph* correspondent despatched a report of Shaw's parting remarks.

When interviewed, he said that natives had far better manners than Europeans and were much more intelligent. They were also, he said, the only people who could do the work that needed doing. Yet thousands of natives were starving.

He spoke scathingly of the 'poor whites'. 'In the Knysna district, where I have been staying amid beautiful surroundings,' he said, 'I came across large numbers of white degenerates, people without intelligence and absolutely hopeless as a stock for South Africa. You ought to shoot them all.'

Dutch country folk generally Mr Shaw found to be a fine, upstanding race, interesting because of their isolation from the world, and needing only education.

'Make them take an intelligent interest in things,' he said, 'and, above all, ban the Bible. Take the Bible away from them. They depend too much on it.' . . .

Finally Mr Shaw advocated a huge Government scheme for enriching the poor soil of South Africa with nitrogen extracted from the air. This, he said, was the solution for all South Africa's troubles.[1]

NOTE

1. In a broadcast relayed throughout South Africa on 6 February Shaw had advanced the same scheme, using 'methods which the Germans were forced by the war to invent and are in operation in England at the gigantic works of Imperial Chemical Industries, Ltd, in which my wife has some shares' (*Cape Times*, 8 February 1932).

South Africa, 1935

From 'Marriages of Black and White', *Daily Telegraph*, 11 June 1935. Shaw revisited South Africa in May 1935 in the course of a voyage round the African continent. In this interview, given on his return to London, he began by speculating whether the climate inhibited the breeding of white settlers, quoting a government minister's appeal for immigrants 'to keep up the white population'.

'I suppose it may be there is too much sunshine for people with white skins. The probable remedy is for them to darken their skins.

'This means, in South Africa, by marrying Bantus.'

'Would not such an idea be highly repugnant to white people?' I asked.

'Well,' replied Mr Shaw, 'there are a great many half-breeds. In Hawaii[1] they told me that the South Sea Islanders were disappearing and that very few pure-bred ones are left.

'In South Africa the mixture of the two colours may provide the solution to the problem. It is not a question of black and white. In the first place there is no such thing as a white man on the face of the earth: the Chinese call us the pinks, very properly.

'The Zulus are a markedly superior type of person, and all attempts to keep them in an inferior position seem to break down before the fact that they are not inferior. Certainly when you see them working you wish you could see British workmen working that way.'

Mr Shaw suggested that the problem was not confined to South Africa, but extended to a very large part of the African continent.

'People,' he said, 'are speaking glibly now about giving the Germans back their colonies. There is Abyssinia on which Mussolini is thinking of laying his hand.[2]

'You may parcel the country out among the European Powers, but at the back of it one day Africa will say, "None of you will have it." Africans, whether Afrikander, black, white, or anything else, will see that Africa belongs to the Africans and not to so many competing European Powers.

'There may be mixture of blood, and so on, but the native has a good deal of capacity; in the long run it may be seen that he has the capacity to live in Africa and the others have not.'

NOTES

1. Shaw had spent three days in Hawaii in March 1933.
2. Germany had been deprived of her colonies (e.g. Tanganyika) after the First World War. For Abyssinia, see above p. 114, n. 1.

World Cruise, 1932–3: I

HIRALAL AMRITLAL SHAH

From Hiralal Amritlal Shah, 'Bernard Shaw in Bombay', *Shaw Bulletin*, November 1956; first published in Gujarati in *Prabuddha Jain* (Bombay), 15 November 1950. On 15 December 1932 the Shaws embarked on the *Empress of Britain* at Monaco for a cruise round the world. Their first port of call after passing through the

Suez Canal was Bombay, where the *Empress* anchored offshore from 8 to 16 January 1933. Shaw had expressed a wish to see the Jain temples and Hiralal Shah took him out in his own commodious, chauffeur-driven Delage touring car. After they had visited one temple, Shah proposed another and Shaw willingly agreed. Jainism,which resembles Buddhism, was an offshoot of the central Vedic religious tradition in India, differing in its belief that one may escape the endless cycle of rebirth, punishment or reward by attaining a true understanding of human life. The first man to do this was the Jina, and he and others who have succeeded are called Tirthankaras. Although Jainism had virtually no mythology in its original pure form, legends and the miraculous soon attached themselves to it.

We proceeded to the Walkeshwar Hills to see the Babu's Jain Marble Temple, built on a hilltop. Mr Shaw expressed delight at the panoramic view that spread before his eyes. Inside, in its sanctum, stood the huge central marble image of Tirthankara (Prophet), and Mr Shaw was able to observe it at close range. I explained to him how the image showed the expressions of Yogi in *Dhyana* (meditation), seated cross-legged in *Padmasana* posture (that is, each leg resting on the other thigh, the palms of the hands opened out and resting one on the other in the centre, above the legs; the gaze of the eyes fixed on the tip of the nose; the body remaining perfectly erect and in a sitting position, while controlling the breath).

Around the central shrine, in the surrounding walls, in individual niches, there were numerous small images of various gods and goddesses. Mr Shaw then directed his attention to the details of these images and observed them intensely, putting several queries to me. I explained to him the different characteristics of these images and of such other types as the God 'Harina Naigameshi',[1] etc. 'When the people see these sculptured images,' he asked, 'do they accept them, in their beliefs and in their thoughts, conceived as such, in concrete form and shape?' I affirmed this.

NOTE

1. Harinagamesi ('the man with the antelope's head'), leader of the heavenly infantry, was entrusted with the task of transferring the Jina's embryo from one womb to another.

World Cruise, 1932–3: II

ATIYA BEGUM

From Atiya Begum, 'Bernard Shaw at Aiwan-e-Rafat', *Dawn* (Karachi), 5

November 1950. Atiya Begum, who had had some earlier acquaintance with
Shaw, recalls in rather different terms the reception described in the previous
extract.

At Aiwan-e-Rafat I had arranged a function for him and he had
made two requests. That I should arrange for Indian dancing and no
autographs should be asked to which I readily consented.

As it happened, Tara, Sitara and Alakhnanda, three exquisite dancers
(sisters) from Nepal, were in Bombay and they gave their best performance
before Bernard Shaw. He left after spending three hours carrying with
him the gold *Kinari* garland I have presented according to custom and a
robe of honour of real *chameli* and *gulab*.[1]

As Shaw was getting into his car, people, in spite of strict injunction,
came with their albums for autographs . . . [*sic*]. Without a word he
collected them all and asked the car to start; just as the car left the gate
he threw the whole lot in the street!

Several months later I received a letter from Bernard Shaw. It started
with saying 'I have discovered that I am a greater fool than I thought.'

The letter went on to say that at the end of their round-the-world
tour every passenger brought out all the rubbish they had collected on
the trip and auctioned the same to get rid of it. When the gold *kinari*
garland was put to auction, he expected to get a dollar or so; instead,
he discovered that a lady was bidding for it and secured the same for
43 dollars. He went up to her and said what a fool she was to throw
away so much money on tinsel; she in return told Shaw that he was a
greater fool than she thought to consider gold as tinsel.

NOTE

1. The *kinari* is the border of a sari, woven out of silver or gold. *Gulab* is a
rose and *chameli* is similar to jasmine.

World Cruise, 1932–3: III

Report in the *Hindu* (Madras) of an impromptu press conference at Colombo on

19 January 1933, reprinted in the *Independent Shavian*, Winter 1965–6. The *Empress of Britain* stayed in port at Colombo until 23 January, Shaw retreating upcountry to Kandy meanwhile.

Mr George Bernard Shaw arrived here this morning by the *Empress of Britain*. He first declined to submit to a formal press interview on account of the relentless persecution to which he was subjected by reporters in Bombay. However, he gave characteristic replies to some questions fired at him. Asked for his views on the political situation in India, Mr Shaw said: 'No politics, please. Only if you give me £50,000 will I answer. This much will I say for nothing, namely, that the political situation in India is not going to be settled by me or in accordance with my ideas.' Asked if he could say anything about the rubber situation, Mr Shaw replied: 'I do not know anything about the rubber situation, but I know that rubber is largely used for the consciences of political statesmen. I suppose you produce that sort of rubber in this country – every country does, you know.' In reply to a question whether he had enjoyed the voyage so far, Mr Shaw said: 'I have not enjoyed my trip so far.' On the subject of travelling, Mr Shaw added: 'It is the most unpleasant thing in the world.' Mr Shaw was asked with what feelings he approached what Mr Lloyd George described as the most wonderful country in the world.[1] Replying, Mr Shaw remarked that Mr Lloyd George had said the same thing about every country he had visited, and hoped the people of Ceylon would not be so stupid as to be taken in by that. When thanked for answering the various questions, Mr Shaw said: 'I have done so with the greatest possible ill-will. Two journalists in Bombay drove me very nearly to physical assault.' Mr Shaw stated that he was going to Kandy and added that there was no use for people trying to see him there.

NOTE

1. David (later Earl) Lloyd George (1863–1945), statesman and former Liberal Prime Minister, had sailed to Ceylon for a holiday a year earlier.

World Cruise, 1932–3: IV

LU HSUN

From 'Lusin looks at Bernard Shaw', trans. from the Chinese version of Hsiu

Hsia by Martin R. Ring, *Shaw Bulletin*, November 1956; first published in
Japanese in *Kaizo*, April 1933. Lu Hsun was the pen name of Chou Shu-jen
(1881–1936), author and social critic, who came to be regarded as China's leading
literary figure. He had lived in Japan from 1902 to 1909, he knew Russian and
he had read a good deal of western literature in translation. Fiercely opposed
to the Kuomintang regime of Chiang Kai-Shek, he became sympathetic to the
Communists c. 1930. On 16 February 1933 he received a telegrammed request
from a Japanese literary group to cover Shaw's visit to Shanghai the following
day. He was unable to locate his quarry until the afternoon, when he was told
that Shaw was with the widow of the revolutionary leader Sun Yat-sen (1867–
1925).

I hastened to Madame Sun's. When I entered a tiny room next to the
living room, Shaw, occupying the seat of honour at a round table, was
eating with five other people. Since his picture had been displayed
everywhere and it was common talk that Shaw was one of the world's
great men, I felt immediately that here was a literary giant. Actually,
though, he had no distinguishing marks. On the other hand, his
snow-white beard, ruddy colouring and amiable countenance would, I
thought, have been extraordinary as a model for a portrait.

Lunch seemed to be half over. It was ordinary vegetarian diet, very
simple. The White Russian newspapers had been reporting that there
were innumerable waiters at Madame Sun's, but there was only one
servant carrying in the dishes. Shaw did not eat very much, but,
perhaps, he had eaten a bit at the beginning of the meal – it was hard
to say. Midway in the meal he started to use chopsticks. He handled
them very awkwardly, unable to get a firm grip on anything. What
made me admire him, though, was that finally he acquired the knack
and, grasping something tightly with them, he very proudly looked
around at everybody. Alas, no one had seen his feat.

I did not feel in the least that the Shaw of the lunch table was a
satirist. His conversation was very ordinary. For instance, he said:
'Friends are better than families. You can have long-term relationships
with friends in which you take them or leave them as you choose.
Fathers, mothers, sisters and brothers are not freely chosen. When you
can no longer stand them you must break away forever.'

When lunch was over, three pictures were taken. Arranging ourselves
for the pictures, I realised how short I was. I thought, 'If I were thirty
years younger, I could do exercises to stretch my body.'

At about two o'clock the Pen Club gave a reception for Shaw and we
all drove over to it in a car. It was held in a big foreign-style building
called the World Academy. When I walked upstairs, the people of the
Arts – the nationalistic writers, social luminaries and bigwigs of the
theatre (about fifty people) – were already gathered around Shaw asking

him all kinds of questions. It was as though they were leafing through the pages of an English encyclopedia.

Shaw spoke a few words. 'You gentlemen,' he said, 'are literary people and so you know all about this folderol. Compared with myself, a mere scribbler of words, you actors know the situation even better, since you engage in folderol as part of your profession. Beyond this I have nothing to say. By and large, today has been something like looking at an animal in a zoo. Now you've all looked. That's all there is to it.' Everybody burst into laughter, probably thinking that this was satire.

World Cruise, 1932–3: V

From 'GBS talks to Japan', *Manchester Guardian*, 28 April 1933. Shaw's visit to Japan consisted of brief calls at Beppu and Kobe and four days at Yokohama (6–9 March). This report on it was supplied by 'a Resident in Tokio', who observed that Japanese political leaders had been apprehensive of Shaw as a 'foreigner with ideas' who might prove unsettling for the regime.

The Prime Minister had a conversation with him, and said it was very interesting. The War Minister, General Araki,[1] had a two-hour chat with him, during which they seemed to agree that earthquakes were a good preparation for air raids. When it was all over the General remarked that Mr Shaw was wonderfully active for his age and not half so wrong-headed as he (the General) had been led to believe. Undoubtedly the prevailing impression in official quarters when the luxury liner with her potentially disturbing cargo went her way was one of pleasant relief.

The expectant Socialists, on the contrary, were not so favourably impressed. Those permitted by law to avow their political complexion assembled to give him tea and take his counsel. 'Are there no Communists here?' asked Mr Shaw. 'No,' was the reply. 'Then you are all Communists,' he said. They continued their denials, and, declaring themselves Fabians, asked for suggestions regarding policy. Mr Shaw brushed this aside and delivered a little lecture on the futility of Parliamentarism and the right of Mr Shaw to change his opinions. This was disconcerting enough, but worse was to come.

The Socialist deputation declared that the ideas embodied in *Fabian Essays* were now making some progress in Japan, but careful readers of *The Intelligent Woman's Guide* had noticed some changes in the doctrine. Had Mr Shaw's opinions changed since then, for his followers in Japan needed an ideology which would stay put? 'No change since the *Guide*,' said Mr Shaw, 'but it may come any day.' The Labour leaders were courteous but distressed. 'It is like trying to be a disciple of a whirlwind,' one of them said to me later. But they were not beaten, for in spite of their disappointment with his failure to preach them a clearly recognisable doctrine they managed to label him in the end. 'Mr Shaw is essentially an artist,' they quickly told the readers of their magazines, 'and not a social and political leader at all.' So now we know.

NOTE

1. Sadao Araki (1877–1966), nationalist soldier and politician, was Army Minister from 1931 to 1934. The Prime Minister at the time was the Admiral Makoto Saito (1858–1936).

World Cruise, 1932–3: VI

WILLIAM ROTHENSTEIN

From William Rothenstein, *Since Fifty: Men and Memories, 1922–1938* (London: Faber & Faber, 1939) p. 281. The artist (Sir) William Rothenstein (1872–1945), who had known Shaw since the 1890s, was more than once his guest at the Malvern Festival. He recalls Shaw there outlining his tactic for getting the peace to write at sea on the 1932–3 cruise. It was a situation Shaw had dramatised in the first scene of *Village Wooing*, written on that cruise, when he also began *On the Rocks*.

He and his wife had recently been on a voyage round the world, when he had managed to write a new play. But wasn't life on a pleasure cruiser disturbing? 'Not a bit,' said Shaw. 'I have an unerring eye for the type of old dear who is flattered to death at the idea of meeting a celebrity – and GBS is not to be met with by every one. Having selected my old dear, I ask her to come and join me one morning, fetch her a chair and a rug, tell her I am setting to work on a new play, and she is so delighted at being given the role of protector of GBS that whenever anyone comes near she makes agitated signs to warn him off, whispering that *Mr Shaw is at work on a new play*. So for the price of a rug and a chair I get perfect peace during the entire voyage!'

World Cruise, 1932–3: VII

EDMUND WILSON

From Edmund Wilson, 'Shaw in the Metropolitan', *New Republic* (New York), 26 April 1933. Shaw's 1933 visit to the United States gave him five days in California at the end of March (spent mainly on the Hearst ranch at San Simeon but also taking in the MGM film studios) and a brisk twenty-four hours in New York. His one public engagement there was a speech given for the benefit of the Academy of Political Science, a little known organisation which he seems to have favoured for its name. It was delivered in the Metropolitan Opera House on 11 April and broadcast live. In the audience was Edmund Wilson (1895–1972), journalist, author and critic, who had been associate editor of the *New Republic* between 1926 and 1931. Shaw's New York stopover was also notable for a satisfyingly symbolic meeting with the daughter of Henry George, the American who had put him on the path to socialism fifty years earlier (see above, p. 32).

Slim and straight, in a double-breasted black coat buttoned up high under the collar with an austere effect almost clerical so that it sets off the whiteness of his beard as his eyebrows against his pink skin look like cotton on a department-store Santa Clause – he walks on and off the platform in his black shiny shoes with the lithe step, all but prancing, of a cavalier; clasps his long tapering hands around his knee, as he leans forward to talk to someone, with a self-consciousness of grace almost feminine; and diversifies his long speech with movements and gestures self-conscious and precise like an actor's. And there are also the reddish nose of the old Irishman, the squared shoulders with arms folded of the schoolmaster, the rare moments of silliness or shyness of the young man who learned to face the public 'like an officer afflicted with cowardice, who takes every opportunity of going under fire to get over it and learn his business'.[1] All these are accommodated to an artistic creation of which Shaw's voice is the supreme expression. This voice has the fine qualities of his prose: with a charming accent, half-English, half-Irish – what the Irish call a Rathmines accent after the fashionable quarter of Dublin, an accent which says 'expawts' when his voice rises, 'exporrts' when it deepens, with a style from eighteenth-century Dublin in which phrases of the most commonplace modern slang start into vulgar relief, in a tone of old-fashioned courtesy which varies between the kindly and the sarcastic, he caresses and enchants the auditor with the music of a master of speech, enmeshing him, though less surely than in his books, by the strands of a skein of ideas of which he reels out the endless thread.

Here in this black arrowy figure, this lovely cultivated voice, is the spirit which for those of us who were young when Shaw had reached the high pitch of his power, permeated our minds for a time, stirring new intellectual appetites, exciting our sense of moral issues, sharpening the focus of our sight on the social relations of our world till we could see it as a vividly lit stage full of small distinct intensely conceived characters explaining their positions to each other. An explanation that burned like a poem. And here is the poet still burning. . . .

[Wilson continues with an evocation of the 'ugly and stale magnificence' of the huge auditorium, filled with a 'vast dumb audience' of supremely dull people.]

Before this demoralising aquarium of blind deep-sea creatures, then – before this awful tribunal of trolls, more terrible because they never pass sentence – poor Bernard Shaw appeared. During the earlier part of his speech, he was driven to comment on the silence which followed his most emphatic points. It was not till about halfway through that he evoked any spontaneous enthusiasm, and this was only from a special quarter. When, after dealing with social-economic issues in rather a gingerly fashion, he finally came out with the assertion that the only justification the capitalist system had been able to put forward was that, in spite of its inequalities in the distribution of wealth, it guaranteed to the working class at least a living wage and that a crisis which left millions unemployed meant the breakdown of the system – a burst of clapping was heard from the highest balcony. Shaw looked up in surprise. 'I confess,' he said, 'the splendour of this building had blinded me to the fact that the majority of my audience apparently belong to the unemployed!'

But it was not the majority of his audience: it was only some radicals in the gallery, where the seats were only a dollar. They broke into applause again when he said that in financing the war America had got 'pretty fair value for her money from the political point of view,' because she had 'achieved the salvation of Russia' – and now and then at similar statements; but when one looked down into the shirt-fronts of the orchestra where the seats had sold for five dollars, one could not see a pair of hands stirring. One man in the next-to-top gallery, where the seats were two dollars, remarked after two or three of these salvos: 'The gallery seem to be having a good time!' as if he had no idea what Shaw was saying nor why the people should clap him nor why he himself should have come, and this man gave the tone of the house. . . . In the beginning, he had not been able to feel out precisely what kind of audience he was up against – he seems to have supposed that the Academy of Political Science was a serious and alert organisation – and by the end he found himself trying to talk to two different and irreconcilable elements: what he evidently imagined, on the one hand, to be a regular after-dinner speaker's audience of conventional after-dinner dodos, and on the other a certain number of radicals. And, tacking between the two, he navigated his course with difficulty – baffled, no doubt, even further by the fog of the radio audience which enveloped him outside, an audience even more mixed, and infused with sufficient hostile sentiment so that it sent in several hundred complaints, while the speech was still going on.

Yet the ambiguity of the occasion was the ambiguity of Shaw himself. Why could he not have spoken under the auspices of some Socialist organisation, to whom he could have talked directly and who would have met him with a definite response? After all, it is not his visit to New York which has taught Shaw his after-dinner manner, made him the idol and prey of the press. . . . Though it is his very dramatist's gift, making it inevitable that he should dramatise himself, which has delivered him into the hands of modern publicity, the effect is a little compromising. After all, why should he be making public speeches in which he has to handle like hot potatoes convictions which were once incandescent? His training as a public speaker has been valuable in giving him what acting on the stage gave Shakespeare, Molière and Ibsen and what every great dramatist seems to have needed: first-hand knowledge of the reactions of an audience. But why should he keep it up? Why should he do it on such a large scale? He can write so much better than he speaks. . . .

Shaw carries his own paradoxes within him; yet it is still his poet's distinction that he can study and understand himself, that through the arguing characters of his plays he can give these paradoxes expression. And even in his public character, less authentic though it is than his literary one, he can still thrill us from time to time as he is able to make the timbre of the old daring, the old piercing intellectual clarity, ring out among the banalities of the lecturer. Even in the pompous opera house, before the dead bourgeois audience which he himself has let himself in for, he continues to stand for something which makes us see audience and theatre as we have never quite seen them before.

NOTE

1. See above, p. 39.

World Cruise, 1932–3: VIII

RITCHIE CALDER

From Ritchie Calder, interview in the *Daily Herald*, 20 April 1933. Ritchie Calder, later Lord Ritchie-Calder (1906–82), journalist and author, had a distinguished career of public service after the Second World War. Stealing a march on his colleagues, he interviewed Shaw in his cabin on the *Empress of Britain* in passage from Cherbourg to Southampton, where they docked on 19 April.

'I am an old man now,' he said to me with a serious wistfulness which was very unlike the old arrogant Shaw. 'When you ask me how I enjoyed this trip do not forget that I am not a young man who has gone round the world living on his emotions. I went on this tour for the rest, principally.

'I wanted to write. I have been writing continually the whole way. I had to, otherwise I should have thrown myself overboard through ennui.

'I have written a new play. At least, I have written enough for six plays and I have not decided yet how I shall deal with it eventually. I shall throw most of it away.

'My receptions were not of my asking. They were too strenuous. I wanted to escape them, but my chief danger was the risk of being mobbed to death. I assure you it was a real danger. . . . [*sic*].

'I did not want to make speeches. I did not want to give interviews. I was forced to, and everywhere I have been misrepresented.

'I visited Hong Kong University. The Chinese fascinated me. The students would keep on shouting for a speech. I gave them one.

'I said what was quite reasonable and quite true: "You young men should be revolutionaries at twenty. If you are not, God help you at forty, for you will be hidebound."

'That went out as "incitement to revolution". The students of Shanghai were planning to give me a similar reception. Because of my Hong Kong speech the "ringleaders" were arrested.[1]

'I had to "give them the slip". Mrs Sun Yat-sen, the widow of the Chinese revolutionary, had to come and take me off in a launch.

'Everywhere I have gone,' Mr Shaw added seriously, 'I have found the civilised peoples unhappy and anxious and, wherever they are uncivilised, they are happy and carefree.

'The natives of Equatorial countries leave you disillusioned about your Europeans, Americans and "civilised" peoples. They are the unspoilt peoples. They are the simple originals of our Smiths and our Browns still unsmudged by the hands of commerce.'

NOTE

1. The *Empress of Britain* was in port at Hong Kong between 11 and 15 February; two days' steaming then took her to Shanghai, for one day only. In a letter to the *Sunday Times* (27 May 1956) Professor Lancelot Forster recalled that in his Hong Kong address Shaw had blasted universities – 'They stereotype the mind' – but conceded that he might have sent a son of his to a university, not to listen to the staff but to argue with his fellow students.

New Zealand, 1934: I

From 'GBS Arrives', *Auckland Star*, 15 March 1934, reprinted in *What I Said in NZ: The Newspaper Utterances of Mr George Bernard Shaw in New Zealand* (Wellington: Commercial Printing and Publishing Company of NZ, 1934) p. 3; hereafter cited as *What I Said in NZ*. The Shaws' tour of New Zealand lasted from 15 March to 14 April 1934. They sailed from London and back again on the *Rangitane*, each voyage taking about five weeks, and at sea Shaw drafted *The Simpleton of the Unexpected Isles*, *The Millionairess* and *The Six of Calais*. In the following extract from the written interview Shaw gave on arrival, the first question has been transposed (it was originally printed after Shaw's answer).

Since New Zealand depends almost entirely upon the Home market, what chance is there for a return to prosperity in the Dominion so long as Britain allows foreign countries to flood the Home market with cheap foodstuffs?

You have no business to let New Zealand remain dependent on what you amusingly call the Home market, or any other overseas market. The real home market for New Zealand is the North Island plus the South. See what happened to the central empires in Europe in 1918. Nature had given them every possibility of self-support and made them impregnable to blockade. Yet they were starved out like rats in a trap because they had made themselves dependent on foreign trade. Keep your wool on your own backs; harness your own water power; get your fertilising nitrates from your own air; develop your own manufactures and eat your own food; and you can snap your fingers at Britain's follies.

What are the feelings of the average Briton towards New Zealanders and towards the Empire generally?

They have none really. The Dominions can indulge in all sorts of imaginative illusions about the British Islands and even call them Home in their sentimental moments; but that side of life does not exist in England. Many Englishmen with astronomical tastes are keenly interested in the moon. Their interest in New Zealand may be guessed from a letter I had before starting from a lady who said she heard I was going to New Zealand and hoped I would stay with her daughter, who has a very nice house in Sydney!

New Zealand, 1934: II

From 'I'm More at Home Here', *Auckland Star*, 2 April 1934, reprinted in *What I Said in NZ*, p. 11. Unlike most of Shaw's written interviews, this was presented without disguise.

Writing to Wanganui from Walrakel. In reply to the question whether he observed that New Zealanders had developed separate national characteristics, Mr George Bernard Shaw said, 'No, it is the other way about. The characteristics of the British Islanders have changed so much in this century. They no longer resemble the Englishmen of the nineteenth century; New Zealanders resemble them very strongly, and consequently there is now a marked difference, but it is the Englishman who has changed, not the New Zealander. I, being an old Victorian, am much more at home here than in London. You are quite natural to me, but to the English visitor born after 1900 you probably appear quaint, foreign and incredible – but that is only my guess, since you ask me for one.'

Mr Shaw said the whole world was being Americanised by Hollywood, which, by the way, was not typically American. 'You must really learn to make your own talkies, or you will lose your souls without even getting American ones,' he said. 'The tendency is no worse in New Zealand than elsewhere, not anything like so strong as in British slums and suburbs.'

New Zealand, 1934: III

From 'Address at Chateau', *Dominion* (Wellington), 4 April 1934, reprinted in *What I Said in NZ*, p. 10. The following extract is taken not from a formal interview, but from the report of a Sunday evening gathering of some 240 people at Chateau Tongariro, at which Shaw invited questions from the floor.

In answer to the question: 'What is your opinion of New Zealand as a tourist country?' Mr Shaw replied:

'I do not think it is going to be a tourist country. It is not as bad as that. New Zealand is a sort of place you should keep for the recreation of your own workers and people and not so much for tourists. The temptation is there because New Zealand has no money to waste.

'You have one advantage in your shows and sights. They are really very curious and interesting. In other parts of the world they have fake sights. People try to manufacture them and tell you something happened there that didn't. In New Zealand I have been taken to see a great many sights, and they are really interesting and extraordinary.

'That is the main thing. The danger is that, when people find out what an interesting place New Zealand is, they may come in crowds and you will be tempted to give up some interesting industry and become waiters (laughter) keeping hotels for tourists; and then when revolutions come in the countries where the tourists come from and they lose their money, where are you? I strongly advise you not to make too much of the tourist sights except for yourselves.'

New Zealand, 1934: IV

From 'The *Dominion* Interview', *The Dominion* (Wellington) 4 April 1934, reprinted in *What I Said in NZ*, p. 14. Although this substantial interview was presented as a live one, given by Shaw at Palmerston North after a long journey from Chateau Tongariro, it is classified as written in Dan H. Laurence's *Bernard Shaw: A Bibliography*, 2 vols (Oxford: Clarendon Press, 1983) vol. II, item C3046.

How do you find the New Zealander of fact comparing with the popular fictional notion of the British colonial?

You may pass over that. That notion is not popular of the colonial at the present time. That you were a colony there was no question. You were playing second fiddle, but the former colonies, United States, Canada and New Zealand, are Dominions now. England went to the Ottawa Conference[1] with a very patronising attitude, but when she got there she found people simply taking her by the scruff of the neck. It was not a case of the dog wagging the tail, but the tail wagging the dog. When I was young the colonies were colonies, but now they have become Dominions. They have now got the right to go direct to the King himself without the intervention of Parliament, and they send their own representatives to international conferences. England is beginning to play second fiddle. They levy protective duties against her and then expect England to give them every possible advantage. They even go to the length of not only asking that we should give a free entry to all of their products, but if any other nation refuses that they want us to retaliate upon that nation on their account. The situation is getting very strained.

NOTE

1. The Ottawa Conference was held from 21 July to 20 August 1932 on a Canadian initiative. Its response to world depression was to adopt trade preference between Britain and her dominions, which was extended to the crown colonies a year later.

New Zealand, 1934: V

From 'Christchurch Arrival', *Christchurch Press*, 9 April 1934, reprinted in *What I Said in NZ*, p. 18. Shaw gave an impromptu press conference in his hotel soon after reaching Christchurch.

Asked whether he had been impressed by the scenery on his way down the coast road from Nelson Mr Shaw remarked that it had been foggy most of the way so that he had not been able to see much of it. 'There's one thing I noticed about you New Zealanders,' he added. 'Wherever I go people say to me that they must take me to see New Zealand's last bit of original bush. I have been driven through miles and miles of it since I have been here, and each bit seems to be just as much the last and just as original as the one before. I must say, though, that it's unlike any bush I have ever seen, the ferns and the other native plants make it delightful.

'But I don't like your stumped paddocks. They look like the old battlefields on the Western Front, with the tree trunks all battered and smashed and burned by the shells. The Government should compel the owners to take them out – no expense should be spared for the sake of appearances.'

New Zealand, 1934: VI

From Ness Mackay, 'Farewell to GBS', *Dominion* (Wellington), 16 April 1934, reprinted in *What I Said in NZ*, p. 28. Ness Mackay interviewed Shaw on the deck of the *Rangitane* just before he sailed for England.

'We want to understand your duo-national views. You know, you have caused much consternation here by criticising ours!'

'Well, then,' he said, 'I did not use the word "sentimental" about you that learnt to call a distant country "Home" before you learnt to speak any other word. I apply the word "sentimental" to those absentee landlords of yours, who lived here, and worked here, and made money here, and now call England "Home" and go and live there, or make long trips there and spend their money there while you in New Zealand are trying to make a living out of what they leave. I have told some of your politicians that there ought to be a law to prevent these people taking all your money out of the country just now while you need it most.'

'Would that be Socialism, Mr Shaw?'

'That, my dear lady, would be sound sense. And there would be more sense, too, if England, which you call "Home" while you make tariff walls against her and then work yourselves to rages about her quotas, just shook you off. You Dominions! You all try to bleed her! I tell you this seriously: A day will come when England will just rebel and get out of "our Empire" as you call the game you play with her. She will, then!' said he with a tinge of a brogue and folded his arms and looked square down at me.

Part 11
Political Opinions, 1919–38

INTRODUCTION TO PART 11

Shaw's major political work in the period between the two World Wars was *The Intelligent Woman's Guide to Socialism and Capitalism* (1928). The arguments in that book were much in line with the ideals and policies of Fabian socialism. The goals of socialism were to be achieved by gradual, non-violent means within the framework of democratic institutions. But there were many signs, in the late 1920s and 1930s, of an increasing disillusionment on Shaw's part with democratic processes. Plays such as *The Apple Cart* (1929) and *On the Rocks* (1933) presented images of democracy in England in a state of almost chaotic disarray. Shaw's earlier fascination with autocratic figures, as exemplified in his portrayal of Caesar in *Caesar and Cleopatra* and Undershaft in *Major Barbara*, came to the surface again in his creation of the impressively intelligent and politically adroit monarch, King Magnus, in *The Apple Cart*. In the meantime, far less benign figures of autocratic power than King Magnus were beginning to emerge as dominant forces on the larger stage of European politics. Shaw was clearly impressed by, and attracted towards, the leaders of the major totalitarian regimes of the 1920s and 1930s, Stalin, Mussolini, Hitler and Franco, and sometimes he displayed a disturbing nonchalance in his attitudes towards their means of gaining and maintaining power. During the 1930s he became more critical of Fascism, especially in his condemnation of the anti-Semitism of the Nazi party; and his much-revised play about international politics, *Geneva* (1938), presents satirical, cartoon-like representations of Hitler (Battler), Mussolini (Bombardone) and Franco (General Flanco de Fortinbras). British domestic politics, the question of reparations after the First World War, movements for self-determination in parts of the British Empire and disarmament were amongst the other topics on which Shaw made public comment in interviews during the period between the wars.

'If Labour Came to Power', 1919

From the *Sunday Chronicle*, 24 August 1919. In the general election of 1918 the

Labour Party gained the second largest representation in the House of Commons and became the official opposition to Lloyd George's Liberal–Conservative coalition government. It was not until 1924 that Labour gained a brief period of office under the Prime Ministership of Ramsay MacDonald. Aleksander Fyodorovich Kerensky (1881–1970), moderate socialist revolutionary, was the head of the Russian provisional government in 1917 before its overthrow by the Bolshevik revolution led by Lenin and Trotsky. Arthur Henderson (1863–1935), chairman of the British Labour Party in 1908–10 and 1914–17 and member of the all-party War Cabinet, visited Russia in 1917 and accepted Kerensky's plan for an international socialist conference in Stockholm. Lloyd George at first favoured the idea but his eventual rejection of it caused Henderson's resignation from the Cabinet on August 12 1917.

(a) *Who are the men in the Labour Party who know anything of foreign affairs?*

(b) *Will not the Labour Ministers be mainly in the hands of permanent officials? Is there an advantage or disadvantage?*

(a) Modesty forbids me to give you a complete list. Have you read my *Common Sense about the War*, published in November 1914? and my *Peace Conference Hints*, published early this year?[1]

All the Labour Party men recognised that these pamphlets gave the simple truth about the diplomacy of the last twenty years. But the others did not recognise it. Of course the men who were behind the scenes knew. They knew even when I was only guessing, though I know the ground and the men so well that I guessed right every time. But outside the little group of statesmen actually implicated, the Unionists and the Liberals talked like schoolboys.

Just look at the mess they made of the Stockholm business! The Labour men, trained in a series of international congresses, know that the Russian revolution must be taken seriously, and that the alternative to Kerensky was not the Grand Duke Nicholas,[2] but Lenin and Trotsky holding Russia together by main force. The silly class-limited Front Benches in the House thought Kerensky was the devil in person, and played into Lenin's hands all through in spite of Mr Henderson.

Now I am myself, as an old Communist, a Bolshevist as far as the word has any sense except what the lawyers call vulgar abuse. To me Lenin is by far the most interesting statesman in Europe, and I foresee that we shall all be up against his problems presently. But it was not England's business to precipitate Bolshevism in Russia; and the Labour Party knew it. But it was the Government that precipitated Bolshevism, in spite of Mr Henderson, through sheer ignorance of foreign affairs, an ignorance quite compatible with the most intimate knowledge of all the gossip of the Embassies.

(b) All Ministers, Labour or Junker, have to depend a good deal on permanent officials. There is nothing in it either way.

Will a Labour Government safeguard the commerce of the country – particularly the overseas commerce?

Will a duck swim? What possible interest has the Labour Party in wrecking our overseas commerce? . . .

Can business men be assured that there will be no threat of unrest or of sweeping changes of a kind tending to paralyse enterprise?

No. They can perhaps be fooled by assurances that cannot be made good. But as long as you have Capitalism you will have industry paralysed as surely as you will have cargoes of fish thrown back into the water to keep up the price of fish, though people may be starving at the time. When the war found out the wretched incompetence of Capitalism, it was Socialism that saved the situation and unchained industry. The increase in production was stupendous; and it was forced on us by the hopeless breakdown of private enterprise. . . .

Will the military and maritime defences, which are vital to a great sea-bound Empire such as ours, be maintained at the pitch of absolute safety?

Of course not. Absolute safety is the dream of a panic-stricken drunkard. The militarists are always clamouring for it. . . .

In view of the dismal failure of the Labour Party now in Parliament is 'Direct Action' advisable?

What do you mean by the dismal failure of the Labour Party in Parliament? The Labour Party is not in Parliament. Mr Lloyd George took care of that. The victory gave him the power to dictate the membership of the House of Commons. He deliberately turned it into a ticket meeting of ignorant nobodies; and now his majority is greater than he can bear – and serve him right! If a man throws away the blade of his sword for fear of its cutting his fingers, and substitutes a leaden imitation, it is no use blaming the discarded steel because the sword won't cut.

If Parliament cannot help the people, the people must help themselves. That is what the cry for Direct Action means. But it is a futile cry, because the people cannot help themselves except by some form of Parliamentary action; that is why the Labour Party, which is nothing if not Parliamentary, came into existence. The people allowed Mr Lloyd George and their own lowest passions to fool them at the General Election; and they must now take the consequences of their folly.

What is this Direct Action that we hear so much of? Strikes. And what is a strike, after all? Just the old oriental trick of starving on your enemy's doorstep until he surrenders. What use is that here in the west, where a man is rich, respected and politically powerful in proportion to the number of people who are starving on his doorstep?

A strike is not direct action; it is direct inaction. Your children go without their dinners on the off-chance of your employer's children running out of strawberry jam five years hence. It is a mug's game, this striking. And even at that, what use is it unless it is powerfully controlled by a political organisation fully responsible to the community?

NOTES

1. *Common Sense about the War* was published on 14 November 1914 as a Special War Supplement to the *New Statesman*. *Peace Conference Hints* first appeared in the *New York American* weekly from 19 January to 23 March 1919 and was published in book form by Constable on 12 March 1919.

2. Nikolay Nikolayevich (1856–1929), a cousin of Tsar Nicholas II and commander of the Russian forces at the beginning of the First World War, was regarded as a possible leader of Russia after the Revolution.

Advice to Welsh Students, 1924

From 'Symposium', *Cap and Gown: the Magazine of the University College of South Wales and Monmouthshire*, November 1924. Under the treaty of Versailles (1919) obligations were imposed upon Germany to make reparations to the Allies for war damages. In August 1924, after the breakdown of many other attempts to devise workable reparations schemes, a conference was held in London under the chairmanship of an American, Brigadier General Charles G. Dawes (1865–1951), and a scheme known as the Dawes Plan was adopted. According to Charles S. Maier (*Recasting Bourgeois Europe* [Princeton: Princeton University Press, 1975] pp. 589–90) the Dawes Plan and the gold-exchange standard it entailed caused in Europe 'a downward pressure on employment' and 'tended to reinforce a corporatist and bourgeois settlement'. In 1922 Shaw had described the reparations as 'simply the plunder of the vanquished' (Anon, 'GBS among Modern Philistines', *Evening Dispatch*, 8 April 1922).

[CAP AND GOWN]: There is a widespread feeling among all faculties in the University of Wales that the payment of Reparations by Germany in accordance with the recent Pact of London will so affect the industrial prosperity of South Wales that students leaving college would be well advised to seek appointments abroad rather than in Wales. This is to them a real problem. Do you consider their apprehension justified?

[GBS]: When a nation condescends to live by plunder instead of honest work, and does not even distribute that plunder fairly, but allows it to be appropriated by its already rich proprietary classes, then its unpropertied students must abandon industrial subjects and qualify themselves to manage expensive golfing and motoring hotels; to trade in furs, jewellery, Rolls-Royce and Hispano-Suiza cars, or in delicacies for Ritz menus and so forth; to act as couriers, valets, gamekeepers, waiters, prizefighters, jockeys, racehorse breeders, specialists in gout and indigestion and cancer and appendicitis, dealers in works of art, fancy stationers, night club entrepreneurs, dancing masters, operatic tenors, and a dozen other employments in the retinue of the idle rich. And as this retinue must have its food and clothing and lodging and doctoring and other necessaries and minor luxuries, there will be plenty of occupation for the less gifted or less ambitious. There is therefore no need for any student to leave the country. What is needed is that the University of Wales should establish Chairs of Parasitism in its various branches, and discontinue all activities based on the assumption that its students are living in a productive and self-supporting country. The attention of its divinity students in particular should be devoted to the justification of Pleasant Ways of Going to the Devil and having a good time, until Germany, putting on muscle whilst we are putting on fat, turns the tables on us.

GBS and Mussolini, 1927

BEATRICE WEBB

From *Beatrice Webb's Diaries, 1924–1932*, ed. Margaret Cole (London, New York, Toronto: Longmans, Green, 1956) pp. 154–5. Benito Mussolini (1883–1945) began his political career as a trade union advocate and journalist, contributing to various socialist papers. His support of Italian participation in the First World War led to his expulsion from the Socialist Party and his leadership of the Fascists, who seized power by a *coup d'état* in 1922. Like many other public figures in Britain, Europe and the United States, Shaw was impressed by Mussolini's success in achieving stable government in Italy in the 1920s and in bringing about various social and economic reforms. He also chose to ignore, or at least seriously underestimate, the ruthlessly repressive character of Mussolini's regime. On 24 January 1927 the *Daily News* published a sympathetic letter by Shaw on Mussolini which a sub-editor had headed 'A Defence'. This drew attacks from many socialists and Italians in exile, including Dr Friedrich Adler, leader of the Austrian Labour Party and Secretary of the Labour and Socialist International. The *Daily News* published an extensive correspondence on the subject between Shaw and Adler on 13 October 1927. In August 1927 the Shaws were holidaying at the luxurious Regina Palace at Stresa.

Meanwhile GBS has created a sensation: he has gone out of his way to testify to the excellence of Mussolini's dictatorship – to its superiority over political democracy as experienced in Great Britain and other countries. Hence an interchange of letters, public and private, between him and Friedrich Adler (the secretary of the Socialist International). This correspondence arose out of an episode last February – an interview with Shaw in the *Daily News*; a telegram from the Italian Socialists objecting to the same; a reply by Shaw to Adler which the International office refused to publish, on the ground that it would appear in the Italian press without any rejoinder. There the matter was allowed to rest. But GBS, fortified in his admiration of Mussolini by spending eight weeks and £600 in a luxurious hotel at Stresa, in continuous and flattering interviews with Fascist officials of charming personality and considerable attainments, handed to the Italian press, in the middle of October, a deliberately provocative answer to Adler's February letter – this letter being broadcast, considerably garbled, throughout Italy. From the published correspondence in the English press and still more from a private correspondence with Adler, it appears that GBS puts forward the Mussolini régime as the *New Model* which all other countries ought to follow! His argument seems to be that either the Haves or the Have-Nots must seize power and *compel* all to come under the Fascist or the Communist plough. It is a crude and flippant attempt at reconstruction, bred of conceit, impatience and ignorance. It will injure GBS's reputation far more than it will the democratic institutions in Great Britain. But it reinforces the Italian tyranny. It is only fair to add that this naïve faith in a Superman before whose energy and genius all must bow down is not a new feature in the Shaw mentality. What is new and deplorable is the absence of any kind of sympathetic appreciation of the agony that the best and wisest Italians are today going through; any appreciation of the mental degradation as implied in the suppression of all liberty of act, of thought and of speech.

Shaw on Fascism, 1931

From 'G. B. Shaw and Fascism', *Daily Telegraph*, 25 February 1931. The following is Shaw's reply to a question put to him by a Bolshevik paper, *Die Welt am Abend*, about the political difficulties of Germany.

The Third Reich (the Hitlerites' name for their proposed State) owes its existence and its vogue solely to the futility of liberal parliamentarism on the English model. What we need now is positive and efficient State control and enterprise and initiative everywhere. What we get is resistance to the State, obstruction and endless talk about liberty – 200 years out of date.

Hence we are being swept into the dustbin by Steel Helmets, Fascists, Dictators, military councils, and anything else that represents a disgusted reaction against our obsolescence and uselessness. The remedy is to reform our political institutions and set to work on social problems with new and effective political machinery so as to outbid the Third Reich in efficiency and rapidity of social change.

If we do this, the Steel Helmets will melt in the sun. If not, no eloquence about democracy, no protest in the name of liberty will help us in the least. We shall simply be kicked out of the way; and serve us right.

'Halt, Hitler!', 1933

From Hayden Church, 'Halt, Hitler! by Bernard Shaw', *Sunday Dispatch*, 4 June 1933. This interview was conducted on Shaw's return from his world tour aboard the *Empress of Britain*. Hayden Church, an American journalist who was a member of the *New York Times* staff in London in the 1930s and 1940s, is the author of numerous interview-articles on Shaw.

MYSELF: Well, Mr Shaw, have you returned a Nazi? You came back from Italy to stand up for Mussolini. You came back from Russia to stand up for Stalin. Have you come back from everywhere to stand up for Hitler?

MR SHAW: The Nazi movement is in many respects one which has my warm sympathy; in fact, I might fairly claim that Herr Hitler has repudiated Karl Marx to enlist under the banner of Bernard Shaw. You can therefore imagine my dismay when at the most critical moment Herr Hitler and the Nazis went mad on the Jewish question.

Herr Hitler has received powers with which only the sanest of statesmen could be trusted; and his first use of them has been to reincarnate Torquemada, who believed that he was saving the world by not only burning live Jews but digging up and burning dead ones.

MYSELF: Why not have it out with him on paper? If anyone can argue Hitler down, you can.

MR SHAW: It is idle to argue against this sort of insanity. Judophobia is as pathological as hydrophobia. A statesman infected with it may go on from persecuting Jews to persecuting Jesuits, Freemasons, witches, Laplanders, and perhaps finally Prussians, against whom our handful of British Jewbaiters express a peculiar animus.

The Ku-Klux outrages on Negroes and Catholics in America are a well-known variety of delirium tremens; but no Kleagle has yet been made President of the United States.

The Nazis are suffering from an epidemic of a very malignant disease; and the result is that the British police had to protect Dr Rosenberg[1] when he came to London, expecting, apparently, to be received with open arms by a friendly England, from being treated as mad dogs are treated.

MYSELF: Well, if you won't argue with Hitler, why not psycho-analyse him? Where did he get this anti-Jew complex? What has it to do with Fascism? Mussolini does not persecute Jews. Why should Hitler?

MR SHAW: Quite true. Judophobia is not a part of Fascism but an incomprehensible excrescence on it.

MYSELF: But where does the persecution of the Jews come in?

MR SHAW: Dr Rosenberg replies that the Jew is a profiteer.

MYSELF: There is nothing peculiar to the Jews in that, is there?

MR SHAW: Nothing whatever, except that the Jew often understands the game better and is cleverer at playing it than the sort of flaxen-haired chump who feels flattered when he is described as Nordic.

There is nothing in Dr Rosenberg's excuse. It is true that as the Nazis are professed Socialists they are pledged to put an end to profiteering. But if there is any lesson that the Socialists have had to learn of late, both from my urgent precepts and from the bitter experience of the Soviets with the Kulaks,[2] it is that a Socialist Government must not expropriate the private employer until it is ready to take his place and do his work.

A silly gaffe like the expulsion of Einstein,[3] recalling the French Revolution's 'the Republic has no need of chemists' when Lavoisier[4] was guillotined, does not matter. Einstein is as great a man out of Germany as in it; and though the colossal laugh which sounded throughout the civilised world at his expulsion was altogether at the expense of the Nazis, still they can pick Einstein's brains as easily when he is beyond the frontier as they can pocket the material property he has had to leave behind him.

But when they ruin their ordinary private employers and put them out of productive action without immediately taking over and carrying on their businesses, they reduce production and presently find the country faced with famine.

MYSELF: As Lenin did in Russia before he saw his mistake and had to undo it.

MR SHAW: Precisely. Even on the ridiculous assumption that the Jews are the only profiteers in Germany, their persecution and expropriation can only transfer their profiteering businesses to the German profiteers, who are just as greedy for profit.

Now if the Nazis are prepared to injure Germany in this useless and cruel way for the sake of destroying the Jew *qua* Jew, it is evident that they are not acting as Fascists or as Socialists, but simply running amuck in the indulgence of a pure phobia: that is, acting like madmen. By doing so they are throwing away all the sympathy they were entitled to from European public opinion.

MYSELF: Had they any?

MR SHAW: Most certainly they had. As Fascists they had the sympathy of Italy. As Socialists, using Bolshevist dictatorial tactics, they had the sympathy of Russia, in spite of the rivalry of Fascism and Communism.

And elsewhere they had the sympathy of the vast mass of public opinion which has turned angrily away from the delays, the evasions, the windy impotence and anarchist negations of our pseudo-democratic parliamentary system. All this sympathy has been turned into angry ill-will in a single day by an explosion of senseless Judophobia.

NOTES

1. Alfred Rosenberg (1893–1946) was a leading theorist and organiser of Nazism. He upheld the idea of German racial purity, and expounded anti-Semitic views. He was found guilty as a war-criminal at the Nuremberg trials, and hanged. Rosenberg paid visits to London in 1931 and 1933.

2. The kulaks were a class of wealthy peasants in Russia who occupied positions of power and importance in the villages. As owners of property and rivals to government-appointed officials, they were seen as a threat to socialist aims, and a campaign to liquidate them was launched in 1929. But the New Economic Policy of 1921 had recognised their significance in the rural economy, and encouraged their managerial activities.

3. Albert Einstein (1879-1955) was subjected to hostile criticism in the pro-Nazi, anti-Semitic sections of the German press whilst on a visit to America in 1933. Although he was not strictly expelled – he made his own decision on the matter – it would clearly have been extremely dangerous for him to have returned to Germany. During his absence in 1933 his possessions were confiscated and his German citizenship cancelled by Nazi authorities.

4. Antoine-Laurent Lavoisier (1743–94), a founder of modern chemistry, was summarily tried by a revolutionary tribunal in May 1794 and condemned to death by the guillotine along with twenty-seven others. He had been a prominent

public servant and member of the main tax-collecting agency, the Ferme
Générale.

The Folly of Disarmament,
1935

From 'That Silly Game – Disarmament', *North Eastern Daily Gazette*, 19 March
1935. During 1934, as tension in Europe was rising and evidence of German
rearmament was accumulating, Ramsay MacDonald became resigned to the fact
that some British rearmament was necessary. A cabinet white paper on the
government's defence policy, recommending increased expenditure on British
armaments, was published on 4 March 1935. The paper, which appeared over
MacDonald's initials, drew angry outcries from Labour and Liberal quarters.

*Do you share the horror of the Left Wing at the Prime Minister's demand for
four million to keep our armaments up-to-date?*

Certainly not. The Prime Minister's position is perfectly correct. If we
are to have an armament at all – and any party suggesting that we
should do without one would give Mr MacDonald a walkover at the
next election even more complete than he had at the last one – it must
be up to the very latest mark.

. The pacifist who calls on Mr MacDonald to disarm the nation is quite
in order, though he is also quite outside politics. But the muddler who
says if we must have guns and battleships let us at least have old-
fashioned and worn-out ones is outside common sanity.

But surely the Left Wing is pacifist before anything?

Surely it is nothing of the sort. You are thinking of Liberalism, with its
peace, retrenchment and reform. And I grant you that it is heart-breaking
to find Parliamentary representatives of Labour falling helplessly into
the old Liberal grooves and putting themselves into unpopular and false
positions because the late Sir William Harcourt held that it is the business
of an Opposition to oppose.[1]

In the modern Parliamentary tug-of-war, where there is a real
opposition between Right and Left, and not a sham one as in Harcourt's
time, the proper tactic, just as often as not, is to give way when the
Government is pulling its hardest. This was a first-rate opportunity for
that simple trick. Mr MacDonald said, 'Let us repair the defences of the
nation.' Instead of saying, 'Certainly,' and giving the Labour Party its
share in the general approval, the Labour Party said, 'We must oppose

because we are the Opposition,' and thereby puts itself hopelessly in the wrong.

Then you think that the Labour Party should take part in the race for armaments?

Do not throw catchwords at me. All the Powers, whatever Christmas cards they may send round to gull the pacifists, will, and indeed must, make themselves as formidable as they can afford to. The only real check on the process is its cost. If this were frankly admitted it would no longer be interpreted as a threat of war. It is the combination of Front Bench hypocrisy with military bugaboo that does the mischief.

Let us build twenty more battleships and 1000 more airplanes and declare honestly that we are doing it because we like to feel strong and can afford it, and that all the rest are welcome to do the same to the limit of their resources, and no harm is done. But if we build one more cruiser and half a dozen new bombers and explain that we are putting the taxpayer to this expense to defend ourselves against a secretly-contemplated attack (by Germany) the fat will be in the fire at once. We shall be not only lying, but asking for another war.

Would you allow Germany to build twenty more battleships and 1000 more airplanes?

I could not prevent her. And I would not if I could. A strong Germany is as important to civilisation as a strong Britain. Every word in Mr MacDonald's White Paper is as true in Germany and of Germany as it is of England. Mr Hitler will not fail to remind Sir John Simon[2] of that when the two meet in Berlin. And Sir John will have too much sense to threaten 'sanctions' which Mr Hitler knows quite well the Allies dare not apply.

It was that knowledge which raised Mr Hitler to his present supremacy in Germany. He will rearm to the very last penny that Germany can afford to spend on that very necessary job.

And when the Powers are all armed to the teeth, what then?

Then they will be strong enough to impose peace on the world. At present they are afraid to do anything but offer to hamstring themselves if all the others will do the same, which of course, the others won't until 'Messieurs les Assassins commencent'. That silly game is called Disarmament.

It amuses the sentimental people who have never had to govern nor to think about government; but the result is that when the League of Nations suffered a long string of slights and insults from the Powers, and was finally kicked into the gutter by Japan, not a hand was raised to help it, and it fell into the negligible position it now holds, and in which it will remain until the United States, England, France, Germany,

Italy and Russia, all fully armed, agree through the League to inflict a complete moral and commercial boycott on any nation or empire that starts dropping bombs, and institute a criminal jurisdiction at The Hague which could issue warrants for the arrest and trial of statesmen and other publicists, including editors of newspapers, guilty of inciting to war or spreading false reports and mischievous libels about foreigners. Anything short of this is poppycock, and will do more to provoke war than to prevent it.

Why do you omit Japan from your list of Powers?

Japan may not care to come in, and we cannot wait for everybody. We must begin with the Powers which are fairly homogeneous psychologically. I have left out not only Japan, but China; and China, especially Communist China, the existence of which our statesmen have either not yet discovered or are trying to ignore like ostriches, is a very important factor in the future of the world.

I have omitted the South American States, which have also to be reckoned with. But those I have named are enough to begin with. Even a majority of them would be enough to impose as much peace and security as we can reasonably hope in our time. I am speaking, of course, of wars between States.

I am not forgetting, and I warn you not to forget, that all the Powers may yet have their hands full with civil wars, except Russia, which has fought its out. It is that possibility which makes a Pacifist Labour Party almost a contradiction in terms.

Thank you, Mr Shaw. I think that is quite enough for today.

Don't mention it. Good-afternoon!

NOTES

1. Sir William Harcourt (1827–1904), Liberal politician, was not the author of this dictum. Edward Stanley, Earl of Derby (1799–1869), said: 'When I first came into Parliament, Mr Tierney, a great Whig authority, used always to say that the duty of an Opposition was very simple – it was, to oppose everything and propose nothing' (*Oxford Dictionary of Quotations*, 3rd edn, 1979, 175:8).
2. John Alsebrook Simon, 1st Viscount (1873–1954), a leading British politician who held the posts of Foreign Secretary and Home Secretary in 1935, was associated with appeasement policies towards Germany. At his meeting with Hitler on 25 March 1934, Simon found that Germany was 'determined to go her own course in rearmament' (Sir John Simon, *Retrospect: the Memoirs of the Rt Hon. Viscount Simon* [London: Hutchinson, 1952] p. 203).

Ireland versus England, 1936

From Elliseva Sayers, 'Bernard Shaw Chooses a Birthplace', *Sunday Dispatch*, 21 June 1936. Elliseva Sayers was an Irish journalist and playwright who wrote for leading Irish, British and American magazines and newspapers. The troubled political relations between Britain and Ireland were aggravated in the 1930s by a tariff war which began in 1932 and caused considerable economic damage to both countries. A trade agreement reached between Britain and the Free State in January 1935 did not remove the economic grounds of hostility, which lay in the penal duties each country imposed on the other.

What do you think of the Irish?

I don't think of them. I am a busy man.

Do you think that there is any hope of a rapprochement between Great Britain and Ireland? Should there be a rapprochement? Would England gain anything from an alliance?

Both of them have to gain by friendly relations. In the event of a war English military and naval forces would have to operate in Ireland.

The main obstacle to good feeling is the fact that the Irish remember past injuries and are vindictive. The English are very easily frightened, and when they are frightened they are capable of any atrocity; but when the danger is past they forget all about it and resume their good humour and their conviction that they are the best and kindest people in the world.

Vindictiveness is thrown away on them, and Irishmen should remember this.

If there were such a possibility, how would you suggest the authorities should go about it?

They need not 'go about' it. If they cast out fear and useless hatred it will go about itself.

Do you think England is as bad as the ardent, extreme Republicans paint her, or do you believe that Ireland herself is largely to blame for her troubles? Or do you believe she has had any troubles at all?

Six of one and three or four dozen of the other – both ways.

If you had the choice, only this choice, to be born in Ireland or England, to be an Irishman or an Englishman, which would you choose? Taking into consideration the dull, prosaic, materialistic Englishman, or the wild, care-free, enthusiastically-minded, almost good-for-nothing Irishman, full of imagination, poetry, fancy, spiritually free.

Nonsense. The DPM Englishman is just as silly a fiction as the WCEM Irishman.

If I could choose my birthplace, I should probably choose neither Ireland nor England, but as between the two I should prefer Ireland, which I may observe, is mainly populated by the descendants of Englishmen and Spaniards who left their native lands to settle in Ireland.

The Empire and Self-government, 1936

From an untitled interview in the form of typed questions and handwritten replies by Shaw given to John Hockin 9 July 1936 (Humanities Research Center, Austin, Texas). In an article written shortly after Shaw's death, John Hockin gives an account of the way in which he gained an interview with Shaw – almost certainly the present one - on the question of self-government for colonial countries and other topics. Hockin had given up a journalist job in Ceylon, and was anxious to establish himself in London. Shaw agreed to provide written answers to Hockin's typed questions. In the year before this interview the Government of India Act had provided a substantial degree of self-government in India though full independence was not achieved until 1947.

On the analogy of 'Ireland for the Irish', do you believe in 'India for the Indians' and 'Ceylon for the Ceylonese'?

You must not ask me whether I 'believe in' this or that. I recognise the existence of an instinct in men called Nationalism which makes them dissatisfied unless they think they are governed by themselves and not by foreigners. They can think of nothing else until this instinct is gratified, just as a wounded man can think of nothing but his wound until he is well.[1] The ablest men in India are being forced to waste their time and energy on demands for self-government, which should be achieved at once, at any cost, to set them free for real service to their country.

Is Japan the 'yellow peril' she is made out to be? Will she eventually dominate the whole of Asia?

All nations and colours are perils if the others do not keep them in check. Except in Soviet Russia the white peril is still the most dangerous in Asia.

Do you defend Empire Trade Preference? Why should an Indian have to pay more for his clothes just to help Manchester cotton mills?

Why not, if he won't make his own clothes? damn him!

Would you have been in favour of granting Home Rule to India and Ceylon, in place of the partial self-government they have got now?

There is no question of 'granting' self-government. England cannot grant separation to India. The Indians must take it. They must create a situation in which only by setting an English soldier with a rifle to stand over every Indian, which is numerically impossible, could British rule be maintained.

Are the people of all countries, however backward according to western standards, entitled to govern themselves?

'Entitled' has no meaning. If they want to govern themselves they must have their way or else live as rebellious slaves to a foreign power. A people set against its government is bound to fall back in civilisation, and its politics to be dominated by national blatherskites.

Don't you think there is some justice in the argument that the East is more advanced than the West considering that the latter relies on rule by force and has only one way of settling an argument – with aeroplanes and guns?

I don't know what you mean by advanced. Asia is the land of great conquerors. Compared to their conquests the British conquest of India was a mere poachers' raid. And they certainly had no scruples about using force. The question suggests that you are getting badly infected with western hypocrisy – a British speciality. Good morning.

NOTE

1. Cf. Shaw's comments on nationalism in the Preface to *John Bull's Other Island*:

Nobody in Ireland of any intelligence likes Nationalism any more than a man with a broken arm likes having it set. A healthy nation is unconscious of its nationality as a healthy man of his bones. But if you break a nation's nationality it will think of nothing else but getting it set again. It will listen to no reformer, to no philosopher, to no preacher, until the demand of the Nationalist is granted. It will attend to no business, however vital, except the business of unification and liberation.

(*Collected Plays*, vol. II, p. 842)

Germany and Europe, 1938

'Bernard Shaw answers Eight Questions', *Daily Express* (London), 26 March 1938. On 13 March 1938 Hitler announced the annexation of Austria as a province of the Third Reich. The next sphere of German territorial expansion was to be Czechoslovakia, the Sudeten areas of which, on its northern, western and southern borders, contained a large population of Germans. Hitler agitated for self-government for these areas and the evacuation of the Czechs. A German protectorate over Bohemia-Moravia was established in March 1939.

Do you regard Czechoslovakia's independence and the existence of her present frontiers as vital for European peace?

All frontiers are dangerous to peace until they are militarily indefensible or undefended, like the Canadian frontier, and until it does not matter which side we live at as far as our personal rights are concerned. A German should not be at any disadvantage in Czechoslovakia, nor a Tyrolese in the Trentino. Lord Astor's speech in the House of Lords the other day was a very wise one on this point.

Do you think that Hitler has solved the Jewish problem in a satisfactory way?

He has not solved it at all. He has created it. It has damaged his intellectual credit to an extraordinary extent. Europe could hardly have been more disagreeably surprised if he had revived witch burning. The exiling of Einstein and the confiscation of his property was Hitler's stupidest single act; and Einstein may yet be the winner.

Have you any personal sympathies for Hitler?

I never met him. His book[1] made a favourable impression on me, though it is a great pity that he did not read my works instead of Houston Chamberlain's.[2] Naturally, I appreciate the political sagacity and courage with which he has rescued Germany from the gutter and placed her once more at the head of Central Europe.

Do you regard the National Socialist contention of 'race pollution' as justified?

It is despicably unscientific. The amazing thing about it is that the anti-Semites do not see how intensely Jewish it is. The fault of the Jew is his enormous arrogance, based on his claim to belong to God's chosen race.

The Nordic nonsense is only an attempt to imitate the posterity of Abraham.

Has Greater Germany, in your view, reached its ultimate frontiers, or are we to expect more surprises?

There is no natural reason why Greater Germany should exist at all, any more than why the British Empire should exist. The Nazis at present are singing that their ultimate frontier is the ends of the earth. In that case, they had better imitate the British Empire in making the ends of the earth much more free and comfortable for the natives than the British Isles are.

Are you in favour of returning the former German colonies (or others) to Germany today?[3]

I see no permanence in the notion that Africa is a huge fowl to be carved for divison among the European Powers. It is bad enough for France to have fifteen million black troops to call upon. To give Germany similar reserves does not appeal to me. My slogan is 'Africa for the Africans!'

Do you agree with some observers who declare that Switzerland has solved the minority problem in an ideal way?

So far the Swiss seem to be getting on in an enviably satisfactory way.

Has Britain – or France – anything to fear from Germany in consequence of the present position of Germany?

All the Powers have everything to fear from their own armaments and their own folly. If Hitler loses his head, and is confronted by enemies who have not any heads to lose, the consequences may be appalling. But sufficient unto the day is the evil thereof; so let us drop the subject.

NOTES

1. *Mein Kampf*, two vols (1925–7).
2. Houston Stewart Chamberlain (1855–1927), an English-born political philosopher, took out German nationality in 1916. Hitler was influenced by his writings on Aryan racial and cultural superiority and his anti-Semitic views.
3. The campaign by Germany for the return of its African colonies, confiscated after the First World War, was intensified in the late 1930s. Shortly before this interview, Hitler had made the most uncompromising of his demands on the issue.

Will there be Another World War?, 1938

Ormsby Lennon,'Thoughts for Today', *Evening Standard*, 11 November 1938. The 1936 and 1937 interviews to which Lennon refers in his opening question here appeared in the *Daily Express* (10 November 1936) and *Evening Standard* (11 November 1937).

On Armistice Eve 1936 I asked you would there be another World War. You replied: 'Not necessarily. Not likely at present. It is such a horrible business the Powers dare not fight each other.' On Armistice Day last year I asked you the same question. You told me your 1936 pronouncement held even better. What is your postscript for 1938?

More than ever. You have seen how Germany went as far as she dared at Munich; but when we dug trenches, mobilised the Mediterranean Fleet, and were within some hours of opening fire very much against our will, Germany precipitately climbed down and sent for Mr Chamberlain.

Mussolini must have told Hitler very urgently that Italy could not afford a war just now. And we were so glad to get out of the mess that we made Herr Hitler a present of Czechoslovakia. The Four-Power Funk was overwhelming. I told you it would be.

If Hitler makes a formal demand for the return of the mandated Colonies, do you think we should hand them back?

The real question is, Will he go to war to recover them? I don't think he will. Then the next question arises. Admitting that Africa is the business of its inhabitants and not a mere stake to be played for by European diplomatists, some African constitution will have to be found that has some decenter fundamental purpose than to provide a reserve of millions of black soldiers for the European Powers to let loose on one another.

What about the Franco-Russian alliance?

Without the Russian alliance and the British alliance France will find herself in Queer Street.[1]

Have you any comment to make upon the situation in Palestine?

When the Balfour declaration was published I said 'A new Ulster'. I have nothing to add.[2]

The Fascist Powers are still busy eliminating Jews from their political, economic and social scheme of things. The British Empire has vast, undeveloped, uninhabited yet fertile spaces. Do you think a tract should be set aside in Northern Australia or elsewhere so that persecuted Jews could settle and form a national State of their own?

The settlement of the Jews anywhere except where they choose to go is a form of persecution. Anti-Semitism is a movement for the extermination of the Jews, not for their organisation as a national State. There is much to be said for their extermination, but not more than for the extermination of the human race.

We did not refuse Hitler his demand for the incorporation of the Sudeten areas of Czechoslovakia within the Reich. By the same token are we justified in refusing Eire the right to absorb Ulster?

Eire has no more right – and no less – to absorb Ulster than Ulster to absorb Eire. But the Ulster captains of industry will find that they need a Catholic agricultural background to defend them against Socialism. That will compel them to join up sooner or later.

Do you think Britain should introduce compulsory military training for all able-bodied males?

No. We are brainless enough already without being completely paralysed by military discipline. Civilians make good soldiers at the shortest notice. Nothing can turn a thoroughly militarised soldier into a capable civilian.

Do you agree with Mr William Randolph Hearst that Britain is so afraid of the future that her present policy is to try and bring the United States of America in on her side? And would the United States be able to keep out of any future World War in which her particular interests were not menaced?

Of course I agree with him, and am glad to find my friend Hearst in his old anti-humbug form. What would have happened to us in the past if the United States had not come in on our side?

No doubt our affection for the States is not disinterested; the bargain must be a good one for both sides; but who has ever supposed that we are a couple of Bands of Hope singing Christian hymns to one another [?].

Where Mr Hearst, like our own governing class, is behind the times, is in his hostility to the USSR. As long as the United States, the British Empire, the French Republic and the USSR stand together, the equilibrium will be too broad for a world war.

The most indispensable of these four factors is Russia; and if the other three persist in combining with Germany and Italy to tell lies about her, the American–Russian axis will be in danger of snapping; and then Heaven help us all!

NOTES

1. A treaty for mutual assistance between France and the USSR was concluded on 2 May 1935. The Anglo-French Entente Cordiale was established in 1904.

2. Arthur James Balfour, 1st Earl (1838–1930), was Conservative Prime Minister of England, 1902–5, and Foreign Secretary, 1916–19. The Balfour Declaration, a statement of British support for 'the establishment in Palestine of a national home for the Jewish people', was issued in 1917.

Part 12
Plays, Players, Films and Filming, 1929–50

INTRODUCTION TO PART 12

Shaw continued to be remarkably active as a playwright during the last twenty-one years of his life. 'I am always writing a new play: it is my profession', the eighty-two-year-old Shaw remarks in one of the interviews in this chapter.[1] The experiments he had made in *Back to Methuselah* with exotic settings, fantastic incident and largely figurative characterisation were further developed in later plays, such as *Too True to be Good* (1932), *The Simpleton of the Unexpected Isles* (1935) and *Buoyant Billions* (1947). Other plays, *The Apple Cart* (1929), *On the Rocks* (1933) and *Geneva* (1938) deal with national and international political themes in unusually direct but extravagantly satirical fashion.

In 1929 the Birmingham director and theatrical entrepreneur, Sir Barry Vincent Jackson (1879–1961), founded the Malvern Festival, with Shaw as patron-in-chief, and the Birmingham Repertory Theatre providing the nucleus of the Festival. Plays by Shaw were the staple dramatic fare at the Festival during the 1930s and 1940s. The 1929 season opened with a production of *The Apple Cart*, with Sir Cedric Hardwicke and Dame Edith Evans in leading roles. The year 1929 was also that of the first production of plays by Shaw (*The Dark Lady of the Sonnets* and *Androcles and the Lion*) at the Old Vic.

During the last thirty years of his life Shaw's theatrical associations were greatly extended through his involvement with the film industry. He had developed a keen interest in the cinema and its possibilities early in the century, and proposals for the production of film versions of his plays began as early as 1913.[2] The first film version of a Shaw play was the filming of a scene from *Saint Joan*, with Sybil Thorndike in the title role, on 27 July 1927. Full-length versions of several of the plays followed in the 1930s and 1940s, the more successful being those undertaken by the Hungarian-born producer Gabriel Pascal (see below, pp. 386–7). During Shaw's lifetime Pascal produced screen versions of *Pygmalion* (starring Leslie Howard as Higgins and Wendy Hiller as Eliza) in 1938, *Major Barbara* (starring Wendy Hiller as Barbara, Robert Morley as Undershaft and Rex Harrison as Cusins) in 1941, and *Caesar and Cleopatra* (starring Claude Rains as Caesar and Vivien Leigh as Cleopatra) in 1945.

NOTES

1. See below, p. 383.
2. See Bernard F. Dukore, ed., *The Collected Screenplays of Bernard Shaw* (London: George Prior, 1980) pp. 2–4.

Shaw and the Malvern Festival

BARRY JACKSON

From Barry Jackson, 'Shaw at Malvern', *Drama*, n.s., no. 20 (Spring 1951). The season at the first Festival, with which Jackson's recollection begins, was made up entirely of plays by Shaw, the newly written play *The Apple Cart* and revivals of *Back to Methuselah*, *Heartbreak House* and *Caesar and Cleopatra*. Distinguished guests at the first Festival in 1929 included the leading theatrical figure Lilian Mary Baylis (1874–1937), manager of the Old Vic Theatre from 1912 and of the Sadler's Wells Theatre from 1931, and Shaw's favourite amongst contemporary English composers, Sir Edward Elgar (1857–1934). Since 1977 the festival (which lapsed after the Second World War) has been revived as a Shaw–Elgar Festival. Shaw was fond of the Malvern district: some years before the Festival began he and Charlotte formed the habit of making annual spring-time visits, staying at the Malvern House Hotel.

GBS threw himself whole-heartedly into the holiday spirit as indeed he did for the succeeding eight years. He was invariably somewhere in the immediate vicinity – about the little town, walking over the hills, at afternoon parties, and frequently in the front of the circle watching the play which, as was his custom, he appeared to enjoy as much as the most loyal Shavian. His participation in all that was going on is amply documented by innumerable photographs and snapshots – talking to Lilian Baylis, the central figure in large groups of the company, chatting to Elgar, cutting young Penelope Drinkwater's birthday cake,[1] busy with his own camera at the bathing pool, studying his own programme in the theatre and talking to impresarios from the USA. . . .

GBS was an infrequent visitor to rehearsals which was perhaps just as well. Our time table was rigid for otherwise the work could never have been accomplished. When he did attend our author would deliver fascinating short-term lectures from which the artists derived intense amusement and satisfaction. The producer, however, seethed with anxiety to get on with his job. There was the dress rehearsal of *Saint*

Joan, for example, with GBS present from beginning to end. Thanks to delightful interludes of discussion by GBS, the rehearsal drifted on until well after midnight. The overtime bill was staggering and GBS was quite surprised when I mentioned the fact to him the next day. . . .

During the last Festival with which I was connected . . . the Shaws stayed with me. One picture I shall always retain is of GBS at the piano, playing and singing an entire act of *Don Giovanni*, with Mrs Shaw, comfortably installed in an armchair, inspecting the daily bundles of Press cuttings, a task which would have occupied the entire attention of a wholetime secretary.

NOTE

1. Penelope Drinkwater (b. 1929), daughter of the poet and playwright John Drinkwater (1882–1937), was born in the year of the Festival's opening. John Drinkwater was the founder, in 1907, of the company which later became the Birmingham Repertory Theatre. Penelope Drinkwater is an author of cookery books.

Shaw at Malvern

HARCOURT WILLIAMS

From Harcourt Williams, 'Enter George Bernard Shaw', *Journal of The Vic–Wells Association*, July 1956. Harcourt (Ernest George) Williams (1880–1957), actor and director, became associated with Shaw's work when he played the parts of Valentine in *You Never Can Tell* and the Count O'Dowda in *Fanny's First Play* in London productions before the First World War. On his appointment as Director at the Old Vic Theatre in 1929, he encouraged Lilian Baylis to introduce plays by Shaw into the repertory. The 1932–3 season opened with a production of *Caesar and Cleopatra*.

That summer I had a long walk with Shaw over the Malvern hills when he was supposed to brief me about *Caesar and Cleopatra*, but he spent the time regaling me with witty stories – some of them mildly scandalous – about stage personalities. But, yes, he did tell me one thing – how once when he was in Egypt he had been out on the desert one night and seen in the distance an Arab fire from which a thin column of smoke ascended silently into the star spangled heavens. It was the utter stillness of that picture he said that suggested the desert scene in which Caesar makes his silent entrance.

Shaw at the Old Vic

JOHN GIELGUD

From John Gielgud, *Early Stages*, rev. edn (London: Heinemann Educational Books, 1974; 1st edn 1939) pp. 110–11. Sir (Arthur) John Gielgud (b. 1904) joined the Old Vic in 1929, at the time when Shaw plays were being introduced into the repertory. *The Dark Lady of the Sonnets* (in which Gielgud played the role of Shakespeare) and *Androcles and the Lion* were presented in the 1929–30 season, and *Arms and the Man* in the 1930–1 season. Gielgud's later Shavian roles included the Inquisitor in a televised version of *Saint Joan* and, also for television, Captain Shotover in *Heartbreak House*.

I had enjoyed myself immensely in [*Androcles and the Lion*], playing the Emperor, with a red wig, a lecherous red mouth, and a large emerald through which I peered lasciviously. Now I was cast for Sergius, the mustachioed conceited major to whom Raina is engaged, in *Arms and the Man*. We were all very much flattered, and considerably awed, when we learned that Mr Shaw had consented to come and read his play to us. We waited for him in the theatre one winter morning. It was bitterly cold, and we sat muffled up in heavy overcoats and scarves. Punctually at 10.30 the great author arrived, wearing the lightest of mackintoshes. His reading of the play was far more amusing and complete than ours could possibly hope to be. He seemed to enjoy himself thoroughly as he illustrated bits of business and emphasised the correct inflexions for his lines. We were so amused that we forgot to be alarmed.

Later Mr Shaw came to a dress rehearsal. We could not distinguish him in the darkness of the stalls, but we saw the light of his pocket-lamp bobbing up and down as he made his notes. He assembled the company in the first interval, produced his written comments, and reduced everybody to a state of disquiet. Then he departed. Unfortunately I was not able to gather from him any hints about my own performance, as Sergius does not appear until the second act.

Playing Bluntschli

RALPH RICHARDSON

From Hal Burton, ed., *Great Acting* (London: British Broadcasting Corporation, 1967; New York: Hill & Wang, 1968) p. 68. Sir Ralph David Richardson (1902–83) played the part of Bluntschli in the Old Vic 1930–1 production of *Arms and the Man*. Another Shavian role played by Richardson was that of William the Waiter in *You Never Can Tell*, at the Haymarket Theatre in 1966.

Shaw came a good deal to rehearsal and he helped me very much indeed. As you remember, when Bluntschli comes on at the beginning of the play, he has escaped from the enemy, and climbed up a drainpipe and in through a window in a terrible state of exhaustion. I tried to act the exhaustion and to show how utterly tired and shot to hell he was. We rehearsed this for a time, and I thought it was rather a good effect, and that I was rather good in it. Then Shaw came to me and he said, 'You know, Richardson, I'd like to have a word with you about your Bluntschli. It's going to be a very fine Bluntschli, I'm sure.' He was a wonderfully courteous, wonderfully polite man, I think perhaps the most polite man I've ever met in my life, especially sensitive to actors. You know, he'd take you aside and talk to you very quietly, very gently, very encouragingly. 'But,' he said, 'you know there's one thing the matter with your Bluntschli. When you come in, you show that you're very upset, you spend a long time with your gasps and your pauses and your lack of breath and your dizziness and your tiredness; it's very well done, it's very well done indeed, but it doesn't suit my play. It's no good for me, it's no good for Bernard Shaw.' He said, 'You've got to go from line to line, quickly and swiftly, never stop the flow of the lines, never stop. It's one joke after another, it's a firecracker. Always reserve the acting for underneath the spoken word. It's a musical play, a knockabout musical comedy.' That taught me a lot about playing in his plays.

The State of the Theatre, 1933

From Leslie Rees, 'GBS Talks about his New Play', *Era*, 31 May 1933. Leslie Rees was the *Era* drama critic. Charles Macdona (1860–1946), actor and theatre manager, formed a group known as the Macdona Players in 1921, which specialised in plays by Shaw and toured widely. In 1933–4, he presented a series of plays at the Prince's Theatre, including a new work of Shaw's, *On the Rocks*.

LR: If you assume, as I do, that the theatre needs its house put in order, needs to be rejuvenated as a thing of the people, rather than kept as a toy for a few toffs in boiled shirts or pearl necklaces, what are the best ways to go about rejuvenating it – apart from putting on Shaw plays? Is Macdona's idea of charging half-prices for the more expensive seats a good one?

GBS: The theatre is continually rejuvenated. At any performance there is somebody in the audience who was never at a theatre before; and on the stage the ingenues, the principal boys, and the leading juveniles last hardly longer than the generations of undergraduates at the universities. Even the old authors have to be replaced by young ones. No! What the theatre needs is what our institutions need; and that is reorganisation and readjustment to fit the new facts as to the distribution of income and of culture in society.

When Bancroft, in the middle of the nineteenth century, abolished the old half-crown pit and substituted half-guinea stalls, he was only trying to make a very small theatre pay; but the effect was to establish a new order of cup-and-saucer drama and drawing-room acting.[1] Shakespeare vanished with the half-crown pit, and was presently known only as an author who spelt ruin for managers. Bancroft's little theatre ceased to be known in the profession as the Dust Hole and became the model for all the new theatres. None of them were quite so small; but they all depended on the half-guinea stall for their success. The old Haymarket alone stuck to the old pit; but presently Bancroft moved in and made an end of it.

Now the half-guinea stall costs much more than half a guinea. You assent because you are thinking of the entertainment tax and the premium charged by the libraries. But that is only a small part of it. Half-guinea stalls mean evening dress, which means a return home from the city to the suburbs to change, and trains, cabs, suppers, tips and sixpenny programmes. A business or professional man who takes his wife to the theatre is very lucky if he gets out of it for thirty shillings if his social position or his desire for a comfortable seat within easy hearing of the actors calls for stalls.

The West End plutocrats to whom money is no object demand a later and later hour of performance because they dine at eight at the earliest and naturally dislike being hurried. And both the suburbs and the West End bring comfortable, even luxurious, homes into competition with nights at the theatre.

No theatre, however spaciously seated and well upholstered, can compete with a rich man's fireside in comfort, to say nothing of the trouble of getting to it. Formerly the need for entertainment drove people into the theatre in spite of all its discomforts and bothers. Today the radio set supplies entertainment at the fireside for the rich and poor alike. There is only one thing that stalls can do that beats the radio and the fireside, and that is to provide an exhibition of fashionable dresses, jewellery, and bare shoulders. The spectator or, rather, spectatress, has become the spectacle.

Consequently the pleasant play lasting two hours and beginning at eight forty-five is now the typical West End play, although the vast majority of us, who can afford only an occasional shilling for entertainment, helped out by smaller sections who can run to half-a-crown or five shillings, want at least three hours' absorbingly interesting drama, or more if they can get it.

Matters have been brought to a crisis lately by the fact that so many of the stall people are now in the upper circle when they are not in the bankruptcy court. And that is where Charles Macdona comes in. Just as Bancroft changed the West End theatre for a century by taking the heart of the auditorium and quadrupling the price of admission to it, Macdona may change it for another century by halving, quartering and tithing Bancroft's prices, and change it for the better. That is why his experiment at the Prince's Theatre is so important.

LR: Charles Macdona has had a good deal to do with presenting your plays. What do you think of him as a manager?

GBS: Well, evidently he is a bit crazy. He took to my plays as a man takes to drink. First one play a week in the provinces; then six plays a week, including *Man and Superman* in its frightful entirety. He has become a hopeless addict. I have remonstrated with him for years for his own sake and that of his wife and family. But I am afraid he is too far gone ever to become a total abstainer.

Possibly my next play will finish him. It is of stupendous length and all about politics. The critics will receive it with a howl of agonised execration. *Too True to be Good* was a mere vaudeville in comparison.[2]

But Macdona will probably think it the greatest play ever written, and ruin himself accordingly.

LR: Would you still, after nearly forty years, say that Sardoodledom was 'claptrap' and 'a bewildering profusion of everything that has no business in a play'?[3]

GBS: Sardoodledom does not last forty years. I have forgotten all about it, except that the stage telegram of which Sardou was so fond has now been superseded by the stage telephone call, which is much more amusing.

LR: Can the realism and primary insistence on logic in the theatre for which you campaigned be exploited still further? Or does not the recent success of a few Victorian revivals – treated usually in burlesque style – show that there was some quality in the nineteenth-century theatre which it is desirable to re-import into the theatre of today – principally an enhanced sense of the stage as stage?

GBS: I never campaigned for realism and logic. My own plays are classically rhetorical and artificial; and my comedy delights in reducing logic to absurdity. But as a critic I had to try to bring the theatre into contact with actual English contemporary life and taste. Nobody nowadays can imagine what the London theatre was before Ibsen knocked it into a cocked hat, except a few dotards like myself.

I do not want any distinctive artistic quality of the nineteenth-century theatre back again. Dramatic art has left that accursed period far behind. For Heaven's sake don't try to exhume it.

NOTES

1. Sir Squire Bancroft (1841–1926), actor–manager, and his wife Marie Effie (née Wilton, 1839–1921) were managers of the elegantly decorated and highly successful Prince of Wales's, formerly a dilapidated theatre known as the Dust Hole. Under Marie Wilton's direction, the theatre was renovated in the mid-1860s and the Bancrofts, who married in 1867, made it a popular venue for drawing-room comedy and drama. In 1880 the Bancrofts took over the Haymarket Theatre.

2. Apart from the playlet *Village Wooing*, *Too True to be Good* was the immediate predecessor to *On the Rocks*.

3. 'Sardoodledom' is a satirical term coined by Shaw in the *Saturday Review* in June 1895 to describe the techniques of the French practitioner of the well-made play, Victorien Sardou (1831–1908).

On Writing Plays

From Hayden Church, 'Bernard Shaw Tells Us All About: My Plays, My Work, My Novels, My Money', *Sunday Graphic and Sunday News*, 17 December 1933.

'How *do* you write your plays?' I asked.

'Just as they come!'

'When you are engaged on a play, have you any regular hours of work?'

'Yes, between breakfast and lunch. Never later.'

'Is any of your plays your personal favourite?' he was asked.

'No, of course not,' Shaw replied. 'My plays are not racehorses. I have no time to bother about them after they are finished and launched.'

'How do themes for plays suggest themselves to you? What, particularly, inspired some of the most famous of them? Have you sometimes had a theme in mind for a long time before utilising it?'

'Plays begin in all sorts of ways. I can sit down without an idea in my head except that I must write a play; and a play comes. A good play, too, provided I do not write anything that bores me, like filling out a plot or anything artificial of that kind.

'Most genuine plays begin with a dramatic situation; the play is only a device for bringing it about. . . .'

'About how long does it take you to write a play?'

'It depends on the length, and on the complication of the stage business. Also on the quality of the writing. The fashionable length of a play for stalls at the highest West End prices is 18,000 words. My plays, written for an ideal audience of shilling stalls and a twopenny gallery, are from a third to half as long again.

'A slosher using ready-made phrases and never stopping to think can write several thousand words a day with the assistance of more or less alcohol. An average thousand words a day is enough for me if I have to think them all out. But that is between breakfast and lunch. . . .

'I can write the dialogue of a long play easily within two months if I stick at it; but it may take me as long again, or longer, to settle the stage business, which is pure drudgery. I had rather write all the dialogue of

Hamlet than decide which side of the stage the Ghost enters, or arrange the necessary time for Ophelia to change her dress.'

'Are your plays, as originally written, subject to a good deal of revision, or not?'

'Of course they are. I have an artistic conscience which makes it impossible for me to let a job go until it is as good as I can make it at the moment. Besides, I now overwrite to such an extent that I have to cut the play down by a full third to pull it properly together and bring it within possible limits of time.

'The publication or performance of a play of mine in the state in which Shakespeare's plays appear in the First Folio would drive me crazy. But I fully admit that Shakespeare's calculation that it was better to spend his time writing *Macbeth* than revising *Hamlet* was justified. But then Shakespeare was a volcano from whom plays burst like lava. I am by comparison a tidy old maid. . . .'

'How lengthy a preface will your new plays have when published? Why do you consider that your plays need prefaces?'

'My new book will contain two prefaces and three plays.[1] If you buy it you will get good value for your money. When you are tired of reading plays to amuse you, you can read the prefaces to improve your mind.

'My plays do not need prefaces; but the people who buy my books need variety and quantity enough to last them at least a week in these hard times.

'Those who like political essays and don't like plays can skip the plays. Those who like plays and don't like political essays can skip the prefaces. In this way everybody in the family is suited.

'The combination of preface-pamphlet and play is a classic tradition in English literature, but nobody has ever given such good measure as I.

'The only trouble is that silly people who are ignorant of the tradition, and who read neither my books nor anyone else's, imagine that the prefaces explain the plays and that the plays are incomplete without them. Of course, they are entirely independent works. . . .'

'Why do you consider it was,' was the final question, 'that your great gift of characterisation, your wit and other qualities did not make your early novels as successful as your later plays have been? Are the two mediums so different, or are they simply not equally congenial to you?'

'How do you know that my novels are less successful?' GBS demanded. 'My plays remain unacted for years at a stretch; but people go on buying my novels and perhaps even reading them.

'As to why I do not go on writing them, do you suppose that anyone who could write a play would condescend to such an easy job as writing a novel? Anybody can write novels; and the worst of it is that nearly everybody does.

'Perhaps when I am ninety I shall become lazy and go back to the old Victorian game. It will be an amusement for my second childhood.'

NOTE

1. The reference is to the volume *Too True to be Good, Village Wooing* and *On the Rocks* (London: Constable, 1934). Prefaces to the first and third of the plays are included.

Shaw as Producer

ALEC CLUNES

From Alec Clunes, 'Bernard Shaw as Producer', *Amateur Producer*, 14 December 1934. Alec Sheriff de Moro Clunes (1912–70), actor, had joined the Old Vic Theatre shortly before the publication of this piece. In the production of *Saint Joan* which opened on the 26 November 1934, he played the part of Gilles de Rais, 'Bluebeard'. In a production of the same play at Malvern in 1938, he played Dunois. In 1947 he played Higgins in *Pygmalion* at the Lyric, Hammersmith, and in 1959 he took over the role of Higgins in *My Fair Lady* and played it for more than a year.

Each scene is rehearsed by the players without interruption. . . . In the centre of the stalls, large loose-leaf notebook in hand, pencil poised, Shaw sits watching (and it is somehow typical of his efficiency that he should make use of shorthand). Spying on him from the circle, one is surprised by the impulsiveness of his expressions, conveying his private opinions, almost with blatancy. (That, however, is probably your own fault for spying on him!)

At the end of each scene, up he clambers on to the stage. And such is his cheery personality that you invariably await his judgement with enthusiasm, no matter how bad you feel you've been. Then, with great excitement in the gruff Irish voice, and the long thin hands that are never still, he proceeds to go through the whole of his notes, taking each person aside in turn to explain to them.

Two things impress themselves upon one immediately – both important factors essential to the would-be perfect producer. Firstly, his genuine practical knowledge of the theatre, which is, to all mortal intents and purposes, infallible. And secondly (for want of a better word), his tact.

If a stress or an inflection is altered, if a position is altered, no matter what change it is he makes, a sort of 'audience-consciousness' is always uppermost in his mind. He has a preference for audibility and a touch of 'theatre', and certainly has no time for the fiddling pseudo-naturalistic cult that is, perhaps, our present-day theatre's greatest enemy. He repeatedly observes the old golden rule of placing his dominant speaking character well up-stage. Always one speaks downstage, and never need one shirk addressing the fourth-wall face to face on climaxes.

His grouping, though in appearance essentially natural, is always decorative. His variation of vocal tempo and pitch, though again seeming natural, is highly coloured, and always calculated to stimulate his audience to mental agility by giving the uttermost clarity to the text.

His method in personally producing each actor is eminently practical, too, and leaves no room at all for misunderstanding. No long-winded dissertations on *how* to do this or that – he just does it! (And only once.) And it is here that his great knowledge of characterisation impresses one. As actor, he is equally convincing (despite his own unique make-up) as Joan, the Dauphin or the Executioner! I am told that his own reading of Lady Cicely at a rehearsal of his *Captain Brassbound's Conversion* once reduced his whole company to a convulsed state of helpless admiration. Whether he is kneeling for Joan, altering an inflection for 'Charlie', or suggesting a type of voice and presence for the Executioner, they are all 'in character' and all almost infallibly correct. . . .

Perhaps I shall best complete this article by two quotations. One, his remark at the conclusion of a long and tiring dress rehearsal, typical of so much of the child-man in him: 'In hops Joan into the Dauphin's bed, and down comes the curtain.' Another, his remark that the play was so good as to be actor-proof. And finally, a very modern young man's remark as Shaw made his final exit from the theatre: 'Well, I suppose that's the nearest to God any of us will ever see!'

'The First Play I Ever Saw'

From Roy Nash, 'The Theatre Today and Yesterday According to George Bernard Shaw', *Manchester Evening News*, 6 December 1938. Tom Taylor (1817–80), dramatist, editor of *Punch*, professor of English and public servant, wrote more than seventy plays in popular nineteenth-century forms for the London theatres. His *Plot and Passion* was first presented at the Olympic Theatre, London, in 1853. Thomas Chiswell King (1818–93), actor, was first engaged at the Theatre Royal, Dublin, in 1851, and became a favourite leading actor there until 1856.

In the 1860s and 1870s he played in various theatres in England and Ireland. *The Corsican Brothers*, a play adapted in 1848 from a novel by Alexandre Dumas (1802–70) by the dramatist, actor, director and theatre manager Dion[-ysius] Lardner Boucicault (1820–90), featured an ingenious device (known as the Corsican Trap) for the appearance and gliding across the stage of a ghost.

What was the first play you ever saw? Where was it produced and who appeared in it? What did you think of it?

The first play I ever saw was Tom Taylor's *Plot and Passion*. I have no idea who acted in it, because it was all real to me. It was followed by *Puss in Boots*, a full-length Christmas pantomime; and in it, too, the fairy queen was a real fairy, and the policeman a real policeman deliciously shot into several pieces by the clown.

The roller skaters who crashed together in the middle of the stage and disappeared shrieking down the grave trap were to me real sportsmen on real ice.

I had to be removed forcibly from the theatre at the end because after the falls of the curtain three times in *Plots and Passion* I could not be persuaded that it would not presently go up again.

I believe the performance began and ended with a farce; for that was the length of entertainment the public expected in those days at the old Theatre Royal, Dublin.

When I next went, I went by myself and saw T. C. King in *The Corsican Brothers*. This time there was illusion, but no deception: I knew that the ghost was a man painted white on a sliding bridge, lighted by a green lantern, and that Chateau Renaud was not really killed, though I enjoyed the fight all the more.[1]

Are you working on a new play? If so, what is it about?

Of course I am.[2] I am always writing a new play: it is my profession. It is not 'about' anything. A play is a play: it is not something about something else.

NOTES

1. Château-Renaud, the villain, is killed in a duel by one of the Corsican brothers at the end of the play.
2. Shaw had recently begun writing *In Good King Charles's Golden Days*.

Shaw and RADA

KENNETH BARNES

From Sir Kenneth Barnes, 'GBS and the RADA', in Stephen Winsten, ed., *GBS 90: Aspects of Bernard Shaw's Life and Works* (London: Hutchinson, 1946) pp. 177–9. Sir Kenneth (Ralph) Barnes (1878–1957) was Principal of the Royal Academy of Dramatic Art from 1909 to 1955. Shaw was elected to the twelve-member Council of the RADA in 1911, in place of Sir William Schwenck Gilbert, who died that year.

GBS had always been the most regular attendant of all the members of the Council at its meetings, and the Academy benefited through the years up to the last war by his sagacity and practical sense of what could, and what could not be done in an institution which had to make its way against prejudices from opposite directions, both lay and professional. His name on the Council has brought more *réclame* to the school than any other name could have done, and all those who know anything about Bernard Shaw recognised that whenever he gave his name he was prepared to give his time and great abilities as well. . . .

When war broke out in 1939 and the blitz started, owing to the small number of students willing and able to continue, a serious financial position resulted. Our friend immediately offered a loan of £1,000, and added that he did not expect to be repaid! He was strongly against closing the institution, as he had been in 1914. He had made up his mind to see it through. In 1941 our Malet Street Theatre was reduced to rubble by a land-mine, and direct hit.[1] He came to see the damage and was, I think, astonished at its extent. He looked silently at it for half a minute, then turned away and said to me, 'Well, they made a good job of it.'

In 1928 the whole Council had tried to persuade Mr Shaw to become their President, and this effort was renewed later on, but he always refused. He thought that position should be occupied by an actor or actress. When, on his eighty-sixth birthday in 1942, he retired from the Council, he was asked to allow himself to be called Honorary President of the Academy, but he replied that he thought no good purpose would be served, although he appreciated the honour. He wished to indicate that his interest in our work had not ceased by remaining as one of the Associate Members. This has enabled me to keep in touch with him in connection with the direction of the RADA but also to realise how greatly we have missed his presence at our meetings.

Although he took such a sustained interest for thirty years in the Academy as an institution, the basis of this interest was a warm, practical sympathy in the welfare of young people who were determined to devote their lives to the Theatre. It is a fact that I never received a refusal when I asked this famous dramatist to superintend rehearsals of any of his plays that were being studied for performance by our advanced students. He usually consented to come for two hours on these occasions, but always ended by staying for three hours and coming again a second and even a third time, when he felt the students so keenly appreciated the unique opportunity of rehearsing under his direction. During these long rehearsals, even when he was over eighty years of age, he hardly ever sat down, but watched every movement and listened to every intonation with his amazing power of concentration. No detail was regarded as unimportant and his comments were gems of lucidity and humour. He had a power of bringing the best out of young people that I have never seen equalled in a long experience. The courtesy with which he treated students was wholly delightful, but of course his critical faculty and prestige assured that no liberty was taken. These rehearsals by Mr Shaw at the RADA remain in my mind as the most significant episode of our working days. At rehearsals he not only explained the dialogue but demonstrated the characters in action; never because he knew he could do this very well, but only if he felt that demonstration would convey the point he wished to make. He regarded good speech as the first and most important qualification for an actor, and he came down hard on mispronunciation and careless diction. A sense of rhythm in speaking dramatic dialogue, an accuracy of timing, were constantly being inculcated. The individual personality of every student was estimated and imitation was never encouraged. He used to imply that acting is full of tricks that the professional performer is bound to know and use, but never to the detriment of sincerity of expression, which meant a keen sense of interpretation of the character drawn by the author.

Every year the annual public performance by the students found GBS in the same gangway seat in the front row of the dress circle. Below in the stalls the audience was largely composed of well-known people of the Theatre, as this event has always been recognised as a kind of meeting-place for actors and managers. The most distinguished person in the house never stirred from his seat and watched the three-hour programme, made up of extracts from plays which included, on many occasions, some act or scene from one of his own plays with which he had helped the performers at rehearsals.

NOTE

1. The Malet Street Theatre was replaced by the Vanbrugh, named in honour of Sir Kenneth Barnes's sisters, the distinguished actresses Irene and Violet Vanbrugh.

Shaw as Scenario-Writer

GABRIEL PASCAL

From Gabriel Pascal, 'Shaw as a Scenario-writer', in Stephen Winsten, ed., *GBS 90: Aspects of Bernard Shaw's Life and Works* (London: Hutchinson, 1946) p. 192. Gabriel Pascal (Gabor Lehöl) (1894–1954), Hungarian-born director and producer, was the major interpreter of Shaw's plays on the screen during the playwright's life. He began his career as a cavalry officer in the Hungarian Hussars. After the First World War he studied acting at the Hofburg Theatre in Vienna, formed his own company in Rome, and worked in films, travelling widely throughout Europe in the 1930s. He claims to have first met Shaw during a naked dawn swim on the French Riviera in 1925. In 1935 he arrived penniless in London, and asked Shaw for the film rights of *Pygmalion*. Shaw consented on 13 December 1935.

When I first asked GBS to write me the reception and bathroom scenes for the *Pygmalion* scenario, he was reluctant to do so, because our understanding was that I should put his plays on the screen as they were, without any of the elaborate Hollywood beauty-parlour treatment described above. Nevertheless, once I had convinced him that they would assist the screen presentation of his play, he wrote these two scenes in no time, and they have the same freshness and vigour as the rest of the play.

For *Major Barbara* he wrote sixteen new sequences for me. I was only able to use six of them for lack of screen time. For my latest picture, *Caesar and Cleopatra*, I needed only three short sequences as transition-scenes to avoid sudden jumps in the action; and GBS was very generous in permitting certain cuts to be made which I thought necessary for the screen adaptation.

These few facts characterise only the week-by-week routine of our collaboration on the actual scenario work. But the great phenomenon of GBS as a screen writer is not only in his writing but in the steady inspiration which he gives to his producer during the whole preparation and making of his picture.

I showed him the still photos weekly and he immediately recognised with his critical eyes the development of the characters by the players; he saw the slightest faults in their make-up or in their portrayal, or the slightest stylistic error in sets and decor; and he became my second artistic conscience, which for a producer–director is more important than all the formula, tradition and technical bravura of which Hollywood is so proud.

Pygmalion and the Film Industry, 1939

From untitled answers to written questions put by the editors of the Association of Cine-Technicians Journal, *Cine-Technician*, September–October 1939. Apart from Pascal's 1938 version, German and Dutch films of *Pygmalion* had been produced in 1935 and 1937 respectively.

Did Pygmalion *lose any of its force in being transferred to the screen?*

No.

Do you think Hollywood could have made a better version of Pygmalion?

No: Hollywood would have murdered *Pygmalion*. That is why Hollywood did not get it.

Which film version of Pygmalion *do you prefer – the earlier Dutch one, or the recent British one? And why?*

I prefer my own version, which is substantially that followed by Mr Gabriel Pascal.

It has been said that on the screen Pygmalion *dates and seems old-fashioned. What is your opinion?*

Anything that is not the latest ephemeral Californian slang seems old-fashioned in that benighted state. I write English – classical and vernacular English.

Are you likely to write directly for the screen? If not, why not?

My stuff is as good on the screen as on the stage.

What is your opinion of screenwriting as a profession? Is the scenario-writer necessary?

PLAYS, PLAYERS, FILMS AND FILMING, 1929–50

That depends on how much the author leaves undone. The author, if a playwright, should do everything except the shooting script.

Would you agree that it is essential for the well-being of the British film industry that it should recognise the organisations representing its technicians, and make agreements with them?

Of course it should.

Have you seen any films which you think are the equal, from artistic or propagandist reasons, of your own work in the theatre?

What do you mean by 'equal'? Nothing, apparently. Pass on.

Do you think the British Board of Film Censors is necessary?

It is only a contrivance to enable timid film firms to give themselves certificates of decency. It has licensed some films that have driven me from the theatre by their dull lubricity, and simultaneously banned a film to which it ought to have given a gold medal for distinguished service to public morals. Such certificates are worthless and sometimes mischievous.

Do you think the British film industry has any future?

Of course I do. Do you think London Bridge has any future?

Now that you have joined your professional organisation (The Screenwriters' Association),[1] are you also going to join your appropriate Trade Union in the film industry – the Association of Cine-Technicians?

I am not a cine-technician. I am a playwright.

Who in your opinion is the second greatest dramatist in the world?

I do not know; and neither do you. You must wait a few centuries for your answer.

NOTE

1. Shaw joined the Association in 1939.

Filmdom's Illiterates

From Dennison Thornton, 'Bernard Shaw Flays Filmdom's "Illiterates"', *Reynolds*

News, 22 January 1939. Dennison Thornton (b. 1909) began his career as a journalist, drama and film critic in Canada (having migrated from his native Ireland) and subsequently become publicist for several major film companies in the UK and America.

If we are to believe what the film producers are always telling us about the low intelligence of the average filmgoer, how do you account for the tremendous success everywhere of Pygmalion, *which has been praised as one of the most intelligent films yet made?*

Only thoughtless people chatter about the low intelligence of the average filmgoer. There is no such person. There are several classes of public entertainment, including several classes of film. And there are several classes of film director, including some who are so illiterate that they cannot conceive anyone being interested in anything but very crudely presented police and divorce court news, and adventures out of boys' journals.

They are usually ranked as infallible authorities on the suitability of scenarios. These gentlemen have never had any use for me; and I cannot pretend that I have any use for them.

Do you think that these filmed versions of your plays will bring about a new type of film – films in which problems of conduct and character of importance to the audience are raised and suggestively discussed?

I don't think *Pygmalion* will bring about anything but the confusion of the idiots who maintain that a good play must make a bad film, and that the musical English of a dramatic poet must be converted into the slang of a Californian bar-tender or it will not be understood in Seattle – where, by the way, they do not speak Californian.

In a note to the stage version of Pygmalion *you deplored what you called 'ready-made, happy endings to misfit all stories'.[1] Yet you allowed such a ready-made happy ending to be substituted in the film version of* Pygmalion. *Why?*

I did not. I cannot conceive a less happy ending to the story of *Pygmalion* than a love affair between the middle-aged, middle-class professor, a confirmed old bachelor with a mother-fixation, and a flower girl of eighteen. Nothing of the kind was emphasised in my scenario, where I emphasised the escape of Eliza from the tyranny of Higgins by a quite natural love affair with Freddy.

NOTE

1. *Collected Plays,* vol. IV, p. 782.

Filming *Major Barbara*

REX HARRISON

From Rex Harrison, *Rex: An Autobiography by Rex Harrison* (London: Macmillan, 1974) pp. 70–1. Rex Carey Harrison (b. 1908), actor, made his first appearance on stage in Liverpool in 1924, and his London debut in 1930. He subsequently divided his time between stage and screen roles. His elegant and engaging style as an actor of comic roles was put to excellent use in the part of Henry Higgins in *My Fair Lady*, which he played for two years on Broadway (1956–8) and in the screen version (1964). He accepted the role of Cusins in Pascal's film of *Major Barbara* in July 1940. *Major Barbara* was filmed in several locations, in Devon, Sheffield and London. Shaw's prologue for American audiences to the film of *Major Barbara* is printed in 'Mr Shaw Speaking', *PM's Weekly*, 19 January 1941 and 'G. B. Shaw's prologue to *Major Barbara*', *Variety*, 13 May 1941. Recordings of the speech are listed by Laurence, *Bibliography* (F27, 1941 and G11, 1940).

George Bernard Shaw came down to the studios one morning, to record a foreword to the film. I was immensely impressed by his appearance. He wore a grey Norfolk jacket, grey knee-breeches, long grey stockings and brogues, and a woollen tie. He was six feet two and very erect, with the most piercing blue eyes I had ever seen. His hair was quite white, and his beard also. With him came his famous secretary, Miss Patch, an old lady who appeared to me to be growing a small white moustache to match his.

All had been made ready for him, and he sat down at the desk he had asked should be provided and, though none of us knew what he was going to say or do, indicated that he was ready. The cameras were started. He sat bent over the desk, then looked up as though surprised to be thus discovered, and embarked on his speech.

It was directed at American audiences, and I can still recall one line: 'You have sent us some of your old destroyers, and I am sending you film versions of some of my old plays.' This was before the United States had come into the war but had made some fifty destroyers available to us, in return for the lease of some of our air bases.

The speech was a delight, and it went on and on until suddenly, as was evident from Gabriel Pascal's worried face, something went awry. Pascal started flapping about: GBS was oblivious. Eventually Pascal crept up to the great man and touched him on the arm – GBS looked round furiously, and Pascal confessed, 'We've run out of film.'

'Run out of what?' roared GBS, who was, I imagine, fairly ignorant of such technical necessities.

It was explained to him that he must stop, to allow the cameras to reload, and then go on. The delay threw him completely. He lost his train of thought, he fumbled, and mumbled and dried up like any novice actor. I was fascinated to see this happen to a self-possessed man of such renowned intelligence. It took several reloads of the camera for him to finish what he wanted to say.

Afterwards, Pascal asked him if he would read through the last scene between Major Barbara and Cusins, and help us to interpret it. Wendy Hiller and I sat on either side of Shaw while he silently read through the long scene. There was a pause. Then he said, almost to himself, and with a strong Irish brogue: 'Ah, what a terrible scene,' and again, 'Ah, what a terrible scene.' It was exactly what we had thought. But there were no further words of wisdom forthcoming from the great man, I think because by then he was thoroughly exhausted.

Filming *Caesar and Cleopatra*

MARJORIE DEANS

From Marjorie Deans, *Meeting at the Sphinx: Gabriel Pascal's Production of Bernard Shaw's* Caesar and Cleopatra (London: Macdonald, [1946]) p. 28. The shooting of *Caesar and Cleopatra*, begun in June 1944 and completed in September of the following year, was carried out at Denham Studios in London and on location in Egypt.

When Bernard Shaw came to Denham to watch the filming of the meeting between Caesar and Cleopatra on the paws of the Sphinx, he stood for a long time in silence, gazing up at the huge crouching image against its background of starry sky; and his expression, though always critical, reflected also the realisation of a fifty-year-old dream.

'What scope! What limitless possibilities!' he said afterwards. 'When I look back on my work as a young man with my colleagues in the theatre, it seems to me we were like children playing with wretched makeshift toys. Here you have the whole world to play with!'

The Film Industry, 1946

From Bernard Shaw, 'What I Think about the Film Industry', *Daily Film Renter*, 1 January 1946.

What in your opinion is the future of the cinema?

I know nothing about the future.

If you had your time over again would you write for the screen rather than for the stage?

Yes.

What is your opinion of Hollywood's treatment of plays as compared with that of British producers?

I do not concern myself with Hollywood. I write for America, a quite different country.

Where in your opinion do the Hollywood and British producers go wrong – in other words, what do you suggest would be the ideal technique for producing motion pictures?

I am sorry, but I cannot take you on as an apprentice.

What do you notice chiefly in British pictures as (1) a shining virtue, (2) a glaring defect?

Whose British pictures? Mine and Gabriel Pascal's or So-and-so's?

Do you think that the enormous popularity of the kinema has been a benefit to the stage? Has it tended to make people more drama-conscious, and so lured many into the flesh and blood theatre who might not otherwise have gone?

Yes, of course it has.

What was your opinion of Henry V?[1]

Quite interesting to theatrical antiquaries as a peep behind the scenes and before them in Shakespeare's day.[2] But you cannot have a play if you destroy the illusion of the stage; consequently no *Henry V*.

Is the propagandist value of the pictures as great as is claimed for it?

Much greater. The world wars were largely Hollywood products.

What would you suggest as the next best advance in kinema technique?

What's wrong with the present technique? It is good enough for anyone who can master it and is a born playwright. The others should peddle baked potatoes.

Can you envisage a time when screen drama will be able to devise its own plots, and so become independent of novels and plays?

There is nothing to prevent its doing both at present except simple incompetence.

Is Saint Joan *going to be filmed?*

Yes.[3]

Which of all your plays do you regard as the most suitable for filming?

All good plays are suitable.

Have you anything printable to say about the average movie on which the fortunes of the industry have been built up? We don't mind what it is.

There is no such thing as the average movie. In fine art there is always trash, mediocrity and treasure. Some of the movies are better than many of the talkies. But drama in its highest reaches cannot exist without speech. When, as at present, there is practically no limit to scenic, vocal and financial possibilities, or to magnification, illumination and audibility, the film leaves the stage nowhere. But that does not prevent the Punch and Judy man from earning a living.

NOTES

1. Lawrence Olivier's film of Shakespeare's *Henry V* opened at the Carlton in London's Haymarket in November 1944, and went on general release in the following summer.

2. By the use of various 'behind-the-scenes' images, Olivier's film attempts to create the illusion that what the audience is seeing is a production at the Globe Playhouse. Olivier hit upon this idea when he was considering the problem of how to deal with the Chorus (see John Cottrell, *Lawrence Olivier* [London: Weidenfeld & Nicolson, 1975] p. 191).

3. This prediction was not fulfilled until after Shaw's death, in 1957, when Otto Preminger produced and directed the first of several screen versions of the play. In June 1935 Shaw completed revisions of a screenplay of *Saint Joan* he had written in October–November of the previous year. The screenplay was immediately censored by the Vatican, and Catholic opposition proved a major obstacle to further progress with the making of a screen version.

An Astonishing Duet

GERTRUDE LAWRENCE

From Richard Stoddard Aldrich, *Gertrude Lawrence as Mrs A: An Intimate Biography of the Great Star by Her Husband* (London: Companion Book Club, 1956) pp. 233–4. Gertrude Lawrence (1898–1952), actress, dancer and revue artist, played Eliza in a highly successful revival of Shaw's *Pygmalion* in 1945. The visit described here occurred in February 1949. In June of the same year, Shaw gave Gertrude Lawrence permission to include a scene from *Pygmalion* in a BBC programme on her success story, in return for another pair of the mittens which she knitted for his use in the winters in his last years.

I went forward and kissed him on the cheek. It seemed a perfectly natural thing to do, and he was a bit surprised although his eyes sparkled as we went into the sitting-room. He sat in his chair and began to talk. That was at half-past three, and at half-past five we were still at it.

We talked about taxation, actors – old school and new. He does not approve of the modern form of underplaying. He thinks it has gone too far and that present-day actors lack gusto and power. This he believes is due to so many of them doing film acting, which restricts their emotions as well as their movements.

We got to pantomime and he said the first one he remembered was *Aladdin*, in which Ada Reeve[1] played Aladdin and sang 'Up, in a Balloon, Boys'. I remembered the song from Granny singing it to me. Shaw and I sang it together, loud and clear, with gestures:

> Come, little girl, for a sail with me,
>   Up in my bonny balloon,
> Come, little girl, for a sail with me,
>   Round and round the moon.
> No one to see us behind the Clouds:
>   Oh, what a place to spoon.
> Up in the sky – ever so high,
>   Sailing in my balloon.

Miss Patch's comment on the performance is worth repeating: Few can have been audience to so astonishing a duet.[2]

NOTES

1. Ada Reeve (1874–1966), British character actress with a long stage and screen career. She played Aladdin frequently in the late nineteenth and early twentieth centuries.
2. See Blanche Patch, *Thirty Years with GBS* (London: Victor Gollancz, 1951) p. 111.

Buoyant Billions: a Garden Rehearsal

From Anon, 'What's He up to Now?', *Picture Post*, 30 July 1949. *Buoyant Billions: A Comedy of No Manners* was produced at a revival of the Malvern Festival in August 1949, by Esmé Percy. The part of Junius Smith was played by stage and screen actor Denholm Elliot (b. 1922) and that of Clementina Alexandra Buoyant by the revue star, Frances Day (Frances Victoria Schenk, b. 1908). Frances Day was also playing the part of the King's mistress in a festival production of *The Apple Cart*. A garden rehearsal of *Buoyant Billions* took place at the home of Shaw's neighbours, the Winstens.

Shaw sipped his apple juice, munched a sandwich and remarked: 'To an old man all things taste alike. That is one of the things old men have to put up with.'

While the players took up their positions, Shaw became aware of what was happening. 'When a playwright finishes writing a play, he doesn't want to read or see it again. He starts a new one. Still,' he added, 'as this is probably the last occasion I can be of use to anybody, I don't mind.'

Esmé Percy brought out his copy of the play: *Buoyant Billions: A Comedy of No Manners*. The scene was set in a tropical landscape, and for this the parched overhanging willows served well enough. Shaw helped without stint; he was old-fashioned enough to insist on clarity of diction, and in his fine musical voice set the pitch and rhythm of each sentence. Above all, he would not permit any stage business to get in the way of the excitement of the words themselves. 'Don't be afraid of being static. I'm a demagogue first and a playwright afterwards. You must remember I am not leading up to a murder, but to a thought. It's the thought first and foremost. And don't play for a laugh. The laughs will come all right. I am not entirely lacking in comedic sense. But it is comedic *sense*, not nonsense.' Again and again he explained his ideas on the play. There was no hint of fatigue.

'Shall we go through it once again?' Esmé Percy asked. But Shaw was sorry for them and advised them to stop. We all gathered round for a chat.

'I'm also doing Orinthia in your *Apple Cart* at the Malvern Festival. I'd like to ask you a terribly intimate question.' Frances Day looked into his eyes, and before she had finished the question Shaw was answering: 'It doesn't matter in the least whether King Magnus and Orinthia slept together. I'm pretty certain they didn't, though of course I don't know all their secrets. No good playwright knows all the secrets of his characters. Judging from my own relationship with women, I am prepared to say it was a platonic relationship. Like finger-prints, all love-affairs are different. You must not confuse the sensual with the enduring relationship of man and wife. All Nature wants is to produce babies, but we are human beings and can order our lives differently. Take Saint Joan. Why did she interest me?'

'I've never read *Saint Joan*. . . . I've seen the film. . . .' Frances Day wondered why her remark brought the biggest laugh of the afternoon.

Why She Would Not

· From Mrs Georgina Musters to Archibald Henderson, 31 October 1955; letter quoted in Henderson, *George Bernard Shaw: Man of the Century* (New York: Appleton-Century-Crofts, 1956) p. 665. Shaw began the writing of *Why She Would Not: A Little Comedy* in the summer of 1950. Mrs Musters, who had previously made a sixteen-page typescript of the play, visited Shaw in company with Lady Astor on 25 October 1950, a week before his death. At the end of the first draft of *Why She Would Not*, Shaw had written, 'End of Scene 5 and of the play'; but there is some evidence that he had thought of adding at least one more scene.

We talked about it [the little comedy]. . . . I had typed it for him and nobody but he and I knew of it – and said with great stress 'It's not worth finishing. . . . It's not good enough.' Then he added 'It's all wrong' and went on to say that hitherto he had considered the important part of marriage the children, but (again with great emphasis) 'NO, it's the companionship that matters.' . . . (I then realised what a very lonely seven years he had had since the death of Charlotte in 1943.)

Part 13
Sundry Topics

INTRODUCTION TO PART 13

Shaw's comments on his attitudes towards such subjects as vegetarianism, dress, female suffrage, religion, love and marriage, are drawn together by the common thread of opposition to the orthodoxies and conventional wisdom of his day. In some cases, as in his condemnation of vaccination, he was swimming against irresistible tides. But many of his opinions, such as those on sexual equality, or the advantages of a vegetarian diet, now seem far from eccentric.

A combination of his impecunious situation as a young man, his reading of Shelley on the evils of the cooking and eating of meat and, finally, a lecture by a journalist colleague, led Shaw to become a strict vegetarian by 1881. In his bachelor days his diet seems to have been rather meagre. In a letter of 10 September 1890, he described his three daily meals as 'Breakfast – cocoa and porridge; Dinner – the usual fare, with a penn'orth of stewed Indian corn, haricot beans, or what not in place of the cow; and 'Tea' – cocoa and brown bread, or eggs.'[1] But under the management of Charlotte and, from 1943, his cook-housekeeper, Alice Laden (a trained vegetarian cook) he enjoyed a sumptuous variety of dishes.[2] During his illness in 1898, when doctors insisted that his condition was exacerbated by his vegetarianism, and tried to persuade him to eat meat extracts, Shaw continued to defend the vegetarian cause, declaring that he had provided in his will that his funeral would be followed 'not by mourning coaches, but by herds of oxen, sheep, swine, flocks of poultry, and a small travelling aquarium of live fish, all wearing white scarves, in honour of the man who perished rather than eat his fellow-creatures'.[3]

Shaw was deeply interested in religion, and many of his plays are centrally concerned with religious themes. He expounded his ideas on this subject in several lengthy prefaces, including those to *Major Barbara*, *Androcles and the Lion*, *Back to Methuselah* and *Saint Joan*, and in numerous speeches which were gathered together in a volume edited by Warren Sylvester Smith.[4] He also explored religious themes in his story *The Adventures of the Black Girl in Her Search for God* (1934). Shaw placed his faith not in established creeds but in the idea of a purposeful divine will, working through evolutionary processes (with which individuals can cooperate) towards the creation of an omnipotent and omniscient godhead. He saw the divine as being expressed in what he called the Life Force, and as a continually evolving phenomenon.

Despite the ambivalence of his treatment of the New Woman in some of his plays (*The Philanderer* and *Press Cuttings*, for example) Shaw was a strong supporter of feminist causes.[5] His ideas on love, marriage and sex were generally in opposition to conventional Victorian sentiment on these subjects.

The opening words of a famous short-wave radio talk which Shaw addressed to America in 1931 were, 'Look, you boob'.[6] The impudence is fairly typical of the tone of Shaw's numerous references to America. But the American response to such barbs has generally been one of delight rather than hostility. His plays have remained extraordinarily popular in that country, and America has long been the major centre of scholarly study of Shaw.

NOTES

1. *Collected Letters 1874–1897*, p. 262.
2. Alice Laden's recipes, with introduction by R. J. Minney and drawings by Tony Matthews, were published under the title, *The George Bernard Shaw Vegetarian Cookbook* (London: Garnstone Press, 1972).
3. 'Wagner and Vegetables', *Academy*, 15 October 1898.
4. Warren Sylvester Smith, ed., *The Religious Speeches of Bernard Shaw* (Pennsylvania: Pennsylvania State University Press, 1963). An excellent working bibliography of writings by and about Shaw on religion, by Charles A. Carpenter, is included in *Shaw and Religion: The Annual of Bernard Shaw Studies*, vol. I, ed. Charles A. Berst (Pennsylvania and London: Pennsylvania State University Press, 1981) pp. 225–46. See also Warren Sylvester Smith, *Bishop of Everywhere: Bernard Shaw and the Life Force* (Pennsylvania and London: Pennsylvania State University Press, 1982).
5. See Rodelle Weintraub, ed., *Fabian Feminist: Bernard Shaw and Woman* (Pennsylvania and London: Pennsylvania State University Press, 1977) *passim*.
6. See Laurence, *Bibliography* (A206).

Vegetarianism

From Raymond Blathwayt, 'What Vegetarianism Really Means: a Talk with Mr Bernard Shaw', *Vegetarian*, 15 January 1898. Raymond Blathwayt (1855–1935), journalist and ordained clergyman of the Church of England, was a special correspondent for *Black and White*, the *Daily News* and other papers. Percy Bysshe Shelley argued the case for vegetarianism in his essays 'A Vindication of Natural Diet' and 'Essay on the Vegetable System of Diet' and in the Notes to his early poem, *Queen Mab*. The references to the Sudan and coloured troops early in this interview would have been prompted by the conflicts in Africa which were to lead in the following year to the outbreak of the Boer War.

'Why are you a vegetarian?' I began.

'Oh, come, Mr Blathwayt! That boot is on the other leg. Why should you call me to account for eating decently? If I battened on the scorched corpses of animals, you might well ask me why I did that. Why should I be filthy and inhuman? Why should I be an accomplice in the wholesale horror and degradation of the slaughter-house? I am a vegetarian, as Hamlet puts it, "after my own honour and dignity".[1] My practice justifies itself. I have no further reasons to give for it.'

'Why is a vegetarian necessarily, apparently, everything else that he shouldn't be?'

'*Is* he?'

'Well, then, is vegetarianism a good thing to fight on, either in the Sudan or Trafalgar Square?'

'You have put your finger on the weak spot in vegetarianism. I regret to say that it is a fighting diet. Ninety-nine per cent of the world's fighting has been done on farinaceous food. In Trafalgar Square I found it impossible to run away as fast as the meat-eaters did.[2] Panic is a carnivorous speciality. If the army were fed on a hardy, healthy, fleshless diet, we should hear no more of the disgust of our coloured troops, and of the Afridis and Fuzzywuzzies at the cowardice of Tommy Atkins.[3] I am myself congenitally timid, but as a vegetarian I can generally conceal my tremors; whereas in my unregenerate days, when I ate my fellow-creatures, I was as patent a coward as Peter the Great.[4] The recent spread of fire-eating fiction and Jingo war worship – a sort of thing that only interests the pusillanimous – is due to the spread of meat-eating. Compare the Tipperary peasant of the potatoes-and-buttermilk days with the modern gentleman who gorges himself with murdered cow. The Tipperary man never read bloody-minded novels or cheered patriotic music-hall tableaux; but he fought recklessly and wantonly. Your carnivorous gentleman is afraid of everything – including doctors, dogs, disease, death and truth-telling; there is no wickedness or cruelty too dastardly for him to champion if only it ends in some dirty piece of witchcraft that promises him immunity from the consequences of his own nasty habits. Don't, in the name of common-sense, talk of courage in connection with the slaughter-house.'

'Let me put you a more personal question. When did you become a vegetarian, and what on earth led you to it?'

'In 1880 or thereabouts. My attention had been called to the enormity of my old habits by the works of Shelley – I am a thorough Shelleyan – but in the seventies the practical difficulties of vegetarianism were very great, as the vegetarian restaurant had not then become an institution.

A lecture by a journalistic colleague of mine, named Lester, since deceased, brought me to the point.[5] During the last seventeen years I have made half-a-dozen separate reputations; and there is not an ounce of corpse in any of them.'

'There is the question of butchers. How would you compensate them for their calling? What would you do with them?'

'Set them up in business as greengrocers and cornchandlers.'

'Has vegetarianism any real *raison d'être* for the present, or hope for the future?'

'Vegetarianism needs no *raison d'être* any more than life itself does. A hundred years hence a cultivated man will no more dream of eating flesh or smoking than he now does of living, as Pepys' contemporaries did, in a house with a cesspool under it. But I do not believe that vegetarianism, as I practise it, is a final solution of the diet question. Man will end by making his food with more care than he makes anything else. Stock-breeding is an advance on the hunter's promiscuous catching and killing. Gardening and agriculture are advances on stock-breeding; but they still mean taking what you find and making the best of it. The human race has not been a very great success on that system. I do not know what the food of the future will be; but it will not be the food of the pigeon, the elephant or the tiger.'

'Another personal question. How do vegetarianism and dramatic criticism blend?'

'A glance at the columns of the *Saturday Review* will enable you to answer that question for yourself without violence to my modesty. The carnivorous output in criticism is very considerable. Just compare the two. Meat-fed criticism is the best for the managers. The vegetarian article is best for the public.'

NOTES

1. Adapted from Hamlet's instruction to Polonius about the Players: 'Use them after your own honour and dignity' (*Hamlet*, II, ii, 525–6).

2. Shaw was present in Trafalgar Square on 'Bloody Sunday', 13 November 1887, when processions of socialist and anarchist organisations protesting against the Government's Irish policy were broken up by police and the Foot and Life Guards. Shaw's boast here is rather at odds with his account of the day in a letter to William Morris (22 November 1887), where he wrote that he and members of the Socialist League, on being charged by police at Clerkenwell '*skedaddled*, and never drew rein until we were safe on Hampstead Heath or thereabouts'. Having been found 'paralysed with terror', he was given a safe conduct to the Square (*Collected Letters 1874–1897*, p. 177).

3. Afridis, Fuzzywuzzies and Tommy Atkins are nicknames for respectively, African, Sudanese and British troops.

4. Peter I (the Great) of Russia (1672–1725). The grounds for Shaw's description of him as a coward are obscure, though he was certainly a bully.

5. Horace Francis Lester (b. 1853), a journalist and author whom Shaw met at a meeting of the Zetetical Society in London between 1880 and 1881, where Lester delivered the lecture, 'Are there any Scientific Objections to Vegetarianism?'.

'Dress and the Writer'

From Maud Churton Braby, 'Dress and the Writer: a Talk with Mr George Bernard Shaw', *World of Dress*, March 1905. Mrs Maud Churton Braby (1875–1932), novelist and author of works on love and marriage, was active in the women's suffrage movement.

'What in the world do I know about dress?' he began.

'Oh, there are lots of things you can tell me. For instance, as a start, do your vegetarian principles allow you to wear kid gloves, fur collars, etc.?'

'I have no principles in that sense. I wear gloves because my hands get dirty in the streets. I never wear fur.'

He threw a glance of horror at my cherished sable stole.

'How can you put such a thing round your neck? Doesn't the smell of it annoy you?'

Considering it was beautifully perfumed with my latest sachet from Paris, I thought this hard, but promptly removed the offending object, to Mr Shaw's great amusement.

In answer to a question about men's dress: 'I like to feel clean,' he said, 'and my great idea of clothes is that they should be clean and comfortable, as far as such a thing is possible in London. This, of course, excludes starch. I couldn't wear a thing which, after having been made clean and sweet, is then filled with nasty white mud, ironed into a hard paste, and made altogether disgusting. To put such a garment on my person, wear it, move in it, perspire in it – horrible! Senseless, moreover – the laundress carefully makes it clean, and then fills it with dirt and hardens the dirt in with an iron. The average man likes it because he doesn't know what cleanliness is. . . .

'He considers a hard, white shirt the cleanest garment possible, because white is to him a symbol of cleanliness, just as the Red Indian paints his face with vermilion as a symbol of bravery; but it doesn't make him brave any more than a white shirt makes a man cleanly dressed.'

'And now about women's clothes?'

'Well, generally speaking, the only thing I have to say about women's clothes is that it's astonishing how women put up with them. Any animal with legs, if fettered with a petticoat, let alone several, would eventually go mad, I should have supposed.'

'They *are* trying,' I murmured. 'It only shows how long-suffering we are.'

'It only shows that you will sacrifice anything sooner than let us see you as you are, instead of letting us imagine you as you are not. But look at the consequences. A human figure with a curtain hung round it from the shoulders to the ankles looks like a badly made postal pillar. You must have either legs or a waist if you are to be bearable by the naked eye. But a waist is not sufficient. Tie a belt round your middle and you look like a sack with its neck in the wrong place. You must have a shape, and that can be produced only by a corset. If I had to wear gowns I should wear a corset in spite of all the surgical diagrams in the Parkes Museum.'[1]

'Then what do you think women *ought* to wear?'

'Anything that will show how they are constructed and allow them the free use of their limbs.'

'You don't advocate bloomers, surely?'

'No: bloomers are an early and revolting form of what is called rational dress, which is not rational at all, but a most irrational, ridiculous and unnatural compromise between male and female attire. You know how ugly a woman looks in a rational cycling dress. But have you ever noticed that if she puts on her husband's Norfolk jacket and breeches, she looks all right at once; they become her perfectly if they are anything like a fit.'

'Then you advise—?' At last we were getting to it!

'I should advise a woman to dress as much as possible like a woman, just as a man dresses like a man. A woman is a biped, built like a man; let her dress like a man.'

NOTE

1. A museum of hygiene named after Edmund Alexander Parkes (1819–76), a distinguished professor of hygiene and a physician. The museum opened at University College, London in 1877.

Votes for Women

From Maud Churton Braby, 'GBS and a Suffragist', *Tribune*, 12 March 1906.
Shaw had some correspondence with Mrs Churton Braby on her novel *Downward*
and on her book *Modern Marriage, and How to Bear It* (see *Collected Letters 1898–
1910*, pp. 785–6, 803).

'The suffrage is nothing to me,' he began. 'I have no opinion on the
subject. I'm not a woman; I've got the suffrage.'

'But if, for the sake of argument, you were a woman—?'

'Of course, if I were a woman, I'd simply refuse to speak to any man
or do anything for men until I'd got the vote. I'd make my husband's
life a burden, and everybody miserable generally. Women should have
a revolution – they should shoot, kill, maim, destroy – until they are
given a vote.'

'And what would you consider the proper qualifications?'

'There's none necessary; the qualification of being human is enough.
I would make the conditions exactly the same as for men; it's no use
women claiming *more* than men, though probably in the end they'll get
more, as they invariably do whenever women agitate for equality with
men in any respect.'

'For example?'

'Take the Married Women's Property Act![1] Since that has been law,
man is a mere insect; he scarcely has the right to live! Women have the
upper hand in every way. Consider their enormous sexual advantage!
Why, even in a court of law no man has a chance in the witness-box
against a woman. It's quite possible, considering the foolish and
sentimental way these things are generally managed, that they will get
more political rights than men in the end.

'What sort of Bill would I introduce, did you say? Simply a short Act
to have the word "men" in all the relevant statutes construed as human
beings – as mankind – though, as you hear people talking of womankind,
I suppose even that would not be understood. It's one of the many
drawbacks to our ridiculous language. We have no word which includes
men and women. It just shows how little we realise men and women
belong to the same species. No one denies that a stallion and a mare
are both horses – they wear just the same kind of harness; but a woman
is looked upon as an entirely different animal to a man. So everything –
costume, coiffer, customs, political rights – everything is arranged as

far as possible to accentuate the supposed difference between two
human beings practically identical. Of course, it's a great advantage to
women to be regarded as a race apart – an advantage which, as usual,
they abuse unscrupulously.'

NOTE

1. The Married Women's Property Act of 1882 provided that all property
acquired by a married woman should become her separate property, free from
her husband's control.

America: I

From Herman Bernstein, '"Why Should I Go to America?" asks Bernard Shaw',
New York Times, 14 May 1911. Herman Bernstein (1876–1935) was a German-
born American journalist who wrote for the *New York Times* between 1908 and
1912. Shaw had many invitations to go to America before making brief visits in
1933 and 1936. Maksim Gorky (Aleksey Maksimovich Peschkov) (1868–1936),
Russian novelist and playwright, author of *The Lower Depths*, attracted much
criticism when he toured America with Maria Fedorovna Andreevna (b. 1872),
an actress with whom he became acquainted at the Moscow Art Theatre. In
1904, having broken off her marriage with a high government official, she had
joined the Bolsheviks and become Gorky's mistress.

'Why should I go to America?' wondered Mr Shaw. 'There is nothing
there that can interest me. When America is a real American Nation,
when the American type becomes fixed, when the American's skin
turns red and his forehead recedes, then it will be interesting to go to
America.

'But at the present time, what are the Americans? An appalling,
horrible, narrow lot.

'Take such a small detail as the incident with the women who wore
harem skirts in New York. They were jeered at and had to run for their
lives. Now, the harem skirt is really a spendid thing, and there is not
the slightest cause for jeering those who wear them. But America is a
land of unthinking, bigoted persecution.

'Take another incident, the Gorky affair. Even if Gorky had come
from a country where divorces are easily granted, the treatment he
received at the hands of the Americans would have been brutal. But
Gorky came from Russia, the land of barbaric laws. Therefore I say

America's outrageous treatment of Gorky put her outside of the pale of civilisation, if she ever was within the pale. This should be said to America. It may do her some good.'

'Are you not interested in the development of the American people – in their achievements?' I asked.

'But they are not developing. That is why they don't interest me. And I am sure they would not be interested in me if I came there. I am not an elephant, so I would not arouse their curiosity. They have much untrained religious enthusiasm, and the trouble with them is that each one is working out his own ideals individually instead of having one common religion or ideal for all.'

'Do you mean to say that you are opposed to individualism, to individual self-perfection?' I asked.

'We must be guided by certain standards. Anything silly or rotten that I write is smashed by public opinion and done for. If I lived on a desert island I would perhaps be writing silly and sentimental romances, which are of no use to anybody. But I am working hard. I argue and debate and weigh every phrase, and work on it and reconstruct it until it is quite simple. It is absolutely true that easy writing is hard reading and hard writing is easy reading.

'Now to return to America, I believe she ought to have a religion of her own. The Pilgrims took the Bible along with them when they emigrated to America. The Christian religion was a real religion in the Middle Ages: then a state of scepticism set in at the time of Shakespeare.

'Since the Pilgrims left their countries because of religious persecution, it was quite natural that they should take their religion along with them. But it would have been much better for them if they had taken the religion of the Indians and developed it. At the present time we all wear clothes that do not fit us. We have the Christian religion, which is the Jewish religion, an Oriental religion – and it does not fit us. It was good for us when we were Orientals, when Judaism and later Christianity came into the world.

'America is overriden with old-fashioned creeds and a capitalist religion. Mr Roosevelt is a typical expression of what I mean.'[1]

NOTE

1. Theodore Roosevelt (1858–1919) was Republican President of the United States from 1901 to 1909.

America: II

From Hayden Church, 'Shaw on What I Eat and Why', *Sunday Express*, 12 October 1930.

I hear that another effort is being made to get you to go to the United States and lecture. Are you going?

I have seen a good many English celebrities after they had returned from lecturing in America, and they all looked like broken-down cab-horses. At my age, the one-night-stands would finish me.

The last man who tried to persuade me to go pointed out that I should be guarded at every point against the exuberance of my admirers, and could travel in such comfort and luxury that I could not fail to have the 'time of my life'.

I reminded him that I had already had the time of my life, and had now to consider the time of my death.

Besides, what man can compete with his own movie-talkie? America has seen me splendidly illuminated and magnified, ten feet high, audible in every corner and visible from every seat.[1] The prosaic reality would be the shabbiest of anti-climaxes.

A very important reason for not going to the United States as a professional lecturer is that by doing so I should spoil a record that I have made for myself. Although I have delivered hundreds, and perhaps thousands, of extemporaneous public addresses during the past fifty years, I have never taken money for one of them.

NOTE

1. Probably a reference to either a 'film interview' made in 1926 or a Fox Movietone Newsreel filmed at Ayot St Lawrence in 1928 (see Laurence, *Bibliography* [G1, G4]).

Religion and Spiritualism: I

From 'Bernard Shaw on Religion', *St Martin-in-the-Fields Review*, May 1922.

Do you believe (a) That there must be 'somebody behind the something'? (b) In a first Cause? (c) That the universe made itself – and that our world is a pure accident?

(a) No: I believe that there is something behind the somebody. All bodies are products of the Life Force (whatever that may be); and to put the body behind the thing that made it is to reverse the order of Nature, and also to violate the first article of the Church of England, which expressly declares that God has neither body, parts, nor passions.

(b) First Cause is a contradiction in terms, because in Causation every cause must have a cause; and therefore there can no more be a First Cause than a first inch in a circle. If you once admit a cause that is uncaused, you give up Causation altogether. And if you do that, you may as well say that everything makes itself. But it can only do that if it is alive; so you are back again at your mystery, and may as well confess that to your ignorance and limited faculty the universe is unaccountable. I daresay every blackbeetle thinks it must have a complete explanation of the world as one of the indispensable qualifications of a respectable cockroach: but it will have to do without it for awhile yet.

(c) All life is a series of accidents; but when you find most of them pointing all one way, you may guess that there is something behind them that is not accidental.

Do you believe that given enough data to go on we could account for everything?

No. As a matter of fact we have data enough, from the Alps to the electrons, to account for everything fifty times over; but we have not the brains to interpret them.

You think the Church has 'failed grossly in the courage of its profession', and therefore you disbelieve in it. But the Labour Party has equally missed its opportunity, yet you believe in it. Why?

The Church has failed infamously: I can hardly imagine how it has the face to exist after its recreancy during the war. But what has that to do with belief or disbelief? The Church of England is only a Society of gentlemen amateurs, half of them pretending to be properly trained and disciplined priests, and the other half pretending that they are breezy public schoolboys with no parsonic nonsense about them. They profess to sustain and propagate religious faith; but their failure or success, their honesty or dishonesty, their sense or their folly, cannot affect the faith: it can only affect the attendance in the buildings in which they pontificate. If a man sells me a bad motor car, I can take my custom away from him, and denounce him as an impostor, without ceasing to believe in the science of mechanics. There are churches where the parson snarls the service and bullies God like a barrister at the Old Bailey. There are churches where he is a duffer, and churches where he is a snob. But that does not prevent people going to St Martin's. The Church is what the parsons make it; and when a man says he does not hold with the Church, and that parsons are frauds, we generally find either that he never goes to church, or else that his particular parson *is* a fraud. The same thing is true of the Labour Party. It, also, is what the Labour men make it. But the truths it stands for remain none the less true.

Do you agree with Voltaire who said 'To believe in God is impossible, not to believe in him is absurd'?[1]

No. Voltaire's remark was witty – that is, true – when he made it; and it is still true of the Omnipotent Personality, with body, parts and passions, which the word God meant in Voltaire's time. But our God, the God who is still struggling with the work of Creative Evolution, and using us as his labourers, having created us for the purpose, and proceeding by the method of trial and error, presents no such difficulty. Unfortunately, many of our people have not yet caught up with Voltaire, much less with the twentieth century; and for them it would be a considerable advance if they were to become Voltaireans.

What effect do you think it would have on the country if every Church were shut and every parson unfrocked? Do you think a Religion is a necessity for the development of a nation? and if so, must it not have some organisation for its development? Or do you believe that nothing can be organised in the realm of the Spirit in this present existence?

A very salutary effect indeed. It would soon provoke an irresistible demand for the Re-establishment of the Church, which could then start again without the superstitions that make it so impossible today. At present the Church has to make itself cheap in all sorts of ways to induce people to attend its services; and the cheaper it makes itself the less the people attend. Its articles are out of date; its services are out of date; and its ministers are men to whom such things do not matter because they are out of date themselves. The marriage service and the burial service are unbearable to people who take them seriously – and please do not conclude that I am thinking now of the current foolish and prudish objections to the sensible and true parts of the marriage service. Your main point is what would happen if the people suddenly found themselves without churches and rituals. So many of them would find that they had been deprived of a necessity of life that the want would have to be supplied; and there would presently be more churches than ever, and fuller ones. The only people who can do without churches are the simple materialists on the one hand, and on the other those who have no use for institutional worship because their churches are their own souls. That is the Quaker position; but you find such people in all circles. They are sometimes artists, sometimes philosophers; and the irony of circumstance has landed one of them in the extraordinary predicament of being a Dean.[2]

Do you think Christ is still a living influence in the present day?

Yes; but there are, as he expected there would be, a good many very unchristlike people trading under his name: for instance, St Paul. The wholesale rebellion against his influence which culminated in the war has turned out so very badly that just at present there are probably more people who feel that in Christ is the only hope for the world than there ever were before in the lifetime of men now living.

NOTE

1. This saying appeared in Voltaire's 'Epître à l'auteur du Livre des trois imposteurs' (10 November 1770).
2. A reference to William Ralph Inge, Dean of St Paul's (see below, p. 474).

Religion and Spiritualism: II

From Hayden Church, 'My Spoof at a Seance: Bernard Shaw Against the Spiritualists – and Why', *Sunday Dispatch*, 13 January 1929.

I asked him if this Life Force, according to his belief, is sentient, or if it works automatically. And if, in the latter case, prayer is a waste of time?

'The Life Force becomes sentient,' he replied, 'by creating organs of sense; your eyes and ears and nose and fingers, for instance. All living things are its organs.

'No,' he continued, 'prayer is not a waste of time except when it is mere begging. Even then it may be a comfort. If you pray that the horse you have backed may win you will not increase his chances of winning, and to that extent you are wasting your time; but if it makes you more hopeful until the race is over, it may be worth your while.

'The praying by which a saint "makes his soul" was said by Mahomet to be a greater delight than perfume or women. Nobody who understands the prophet will ever say that this kind of praying is a waste of time.'

That Shaw believes in survival after death is clear. . . . But he made it equally clear to me that he does not believe that our individualities survive eternally, nor does he consider it desirable that they should.

'If you want to live for ever,' he said, 'if you want to carry your memories of your blunders and infirmities and defects and meannesses and mistakes and humiliations and sins and illnesses with you to the last syllable of recorded time, you must be on better terms with yourself than I have ever succeeded in establishing between myself and Bernard Shaw.

'Combine my advice with Dogberry's: die like a gentleman, and thank God you are rid of a knave.[1] Anything that is worth keeping in you will be worked up into some better attempt at a man than you are.

'All the people I know who look forward to an eternity of themselves stipulate that they shall be angels in the next world.

'As in that case they certainly will not recognise themselves, nor be recognised by any of their friends, they might just as well go the way of all flesh without murmuring, and believe in the life to come without insisting that it should retain their names and addresses.

'Tennyson told them to rise on stepping stones of their dead selves to higher things;[2] and I tell them the same. But no: they want their dead selves to be kept as my grandmother used to keep old wax candle ends. I have no patience with such conceit.'

This brought us inevitably to Spiritualism, upon which subject, up to the present, he has never publicly expressed his views.

'My experience of Spiritualism,' he said, 'began when I was a small boy. My mother amused herself in her old age by making what she called spirit drawings (I have a bundle of them somewhere) and holding conversations with the dead.

'She was as game and shrewd as Sir Oliver Lodge,[3] which proves that if a belief in Spiritualism is a craze, it is one which a thoroughly soundheaded person can keep in a thought-tight compartment without injury to the general mental health.

'I noticed that my mother soon got bored by the spirits of people she had known, including the relatives for whose sake she had taken up the practice. She communicated almost entirely with a sage whose date was 6,000 BC.

'I have never before said anything about this in public. I held my tongue because I did not like to say anything that could worry my mother; and I have kept it up since her death because Oliver Lodge and Conan Doyle[4] are friends of mine; and there is a fact in my past that makes it impossible for us to be in sympathy on the subject.

'I am quite sure that neither of them has ever cheated at a séance. Well, I have. I used to say that unless everybody cheated as hard as they could, and the results obtained went beyond those that could be obtained by cheating, the séances could prove nothing.

'Accordingly I cheated, and was amazed by my success (I am no conjurer) and by the discovery that the more cultivated, clever and imaginative my victims were the more easy it was to cheat them – or rather to induce them to cheat themselves.

'Even when I owned up they would hardly believe me. I thus lost my innocence, and could not feel about the experiences of Lodge and Doyle as they did themselves.

'You see, there is the terrible difficulty that almost all the believers who are not mere miracle gapers have lost somebody they are fond of; and one cannot shatter a consolation and a hope as one could criticise a scientific experiment.'

NOTES

1. Part of Dogberry's advice to a Watchman who asks what to do if a suspect will not stand in the Prince's name is to 'presently call the rest of the watch together and thank God you are rid of a knave' (*Much Ado About Nothing*, III, iii, 29–30).

2. Alludes to 'In Memoriam A. H. H.', I, 3–4.

3. Sir Oliver Joseph Lodge (1851–1940), mathematician and physicist, was appointed Professor of Physics at University College, Liverpool, and subsequently became the first principal of Birmingham University. He did important work in the field of wireless telegraphy and developed a deep interest in psychic phenomena. He was a President of the Society for Psychical Research. Writing to Lodge on 14 June 1924, Shaw reported that his own 'spiritualistic life' began when he was about six years old 'with the arrival at our house of the first planchette [device used to record supposed spirit messages] imported into Ireland'. In the same letter Shaw writes that he suffered 'pangs of conscience' every time he remembered his cheating experiment (see *Collected Letters 1911– 1925*, pp. 878–9).

4. Sir Arthur Conan Doyle (1959–1930), creator of Sherlock Holmes, wrote several works on spiritualism, including a history of the subject published in 1926.

On Hurting Feelings

From St John Adcock, 'GBS at Home', *Bookman*, LXVII, no. 399 (December 1924).
Arthur St John Adcock (1864–1930), novelist, essayist and journalist, was editor
of the *Bookman*. Quoting a critical remark about Shaw that he had 'often written
in order to hurt', Adcock asked was the accused 'conscious of having been
guilty of such cruelty'.

'A dentist may be the kindest of men,' said he, 'but if he wants to drill
the rot out of a tooth he can't always help hurting the patient. I may
have hurt as the dentist does, but never from any desire of hurting. I
think I may claim that I take as much trouble as any dentist to make the
operation as painless as possible. But you must remember that in all
operations a critical writer can perform, there is nothing more offensive
and hurting than an obvious attempt to spare the subject's feelings. The
real way to spare his feelings is often by an apparently brutal disregard
of them. I had much rather infuriate a man than humiliate him or
discourage him – or even merely dissatisfy him. Fury is a breezy,
cheerful sort of emotion which rather bucks a man up than lets him
down; and after he has expressed his feelings with appropriate violence
he very seldom bears malice. But there are certain ways in which people
feel hurt that are entirely beyond the control of the person who inflicts
the hurt, for they are really outside his consciousness. A big policeman
may terrify a little child most cruelly by the mere fact of his visible
existence. The policeman may be the most amiable of men and may
endeavour to wreathe his countenance in the most ingratiating smiles,
but he may frighten the child into fits for all that. In literature, a great
deal of alarm and suffering are caused not by any ill will on the part of
the big policemen of letters but simply because big people are terrifying
to little people.' . . .

I asked whether they were right who described him as a pessimist
and an 'anti-idealist'.

'I am no pessimist,' said he, 'but a meliorist. I don't think we are
doing well, and am anxious we should do better. As a nation, we are at
present attempting to manage an empire before we are able to manage
a village decently. The question is shall we ever be capable of managing
both the village and the empire? If we are not, our empire goes to smash
as all previous empires have gone. But even if we collapse, we shall try
again. If we end as Rome and Egypt ended, we shall begin again. The

menace of the barbarians may precipitate matters, but I do not believe in the barbarian conquest. All empires collapse really from within – thus giving the barbarians their chance. So long as an empire remains sound it can always keep the barbarians out. So long as a man remains healthy he can defy all infections, but the moment he begins to crack up they get hold of him. Civilisation has collapsed over and over again, at the very corner we are trying to get round. I am doubtful whether we shall get round it; but even if we fail and are wiped out completely, as by the return of the ice age, life will presently begin afresh – begin perhaps with some new being – some improvement on man.

Vaccination Condemned

From G. S. Viereck, 'Are Doctors Humbugs? The Crime of Vaccination. George Bernard Shaw Interviewed', *Tit Bits*, 16 October 1926. George Sylvester Viereck (1884–1962) was a German-born American playwright, poet and novelist.

'In England,' Shaw declared, 'the battle against compulsory vaccination lasted almost half a century. I myself had smallpox in 1881.[1] That is how I became interested in the subject.'

'How were you cured?' I asked.

'I cured myself.'

'What did you do?'

'Nothing. I went to bed, rested, lived sensibly, and my own body, not tainted by vaccination, conquered. In a few days I was again on my feet.' . . .

'Vaccine,' Mr Shaw explained, 'comes from the French for *la vache*, the cow. It is a term applied indiscriminately to all forms of inoculation, irrespective of their source.

'Vaccines prepared in the laboratory are, on the whole, less objectionable than the scab from the wound of diseased animals, but everybody who introduces poisons into the human system is playing with fire. His experiment may do incalculable harm to the organism.

'Vaccination kills more persons than smallpox. General vaccæmia, which sometimes results from vaccination, is the worst imaginable disease. It occurs when something goes wrong with the inoculation. In former years, when this dread malady occurred among poor people, the doctors attributed the disease to venereal taint in the parents. The poor people had no remedy – until somebody had the spunk and got the money together to sue the doctors for libel.' . . .

'But,' I said, 'does not vaccination increase resistance to the disease?'

'That,' Shaw replied, 'is the worst of it. Vaccination increases the resistance of the system, but it does not stop the disease. The vaccinated child gets the disease worse than others, because it penetrates the entire system before the patient collapses. In the early stages the child still walks about and gives the disease to other children.

'This phase of vaccination is admitted by many doctors.' . . .

'How do you explain the fact that the ravages of smallpox have almost ceased?'

'Sunshine and common sense, cleanliness and sannitation, diet and exercise, drive out the plague. They, not inoculation, deserve the credit for vanquishing smallpox.'

NOTE

1. Shaw contracted smallpox late in May 1881, and refers to his illness as 'a thing of the past' in a letter dated 23 August 1881 (see *Collected Letters 1874–1897*, pp. 38, 40).

A Meeting with Strindberg

From Judge Henry Neil, 'Bernard Shaw – as Few Know Him. An Intimate Study of the Man Himself', *Pearson's Magazine*, February 1927. Judge Henry Neil is described by Dan H. Laurence as 'a Chicago eccentric who devoted most of his life to the advocacy of pensions for mothers and other social causes' (*Collected Letters 1911–1925*, p. 470). The following recollection is drawn from an account of a lunch at the Savoy Hotel attended by Neil, the novelist Sir Hall Caine (1853–1931) and Shaw. Shaw met the great Swedish dramatist August Strindberg (1849–1912) during a visit to Stockholm in July 1908.

'When I was in Stockholm,' he said, 'I wrote to Strindberg saying that I was in town and that I should value the privilege of calling on him. By return mail I got a very long and keen letter written one third in French, one third in German, and the remaining third in English.

'He said he was living in complete seclusion; that he never went out except between three and four in the morning when no one was about; that it was impossible for him to meet anyone; that he was dying of a mortal disease, and that as we did not speak one another's languages, an interview between us would be a conversation of the dumb with the deaf. Next morning I got an urgent letter asking me to come to see him at his little Intimes Theatre.'[1]. . .

'My wife came with me,' Shaw continued. 'We found Strindberg in a mood of extreme and difficult shyness; but his sapphire-blue eyes were irresistible; the man of genius was unmistakable. He had lived longer in France than in any foreign country; so I thought French would be the best language, and I had carefully prepared a few sentences as I am a villainous linguist. Then he declared that he preferred German. My wife talked to him and jollied him a little; and finally he smiled and became quite at ease.

'He was in love with his Little Theatre, where we saw his *Froken Julie* next night;[2] but I said it was too small; his works needed the Opera House. We were getting on capitally when he suddenly took out his watch, looked at it, and announced in a solemn voice, *'Um zwei Uhr werde ich krank sein!'* At two o'clock I shall be sick.'

'I could hardly believe my ears, or trust my knowledge of German. But as it was a quarter to two then, and, as he had evidently quite made up his mind to be sick, there was nothing for us to do but to leave. That was the mortal disease from which he was suffering.'

'Was he really sick?' I inquired.

'No! He was the greatest hypochondriac on earth,' Shaw said. 'He seemed full of life. Still, I am bound to admit that he died soon after.'

NOTES

1. The Intima Teatern was established in Stockholm in 1907 for the exclusive presentation of plays by Strindberg, who was closely associated with the theatre from 1907 to 1910.

2. I.e. the play known as *Miss Julie* in English.

Tea with Isadora

From Sewell Stokes, *Hear the Lions Roar* (London: Harold Shaylor, 1931) pp. 35–7. Sewell Stokes (b. 1902), author, journalist and broadcaster, was a member of the editorial staff of the *Sunday Times* from 1920 to 1922, and London theatre critic for the *Theatre Arts Monthly* from 1944. Isadora Duncan (1877–1927), the American dancer and teacher, is one of the founders of modern dance. Rejecting the conventions of classical ballet and popular theatrical dance, she encouraged natural, spontaneous movement which arose out of the inspiration of the music. Lady Kathleen Scott (later Mrs Edward Hilton Young, later Lady Kenneth)

(1878–1947) was a sculptor, and widow of the Antarctic explorer, Robert Falcon Scott. She made a bust and a full-length figure of Shaw in bronze.

'My one meeting with Isadora, and I never saw her dance, was a curious one,' he said. 'At the time I did a thing which it is very rare for me to do, I went into Society. I went to a tea-party given by Lady Scott.

'I was sitting on a sofa, I remember, when suddenly a woman who was quite unknown to me sat down by my side and asked:

'"Are you Shaw?"

'"I am", I replied.

'Then, holding out her arms, the woman said: "Come to me, I have loved you all my life!"'

As Shaw repeated this story, he chuckled; the recollection of it seeming to please him enormously.

'And what did you do next?'

'I performed the second act of *Tristan and Iseult*,'[1] replied Shaw. 'For about an hour Isadora and I kept it up. I can't remember all we said to one another, but I know the audience, which listened to every word, was very much amused. I think at first my hostess was a little nervous of how I would take the situation!'

'I can well imagine it. Isadora was always telling me that she ought to have married either you, or Augustus John. What impression did she make on you?'

'The odd thing is that I cannot remember her as looking in the least like any of her photographs; which is curious, because in all of them she appears to have very distinctive features. To me she appeared fat, and . . . rather like a piece of battered confectionery.'

I told Shaw that the description fitted poor Isadora perfectly. At the time he met her she had ceased to care about her personal appearance, and the tragedies she had passed through had already begun to find their reflection in her features.

'She had the cheek of the devil,' added Shaw. 'She said just what she liked. Yet there was more in her than that. Somehow one didn't feel like telling her to go to the devil.'

Now – with Shaw in an excellent mood, sitting opposite to me – was the time to settle once for all the question of that celebrated anecdote so often repeated about the dramatist and Isadora.

According to this anecdote, Isadora, at a time when her figure was considered by sculptors and artists to be one of the most graceful in the world, wrote to Shaw asking him if he would consent to have a child by her. She was supposed to have said: 'You have the greatest brain in the world, I have the most graceful body. Let us, then, produce the perfect child.' To which Shaw is said to have replied: 'But what if the child turned out to have my body and your brain?'

'Actually,' said Shaw, 'it was not Isadora who made that proposition to me. The story has been told about me in connexion with several famous women, particularly Isadora Duncan. But I really received the strange offer from a foreign actress whose name you wouldn't know, and which I've forgotten. *But I did make that reply.'*

NOTE

1. An allusion to the love-duet sung by Tristan and Isolde in Act II of Wagner's opera.

Sex, Love and Marriage: I

From A. Emil Davies, *I Wander* (London: Watts, 1942) pp. 77–9. Davies here recounts the conversation he had with Shaw and two companions on a night walk at Hindhead in May 1914 (see above, pp. 153–4).

I really do not know how we came to discuss the question of incest, but I recollect Shaw telling us that he was much struck by reading in Plutarch the story of Caesar relating how he had dreamt of having incestuous relations with his mother and regarded it as a good omen and went on to a magnificent victory.[1]

Shaw said that while his dreams had not gone quite so far, he had often had dreams of a somewhat similar nature with regard to his own relations; whereupon one of us asked him whether he attributed his success to that fact. He went on to say that it was strange, this general idea among us that incest was peculiarly abhorrent or unnatural. He attributed its comparative infrequency (leaving out of account the well-known effects of overcrowding – families living in one room, etc.) to the fact that daily intercourse and close familiarity with persons of the opposite sex did not conduce to a feeling of passion towards them, but that of course in incest there was nothing inherently immoral.

Upon my remarking that the feeling against incest might have its basis in knowledge of the fact that inbreeding had bad physical results, I was somewhat taken aback to find that all three stated that modern scientific opinion was against that theory. Of course, said Shaw, if there are bad qualities in families they are more likely to be perpetuated in that fashion, but so are good qualities.

Someone remarked that there was a little-known play of Euripides in which the hero unknowingly marries his mother, who has a daughter. The hero then goes to the wars, disappears for many years, goes back, meets the girl, falls in love with her and marries her, the girl being his daughter. The tangle of relationship was peculiar.[2]

This led Shaw to ask if we had noticed how in the classical play on that subject – *Oedipus* – Sophocles is painfully conventional. When Oedipus discovers that he has murdered his father and married his mother he is overcome by the painfulness of the episode. Shaw said that he had long harboured the desire to write a fresh *Oedipus*, in which the hero, on ascertaining what he has done, would turn to the crowd and say: 'Gentlemen, I am sorry to discover that the gentleman I have slain happens to be my father, and the further news that you tell me – namely, that the lady who is my wife is also my mother – is most interesting, and makes me regard that lady with redoubled affection'!

From this we went on to more general discussion of the perpetual sex problem. Shaw said we never would get clear with regard to it, because it was the one thing that we do not know about each other – for people do not tell. He seemed to regard this as an insuperable difficulty in the way of a solution of the much-vexed question. He said, 'If people only knew the truth! A girl ought to be told that she is capable of rousing certain emotions in any young man, which do not, however, justify her, as she believes, in thinking that he is on that account prepared to undertake a most dreadful responsibility; that it does not necessarily mean that they are twin souls and suitable life companions.'

He then went on in his most characteristic vein – viz., a stream of witty and humorous exaggeration. When in the mood he could go on in that strain for half-an-hour without a break.

NOTES

1. Plutarch's 'Life of Julius Caesar' places this dream on the eve of Caesar's crossing of the Rubicon (49 BC), which launched the war that was eventually to make him master of the Roman empire. The reference (in North's translation) is brief: 'It is said, that the night before he passed over this river, he dreamed a damnable dream, that he carnally knew his mother.'
2. No surviving play of Euripides answers to this description.

Sex, Love and Marriage: II

From G. S. Viereck, 'Shaw Looks at Life at 70', *London Magazine*, December 1927. The story about the Wandering Jew to which Viereck refers in this interview was published the following year under the title, *My First Two Thousand Years*. Viereck was co-author of three books with the New York novelist, poet and short-story writer, Paul Eldridge (1888–1982).

'What is your testament on love?'

'Love,' Shaw replied, somewhat contemptuously, 'lacks personal interest. Love is the most impersonal of all passions. It is a vital experience in actual fact; but on paper it is redeemed from intolerable boredom only as a subject of biological science.

'Even Shakespeare could not make love interesting. Everybody yawns in *Romeo and Juliet* when Mercutio and the Nurse leave the stage.

'All the great love stories, like 'Francesca da Rimini,'[1] are equally tiresome. Every man is the same sort of idiot when he is in love.'

I confessed that I was working with Paul Eldridge on a novel having as its subject the life story of the Wandering Jew.

'This,' I explained, 'gives us the opportunity to write the history of love.'

'It is not worth writing,' Shaw advised. 'Eliminate the erotic element entirely from your novel.'

He yawned, slightly bored by the thought of 2,000 years of love!

'How, by the way,' he asked, 'do you dispose of your hero?'

'His fate remains in doubt,' I replied.

'Why don't you kill him by meeting that impressive intellectual vacuum, the late Mr Bryan?'[2] . . .

'Do you think marriage will develop along the revolutionary lines evolved by the Russians?'

'The Russians have not evolved any revolutionary lines as far as I know. They have tightened up the Russian marriage law so as to force people who live together to marry one another, even if they have to divorce their wives and husbands to make that possible. Instead of our tolerated polygamy whitewashed with sacramental monogamy, they have instituted dissoluble monogamy, but monogamy at all costs. Whether it works I do not know.

'The relations of the sexes,' Mr Shaw insists, 'can never be really wholesome until woman achieves complete economic emancipation.

Not merely the woman, but the man must be emancipated from economic toils.

'Successful households are based on mutual liking and congeniality, but successful families in the eugenic sense may be the fruit of purely sexual and hideously unhappy unions. The sentimental fiction-mongers connive with the preachers to falsify the facts. The marriage ceremony effects no sudden change in the biology of two human beings. A happy marriage may last fifty years; a sex infatuation cannot be depended on to last fifty minutes.

'Until we free the marriage relation from economic entanglements and from sentimental hocus-pocus, the revolting custom of husband-hunting cannot be eradicated. Suffrage, while giving political freedom to woman, does not break her economic chains.

'Until we sublimate the marriage relation, the difference between marriage and Mrs Warren's profession[3] remains the difference between union labour and scab labour.'

'Do you advocate monogamy?'

'Monogamy,' the grey poet-prophet continued, 'is imposed by the economy of nature, which more or less equalises the birth rate of the two sexes. If a war upset it you would have polygamy without question in ten minutes. The Mormons were the most narrowly straitlaced monogamic moralists on earth; but when they had either to multiply rapidly or be wiped out by their persecutors in Missouri, they were almost instantaneously converted to polygamy in spite of their horror when their prophet first broached it to them.'

'What is your attitude towards the dissolution of marriage? Do you favour easy divorces?'

'I do not know what you mean by easy. Brieux[4] has pointed out that it is sometimes harder to escape from an illicit alliance than from a legal marriage. But if you mean legally easy, I think divorces should be granted for the asking, without any further reason. The present legal reasons are ridiculous. Bad temper is a better ground for divorce than adultery. . . .

'I cannot conceive of anything more hideous than to compel two human beings to live together against their wills. If a woman can reject a suitor because she does not love him, why should she be forced to live with a man whom she no longer loves?'

'The children make a difficulty, don't they?'

'They do now,' Shaw replied promptly.

NOTES

1. The famous story (referred to in Dante's *Inferno*) of the illicit love of Francesca, daughter of Giovanni da Polenta, Count of Ravenna, for her

husband's brother, Paolo. In referring to the story here Shaw employs a version of the title of Tchaikovsky's symphonic fantasy, *Francesca da Rimini* (1876).

2. William Jennings Bryan (1860–1925), a fiery and indefatigable orator, was an unsuccessful candidate for the American presidency on three occasions. His fundamentalist religious views led him to assist the prosecution in the famous Scopes trial of 1925, in which a schoolteacher was accused of teaching Darwinian evolutionary theories instead of divine creation.

3. In Shaw's early play, *Mrs Warren's Profession*, Mrs Warren is the owner of a chain of brothels.

4. Eugène Brieux (1858–1932), a French dramatist in the naturalist tradition whose social problem plays were much admired by Shaw.

Sex, Love and Marriage: III

From Hayden Church, 'Myself and Love. By G. Bernard Shaw in the Most Remarkable Interview He has Ever Given', *Sunday Dispatch*, 6 January 1929.

How great (or how small) a part has love played in the life of George Bernard Shaw? Before, at the age of forty-two, he surprised everybody by marrying, he was generally regarded as a misogynist. Some people persist in regarding him as something like that even now! Among these is one of the cleverest women of my acquaintance, and she, on hearing that I was to interview Mr Shaw, remarked: 'The question *I* should most like to ask GBS is, "Have you ever been in love?" But I think,' she added, 'that I could answer it myself with one word: Never!'

I asked Shaw to say if she was right or wrong. His reply was:

'Your circle of female acquaintances must be an extraordinarily stupid one if the cleverest of them cannot guess. What does the question mean?

'A love-affair may mean anything from a correspondence continued for years between people who have hardly ever met, to one of those inevitable results of a drunken orgy which you described as characteristic of American girls under the spell of Prohibition.

'The truth is, all the cases worth counting are different. I could tell you that I have never been in love. I could tell you I have never been out of it. And you would be no wiser than you were before. Therefore I shall not tell you anything at all. Next question, please.'

Part 14
At Home

INTRODUCTION TO PART 14

After their marriage in June 1898, the Shaws lived in Surrey for a year before setting off for a holiday in Cornwall, followed by a Mediterranean cruise on the S.S. *Lusitania*. In October 1899 they moved into Charlotte's flat at 10 Adelphi Terrace, which was to remain their London residence for almost thirty years. Adelphi Terrace was a row of houses on the Thames Embankment built by the Adam brothers in 1768–72. The Shaws lived on the two top floors of no. 10, the lower floors being occupied by staff of the *Nation*. The house had spectacular views, but was rather cramped, and lacked a bathroom (the Shaws bathed in saucer-shaped tin tubs). In 1928 they transferred their London residence to a larger apartment at Whitehall Court, a block of service flats next to the National Liberal Club.

In November 1906 the Shaws established a second residence at a former rectory in the tiny Hertfordshire village of Ayot St Lawrence, having rented, since the spring of 1904, a house at Harmer Green in nearby Welwyn. The house at Ayot, later named 'Shaw's Corner', is a substantial two-storey late Victorian house set in a pleasant garden overlooking fields. At the bottom of the garden Shaw had a small hut which he used for writing, and which could be revolved to catch the sun. The house was bequeathed by Shaw to the National Trust in 1944, and now attracts some 10,000 visitors each year.

The Shaws entertained frequently at both their London and Ayot houses. Charlotte, by all accounts an exceptionally capable household manager, remained unconverted to her husband's vegetarian and teetotal diet. The generous fare at the Shaw table included meats and wines, as well as a great variety of vegetarian dishes.

Like his hero Jack Tanner in *Man and Superman*, Shaw lived in a style to which few socialists are accustomed. From 1907 he employed several private secretaries, of whom the formidable and highly efficient Miss Blanche Patch was the longest serving. The household staff at Ayot St Lawrence included a cook–housekeeper, a parlourmaid, a chauffeur and two gardeners.

10 Adelphi Terrace

From 'Celebrities at Home. No. MCLIII. Mr George Bernard Shaw in Adelphi Terrace, Strand', *World*, no. 1359 (18 July 1900).

For variety and architectural beauty, no view in London surpasses that obtainable from Mr Bernard Shaw's rooms in the Adelphi Terrace, especially when, under the conditions of a westerly wind, the smoke and the undefinable haze incident to a great city have been rolled away. Then the picture presented is at its best. The fair green hills of Kent and Surrey, the latter jewelled with the sunlit Crystal Palace, demarcate the horizon; and the flowing Thames, flanked east and west by St Paul's and the Houses of Parliament, agreeably fill the middle distance; while at your feet the fresh verdure of the Embankment Gardens vividly contrasts with the grey antiquity of Cleopatra's Needle.

'These chambers in Adelphi Terrace constitute the real centre of my domesticity,' Mr Shaw explains, 'because my wife lives here. My official residence, qualifying me as a vestryman, is in Fitzroy Square; my mother lives there. I live nowhere.' . . .

'In fact,' as he remarks, 'any place that will hold a bed and a writing table is as characteristic of me as any other; and as I never keep or collect anything, I have no more home instinct than a milk-can at a railway station. I am always content wherever I may happen to be – not like most people, who, wherever they are, want to be somewhere else, and are always convinced that their happiness lies round the corner.' This contented spirit may strike you as being scarcely surprising as you turn from the open window and survey the drawing-room where your host has received you. Delicate landscapes by the Italian pastellist, Sartorio,[1] decorate the sage-green walls which the white furniture charmingly relieves; and one *chef d'œuvre* has been deftly inserted in the setting of the overmantel. This is the camping-ground of a crowd of nicknacks – carved ivories, bronzes and curios mostly collected by Mrs Shaw during a tour in India;[2] indeed, the spoils of the East are as much a feature of this artistic room as the great bookcase which monopolises one side of it, and which is the repository of such heterogeneous strains of thought as are indicated by mention of the names of Ruskin, Nietzsche, Balzac, Sidney Webb, Stanley Jevons, William Morris – a miscellany of literary labour which is well reflected on the facets of your

host's mind as dramatist, novelist, journalist, economist, critic and
political pamphleteer. He is, however, impatient of books, and declares
that the only author from whom a dramatist can learn anything is
Bunyan, for whom he has an unbounded and somewhat unexpected
admiration, quoting his best passages as superior to Shakespeare's. The
little Bechstein piano, a relic of the first Arts and Crafts Exhibition, is to
Mr Shaw what the armchair by the fireside is to other writers. Instead
of reading novels and poems, he goes to the piano, attacks an opera or
symphony, and is his own Melba, his own Plançon,[3] and his own
orchestra, thanks, as Mrs Shaw rather pathetically explains, to 'a
remarkable power of making the most extraordinary noises with his
throat.' . . .

After luncheon your host may take you to his writing-room, where
Walter Crane's 'Triumph of Labour'[4] and some Albert Dürer prints
decorate the Morris 'Woodbine' papered walls. Mr Shaw possibly
apologises for the untidiness of the room; however, his marriage has
reformed him more than he suspects, for the room is fairly in order,
and there is plenty of method about the neat little silken bags full of
press cuttings, which, like 'sweet herbs' hung up to dry, may serve as
a savour to his literary work – 'every original writer,' he observes,
'should keep a foolometer of this kind' – and there is indisputable
neatness of arrangement to be found in a little bureau, wherein labelled
memoranda recall those *Plays Pleasant and Unpleasant*, some of which
have been very recently performed at the Crystal Palace and the Strand
Theatre, to the no small interest of a large number of cultured playgoers.
He confesses that he delights in driving bargains and drawing up the
most methodical agreements. 'The other parties never keep them,' he
adds, 'but it amuses me to make them.'

NOTES

1. Aristide, or Giulio Aristide, Sartorio (1860–1932) was one of the foremost of
the modern Italian painters who were active in the period dominated by
Symbolism. He was inspired by the work of the English Pre-Raphaelites,
especially that of D. G. Rossetti. On a visit to Rome before she met Shaw,
Charlotte commissioned a pastel portrait of herself by Sartorio.
2. Charlotte toured India in 1892.
3. Dame Nellie Melba (1861–1931), the Australian-born opera singer, was the
outstanding prima donna of her day. Pol (Henri) Plançon (1851–1914), French
operatic bass, became a favourite with English audiences.
4. Walter Crane (1845–1915), illustrator, designer and theoretician, was a
forerunner of the English Art Nouveau. He worked with Morris and Burne-
Jones and was a member of the Socialist League. 'The Triumph of Labour',
issued in 1891, is a large wood-engraving showing 'a procession of workers of
all kinds, both manual and mental, marching out to celebrate the International

May Holiday, and bearing banners and emblems declaring their ideals' (Walter Crane, *An Artist's Reminiscences* [London: Methuen, 1907] p. 354).

Shaw's Arrival at Ayot St Lawrence, 1906

EDITH REEVES

From Allan Chappelow, ed., *Shaw the Villager and Human Being: A Biographical Symposium* (London: Charles Skilton, 1961) pp. 165–7; hereafter cited as *Shaw the Villager*. Allan Chappelow, photographer and author, is the editor of two extensive works, *Shaw the Villager* and *Shaw, the Chucker-out* (1969). He made many striking photographic studies of Shaw in old age. *Shaw the Villager* is a gathering of recollections by servants in the Shaw household at Ayot, local officials, tradespeople and neighbours. Mrs Edith Reeves and her husband ran a farm on the estate adjoining the Shaws' property. They had been residents in the village, since 1899. Harry Higgs was the Shaws' head gardener from 1901 to 1943. His wife, Clara, was housekeeper during the same period.

The villagers used to call Bernard Shaw 'Old Hair and Teeth' in those days, because his red hair and grinning white teeth were his most prominent features.

When Bernard Shaw first arrived in the village there was an awful lot of gossip. The villagers all thought he was a rum one – a *very* rum one. Later, during the First World War, everyone thought he was a German, because he kept a light burning in a window at the top of his house – just as Otto Beit did in the neighbouring village of Codicote.[1] We thought they wanted to show the German planes the way.

My husband and I saw Mr Shaw frequently from the day when he first came to live in our village, and we lived next door; but he kept himself to himself a lot in those days, and it was not until 1915, during the terrible Hertfordshire Blizzard, that the village in general got to know him more closely. He came out and worked hard with the other menfolk for days on end, sawing up trees which had been torn up by their roots and lay blocking the road.

During the First World War the Shaws said we could go down into their cellar if there were local air-raids: there was an anti-aircraft station in the district. But my husband didn't accept because he thought that if a bomb *did* fall near, the whole house would come down on top of us.

Mr Shaw would always sit bolt upright when motoring. He used to drive his cars very fast through the village, and some people grumbled about this; but though fast, he was careful, I think. I never heard of him knocking anybody down in the village. He used an ordinary cycle also, and often journeyed by foot.

He was fond of animals, and when we loaded pigs into the cart for market they squealed a lot, as they always do, and we thought he would complain and accuse us of cruelty. But he always minded his own business.

GBS used to put the mown grass from his extensive lawn over our wall for fodder for our cows and livestock, and he would give us cabbages and other vegetables from his garden – while we gave him raspberries and cherries from ours. He paid us for these, but would never accept anything for the vegetables he gave us. I think his view was that fruit and vegetable growing was part of our business as farmers, but only a hobby with him. But my husband made it right by helping Harry Higgs, Mr Shaw's gardener, with the mowing.

Bernard Shaw was particularly fond of White Hart cherries and bought a lot from us, and got Mrs Higgs, his housekeeper, to bottle them. He had a special kind of milk supplied in screwtop bottles and she used these bottles afterwards for bottling fruit. We did a regular milk round, but never delivered to the Shaws. Mr Shaw liked to distribute his custom evenly and must have got his milk from some other local supplier.

I named one of my sons Bernard after Mr Shaw, who was fond of children – as also was his wife. Mrs Shaw was always very anxious not to disturb my babies when they were asleep, and I had a special window made in the hood of the pram so that she could peep at them without their being awakened. My first daughter used to cry out when Bernard Shaw looked into the pram: she was afraid of his red beard. So I got him, too, to look at her only through the window in the hood.

Mrs Shaw told me once that she would very much like to have children. My husband and I reckoned that the reason Mr Shaw never had children was because Mrs Shaw was very asthmatical and he didn't want her to have the hurt of it. Child-bearing was much more painful half a century ago than it is nowadays.

NOTE

1. Sir Otto Beit (1865–1930) and his brother Alfred (1853–1906), sons of a Hamburg merchant, were British financiers and philanthropists.

Weekends at Ayot

LILLAH McCARTHY

From Lillah McCarthy, *Myself and My Friends* (London: Butterworth, 1933) p. 86. Lillah visited the Shaws at Ayot St Lawrence during rehearsals for *The Doctor's Dilemma*, in which she played Jennifer Dubedat, with Granville Barker as Dubedat, and which opened on 20 November 1906 at the Court Theatre.

I have often been asked by people who admire or who dislike Shaw to give them a picture of Bernard Shaw at home. The admirers are pleased and the hostile disappointed to see what a charming picture it is. It began to paint itself in my mind during the fine weekends of 1906 when I used to stay with Mr and Mrs Shaw at Ayot. They were weekends of rest and quiet. Shaw would run round the garden in the morning, doing his breathing exercises the while. After breakfast we would walk, and sometimes we would carry on our conversation with quotations from Shakespeare or Dickens. His memory was amazing and mine was not so ill, so we enjoyed ourselves and fed a harmless vanity at the same time. In the afternoon, he would play his pianola or read a book. There were no hectic discussions and no displays of cleverness. Sometimes there might be leisurely talks about our friends, the Sidney Webbs, of the work of the Fabian Society, or of the vagaries of the new member, H. G. Wells.

'Squire' Shaw

FRANCIS HOPKINS

From Francis Hopkins, ' "Squire" Shaw: Being an Unconventional Interview with one of the Most Written-about Persons in the Public Eye', *Lady's Realm*, October 1909.

Everybody in Ayot St Lawrence knows Mr Shaw as the village squire, and as none other. The working-man villagers raise their hats as he passes in token of their admiration of the Squire. They know nothing of his plays, or his books or his Socialism. He is Squire Shaw – and an excellent type of squire he is, quiet, dignified, but not in the least haughty, ready always to help the village children to pick buttercups and daisies and to tell them enchanting tales of lions and tigers, and big elephants. He dresses as a well-conducted squire should dress – quite neatly and conventionally. We walked along lanes which had been trodden for centuries, across meadows as level and as short-cropped as bowling-greens, and through creaking gates, and so to the fourteenth-century ruin and the modern ecclesiastical temple.[1]

'Civilisation took a jump over Ayot St Lawrence,' observed Squire Shaw, forgetting amid these heavenly surroundings that he is a Socialist. 'We are two miles from the main road. We get no dust from motor-cars. People do not come this way unless they want to, and so we are left undisturbed and happy.' We were among the church ruins.

'Beautiful example of fourteenth-century architecture,' commented the Squire. 'Look at the remains of the fine old timbered roof. Owls get up there and screech. See the beauty of that fragment of ornamentation. Pity some fool laid violent hands on it. . . .'

The labouring villagers of Ayot St. Lawrence do not know George Bernard Shaw. They only know Mr Shaw, who lives in 'that new house just in the turning of the lane there'. I spoke to one worthy man and asked him if he knew what Mr Shaw did for a living.

'He does something in London, I think,' he said, 'but dashed if I know what. He doesn't tell the likes of us. But I do know as he's a darned good sort. My wife was very ill and he sent her some eggs, and Mrs Shaw called and made the missus feel quite well again. Of course, it isn't for me to ask him about his trade, is it?'

NOTE

1. The fourteenth-century abbey church of Ayot St Lawrence was partly pulled down in the seventeenth century by the lord of the manor at the time, Sir Francis Lyde. Indulging his enthusiasm for Palladian architecture, he commissioned the building nearby of an incongruous classical temple, which then served as the parish church.

'A Great Hero'

LOUISE RUMBALL

From *Shaw the Villager*, p. 161. Louise Rumball's mother taught at a school in Ayot from 1905 to 1930.

Bernard Shaw sent my mother cheques every year to be spent on sweets for the school-children in Ayot. She passed the money over to the village post-office and shop, and the children could then get sweets there without paying, to the extent of a shilling each. This sum was, in those days when golden sovereigns were common tender, the equivalent of perhaps seven or eight shillings today – quite a lot of money for a child to buy sweets with. As a result, Mr Shaw became a great hero with the school-children. How many schools are there with benefactors of this kind – which are so truly appreciated by the pupils? Certainly Bernard Shaw was the only person in the village who did this, and I have not heard of anyone else at any time or place with the same original idea.

On Being Shaw's Private Secretary, 1912–20

ANN JACKSON (née ELDER)

From *Shaw the Villager*, pp. 263–4. Ann M. Jackson (*née* Elder) succeeded Mrs Georgina Musters as Shaw's secretary in 1912. She had been recommended by Mrs Musters herself, and remained in the position, with one interruption of service in 1918–19, until 1920, when she married and left to join her husband in India. Margaret Bilton was the Shaws' cook–housekeeper at Adelphi Terrace until her retirement in 1927.

I enjoyed every minute of my period with Bernard Shaw as his Secretary. I was in my twenties at the time, and although Mr Shaw was in his late fifties and early sixties he was full of zest for life. I've always had a good sense of humour, and I think you had to have that to understand him. . . .

I remember once Mrs Bilton, Shaw's housekeeper at the time, came to me in the study saying: 'Don't you think Mr Shaw is such a *Christ-like* man?' On another occasion she asked Mr Shaw's advice on whether she should listen to a particular preacher at a church in London. Shaw – the alleged atheist – replied: 'Yes, of course, go ahead!' He always respected other people's convictions, if sincere and not humbug. . . .

Another incident I remember was during the First World War. Mrs Bilton came rushing up the stairs shouting, 'Mr Shaw would like you to come down immediately, Miss Elder.' I ran down the steps, rather alarmed – only to find that Mr Shaw didn't want me to miss the sight of the first daylight air raid on London. He was very excited and counted the planes: there were twenty-two bombers.

Table-talk

LADY GREGORY

From *Lady Gregory's Journals 1916–1930*, ed. Lennox Robinson (London: Putnam, 1946) pp. 199–200. Lady Gregory recalls some lunch-time conversation at Adelphi Terrace on 19 November 1916. Matthew Haffigan is mistaken here for Tim Haffigan, a character in *John Bull's Other Island* who in Act I passes himself off as a typical Irishman, but who is later discovered to have been born in Glasgow. Matthew Haffigan is his Rosscullen cousin.

There was some talk at lunch of Spiritualism. GBS said his mother had been very much given to table-turning, and that a spirit used to come who gave his name as Matthew Haffigan – a name he has used later in *John Bull*, and who was a most awful liar. They tried to verify some of his statements, and they were always false. His mother, however, went on quite happily. GBS himself became an adept at cheating at séances and gave no belief to anything in them.[1] He says his mother's real love was for gardens, that if he were run over by a dray she would say, 'Oh, poor fellow!' but if a beautiful rose had been crushed she would go out of her mind with grief!

NOTE

1. See above, pp. 411–13.

The Shelter, and Tools of Trade

BLANCHE PATCH

From Blanche Patch, *Thirty Years with GBS* (London: Victor Gollancz, 1951) pp. 40–1. Blanche Patch (1879–1966) was Shaw's private secretary from 1920 until his death. Born in Winchelsea, the daughter of a clergyman, she was introduced to Shaw by Beatrice Webb. She was a woman of strong character, described by her employer as 'Shaw-proof', and very much admired and valued by him: 'The trouble you have NOT given me and the help you HAVE given me are immeasurable' (*Thirty Years with GBS*, p. 236).

What Shaw did resent, wherever he might be, was the inquisitive intruder, whether in a railway carriage, or on board ship, or at Ayot, where his shelter, hidden among the bushes, gave him the solitude which he preferred. There he would sit all morning in his wicker chair by the window at a simple flap table fixed into a corner, with a thermometer on the wall and his paste pot, paper clips, red ink and alarum clock tidily deployed in front of him as he wrote his neat shorthand. He loved his red ink, paste pot and paper clips; to make a correction he would type the altered line or two on a slip of paper and paste it over the deletion. Although he carried a watch, the alarum clock was set each day to remind him when it was time for lunch. He never took any notice of it, and had always to be summoned. For this purpose a hand-bell such as porters used to clang on railway stations was installed, not without feeling in the village during the early days of the war when all other bells were banned. . . .

In the shelter on another small table stood Shaw's portable Remington. He had always played about with a typewriter. I imagined that he got one in his early London days as soon as typewriters were to be had and he had the money to spare: he was ever curious about any new device, whether typewriter or atom bomb. He toyed with the idea of a dictaphone, and at one time looked forward to a day when an author would speak into a dictaphone and the dictaphone would work a linotype without the intervention of a compositor. Then he decided that meantime his own shorthand was more fascinating. . . . Before he had a secretary, he did for some time do his own typing. He did not 'touch' type: he used two fingers. Latterly, for personal letters, or, to save time, he might want to add an extra page when revising a script. Before deciding to buy his last machine he went round a trade exhibition. 'Could that typewriter type a play?' he asked a young woman demonstrator, perhaps somewhat unnecessarily. 'Of course it could,' said she, rather annoyed. 'It could type anything.' For all his interest in the most up-to-date mechanical devices, GBS himself was baffled when faced with having to put a new ribbon on his machine: he had actually to bring it up to London to let me fix it for him.

Perambulations

FRED DRURY

From *Shaw the Villager*, pp. 51–5. Fred Drury came to Ayot St Lawrence at the age of nineteen as a temporary help, and stayed on as under-gardener.

Mr and Mrs Shaw used to walk around the garden together quite often. . . . They used to put stones in a heap in a certain spot to mark every mile. They had a special route round the garden which was just about a mile, and they put one stone down every time they passed it. Both their initials were engraved on the glass of the greenhouse, framed around with shamrocks. One can only speculate as to what went on between the two as they walked and talked together.

Mrs Shaw *made* Mr Shaw. She used to help him a lot with his work. She used to read his drafts and proofs and make suggestions and criticisms. She was a real helpmate and constant companion in all aspects of his life. Theirs was that sort of marriage.

Mr and Mrs Shaw were born within a month of each other in 1856[1] – and their handwriting was very similar too, but she was the more sociable. She liked London life and used to go up to London regularly every Wednesday, in the Rolls. He'd go up on the Thursday, by train – mainly to attend to business – and they'd come back together in the car on Saturdays. . . .

He was very fond of his garden – used to walk round it a lot. It gave him exercise without the need for going outside the gates. And of course he used to go down to his little wood hut to work regularly every day till his last year or so – when he went only when it was fine, or when he was in the mood, but he never laid out new flower beds or anything like that.

We grew some large red poppies at the bottom of the garden. Mr Shaw asked me once during the war if the seeds were poisonous. I said 'Yes'. He remarked: 'We must get a packet and send them off to Hitler,' and stalked off. He used to love bonfires and would often stand watching them. I think he was more sympathetic to Mussolini than Hitler. Once when we had a bonfire going he said he'd like to put Hitler on top of it with all the other weeds and things.

[Chappelow asked: 'But he liked flowers, didn't he?']

Well – not specially, really. He didn't notice them very much. He was more interested in his fruit – especially the strawberry beds. He loved strawberries and cream. It was the greengage tree near the strawberry bed that he was pruning when he fell and broke his thigh. It was always a bad tree that one – its fruit was always hard, and it did him in, in the end.

Pruning with the secateurs was his chief interest. He was lost in thought most of the time, thinking about his plays. He always had his notebook with him, and used to fetch it out and write down things in it, as he walked along. I remember Mr Shaw once lost his secateurs and told the keeper on the estate nearby on which he'd lost them: 'I'll give you £5 if you find them; they were a present from my wife.' The price of the sacateurs in the shops was only about 5/-. I thought that incident was a touching indication of his feelings for Mrs Shaw. . . .

Mr Shaw was a very nice gentleman – all bark and no bite. And Mrs Shaw was one of the best. No better pair one couldn't have wished to have worked for.

NOTE

1. Charlotte was born about six months after Shaw, on 20 January 1857.

Postal Affairs

JISBELLA LYTH

From *Shaw the Villager*, p. 81. Mrs Lyth became postmistress at the combined village shop and post office at Ayot in 1931.

Before the war Mr Shaw spent only part of the week here – the rest at his London flat in Whitehall Court, but no matter where he was, he always wrote to me for all his stamps, even though when in London he could have obtained them very easily on the spot. I had hundreds of letters from him – with orders for stamps – during the twenty years or so I knew him.

I was getting 10/- per week widow's pension, and 12/- per week for running the sub-post-office at that time. I once asked GBS why he bothered to write to me for stamps when I lived next door and he could so easily have sent out for them, or ordered them in quantity from London. He replied: 'My dear woman, you shouldn't complain. You will be able to sell them for 2½d each when I am dead.' 'Tuppence ha'penny each, indeed.' I told him. 'Why, I sell them for 10/6d now you're alive!' And the price I was able to charge rose steadily over the years till it reached two to three guineas. . . .

Mr Shaw used to come up to my post office regularly every day until his last year or two, and I used to watch out for him. Many's the time he's helped me with my crossword puzzles. I shall always remember one occasion when the clue word was 'fret'. It had to do with Shakespeare – something about 'strut and fret across the stage'. I remember Mr Shaw was exceptionally interested and quite excited and gave me a whole lecture on it!

One day Mr Shaw came into my shop, and asked me if I would like to have a picture of his house for sale in my shop. I replied that I would, very much, but should have to give it a name. 'Call it "Shaw's Corner" and I will pose with it,' he said. But the next day he came in again and said: 'I won't pose *with* the house – you can have me separately, and then you will sell two postcards instead of one.' He brought a large assortment of pictures of himself which I still have. One of the photos he showed me was of himself on a raft – almost in the nude. 'What could I do,' he said, 'I couldn't *shoot* the photographer because I hadn't got a gun!' ('So much for your pacifism,' said I!)

'The Choicest of Dishes'

SIEGFRIED TREBITSCH

From Siegfried Trebitsch, *Chronicle of a Life*, trans. Eithne Wilkins and Ernst Kaiser (London: Heinemann, 1953) p. 276. Trebitsch visited Ayot in October 1925 and in the same month of 1926. The following recollection probably refers to the second visit.

In Ayot I was once again to meet with the blessings of vegetarian cookery. There, more than in his London home, I had the opportunity of observing the strange division of diet that this couple had instituted. I was no longer sorry for Shaw as a vegetarian, for he used to get two extra helpings of macaroni au gratin, twice as many potatoes as anyone else, a large piece of Emmenthal cheese afterwards, three oranges instead of one – and I could go on in this way for a long time – while Mrs Shaw served her guests and herself with the choicest of dishes but not with so much of them. Even at breakfast there was tea and coffee, ham, cold partridge, and masses of all kinds of cheese and butter. We, who were naturally not used to such luxurious breakfasts, had to our great regret, feasting our eyes more than our stomachs on these delicacies, to renounce most of this delicious fare. Mrs Shaw herself did not eat much of any of these many titbits, but there they were, after all, and it seemed to be a point of pride with her that all these things were to be had in her house in the country. When I consider what quantities of food Shaw devoured instead of the small slice of meat that we ate, I rather doubt whether the vegetarian way of living is to be regarded as particularly abstemious or ascetic.

'Lunch with Mr and Mrs Bernard Shaw'

FRIEDA LAWRENCE

From *Frieda Lawrence: the Memoirs and Correspondence*, ed. E. W. Tedlock (London, Melbourne, Toronto: Heinemann, 1961) pp. 147–8. Frieda von Richthofen Lawrence (1879–1956) eloped with D. H. Lawrence in 1912, and married him in 1914. They had a tempestuous, but happy and productive relationship which lasted until Lawrence's death in 1930. Frieda's visit to the Shaws may have been that referred to in a letter she wrote to Martha Gordon on 7 November 1932, in which she says: 'Went to the G. B. Shaw's, liked *her* so much' (Henry T. Moore and Dale T. Montague, *Frieda Lawrence and Her Circle* [London: Macmillan, 1981] p. 63). Before receiving her invitation to lunch Frieda had come across an article which said that Shaw had been mean in giving only £10 to Lawrence when asked for help by their mutual friend, Lady Ottoline Morrell. Frieda wrote to Charlotte to say how sorry she was about the article and to say that she did not think Shaw's gift mean.

The Shaws asked me to lunch. I went, and going up the stairs a slim figure sprinted past me up the steps like a young hound. 'Maybe this is

Shaw.' From their spacious apartment you could see through the big windows the boats and barges going past on the Thames. For lunch there were several people: Lady S., a feminist, and a famous bookseller and another man, I think a general.[1] We had chicken for lunch, but Shaw, who sat beside me, only had vegetables. A footman waited on us, we had wine, but Shaw did not. On the way to the lunch in the taxi I had said to myself: 'Now look out and don't make a fool of yourself for Lawrence's sake. Shaw is too clever for you.'

Lawrence and Shaw were such worlds apart. Shaw and Lady S. talked about a Welsh miner who had just written a book. 'Do they put Lawrence on the same level with this man?' I thought. Then Lady S. asked me: 'Don't you think we all like to belong to a class, Mrs Lawrence?' Class? after all I had married a miner's son. 'No,' I told her, 'I would like to be a Hottentot.' 'I think you are an aristocrat,' said Shaw to me.

Suddenly Shaw turned to me: 'Is it true that you broke a plate over your husband's head?'

'Yes, it is true.'

'What did you do that for?'

'Lawrence had said to me women had no souls and couldn't love. So I broke a plate over his head.'

This Shaw thought over. Such a quick, violent response was alien to his make-up.

Then he asked about the ranch in New Mexico.[2] I told them about the cabins high up among the pines, we only had horses and a buggy, and how Lawrence milked the cow Susan and looked after the chickens and split the wood for the stove and the big fireplace that he had built with the help of the Indians. How we had no civilised comforts and how wild and far away from everything the place was and how we loved it. He listened and said: 'And that man wrote.' I wanted to say: 'Yes, but not like you,' but didn't. Then they both said: 'We will visit you at the ranch.' But that never happened.

After lunch I told Mrs Shaw: 'I am so glad to meet you.'

She opened her eyes wide: 'Me, they always want to meet Shaw.'

I laughed: 'I also have been a writer's wife, I know.'

There was such a wonderfully free atmosphere about, you were sure that nothing you said or did would shock or surprise them. If you had suddenly turned a somersault they would have taken it along with the rest. Because of this freedom Shaw and Lawrence might have liked each other, I am sorry they never met.

I am glad I had lunch with the Shaws.

NOTES

1. The feminist 'Lady S.' was possibly Lady Shena Simon, wife of a Manchester expert on housing education and local government, Sir Ernest Simon, 1st Baron

of Wythenshawe (1879–1950), a shareholder and board-member of the *New Statesman*. Lady Simon collaborated with her husband in local government work, and had interests in feminist causes. They were known as 'The Webbs of the North'.

2. From 1922, the Lawrences made extended visits to a lonely ranch in the Lobo mountains, fifteen miles from Taos in New Mexico. Frieda returned to live there with Angelo Ravagli in 1931.

'Nothing Flourished'

VIRGINIA WOOLF

From *The Diary of Virginia Woolf*, vol. IV: *1931–35*, ed. Anne Olivier Bell assisted by Andrew McNeillie (Harmondsworth, Middx: Penguin, 1982) pp. 163–4. The association with the Shaws of (Adeline) Virginia Woolf (1882–1941) and her husband Leonard Sidney Woolf (1880–1969), author, political worker and journalist, began shortly before the First World War. In 1913 Sidney and Beatrice Webb, impressed by an article that he had contributed to the *Manchester Guardian*, invited Leonard Woolf to lunch and urged him to become a member of the Fabian Society. He subsequently carried out work for the Society, and wrote for the *New Statesman*. Leonard records a meeting with Shaw at a Fabian Society conference in July of the following year.[1] The Woolfs spent the weekend of 17–19 June 1916 with the Webbs and the Shaws at a house which the Webbs had taken near Turners Hill, Sussex.[2] According to Shaw, in a letter to Virginia Woolf on 10 May 1940, it was there that he conceived *Heartbreak House*.[3] This extract from Virginia Woolf's diary entry for 16 June 1933 provides an account of a lunch party at Whitehall Court on the previous day.

Figure to yourself lunch on a hot day at the Shaws. Long narrow room overlooking river & white sepulchral buildings. The Binyons. He a plethoric bolt eyed congested little man; she, washy watery.[4] Mrs Shaw small gimleteyed. In comes Shaw, alert for business, but not in the mood. No one in the mood. Lunch in another long narrow room. Unreal hotel lunch. butlers. Service Kitchen. Shaw's paddle actually out of the water. Cutting no ice. Had to make a speech to friends of the Nat. Libraries that afternoon; didnt know what their object was; but hoped to say something unpleasant about the conference.[5] And I talked. And I said This is d—d dull. I said it at intervals. Nothing flourished. Every saying died as spoken. All I retrieved was: Shaw does not visualise. I think of the sharp key as brass [?] – thats all. I never see my characters. I feel them in another way. Also, he had been ɔunded about the O. M. Baldwin said, he'll only guy us. 'I said I have already conferred the Order of Merit on myself'.[6] Stories – about China: some he'd told

already.[7] L[eonard]'s hand clattered.[8] Story about his fathers love,
which I share, of anti-climax.[9] Throw them all into the Liffey – of his
ancestors bones, when they wanted to make a new church. And I kept
saying no the drug won't work. Never once did it work; & we were all
glad – Shaw glad – when Mrs S. whose mild babble is continuous –
moved; & we never sat down, but had one look at the river, & Shaw
escorted us along the black & white passage – very jaunty, upright –
sea green eyes red face to the lift. A man of perfect poise – spring –
agility – never to me interesting – no poet, but what an efficient, adept,
trained arch & darter! His wires, his spring, at seventy-six entirely
astonishing. And the hands flung out in gesture: he has the power to
make the world his shape – to me not a beautiful shape – thats all. So
home.

NOTES

1. See Leonard Woolf, *Beginning Again: An Autobiography of the Years 1911–1918*
(London: Hogarth Press, 1964) p. 167.
2. See *The Question of Things Happening: The Letters of Virginia Woolf*, vol. II:
1912–1922, ed. Nigel Nicolson (London: Hogarth Press, 1976) p. 101.
3. See Leonard Woolf, *Beginning Again*, p. 126.
4. (Robert) Lawrence Binyon (1869–1943), poet, playwright and art historian,
entered the British Museum after graduating from Trinity College, Oxford. In
1932–3 he was Keeper of Prints and Drawings at the Museum and later in 1933
succeeded T. S. Eliot as Charles Eliot Norton Professor of Poetry at Harvard.
5. Shaw addressed a conference of the Friends of the National Libraries in the
rooms of the British Academy, Burlington House on 15 June. He did not say
unpleasant things about the conference.
6. Stanley Baldwin, 1st Earl, Baldwin of Bewdley (1867–1947), Conservative
leader, had terms of office as Prime Minister in the 1920s and 1930s. From 1931
to 1935 he served as Lord President of the Council in Ramsay MacDonald's
national government. It was MacDonald, a great admirer of his work, who
sounded Shaw out concerning the Order of Merit.
7. See below, pp. 499–500.
8. Leonard Woolf 'suffered from a congenital nervous tremor of the right hand,
which increased markedly under stress' (editorial note on this passage in *The
Diary of Virginia Woolf*).
9. Cf. Shaw, Preface to *Immaturity* (London: Constable, 1930) p. xxi.

Shaw and Keynes at Lunch

ROM LANDAU

From Rom Landau, *Personalia* (London: Faber & Faber, 1949) p. 161. Rom Landau (1899–1974), British-born educator and author, wrote books on Morocco and the Near East, where he spent much time. He was Professor of Islamic and North African Studies at the University of the Pacific from 1952 to 1967. John Maynard Keynes, 1st Baron (1883–1946), the eminent and influential British economist, was a Fellow and Bursar of King's College, Cambridge and a member of the Bloomsbury Group. Charlotte invited Landau to lunch after the publication of his best-selling work, *God is My Adventure* (1935).

GBS himself, I suppose, could not help being witty most of the time, often brilliant, and persistently provocative. But because I had never expected him to be anything else, there seemed nothing outstanding about it. What struck me far more was the air of gay benevolence and quiet enjoyment that he radiated, and the undercurrent of an obviously very genuine modesty: never a dogmatic statement, pontifical judgement, or intolerant word. And not a single reference to his own work, or to his position in the world. Yet since conversation ranged wide, over politics, economics, literature and social problems, there were countless excusable opportunities for making a show of his egotism.

Although *ami de famille*, Keynes appeared shy at first, but soon became voluble, with the eagerness of an overgrown boy whose mind worked too fast to permit his lips to follow the torrent of ideas. However well he expressed himself – and he was a master of the English tongue – I had the feeling that he could have done it far better if his ever-rushing mind had left him the time to give his ideas final form.

It was this characteristic that most distinguished his talk from that of our host. For however brilliant GBS might be, it was not the unexpected facet of a subject upon which he had turned the keen beam of his mind, nor his quixotic assessment of it that was most impressive: rather was it the wonderful co-ordination of thought and expression, and his skill in communicating these. Not only did each word seem the only right one for the particular purpose, but his talk was completely free from the impediments of little hesitations, repetitions, withdrawals and stammers, the dross of which so often cloys the conversation of even the most experienced speakers. Not a few people have ideas that are brilliant or profound. But how many of them are capable of translating those ideas into words that are their only faithful mirror? There were many occasions during our meal when I suspected that the mind of Maynard Keynes was both more original and deeper than that of our host. Yet GBS scored every time, thanks to what I should call his greater articulateness.

Lunch with Shaw and Wells

ZSA ZSA GABOR

From Zsa Zsa Gabor, article in the *People*, 15 August 1954. Sari (Zsa Zsa) Gabor (b. 1919?), exotic international leading lady, was crowned Miss Hungary in 1936, and starred in numerous British and American films. Zsa Zsa Gabor visited London with her husband and a party of Turkish journalists as guests of the British Council in the summer of 1939.

As we drove to Shaw's house I expected I might be a little bored. I was prepared to be neglected while the talk flowed on a level away above my head.

I didn't know then that Shaw and Wells were by no means blind to feminine attractions.

Sitting between them at lunch, I was plied with attention and flattery. Shaw talked knowledgeably about Kemal Atatürk[1] – a subject I could discuss too.

When Shaw told me for the tenth time that I was an attractive woman, Wells said:

'You're much too old for philandering.'

Shaw replied: 'A man is never too old. But anyway, you're mistaking gallantry for philandering.'

At one stage of the luncheon, I dropped my napkin. Shaw and Wells both bent down at the same time to pick it up. There was a lot of groping, and they almost bumped their learned heads together.

Wells got the napkin, and, as he lifted it he touched my ankle. I have always tried to convince myself that it was an accident.

After luncheon the great men agreed to pose for me. They looked like two rather naughty schoolboys as they stood side by side while I took their picture with my new camera.

NOTE

1. Kemal Atatürk (Mustafa Kemal Pasa) (1888–1938), soldier, statesman and

reformer, was the first President of the Republic of Turkey (1923–38). He modernised legal and educational systems in Turkey, and set aside traditional laws which prevented equality between the sexes.

Mixed Feelings

DAVID GARNETT

From David Garnett, *The Familiar Faces: Being Volume Three of the Golden Echo* (London: Chatto & Windus, 1962) pp. 113–14. David Garnett (1892–1981), novelist and critic, made several visits to the Shaws at Whitehall and Ayot in the course of preparing his edition of the letters of T. E. Lawrence (1938). His view of the Shaws may have been coloured by the difficulty he had in persuading Charlotte to release Lawrence's letters to her for publication.

Once I drove over from Hilton[1] to lunch with them at the vicarage at Welwyn which was their resort in the country. It is a disagreeable late Victorian brick house hidden behind shrubberies – a house the outside of which nothing could make beautiful. But the Shaws had made it as ugly as it is possible to imagine inside as well. It revealed in both of them an absolute absence of any visual taste. In the narrow entrance hall there was a bust of – if my memory is to be trusted – Mr Sidney Webb. In none of the rooms I entered did I notice a single piece of good furniture. Carpets and wallpapers were hideous, mantelpieces and tables crowded with a clutter of souvenirs and bric-à-brac. In Bernard Shaw's workroom pride of place was taken by an enormous photograph of a grey donkey. Charlotte Shaw who was showing me the room told me that it was an enlargement of a snapshot taken by Bernard in the West of Ireland and that he had been much attached to the animal, going out to see it once every day from their hotel in the field where it was pastured. At lunch Shaw talked freely about old friends, such as the Oliviers,[2] but, as always, in everything he said I detected a curious spiritual itchiness, the uneasiness of a man whose vanity will never allow him to forget himself in the interest of the subject under discussion. Yet he was obviously very kind and good as well as being a cultured gentleman with an Irish accent, who could tell plenty of amusing stories. Indeed he was amusing and charming in describing his affection for the donkey.

NOTES

1. Garnett lived at Hilton Hall in the village of Hilton, Huntingdonshire.
2. I.e. the Sydney Oliviers (see above, pp. 40–1).

Unhappy Memories

LORD GRANTLEY

From *Silver Spoon, Being Extracts from the Random Reminiscences of Lord Grantley*, ed. Mary and Alan Wood (London: Hutchinson, 1954) p. 209. Lord Grantley (Richard Henry Brinsley Norton, 6th Baron, 1892–1954) divided his career between international finance and films. As Managing Director of Pinewood Studios and Chairman of the British Film Producers Association, he was sometimes referred to as 'The Wicked Uncle' in the film world because of his monocle and sinister expression. He had a reputation as a witty raconteur. His connection with Shaw began when Gabriel Pascal approached him about the making of the film version of *Pygmalion*.

I can remember a number of meetings with him in his awful little house at Ayot St Lawrence, which I came to know so well. It was thoroughly suburban, in some ghastly Edwardian style with little bay windows, and had the most tasteless furnishings; the general impression being of a boarding house sprinkled with the souvenirs of a great man. There were doyleys under the cakes, thin bread and butter in rolls for tea, and all that sort of thing. It was only redeemed by the books and by Shaw himself.

Ayot St Lawrence had a special purgatory for me in never being allowed to smoke. Once, when I could not bear it any longer, I excused myself, left Gaby and Shaw talking inside, and went out to light a cigarette. I had a walk and a smoke, and the next thing I knew was that Shaw came charging out of the house, and started abusing me because I had thrown the cigarette end away on one of the flower beds. He was so vehement that his accent grew more and more Irish.

'I thought you told me you were a gardener,' he said.

'Well, so I am . . .'

'And look at you polluting me beautiful flowers!' (referring to one or two tattered antirrhinums).

It is hard to know what to do with a rude old man who is very old indeed, and very great. So far as I can remember, I just picked up the cigarette end, and I suppose put it in my pocket.

Two Visits to Ayot

THOMAS JONES

From Thomas Jones, *A Diary with Letters 1931–1950* (London: Oxford University Press, 1954) pp. 496–7, 518–19. Thomas Jones (1870–1955), economist and civil servant, established associations with leading Fabian socialists after graduating from the University College of Wales, Aberystwyth. Having held a Chair of Economics at The Queen's University, Belfast and several other posts, he arrived at Whitehall in 1916 to join the new Cabinet Secretariat under Lloyd George, the first of four Prime Ministers to whom he acted as adviser. With Professor Gwyn Jones, he translated the eleven Welsh stories known as *The Mabinogion*. He was associated with the Gregynog Press, and with the bringing out by that company of the collection of autobiographical writings of Shaw entitled *Shaw Gives Himself Away* (1939). The visits described below were made in the company of Nancy Astor.

[*February 1942*] Then away we went for half an hour's run to see the Bernard Shaws at Ayot St Lawrence. . . . Miss Patch, their companion, had taken a day off and gone to London, much to Nancy's relief, who thinks she is a tyrant and probably is a very efficient caretaker. GBS still retains great vitality, dresses perfectly, talks whenever he is given a chance, and often when he is not. Nancy and he both want to talk at once, and I cannot keep – though I try – a conversation going with Charlotte because she is deaf and we are drowned anyway by the other two. The two Shaws are enormously pleased with the Russian advance.[1] GBS would like to do a broadcast on the end of the British Empire. The Russians would defeat Germany; the Italians will take Malta; Franco Gibraltar; China will take Hong Kong; the Japs Australia; pity the Maoris could not have New Zealand – they had the advantage as fighters that they ate their enemies after defeating them. And so on with gusto. . . .

Of course all talks with GBS lead sooner or later to money and taxation. He growled that the £29,000 which he made out of the *Pygmalion* film had all been taken from him by our tax collectors. He would have talked all afternoon of this grievance had we let him. . . .

[*June 1944*] We found GBS in a garden hut making out cheques for domestic bills. Since Charlotte's death he won't have Miss Patch, the PS [Private Secretary], down. She is at Whitehall Court. Higgs the gardener and Mrs Higgs the housekeeper, who have been with the

Shaws for forty-two years, look after him, but feel that now they are over seventy they ought to have a 'bit of life of their own' and want to leave. Nancy wants him to give them a cottage in Cornwall. We went into the house for tea – for us – milk for him. He is ever so much better since Charlotte died. I noticed that when talking he gripped the arm of the chair with both hands, steadying himself while sitting erect, and talking with his usual clarity and emphasis, mainly about money, taxes, property and his will. I chaffed him about the reform of the alphabet – a dying jester's last joke, but he was quite firm and serious. 'I'm the first to have approached the problem from the economic side.' . . .

I mentioned Passfield's OM.[2] 'I have made my own Order of Merit. I discovered Webb sixty-five years ago, otherwise no one would have noticed him. He lacks humour. He has all the information and is willing to dispense it to the needy, but does so in a graceless fashion, implying all the time that "you ought to have known it".'

He talked most tenderly of the last thirty or forty hours of Charlotte's life when she grew so extraordinarily young and beautiful to look upon that he phoned to Nancy to hurry up from Plymouth to see her. He had never seen her so beautiful and told her so. 'We had a nurse trained to be always cheerful, and one morning she came to me and said "Your wife died at half-past two, but I thought it was no good disturbing you."' He sold Charlotte's personal jewellery in a heap for six pounds! Nancy was furious at this, and on the afternoon we were there GBS gave her Charlotte's box with bottles, scissors etc., a case of Irish origin, which Nancy took away with her, but will return later.

NOTES

1. From late December 1941, through the early months of 1942, the British press carried almost daily reports of the Russian advance, their descent on the Crimea and routing of German forces on several fronts.
2. Sidney Webb (Lord Passfield) was awarded the Order of Merit in 1944 in recognition of the work of the partnership.

A Tidy Man

MARGARET SMITH

From *Shaw the Villager*, pp. 48–9. Margaret ('Maggie') Smith was Shaw's parlourmaid from 1944 until about six months before his death in November 1950, when she left his service to get married.

He never bore malice to anybody. If an article or play of his was criticised he'd only laugh at it. He didn't care – he was too big a person – very charitable and good-natured and charming.

Mr Shaw was a very tidy man. He always put chairs back in place, and his pyjamas on his bed in his room, neatly folded. That's more than many a younger person would do. He always put all his things back where they came from and knew exactly where everything was. I remember once I began to tidy up his books. He said, 'Maggie – what are you doing? *You* may be tidying up, but you're untidying what *I'm* doing.'

Mr Shaw was very particular about his erectness and appearance – proud of his person and figure. He used to dress himself and bathe himself. He normally had a bath every day, but during the war when we were urged to save water, he made it once a week. He always changed for the evening meal regardless of whether anyone was coming to see him or not.

He sometimes had to be called several times before getting up. He'd say to me, 'Why didn't you call me?' I'd reply, 'I did.' 'Well, I never heard you,' he'd answer. 'You should have come right up and shouted in my ear.'

He was a bit slower in his last years – otherwise I didn't notice much difference in him. He received far fewer visitors, and was very much against being photographed in case he should look his age.

'A Vur-r-r-ee Fine Man'

ALICE LADEN

From *Shaw the Villager*, pp. 27–36. Mrs Laden, a Scottish-born trained nurse who had looked after Charlotte Shaw in her last illness at Whitehall Court, came to Ayot as housekeeper in 1943 and stayed until Shaw's death in 1950.

'I looked after Mr Shaw as I would a piece of rare Dresden China,' was how Mrs Laden summarised her attitude to the great man. 'When Mr Shaw first offered me the job he said, "I don't want a housekeeper who is a Shaw fan, but one who is a good *housekeeper*." "Well," I said to him,

"I am a rank Tory and I heartily disagree with all Socialist views." So Mr Shaw and I knew where we were from the start.

'I was never afraid of George Bernard Shaw like so many were. On the contrary, I think *he* was a little afraid of *me*! He was a vur-r-r-ee nice man, but he was queer and cantankerous at times, and I wouldn't stand any of his nonsense. His nickname to some was 'The Saint of Ayot'; I told him he was St George to my Dragon! We had many battles. . . .

'Mr Shaw was often up before the rest of us, and was the last to retire. When Mrs Shaw was alive he used to go to bed at eleven, but after her death, it was seldom before twelve or after. "My mother never went to bed before midnight, and I won't either," he used to say. He often played the piano and sang late at night after the rest of us had gone to bed. He played Beethoven and Mozart and other composers, and sang excerpts from operas, especially Wagner's, and Irish songs. He had a good voice for a man of any age and was never out of tune. He always went out in the garden to look up at the stars before going upstairs to bed, and would often forget to lock up the house after him. Once he was singing late at night at the top of his voice after I'd gone to bed. I looked out from the top of the stairs and he shouted: "Get back to your bed," but I *had* to remind him to lock up because we'd had two burglaries in the village at that time. Then in the morning he'd always be dressed and fully ready for work by eight o'clock or earlier, even at the age of ninety-four. He sang in the mornings too, sometimes, before breakfast.

'He used to take two or three hours over his midday meal. He had his letters spread out on the table with his food, and he used to read through them all and decide which ones he'd reply to before leaving the table. He lived on soups, eggs, milk, honey, cheese, fruit, cream and lemon juice. He had difficulty in eating nuts in his later years. After lunch he would lie down to rest for an hour or two – always in exactly the same position. . . .

'Mr Shaw was a prisoner in his own house. He could not even poke his head out of the window without someone spotting it. Then news would travel and a collection of people would gather. That explains why Mr Shaw kept to the house more in his last years. He'd still sometimes go out into the village, but never at weekends – only during the week when things were quiet. He came to the village for peace and quiet in the first place: Mr Shaw was a retiring man by nature. I once asked him, "Why did you originally come to live in this out-of-the-way spot?" He replied, "People bother me. I came here to hide away from them." When the phone rang he'd shout to me: "I don't want to speak to anybody, alive or dead." . . .

'I grew vur-r-r-ee attached to Mr Shaw while I was serving him, and was vur-r-r-ee proud to have been his housekeeper. I didn't know all his plays or other writings, but I *did* know Mr Shaw. I knew him as a human being. He was a remarkable man, a vur-r-r-ee fine man, and much more human and like other men than was generally supposed. A bit queer and cantankerous, and he used to need humouring, but oh! such a nice man he was – so generous and kind, and a charming man to the last. There'll never be another Ber-r-r-nard Shaw.'

Part 15
Second World War and After

INTRODUCTION TO PART 15

Shaw opened his commentary on the Second World War with a salvo in the *New Statesman* which, both in title and spirit, recalled his critical attack on British attitudes at the outbreak of the First World War. He made a scathing attack on Chamberlain and Churchill for their explanations of Britain's entry into the war, and castigated a leading churchman for blessing the troops.[1] In a radio talk which he prepared for the BBC, but which was immediately banned, he made some provocatively complimentary remarks about Hitler before roundly condemning him for his racist policies: 'We ought to have declared war on Germany the moment [Hitler's] police stole Einstein's violin.'[2] Shaw's summary verdict on Hitler, delivered in an interview published in December 1945, was as follows:

He may not be treated by history, if at all, as a serious character. He began well; but power turned his head and destroyed him. He will hardly be ranked with Caesar, William the Conqueror, Cromwell and Napoleon. But, so far, we know a great deal of the worst of him and nothing of the best of him. He may be remembered mainly as a pathological case.[3]

Despite some prevarications Shaw was in no doubt about the necessity of defeating Hitler's Germany.[4] After the initial outburst in the *New Statesman*, his comments on the Second World War tended to be focused on specific issues of strategy, and speculations about the outcome of various phases of the struggle. Some journalists of the period seem to have regarded him as a father figure to whom anxious appeals for reassurance could be addressed. Until almost the eve of the outbreak of war he remained optimistic about the success of the Chamberlain policies of appeasement. During the war and after, his opinions were strongly coloured by his admiration for Stalin, and for the Stalinist forms of communism, which he continued erroneously to regard as Russian versions of Fabian socialism. Ireland's neutrality, India's struggle for independence, the A-bomb and the Korean War were amongst the other topics of the day which Shaw commented upon in interviews published in the last decade of his life.

NOTES

1. Bernard Shaw, 'Uncommon Sense about the War', *New Statesman*, 7 October 1939. An extract from this article was published as a circular, with the title *Sacrifice - for What?*, by the Peace Pledge Union early in 1940. Readers of the circular were urged to press politicians for 'an immediate truce and a world conference to make a constructive peace' (Laurence, *Bibliography* [A238]).

2. Bernard Shaw, 'The Unavoidable Subject', in Anthony Weymouth, *Journal of the War Years (1939–1945) and One Year Later Including 'The Unavoidable Subject' by George Bernard Shaw*, 2 vols (Worcester: Littlebury, 1948) I, 263. For his account of the invitation to Shaw to give the talk and its subsequent banning, see Weymouth, *Journal of the War Years*, pp. 254–5, 258–60.

3. Cedric Ray, 'Shaw on Soldiers', *Parade*, 22 December 1945.

4. In May 1940 he said: 'When Germany made its move to conquer the world . . . someone had to bell the cat. We took on the job, and now for one or both of us the hour has come. We're in a very tight corner, but what can we do? We can either practically surrender or we can die in the last ditch. I think we should die in the last ditch' ('Mr Shaw's Advice', *Manchester Guardian*, 24 May 1940).

'We Will Have Peace'

From E. M. Salzer, 'Bernard Shaw (Who is Eighty-three Today) says We Will Have Peace', *Daily Express*, 26 July 1939. This interview was published a little over a month before the outbreak of the war, precipitated by Hitler's issuing of the command to invade Poland on 31 August. Before the war Germany had been demanding the removal of the Polish Corridor, which separated East Prussia from Germany, and the reunification of Danzig with the Reich. In pursuing his policies of appeasement towards Hitler, the British Prime Minister (Arthur) Neville Chamberlain (1869–1940) made three visits to Germany in September 1938. On 30 September Germany, Britain, France and Italy concluded the Munich Agreement which provided for the annexation by Germany of the Sudetenland of Czechoslovakia.

Has war become more imminent now that all Europe is armed to the teeth and Britain so determined to safeguard Europe's present frontiers?

No. The peace at present is maintained by funk; anything that intensifies funk makes for peace. The polite name for funk is common sense.

But rearmament safeguards peace. And it gives employment instead of the dole.

A lasting peace is a dream. But any statesman who is not desperately afraid of starting a cannonade should be sent to a mental hospital.

Do you think Danzig will provide the spark to set the European powder barrel on fire?

Danzig by itself is not worth a war to Germany or any other Power except Poland. All the Powers want to settle the Danzig question without a fight; therefore it will probably be peacefully settled – or left unsettled. But, of course, if Germany went mad enough to want to fight, Danzig would be as good an excuse as another.

Is Dr Goebbels right when claiming that the present 'encirclement' of Germany provides a simile to 1914?[1]

Yes, as far as the encirclement is concerned. But there is no secrecy about the present situation. If that had been the case in 1914 there would have been no war.

What would be the most sensible thing for Herr Hitler to do now that he is faced by the determined attitude of the democracies?

Nothing.

We are all so desperately frightened of a full-sized war that we are all wanting peace, including Herr Hitler and Signor Mussolini.

Mr Chamberlain did the right thing at Munich. The alternative was to bomb Berlin and have London bombarded next day. We have never given in to the dictators. We made a wicked treaty in 1918 and covered Central Europe with military frontiers instead of geographical ones. Thereby we put ourselves in the wrong and mutilated Germany in the right. That is what has beaten us.

Can propaganda, such as is broadcast in German by the BBC today, help to overcome the conflicts that threaten to incite war?

I don't know. It all depends on the propaganda. If it is sufficiently emollient it may do good. If, as is quite possible, it is self-righteous and irritant, it may make matters worse.

Herr Hitler places immense value on the weapon of propaganda both at home and in the enemy camp. Do you agree?

Propaganda is a necessary means of achieving any political purpose that is fit for publication. But Herr Hitler is terribly handicapped by his anti-Semitism, which is a crazy fad and not a political system.

The Jews will be his ruin in the long run, even if they perish with him – especially if enough of them perish with him.

NOTE

1. Joseph Goebbels (1897–1945), Nazi leader and propagandist, frequently invoked historical parallels such as this in his speeches.

The Russo-Finnish Peace

From E. M. Salzer, 'What Shaw Thinks of Russia and Finland', *Leader*, 6 April 1940. In March 1940 Finland sought peace from Russia, after having resisted the Russian invasion launched in November of the previous year. The peace involved the ceding of several Finnish territories to Russia.

Do you agree with those who deplore the Russo-Finnish peace as another Munich, or do you think the Finns had no other choice?

Why ask me? I was explicit enough, I think, when I warned our people that we were backing the wrong horse in the Baltic. The Russo-Finnish treaty is the best news we have had since the war began and the narrowest escape from the frightful mistake of letting ourselves be dragged into class war on Russia, which is the dearest wish and insanest dream of our maddest old reactionaries.

Will Stalin penetrate further westwards now that he has the key to the West?

Why should he? Do you think he has not enough on his hands as it is? All he has done in Finland now that it is at his mercy is to secure the key of his front door. If the Nazi Reich or the British Empire had been in his place they would have annexed all Finland and probably forced their way into Norway as far as Narvik. But you cannot convince Imperialists that Communists are not just like themselves.

Will war spread now?

Well, as the first serious attempt to spread it has just failed, let us hope for the best: that is, for the triumph of wholesome funk and common humanity.

Do you see a possibility of stopping the war without 'giving in' and would it only mean a German victory?

Both sides will have to 'give in' very ingloriously if common sense does not stop the war first. What good would a victory do either way? We won one in 1918. It ended in the enemy winning the peace.

Will Hitler Invade?

From E. M. Salzer, 'George Bernard Shaw on Will Hitler Invade?', *Daily Express*, 24 September 1940. Hitler's plans for the invasion of the British Isles, prepared in July 1940, were frustrated by British resistance to German air-raids in the Battle of Britain and retaliatory bombing of German troop concentrations in Western Europe and of German cities. Massive attacks on British air bases and cities by the Luftwaffe had begun in August. At the outbreak of the war Spain declared its neutrality, but subsequently adopted a policy of non-belligerent support for the axis powers. In 1943 Franco returned to neutrality and later broke off diplomatic relations with Germany and Japan.

1. Do you think that Hitler is going to invade Britain? If not now, when?

How do I know? How does anybody know? He does not know himself. If a walk-over had seemed possible he would have attempted it before now. It has not seemed possible so far; and it is our business to keep it so.

2. Can he be successful?

Do not ask questions which you know I cannot answer. But suppose he lands a force in England – or Ireland? How much further does it get him? Possibly as far as Napoleon got at Waterloo.

3. In any event, what should we do next?

Wait until we find out – or guess – what he is going to do next. Or else do something that will astonish *him*.

4. What in your view are our chances for an invasion of Germany and occupied territory?

If our peace terms, when we are in a position to dictate them, are to mean only that we are to do to France, Holland, Germany and Poland what Mr Hitler has done to them and to us: that is, overrun them with a devouring foreign army, we shall only make a bad business worse. The real settlement when the killing is over will be made at Geneva. And this time we shall have to stick to our professions.

5. What help do you think we will get from our Fifth Column in Nazi-occupied territory?

None, until we no longer need it. The real Fifth Column means to exploit Mr Hitler. To be its slave driver would not be much of a catch for him, would it? But when the fate of all upstart autocrats overtakes him he will still be a great attraction in whatever museum he ends in.

6. What should we do now to win the support of the 100 million potential allies on the Continent?

Win the war for them. So far their support of us has been their ruin. We owe them an apology and an energetic demonstration that they were right, after all.

7. What, do you think, will General Franco do next? Or, what could we do to prevent him from joining the Axis?

He has not told me. Besides, he doesn't know until the cat jumps. To prevent him from joining the Axis we have got to make the cat jump our way. Meanwhile he has plenty to do at home.

8. Is Italy's position in the Mediterranean strong enough to frighten us?

Of course it is strong enough to frighten us. The snag in it for Italy is that frightened animals are dangerous.

9. Do you agree with those who call Mussolini Hitler's stooge?

I do not concern myself with that sort of mischievous small talk.

10. How do you view the position of Eire today?

I am not allowed to say. I have done my best to make the IRA understand that as the Irish are too few to have a dog's chance against a first-class foreign Power, it must in case of a German invasion call upon the British Empire to fulfil its bargain under the treaty and undertake the defence of Ireland. It must, anyhow, whether the IRA likes it or not. But I am muzzled, both in London and Dublin.

11. Will the USA have the last say in this war, as in the last?

Yes. At least I hope so. A single-handed victory would not be as good for us as an Anglo-American one.

Advice to Ireland

From 'Bernard Shaw's Advice to Ireland', *Forward*, 30 November 1940. At the outbreak of the war the Irish President Eamon de Valera (1882–1975) immediately declared the neutrality of Ireland and refused Great Britain permission to use Irish ports. In an interview with W. R. Titterton in the *Sunday Graphic*, 17 November 1940, Shaw had criticised de Valera's position on the matter of the ports, repeating what he had said before that 'the British Isles are one military unit, and that it was out of the question for one fraction of the unit to maintain effective neutrality when the other fractions are at war'. Shaw's *Forward* interview drew an angry response from de Valera in the *Irish News* of 12 December 1940.

1. Do you think Ireland should remain neutral?

This is covered by my interview in the *Sunday Graphic*, which, by the way, omitted all the parts that would have convinced the Irish that I am not merely a conventional Anglicised Protestant. The British idea of propaganda is simply fulsome eulogy of England. It only exasperates foreigners.

2. What would be your advice to de Valera?

To stop talking obvious nonsense about Ireland defending herself – 4 million disunited Irish against 40 million British, 80 million Germans, 44 million Italians and 130 million Americans! For if Germany invades her, and Ireland becomes the cockpit of the war, she will have to defend her neutrality against the lot. Until Mr de Valera admits that Ireland can do nothing for herself by herself except commit suicide nobody will waste time listening to him.

3. And to the Government of Ulster?

Nothing but OK: go ahead. The Protestant boys are carrying the drum all right.

4. What would you think should be done if Eire persists in her refusal to allow the British Navy to use the ports it requires?

The British MUST take the ports if the German submarine campaign threatens to starve them out. They took Eubœa from the Greeks in 1914 to secure their supply of a mineral needed for their blast furnaces. Do you suppose they will hesitate to take the Irish ports to secure their supply of bread?

5. What do you think would happen to Eire if Hitler won the war?

I don't know. Probably the Führer will adopt the view that the Irish are the lost tribes of Israel and treat them accordingly. At any rate neither Protestants nor Catholics of the Irish variety can expect any mercy from him.

6. Would Ireland stand to gain by coming in on our side?

No country stands to gain in the long run by war. Ireland would be right to keep out of the war if that were possible. If she were to come in and choose the German side it would mean that she had turned Nazi or else was simply backing Germany to win – on terms, of course. In that case, as the odds are at present, it looks as if she would be backing the wrong horse. She could not possibly unite the Irish on it. It would mean civil war.

American Involvement

From W. R. Titterton, typescript of an interview held at the Humanities Research Center, Austin, Texas. (Shaw's replies were published by Titterton, under the title 'Bernard Shaw Explains the War', in the *Sunday Dispatch*, 6 April 1941.) In September 1940 the American Congress enacted legislation which provided for the lending to Britain of fifty US destroyers and the granting by the British to the US of leases of naval and air bases in British Guiana, several West Indian Islands and Newfoundland.

Is the Lease and Lend Act of vital importance? Has German diplomacy been trying every dodge to stop the passage of the Bill? And is its enactment a major defeat for Herr Hitler?

As the Lease and Lend has passed and is now an Act, leaving the USA virtually at war with the Reich, these questions are out of date. Do not let us waste our time looking behind us.

What about looking before us?

That is dangerous: it might land both of us in prison. America or no America, we are not going to have things all our own way. Neither are the Germans. We are both up to the neck in two campaigns. One is burning and bombshelling each other's cities from the air. The other is sinking ships to starve one another: the blockade, in short. City bombing is inconclusive, because, as the bombed cannot surrender and the bomber has to run away when he has shot his bolt, neither victory nor defeat is possible: there is nothing for it but retaliation; and of that there is no end as long as there are cities and explosives left. Blockade on the other hand can be decisive: it decided the American Civil War eighty years ago; and it decided the Four Years War. But it is such an intolerable nuisance to the neutral countries . . . that it will sooner or later have to be ruled out as a method of warfare by whatever combination of Powers may be left in command of the situation. As far as we can see at present, that command will be with the USA and the USSR. The war will force them to shake hands. If and when the combatants, after doing their utmost to destroy one another, are left exhausted and stalemated, these two great Powers may say to them, Ulster fashion, 'We won't have it',[1] meaning the blockade, or possibly war as such. Russia is in earnest about this; and neither Russia nor the USA wishes either Britain or Germany to finish cock of the walk. You see what comes of looking ahead. So we had better drop it.

NOTE

1. A reference to the refusal of Ulster to accept Home Rule, which led to the formation in 1920 of the state of Northern Ireland.

To Bomb or Not to Bomb

From W. R. Titterton, 'To Bomb or Not to Bomb', *Sunday Chronicle*, 4 May 1941. On 28 April 1941, the London *Times* published a letter signed by Shaw and Gilbert Murray proposing that an understanding be reached between Germany and Great Britain that neither side would bomb metropolitan cities. In this interview Shaw elaborated his views on this subject.

In the letter to The Times it is said: 'Whatever may be said from the military point of view for our treatment of Bremen, Hamburg and Kiel, there is nothing to be said for the demolition of metropolitan cities as such.'

We say that there are military objectives in Berlin; the Germans say that there are military objectives in London.

Where is the line to be drawn?

You can say what you like. The letter said nothing about military objectives.

We have suffered badly from aerial bombardment while the enemy has had the numerical predominance in aeroplanes. Are we to be asked to surrender the advantage when we shall soon reach equality and even supremacy?

What advantage? Our point is that by this new method of warfare there is nothing to be gained.

If all the cities in British, German, Italian and American occupation were smashed into heaps of debris, as many of them will be at the present rate, and some are already, would any of the belligerents be a day nearer a decision? All these acts of diabolical wickedness would have done nothing but gratify at enormous cost passions which civilised nations should not gratify.

Some people hold that, while the effect of air raids upon London has been to infuriate Londoners, it would have ultimately the effect, in the case of Berlin, of cowing the Berliners and making them yell for peace. Do you agree?

The shortest way to disgrace and defeat is allowing tactics to be dictated by fools who talk like that. We have done our very damnedest to Berlin and the Germans have done their very damnedest to London. The effect has been the same in both places.

The people who are not in bed run for the nearest shelter. They do not yell for peace, as for Berlin, Hamburg or Southampton.

In London in peace-time between 300 or 400 people die every day in the course of nature and nothing like that death-rate has yet been achieved, or is likely to be achieved by bombing raids.

Nobody knows the full extent of what is happening; no man can see further than his own street, and for the rest he is told next morning that there were 'a few casualties'.

There is demoralisation of course – all war is demoralising. But as the demoralisation takes the shape of 'Give it them back', 'Let them have a taste of their own medicine', the flames are fanned instead of being extinguished.

An endless series of retaliations finally exhausts both sides, leaving them not a step nearer to victory. Can any sort of warfare be more senseless?

Hitler has a habit of breaking pledges. He has threatened to invade us and may keep that pledge if it were to his advantage.

But in that case is it likely that he would keep any pledge he might make not to bomb London and other metropolitan cities?

There is no question of pledges. What the letter suggests is that both sides might consider whether retaliatory bombing is any good to either of them and agree to drop it.

Neither party will give up an advantage, but both may [come to acknowledge that the sup]posed advantage is, in effect, a very costly disadvantage.

Does Rome mean as much to the ordinary Briton as the city in which he lives? Does the freedom of Rome from attack arouse some natural irritation, and, in fact, has the threat of our War Cabinet had something to do with the mild treatment of Athens?

There has been no mild treatment of Athens. Athens was bombed until the Germans took it. Now that they are there, our screamers will want us to bomb it ourselves.

As to Rome, there is a sense in which Rome means less to the ordinary Briton than the city in which he lives.

To the rest of us who are good Europeans Rome is a priceless possession. What should we gain by bombing it? Unbomb Athens or Cairo?

It would simply provoke more mischief of the same kind. Let us forget that unfortunate threat of ours.

It was only a flash of British spleen and is already repented of.

When you hear people howling for retaliation, you must conclude that they are not intelligent enough to listen to Gilbert Murray or to me.

The War Strategy

From 'GBS – If I Were Churchill', *Cavalcade*, 1 November 1941. When Hitler launched his attack on the Soviet Union in 1941, Churchill immediately pledged British aid. But when Stalin called for the creation of a Second Front in the West, Churchill responded that this was beyond the range of possibilities. Instead he suggested launching naval operations in the North to protect the sea routes to Murmansk and Archangel. Arms and supplies were made available to Russia. Contrary to Shaw's statement in this interview, the idea of launching an Indian army against the Germans in Russia does not seem to have been favoured by Churchill.[1]

What would you do if you were in Mr Churchill's place at the moment in regard to (a) the influences which operate against a free and full policy of aid to Russia? (b) the growing body of popular feeling which demands a decisive policy of action?

(a) Put me in it, and I shall know but probably not tell you. There are no intelligent influences operating against all the aid to Russia we can afford. . . .

(b) What action? The alternatives are: (1) seizure of the Channel and North Sea ports, involving considerable damage to our Allies; (2) launching an Indian army, potentially 30 million strong, at the Germans from the East; (3) smashing the Axis by a ruthless conquest of Italy.

None of these can be carried out in five minutes, which is what the clamour for an offensive means. Mr Churchill has given more than a hint that he is for no. 2. That, I suspect, would be my own choice if I were Prime Minister. The Moslems of North-west India are the Protestant Boys of the East, as convinced as any Belfast Orangeman that the

Protestant Boys shall carry the Drum, and much better fighters, I should say, than either we or the Germans. They think so themselves.

No. 3 is aesthetically objectionable and uselessly mischievous. Our Philistine rulers cannot imagine that aesthetic considerations can enter into foreign policy or military tactics; but that is just their ignorance.

Do you think the financial and economic system of Britain and America will survive the war, and, if not, what measures would you advocate to replace it – and what would be their advantages?

Financial systems are in continual flux, and don't survive anyhow, war or no war. Economic systems all depend on the balance of power between the holders of private property with their parasites and the really productive proletariat. Mr Churchill and Mr Anthony Eden are for private property and oligarchy. Stalin is for public property and democracy. So am I. Therefore, I cannot give you an unbiased opinion. All I can tell you is that when the war is over there will be wigs on the green.[2]

Do you think that behind the façade of public utterances by members of the Cabinet, Foreign Office diplomacy is heading for a new Balance of Power, in which the British Empire will attempt to make the best of two worlds – a Hitlerised Europe and Asia on the one hand, and a frightened America on the other? In other words, appeasement on a grand scale?

Foreign Office diplomacy is mostly nothing but an indulgence in bad habits tempered by fits of panic when the consequences threaten disaster. Please don't talk about that obsolete nuisance, the British Empire. The existing fact is officially and intentionally the British Commonwealth, and should always be called so. Appeasement on a grand scale is what we are fighting for; and if the Foreign Office is aiming at making the best of two worlds it has more horse-sense than we give it credit for. Think of the meaning of the word appeasement and not of its accidental association with unpopular bygones at Munich and elsewhere.

NOTES

1. In a letter to Sir (Richard) Stafford Cripps, Labour statesman (1889–1952), of 28 October 1941, he wrote: 'We will do anything more in our power that is sensible, but it would be silly to send two or three British or British–Indian divisions into the heart of Russia to be surrounded and cut to pieces as a symbolic sacrifice' (Winston Churchill, *The Second World War: The Grand Alliance* [Boston: Houghton Mifflin, 1950] vol. III, p. 473).

2. 'A colloquial expression (originally Irish) for coming to blows or sharp altercation (wigs being liable to fall or be pulled off in a fray)' (*OED*).

Democracy Indestructible

From 'Democracy is Indestructible – Says Bernard Shaw', *Cavalcade*, 28 March 1942. The strong notes of optimism in this interview seem scarcely to have been justified by the circumstances at the time. In 1941 Britain had suffered a number of serious reversals. They were driven out of Greece and Crete; Hong Kong had fallen; the Malay Peninsula was overrun; India was threatened; the Battle of the Atlantic had worsened. Churchill was not optimistic in March 1942 about an early conclusion to the war. On 26 March he said at a Conservative Party Central Council Meeting: 'I cannot offer this morning any guarantee that we are at the end of our misfortune.'[1]

Do you think that, in the event of the complete victory of Great Britain, the USA, Russia and China, the form of National Socialism called Nazism or Fascism would be entirely destroyed in Germany and Italy?

If victory comes our way it will be a victory of the United States, Russia, China, Australasia, Free France, as well as of Great Britain. Russia is up to the neck in National Socialism, and all the rest are up to the knees in it. None of them could exist for a week without a good deal of National Communism. The war has imposed military communism on them all. Any attempt to destroy National Socialism and replace it by plutocratic oligarchy of the British–American sort, which I am afraid is what Colonel Blimp is dreaming of, would throw Russia and China into the arms of Germany and Italy, all four convinced that their next job must be to smash the British Empire and send the Colonel to join Hitler and Mussolini in whatever exile may be their doom.

Assuming that the war lasts some years longer than Winston Churchill anticipates, do you think it possible that, all the belligerents becoming war weary, a negotiated peace will result?

Any peace must be a negotiated peace, unless it is the peace of extermination of the vanquished. What you mean by a negotiated peace is a surrender, or at least a Cease Fire, made while we are winning and can win still more if we go on.

But military winnings may cost more than they are worth; and both sides may be afraid that another year's fighting, however victorious, will leave them bankrupt or provoke home revolution. There is also such a thing as stalemate. But in any case a peace to which nine or ten belligerents are parties must be elaborately negotiated. Even Versailles, where the vanquished were pitilessly steamrollered, had to be negotiated.

Assuming the almost impossible happening, would the defeat of the Allies result in the disintegration and downfall of the British Empire? Would this mean the enslavement of Europe and the destruction of democracy?

In war nothing is impossible; and its results are never those expected by the belligerents. If the Allies are defeated we shall have to do what the German Führer orders: that is all. But at this moment the old British Empire is already disintegrated in the Far East and badly cracked in the nearest West, now called Eire.

If the peace is to be negotiated on the old Imperialist lines what will happen at the Peace Conference? If China recaptures Hong Kong, Singapore and Burma, she can hardly be expected to make us a present of them; and China, as an eastern Power, may refuse to sell them back to the west on any terms. If Australia is saved by the United States she may feel it safer to federate with them than with us. We may have to drop India as we have had to drop Eire, and leave her to become an independent federation like the USA or the USSR.

These are all possibilities; and some of them are at this moment pretty strong probabilities. If they are realised, the fat will be in the fire again, with Roosevelt and Churchill *contra mundum*. The only alternative to the old Imperialism of conquest and garrison is democracy, which means that finally the world must regroup itself politically in federations chosen by the inhabitants, in which case the States which are not strong enough to stand alone will choose the federations which are likely to treat them best. Democracy is indestructible; but the world is strewn with the ruins of empires. . . .

If Russia wins a complete victory over Germany and thereby ends the war as far as Europe is concerned, do you think that the various countries will adopt Communism and federate with the Soviets, or will they continue as kingdoms and republics under capitalistic conditions?

Each country will have its own problem, its own readiness for more or less communism. Without a good deal of communism no State, no tribe even, can exist at all. As to federation, all the great Powers are now federations; and the detached States will have to choose; but their choice will be limited not only by geographical considerations, but by the willingness of the desired federation to accept them.

The USSR cannot take on the whole world. It is already carrying one-sixth of it, which is quite enough for one centre of organisation. As to capitalistic conditions they no longer exist in their integrity. Each State must decide how much capitalism and how much socialism it can manage with. Even in Russia there is still a considerable mixture.

Whom do you think is the greatest man this war has yet produced?

Stalin, of course; but then he is not a product of this war. No other living statesman has been through such a terrific apprenticeship. Others who went through it have been killed by it or had their heads turned. Stalin alone has taken it easily without losing his sense of humour.

NOTE

1. *Winston S. Churchill: His Complete Speeches, 1897–1963*, ed. Robert Rhodes James (New York and London: Chelsea House, 1974) VI, 6605.

On Peace and War

From Octavio Novaro, 'Bernard Shaw on Peace and War', *World Review*, November 1943. Octavio Novaro was a Mexican journalist who had recently been a guest of the British Council.

When this war is over, will it have been useless?

Until a war has produced its final results, no one can tell whether it has been worth while or not. War is always wasteful, cruel, mischievous, destructive, demoralising and detestable to every humane instinct; yet it is not always avoidable; and often it effects social changes that occur only under its terrible pressure. The war of 1914–18 made an end of four empires which might have endured for four centuries more at peace. Whether it was worth the bloodshed and devastation it cost, depends on whether the new republics make their citizens better than the old empires did. But if they do, it still remains true that it would have been wiser to make the change reasonably rather than violently.

Will social revolution come in England, or in all countries, at the end of this war?

Not necessarily. If the ruling and propertied classes give way to the proletariat sufficiently to offer an acceptable ransom for their privileges, then there will be no disturbance big enough to be called a revolution. But if not, the Marxian class struggle may break out into civil war, as it did in Spain.

Is Communism now the only door open to mankind?

Communism has a hundred doors; and they do not all open and close at the same moment. Everywhere already we have communism in roads, bridges, street lighting, water supply, police protection, military, naval and air services. These can be added to item by item without communising everything at one blow. In the USSR Communism is the official policy; yet there is more personal property and private enterprise in Russia today than there was under the Tsars. . . .

Ought the Germans to disappear as a Nation?

Perhaps. Perhaps also the human race ought to disappear as a species. But as there is no likelihood of their doing anything so sensible, the question is an idle one.

Calm Under Fire

From Blanche Patch, *Thirty Years with GBS* (London: Victor Gollancz, 1951) pp. 38–9. From June 1944 the Germans began launching their new V-1 and V-2 flying missiles against Britain. During the latter part of 1943 and the first half of 1944, Miss Patch had been working at Whitehall Court. When the V-bombs began, and the blast from one which fell near Charing Cross had blown out the study window at Whitehall Court, shattering a grandfather clock and covering everything with dust, she retreated to Ayot, where, soon afterwards, a similar incident occurred.

I had only been there a few weeks – in fact just before midnight on the eve of Shaw's eighty-eighth birthday – when I awoke suddenly, thinking that something had struck the wall under my room. I got up and went out of the room to see what had happened, but GBS, for all his eighty-eight years, was there before me, reconnoitring in his dressing gown. A V-bomb had fallen some half a mile away in a coppice and the blast had blown in the glass of one of his windows. The glass flew clear of his bed, to which, finding that the rest of the household were safe, he retired unruffled.

All through the war his nerve remained steady, and often in the late evening when we heard the wail of the Alert siren, and the planes were droning overhead, he would sit down at the piano and play and sing the old Italian operas. The piano was an ordinary upright; he hated grand pianos, as, so he told me, did William Morris. It was always in the hall because Charlotte liked to lie in her room upstairs and listen to him. One day he asked me if his playing disturbed me and I said it did not, although it really did for I used to try to hear the planes and the banging of the raids on London, which were quite audible from my room.

What to do with Germany

From 'Break Germany for Ever? – Nonsense Says Bernard Shaw', *Sunday Pictorial*, 13 August 1944. At the conclusion of the Franco-Prussian War of 1870–1, Wilhelm I, King of Prussia, was crowned emperor of a new German Reich. During the war the southern states had joined the North German Confederation established by Bismarck in 1867. Before this time the thirty-six states of Germany were collected loosely together in a confederation dominated by the Hapsburgs.

1. Many politicians advocate the breaking up of Germany into small unfederated states, such as existed before the war of 1870, as a means of breaking the power of the Reich to organise and maintain another large scale war. Do you think this plan would be successful?

We cannot break the power of sixty million German-speaking people to organise and maintain their military resources. We tried in 1919 and failed. The attempt produced Hitler and a renewal of the war. It was the outcome of the cry for security which war always provokes.

Well, there is no such thing as security in a world dominated by mankind, which is a dangerous species. Man, being a dangerous animal, must live dangerously. When Hitler tore up the Treaty of Versailles clause by clause and threw the bits in our faces, we dared not lift a finger to prevent him; and if a German group of little states bred another Bismarck and federated into a new Reich we should find ourselves equally impotent.

We can do nothing permanent to disable Germany militarily unless we are willing to accept it reciprocally for ourselves.

2. It is commonly believed that the Germans as a people are so imbued with the idea of dominance that they must be crushed as a power and prohibited from engaging in the heavy and chemical industries that are essential for modern warfare. Do you agree?

There is no power in the world more completely imbued with the idea of its dominance than the British Empire. Even the word Commonwealth as a substitute for the word Empire sticks in Mr Churchill's throat every time he tries to utter it. If he starts discussing with Hitler which is to be 'The Chosen Race' they will presently be fighting again.

As to chemical industries, are you aware that I, at the cost of a shilling or two for apparatus and a few pence for chemicals, can in fifteen minutes make an explosive that could blow you to smithereens more violently than all the gunpowder of Guy Fawkes?

You should learn a little chemistry before asking questions about chemical industries.

3. *If you had the framing of the Peace Treaty, what would you consider to be the six fundamental clauses necessary in it to ensure the peace and prosperity of Europe and the world?*

If you give me the job and pay me handsomely for doing it, perhaps I may be tempted to tackle it. But had you not better try a younger man? Even when I was in my prime I was not God Almighty.

4. *In your opinion, would a peace that imposed conditions on Germany that reduced its population to poverty for a long time be injurious or otherwise to the Allies and the rest of Europe?*

Of course, it would be injurious. We are Europeans as well as Britishers, are we not? When we capture a German soldier after wounding him, we have to nurse him back to health exactly as we nurse and cure an Allied soldier. Otherwise, all prisoners of war, wounded or not, would be killed.

Having smashed the German cities with our bombs, we shall have to help to rebuild them for our own sakes. Formerly when we took a city we had it for our pains. Now we have only an artificial Pompeii.

Which means, happily, that war has reduced itself to absurdity, as we shall perhaps realise in another century or so.

5. *When Germany is defeated and forced to accept the Allies' terms of 'unconditional surrender', would you advocate the inclusion of any Nazis who have not committed criminal acts in the negotiations for the provisional government?*

What a question! What do you mean by Nazi? What do you mean by criminal acts? Why do you start with unconditional surrender and then end with negotiated surrender?

Nazi is short for National Socialism and not for every bee in Führer Hitler's bonnet. Without a good deal of National Socialism and Communism no modern State could exist for a week.

What to do about India, 1944

From 'G. B. Shaw Gives Churchill a Tip about India', *Reynolds News*, 1 October 1944. In mid-1942 when a Japanese invasion of India seemed imminent, the leader of the Indian nationalist movement Mohandas Karamchand (Mahatma) Gandhi (1869–1948) urged the British to leave the country so that the invasion could be met by non-violent methods. The British refused a demand for their departure made by the Indian Congress Committee in August 1942, and Congress leaders were interned. The prisoners were gradually released from 1944. The independence of India, together with its partition and the establishment of the Islamic Republic of Pakistan, was completed on 15 August 1947. Ghandi and Shaw had a meeting and conversation in London in 1931. They may have met much earlier, during Gandhi's days as a law student in London from 1888 to 1890.

Mahatma Gandhi's birthday falls on 2 October. What would be your birthday message to him?

I never send messages to people on their birthdays, and I wish they wouldn't send them to me.

Indian National Congress leaders are still detained. Would you advocate their release?

Of course I do. They should never have been arrested.

Supposing you were a national leader of India. How would you have dealt with the British? What would have been your methods to achieve Indian Independence?

Please do not suppose a situation that can never happen. The achievement of Indian Independence is not my business.

Gandhi and Jinnah[1] were engaged in devising a plan for the partition of India into Hindu and Moslem States – Hindustan and Pakistan. Do you think India should be divided?

A partition is possible, and may be inevitable, as in the case of Ireland. But India cannot be 'divided' by a pair of scissors. Is Pakistan to be an Ulster, a Baltimore or a Canada?

What do you think is the most effective way of getting the British out of India? What should the Indian people do?

Make them superfluous by doing their work better. Or assimilate them by cross-fertilisation. British babies do not thrive in India.

Britain owes India about £800,000,000.[2] *India fears that Britain is going to repudiate this debt. How can we get this money?*

Do not waste your time on paper figures. The money is spent and done with. Clean the slate and get to business.

What advice would you give to Mr Churchill concerning India?

TO KEEP OUT OF IT.

Do you agree that all Asiatic peoples should be free from European domination?

My agreement is not called for and would be of no importance anyhow. Europeans can be useful in Asia. What would Siberia now be without Moscow? The British Indian Civil Service has had its uses. Remember the old saying 'The stranger does justice.' A Judge who despises both suitors equally is better than one who has an axe to grind or is bribable.

NOTES

1. Muhammed Ali Jinnah (1876–1948), Indian Muslim leader, was the first governor-general of Pakistan. He joined the Indian National Congress in 1906 and the Muslim League (established to protect Muslim interests against the Hindu majority) in 1913. Disagreeing with its stance towards the British, he resigned from the Indian National Congress in 1920. In 1940 he presided over the Muslim League meeting which made the first demand for the partition of India and the creation of Pakistan.

2. The £800,000,000 loan was agreed to as part of India's contribution to the war effort. According to Churchill the rates of exchange employed in the contracts were very unfavourable to Britain, a country which played a major role in protecting India from invasion: 'enormous so-called "sterling balances" – in other words, British debts in India – were piled up. Without sufficient scrutiny or account we were being charged nearly a million pounds a day for defending India from the miseries of invasion' (Winston S. Churchill, *The Second World War: the Hinge of Fate* (Boston: Houghton Mifflin, 1950) IV, 202–5.

The Future of Europe

From Dorothy Royal, 'Capitalism in the Future by G. Bernard Shaw', *Sunday Express*, 8 October 1944. William Ralph Inge (1860–1954), Anglican theologian and author, was Dean of St Paul's from 1911 to 1934. He was a personal friend of the Shaws. In a speech to the Ruskin Society on 8 February 1944, Inge had expressed the view that England had come to the end of the period when it was a great and wealthy nation, and said that it should 'gradually slide back into the pre-industrial England with a population of 20,000,000 consisting mainly of agriculturists [sic] working healthily in the open air, and a number of small tradesmen in the towns' (*The Times*, 9 February 1944).

Are you of the opinion that the war has caused so much devastation and social upheaval that it will result in the general impoverishment of Europe, and that England will become, to quote the Right Rev. Ralph Inge, DD, 'a poor agricultural country of 25,000,000 inhabitants without foreign or invisible trade'?

No. The war will stop when it has destroyed enough capital to make the rebuilding of Europe lucrative, and further destruction dangerous.

Capitalism has hitherto always stopped short of suicide; and there is no reason to fear that it will lose its head completely this time, especially as it is now State-financed: that is to say it is no longer old Cobdenite Capitalism[1] but modern Fascism, which is now firmly established in big business.

In Cobden's time the Capitalists provided their own ships and factories and dug their own mines. Nowadays the State builds the ships and factories and makes a present of them to the Capitalists; and mines are dug as public utilities with public money. Consequently no enterprise is now too big for Capitalism.

So you need not be anxious. Fascism will pull Europe through, and give us a Beveridgian[2] scrap of the plunder at the same time by way of ransom; and we shall go on denouncing it as the blackest of tryannies whilst plunging into it up to the neck.

Would you prefer to see the European nations formed into the United States of Europe, with equal citizenship, a common currency and free trade within its border, similar to the USA, in preference to the continuance of separate sovereign States, guaranteed from aggression by the Allies as laid down in the Atlantic Charter?[3]

I should if I could see the faintest prospect of such a paper Utopia being set up, or lasting longer than a house of cards. The States will not give up their sovereignties all together in a lump, but bit by bit very reluctantly.

Do not deceive yourself: the world is not going to be a new world; you will have to put up with the old one with occasional spring cleanings in which a good deal of the dirt will be swept under the furniture instead of being removed.

It is easy to draft Atlantic Charters and hold Quebec Conferences[4]; but when you want to abolish a custom house or move a frontier, or even introduce so simple and obvious a reform as Summer Time, it costs a war to get a move on.

Will there be a tendency of the various nations of Europe, especially the smaller ones like the Balkans, to imitate Russia and form themselves into Soviets, or will they, like Eire and Switzerland, remain as improved democracies retaining Capitalism with a substantial leavening of Socialism and possibly Communism, without which no community can exist?

It is the big Powers that will have to imitate Russia. Success is always imitated willy nilly. Russia's success now that the Soviet has got rid of Trotsky's All-or-Nothing catastrophism[5] and settled down to Fabian Socialism and collective farming has been so stupendous, and so utterly beyond the possibilities of Capitalism – even Fascist Capitalism – that her rivals, for the moment her reluctant allies, dare not let her get so far ahead of them in civilisation as she is at present. What the small States do does not matter.

Stalin is reported to have said recently: 'There are two theories: 1, to every man according to his needs – that is Communism; 2, to every man according to the value of his work – that is Socialism. We have chosen the second.' Do you consider it likely that the Soviets will drift into Capitalism, and can you explain briefly the difference between a system of Government based on the 'man value' theory and the Governments that exist in England and the USA?

What Stalin means by his remark is plain enough. How are you to give men what they need unless they also produce what they need? Production must come first before you can have anything to give. Yet you must feed babies, who produce nothing, soldiers who destroy everything, and artists and philosophers and employers, who tell others how to produce, or amuse them, but have to be fed by those whom they direct or amuse.

Therefore the Soviet must put production before need, and by piece work and every other honest device stimulate the baker to bake two loaves though one is enough for his own need, and so on all through the industries. And it must not tolerate unserviceable idleness on any terms as we do. This is not a move back to Capitalism. It is a repudiation of it.

Do you believe that after Germany is defeated, as many advocate, fifty years of resolute government by the Allies will be necessary before she will be able and fit to be permitted to govern herself without preparing for another war of conquest and revenge?

No nation can be resolutely governed except by itself. The old Ascendancy in Ireland was always clamouring for twenty years of resolute government; but it never achieved it. The little finger of the Irish Free State proved thicker than Dublin Castle's loins.

All this talk of governing Germany when we cannot even govern ourselves is childish nonsense. Leave Germany to itself, and there will be a reaction against Hitlerism as surely as there was a reaction after Cromwell's major generals.

When a horse is down you may have to sit on his head for a minute or two before helping him up; but you cannot sit on his head for fifty years. Both horse and man must get on their own legs again pretty quickly if they are to survive.

In the second League of Nations which is being planned in America,[6] and which will certainly be formed, Germany and Japan will have to be represented equally with Britain, the USA, the USSR and China, or the League will be only a military alliance to keep these two great nations crushed.

You take my breath away, Mr Shaw. What is the next thing you would do if you were Mr Churchill?

I would secretly guarantee Hitler a palatial residence free of rent and rates, and £20,000 a year free of Income Tax, to begin when Germany surrenders, not unconditionally, but on conditions dictated to me. Good morning.

NOTES

1. Richard Cobden (1804–65), politician and essayist, successfully agitated for the repeal of the British Corn Laws in 1846. He was a strong advocate of *laissez-faire* economic policies, and known as the Apostle of Free Trade.

2. William Henry Beveridge, 1st Baron (1879–1969), economist, was one of the key architects of the post-Second-World-War British welfare state. His *Social Insurance and Allied Services* (the 'Beveridge Report', 1942) outlined his welfare policies.

3. The renunciation of territorial aggression was the first of eight principles of international relations set forth in the Atlantic Charter issued by Winston Churchill and Franklin D. Roosevelt on 14 August 1941, and endorsed by twenty-six of the allied nations on 1 January 1942.

4. Anglo-American conferences were held in Quebec in 1943 and 1944 to discuss strategies for the war.

5. Leon Trotsky (1879–1940), Russian revolutionary, was in favour of permanent revolution and the spread of communism throughout the world. He clashed with Stalin, who favoured the consolidation of socialism within Russia itself. Trotsky was expelled from the Communist Party in 1927, and exiled from Russia in 1929.

6. Plans for a revived League of Nations were discussed by representatives from the United Kingdom, America, the USSR and China in Washington from 21 August to 7 October 1944. The United Nations Organisation came into being on 24 October 1945.

World Questions, 1945

From Dorothy Royal, 'The Future of the World – Stalin – Russia – the Beveridge Reports – and Socialism', *Sunday Express*, 4 February 1945.

Supposing Russia and China become the dominant Powers in Europe and Asia, will it affect the British and American democracies for better or worse?

There are no such things in the world as British and American democracies. The United States and the British Commonwealth are plutocracies; and there is no future permanence for plutocracy.

Both have passed through feudal plutocracy, maintained by a vast majority of serfs, to a Cobdenist or capitalist plutocracy maintained by a vast majority of wage slaves, merchants, financiers, and suburban snobs, and are now passing headlong into Fascist or Nazi plutocracy depending on the same majority, but abandoning Cobdenism and equipping private enterprise with public capital and protecting it by State regulation.

Hitherto, all civilisations have got this far and then collapsed.

The development of Fascism into sufficient Communism to abolish classes by making the whole population intermarriageable has never been achieved.

The USSR is making a prodigious and not unpromising attempt at it; but in the west plutocracy is still firmly established on the votes of the poor.

That is the present situation: and nobody can say what it will be even five years hence. So please don't ask me to prophesy. Ask the popular politicians, who think they know. I don't.

Commander Bower, MP,[1] said recently: 'Marshal Stalin is a cold-blooded realist, and as a good Communist he naturally believes that truth, honour, straight dealing, and so on are bourgeois prejudices to be made use of if to do so is to the advantage of Communism. . . .'
What do you think of that statement?

Commander Bower, having presumably begun by assuming, heaven knows why, that Communists have no consciences, is put into a difficulty by the fact that Stalin, the Arch-Communist, behaves exactly as if he were stuffed with conscientious scruples from some of the most important of which his Western Allies are free.

So the commander explains that this is not because the Marshal is a truthful, honourable man and a bluntly straight dealer, but because he has found that these qualities are favourable to Communism.

Clearly the next logical step for the commander is to join the Communist Party, and practise the virtues which he thinks Stalin only affects. I wonder does he suspect Hitler of being a saint pretending to be a tyrant.

Do you regard Russia as a really democratic Power, and are the Soviets ruled by the people?

A country ruled by the people is never democratic, and never can be. Government is a highly skilled art founded on a very complicated social science, which only a small percentage of the human race is capable of exercising.

If the necessary schooling and culture is within the reach of everybody, the percentage will be large enough to give the electors a sufficient choice of their rulers. But ruling must be done by those capable of ruling, just as ships must be built by shipbuilders and not by confectioners.

Give the job to Tom, Dick and Harriet, and they will begin by printing unlimited paper money, executing one another, and making war on the slightest provocation, besides nationalising land and capital which they are unable to use and just sterilise. They end by throwing themselves and the country at the feet of the first adventurer who promises to set everything right for them.

In France we have just seen men sentenced to forty years' imprisonment for stealing cigarettes. Quite a typical example of popular justice. But you need go no further than some of the fines lately inflicted by our own local Dogberries for native samples.

Do you think that the Beveridge Reports, the White-papers and the numberless promises of a 'Brave New World' after the war are killing the ideal of 'Socialism in our time' that was so strenuously advocated by Socialists before the war as an election slogan?

Not at all; they are making very lively propaganda of Socialism, and are all advocating instalments of it. And they are helping to get rid of the childish notion that Socialism is a paradise into which the world will change from an inferno called Capitalism in a single day with an old world on Saturday and a new one on Sunday. The Conservatives are obsessed with this silliness as much as the greenest young Socialist.

No modern State can get on without an enormous foundation of Communism in roads, streets, bridges, police, fire brigades, water supply, electrification, armed forces, judiciary, clergy and schools. The people who bleat about Communism as a crime do not know what they are talking about. If bread and milk and utility clothing were communised tomorrow, as they might quite wisely be, it would be only an extension of our existing practice.

But everything cannot be communised. Bread and milk and clothes can be communised because everyone eats and drinks and dresses. But as everyone does not play the trombone you cannot communise trombones; you can only socialise their production and make those who want them pay cash for them as they now pay for postage stamps.

Well, suppose you communise and socialise until everyone can earn a handsome livelihood by working four hours a day for five days a week, they will not spend all their leisure at dog races or in cinemas. There will be a huge increase of private activities: much more than is now possible.

You will have Communism, Socialism, Private Enterprise, and a mixture of them all going at the same time in changing proportions which will be continual subjects of political controversy. But the politicians will know what they are talking about, which none of them do at present.

Even if the coming general election resulted in an overwhelming Socialist and Labour majority, do you think that it would be possible for Britain to have collective ownership of land, industries and finance unless the Empire, the US and other great capitalistic countries adopted a similar Constitution?

That question has been settled in Russia. Trotsky held that Socialism in a single country was impossible. Stalin said it must begin somewhere, not everywhere; and he would try. He tried, and succeeded conclusively.

Collective farming in Russia has succeeded without the smallest hindrance from peasant proprietorship in France or landlordism in England.

Russia is ruled by several Cabinets, with a Cabinet of thinkers at the top. In Britain we have one Cabinet of talkers, who have no time to think. No difference could be more profound; but it exists for all that. What is really impossible in a single country is capitalist trade and finance.

NOTE

1. Commander Robert Tatton Bower (1894–1975) had extensive experience in the Royal Navy in both World Wars, and was Unionist MP for Cleveland, Yorkshire, from 1931 to 1945.

Questions of the Hour, June 1945

From 'GBS Mounts the John Bull Platform to Answer these Questions of the Hour', *John Bull*, 23 June 1945. The German High Command accepted the Allies' terms of surrender on 7 May 1945. The war against Japan ended in August. On 26 July 1945 the British Labour Party under Clement Richard Attlee, 1st Earl, Viscount Prestwood (1882–1967) scored a decisive electoral victory over the Conservatives under Churchill.

What do you consider, Mr Shaw, are the chief perils presented by peace to the prosperity of our population?

There are no chief perils. In the Ship of State the cabin boy is as necessary as the admiral, and in its machinery the cook's stopcock as indispensable as the propeller. The practical question is one of priority for repairs and reforms, and the decisions must be according to the pressure of circumstances at the moment. The point for Utopians to remember is that the State cannot be put into complete repair in a single day, nor its machinery stopped for a single hour. All repairs must be running repairs; for a government can no more stop functioning than an animal can stop breathing.

Assuming that the Labour Party comes into power in July, will its programme of Socialisation abolish unemployment and poverty in this country unless its export trade is greatly increased, which in turn will depend upon the comparative wealth or poverty of foreign purchasing countries?

No country should be dependent on export or import trade. Traders urge that the country cannot live without foreign trade. Hangmen probably believe equally that the country cannot live without murders. From the traders' point of view the oftener an article has to be exchanged and shipped or carried long distances before it is consumed, the better. This is pure gammon: the truth is just the reverse. At present it costs more to sell an article than to produce it. The ideal is production and consumption on the same spot and no trade at all.

Do you think that if there is an overwhelming Conservative majority at the forthcoming election the Government will be able to restrain Socialistic legislation with its trend towards Communism which has been in evidence since the first Poor Laws were passed in the reign of Elizabeth?

No. But the issue now is between Fascism and Communism. Fascism is profiteering with State-provided capital and protection. We have plenty of it already and Conservatives want more of it. Communism is public enterprise without profiteering, all goods and services being either open to all users without direct payment on the spot, like London Bridge, or purchasable at their averaged cost, like postage or municipal electricity. Both can and must co-exist. Banking and insurance should obviously be communised; but inventive and experimental private adventure should be not only tolerated but encouraged and even subsidised by the State.

Do you consider that the underground propaganda of influential and wealthy individuals in the USA and this country against Russia is likely to produce an atmosphere of unfriendliness, which might develop into war?

Yes; but why underground? We had twenty years of the fiercest overground propaganda against Russia after 1917, with daily British and American denunciations of Stalin as a ruthless dictator and bloodstained monster, accompanied until 1939 by the politest compliments to Mussolini and Hitler; yet it has produced our victorious military alliance with Russia, ending with the lynching of Mussolini and the suicide or Neronian murder of Hitler[1] with our full approval. Both these dead dictators had banked on our joining them in a British–American crusade against Russian Communism. Such a crusade would not be at all unpopular with our Fascists and Capitalists. The situation needs very careful watching; and Stalin knows it.

NOTE

1. It is generally assumed that Hitler commited suicide in his underground headquarters in Berlin early in May 1945. But there was some speculation at the time that he may have fled (see *The Times*, 2 May 1945, p. 40). It is not known whether the Roman Emperor Nero (AD 37–68) committed suicide or, having fled to the Greek islands, was recognised and executed under an earlier edict of the Senate. There is no evidence for the idea that Hitler may have been murdered.

Self-government for India

From H. C. Miller, 'Shaw on India's Demand', *Hindu*, 28 March 1946. H. C. Miller was a member of the London staff of the *Hindu*. When Labour came into power in 1945, the Attlee government was committed to independence for India;

but there remained concern, both in India and Britain, about provinces having independence forced upon them without safeguarding of minority rights. By 1946 Jinnah had the overwhelming support of the Muslim League for the partition of India into Hindu and Muslim states. In March 1946 the British government sent a cabinet mission to Delhi to work out constitutional proposals with the Indian leaders. The members of the mission were Frederick William Pethick-Laurence, 1st Baron (1871–1961), Secretary of State for India and Burma; Sir Stafford Cripps, President of the Board of Trade; Albert Victor Alexander (Alexander of Hillsborough, 1st Earl, 1885–1965), First Lord of the Admiralty; and Archibald Percival Wavell, 1st Earl (1883–1950), Field Marshal and Viceroy of India, 1943–7. Sir Stafford Cripps had led an unsuccessful mission to India in 1942.

The common argument voiced in this country against self-government for India is that left to themselves Indians would allow religious differences so to influence them as seriously to impede that degree of co-operation necessary for successful Government. Indians strongly resent this suggestion. What do you think of it?

Don't let us begin by talking nonsense. Self-government is not a schoolchild's prize for good conduct – it is a human passion that demands unconditional satisfaction.

It has been said that in a free India there could be no democracy as we in the West know it owing to the vast Hindu majority. Would you agree with this?

There is no democracy in the West owing to the vast labour majorities. Indians will not be free under any government; but they will never be satisfied until they govern themselves, well or ill.

Pakistan is the positive ultimatum of Mr Jinnah and the Muslim League. Do you think Pakistan is a rational and practical proposal and, as Mr Jinnah suggests, is the only possible solution of India's constitutional problems?

Pakistan is not rational: it is national and natural, like Ulster in my native country. Do not wrangle about it, give it a trial; and Pakistan will rejoin the peninsula as Ulster, I prophesy, will rejoin Eire.

With India's population increasing at the present rate grave problems of food and employment and hygiene must inevitably arise in the near future. Do you think India could support her population if the increase continues and what methods for dealing with the problem would you suggest?

There is no inevitability about it. A well-governed India could feed itself and control its birth-rate. An ill-governed one will starve anyhow.

A great majority of Indians are and always have been in a state of semi-starvation. Now a new and terrible famine has been 'forecast'. Do you think this problem could be dealt with by (a) Great Britain, (b) India herself under self-government, or (c) by the United Nations?

India has suffered several famines during my lifetime. That fact disposes of the notion that India can be governed from Downing Street or that if it could England would. India must do its best for itself. As to the United Nations, that question does not arise as the nations are not united.

For some twenty-five years India's demand for self-government has been repeatedly deferred by promises from this country and by sending to India endless delegations and missions. Now in a new Mission three Cabinet Ministers have gone to India. What do you imagine will happen if the result of this mission be anything but a complete acceptance of India's demands?

It does not matter what will happen: perhaps a dozen civil wars in the peninsula plus a foreign war, with Downing Street forcing those engaged in civil war to unite in their common defence; perhaps only angry speeches and letters in the newspapers; but Home rule anyhow.

The US Elections, 1948

From 'GBS and US Elections', *New Cavalcade*, 15 May 1948. The 1948 election was won by the Democratic candidate Harry S. Truman (1884–1972). Truman had been elected Vice-President in 1944, and began his first term as President on the death of Roosevelt in 1945. His postwar policies of confrontation with the USSR contributed to the development of the cold war. Henry Agard Wallace (1888–1965), Vice-President of America, 1940–4, ran as a presidential candidate in 1948 for the Progressive Party, advocating social reform, reduction of armaments and friendly relations with the USSR.

If you were an American Democrat, Mr Shaw, would you be likely to vote for Mr Henry Wallace?

Of course I should vote for him. I was the first to propose his candidature in the British Press.

Would you agree with his pronouncement: 'There is no real fight between Truman and the Republican. Both stand for a policy which opens the door to make war in our lifetime and a certainty for our children'?

I agree. But the door is always open for war. Mr Wallace's policy no less than President Truman's. But Mr Wallace's mental capacity is that of a citizen of the world, not that of an American ward boss.

Do you think Mr Wallace's appeal 'to come out boldly and vote for the new party, that will bring peace for ourselves and our children's children' likely to receive a great response?

Do stop canting about peace for ourselves and our children's children. Keep it for Christmas cards. The point in question at the election of President is whether he understands that Russia cannot afford another war, and that Stalin knows this better than any other ruling statesman on earth. Mr Wallace knows it, too; but all his rivals are more or less under suspicion of being more afraid of Russia, instead of less, than of the other States.

The A-bomb and North Korea

From Hayden Church, 'GBS on the A-bomb', *Reynolds News*, 6 August 1950. According to Dan H. Laurence, this interview – the last to be published in Shaw's lifetime – was entirely written by Shaw, except for the first question.[1] After the outbreak of the Korean War (25 June 1950) Truman did not rule out the possibility of employing the atomic bomb against North Korea; and he caused consternation by his statement at a press conference in November that 'there has always been active consideration of its use'.[2]

The Americans have been urged frequently of late to drop the atom bomb on the North Koreans. Do you consider that the use of this bomb is ever justifiable?

In war the word justifiable has no meaning. There is only one rule of conduct: kill the other fellow or he will kill you. Kill him as best you can even at the risk of being killed yourself.

But the atom bomb will not be used unless the combatants go stark mad with Jingo war fever, because the bomb is a boomerang, fatal alike to the bomber and his victim. A Field Marshal is not 'the priest that slew the slayer and shall himself be slain'.[3]

The bomb will be disused in the next war just as poison gas was disused in the last.

Do you approve of the Government sending British troops to take sides with the USA in fighting North Korea,[4] and of the enormous expenditure at home on rearmament with the heavy taxation it involves?

You are mixing up two entirely different questions. As long as war persists as an institution every nation must to the utmost of its resources keep its armed and drilled forces up to the level of its most formidable rivals.

It must make alliances and watch the balance of power jealously. It must propagate Jingo patriotism while professing peace on earth and goodwill among men to be secured by military preparedness for adequate defence. There is no use approving or disapproving: circumstances impose it on all Governments.

Stalin knows that Russia cannot afford another war; all the same he has to prepare for it just as Mr Shinwell has,[5] or President Truman.

But this is an entirely different question from that of the so-called United Nations disunitedly making war on North Korea in support of South Korea, and calling it a war on Communism as a transparent disguise for a war on Russia.

Pandit Nehru declares that he would go to any length to avert such a war.[6] So would I. Winston Churchill says virtually the same.[7] No more horrible calamity could be conceived. But an epidemic of Jingo fever has already set in; and President Truman is showing symptoms of it.

It struck down Woodrow Wilson when he was the most popular figure in America as the man who kept his country out of the 1914–18 war. When he plunged his country into it, he was cheered to the echo for the moment, and then utterly and finally extinguished.[8]

Are you a Communist, Mr Shaw?

Yes: of course I am. A war on Communism is ignorant blazing nonsense. Without its present immense basis of Communism and Socialism our civilisation could not exist for a week. Our strength is in that basis.

If Mr Shinwell announced that he would leave the defence of the country to private enterprise he would be certified and stowed in a mental hospital next day.

The future is to the country which carries Communism farthest and fastest. Russia has civilised the Siberian desert miraculously by it, outstripping us all by borrowing the English methods invented by myself and my Fabian colleagues.

Thank you, Mr Shaw: that is as much as I can swallow in a day. May I congratulate you on what The Times *described as your restful birthday?*

Restful!!! Restful, with the telephone and the door bell ringing all day! With the postmen staggering under bushels of letters and telegrams! With immense birthday cakes, uneatable by me, falling on me like millstones!

With the lane blocked by cameramen, televisors, photographers, newsreelers, interviewers, all refusing to take No for an answer. And I with a hard day's work to finish in time for the village post. Heaven forgive *The Times*, I cannot. Good day to you.

NOTES

1. See Laurence, *Bibliography* [C3928].
2. See David Rees, *Korea: The Limited War* (New York: St Martin's Press, 1964) p. 167.
3. Slightly misquoted from stanza x of 'The Battle of Lake Regillus', by Thomas Babington Macaulay (1800–59).
4. After the outbreak of the war, British vessels in Japanese waters were placed under American command. On the 29 August 2,000 men from the British 27th Infantry Brigade landed at Pusan. Later in the year Attlee pledged Britain to an extensive rearmament programme.
5. Emanuel Shinwell (1884–1986), British Labour Party and trade union activist, was Minister of Defence at this time.
6. Jawaharlal (Pandit) Nehru (1889–1964), first Prime Minister of India after Independence, condemned the North Korean aggression, but refused active participation by India in the war.
7. Churchill unequivocally supported US military intervention in the Korean War, though he expressed anxiety about the possibility that the struggle might lead to another world war.
8. (Thomas) Woodrow Wilson (1856–1924) was American President from 1912 to 1921. After the outbreak of the First World War he fought successfully to preserve American neutrality and to keep trade channels open. But when, in January 1917, Germany renewed unlimited submarine warfare he severed diplomatic relations, and in the following April he sought and received Congress approval for a declaration of war.

Part 16
Later Recollections

INTRODUCTION TO PART 16

The last twenty-five years of Shaw's career began on a high plane of international recognition and fame. His new play, *Saint Joan*, had been produced with triumphant success on both sides of the Atlantic in the 1923/4 season. In the wake of this success he was awarded the Nobel Prize for Literature for 1925. Shaw jokingly told Archibald Henderson that he presumed the honour had been awarded 'as a token of gratitude for a sense of world relief – as he had published nothing in 1925'.[1] There were grains of truth and prophecy in this jest. Shaw's fame, and the attention of the media to his every public word and action, continued without abatement. But, especially in some literary and academic circles, his reputation suffered a substantial decline in the period from 1925 to his death, and beyond into the two following decades. His ambiguous attitudes towards European fascist leaders, not entirely corrected by his lampooning of them in his play *Geneva* (1938),[2] and his unwavering and uncritical admiration for Stalin, were sources of disquiet and animosity. Some of the late plays have now gained more respect in the theatre and in academic study. But generally their reception by contemporary theatre critics was not strongly favourable, and often showed signs of impatience.

T. S. Eliot, whose critical pronouncements profoundly influenced literary taste and judgement in the English-speaking world, made unfavourable comments about Shaw in writings published in the late 1920s.[3] Shaw's work was virtually ignored by the influential Cambridge school of criticism in the 1930s, 1940s and 1950s, and by a great many of the rapidly burgeoning and multiplying university departments of English in the post-Second World-War period. The rising star of modern drama according to Raymond Williams's book, *Drama from Ibsen to Eliot*, was Eliot, and its falling star was Shaw. Theatrical history has shown this judgement to be quite untenable; but Williams's narrowly selective, tendentious and unfavourable analysis of Shaw continues to be influential.[4] In a wildly polemical review published in the *Spectator* in 1955, F. R. Leavis described Shaw as 'boring and cheap'.[5]

A counter-movement, of critical rehabilitation of Shaw, began in 1947 with the publication of an important study by Eric Bentley.[6] Since then a steady succession of more than thirty full-length critical studies, together with a large amount of periodical literature, has helped to promote more informed understanding of Shaw's work and greater recognition of his achievement as a dramatist. The revival of interest in Shaw's plays in England which began in the 1970s has been a major and continuing phenomenon in the theatre world. It now seems clear that many of this plays are established as part of the classical tradition of English comedy. The recent editions of his music criticism and of his remarkably lively and entertaining correspondence have further enhanced Shaw's current reputation. Yet he remains a controversial figure who still arouses conflict and uncertain responses. The recollections of this part, which supplement those relating to particular topics elsewhere in this volume, testify to the extraordinary mixture of fascination and reserve which Shaw has inspired, particularly in the land to which he was chief jester for more than half a century.

NOTES

1. Archibald Henderson, *George Bernard Shaw: Man of the Century* (New York: Appleton-Century-Crofts, 1956) p. 838.
2. See above, p. 349.
3. T. S. Eliot made critical attacks on Shaw in a review of a book on *Saint Joan* by John Mackinnon Robertson, 'Shaw, Robertson and "The Maid"', *Criterion*, IV (April 1926) 389–90; and in his 'A Dialogue on Dramatic Poetry' (1928), rpt. in *Selected Essays*, 3rd edn (London: Faber & Faber, 1951).
4. Raymond Williams, *Drama from Ibsen to Eliot* (London: Chatto & Windus, 1952) pp. 138–53 (revised as *Drama from Ibsen to Brecht*, 1968). Williams leaves out of account the entire corpus of Shaw's dramatic writings of the middle period, from *Man and Superman* to *Heartbreak House*, and all of the late plays after *Saint Joan*, and deals briefly with only a few of the early plays.
5. F. R. Leavis, 'Shaw against Lawrence, *Spectator*, CXCIV (1 April 1955) 397–9; rpt. in *D. H. Lawrence: A Critical Anthology*, ed. H. Coombes (Harmondsworth, Middx.: Penguin, 1973) pp. 381–4. Leavis was reviewing *Sex, Literature, and Censorship*, ed. Harry T. Moore, with Introduction by H. F. Rubinstein.
6. Eric R. Bentley, *Bernard Shaw* (Norfolk, Conn.: New Directions Books, 1947).

Shaw and Lady Astor

A. E. JOHNSON

From A. E. Johnson, 'Encounters with GBS', *Dalhousie Review*, Spring 1951. A. E. Johnson held the post of Professor of English at Syracuse University, New York. The scene of Johnson's recollection was a reception given by Lady Astor at her town house, 4 St James's Square, on 5 July 1928. Johnson and others had been invited to meet the Shaws.

Lady Astor who, so far from treating Shaw as an idol, jollied him as if he were a bright spoiled boy, began the discussion by asking him why he wrote *Saint Joan*. GBS said he thought the Maid inspired him, so that the various legends floating about might be overridden. He opined that in a sense he, GBS, didn't do it: he just happened to know how to arrange it, that was all.

He went on to speak of Russian spirituality, and thought we should follow their example, and cease to worship the idle rich. America had but exchanged black slaves for white; all of which called forth the banter and rebuke of Lady Astor who did everything short of bearding Shaw with the loose arm of her antique chair, which she actually at one point removed. Finally, with that fearlessness which made her a terror in the House of Commons, she turned to him and said, very spiritedly: 'The trouble with you, G.B., is that you think you're clever: you're not clever, you're only *good*! Isn't he, Mrs Shaw?'

At this delicious pantomiming, which made me wonder – even then – if I were dreaming, the much-amused Shaw laughingly threw back his head and began to quote Kingsley's famous quatrain: 'Be good, sweet maid, let who will be clever!'[1] We all joined in the merriment, and Mrs Shaw smiled serenely at Nancy Astor as if to tell her that she was right. I gained the impression that Shaw did enough talking for them both, and that his wife had long ago decided that this was so.

After the somewhat rambling, but never for one moment dull, talk, we adjourned for refreshment. G.B. took some orange juice, but literally could not consume it for chattering with a little knot of us. I chanced to be clean facing him, and might have been his microphone. It would have been impossible for me to talk back at him, even had I either the information or the courage. He spoke, I recall, of fascism and communism, and explained the Matteotti murder.[2]

Lady Astor interrupted us – or rather him – with a platter, and tried to make Shaw have a piece of bread and butter. Shaw refused, saying, like an actor: 'Bread and butter? From *you*? You ought to give me nightingale's tongues!' I still wondered if I were dreaming; and there is a sense in which I still do.

Mr J. J. Mallon,[3] whom Lady Astor twitted a good deal, quoted the definition of England as 'an island lying off the east coast of the Irish Free State entirely inhabited by Bernard Shaw and Lady Astor'.

'Why drag in Lady Astor?' tallied the impish Shaw, at his Shavian best.

NOTES

1. The line from 'A Farewell to CEG' by Charles Kingsley (1819–75) should read: 'Be good, sweet maid, and let who can be clever.'

2. Giacomo Matteotti (1885–1924) was secretary general of the Italian Socialist Party. He was abducted by Fascists on 10 June 1924, and his murdered body was found on 18 August 1924 near the Via Flaminia outside Rome.

3. James Joseph Mallon (1875–1961), sociologist and educator, was for thirty-five years the Warden of Toynbee Hall, an educational centre in the East End of London founded with the purpose of exploring and improving local social and economic conditions. He was an executive member of the Workers' Educational Association.

'Bright, Nimble, Fierce, and Comprehending'

WINSTON CHURCHILL

From Winston Churchill, 'Bernard Shaw – Saint, Sage and Clown', *Sunday Chronicle*, 13 April 1930. Apart from the opening paragraphs, which are reprinted here, Churchill's article is more of a general essay on Shaw and his work than a recollection. The article was published again in Churchill's *Great Contemporaries* (1937) and, with some cuts, in the *Sunday Dispatch*, 2 March 1941.

Mr Bernard Shaw was one of my earliest antipathies. Indeed, almost my first literary effusion, written when I was serving as a subaltern in India in 1897 (it never saw the light of day), was a ferocious onslaught upon him, and upon an article which he had written disparaging and deriding the British Army in some minor war.

Four or five years passed before I made his acquaintance. My mother, always in agreeable contact with artistic and dramatic circles, took me to luncheon with him.[1] I was instantly attracted by the sparkle and gaiety of his conversation, and impressed by his eating only fruit and vegetables, and drinking only water.

I rallied him on the latter habit, asking: 'Do you really never drink any wine at all?' 'I am hard enough to keep in order as it is,' he replied. Perhaps he had heard of my youthful prejudice against him.

In later years, and especially after the war, I can recall several pleasant and, to me, memorable talks on politics, particularly about Ireland and about Socialism. I think these encounters cannot have been displeasing to him, for he was kind enough to give me a copy of his Magnum Opus, *The Intelligent Woman's Guide to Socialism*, remarking (subsequently), 'It is a sure way to prevent you reading it.'

At any rate, I possess a lively image of this bright, nimble, fierce, and comprehending being, Jack Frost dancing bespangled in the sunshine, which I should be very sorry to lose.

NOTE

1. This meeting seems to have taken place in late January 1912. On 23 January 1912 Shaw wrote to Lillah McCarthy inviting her to be present on the occasion: 'Will you come to lunch on Friday and help us to entertain Winston Churchill, who will not find *my* beaux yeux much of a treat. Harley [Granville Barker] can entertain Winston's mother' (*Collected Letters 1911–1925*, p. 73).

Three Meetings

LEONARD WOOLF

From Leonard Woolf, *Beginning Again: An Autobiography of the Years 1911–1918* (London: Hogarth Press, 1964) pp. 120–2. The occasion of the first of the meetings described here was the cremation of H. G. Wells's second wife, Amy Catherine ('Jane') Wells (d. 1927). Amy met Wells as one of his pupils in a biology class at William Briggs' Tutorial College for the students of London University. She became well known in literary circles and in the Fabian Society, of which she was Secretary in 1906. Shaw was fond of her. He wrote to Wells on 24 March 1906: 'Give my love to Jane, that well-behaved woman. Why she married you (I being single at the time) the Life Force only knows.'[1] Woolf does not supply a date for the second meeting, in the House of Commons. The chance meeting in Kensington Gardens occurred on 28 April 1933. The Shaws had recently returned from their world cruise aboard the *Empress of Britain*.[2]

One of the strangest things about him was that he was personally the kindest, most friendly, most charming of men, yet personally he was almost the most impersonal person I have ever known. He was always extremely nice to Virginia and me. If one met him anywhere, he would come up and greet one with what seemed to be warmth and pleasure and he would start straight away with a fountain of words scintillating with wit and humour. You might easily flatter yourself that you were the one person in Europe to whom at that moment the famous George Bernard Shaw wanted to talk, but if you happened to look into that slightly fishy, ice-blue eye of his, you got a shock. It was not looking at you; you were nowhere in its orbit; it was looking through you or over you into a distant world or universe inhabited almost entirely by GBS, his thoughts and feelings, fancies and phantasies. Writing this, I remember three more or less casual meetings with him which seem to me wonderfully characteristic. The first was at Golders Green; Virginia and I went to the cremation of H. G. Wells's wife. When we came out, Maynard and Lydia Keynes came up to speak to us. Lydia was in tears. Then Shaw came up and put his hand on Lydia's shoulder and made a kind of oration to her telling her not to cry, that death was not an event to shed tears upon. It was a kindly, even a beautiful and eloquent speech, and yet, though he knew Lydia well and certainly liked her, one felt that it was hardly addressed to this highly individual and warm-hearted woman, who had danced as Lydia Lopokova in Diaghilev's Russian Ballet and out of it into marriage with John Maynard Keynes, but rather to 'someone in tears', who indeed might have been any woman in tears.

The second was in a Committee Room in the House of Commons. It was, I think, a Fabian Committee of which Webb was chairman and I was secretary. Shaw was sitting next to me; on committees he was just like the Shaw not on a committee; he loved to talk paradoxically and amusingly and at considerable length. If Webb was the chairman, GBS was never allowed to get going; he was kept to the point or to silence, and it was usually to silence. On this afternoon, he had been allowed scarcely two sentences, and when the proceedings came to an end, he must have been bursting with words and ideas. He turned to the man sitting on his left, who was an MP and one of the dullest and stupidest men I have ever known, and began an extraordinarily brilliant and amusing monologue. I had to discuss some matter of business with Sidney Webb, who was sitting on my right, and, when I had finished, I found that Shaw's splendid display was still going on. Indeed the fireworks went on for another five or ten minutes; it was superb, but I don't think that the MP understood, let alone appreciated, a single one of Shaw's squibs, crackers or rockets. But it made no difference to GBS; it made no difference to him whether he talked to the dummy MP or the cleverest man in Europe – the ice-blue eye went through or over the MP, fixed upon the universe of GBS.

The third occasion was in Kensington Gardens. One fine Sunday afternoon Virginia and I went for a walk in the Park and we had just crossed from Hyde Park into Kensington Gardens and were making for the Flower Walk when we met Shaw coming from the opposite direction. He stopped and immediately began to tell us about his voyage round the world in a 'luxury' liner from which he had just got back. For the next quarter of an hour or twenty minutes he stood in front of us in the characteristic GBS attitude, very erect with folded arms, his beard wagging as he talked, and gave us a brilliant unflagging monologue, describing the ship, the passengers, his audiences, what he said to them, his triumphs. When the fountain of words at last died down and we parted, I found that we were the centre of a wide circle of fifteen or twenty people; they had recognised Shaw and had stopped to listen to his oration as though it were a public entertainment. And it struck me then that that was just exactly what it was. Although we were fond of him and he, I think, in his curious way really liked both of us, the sparkling display to which we had just listened might just as well have been addressed to the twenty strangers gaping at him as to us.

Though Shaw had, quite rightly, a very high opinion of Shaw, he was entirely without the pretentiousness and personal prickliness which nearly always make the great or still more The Very Important Person such an intolerable nuisance. Like the Webbs, he seemed never to resent or to be offended by anything which a younger person said or did to him.

NOTES

1. *Collected Letters 1898–1910*, p. 614.
2. The date is provided by Virginia Woolf in her diary. See below, p. 499.

Meeting, 1932

VIRGINIA WOOLF

From *The Diary of Virginia Woolf*, vol. IV: *1931–35*, ed. Anne Olivier Bell assisted by Andrew McNeillie (Harmondsworth, Middx: Penguin, 1982) pp. 106–7. The occasion of this recollection was a lunch party held at the home of Maynard Keynes on 2 June 1932.

My comment upon the Shaws: he said 'I am not sufficiently fond of myself to wish for immortality. I should like to be different. I should like to be a performer in music, & a mathematician. So I dont keep a diary. I destroy all my letters.[1] So did [*blank in* MS]. He had had letters from every great man. He took them out in the garden & burnt them. But I couldnt burn Ellen Terry's.[2] They were works of art. It would have been like burning a page of the Luttrell psalter.[3] The handwriting was a work of art. She scribb[l]ed them – never thought of a phrase. But I admit that when our correspondence was published I thought – I admit – I shall be the hero: not a bit of it: I have to admit that Ellen was the superior. She comes out far the better of the two. Frank Harris – his life of me was a life of himself.[4] Theres no truth in it about me. No life of me has a word of truth in it. They say my father was persecuted, & that I was persecuted, as a boy – sent to a Wesleyan School. Desmond MacCarthy says he's going to write my life – well, he may say so.[5] He comes & talks – I cant tell the truth yet, about myself. The Webbs looked lonely somehow going off to Russia.[6] He's not growing old – no, I dont find that. I've always quarrelled with the Webbs. You see Webb has a gigantic faculty for absorbing information. He could have gone to Oxford – found some flaw in the statutes – proved it to the examiners. But didn't go: only wanted to be in the right. And so, when I first knew him, I had to overcome an immense amount of useless knowledge. He had to forget things he had learnt. I always tell a story to illustrate this. When I was a boy I asked my father 'What is a Unitarian' And he thought for a time & then he said, 'Unitarians believe that after Christ was crucified he got down off the Cross & ran away on the other side of the hill.' Years later, when I was thirty or so, I was staying with the Trevelyans at Wellcomb;[7] & the talk got upon Unitarians, & it flashed upon me, this cannot be the true story – but I'd always seen Christ running down the hill all those years. Webb would be much more effective if he'd one drop of the artist. But he has, not one. Beatrice is in despair about it. Cant make a good speech therefore. People think my style as speaker is spontaneous, colloquial. Its the most artificial ever known. I've taken long railway journeys & spent them saying the letters of the alphabet aloud so as to make my vowels strike out. Then they forget I'm an Irishman – I think quicker than the English. No I dont mug things up – when I write history I dont read it. I imagine the sort of things people would have done & then I say they did them & then I find out facts – one always can – that prove it. The great pleasure of the Broadcasting to me is that I can sit at home & conduct *The Meistersinger*[8] myself. I sit with the book of the score & conduct & I'm furious when they dont follow me. That way one finds how often the singers make howlers – come in a bar early or late. Beecham[9] – (here he sang a piece of the *Magic Flute*) turned *that* – which is solemn, slow, processionly [?] – into a hornpipe. I leapt in my seat (he leapt up his knees & clasped them in agony – he is never still a moment – he clenches his fists – he flings himself this way & that; he sprang up to go, as if he were twenty, not seventy-four as L[eonard] remarked. What life, what vitality! What immense nervous spring! That perhaps is his genius. Immense vivacity – & why I dont read him for pleasure. His face is bright red; his nose lumpy: his eyes sea green like a sailors or a cockatoos. He doesnt much notice who's there.

NOTES

1. Shaw did keep diaries, and extensive files of correspondence.

2. The correspondence between the celebrated actress Ellen Alice Terry (1847–1928) and Shaw had recently been published (*Ellen Terry and Bernard Shaw: A Correspondence*, ed. Christopher St John (New York: Fountain Press; London: Constable, 1931). Laurence (*Bibliography* [A205]) points out that Shaw had silently edited out sensitive passages in the correspondence for this edition.

3. A famous illuminated psalter (c. 1340) by Sir Geoffrey Luttrell of Irnham, Lincolnshire.

4. Frank Harris, *Bernard Shaw: An Unauthorised Biography* (London: Victor Gollancz, 1931).

5. This intention was not carried out.

6. The Webbs departed in May for a three-month visit to Russia.

7. Welcombe House, near Stratford-on-Avon, was one of the houses belonging to the Trevelyan family. Shaw corresponded with Sir Charles Trevelyan (1870–1958), a Liberal MP who changed his allegiance to Labour (see *Collected Letters 1911–1925*, pp. 529, 787).

8. I.e. Wagner's opera *Die Meistersinger von Nürnberg*.

9. Sir Thomas Beecham (1879–1961), celebrated British conductor and director of operatic productions.

Meeting, 1933

VIRGINIA WOOLF

From *The Diary of Virginia Woolf*, vol. IV: *1931–35*, ed. Anne Olivier Bell assisted by Andrew McNeillie (Harmondsworth, Middx: Penguin, 1982) pp. 152–3. The following extract from her diary, dated 28 April 1933, records Virginia Woolf's reaction to the same chance meeting with Shaw in Kensington Gardens of which Leonard provides an account (see above, p. 496).

A mere note. We got out of the car last night & began walking down to the Serpentine. A summer evening. Chestnuts in their crinolines, bearing tapers: grey green water & so on. Suddenly L[eonard] bore off; & there was Shaw, dwindled shanks, white beard; striding along. We talked, by a railing, for fifteen mins. He stood with his arms folded, very upright, leaning back; teeth gold tipped. Just come from the dentist, & 'lured' out for a walk by the weather. Very friendly. That is his art, to make one think he likes one. A great spurt of ideas. 'You forget that an aeroplane is like a car – it bumps – We went over the great wall – saw a little dim object in the distance. Of course the tropics are the place. The Ceylon[?] people are the original human beings — we are smudged copies.[1] I caught the Chinese looking at us with horror – that we should be human beings! Of course the tour cost thousands; yet to see us, you'd think we hadnt the price of the fare to Hampton Court. Lots of old spinsters had saved up for years to come. Oh but my publicity! Its terrifying. An hours bombardment at every port. I made the mistake of accepting [*blank*] invitation. I found myself on a platform with the whole university round me. They began shouting We want

Bernard Shaw. So I told them that every man at twenty-one must be a revolutionary. After that of course the police imprisoned them by dozens. I want to write an article for the Herald pointing out what Dickens said years ago about the folly of Parliament. Oh I could only stand the voyage by writing. I've written three or four books. I like to give the public full weight. Books should be sold by the pound. What a nice little dog. But aren't I keeping you & making you cold (touching my arm) – Two men stopped along the path to look. Off he strode again on his dwindled legs. I said Shaw likes us. L. thinks he likes nobody. What will they think of Shaw in fifty years? He is seventy-six he said; too old for the tropics.

NOTE

1. In his play *On the Rocks* (1933) Shaw has an elderly Sinhalese, Sir Jafna Pandranath say: 'Look at your faces and look at the faces of my people in Ceylon, the cradle of the human race. There you see Man as he came from the hand of God, who has left on every feature the unmistakeable stamp of the great original creative artist. There you see Woman with eyes in her head that mirror the universe' (*Collected Plays*, vol. vi, p. 713).

'In the Vortex'

VINCENT BROME

From Vincent Brome, *Confessions of a Writer* (London: Hutchinson, 1970) pp. 111–12. Vincent Brome (b. 1910), biographer, novelist, playwright and journalist, visited Shaw in the hope of interviewing him about a proposed biography of H. G. Wells. Brome's biography of Wells was published in 1951. The mention of Shaw's age suggests that this visit took place in 1934.

Blanche Patch answered the front door, escorted me to a second door, opened it and almost at once like the spinning centre of a whirlwind I was caught up in the vortex of an extraordinary personality and set down again on a sofa to confront a very tall man with a leonine head, wearing old-fashioned knickerbockers and big brogue shoes. I knew this man to be at least seventy-eight years old but he emanated enormous energy and immediately poured a flood of words over my head. His movements were jerky and crackling. It was like encountering a very attenuated marionette whose legs and arms made quick spasmodic movements from some hidden mechanism which also fed electricity into the joints so that I expected them to emit sparks at any moment.

The tables were now completely turned. I had come to interview George Bernard Shaw but he at once proceeded to interview Vincent Brome. How old was I, what did my father do, what education had permanently crippled my view of life? No education! Marvellous. Thank goodness I had escaped that final horror of the mass-produced mind – an academic training. Did I have ambitions? *Small* ambition! But that was madness. Ambition had to be large, overwhelming, intolerant. Why did I suffer from that middle-class disease of misplaced modesty? It ought to be an indictable offence. It was no less a piece of lying hypocrisy to underestimate one's talents than it was to overestimate them.'Now come on, young man – you can't deceive me – you have big ambitions haven't you? – admit it – big ones – somewhere hidden away!' Under this steadily mounting pressure I at last timidly admitted that I too hoped to become a writer. Whereupon the electrically alive marionette jerked from one end of the room to the other in two gigantic strides and boomed: 'So you want to compete with me, do you! Now let me tell you. This year in the theatre I have produced . . . [sic]. And this year I am publishing . . . [sic].'

If my memory serves me correctly there were three plays and three books appearing that year and he finished the catalogue with an accusative roar: 'And you hope to compete with that do you?'

I admitted that I didn't. Whereupon the torrent of questions renewed itself. What kind of writing, for what kind of purpose – did I want to undertake? Not another of those interminably earnest novels exposing the shallowness of everything except the author; not another frilled and pantalooned bedroom farce which kept decent stuff off the stage; above all not a Shavian play with a Shavian message!

I remember the flood of words seemed to fill the room and silence me but I managed to stammer out at last, 'I was thinking of writing a biography.'

'A biography! Now I see through you, sir – now I realise why you have forced your way in here under false pretences. So you want to write a biography of me do you? Let me tell you, young man, you are the twentieth person who has dedicated his life to that imbecile purpose . . . [sic].'

Once again there were at least three minutes of flawless invective, the flow of which I was quite incapable of stopping, but at last I ventured to correct him.

'A biography of H. G. Wells, not yourself.'

He received this with a prolonged guffaw of laughter.

'You must be madder than I thought. No one will ever contain H. G. between the covers of a book. Wait till he hears of this!'

'Do you think he would object?' I said.

'Object!' Shaw roared. 'He'll bring the house down round you. I never met such a chap. I could not survive meeting such another.'

Portraying Shaw

SIR JACOB EPSTEIN

From Sir Jacob Epstein, *Epstein: An Autobiography* (London: Hulton Press, 1955) pp. 82–3. The bust of Shaw by the famous sculptor, Sir Jacob Epstein (1880–1959), was cast in 1934. Shaw wrote of the work: 'Show it to anyone who knows nothing about me and ask them to guess the subject and the reply will be: "Legree the slave trader, or half civilised cave man, or somebody ferocious and sensual, all mouth and jaws and hair with a negligible brow. In short, a Neanderthal Shaw." '[1]

Shaw sat with exemplary patience and even eagerness. He walked to my studio every day, and was punctual and conscientious. He wise-cracked of course. In matters of Art he aired definite opinions, mostly wrong, and I often had to believe that he wished to say smart, clever things to amuse me. On seeing a huge block of stone, unworked in the studio, he asked me what I intended to do with it. Not wishing to tell him exactly what my plans were, I merely remarked that I had a plan. 'What,' he exclaimed, 'you have a plan! You shouldn't have a plan. I never work according to a plan. Each day I begin with new ideas totally different from the day before.' As if a sculptor with a six-ton block to carve could alter his idea daily! Shaw believed that sculptors put into their portraits their own characteristics, and of a bust done of him by a prince, he remarked that it contained something very aristocratic. This was amusing in view of the fact that this particular bust was peculiarly commonplace.

One day Robert Flaherty[2] brought along the Aran boatman, Tiger King,[3] who was the chief character in the film, *Man of Arran* [sic], written about fishermen. In the studio, when Tiger King was introduced, Shaw immediately started talking to him on how to sail a boat, what happened in storms, and generally instructed him in sea-lore.

Shaw was puzzled by the bust of himself and often looked at it and tried to make it out. He believed that I had made a kind of primitive barbarian of him. Something altogether uncivilised and really a projection of myself, rather than of him. I never tried to explain the bust to him, and I think that there are in it elements so subtle that they would be difficult to explain. Nevertheless, I believe this to be an authentic and faithful rendering of George Bernard Shaw physically and psychologically. I leave out any question of aesthetics, as that would be beyond Shaw's comprehension. When the bust was finished, we were filmed, and Shaw was wonderful as an actor, taking the filming very seriously.

In 1934, when the work in bronze was done, I offered Shaw a copy of the bust through Orage,[4] but was told that Shaw could not think of having it in his house. This, I believe, was due to Mrs Shaw's dislike of it.[5]

Throughout my life in England, Shaw was an outspoken champion for my work, on several occasions giving the great British public lively smacks on my behalf.[6] I will not say that he understood what I have made. He seemed deficient in all sense of the plastic, but had a lively notion of how stupid the newspapers can be over new works of sculpture or painting. He was generous to young talent, but always likely to be taken in by cleverness or pretence. I would say that Shaw was not really interested in the plastic arts, although he could be got to take a passing or journalistic interest in controversial work. On one occasion, on visiting an exhibition of paintings of Epping Forest, not knowing what to say, he asked me if I had done the paintings with brushes.

NOTES

1. See Archibald Henderson, *George Bernard Shaw: Man of the Century* (New York: Appleton-Century-Crofts, 1956) p. 846.

2. Robert Joseph Flaherty (1884–1951), film director, is considered the pioneer of the documentary film, and is noted for his presentation of Eskimo life in *Nanook of the North* (1922), of Samoan life in *Moana* (1926) and for the much praised *Man of Aran* (1934) about the lives of the people of the Aran Islands off the coast of Galway, Ireland.

3. Tiger King was an expert on boats and sea-lore. He is described by Robert Flaherty's wife as 'a great tall figure with dark, curly hair like a Spaniard' who 'looked something like a gypsy and had a fey air about him' (Frances Hubbard Flaherty, *The Odyssey of a Film Maker* [Urbana, Ill.: Beta Phi Mu, 1960] p. 28).

4. Alfred Richard Orage (1873–1934), journalist and psychologist, who bought, and became editor of the *New Age* (1907–22) with the aid of £500 from Shaw.

5. Charlotte said of the bust: 'If that thing enters the house I leave it' (see *Shaw: an Autobiography, 1898–1950*, selected from his writings by Stanley Weintraub [London, Sydney, Toronto: Max Reinhardt, 1971] p. 253).

6. For instances of this, see Henderson, *George Bernard Shaw*, p. 175 and Epstein, *Let There Be Sculpture* (London: Michael Joseph, 1940) p. 68.

'Shaw's Hidden Qualities'

LADY ASTOR

From Lady Astor, 'Shaw's Hidden Qualities', *Observer*, 5 November 1950.

GBS would not have called himself a Christian, but those who knew him most intimately could not have called him anything else. His purity, his patience, his great kindness and charity, his moral courage and his control of the carnal by the spiritual proved up till the end that he had the 'peace that passeth all understanding'. His weapons, like St Paul's, were never carnal, but 'mighty through God to the pulling down of strong holds'.

To write of GBS without writing of his wife, Charlotte, would really not be writing about the whole man. She, in her way, was just as remarkable as he was. No two people ever had a better understanding than those two, or a happier life. Her judgement about people was far better than his, but her faith in his vision was unshakable. She laughed at his weakness and vanities, but often said to me, 'GBS is nearly always right'. He was tender and thoughtful as a husband, and although he wrote a lot of nonsense about women and matrimony, nobody ever kept the rules so sacredly and kindly as this playboy of the Western World.

It was only when she went that I fully realised what she meant in his life, both for his happiness and for the discriminating guidance which she often gave him. I don't believe that alone he could have done what he did, and when he told me he wanted his ashes mingled with Charlotte's, I realised that in purpose and outlook their lives had always been one.

GBS was a great actor, and he knew how to hide from most of the world two things – his deep spirituality and his complete happiness with Charlotte.

What Shaw was Like

ST JOHN ERVINE

From St John Ervine, 'Bernard Shaw', *Spectator*, 10 November 1950.

What was Bernard Shaw *like*? This is the question I have been most often asked, and it is the question I find hardest to answer. What *was* he like? He was, at one and the same time, the most engaging and the most infuriating man I have ever known; but he was infuriating only as a public figure, never, in my knowledge of him, as a personal friend. He could be terrifyingly frank, and some people, whose vanity he disturbed, thought him cruel; but he was not cruel, though I can understand touchy and pretentious people believing that he was. Those who detested him were seldom personally acquainted with him. I sometimes heard from a man in America who never in his life saw Shaw, but foamed at the mouth when his name was mentioned. Those who knew him well allowed none of his quirks and intellectual acrobatics to diminish their regard for him. Almost all his friends were of long standing, though his interest in life was strong enough to make him eager to meet young people and to make new acquaintances. He was exceptionally kind, but kind without being sentimental, and he did not demonstrate his emotions. I remember hearing a foolish fellow charge him with meanness. 'You never see his name in a public subscription list!' 'No, indeed you don't,' I replied, 'but you'll see it at the foot of many an unadvertised cheque for a man in need!' Shaw, I haven't the slightest doubt, gave away far more than a tithe of his income, but only the recipients of his charity knew about it. He was indiscreet in his conversation, revealing many things that ought not to have been revealed, but he was silent as the grave about his benefactions.

He sometimes seemed to be cruel, because he had scarcely any reticence about what are called private feelings. He seemed to think that reticence was an unworthy thing, that to hoard up one's life to oneself was almost as mean as if a scientist, having discovered, say, a cure for cancer, should use it only for the benefit of his relatives. Shaw was intensely interested in people, and the things they did, and eager to learn why they behaved as they did. It is true that he sometimes used a person's confidences for the purpose of pleasantry – he could not resist a good story, and was apt to embellish it – but he did not do this for any mean reason. There was no meanness in Shaw, absolutely none. He is the only man I have ever known of whom that could be said. When he told a story that might have wounded the person about whom it was told, he did so, not to mock the man or hurt him, but to point a tale or to add to the gaiety of conversation. He simply could not understand anybody resenting an entertaining revelation. His frankness was almost scarifying; but he was frank because he thought it better to tell people the truth than to involve them in long, obscure dodgings of it.

His mind was terribly tidy – old-maidish, he himself called it – and he was scrupulously clean both in body and in mind. In bodily cleanness he was as fastidious as General Booth:[1] in mental cleanness he was far more fastidious than Tolstoy. During more than forty years' knowledge of him I never heard him use an improper word or tell what is called a dirty story. He himself declared that he was deeply shocked by some of the words used by James Joyce in *Ulysses*.[2] *Lady Chatterley's Lover*, if he had read it, would have horrified him.[3] But he was not addicted much to novels. He liked to read plays, but was bored by novels. In spite of his fastidiousness, however, he was the most shocking conversationalist I have ever listened to, and would say things that might be expected to throw routine people into convulsions without, however, appearing to know that he was saying anything unusual. It is true that he made disrupting remarks in a highly entertaining way, and could leave you, if you were not a mass of unsavoury inhibitions and routine thoughts, immensely interested. He was exceptionally stimulating in his talk, even when he was unconvincing and flippant, and he enjoyed his own conversation as much as did his audience, though he was a better listener than is commonly believed. . . .

He was a shy man. I remember, early in our acquaintance, seeing him enter a room which he had expected to find unoccupied and, discovering several people in it, blushing like an embarrassed girl. He was always a little ungainly at first meetings. That was because he was essentially solitary. His recreations – reading, swimming, long walks – were all solitary recreations. It was no trouble to him to be alone: it was sometimes a trouble to him to be with other people. But anyone who concludes from that statement that he had no gift of friendship will conclude very wrongly. He had many friends, and they were devoted to him. But he did not need people. His friends were seldom such as one might expect the friends of a dramatist to be. He cared little for the company of authors and had few friends among them. Those writers he knew and liked best were people of his own sociological sort.

He liked H. G. Wells immensely, despite the frequency with which Wells quarrelled with him. They proved beyond a doubt that it does *not* take two to make a quarrel. Shaw never quarrelled with anybody. People quarrelled with him. He had no rancour, and rarely harboured resentment, though he maintained his argument and firmly defended his faith. Indeed, I only knew him to express resentment once: he had hoped to be made a member of the Irish Convention in 1916, and was bitterly angry with Asquith for not appointing him; a foolish failure by Asquith, for Shaw in his middle years was a very good committee man.[4] Considering how nervous his temperament was, he had extraordinary control of himself and seemed imperturbable. Yet he was a nervous man and a very sensitive man. He was ashamed of his sensitive feelings, and created a great deal of antipathy to himself by his efforts to conceal his pain. I *know* that Shaw was deeply moved when, during the first war, he visited France and saw the headless body of a soldier. But he would not admit that he had been moved, and on his return to London wrote a flippant article in the *Daily Chronicle* about 'a gentleman who had lost his head',[5] which gave great pain and offence to thousands of readers. Shaw often did that sort of thing: laughed, lest he should be found in tears; a foolish habit which brought him much misunderstanding and dislike.

Of all the people he knew, I think he liked most Sidney and Beatrice Webb, William Archer and G. K. Chesterton. He loved Chesterton, as who didn't? These four were totally unlike himself in every respect; but his affection for them, and their affection for him, was immeasurable. He greatly admired T. E. Lawrence, and got on with J. M. Barrie and Arthur Pinero better than might reasonably have been expected. He was not fond of Irish authors, generally speaking, and had illimitable contempt for George Moore. Wilde was never a friend of his – they rarely met, not more than, perhaps, half a dozen times – and he had a temperate liking for Yeats. He was more akin to 'A. E.' than to any other Irish author. But the Irishman he liked most was Sir Horace Plunkett. His happiest associations were with people of that sort, men and women who were trying to remake their world. He seemed indifferent to the loss of his friendship with Granville Barker, for which he was entirely to blame, but I remember once, when I was taking him to lunch with Clemence Dane in Devonshire,[6] that as we passed the end of a road, and I said to him, 'Harley Granville Barker lives up there,' he looked along it a little wistfully and said, 'Oh, Harley!' in a tone I'd never heard him use before. He had never been inside that house.

NOTES

1. William Booth (1829–1912), founder and general of the Salvation Army, had an intense dislike of dirt and squalor.

2. This rather oversimplifies Shaw's reaction to *Ulysses*. It is true that Shaw said to Archibald Henderson: 'I could not write the words Mr Joyce uses: my prudish hand would refuse to form the letters' (Henderson, 'Literature and Science', *Fortnightly Review*, CXXII (October 1924) 519–21). The novel evoked for Shaw unpleasant memories of his youth in Dublin, but he nevertheless recognised its outstanding distinction. In a letter to *Picture Post* of 3 June 1939, he wrote as follows:

> In your issue of the 13th Mr Geoffrey Grigson . . . states that I was 'disgusted by the unsqueamish realism of *Ulysses*, and burnt my copy in the grate'.
> Somebody has humbugged Mr Grigson. The story is not true. I picked up *Ulysses* in scraps from the American *Little Review*, and for years did not know that it was the history of a single day in Dublin. But having passed between seven and eight thousand single days in Dublin I missed neither the realism of the book nor its poetry. I did not burn it; and I was not disgusted. If Mr Joyce should ever desire a testimonial as the author of a literary masterpiece from me, it shall be given with all possible emphasis and with sincere enthusiasm.

3. But Ervine himself records that Shaw said to an uncomprehending General Smuts that 'every schoolgirl of sixteen should read *Lady Chatterley's Lover*' (St John Ervine, *Bernard Shaw: His Life, Work and Friends* [London: Constable, 1956] p. 522).

4. The Irish Convention was established by the Lloyd George government in 1917, with a view to solving problems of the relations between Ireland and England. Shaw made several attempts to have himself appointed as one of the fifteen eminent Irishmen who formed the nucleus of the Convention, under the chairmanship of Sir Horace Plunkett (1854–1932), who was the founder of the Agricultural Co-operative Movement in Ireland. In a letter written in 1914, Shaw described Plunkett as 'about the ablest, honestest and whitest man in practical politics at present' (*Collected Letters 1911–1925*, p. 276). Asquith's role in the matter of Shaw's application for membership of the Convention is not clear.

5. 'A man lying by the roadside was not a tramp taking a siesta, but a gentleman who had lost his head.' This sentence occurs in the first section of a remarkably candid and graphic account which Shaw wrote of his experiences when he visited the Front early in 1917 (see above, pp. 244–51). The account was published as a three-part article under the title, 'Joy Riding at the Front' (*Daily Chronicle*, 5, 7 and 8 March 1917).

6. Clemence Dane was the pseudonym of Winifred Ashton (1888–1965), playwright and novelist.

'Thoughts on Shaw'

J. B. PRIESTLEY

From J. B. Priestley, 'Thoughts on Shaw', *New Statesman and Nation*, 28 July

1956. John Boynton Priestley (1894–1984), novelist and critic, wrote this article to mark the centenary of Shaw's birth. Priestley wrote about Shaw in more complimentary vein in an earlier essay, which concluded with the words: 'Some of the air we breathe now has GBS in it, a little mountain oxygen that has somehow penetrated the fog. And where this mountain air comes from there is nothing small, nothing mean, nothing vindictive and cruel; it knows the sun of wit and wisdom and great cleansing winds of doctrine' ('GBS – Social Critic', in Stephen Winsten, ed., *GBS 90: Aspects of Bernard Shaw's Life and Work* (London, New York, Melbourne, Sydney: Hutchinson, 1946) pp. 50–4).

When I was a boy, ordinary stupid people thought him a self-advertising intellectual clown, who would say anything to attract attention. This view of him was dismissed with contempt even by those like Chesterton who sharply disagreed with him. And, of course, it was nonsense. Yet there was in it, as there often is in the judgements of ordinary stupid people, a valuable grain of truth. He held many beliefs but he did not hold them as most of us do. He never appeared to be emotionally committed to them. He could advance or defend them without anger. His warmest admirers tell us that this was because he was almost a saint. The opposite party say it was because he had a great deal of the charlatan in him. What is certain is that his peculiar relation to his beliefs gave him both the strength and the weakness characteristic of him.

He and Wells, whom I knew better than I did Shaw, offered some valuable contrasts. Wells always behaved far worse than Shaw; he was too impatient; he made mischief; he lost his temper and screamed insults and slanders. (Belloc once said that Wells was a cad who didn't pretend to be anything but a cad; that Bennett was a cad pretending to be a gentleman; that Shaw was a gentleman pretending to be a cad.) These tantrums threw into relief Shaw's patience and good humour and courtesy; and in any debate between these two, GBS would win easily on points. Yet for my part I was always admiringly and affectionately aware of H. G.'s honesty of mind, his frankness, his raging desire to discover and to announce the truth. To those redeeming qualities it seemed to me that Shaw opposed something personally attractive and polemically formidable, but disingenuous and dubious.

Thus, Shaw might win the argument about Stalin and the Soviet Union, but it was Wells who was nearer the truth, and was not playing any monkey tricks with his own values. Sometimes, both when I read him or heard him in private, I felt that Shaw deliberately switched off his imagination when dealing with certain topics. It is not that he was downright dishonest, but that he refused to follow his debating points into the world of flesh and blood. So he could defend or even admire dictators when he must have known that he could never have endured their authority. He could cheerfully advocate the 'liquidation' of anti-social types, as if they were merely being barred from a summer school.

He did not see them as real people, shrieking and bleeding, but as creatures of paper and ink, characters with no entrances in the third act.

'The Shavian Mask' and some Recollections

LADY RHONDDA

From a series of three articles on Shaw by Lady Rhondda, published in the 'Notes on the Way' column of her magazine *Time and Tide* for 28 July, 4 August and 11 August 1956. The articles were entitled 'The Shavian Mask', 'Holding the Mask in Place' and 'The Man behind the Mask'.

Most shy people have some kind of defence mechanism with which to confront the world, and, oddly enough, it not unusually takes the form of trying to make themselves out to be very much more unpleasant people than they really are. That was the form which it took with Shaw. He had the kind of pride that intensely dislikes being laughed at. If he was to be sneered at he wished to be foremost among the sneerers. He did not propose that the world should know anything about the private man. Add to that that he very much enjoyed shocking it. He proceeded to paint a completely false and in many respects extremely unattractive public portrait of himself.

He was, I think, inclined to despise the world. That, incidentally, is very often part of the defence mechanism of a shy man. By the time Shaw was famous no one thought of him as shy, indeed he no longer was. But the habits that had been formed when he was young remained. He had learnt his tricks so well that he continued to play them quite unconsciously when he no longer knew he was doing it. And to feel despised is a thing that few men forgive.

There may have been other reasons for the dislike of course. He had all the usual artist's faults. He was a showman – and an extremely good one. He had the artist's vanity. But he never, so far as I could see, allowed his vanity to interfere with his sense of justice, to give him a rose-coloured picture of himself, to make him denigrate unfairly any of his colleagues, or to make him anything less than universally generous. Most vanity does all these things. In fact, most vanity corrodes. Shaw's corroded him comparatively little.

Still, there it is. Seldom has a man had in so great a measure the capacity for arousing irritation and even dislike in those who did not really know him. It made no difference whether they were writers themselves or simply members of the general public. The reaction was the same. I happened to meet recently two men on succeeding days, one a man of letters, the other a business man. They were as unlike each other in every way as any two men could be, save for one thing. They had each met Shaw once for a few minutes and they had each quite obviously taken a strong dislike to him. He had got under their skins. . . .

Amongst the qualities that Shaw enjoyed showing to the world and which are already known to be false were meanness and an inordinate love of money. To take two often quoted examples, he was, as I have said, unusually generous in every way. He pretended to be mean and hard. He was completely devoted to his wife. He tried to give the impression that he had married her for her money. One could easily give half a dozen other examples. Anyone who knew him well knew how false they were, and certainly one that has already been dispelled was the legend of his hardness. He was, on the contrary – how could he otherwise have been an artist? – extremely sensitive.

An occasion when I was conscious of this stays in my mind. One weekend, when the Shaws were staying with my mother, one of my uncles, who had read something I had written and completely misunderstood it, called across the table to accuse me of having said the exact opposite to what I had in fact written. I explained. 'The trouble with you, Uncle X,' I added, 'is that you can't read.' It was the fashion in my numerous family for half-meant laughing insults to be hurled from one to another and to be countered in the same spirit, and Uncle X was in no way perturbed. In the first place, he didn't believe me; but even if he had, he would not have minded very much. If he had been accused of not knowing how to fish it might have been another matter. Shaw, however, who was sitting beside me, was most distressed. He felt that I must have hurt my uncle's feelings and he couldn't bear it.

Part 17
Old Age and Death

When Shaw reached the age of sixty in July 1916, he still had before him an extraordinarily extensive career as playwright, essayist, controversialist and public figure. He had begun writing *Heartbreak House* earlier in the year; but that play, with its fascinating portrait of an old sea captain as its central character, and two other of Shaw's most ambitious works, *Back to Methuselah* and *Saint Joan* were yet to be completed as was the entire series of political satires, extravaganzas, allegorical and philosophical plays which he wrote between the late 1920s and his death in 1950. Two of Shaw's major political works, *The Intelligent Woman's Guide to Socialism* and *Everybody's Political What's What* also belong to this last phase of his career. As birthday after birthday passed with no sign of flagging vigour on Shaw's part, joking speculation increased that he might personally achieve the miracle of extreme longevity attained by some of the characters in *Back to Methuselah*. He himself, however, had no such delusions or ambitions: 'An eternity of GBS would be the most appalling prospect', he remarks in one of the interviews below (p. 520), and in the days of his last illness he is reported to have expressed an intense longing for death.

Shaw's last illness and death attracted enormous media attention. After the fall in the garden which brought about his final illness, newspapers carried daily bulletins about his health; and his death, seven and a half weeks later, was front-page news around the world. Theatre audiences stood in silence, and the lights of Broadway were dimmed in farewell.

Growing Old

From James Douglas, 'Secrets of his Next Play . . . GBS's Guardian Angel', *Daily Express*, 26 July 1933. James Douglas (1867–1940), journalist, poet, novelist and critic, was editor of the *Sunday Express* from 1920 to 1931. A few weeks before the publication of this interview Shaw completed the writing of his dramatic portrait of British democracy in chaos, *On the Rocks*.

'Tell me,' said I, 'how does it feel to grow old?'

'I don't know,' he laughed. 'In London sometimes I stop after walking an hour or two and take a cab. I suppose that is a sign of old age.'

'Arnold Bennett,' I said, 'told me that his first sign of age was sitting down to brush his hat.'

Shaw laughed, 'Well, I don't do that yet!' . . .

His clear blue eyes are young. His skin is like a child's – smooth, soft and unwrinkled. His voice rings out like a bell. His laugh is uproarious. . . .

'What keeps you so young?' I asked.

'Well,' he said, 'there is something in the mind that goes on growing and developing. Of course I know I am an old dodderer, but there is a mind spot or speck in me that really goes on and on, and the changes in it keep it young.'

Then he talked of the great changes in his mind.

'When you and I were young – a pair of Irish adventurers – we believed that civilisation went on progressing. But Flinders Petrie has shown that six or seven other unknown civilisations went through the same phases as Greece, Rome, and our own age, and then perished utterly.[1]

'And they perished after they had arrived at about the same point that we have reached! They could not get round the corner.'

NOTE

1. Sir William Matthew Flinders Petrie (1853–1942), leading British archaeologist, was Professor of Egyptology at the University of London from 1892 to 1933. Petrie was a pioneer in establishing methods of tracing the evolution of cultures by investigating sequences of types of pottery.

Passages

JAMES DRAWBELL

From James Drawbell, *The Sun Within Us* (London: Collins, 1963) pp. 290–1. James Wedgwood Drawbell (1899–1979), journalist, was editor of the *Sunday Chronicle* (1925–46) and managing editor of George Newnes Ltd (1946–64). Drawbell and the Shaws were fellow passengers on the *Llangibby Castle* in the spring of 1936, Drawbell being bound for Italy and the Shaws for South Africa.

He was on his feet now, his spindly legs sustaining the frail body. We were having a rough voyage; it did not daunt Shaw. As we moved cautiously along, the deck falling from us at a dizzy angle, he continued to think aloud. The wind threw his words at me.

'I believe that every hard-working man, when he reaches the age of forty should be put to bed for fifteen months. History is full of the names of men who died in their late thirties or early forties. If they'd had a year in bed, or rested completely away from work, they might have gone on working to a ripe old age.'

I glanced at him in astonishment. Go to bed for a year! I did not understand then that what he meant was not bed, literally, but a break, a sabbatical year of doing nothing. I thought I was listening to the gay nonsense, the privileged clowning, of a great man. If ever there was a time in my life when I should have stopped and listened, this was it.

He saw my smile.

'I'm not joking,' he said, 'I'm talking from experience. The most troublesome time in a man's life is round the age of forty. I had an awful time. Most men go through the same thing. You realise at forty that you'll never be young again. Naturally you want to resist the knowledge, and instead of making all the sensible physical and mental adjustments to fit you for the future you go ahead trying to beat nature, stirring up trouble. The fifties find you out. The tired body creaks and groans. You nearly give up the ghost.'

He certainly had not given up the ghost. He laughed right out in the face of the storm. He was far from finished, either with his life or his admonition to me.

'And then after sixty comes the resurrection! You take on a quite remarkable new lease of life. The past drops away from you and you feel well and carefree and almost reckless. Nothing seems to affect you. It's a wonderful period in living. It has continued with me until now. But at eighty I'm beginning to feel the wear and tear. Of course I put up a bit of stage-front about it for my own benefit. I try to walk with a springy step, and all that sort of thing, but I can't hide from myself any longer that I'm growing old.'

'A Man All Light'

JAMES AGATE

From James Agate, *Ego 3: Being Still More of the Autobiography of James Agate*

(London: Harrap, 1938) p. 296. James Evershed Agate (1877–1947), dramatic critic, wrote for the *Manchester Guardian* from 1907) and later the *Sunday Times*. His autobiography, written in nine parts, is in the form of a diary. The following is the entry for 3 March 1938. Agate had visited the Shaws, taking Charlotte a basket of spring flowers.

We talked a little about *The Three Sisters*,[1] which they had just seen, and I recommended F. L. Lucas's *Land's End*.[2] GBS said, 'But he's an old man!' I said, 'Oldish men have written goodish plays.' And except for a short, musical bark answer came there none. We were standing in the middle of the room, Shaw with his back to the window and intercepting a shaft of brilliant March sunshine. He has become so insubstantial that even in ordinary light he looks like a figure in stained-glass. As he stood against the window I saw the outline of head and chin. William Archer once said mischievously that if you could see Shaw's face without the beard it would be hatchet-shaped and mean. Archer was wrong. Today I clearly saw the chin, and it juts nobly. The point about the shaft of sun is that it stressed the unreality of one who is rapidly turning into a saint. Which I expect will make it very uncomfortable for some other saints. The sun streaming through the white hair made a halo of it, and I thought of Coleridge's 'a man all light'.[3]

NOTES

1. The play by Chekhov.
2. *Land's End* by Frank Lawrence Lucas (1894–1967), scholar, critic and poet, was included in his *Four Plays* (Cambridge: Cambridge University Press, 1935).
3. 'A man all light, a seraph-man/On every corse there stood' (*The Ancient Mariner*, ll. 490–1).

At Cliveden, 1941

JOYCE GRENFELL

From Joyce Grenfell, *Joyce Grenfell Requests the Pleasure* (London: Macmillan, 1976) pp. 160–1. Joyce Irene Grenfell (1910–1979), theatrical entertainer, songwriter and mimic, had known the Shaws since she was fifteen. She was a niece of Lady Astor and stayed frequently at Cliveden, the Astors' palatial residence on the Thames near Maidenhead. She was there during a visit by the Shaws in August 1941, and sent the following report to her mother. At the time of the visit Stephen Potter (1900–69), author, and, from 1938, writer–producer with the BBC, had been endeavouring to arrange for Shaw to do a radio programme with him.

GBS won't do the programme because he says he is too old, which, being translated, means his teeth don't fit and make rude noises that would be particularly exaggerated on the air and his vanity won't stand for such a thing. And I think he is right. He *is* older but he is incredible for eighty-five. Looks wonderfully pink and white and fresh and beautifully dandified. I do like attractive old people. Both the Shaws take trouble over their appearance. The more I see of them the more I like them and find their company stimulating. When he isn't putting on his act, is not being the contradictory small boy who must take the opposite view – then he is a charmer and what he has to say is worth hearing. I've had several quiet meals with them and we have talked of books, of Barrie, of music, of Elgar; of the stage and Mrs Pat, of the English, eugenics and food. Mrs Shaw is very deaf, which means that conversation takes time and must be executed *fortissimo* and that can make almost anything one says sound worthless! We left most of the talking to GBS.

'Dodging his Dotage'

W. R. TITTERTON

From W. R. Titterton, 'Dodging his Dotage', *Strand Magazine*, July 1943.

A man who was with me, and did not understand that Shaw hates to be interviewed as if he were Greta Garbo or the Oldest Inhabitant, here remarked, 'To what do you attribute your longevity?'

Shaw gazed at him smiling with his eyebrows raised, as if in doubt whether he would reduce him to ashes or reply, 'I attribute it to the grace of God and the provisions of the Fabian Society.'

What he did say was, 'Mainly to the fact that I have never taken part in any form of athletics.'

He put his thumb in the armhole of his waistcoat in the old familiar way, and went on:

'Sandow tried to get hold of me once. I told him, "I know what you can do. You can lift three elephants, half a dozen pianos, and twenty men on your chest. That's no use to me. I want to keep them off my chest."' Shaw added reflectively: 'He died young.'[1]

Throwing off the melancholy reflection, he said: 'I like what the centenarian said to his interviewers – "I attribute my longevity to the fact that I abstained from spirit, wines, and beers, and from traffic with women until I was fourteen."'

NOTE

1. Eugen Sandow (1867–1925), German professional strong man and film actor, died of a cerebral haemorrhage in London.

'Life, Death and the Hereafter'

From Hannen Swaffer, 'Bernard Shaw's Final Words on Life, Death and the Hereafter, his Failures, Doubts and Hopes', *Daily Herald*, 18 November 1943. Hannen Swaffer (1879–1962), journalist and dramatic critic, one of Fleet Street's best-known characters in his day, had a strong interest in the subjects of spiritualism and life after death.

'What do you think you are facing when you die?' I asked.

'Oh, when I die, I go,' he replied. 'I never did, and I do not believe in individual survival. I do not think anybody could believe in it and realise what it means.

'An eternity of GBS would be the most appalling prospect. Like the Wandering Jew, I would give £5 to anyone who would shoot me.'

'But it wouldn't be the same GBS always,' I explained, as the Spiritualist that Shaw knew me to be. 'He would endure. He would progress. Eventually, gradually losing his earth personality, he would become merged more and more in the great spirit of Creation.'

Shaw did not deny that. He tried to explain it, though, another way.

'I believe in the Life Everlasting, as in the Creed,' he said, although orthodoxy of any kind he would deny. 'It is life force.

'What you see here,' – and he pointed to his body – 'is a combination of carbon, potash and a lot of chemicals.

'Here is a life that has organised itself in an extraordinary manner and made a tremendous machine on top of my shoulders.

'The time will come when that will suddenly stop, and I get myself burned as soon as possible or otherwise tumble into a heap.

'The life goes on. The individual perishes. Life still goes on. New people come into the world. They will be using the same life.

'The carbon which is the individualism of that life force you get rid of, and the life force becomes somebody else. You may regard me as an incarnation of anybody you like. That is all right. That is not individual survival.' . . .

Yet he added the amazing words: *'I am talking about something I know nothing about.'*

Nothing was known about it, he declared. He had asked physiologists and biologists, but they could not answer the very first question, 'What is the difference between a dead body and a live one?'

It was something chemical and something visual, but no one could tell him.

'The Elderly Gentleman'

JOHN MASON BROWN

From John Mason Brown, 'Back to Methuselah: a Visit to an Elderly Gentleman in a World of Arms and the Man', *Saturday Review of Literature*, 22 July 1944. John Mason Brown (1900–1969), drama critic, was serving in the United States Navy at the time of this visit to Shaw. His companions were Nancy Astor and Lieutenant MacGeorge Bundy, military aide to Rear-Admiral Alan G. Kirk. The Elderly Gentleman is the principal character in Part IV of *Back to Methuselah*, 'Tragedy of an Elderly Gentleman'.

By the time we had followed him back to the house, he had already lunged into sex, marriage, primogeniture, cattle, the English clergy, Norman architecture and Victorian bad taste.

'Sit down, sit down,' he exclaimed when we had come into the living room which was all windows and sunlight and shadowless, and highly polished furniture and books, 'No special chairs here.'

Then tea was served to us – delicious tea, beautifully served – while he took a glass of hot milk. The talk continued, wobbling from subject to subject much as he had swayed in his walking. As he talked he pinkened, gathering strength with his thoughts. . . .

With the speed, and often with the brilliance with which he hedgehops from subject to subject in the subdivisions of his prefaces, the Elderly Gentleman held forth. On Lunachevsky.[1] On Mrs Shaw's will. On his disappointment in the man known to the world as Uncle Jo.[2] On his visits to the Front in the last war. On General Haig.[3] On Mrs Patrick Campbell. On Hesketh Pearson. On Mr Shaw – 'the historic Shaw, the man of my middle years, the Shaw the world will remember,' as he put it. On the movie of *Caesar and Cleopatra*. And as casually as you mention a friend seen last week, on Stanley, the Stanley of Mr Livingstone, I presume.[4] 'I remember Stanley telling me that only five per cent of the men under him were ever equipped to take over his command, if he had to delegate authority. That's how rare real leadership always is.'

'My actuarial expectancy,' said the Elderly Gentleman, sipping his hot milk, and smiling as wholeheartedly as at the best of jokes, 'is three days. As a matter of fact I may die while you are sitting here. Death has no terrors for me.' . . .

By the visit's end, the Elderly Gentleman, so frail and mortal behind his prophet's beard, seemed tired. Slowly and unsteadily, though erect as an exclamation point, he had preceded us to the gate. As he stood there in the road while we drove off, with the breeze ballooning his cap, with the sun hallowing his beard, and an arm upraised, the saintly old satan, or, more accurately, the satanic old saint looked more alone than any man I have ever seen. He was as alone as only old age and such a mind as his can make a man.

NOTES

1. Probably Anatoly Lunacharsky (see above, p. 324, n.1).
2. I.e. Joseph Stalin.
3. Sir Douglas Haig, 1st Earl (1861–1928), Field Marshall, was Commander-in-Chief of the British forces in France during the First World War.
4. Sir Henry Morton Stanley (1841-1904), journalist and explorer of Central Africa who rescued the Scottish missionary and explorer David Livingstone (1813–73), greeting him with the now famous words, 'Dr Livingstone, I presume'.

Wood-chopping at Eighty-eight

From 'Bernard Shaw, at 88, Gives His Home to the Nation', *News Chronicle*, 26 July 1944.

'Mr Shaw is in the garden chopping wood,' said his Irish maid,[1] when I called at his country home at Ayot St Lawrence yesterday afternoon. I found him under the apple trees, wearing an amazing style of headgear with a talc eyeshield, sawing away vigorously, surrounded by a pile of logs.

'This is a miner's helmet,' he said when he saw me. 'A very good thing for chopping wood. It keeps the chips out of your eyes.'

He looked a little frailer than when I saw him last, but his actions belied his looks.

'Are you going to chop wood on your birthday tomorrow?' I asked him.

'Is it tomorrow?' he said. 'I'd forgotten all about it.'

'How are you going to keep your birthday?'

'Well, so many other people are keeping my birthday for me – taking up my time and preventing me from working – the less I do about it the better.'

NOTE

1. Mrs Margaret ('Maggie') Smith.

'A Rather Dangerous Bird'

R. da COSTA

From R. da Costa, 'Pilgrimage to Bernard Shaw', *Palestine Post*, 14 November 1947.

We turned right from the lawn to the group of tall trees, and found ourselves suddenly in front of the famous wooden hut. The maid looked in and said: 'Here is the gentleman. And also the lady.'

There he sat, like a shrivelled Mexican idol, with a gardener's hat on. An idol he resembles, or a very old and rather dangerous bird, ready to jump out and peck. And, presently, he pecks:

'Why did you come out all this way? I don't know more about Palestine than anybody else! Why didn't you send the questions?'

The voice is high-pitched, angry, quarrelsome and amazingly loud. The old, dangerous bird looks for a moment as if it would fly at me. I almost retreat a step. Then I say: 'I walked all this way because I very much wanted to meet you.'

He mellowed visibly and said, with only a pretence of anger: 'Did you? Well, now you can see the animal!' It sounded as if he had said it often before.

But the smile was striking indeed. The wooden hut, tiny and cage-like, and in its centre the withered figure, perched on a stool. Shaw is shockingly thin now. The famous beard has shortened considerably and is almost a goatee. His skin is like parchment. The whole figure seems more like an echo of itself and a reflection of a famous picture.

But there are the ninety-one-year-old eyes.

Above dangling spectacles with halved glasses you see the eyes of a youth. Blue, radiating, quick and alert, they are the real Bernard Shaw. You realise at once that you stand in front of the great firebrand, the fighter with the superb brain who for over half a century has shocked and stirred and stunned, first his country and then the world, who has gradually become an object of admiration and love, first in the world and then in his country.

[da Costa goes on to record an unsuccessful attempt to elicit from Shaw a comment about the recent deportation from Palestine to Germany of 4500 Jews]

There was nothing doing. He led the conversation to the countryside, through which we had passed. And, with a jerk, he turned his head to my companion, who had stood there wide-eyed all the time. 'Why did *you* come here all the way?' She stammered.

'She also wanted to see you,' I answered for her. 'In fact, she pestered me so long until I had to take her with me.' He gave her a huge wink. 'She studies acting, and only recently Tyrone Guthrie[1] granted her an audition at which she gave Saint Joan.'

'Tyrone,' said Shaw, pronouncing it the Italian way and laughing lustily. He suddenly seemed extremely pleased and, while he was busy starting a veritable flirtation with the girl, I remembered why I was here and glanced at the interior of the hut.

On the right is a sort of camp-bed, as narrow as the figure for which it is built is slim. To the left is the writing-table, heaped high with papers. On top are a number of blue sheets with the familiar handwriting. I can see where he had been interrupted when we arrived. No wonder he was rude at first.

NOTE

1. William Tyrone Guthrie (1900–1971), actor, director and playwright.

Shaw's Ninety-fourth Birthday

F. G. PRINCE-WHITE

From F. G. Prince-White, 'Bernard Shaw is 94 Today', *Daily Mail*, 26 July 1950. Frederic George Prince-White (1894–1975), journalist, was on the editorial staff of the *Daily Mail* for over forty years. The short play to which Prince-White refers was finally entitled *Why She Would Not: A Little Comedy* (see above, p. 396).

'I've got a piece of news for you,' he told me yesterday, when I talked with him in his study at Ayot St Lawrence.

'I thought something might be expected of me to mark my birthday, as usual, so I've written another play. I've labelled it 'a little comedy', and called it *The Lady She Would Not*. It is in five scenes. I wrote the whole thing in seven days.'

He beamed triumphantly as he repeated: 'Yes, *in seven days*.'

'People seem to think,' he went on, 'that I ought to go on writing big plays like *Back to Methuselah* and *The Doctor's Dilemma* – but why should I? I've said all I wanted to say; now I can write little things to amuse myself.'

He grumbles fiercely about people who 'pester' him when his birthday comes round.

'I *don't* want to be asked how I am,' he insisted angrily. 'There's so much nonsense in this "How are you?" business. People are always saying "You look younger than ever", when the truth is they are thinking how damned awful you look and wondering that you manage to keep alive, anyhow.'

Presently he smiled (there is a world of charm in that rare smile of his) and said: 'Anyway, I'm past my second childhood now; now I'm really beginning to grow up. I still maintain that a man needs to live to be 250 if he is to make full use of the knowledge and wisdom he acquires. That is the ideal. I don't say I'm going to soar to it.'

The Fall

'MAGGIE' SMITH

From *Shaw the Villager*, pp. 49–50. Shaw's final illness was precipitated by a fall which occurred in his garden at Ayot St Lawrence on Sunday 10 September 1950, while he was pruning a tree. He suffered a fractured thigh, and was admitted to the Luton and Dunstable General Hospital. The doctor who attended Shaw in his last illness was Thomas C. Probyn, of the nearby village of Kimpton. At the time of the fall Mrs Smith had returned to Shaw's service to replace Mrs Laden who was on holiday.

It was a terrible moment for me when I heard him whistle on my first day back with him. He carried a whistle with him always, to blow if he fell over or anything like that. He was a bit shaky on his feet sometimes. He was ninety-four, remember. I ran out into the garden and found him on the ground. I had him sitting on my knees for fifteen minutes. 'Put me down and go and fetch someone,' he said, but I wouldn't put him on the wet grass and blew and blew at the whistle till my husband, who happened to be near, came and helped Mr Shaw into the house. Then the doctor arrived a little later.

Mr Shaw had had enough – he didn't want to recover. He was a very determined man and no one could make him do anything he didn't want to.

Last Days: I

F. G. PRINCE-WHITE

From F. G. Prince-White, '"I Would Like to Go into My Garden," said Shaw', *Daily Mail*, 13 October 1950. Shaw returned home twenty-four days after his accident, on 4 October. In hospital he had successful operations on his thigh and kidney, but refused a second kidney operation which had been prescribed. On his return home, Shaw was nursed by Sisters Gwendoline Howell and Florence Horan.

George Bernard Shaw looked wistfully out of his bedroom window at Ayot St Lawrence yesterday and saw the sun shining warmly on his wide lawns and casting a deep shadow in the little dell where Saint Joan stands pondering on the folly of men.[1]

'I would like, more than anything,' he said, 'to go into the garden.'

'And so you shall,' his day-nurse, Sister Horan, told him.

Presently she and Shaw's housekeeper, Mrs Alice Laden (he calls her 'My Scots manager'), had got him out of bed, wrapped him up very snugly, put him into his new wheel-chair, and pushed him out on to his gravelled terrace.

He would not wear a hat, but called for his old grey cap. 'It's much warmer,' he said.

He turned his face gladly to the sun, for it was the first time he had been in the open air since his return from hospital.

Looking across the garden to the woods and fields of Hertfordshire beyond, all agleam in the mellow afternoon, he murmured: 'It's all very beautiful.'

Shaw is not now the scintillating sage we knew even a few months ago. The fall that broke his thigh would seem to have shattered at the same time something intangible in him – that peculiar brittle quality in his make-up that was expressed by the caustic side of his tongue, a quality that was the main source of his barbed and brilliant wit.

I had not until yesterday seen him since his accident, and I missed the old humorous irritability and impatience with which he regarded the world and all in it.

A gentleness is on his face now, a softness in his once-piercing glance.

I saw him first in his bedroom, sitting at the window, with the sunlight emphasising the almost transparent texture of his skin.

He greeted me with a smile.

We talked of his last play – a comedy he was writing just before his ninety-fourth birthday in July. He had called it *The Lady She Would Not*.

I asked him when it was likely to be produced.

He shook his head. 'I didn't complete it,' he said. 'There was more work to be done on it – and now it will never be done. The truth is I *can't* do it. That play will be another "Unfinished Symphony".'

He was silent for a while. Then he said, quietly:

'I don't think I shall ever write anything more.'

He fixed his gaze on the autumnal vista of sunlit countryside merging into mist, and mused: 'I suppose it is something that I can sit here at this window and look on the shining grass and the trees.'

Out on the terrace in his wheel-chair the world's greatest living playwright looked lingeringly round the garden.

He stayed there only a few minutes. A cloud passed over the sun, and he said to Sister Horan: 'I think I ought to go in now. The sunshine was beautiful, but I don't like the shadow.'

NOTE

1. A bronze statue of Saint Joan was cast for Shaw by his neighbour, Clare Winsten, and placed on a lawn-covered bank in the garden at Ayot St Lawrence.

Last Days: II

ESMÉ PERCY

From Esmé Percy, 'Memories of Bernard Shaw', *British Peace Committee News Letter*, March–April 1956.

My last visit to Bernard Shaw was a week before his death – a memorable milestone in my long life, an end of an epoch indeed. He was lying in his bed, which had been brought down to his study on the ground floor of his house at Ayot St Lawrence.

His hair and beard were longer and thicker than I had ever seen them – but his eyebrows seemed less Mephistophelian; doubtless he had given up the impish coquetry of combing them from right to left and left to right (he always carried a minute tortoiseshell comb for that purpose).

He was wearing what I took to be a nightgown of heavy woven fabric of light saffron shade with monk-like wide sleeves – a Blake-like figure indeed.

We talked for quite a long time, just we two. It was an afternoon of autumn in all its glory, hyacinth and gold. We talked about the theatre, about myself, about Barker. 'The trouble with Barker,' Shaw said, 'was that he never really understood my plays; he produced them as if they'd been written by Galsworthy!' A bewildering *volte-face* indeed in view of their long association at the Court Theatre.

He told me how he no longer wanted anything but death. 'I could resign myself to being confined to physical inactivity, but to have no more control of my bodily functions, to be like a baby in swaddling clothes – no.' The sudden, unexpected vehemence and force with which he pronounced the word 'no' was startlingly irrevocable.

The sister who was then attending on him came in at that moment and signified that it was time for me to go. I rose and left; he seemed not to notice my departure.

I was just about to get into my car when the nurse rushed over to me to tell me Mr Shaw wished to see me again. 'I forgot, I forget everything now,' he said. 'You are about to go to America?' Yes, I replied.

He took my hand and pressed it against his heart. How thin his body was. He just said, 'Good luck, good-bye', and then a brief but heartrending pause, and 'Now get along with you.' That was the second time I noticed what looked like a tear.

Last Days: III

EILEEN O'CASEY

From Eileen O'Casey, *Sean*, ed. J. G. Trewin (London: Macmillan; Dublin: Gill & Macmillan, 1971) pp. 209–10. Eileen O'Casey (née Carey), actress, married Sean O'Casey in 1927.

On arrival I found Shaw dozing and very pale indeed. Before he woke I had time to study the room in detail; except for its pictures of Stalin and Gandhi, it did look like a small room in a hospital, with its collection of medicine bottles by the bed. Finally GBS opened his eyes. Turning to me, he said, 'I really think I am going to die.' His voice was weak and he spoke softly; one had to move close to him to hear what he was saying. But he rallied for a moment and began to talk in his old humorous way, asking what was going to happen after death and whom he would meet, treating it as a new experience instead of being in any sense frightened: 'If there's an Almighty, Eileen, I'll have a hell of a lot of questions to ask Him.' I said that perhaps he would be able to tell Sean what there was to meet. Sean, he answered, would have to carry on. 'No,' I said, 'Sean is too old'; and he replied, 'It's up to one or both of the boys if their lives aren't wasted in another war.' His long white hands on the coverlet, he stole back to sleep again, first asking me not to go yet. Though he was so sick, his brain was as clear and bright as ever.

I crept from the room, believing I ought to go. I was talking to the nurse when the bell that was fastened to GBS's shoulder suddenly rang. He asked if I had gone, for he would like to say goodbye. Though a little reluctant, the nurse whispered to me: 'Yes, if you are not too long with him this time; he was so anxious to see you.' On my return he gave one of his lovely smiles, and said that his head was aching always. Would I stroke his forehead? Feeling that he was back again as a small child wanting a mother's comfort, I spoke to him very gently. It was wonderful, he murmured, to have the soft touch of a woman's hand and the sound of a gentle voice. Then I stroked his forehead until he dozed off, practically to sleep. 'Kiss me goodbye,' he asked. I kissed him; he smiled quietly; and when I said 'Goodbye and God bless you,' he answered, in his old quick manner, 'He has blessed you already.' He sank back into sleep. When I left I knew I should never see him again.

Last Days: IV

LADY ASTOR

From a letter by Lady Nancy Astor to Archibald Henderson, 25 September 1951 in Henderson, *George Bernard Shaw: Man of the Century* (New York: Appleton-Century-Crofts, 1956) p. 874. Adelina Patti (1843–1919), the famous coloratura soprano, married three times. With her second husband (her tenor partner in *La Traviata*) Ernest Nicolini, whom she married in 1886, she purchased a Victorian castle, known as Craig-y-nos, on the northern side of Swansea Valley. In 1899, after the death of Nicolini in the previous year, she married the Swedish Baron Rolf Cederstrom, and continued to live for a time at Craig-y-nos. It is difficult to determine which of the two husbands is meant to be the hero of Shaw's no doubt apocryphal story. One of Nancy Astor's maids, Rosina Harris, remarks in her biographical work, *Rose: My Life in Service* (London: Cassell, 1975) p. 136, that 'Mr Shaw's death, . . . comes as a shock to my lady, and which she took badly'.

I think I wrote you that one of the reasons GBS was so fond of me was because of Charlotte. He missed her very much in those last few days before he went, and he told me that he kept dreaming about her. I will try to describe the last two or three hours I spent with him. I said to him:

'Well, GBS, I am going to rub your head.'

He said: 'How do you know if I want it rubbed?'

I said: 'I don't, but I think it would be good for you.'

He asked me if I had healing hands and I told him that some people thought so, 'Anyhow, we'll try.' So healing were my hands that he told me that I could go on rubbing his head all night. Soon after that he perked up and said:

'You must meet my night nurse, she is a Card! She nursed Adelaide Patty's [Adelina Patti] husband. Did you know Adelaide Patty?' I replied that I did not. 'Well,' he said, 'they were a most extraordinary couple' and then he told me this story.

Adelaide Patty you know married a foreigner who bought an estate in Wales. He gave a party to all the nobility, the Lord Mayor and so forth and in the midst of the Ball he rushed into the room and said:

'Stop ze music, put out ze lights, and all go 'ome. A terrible thing has happened, I went upstairs and found my wife in bed with a man. Stop ze music, go 'ome.'

In fifteen or twenty minutes as the guests were departing, he came back and said: 'Do not go, put up ze lights, start ze music, dance, enjoy yourselves. He has apologised.'

When he had told this story GBS roared with laughter. . . .

Then I told him the story of a coloured woman who in Hospital was questioned as to how many husbands and children she had; she answered,

'I'se had two husbands and six children, two by John, two by Mose and the last two by myself.'

Those were my last words with him and he then went to sleep. That was the end of my beloved friend. I knew I would miss him but I did not know how much.

Shaw's Death

F. G. PRINCE-WHITE

From F. G. Prince-White, 'GBS Begged to be Allowed to Die', *Scottish Daily Mail*, 3 November 1950. Shaw died in the early morning of 2 November 1950.

George Bernard Shaw died longing for death. With all the waning strength of his great mind he resented the last infirmities that beset his body, and regarded his helpless state as a degradation.

He made this very clear only a little while before he lapsed into the coma that lasted twenty-six hours and from which he was never to emerge.

He said to Sister Gwendoline Howell, who, with Sister Florence Horan, had nursed him since his return from hospital a month ago: 'I am weary – utterly weary of everything. I want most intensely to die.'

And he begged that nothing should be done that might prolong his life. 'It is not worth doing,' he said. 'Let me die.'

This mood was not a sudden one. It was plain to those who knew him that he had as it were, closed the book of his life on the day he fell in his garden and fractured his thigh.

I myself at once became aware of this when I visited him a week after he was brought home in a motor-ambulance. I saw that he had come home to die.

He said to me very quietly, but in a tone of absolute certainty: 'I am finished. I've shot my bolt.'

I murmured something about the beauty of the day.

'It may be beautiful – *for you*,' he said.

The emphasis on those last two words conveyed a significance which could not be misunderstood.

Nevertheless, up to a few days before his death Shaw's impatience with life at moments subsided under small upwellings of his old playful, mischievous spirit.

He would cock one bushy eyebrow and remark to his nurses: 'You treat me as if I were a new-born baby – an outsized one'; or he would comment chaffingly on what he called the absurdity of trying to repair a broken-down 'ancient monument' – one of his favourite descriptions of himself.

The final disintegration of his vital forces began with the onset of fever that rapidly raised his temperature to danger-pitch, and a pounding pulse shook his wasted frame.

Yet that astonishingly stout heart of his held out unfalteringly until only a few hours before it ceased to beat.

The failure was so gradual that it was almost imperceptibly that he breathed his last.

Summoned by telephone, Shaw's own medical attendant, Dr Thomas Probyn, hastened from the neighbouring village of Kimpton and confirmed that the sage of Ayot St Lawrence, the greatest playwright of his time, was dead. He defined the cause of death as 'kidney failure'.

The two nurses had been at Shaw's bedside almost constantly for more than forty-eight hours.

They declared it had been no hardship: said they had been proud to have such a 'great and courageous gentleman' in their care.

Sister Howell was due to attend another patient the day before Shaw died, but decided to stay on another day. 'I knew Mr Shaw could not last very long,' she said.

When she told him at the beginning of this week that she would have to leave him, Shaw said: 'I shall be dead before you go.'

'I felt then with even greater certitude, that Mr Shaw was *willing* himself to die, and would have his way,' Sister Howell told me.

This announcement, in bold handwriting, was affixed to the wrought-iron gates of 'Shaw's Corner': –

'Mr Bernard Shaw passed peacefully away at one minute to five o'clock this morning, November 2.

'From the coffers of his genius he enriched the world.'

Slowly the words grew visible in the dawn light that spread, gentle as a benediction, over the lawns and walks and shadowy spinneys of Shaw's garden. A rainstorm had lately passed, and grass and colouring leaves were all agleam.

A few villagers approached and peered: hats were raised, caps pulled off in rustic regret at the passing of one whose fame, though it had encompassed the world, was in his own small village of less account than his long-familiar self.

In the cream distempered dining-room that had served as his bedroom for the last four weeks of his life Shaw lay in his wood-framed bed in the dignity of ultimate serenity.

On the wall behind him hung the scrolls presented to him when he received the freedoms of St Pancras and Dublin; in a corner hung the virile portrait of him by Mr Augustus John; on the window-sill a photograph of his late wife was propped up.

Looking on his face, which had been for half a century as readily recognised in Timbuctoo and Tahiti as in Tooting and Totnes, I discerned in it a content deeper by far than I had ever known it to hold.

Was it mere fancy that a ghost of a smile flittered about the snowy-whiskered mouth – a smile of quiet but determined triumph?

He had, it was certain, gained the peace he so imperiously desired. He had not shot his bolt in vain.

They had put on him his favourite mauve-silk pyjamas, but not until a missing button had been sewn on.

'Mr Shaw would have hated to wear a pyjama jacket that had a button off,' said Mrs Alice Laden, his housekeeper.

The other day Shaw talked freely to her of his expected death. 'Mrs Laden,' he said, 'you must see that I'm put into a plain, ordinary coffin, like any other man.

'I don't want anything expensive.'

'And another thing,' he added. 'Don't keep me cluttering up the house longer than necessary when I'm dead.

'Get me out quick. Have me put somewhere quiet until they cremate me.'

Last Rites

SYDNEY COCKERELL

From Wilfrid Blunt, *Cockerell* (London: Hamish Hamilton, 1964) p. 211. Shaw was cremated at the Golders Green Crematorium, London. He had specified in his will that there be no service which would suggest that he accepted the tenets of any established church or denomination. Cockerell made attempts to have Shaw's ashes placed in either Westminster Abbey or St Patrick's Cathedral in Dublin. But Shaw's request was that his ashes, mingled with those of Charlotte, should be inurned or scattered in the garden of the house at Ayot St Lawrence. The ashes were scattered by his doctor, Thomas C. Probyn, at a simple ceremony attended by the Public Trustee, F. Wyndham Hirst, and others.

There was no religious ceremony. The organist played Elgar's 'We are the Music Masters' (from the *Enigma Variations*)[1] and 'Libera me' from Verdi's *Requiem*, in accordance with a wish expressed by Shaw to Lady Astor, and between these performances I read (very badly) the final words of Mr Valiant for Truth from *The Pilgrim's Progress*, a book greatly admired by GBS all his life, with the following passage ending 'and all the trumpets sounded for him on the other side'.[2] I think nothing could be more appropriate for the occasion.

NOTES

1. The Elgar piece sung at the ceremony was one from his 'The Music Makers', a setting of an ode by Arthur William Edgar O'Shaughnessy (1844–81), 'We are the Music Makers'.
2. The passage Cockerell read was that beginning with the words, 'My sword I give to him that shall succeed me in my pilgrimage' (see Archibald Henderson, *George Bernard Shaw: Man of the Century* [New York: Appleton-Century-Crofts, 1956] p. 877).

Shaw's Corner, 11 December 1950

HAROLD NICOLSON

From Harold Nicolson, *Diaries and Letters 1945–1962*, ed. Nigel Nicolson (London:

Collins, 1968) pp. 196–7. Sir Harold George Nicolson (1886–1968), man of letters, spent many years in the diplomatic service before settling down to life as an author, lecturer and journalist. Nicolson was appointed Vice-Chairman of the National Trust in 1947. His lifelong friend, James Lees-Milne (b. 1908), architectural historian, was Secretary of the Historic Buildings Committee for the National Trust from 1936 to 1951. John Francis Warre Rathbone (b. 1909), solicitor, was Secretary of the National Trust for Places of Historic Interest or Natural Beauty from 1949 to 1968.

I go down to Hertfordshire with Jim Lees-Milne and Jack Rathbone to see Bernard Shaw's house which he left to the Trust. We first go into the garden. A sloping lawn and rough grass intersected by a few rose-beds. A bank, with a statue of Saint Joan. A hut in which he worked. Everything as he left it. Postcards, envelopes, a calendar marking the day of his death, curiously enough a Bible and prayer-book and Crockford's Directory,[1] a pair of mittens. The grass path and the bed around the statue of Saint Joan are still strewn with his ashes and those of Mrs Shaw. The Trustees and the doctor got both urns and put them on the dining-room table. They then emptied the one into the other and stirred them with a kitchen spoon. They went out into the garden and emptied spoonfuls of the mixture on to the flower beds and paths. All this some fifteen days ago, but the remains are still there. Just like the stuff Viti[2] puts down for slugs.

We see the housekeeper, a nice Scotch body.[3] She would like to stay on, but how can we afford her? Shaw has left us nothing at all. The house is dreadful and not really lettable. It will, moreover, be difficult to show to tourists as it is so small. It will be essential to keep the furniture exactly as it is. All his hats and coats and nailbrushes etc. are here. His long woollen stockings and his thick underclothes. The pictures, apart from one of Samuel Butler and two of Stalin and one of Gandhi, are exclusively of himself. Even the door-knocker is an image of himself.

We decide that morally we must accept Shaw's house. I am not happy about it. I do not think that Shaw will be a great literary figure in 2000 AD. He is an amazingly brilliant contemporary; but not in the Hardy class.

NOTES

1. Church of England Clerical Directory.
2. The Hon. Victoria Mary ('Vita') Sackville-West (1892–1962), poet and novelist, who was Nicolson's wife.
3. Mrs Alice Laden.

Index